ARIUS DIDYMUS

**Rutgers University Studies
in Classical Humanities, vol. 20**

Series Editor: William W. Fortenbaugh
Advisory Board: Tiziano Dorandi
David C. Mirhady
Stefan Schorn
Eckart Schütrumpf
Stephen A. White

On Stoic and Peripatetic Ethics: The Work of Arius Didymus I

Theophrastus of Eresus: On His Life and Work II

Theophrastean Studies: On Natural Science, Physics and Metaphysics, Ethics, Religion and Rhetoric III

Cicero's Knowledge of the Peripatos IV

Theophrastus: His Psychological, Doxographical, and Scientific Writings V

Peripatetic Rhetoric after Aristotle VI

The Passionate Intellect: Essays on the Transformation of Classical Traditions presented to Professor I.G. Kidd VII

Theophrastus: Reappraising the Sources VIII

Demetrius of Phalerum: Text, Translation and Discussion IX

Dicaearchus of Messana: Text, Translation and Discussion X

Eudemus of Rhodes XI

Lyco of Troas and Hieronymus of Rhodes XII

Aristo of Ceos, Text, Translation and Discussion XIII

Heraclides of Pontus, Text and Translation XIV

Heraclides of Pontus, Discussion of the Textual Evidence XV

Strato of Lampsacus: Text, Translation, and Discussion XVI

Aristoxenus of Tarentum: Texts and Discussion XVII

Praxiphanes of Mytilene and Chamaeleon of Heraclea: Text, Translation and Discussion XVIII

Phaenias or Eresus: Text, Translation and Discussion XIX

Arius Didymus on Peripatetic Ethics, Household Management, and Politics
Text, Translation, and Discussion

William W. Fortenbaugh
Editor

NEW YORK AND LONDON

First published 2018
by Routledge
711 Third Avenue, New York, NY 10017

and by Routledge
2 Park Square, Milton Park, Abingdon, Oxon OX14 4RN

Routledge is an imprint of the Taylor & Francis Group, an informa business

© 2018 selection and editorial matter, William W. Fortenbaugh; individual chapters, the contributors

The right of William W. Fortenbaugh to be identified as the author of the editorial material, and of the authors for their individual chapters, has been asserted in accordance with sections 77 and 78 of the Copyright, Designs and Patents Act 1988.

All rights reserved. No part of this book may be reprinted or reproduced or utilised in any form or by any electronic, mechanical, or other means, now known or hereafter invented, including photocopying and recording, or in any information storage or retrieval system, without permission in writing from the publishers.

Trademark notice: Product or corporate names may be trademarks or registered trademarks, and are used only for identification and explanation without intent to infringe.

British Library Cataloguing in Publication Data
A catalogue record for this book is available from the British Library

Library of Congress Cataloging in Publication Data
A catalog record for this book has been requested

ISBN: 978-1-4128-6553-1 (hbk)
ISBN: 978-0-203-70385-4 (ebk)

Typeset in Minion Pro

Contents

Preface		vii
Contributors		xi
1	Didymus' Epitome of Peripatetic Ethics, Household Management, and Politics: An Edition with Translation *Georgia Tsouni*	1
2	The Quest for an Author *David E. Hahm*	69
3	Moral Virtue in Didymus' Epitome of Peripatetic Ethics *William W. Fortenbaugh*	75
4	Intrinsic Worth of Others in the Peripatetic Epitome, Doxography C *Stephen A. White*	123
5	Two Conceptions of "Primary Acts of Virtue" in Doxography C *Jan Szaif*	161

Contents

6	Bodily and External Goods in Relation to Happiness *Myrto Hatzimichali*	205
7	Didymus on Types of Life *William W. Fortenbaugh*	227
8	Didymus' Epitome of the Economic and Political Topic *Eckart Schütrumpf*	255
9	Von Arnim, Didymus and Augustus: Three Related Notes on Doxography C *Peter L. P. Simpson*	293
10	Seneca's Peripatetics: *Epistulae Morales* 92 and the Stobaean Doxography C *Margaret R. Graver*	309

Subject Index to Chapters 2–10   343

Preface

The present volume is the twentieth in the series Rutgers University Studies in Classical Humanities, frequently referred to as RUSCH. With this volume the series returns to its roots. In March of 1981, a conference was held at Rutgers University on an epitome of Stoic and Peripatetic ethics that is preserved for us by Stobaeus and commonly attributed to Arius Didymus, the court philosopher of Caesar Augustus. The proceedings of the conference became volume I in the RUSCH series. It was published in 1983 and carried the title *On Stoic and Peripatetic Ethics: The Work of Arius Didymus*. Now thirty-three years later, RUSCH has returned to the work of Didymus. Volume XX contains the proceedings of a second conference on Didymus held at Rutgers in 2014. This time the conference narrowed its focus to the Peripatetic portion of Didymus' epitome. That is announced in the title of the present volume: *Arius Didymus on Peripatetic Ethics, Household Management, and Politics*. Nevertheless, issues concerning the Stoa are not entirely ignored. Indeed, how could they be, since Zeno founded the Stoa c. 301–300, when Theophrastus had succeeded Aristotle as head of the Peripatos. Interaction, even rivalry, between the two schools was inevitable and is reflected in what Didymus records concerning Peripatetic doctrine.

A special feature of this volume is the inclusion of a text-translation of the Peripatetic epitome. Since 1999 persons interested in the Stoic portion of Didymus' work have been able to consult the edition-translation by Arthur Pomeroy. Persons interested in the Peripatetic portion have not been so fortunate. To be sure there are new translations by Robert Sharples, 2010, and Peter Simpson, 2014, but for the Greek text one must still work with the 1884 edition of Curt Wachsmuth. The present volume offers both a new text and a new translation, which are printed on facing pages in order to facilitate comparison. The prime mover in creating this text-translation is Georgia Tsouni. Her initial drafts were more than a beginning and revisions went smoothly. I personally enjoyed working with Georgia and have appreciated the way in which she responded to suggested improvements: some on the mark and some off the mark. In addition, both of us are grateful for valuable corrections and suggestions that came from other contributors to this volume. Also to Tiziano Dorandi, who has not contributed an essay but has nonetheless contributed by reading through and commenting on Georgia's text. I like to think that we are all team players.

As editor of the present volume, I have made a number of decisions that are best mentioned here. The first concerns the name Arius Didymus, which appears in the title to this volume. That reflects the majority opinion among scholars today: the epitome preserved by Stobaeus was composed by a Stoic named Arius Didymus, the court philosopher of Caesar Augustus. The trouble is that the opinion is not clearly supported by the text of Stobaeus. In particular, a portion of text preserved apart from the epitome proper refers to Didymus and not to Arius Didymus. That opens the door to doubt, which has found expression in recent scholarly literature. Accordingly, Georgia Tsouni has exhibited caution, I would say prudence, in referring to Didymus *simpliciter* in the title to her text-translation. I have, however, preferred a compromise. On the one hand, I have included Arius in the title to the present volume, for without Arius not a few scholars may fail to make the connection with the epitomist, whom they know as Arius Didymus. On the other hand, I have respected Georgia's judgment in printing the titles to the several articles: all refer to Didymus without the addition of a forename. That takes account of the Stobean evidence, while leaving open whether the epitomist was in fact a Stoic philosopher closely associated with the Emperor Augustus.

In regard to style, I am no stickler. Concerning references to the scholarly literature and cross references within the volume, I have encouraged but not insisted on consistency. Occasionally, I have asked authors to shorten sentences and to introduce commas and semicolons, but I have let the authors decide. In regard to citations in Greek, I have allowed both the use of Greek font and the use of transliteration. Several considerations may be mentioned. On the one hand, the transliteration of individual words and phrases has gained wide acceptance; it makes easier the preparation of a finished manuscript; the reader who has little Greek but is familiar with individual words is not put off by transliterated words and phrases. Indeed, he is apt to welcome them as informative in a given context. On the other hand, long stretches of transliterated Greek may have a negative effect not only on the Greekless reader but also on persons who have a decent command of ancient Greek. Better to print the Greek in full and add a translation. The addition may seem unnecessary to the person who prides himself on his command of ancient Greek, but as editor I am aiming at a wide audience: not only philologists but also educated persons who have a healthy interest in Greek ethics, household management and politics.

Special thanks goes to the Loeb Classical Library Foundation, which provided funding for the publication of this volume. Also to Brad Inwood who attended both the 1981 and the 2014 conferences and supported our application for funding to the Loeb Foundation. So too heart felt thanks go to my long time friend, Diane Smith, who prepared this volume for publication, creating the facing pages and arranging the *apparatus criticus* as well as that of parallels texts.

WWF

Contributors

William W. Fortenbaugh, Department of Classics, Rutgers University, New Brunswick New Jersey 08901, USA

Margaret R. Graver, Department of Classics, HB 6086, 3 Bridgman Road, Dartmouth College, Hanover, New Hampshire 03755, USA

David E. Hahm, Department of Classics, Ohio State University, Columbus Ohio 43210, USA

Myrto Hatzimichali, Department of Classics, Homerton College, Cambridge CB2 HP, UK

Eckart Schütrumpf, Department of Classics, University of Colorado, Boulder CO 80309, USA

Peter L. P. Simpson, Department of Philosophy, Graduate Center, City University of New York, NYC NY 10003, USA

Jan Szaif, Department of Philosophy, University of California at Davis, 1 Shields Ave, Davis CA 95616, USA

Georgia Tsouni, Institut für Philosophie, Längassstrasse 49a, Universität Bern 3012, CH

Stephen A. White, Department of Classics, University of Texas at Austin, 2210 Speedway, C3400, Austin TX 78712, USA

1

Didymus' Epitome of Peripatetic Ethics, Household Management, and Politics
An Edition with Translation

Georgia Tsouni

Introduction

1. Authorship[1]

The work of a certain philosopher named Didymus figures among the numerous sources that Ioannes Stobaeus used to compile his anthology of ancient wisdom in the fifth century AD.[2] This evidence is supported by a lemma in Stobaeus' *Anthology* 4.39.28 (918.15–919.6 Hense) which is introduced by the words "From the Summary of Didymus" ('Ἐκ τῆς Διδύμου Ἐπιτομῆς). Since the part prefaced with these words appears also in the Peripatetic doxography of ethics in book 2, chapter 7 of Stobeaus' work (in the part where the Peripatetic conception of *eudaimonia* is treated), Didymus may be securely identified with the author of the whole doxographical piece on Peripatetic ethics entitled *Of Aristotle and the Other Peripatetics*

---

[1] The chapter on the authorship of the doxography is a slightly altered version from the corresponding section in Tsouni, "Peripatetic Ethics in the First Century BC: The Summary of Didymus," in Falcon A. (ed.) *The Brill's Companion to the Reception of Aristotle in Antiquity* (Leiden [2016]: 120–37).

[2] Didymus figures as one of Stobaeus' (philosophical) sources in the list of authors provided by Photius in his *Library* (cod. 167.114a).

on Ethics (Ἀριστοτέλους καὶ τῶν λοιπῶν Περιπατητικῶν περὶ τῶν ἠθικῶν) in Stobaeus' *Selections* book 2.[3]

Since the publication of Diels' *Doxographi Graeci*, the prevailing hypothesis has been that the author of the Peripatetic and Stoic doxographies in Stobaeus' *Selections* 2.7 is Arius Didymus, a Stoic philosopher contemporary of Augustus.[4] This Arius Didymus would be the same person as the Stoic Arius who appears in the so-called *index locupletior* of Diogenes Laertius,[5] and as Arius Didymus, the author of an epitome of Stoic philosophy referred to in Eusebius' *Preparation for the Gospel*.[6]

Although it has remained unchallenged for a long time, this hypothesis does not rest on evidence that is beyond dispute. In the *index locupletior*, the Stoic Arius (who on Diels' hypothesis is identical with the writer of the ethical doxography) is not listed as Arius Didymus, but only as Ἄριος without the accompanying cognomen. One could still argue that Eusebius provides a secure basis for the identification of Didymus with the Stoic Arius. However, there is a further complication: while Eusebius recalls Arius Didymus as the writer of an epitome of Stoic philosophy, he mentions only a certain Didymus as the author of a work on the doctrines of

---

[3] The title of the Peripatetic account of ethics in book 2 is elliptical and calls for comment. Sharples (2010) 111 translates the title "From Aristotle and the Other Peripatetics on Ethics." That translation invites comparison with the lemma in Stobaeus book 4, which translates "From the Summary of Didymus" (see above). Nevertheless, an alternative is preferred by Fortenbaugh, who points to the title of the account of Stoic ethics earlier in book 2. The syntax is quite similar (n.b., the use of double genitives, with which both titles begin, and the Stoic title makes explicit reference to opinions, *dogmata* [57.13–14]). Understanding *dogmata* in the Peripatetic title gives the translation "[The Opinions] of Aristotle and the Other Peripatetics on Ethics," which suits the doxography. That translation will appear in the text translation below on p. 15.

[4] See Diels *Doxographi Graeci*, Berlin: Weidmann (1869), 80. Diels followed Meineke on this point. Cf. Meineke *Ioannis Stobaei Eclogarum Physicarum et Ethicarum Libri Duo*. Leipzig, 1860, CLV. This hypothesis is taken for granted in most modern bibliography after Diels. See, for instance, Moraux *Der Aristotelismus bei den Griechen. Von Andronikos bis Alexander von Aphrodisias* Bd. I (Berlin, 1973), 259; and Hahm, "The Ethical Doxography of Arius Didymus," in *Aufstieg und Niedergang der Römischen Welt* 36.2, edited by W. Haase and H. Temporini (Berlin/New York: De Gruyter, 1990), 3047. The only exception known to me is Göransson, *Albinus, Alcinous, Arius Didymus* (Göteborg: Acta Universitatis Gothoburghensis, 1995), 203–18.

[5] The *Index locupletior* refers to a lost part of book 7 of Diogenes Laertius' text. See also the reference to the Stoic Ἄριος in Strabo, *Geography* 14.5.4.

[6] Eusebius, *Preparation for the Gospel* 15.15: Ταῦτα μὲν ἡμῖν ἀπὸ τῆς Ἐπιτομῆς Ἀρείου Διδύμου προκείσθω; ibid. 15.20: Τοιαῦτα καὶ τὰ τῆς Στωϊκῆς φιλοσοφίας δόγματα ἀπὸ τῶν Ἐπιτομῶν Ἀρείου Διδύμου συνειλεγμένα.

Plato (Περὶ τῶν ἀρεσκόντων Πλάτωνι συντεταγμένων) and refrains from using the full version "Arius Didymus."[7]

There is also the possibility that "Arius" has been falsely attached to Didymus in Eusebius as the result of scribal error. That is suggested by the *Suda* in which reference is made to an Academic philosopher Didymus with the cognomen Ateius who wrote "*Solutions of Plausible Arguments and Sophisms* in two books, and many other things."[8] He could provide an alternative authorship for the text, and one which would connect the writer of the epitome with the Academic *milieu*. Since I wish to keep the question of the authorship of the text open, I will refer to the writer of the doxography as Didymus, and not, as has been customary until now, Arius Didymus.

2. The Manuscript and Editorial Tradition

The anthology to which Didymus' *Epitome of Peripatetic Ethics* belongs was put together in the fifth century AD by Ioannes of Stobi and was dedicated to his son Septimius. The most important and oldest evidence stems from the ninth century, from Patriarch Photius' *Myriobiblos* or *Bibliotheke* (Bibl. Cod. 167), where among the 279 books read for the compilation of the *Library*, we read the title Ἰωάννου Στοβαίου ἐκλογῶν ἀποφθεγμάτων ὑποθηκῶν βιβλία τέσσαρα. We may assume that Photius had an archetype of the anthology written in the newly established minuscule from which the surviving manuscripts containing the Didymus' text derive. In addition, Photius drafted a catalogue listing the titles of the 208 chapters of the four books, which comprise the anthology, and also a list of the authors who were the sources of the material. Already from the beginning of the tradition, the material of the four books of the anthology was separated into two volumes,[9] which subsequently developed into two independent manuscript traditions, the more impoverished one of the *Eclogai* and the richer one of the *Florilegium*. It is suggestive that the oldest manuscript of the entire compilation (ms. Vindobonensis, dating from the tenth century) contains only the latter.

---

[7] Cf. also a reference by Clemens of Alexandria in *Stromata* 1.16.80.4 (perhaps to the same Didymus who appears to have written on Pythagorean philosophy as well).

[8] *Suda* s.v. "Didymus" (δ 871 Adler) reads as follows: Δίδυμος, Ἀτήϊος ἢ Ἄττιος χρηματίσας, φιλόσοφος Ἀκαδημαϊκός. Πιθανῶν καὶ σοφισμάτων λύσεις ἐν βιβλίοις β'. καὶ ἄλλα πολλά.

[9] See also Photius' comment that he read Stobaeus' work in "two volumes" (ἐν τεύχεσι δυσί), *Library* 167.112a.

The doxography of Didymus survives in the first strand of the tradition which comprises the first two books of the anthology, forming part of the so-called *Eclogai* [*Selections*]. The second book, which contains the Peripatetic doxography, has survived incomplete with 37 out of its 46 chapters missing. Only the first nine chapters of the second book survive in the manuscript tradition. Some of the missing parts of the second book (chaps. 15, 31, 33, and 46) have, however, been recovered from a fourteenth-century gnomology (Laurentianus plut. 8.22).

The two manuscripts on which the present edition is based (Farnesinus III D 15 and Parisinus Gr. 2129) belong to the group of the oldest known manuscripts of the *Eclogai* and go back to the same archetype. They are not earlier than the fourteenth century.[10] The older manuscript is Farnesinus (*F*) III D 15, written on occidental paper, stemming probably from the fourteenth century. A characteristic feature of the manuscript is that initial terms and titles are colored with a different ink from that of the rest of the text. *F* also contains a transposition of pages after the word θηριώδη in 119.24, which is reflected in other known manuscripts of the *Eclogai* as well.[11]

The second manuscript collated for the present edition is Parisinus (*P*) 2129, probably from the fifteenth century, written on oriental paper and now found in the Bibliothèque Nationale de France. For the later dating of the Parisinus speaks the handwriting characterized by many abbreviations and ligatures. There is evidence of a second hand, which introduced some corrections (this is noted with the siglum P^2 in the *apparatus criticus*). That *P* is independent of *F* is suggested not only by the presence of different readings in a number of cases but also in that it preserves the correct order of pages of the text in the place where *F* and dependent manuscripts witness a transposition of the text.

The *editio princeps* of the text of the *Eclogai* took place in the year 1575 by Gulielm Canter[12] (*Ioannis Stobaei Eclogarum Libri Duo: Quorum prior Physicas, posterior Ethicas complectitur Graece editi interprete Gulielmo*

---

[10] Both manuscripts were studied by means of digitized copies (jpeg files); copies for Farnesinus III D 15 were granted by the Biblioteca Nazionale di Napoli "Vittorio Emanuele III" (Laboratorio Fotografico) and for Parisinus gr. 2129 by the Bibliothèque Nationale, Paris, France. I point to the fact that my report on some readings of F and P depart from the one found in the Wachsmuth edition.

[11] Other known manuscripts of the *Eclogai* (Vaticanus gr. 201, Augustanus, Escurialensis) seem to derive from *F* since they contain the same transposition of pages after the word θηριώδη in 119.24.

[12] The *editio princeps* of the *Florilegium* dates back to 1536 (by the humanist Vittore Trincavelli).

Cantero. Antverp. Ex bibliotheca c.v. I. Sambuci). It contained the Greek text without apparatus criticus and a parallel Latin translation. This was superseded by the edition of Heeren, *Ioannis Stobaei Eclogarum Physicarum et Ethicarum Libri Duo*. Gottingae 1792–1801, the first edition of the text to add an apparatus criticus alongside a Latin translation. Heeren collated all the known manuscripts of the *Eclogai* (except Farnesinus III D 15) and proposed in some cases readings that made the text more intelligible. Subsequently Thomas Gaisford offered a new edition, *Ioannis Stobaei Eclogarum Physicarum et Ethicarum Libri Duo* (Oxford 1850), which in almost all cases adopted the text of Heeren and his apparatus. Meineke, *Ioannis Stobaei Eclogarum Physicarum et Ethicarum Libri Duo* (Lipsiae 1860–1864) offered a new text without, however, an *apparatus criticus*. The most complete and satisfactory edition of the text is the work of Curt Wachsmuth: *Ioannis Stobaei Anthologii libri duo priores, qui inscribi solent Eclogae Physicae et Ethicae*, volumen I (Berolini 1884). Wachsmuth was the first to take into account the readings of the oldest known manuscript of the *Eclogai*, namely Farnesinus III D 15. He also added an extensive *apparatus criticus* and adopted many corrections proposed, in both published and unpublished form, by Usener, Meuer, Spengel, and Trendelenburg.

My methodological guideline in this new edition has been the attempt to keep the readings of the two major manuscripts of the *Eclogai* and their order of the original text intact, whenever this is possible. The English translation of the text reflects this guideline. In the *apparatus criticus*, I have taken into account, apart from all the modern editions of the text of Didymus, also readings appearing in modern studies of the text, such as in Moraux's *Der Aristotelismus bei den Griechen*, Band I (Berlin, 1973). That said, I have tried to be judicious in reporting conjectures, thereby avoiding an inflated apparatus in favor of one that exhibits economy.[13]

3. Divergencies from Wachmuth's Edition

The textual divergencies of the present edition from Wachmuth's text (with the exception of changes in punctuation) are presented in the following table. The left hand column lists the readings found in the present edition and the right hand column lists what occurs in Wachmuth's 1884 edition.

---

[13] Throughout the preparation of the translation and the apparatus, I have profited greatly from the comments of Bill Fortenbaugh and David Sedley to whom I owe great thanks. I also thank Tiziano Dorandi for providing comments on editorial matters.

117.15	τὰ πρακτὰ	τὰ <φθαρτὰ> πρακτικὸν
118.1	καὶ <πρὸς> ταῦτα πεφύκαμεν	κατὰ ταῦτα πεφυκέναι
119.1	ἡμῶν	ἡμῖν
119.2	ὧν	<δι'> ὧν
119.8	ἐπιζητήσαιμεν	ἐπεζητήσαμεν
119.10	ἀπατώμεθα ... παραπέμπομεν	ἠπατώμεθα ... παρεπέμπομεν
119.11	ἐντυγχάνομεν	ἐνετυγχάνομεν
119.14	μόνως	δαιμονίως
120.12	δι' αὐτοὺς	δι' αὐτοὺς
120.17-18	<τὴν> ... φιλίαν ... αἱρετήν	ἡ ... φιλία ... αἱρετὴ
121.2	κατ' ἀξίαν	πρὸς ἀξίαν
121.3	ἐξελέσθαι	ἐξελεῖσθαι
121.7	νάμασι	νάματι
121.22	ἐπειδὴ	ἐπεὶ δὲ
121.24	αἱρετόν	αἱρετός
122.7-8	τὰ λεγόμενα	τὰ γινόμενα
123.1	ἄλλως	ὅλως
123.14	περὶ	ἐπὶ
125.22-23	ἐπειδὴ γὰρ	ἐπειδὴ δὲ
126.2	ᾠκειῶσθαι ... αὐτὴν	ᾠκείωται ... αὐτή
126.6	καὶ	κακῶς
126.16	αὐτῶν	ἁπάντων
126.20	προηγουμέναις	χορηγουμέναις
127.5-6	ὅ τε φιλόπατρις καὶ φιλοπάτωρ καὶ φιλοίκειος	τό τε φιλόπατρι καὶ φιλόπατορ καὶ φιλοίκειον
127.18-19	τῆς ὁρμῆς	ταῖς ὁρμαῖς
128.8	<ἀρετῶν> post ἄλλων	
128.16	ἀρετὴ	ἀρετῆς
128.27	ἐφ' ἑαυτοῦ	ἐφ' ἑαυτὸ
129.14	τὰς αὐτῶν χρήσεις	τὰς χρήσεις αὐτῶν
130.5	τελειότητα	τελείωσιν
130.19	προηγουμένην	χορηγουμένην
131.11	τῶν οὔτ' ἀγαθῶν οὔτε	οὔτε τῶν ἀγαθῶν οὔτε τῶν
132.2	πλεῖστον	τὸ πλεῖστον
132.8	προηγουμένην	χορηγουμένην
132.22	οὔτε	οὐδὲ
133.21	ἀλλ' ὅτε	ἀλλ' ὁπότε
Ibid.	προηγούμενον	χορηγούμενον
134.2-3	<οὕτως τὸν κακὸν τἀγαθὰ ἔχειν καὶ αὐτὸν βλάπτειν καὶ τοὺς ἄλλους> post ἄλλοις	
134.8	ἐπεὶ δὴ μὲν	ἐπεὶ δ' ἡμῖν

134.12	θεὸν εἶναι τὸ πρῶτον	θεῖον εἶναι τὸ πρῶτον
134.24	<γυμνάσια> ante ὑγιείας	
135.5	ἃς	ἂν
135.6	ἀγαθὰ	ἀγαθὸς
136.3	χρωμένοις	χρωμένους
136.24	εὐτυχίαν ... ἀθανασίαν	εὐψυχίαν ... ἀθαυμαστίαν
137.1-2	ὡς τὸ ζῆν	καὶ τὸ ζῆν
137.18	λογικόν	λόγον
138.2-3	<περὶ> τῶν ἀφανῶν	<ὑπὲρ> τῶν ἀφανῶν
138.15	ταῦτ'	ταῦτ'
139.13	μήτε	μηδὲ
139.23	δὲ	δὴ
140.20	<πλεονεξία, μειονεξία> post δικαιοσύνη	
141.12	οὔτε τὸν ἀνάλγητον	οὔτε τὸν ἀνάλγητον καὶ μηδενὶ μηδέποτε ὀργιζόμενον
141.20	ἀνελεύθερον	ἀπρόετον
143.10	διὰ τι τούτων	δι' ἕν τι τούτων
143.20-21	διὰ τοῦδε	διὰ τοῦτο δὲ
144.1	ἐπὶ	τινὶ
145.15	δοξαστικοῦ καὶ ἠθικοῦ	δοξαστικῆς καὶ ἠθικῆς
145.17	τοῦ δὲ διανοητικοῦ	τὴν δὲ διανοητικὴν
145.21	ἢ καλά	ἢ ἀγαθὰ καὶ καλά.
146.2	<ἡδονῶν καὶ λυπῶν> post φυγῇ	
148.4	ἄνθρωπος	ἄνθρωπος
148.6	γενέσει	γεννήσει
149.9	αὐτοῦ τε	αὐτοῦ τε οἴκου
150.13	αὐτοῦ τε	αὐτοῦ τε οἴκου
151.1	πολιτειῶν ἀρχὴν	πολιτείαν ἀρίστην
151.11	ἄνισα ἔχειν	ἄνισα, οἱ δὲ ἄνισοι ὄντες ἴσα ἔχειν
152.8	ἄπαν	ἁπάντων
152.11	πολιτικῶν	πολιτικὸν

The most important divergence from Wachsmuth's edition consists in the preservation of the word προηγούμενος in a number of cases. The word means not only what is primary in a chronological sense ("what comes first") but also what is primary in an evaluative sense, what is preferential in relation to something else. In Stoic ethical philosophy, the term acquired a special meaning applying to things or actions which have a higher selective value compared to things which are chosen only under special circumstances. Accordingly, in its adverbial use (προηγουμένως), the word denotes what happens "under normal or favorable conditions," as opposed to what happens in "special or exceptional circumstances" (κατὰ περίστασιν).[14]

In Stoicism the value priority expressed through the use of προηγούμενος signifies a relative value in comparison with the absolute value of moral goodness. For example, objects of desire which are sought on the basis of the natural process of "affinity toward oneself" (οἰκείωσις) and are thereby "according to nature" (κατὰ φύσιν) are deemed προηγούμενα in the Stoic Antipater's definition of happiness.[15] The higher selective value of certain objects of impulse grounds the priority of corresponding appropriate actions (καθήκοντα) as well. In this sense we encounter the word in an excerpt from Hierocles' *On Marriage* which survives in the fourth book of Stobaeus' *Anthology*.[16]

Didymus seems to have used the Stoic term προηγούμενος in order to convey Peripatetic teaching, and more specifically the priority of a (virtuous) life among a moderate amount of external goods. Wachsmuth in his 1884 edition thought that the word should be excised from the text: with the exception of its adverbial uses, προηγούμενος has been consistently replaced by χορηγούμενος in an attempt to make the text comply with surviving Aristotelian texts.[17] Wachmuth's inspiration were passages where Aristotle talks about the value of external goods for the attainment of the happy life and uses in relation to these external conditions the terms χορηγία, χορηγούμενος or κεχορηγημένος (deriving from the verb χορηγέω, meaning, in its more general sense, "to furnish" or "to supply with means"). Such texts include *Nichomachean Ethics* 1.1099a32–33: ἀδύνατον γὰρ ἢ οὐ ῥᾴδιον τὰ καλὰ πράττειν ἀχορήγητον ὄντα; and ibid. 1101a14–16: τί οὖν κωλύει λέγειν εὐδαίμονα τὸν κατ' ἀρετὴν τελείαν ἐνεργοῦντα *καὶ τοῖς ἐκτὸς ἀγαθοῖς ἱκανῶς κεχορηγημένον* μὴ τὸν τυχόντα

---

[14] For the adverbial form προηγουμένως as opposed to κατὰ περίστασιν, see Epictetus, *Diatr.* 3.14.7. For other instances of this terminology, see *SVF Index sub verbis*.

[15] Stob. *Selections* 2.75.11 W. = *SVF* 3.57: πᾶν τὸ καθ' αὑτὸν ποιεῖν διηνεκῶς καὶ ἀπαραβάτως πρὸς τὸ τυγχάνειν τῶν προηγουμένων κατὰ φύσιν. Cf. the phrase κατὰ προηγούμενον λόγον attributed to Zeno in Stob. *Selections* 2.84.21 W. = *SVF* 1.192: Τὰ μὲν οὖν πολλὴν ἔχοντα ἀξίαν προηγμένα λέγεσθαι, τὰ δὲ πολλὴν ἀπαξίαν ἀποπροηγμένα, Ζήνωνος ταύτας τὰς ὀνομασίας θεμένου πρώτου τοῖς πράγμασι. Προηγμένον δ' εἶναι λέγουσιν, ὃ ἀδιάφορον ὂν ἐκλεγόμεθα κατὰ προηγούμενον λόγον.

[16] Hierocles apud. Stob. *Florilegium* 4.22a22 (4.502.8–503.10 Hense): Οὐκοῦν ἔχομεν ἐν τοῖς περὶ οἴκων ἀποδεδειγμένον, ὡς τῷ σοφῷ προηγούμενος μέν ἐστιν ὁ μετὰ γάμου βίος, ὁ δ' ἄνευ γυναικὸς κατὰ περίστασιν.

[17] Still, the term has been preserved by Wachsmuth in the following passages: Τὴν δ' εὐδαιμονίαν ἐκ τῶν καλῶν γίγνεσθαι καὶ προηγουμένων πράξεων in 129.19–20 and 134.18–19: τελικὰ (sc. ἀγαθά) μὲν τὰς κατ' ἀρετὴν προηγουμένας πράξεις.

χρόνον ἀλλὰ τέλειον βίον. In *Politics*, book 7 (1323b40–1324a2), the participle κεχορηγημένος features in a definition of the best life for both the individual and the city: νῦν δὲ ὑποκείσθω τοσοῦτον, ὅτι βίος μὲν ἄριστος, καὶ χωρὶς ἑκάστῳ καὶ κοινῇ ταῖς πόλεσιν, ὁ μετ' ἀρετῆς κεχορηγημένης ἐπὶ τοσοῦτον ὥστε μετέχειν τῶν κατ' ἀρετὴν πράξεων ("Let us assume then that the best life, both for individuals and states, is the life of virtue, when virtue has external goods enough for the performance of actions according to virtue").

In Didymus' outline the word προηγούμενος underlines the importance of external goods for the attainment of the happy life by qualifying the use or activity of virtue which results in happiness. This becomes evident from passages in the doxography where the *telos* formula containing the word προηγούμενος appears next to other formulations of the final end. Thus, a προηγούμενος use of complete virtue in a complete lifetime (χρῆσιν ἀρετῆς τελείας ἐν βίῳ τελείῳ προηγουμένην) is in 130.19 equivalent to "the unimpeded use of virtue among things in accordance with nature" (χρῆσιν ἀρετῆς ἐν τοῖς κατὰ φύσιν ἀνεμπόδιστον). Also, in 132.8–9 the adjective qualifies the activity of virtue which takes place among "natural goods" and is for this reason preferable ("Προηγουμένην" δὲ τὴν τῆς ἀρετῆς ἐνέργειαν διὰ τὸ πάντως ἀναγκαῖον ἐν τοῖς κατὰ φύσιν ἀγαθοῖς ὑπάρχειν). The priority of a life supplied with external means is expressed again in 126.19–20 according to which the happy life is manifested in actions which are "primary as one would wish" (Ὅθεν ἐνέργειαν εἶναι τὴν εὐδαιμονίαν κατ' ἀρετὴν ἐν πράξεσι προηγουμέναις κατ' εὐχήν). It transpires that the use of the Stoic term προηγούμενος in this Peripatetic source follows upon that of "goods according to nature" (κατὰ φύσιν ἀγαθὰ) and is adjusted to the Peripatetic value theory. Contrary to the Stoics, the term προηγούμενος denotes the necessity of the presence of a category of goods (deemed "natural") for the attainment of happiness. The preservation of the manuscript reading is supported by the presence of the expression ἐν προηγουμένοις in formulations of Peripatetic happiness in other exegetical texts which postdate Didymus: these passages are found in Aspasius and Alexander of Aphrodisias,[18] and suggest, similarly to its use in Didymus, the need for the presence of "primary and choiceworthy conditions" for the attainment of complete happiness.

The case of προηγούμενος suggests that what informed Wachsmuth's edition was a belief that Didymus contaminated his Peripatetic material

---

[18] Alexander of Aphrodisias *Ethical Problems* 4.25 (p. 148.30–34 Bruns) and Aspasius (*Commentary on Nicomachean Ethics*, p. 151.11 Heylbut).

with alien terms, in a way that altered the original meaning of the text. The hermeneutical fallacy that underlies this is that the use of common vocabulary means also identity in doctrine. This however does not do justice to the spirit of the author of the doxography; he might not have intended to reconstruct the ethical teaching of the Peripatos according to modern (historical) standards, but may well have wanted to convey an updated view of Peripatetic ethics by use of terminology which had become in his time common currency.

Sigla

Codices

F	Farnesinus III D 15, Biblioteca Nazionale, Napoli, ms. chart. xiv saec.
P	Parisinus gr. 2129, Bibliothèque nationale de France, ms. chart. xv saec. (P^2 codicis *P* corrector)

Editiones et adnotationes ad textum

Arn.	Arnim, von H., *Arius Didymus' Abriß der Peripatetischen Ethik*, Akademie der Wissenschaften in Wien, Philosophisch-historische Klasse, Sitzungsberichte, Bd. 204, 3. Abhandlung, Wien, 1926
Cant	*Ioannis Stobaei Eclogarum Libri Duo*. Interprete Gulielmo Cantero. Ex bibliotheca c.v. I. Sambuci. Antuerpiae. 1575
Flor.	*Ioannis Stobaei* Anthologii Libri duo posteriores, qui inscribi solent Florilegium, recensuit O. Hense. Berolini, 1894–1909
Gaisf.	*Ioannis Stobaei Eclogarum Physicarum et Ethicarum Libri Duo.* Recensuit Thomas Gaisford, vol. II. Oxonii 1850
Görg.	Görgemanns H., "*Oikeiosis* in Arius Didymus," in W. Fortenbaugh (ed.), *On Stoic and Peripatetic Ethics: the Work of Arius Didymus, RUSCH* vol. 1, 1983, pp. 165–89
Heer.	*Ioannis Stobaei Eclogarum Physicarum et Ethicarum Libri Duo.* Editi ab Am. Hem. Ludov. Heeren Gottingae 1792–1801
Henk.	Henkel H., *Zur Politik des Aristoteles*, Stendal 1875

Madv.	*M. Tulli Ciceronis De Finibus Bonorum et Malorum. Libri Quinque.* Recensuit N. Madvig, Hauniae (Copenhagen) 1876
Mein.	*Ioannis Stobaei Eclogarum Physicarum et Ethicarum Libri Duo.* Recensuit Augustus Meineke. Leipzig 1860–1864
Meur.	Meurer H., *Peripateticorum philosophia moralis secundum Stobaeum enarratur*, Weimar 1859
Mor.	Moraux P., *Der Aristotelismus bei den Griechen. Von Andronikos bis Alexander von Aphrodisias*, Bd. I. Die Renaissance des Aristotelismus im 1. Jh. V. Chr. Berlin 1973
Mull.	Mullach F., *Fragmenta Philosophorum Graecorum*, vol. II. Paris 1867
Rass.	Rassow H., *Observationes criticae in Aristotelem*. Berlin 1858
Speng.	Spengel L., Review of Meineke in *Gelehrte Anzeigen*, hrsg. von Mitgliedern der kaiserlichen bayerischen Akademie der Wissenschaften. München 1850
Strach.	Strache H., "De Arii Didymi in Morali Philosophia Auctoribus," Ph.D. Diss. Göttingen 1909
Trend.	Trendelenburg F. A., "Über die Darstellung der peripatetischen Ethik beim Stobaeus. (Eclog. II. 7.)," in *Monatsberichte der Königlich Preußischen Akademie der Wissenschaften zu Berlin*, 1858, pp. 155–58
Ts.	Tsouni 2017
Usen.	Usener H., apud Wachsmuth 1884
Wachs.	*Ioannis Stobaei Anthologii* Libri duo priores, qui inscribi solent *Eclogae physicae et ethicae*, recensuit C. Wachsmuth. Berolini 1884
Wilam.	Wilamowitz-Moellendorff U. von, "Parerga," *Hermes* 14, 1879
Zell.	Zeller E., *Die Philosophie der Griechen in ihrer geschichtlichen Entwicklung*, III—*Die nacharistotelische Philosophie*. Leipzig 1880[3]

Auctores antiqui vel opera quae in apparatu occurrunt

Arist. *EN*	*Aristotelis Ethica Nicomachea*. Ed. I. Bywater. Oxford, 1894
Arist. *EE*	*Aristotelis Ethica Eudemia*. Eds. R. R Walzer and J. M. Mingay. Oxford, 1991

Arist. *Pol.*	*Aristotelis Politica.* Ed. W. D. Ross. Oxford, 1957
Arist. *MM*	Aristotelis *Magna Moralia.* Ed. F. Susemihl. Leipzig, 1883
Arist. *Virt. et Vit.*	Aristotelis *De Virtutibus et Vitiis.* Ed. I. Bekker. Berlin, 1831. Repr. 1960
Cic., *Ac.*	*Cicero Academica.* Ed. O. Plasberg. Leipzig, 1922
Cic., *Fin.*	*Cicero De Finibus Bonorum et Malorum Libri Quinque.* Ed. L. D. Reynolds. OCT, 1998
Cic., *Off.*	*Cicero De Officiis.* Ed. M. Winterbottom. OCT, 1994
Critol. fr.	Critolaus, *Fragmenta.* Ed. F. Wehrli. Basel/Stuttgart, 1967–69
Men. fr.	Menander, *Fragmenta.* Ed. R. Kassel and C. Austin. Poetarum Comicorum Graecorum (PCG), vol. VI.2. Berlin, 1983
Pind. *Nem.*	Pindarus, *Nemea.* Ed. H. Maehler (post B. Snell). Leipzig, 1971
S.E. *PH*	Sextus Empiricus, *Pyrrhoniae hypotyposes.* Ed. H. Mutschmann. Leipzig, 1912
SVF	*Stoicorum Veterum Fragmenta.* Ed. J. von Arnim, vols. I–III, Leipzig, 1903–24; vol. IV (indexes) by M. Adler
Theophr. fr.	Theophrastus, *Fragmenta.* Eds. W. W. Fortenbaugh, P. M. Huby, R. W. Sharples, and D. Gutas. Leiden, 1992 = FHS&G
TrGF	*Tragicorum Graecorum Fragmenta.* Ed. R. Kannicht and B. Snell. Göttingen, 1971–2004

Breviata

<αβγ>	littera suppleta/addenda
[αβγ]	littera spuria/eliminanda
add.	addidit
ap.	apud
cf.	confer
coni.	coniecit
corr.	correxit
del.	delevit

fort.	fortasse
fr.	fragmentum
ind.	indicavit
in mrg.	in margine
inser.	inseruit
iter.	iterat
lac.	lacuna
om.	omisit
secl.	seclusit
sec.	secutus
suppl.	supplevit
transp.	transposuit
vid.	vide

N.B. Section numbers (marked by W) as well as page and line numbers appearing in the right hand margin of the Greek text refer to Wachmuth's 1884 edition. Vertical lines in the body of the text mark line divisions in Wachsmuth's text. When a division involves dividing a work into two segments, that is indicated by the use of a hyphen in Wachsmuth. See, e.g., the division between 117.9 and 117.10. In the lefthand margin are my section numbers (marked by Ts). The line numbers in the apparatus to the text refer to Wachsmuth's edition.

Sec. 1 Ts   Ἀριστοτέλους καὶ τῶν λοιπῶν Περιπατητικῶν   Sec. 13W
                               περὶ τῶν ἠθικῶν   116.19

Τὸ μὲν οὖν ἦθος τοὔνομα λαβεῖν φησί ἀπὸ τοῦ ἔθους·
ὧν γὰρ ἐκ φύσεως ἀρχὰς ἔχομεν καὶ σπέρματα, | τούτων τὰς   117.1
τελειότητας περιποιεῖσθαι τοῖς ἔθεσι καὶ ταῖς ὀρθαῖς ἀγωγαῖς.
Διὸ καὶ τὴν ἠθικὴν ἐθικὴν εἶναι καὶ περὶ μόνα τὰ ζῷα γίνεσθαι
καὶ μάλιστα περὶ ἄνθρωπον. Τὰ μὲν γὰρ λοιπὰ ἐθισθέντα
οὐ λόγῳ ἀλλὰ τῇ ἀνάγκῃ | γίνεσθαι ποιὰ ἄττα, τὸν δ' ἄνθρω-   .5
πον τῷ λόγῳ πλαττόμενον ἐκ τοῦ ἐθισμοῦ, <τοῦ ἀλόγου>
μέρους τῆς ψυχῆς διακειμένου κατὰ τὸν λόγον. Ἄλογον δὲ
λέγεσθαι ψυχῆς μέρος οὐ τὸ καθάπαξ ἄλογον ἀλλὰ τὸ οἷόν τε
πείθεσθαι λόγῳ, ὁποῖόν ἐστι τὸ παθητικόν, τοῦτο καὶ τῆς ἀρε-
| τῆς δεκτικόν.   .10
    Τῆς γὰρ ψυχῆς τὸ μὲν εἶναι λογικόν, τὸ δ' ἄλογον· λογικὸν
μὲν τὸ κριτικόν, ἄλογον δὲ τὸ ὁρμητικόν. Τοῦ δὲ λογικοῦ
τὸ μὲν περὶ τὰ ἀΐδια καὶ τὰ θεῖα θεωρητικὸν ἐπιστημονικὸν
καλεῖσθαι, τὸ δὲ περὶ τὰ ἀν | θρώπινα καὶ τὰ πρακτὰ βουλευ-   .15
τικόν. Καὶ τοῦ ἀλόγου τὸ μὲν ὀρεκτικὸν τῶν ἐφ' ἡμῖν ἐπιθυμητικόν, τὸ δὲ πρὸς τοὺς πλησίον οἷον ἀμυντικὸν θυμικόν.
Ὥστε διττὸν εἶναι καὶ τῶν ἀρετῶν τὸ εἶδος, τὸ | μὲν λογικόν,   118.1
τὸ δ' ἄλογον, ἐπειδὴ καὶ <πρὸς> ταῦτα πεφύκαμεν, θεωρίαν
καὶ πρᾶξιν. Ὅθεν καὶ τὴν ἠθικὴν ἀρετὴν οὐκ εἶναι μὲν
ἐπιστήμην, προαιρετικὴν δὲ τῶν καλῶν ὑπάρχειν <ἕξιν>.
| Ἐκ τριῶν δὲ συμβεβηκέναι τὴν ἀρετὴν τελειοῦσθαι, φύσεως,   .5
ἔθους, λόγου. Τὸν γὰρ ἄνθρωπον διαφέροντα κατά τε σῶμα
καὶ ψυχὴν τῶν ἄλλων ζῴων διὰ τὸ μεταξὺ τῶν ἀθανάτων ὄντα
καὶ τῶν θνητῶν κοινωνίαν ἐξῆφθαι πρὸς ἄμφω, πρὸς μὲν τὰ
λογικὰ τῷ κατὰ τὴν | ψυχὴν θείῳ, πρὸς δὲ τὰ ἄλογα τῷ κατὰ   .10
τὸ σῶμα θνητῷ, κατὰ λόγον ἀμφοῖν τῆς τελειότητος ἐφίεσθαι.

116.21-22 Arist. EN 2.1103a17-18, 6.1144b4-9, EE 2.1220a40-b2, MM 1.1186a1-2   117.7-10 EN 1.1102b13-14, 28-31, MM 1.5.1185b12-13   117.11-12 EN 1.1102a27-28, 6.1139a4-5, MM 1.1185b4-5   117.13 EN 6.1139b23-24   117.11-15 MM 1.1196b16-18 118.9-10 EN 10.1177a15-16

116.19 Ἀριστοτέλους P in mrg. καὶ om. P   117.3 ἐθικὴν om. P   117.4 λοιπὰ om. P   117.5 ἄττα FP: ἄττα Heer.   δ' ante ἄνθρωπον om. P   117.6 ante μέρους add. τοῦ ἀλόγου Usen.   117.7-8 ἄλογον δὲ ... ἄλογον Heer.: λόγον δὲ ... ἄλογον F: λόγον δὲ ... λόγον P   117.9 post τοῦτο add. δὲ Heer.   117.13 ἀΐδια Speng.: ἴδια FP   117.15 τὰ πρακτὰ Ts.: τὰ πρακτικὰ FP: τὰ <φθαρτὰ> πρακτικὸν corr. Speng.   117.16 ἐφ' ἡμῖν Meur.: ἐν ἡμῖν FP   118.1 καὶ <πρὸς> ταῦτα πεφύκαμεν Ts.: καὶ ταῦτα
→

(The Opinions) of Aristotle and the Other Peripatetics on Ethics

He says that moral character (*ēthos*) receives its name from habit (*ethos*). For the things whose beginnings and seeds we have from nature are perfected through habits and the right upbringing. That is also why ethics (*ēthikē*) is the discipline of habits (*ethikē*) and occurs only in living beings and, above all, in humans. For other beings acquire their qualities by being habituated not by reason but by necessity, whereas human beings on the other hand are formed by reason through habituation, when the irrational part of their soul is disposed according to reason. The part of the soul which is called irrational is not the one that is absolutely deprived of reason but the one which can obey reason; of this kind is the emotional (part of the soul) and, as such, it is also capable of receiving virtue.

For the soul has a rational and an irrational (part); rational is the judging (part of the soul), irrational the impulsive one. The part of the rational (soul) which contemplates eternal and divine things is called scientific, whereas the one which is concerned with human things and actions is the deliberative. And of the irrational part, the one which desires things that are in our power is the appetitive part, whereas the one which is, as it were, defensive toward one's neighbors is the spirited (part). Therefore, there are also two kinds of virtues, the rational and the irrational, since we are by nature inclined toward both contemplation and action. That is also the reason why moral virtue is not a science but a disposition of choosing noble things.

And virtue is perfected through three things: nature, habit, reason. For as humans are different from other living creatures in body and soul by being between the immortal and the mortal, they form a community with both: with rational beings by the divinity of their soul and with the irrational by the mortality of their body; accordingly, they desire the perfection of both (i.e., body and soul).

πεφύκαμεν *FP*: επειδὴ καὶ ταῦτα πέφυκε μὲν κατὰ θεωρίαν καὶ πρᾶξιν *Heer.*: κατὰ ταῦτα πεφύκαμεν κατὰ θεωρίαν καὶ πρᾶξιν *Speng.*: κατὰ ταῦτα πεφυκέναι *Usen.* 118.4 *post* ὑπάρχειν *add.* ἕξιν *Wachs.*   118.11 τῆς τελειότητος *F*: τὴν τελειότητα *P*

Sec. 2 Ts   Καὶ πρῶτον μὲν ὀρέγεσθαι τοῦ εἶναι, φύσει γὰρ ᾠκειῶσθαι πρὸς ἑαυτόν· διὸ καὶ προσηκόντως ἀσμενίζειν μὲν ἐν τοῖς κατὰ φύσιν δυσχεραίνειν δ᾽ ἐπὶ τοῖς παρὰ φύσιν. | Τήν τε γὰρ .15 ὑγιείαν περιποιεῖσθαι σπουδάζειν καὶ τῆς ἡδονῆς ἔφεσιν ἔχειν καὶ τοῦ ζῆν ἀντιποιεῖσθαι τῷ ταῦτα μὲν εἶναι κατὰ φύσιν καὶ <δι᾽> αὕθ᾽ αἱρετὰ καὶ ἀγαθά, κατὰ δὲ τἀναντία τὴν νόσον καὶ τὴν ἀλγηδόνα καὶ τὴν φθορὰν διακρούεσθαι καὶ παρακλίνειν τῷ παρὰ φύσιν | ὑπάρχειν καὶ δι᾽ αὐτὰ φευκτὰ καὶ κακά. Φίλον .20 γὰρ εἶναι | ἡμῶν τὸ σῶμα, φίλην δὲ τὴν ψυχήν, φίλα δὲ τὰ 119.1 τούτων μέρη καὶ τὰς δυνάμεις καὶ τὰς ἐνεργείας· ὧν κατὰ τὴν πρόνοιαν τῆς σωτηρίας τὴν ἀρχὴν γίνεσθαι τῆς ὁρμῆς καὶ τοῦ καθήκοντος καὶ τῆς ἀρετῆς.

Εἰ μὲν γὰρ περὶ | τὰς τῶν εἰρημένων αἱρέσεις καὶ φυγὰς .5 μηδεμία συνέβαινε πλάνη καθάπαξ ἀλλὰ τῶν μὲν ἀγαθῶν ἐπήβολοι τῶν δὲ κακῶν ἄμοιροι διετελοῦμεν ὄντες, οὐδέποτ᾽ ἂν τὴν ὀρθὴν καὶ ἄπταιστον ἐν τούτοις ἐπιζητήσαιμεν ἐκλογήν. Ἐπεὶ δὲ πολλάκις δι᾽ ἄγνοιαν περὶ τὰς αἱρέσεις καὶ φυγὰς | ἀπατώμεθα καὶ τὰ μὲν ἀγαθὰ παραπέμπομεν, τοῖς κακοῖς δ᾽ ὡς .10 ἀγαθοῖς ἐντυγχάνομεν ἀναγκαίως τὴν τῆς ἐπικρίσεως βέβαιον εἴδησιν ἐπεζητήσαμεν, ἣν καὶ συνῳδὸν εὑρόμενοι τῇ φύσει, διὰ τὸ τῆς ἐνεργείας μεγαλοπρεπὲς ἀρετὴν προσηγορεύσαμεν καὶ μόνως θαυμάσαντες ἔτι | μήσαμεν πρὸ τῶν ἄλλων ἁπάντων. .15 Τὰς γὰρ πράξεις ἀπό τε τῆς τῶν κατὰ φύσιν ἐκλογῆς καὶ τῆς ἀπεκλογῆς τῶν παρὰ φύσιν τὰς ἀρχὰς ἔχειν συμβέβηκε καὶ τὰ λεγόμενα καθήκοντα. Διὸ καὶ τάς τε κατορθώσεις καὶ τὰς ἁμαρτίας ἐν τούτοις καὶ περὶ ταῦτα γίνεσθαι. | Σχεδὸν γὰρ τὴν .20 ὅλην τῆς αἱρέσεως ὑπογραφὴν ἀπὸ τούτων ὁρμῆσθαι, καθάπερ ἐπιδείξω διὰ βραχυτάτων.

Sec. 3 Ts   Ὅτι γὰρ οὐ μόνον αἱρετὰ τὰ τέκνα τοῖς γειναμένοις ἐστὶ διὰ τὰς χρείας ἀλλὰ καὶ δι᾽ ἑαυτὰ γνώριμον ἐκ τῆς ἐναργείας· οὐδένα γοῦν οὕτως ὠμὸν εἶναι καὶ θηριώδη | τὴν φύσιν, ὃς 120.1 οὐκ ἂν σπουδάζοι μετὰ τὴν ἑαυτοῦ τελευτὴν εὐδαιμονεῖν τὰ

119.2–4 *Cic. Ac. 1.23*

118.13 ἐν om. Mein.   118.16 ἔφεσιν *Mein.*: φύσιν F: πόθον P   ἀντιποιεῖσθαι P²: ἀναποιεῖσθαι FP¹   118.17 δι᾽ αὕθ᾽ αἱρετὰ *Mein.*: αὐθαίρετα F: αὐθέρετα P   118.19 παρακλίνειν *Speng.*: περικλίνειν FP   118.20 δι᾽ αὐτὰ *Speng.*: διὰ ταῦτα FP   119.1 ἡμῶν FP: ἡμῖν *Meur.*   119.2 ὧν FP <δι᾽> ὧν *Usen.*   119.5 εἰρημένων FP²: ἐρημένων P¹   119.6 ἐπήβολοι FP: ἐπίβολοι *Heer.*   119.7 διετελοῦμεν FP²: διατελοῦμεν P¹   119.8 ἐπιζητήσαιμεν *Heer.*: ἐπεζητήσαμεν F   119.10 ἀπατώμεθα P: ἠπατώμεθα F

Didymus' Epitome of Peripatetic Ethics—An Edition with Translation 17

Sec. 2 Ts And first of all, they desire existence, for they have an affinity toward themselves by nature; that is why they experience a suitable enjoyment among things according to nature and are annoyed by things which are contrary to nature. For they take care to preserve their health and they desire pleasure and strive for life, because these things are according to nature and choice-worthy and good for their own sake. Conversely, they reject and avoid illness, suffering and destruction because they are against nature and in themselves to be avoided and bad. For our body is dear, and our soul is dear, and so are their parts and their capacities and activities dear; in forethought for the preservation of these lies the origin of impulse, appropriate action and virtue.

For if there were absolutely no possibility of error regarding our choices and avoidances of the things mentioned, and we were constantly achieving good things and never had to share in bad ones, we would never have sought the right and infallible selection among these. But, since frequently out of ignorance we are deceived in relation to the choices and avoidances and we dismiss good things while we approach bad ones as though they were good, we necessarily had to seek for a secure knowledge for our judgment; since we found it to be consonant with nature, on account of the magnificence of its activity, we named it virtue and admiring it as unique, we valued it above all other things. Our actions and the so-called appropriate actions have their origin in the selection of things according to nature and the rejection of things contrary to nature; that is why also the right actions and the mistaken ones occur among these and relate to them. For nearly the whole outline of (the ethics of) this school derives from these, as I will show very briefly.

Sec. 3 Ts For it is known from manifest facts that children are choice-worthy for their parents not only out of need but also for their own sake. At any rate, no one has such a cruel and brutal nature as not to take care of the happiness of one's children and of their

---

παραπέμπομεν *FP*: παρεπέμπομεν *Usen.*   119.11 ἐντυγχάνομεν *P²*: ἐνετυγχάνομεν *FP¹*   119.14 προσηγορεύσαμεν *F*: προσαγορεύσαμεν *P*   καὶ μόνως *Mein.*: καὶ μόνοι ὡς *F*: καὶ μόνοις ὡς *P*: καὶ μόνως, ὡς *Heer.*: καὶ νόμοις *Speng.*: καὶ δαιμονίως *Wachs.*   119.14–15 ἐτιμήσαμεν *Speng.*: ἐπετιμήσαμεν *FP*: εἴτ' ἐτιμήσαμεν *Mein.*   119.21 ὁρμῆσθαι *P*: ὡρμῆσθαι *F*   119.24 ἐναργείας *Usen.*: ἐνεργείας *FP*

τέκνα καὶ καλῶς ἔτι διάγειν μᾶλλον ἢ τοὐναντίον. Ἀπὸ ταύτης γοῦν τῆς φιλοστοργίας καὶ διαθήκας τελευτᾶν μέλλοντας τίθεσθαι καὶ τῶν ἔτι κυοφορουμένων φροντίζειν ἐπιτρόπους ἀπολείποντας καὶ κηδε- | μόνας καὶ τοῖς φιλτάτοις 120.5 παρατιθεμένους καὶ παρακαλοῦντας ἐπικουρεῖν αὐτοῖς καί τινας μὴν ἀποθνήσκουσι τοῖς τέκνοις συναποθνήσκειν.

Τῶν δὲ τέκνων οὕτως ἀγαπωμένων κατὰ τὸ <δι'>αὐθ' αἱρετόν, ἀναγκαῖον καὶ | τοὺς γονεῖς καὶ τοὺς ἀδελφοὺς καὶ .10 τὴν τοῦ λέχους κοινωνὸν καὶ τοὺς συγγενεῖς καὶ τοὺς ἄλλους οἰκείους καὶ πολίτας ὡς δι' αὐτοὺς φιλίας τυγχάνειν. Ἔχειν γὰρ ἐκ φύσεως ἡμᾶς καὶ πρὸς τούτους τινὰς οἰκειότητας· φιλάλληλον γὰρ εἶναι καὶ κοινωνικὸν ζῷον τὸν ἄνθρωπον. | Εἰ δὲ τῶν φιλιῶν τὰς μὲν εἶναι πόρρω συμβέβηκε, τὰς δὲ .15 προσεχεῖς ἡμῖν οὐδὲν πρὸς ἔπος· πᾶσαν γὰρ δι' αὐτήν αἱρετήν δ' ὑπάρχειν καὶ μὴ μόνον διὰ <τὰς> χρείας.

Εἰ δὲ <τὴν> πρὸς τοὺς πολίτας φιλίαν δι' αὐτήν αἱρετήν ἀναγκαῖον εἶναι, καὶ τὴν πρὸς ὁμοεθνεῖς καὶ ὁμοφύλους, ὥστε καὶ | τὴν πρὸς πάντας ἀνθρώπους. Καὶ γὰρ δὴ πάντας .20 | τοὺς σῴζοντας οὕτως ἔχειν πρὸς τοὺς πλησίον, ὥστε μὴ 121.1 κατ' ἀξίαν ἀλλὰ κατὰ τὸ δι' αὐθ' αἱρετὸν τὰ πλεῖστα δρᾶν. Τίνα γὰρ οὐκ ἂν ἐξελέσθαι θεασάμενον ἄνθρωπον ὑπὸ θηρίου καταδυναστευόμενον, εἰ δύναιτο; Τίνα δ' οὐκ | ἂν .5 ὁδὸν πλανωμένῳ μηνύσειν; Τίνα δ' οὐκ <ἂν> ἐπαρκέσειν ὑπ' ἐνδείας ἀπολλυμένῳ; Τίνα δ' οὐκ ἂν ἐπ' ἐρημίας ἀνύδρου νάμασι περιτυχόντα γνωρίσμασι διαδηλώσειν τοῖς τὴν αὐτὴν ὁδὸν βαδίζουσιν; Τίνα δ' οὐ τῆς μετὰ τὸν βίον εὐφημίας πολὺν ποιεῖσθαι λόγον; Τίνα δ' οὐκ ἀποστυγεῖν | τὰς τοιαύτας φωνὰς .10 ὡς παρὰ τὴν ἀνθρωπίνην οὔσας φύσιν: «Ἐμοῦ θανόντος γαῖα μιχθήτω πυρί», «οὐδὲν μέλει μοι, τἀμὰ γὰρ καλῶς ἔχει».

120.3–4 Cic. Fin. 3.65   121.12 TrGF fr. 513 Kannicht/Snell, Cic. Fin. 3.64

120.2 ἔτι διάγειν Wachs.: ἐπανάγειν FP   120.5 ἀπολείποντας P: ἀπολίποντας F   120.7 μὴν Mein.: μὲν FP   120.8 δὲ Heer.: δὴ FP   120.9 <δι'>αὐθ' αἱρετόν Wachs.: αὐθαίρετον FP   120.12 αὐτοὺς FP: αὐτοὺς Mein.   120.16 δι' αὐτήν P: δι' αὐτήν F   120.17 αἱρετήν Heer.: ἀρετήν F: om. P   δ': om. P   μόνον P: μόνη F   ante χρείας suppl. τὰς Wachs. post δὲ suppl. τὴν Ts.: ἡ Wachs.   120.18 φιλίαν ... αἱρετήν FP: φιλία ... αἱρετή Wachs.   120.19 ὁμοεθνεῖς P²mrg: ὁμοσθενεῖς FP¹ ὁμοφύλους Heer. ex cod. Aug: ὁμοφίλους FP   121.2 κατ' ἀξίαν Ts.: τὰς πράξεις FP: τὰς πράξεις χρείας ἕνεκα Speng.: κατὰ χρήσεις Heer.: πρὸς ἀξίαν Usen.   δι'
→

continuing to live finely after his own death, rather than the opposite. This affection (toward one's own children) at any rate is the reason why when about to die parents both draw up wills and make provisions for those who are not yet born by leaving them trustees and protectors and entrusting them to the persons most dear (to themselves), and calling on them to stand by them (the children), and even in some cases, when the children die, they die with them.

Since there is such an affection toward the children as being choiceworthy for their own sake, necessarily also parents and brothers and one's wife and relatives and other close persons and fellow-citizens are befriended for their own sake; for we have from nature certain kinds of kinship with them too, for humans are social living beings with affection for each other. If some of these affective relations happen to be a bit more distant or closer to us, that does not change what we say, as all of them are chosen for their own sake and not only out of need.

If affection toward one's fellow citizens is necessarily choiceworthy for its own sake, then so is that toward people of the same nation or race and, therefore, also that toward all human beings. For also all those who save (someone) have manifestly such a disposition toward their neighbors as to act in most of the cases not according to the merit (of each person) but according to what is choiceworthy for its own sake. For who wouldn't rescue, if one could, someone who is seen being overpowered by a beast? Who wouldn't indicate the way to someone who is lost? Who wouldn't assist someone who is dying through lack of means? And who, if he came upon a spring in the middle of a waterless desert, wouldn't use signs to reveal its whereabouts to those who travel the same route? Who wouldn't put much value on their good repute after death? Who wouldn't condemn violently the following sayings as being against human nature: "When I die, let the earth mix with fire," "Since my affairs are doing fine, I couldn't care less about anything else." It is obvious,

αὐθ'αἱρετὸν *Wachs.*: διαυθαίρετον *FP*   121.3 ἐξελέσθαι *FP*: ἐξελεῖσθαι *Speng.*
121.5 πλανωμένῳ *Mein.*: πλαζομένῳ *F*: πλανομένῳ *P*   ante ἐπαρκέσειν suppl. ἂν *Heer.*   121.7 νάμασι περιτυχόντα *F*: νάματι τυχόντα *P*: νάματι περιτυχόντα *Wachs.*
121.14 οὐδὲν *Kannicht/Snell v. supra, Wachs.*: οὐθὲν *FP*

Φανερὸν οὖν ὅτι πρὸς πάντας ἐστὶν ἡμῖν εὔνοια φυσικὴ καὶ φιλία τὸ δι' αὑθ' αἱρετὸν ἐμφαίνουσα καὶ τὸ κατὰ λόγον· «ἓν» γὰρ «ἀνδρῶν, ἓν θεῶν γένος ἐκ μιᾶς δὲ πνέομεν | ματρὸς ἀμφότεροι», τῆς φύσεως.

Ἐπειδὴ κοινή τις ἡμῖν ὑπάρχει φιλανθρωπία, πολὺ μᾶλλον πρὸς τοὺς ἐν συνηθείᾳ φίλους τὸ δι' αὑθ' αἱρετὸν φανερώτερον. Εἰ δ' ὁ φίλος δι' αὑτὸν αἱρετόν, καὶ ἡ φιλία | καὶ ἡ εὔνοια καὶ ἡ παρὰ πάντων τῶν τοῦ βίου κοινωνούντων καὶ <ἡ> παρὰ τῶν πλείστων ἀνθρώπων. Ὥστε καὶ τὸν ἔπαινον εἶναι δι' αὑτὸν αἱρετόν· οἰκειοῦσθαι γὰρ ἡμᾶς πρὸς τοὺς ἐπαινοῦντας. Εἰ δ' ὁ ἔπαινος δι' | ἑαυτὸν αἱρετὸς καὶ ἡ εὐδοξία· καὶ γὰρ οὐδὲν ἕτερον τὴν εὐδοξίαν κατὰ τὴν ὑπογραφὴν παρειλήφαμεν, εἰ μὴ τὸν παρὰ τῶν πολλῶν ἔπαινον. Ὥστε ταύτῃ μὲν τὰ λεγόμενα τῶν ἀγαθῶν ἔξωθεν ὅτι δι' αὑθ' αἱρετὰ πέφυκεν ἐπιδεδεῖχθαι σαφῶς.

Sec. 4 Ts   Πῶς οὖν οὐ πολὺ μᾶλλον τὰ περὶ | ἡμᾶς καὶ ἐν ἡμῖν, λέγω δὴ τὰ περὶ σῶμά τε καὶ ψυχήν. Εἰ γὰρ ὁ ἄνθρωπος δι' αὑτὸν αἱρετὸς καὶ τὰ μέρη τοῦ ἀνθρώπου δι' αὐτὰ ἂν εἴη αἱρετά, μέρη δ' ἐστὶν ἀνθρώπου ὁλοσχερέστατα σῶμα καὶ ψυχή. Ὥστε καὶ τὸ σῶμα δι' αὑτὸ ἂν αἱρετὸν εἴη. Πῶς γὰρ τὸ μὲν τοῦ | πλησίον σῶμα δι' αὑτὸ αἱρετόν ἐστιν ἡμῖν, τὸ δ' ἡμέτερον οὐκέτι; Ἢ πῶς ὁ μὲν πλησίον ἄνθρωπος δι' αὑτόν ἐστιν αἱρετός, οὐχὶ δὲ καὶ ἕκαστος ἡμῶν αὑτῷ δι' αὑτὸν αἱρετός;Ἢ πῶς τοῦτο μὲν, οὐχὶ δὲ καὶ τὰ μέρη τὰ τοῦ σώματος καὶ αἱ τῶν μερῶν ἀρεταί, καὶ αἱ τοῦ ὅλου σῶ | ματος ἂν εἶεν αἱρεταί; Ὥστε δι' αὐτὰ αἱρετὰ ἡμῖν εἶναι τὴν ὑγείαν, τὴν ἰσχύν, τὸ κάλλος, τὴν ποδώκειαν, τὴν εὐεξίαν, τὴν εὐαισθησίαν, καθόλου πάσας ὡς ἔπος | εἰπεῖν <τὰς σωματικὰς ἀρετάς>. Καὶ γὰρ ἄλλως οὐδεὶς ἂν εὖ φρονῶν δέξαιτο ἄμορφος καὶ λελωβημένος εἶναι κατὰ τὸ εἶδος, κἂν εἰ μηδεμία μέλλοι δυσχρηστία τὸ παράπαν ἐπακολουθεῖν διὰ

121.19–20 Pindar Nem. 6.1–2   122.16–20 Cic. Fin. 5.37, 5.46.

121.17 δι' αὑθ' αἱρετὸν Speng.: διαυθαίρετον F: τ' αὐθαίρετον P   121.20 ματρὸς Pind. γαστρὸς FP   121.21 φύσεως P: πίστεως F   121.22 ἐπειδὴ FP: ἐπεὶ δὲ Heer.: ἐπειδὴ δὲ Mein.   121.23 δι' αὑθ' αἱρετὸν Mein.: διαυθαίρετον FP   121.24 εἰ δ' ὁ F: ὁ δὲ P   αἱρετὸν FP: αἱρετός Heer.   122.1–2 παρὰ πάντων τῶν τοῦ βίου κοινωνούντων: iter. F   122.2 ante παρὰ suppl. ἡ Wachs.   122.3 δι' αὑτὸν P: δι' αὑτὸν F   122.7 ταύτῃ Heer.: ταύτην FP: ταῦτα Speng.: ταυτὶ Mein.   122.7–8 λεγόμενα FP: γινόμενα Usen.   122.8 ἔξωθεν Wachs.: ἐξ ὧν FP: ἔξω Heer.   δι' αὑθ' αἱρετὰ Mein.: δεῖ αὐθαίρετα FP   122.10 σῶμά τε F: σώματα P   122.11 δι' αὑτὸν P: δι' αὐτὸν F   122.12 δι' αὐτὰ P: δι' αὐτὰ F   122.14 δι' αὑτὸ P: δι' αὑτὸ F   αἱρετὸν →

therefore, that we have a natural goodwill and affection toward everybody, which reflects the things that are chosen for their own sake and are according to reason; for "there is one race of men and gods and we both draw breath from the same mother," namely from nature.

Whereas a common affection for humankind exists in us, it is clearer that the choiceworthy for its own sake exists to much greater degree when it is directed toward intimate friends. If the friend is choiceworthy for his own sake, then so are friendship and the goodwill of all the people, with whom we have intercourse in our life, as well as of the majority of people; therefore, praise too is choiceworthy for its own sake, as we have an affinity toward those who praise us. If praise is choiceworthy for its own sake, so is good reputation; for we understand by good reputation in this outline nothing else but praise from the majority of people. So in this way, it has been clearly shown that the so-called external goods are by nature choiceworthy for their own sake.

Sec. 4 Ts Aren't therefore the goods which relate to us and are inside us much more choiceworthy? I mean the goods related to our body and soul. If human beings are choiceworthy for their own sake, so also would their parts be choiceworthy. The most general parts of a human being are body and soul; therefore, the body also would be choiceworthy for its own sake. For how could the body of our neighbor be choiceworthy to us for its own sake, yet not also our own? Or how is our fellow human being choiceworthy for his own sake yet not also every one of us choiceworthy to himself for his own sake? Or how could this be so, yet the parts of the body and the virtues of the parts and of the whole body not also be choiceworthy? Therefore, health, power, beauty, swiftness of foot, good state of health, soundness of the senses and generally all the bodily virtues, so to speak, are choiceworthy for their own sake. And besides no well-judging person would welcome being misshapen and mutilated in appearance, even if no disadvantage at all would result from

εἴη *F*: ἂν εἴη αἱρετὸν *P*   τὸ *Heer.*: τοῦ *FP*   122.15 δι' αὑτὸ *P*: δι' αὐτὸ *F*   122.16 *ante* πλησίον *iterum* ὁ *F*   122.17 αὑτῷ *Wachs.*: αὐτῷ *FP*   122.19 ἀρεταί *Cant.*: αἱρεταὶ *FP*   122.20 δι' αὑτὰ *P*: δι' αὐτὰ *F*   123.1 *post* εἰπεῖν *suppl.* τὰς σωματικὰς ἀρετάς *Wachs.*   ἄλλως *P*: ἄλλος *F*: ὅλως *Usen.*   123.3 μέλλοι *Cant.*: μέλοι *FP* δυσχρηστία *F*: εὐχαριστία *P*

τὴν τοιαύτην εἰδέχθειαν. Ὥστε καὶ δίχα | τῆς δυσχρηστίας 123.5
εὔλογον φυγὴν φαίνεσθαι τοῦ αἴσχους. Εἰ δὲ δι'αὐτὸ φευκτόν
ἐστι τὸ αἶσχος καὶ τὸ κάλλος οὐ μόνον διὰ τὴν χρείαν αἱρετόν
ἀλλὰ καὶ δι'αὐτό. Ὅτι γὰρ ἐξ αὐτοῦ προσκλητικόν <τι> ἔχει
τὸ κάλλος ἐμφανές· πάντας γοῦν φυσικῶς οἰκειοῦσθαι τοῖς
καλοῖς χωρίς πά | σης χρείας· καὶ γὰρ πρὸς τὸ εὖ ποιεῖν αὐτοὺς .10
καὶ εὐεργετεῖν ἑτοίμως ἔχειν, ὅθεν δὴ καὶ δοκεῖν εὐνοίας εἶναι
παρασκευαστικόν. Ὥστε καὶ κατὰ τοῦτον τὸν λόγον τὸ μὲν
κάλλος τῶν δι' αὐτὰ αἱρετῶν ὑπάρχειν, τὸ δ'αἶσχος τῶν δι'
αὐτὰ φευκτῶν. Τὸν δ'αὐτὸν λόγον καὶ περὶ ὑγείας | εἶναι καὶ .15
νόσου καὶ ἰσχύος καὶ ἀσθενείας καὶ ποδωκείας καὶ βραδυτῆτος
και αἰσθήσεως καὶ πηρώσεως.

Sec. 5 Ts   Ὥστε εἰ καὶ τὰ σωματικὰ τῶν ἀγαθῶν δέδεικται δι'
αὔθ' αἱρετὰ καὶ τἀναντία τούτων κακὰ δι' αὐτὰ φευκτὰ καὶ τὰ
τῆς ψυχῆς ἀναγκαῖον μέρη δι'αὔθ' αἱρετὰ ὑπάρ | χειν καὶ τὰς .20
ἀρετὰς αὐτῶν καὶ <τὰς> τῆς ὅλης ψυχῆς. Τὴν γὰρ εἴσοδον ἡ
ἀρετὴ λαβοῦσα, καθάπερ ὑπεδείξαμεν, ἀπὸ τῶν σωματικῶν
καὶ τῶν ἔξωθεν ἀγαθῶν καὶ πρὸς ἑαυτὴν ἐπιστρέψασα καὶ
θεασαμένη, διότι καὶ αὐτὴ τῶν κατὰ φύσιν πολὺ μᾶλλον
τῶν τοῦ σώματος ἀρε | τῶν, ᾠκειώθη πρὸς ἑαυτὴν ὡς πρὸς .25
δι'αὐτὴν αἱρετὴν καὶ μᾶλλον γε πρὸς ἑαυτὴν ἢ πρὸς τὰς τοῦ
σώματος ἀρετάς· ὥστε παρὰ πολὺ τιμιωτέρας εἶναι <τὰς> τῆς
ψυχῆς ἀρετάς.

| Οὐ μὴν ἀλλὰ καὶ ἀπὸ τῶν προεφωδευμένων τοῦτ' ἄν τις 124.1
ἐπιλογίσαιτο. Εἰ γὰρ ἡ τοῦ σώματος ὑγίεια αἱρετὴ δι' αὑτήν, καὶ
πολὺ μᾶλλον ἡ τῆς ψυχῆς· <ὑγίεια δὲ ψυχῆς ἐστιν> σωφροσύνη
τῆς σφοδρότητος ἀπολύουσα τῶν | παθῶν ἡμᾶς. Καὶ εἰ ἡ ἰσχὺς .5
ἡ σωματικὴ τῶν ἀγαθῶν ἐστί, πολὺ μᾶλλον ἡ ψυχικὴ δι' αὑτὴν
ἂν εἴη αἱρετὴ καὶ ἀγαθόν· ψυχῆς δέ ἐστιν ἰσχὺς ἀνδρεία καὶ
καρτερία, εὐρώστους τὰς ψυχὰς κατασκευάζουσα, διόπερ ἂν
εἴη καὶ ἡ ἀνδρεία δι' αὑτὴν αἱρετὴ καὶ ἡ καρτερία. Κατὰ τὸ

123.6 δι'αὐτὸ P: δι' αὐτὸ F   123.7 δι'αὐτὸ P: δι'αὐτὸ F   123.8 αὐτοῦ Heer.: αὐτοῦ
P   προσκλητικὸν P²: προκλητικὸν FP¹   τι suppl. Heer.   123.13–14 δι'αὐτὰ ...
δι'αὐτὰ Speng.: δι'αὐτὸ ... δι'αὐτὸ FP   123.14 αὐτὸν F: αὑτὸν P   περὶ FP: ἐπὶ
Mein.   123.17–18 δι' αὔθ' αἱρετὰ Mein.: καὶ αὐθαίρετα FP   123.19 δι' αὔθ' αἱρετὰ
Mein.: δι' αὐθαίρετα FP   123.20 ante τῆς ὅλης ψυχῆς suppl. τὰς Wachs.   123.24
αὑτὴ Mein.: αὕτη FP   123.25 δι'αὐτὴν P: δι' αὐτήν F   123.27 ante τῆς ψυχῆς
→

such repulsiveness. So, even without considering any inconvenience, it seems to be reasonable to avoid ugliness. And if ugliness is to be avoided for its own sake, beauty is also to be chosen not only for its utility but also for its own sake; for it is obvious that in itself beauty has something attractive about it. At all events, everybody has by nature an affinity toward beautiful people apart from any profit, and is willing to benefit and do good services to them, whence the impression arises that beauty generates goodwill; so, according to this argument, beauty too belongs to the things to be chosen for their own sake, ugliness to the things to be avoided for their own sake. The same argument applies to health and disease and strength and weakness and swiftness and slowness and perception and handicap.

Sec. 5 Ts   Therefore, if the bodily goods have been shown to be for their own sake choiceworthy and their opposite evils to be avoided for their own sake, it is necessary also that the parts of the soul are to be chosen for their own sake and their virtues and those of the whole soul. For after virtue was introduced, as we showed, by the bodily and external goods and turned to view itself, because it too belongs to the things which are according to nature much more than the bodily virtues, it became akin to itself as to something choiceworthy for its own sake and more so to itself than toward the bodily virtues; therefore, the virtues of the soul are much more valuable (than the virtues of the body).

Not only that, but also from the things gone over before, one could reach the same conclusion. For if the health of the body is choiceworthy for its own sake, then much more is that of the soul; but the health of the soul is temperance setting us free from the violence of the affections. And if bodily strength belongs to the goods, even more would the strength of the soul be choiceworthy for its own sake and a good; but strength of the soul is bravery and endurance which strengthens souls. Therefore, bravery and endurance would be choiceworthy for their

---

suppl. τὰς Heer.   124.2 ἐπιλογίσαιτο FP: ἀπολογίσαιτο Heer.   124.3–4 ante σωφροσύνη suppl. ὑγίεια δὲ ψυχῆς Heer.   124.5 εἰ: om. P   ἡ σωματικὴ Heer.: ἢ σώματι FP   124.6 ἡ ψυχικὴ Cant.: ἢ ψυχῇ· καὶ FP   δι᾽ αὑτὴν P: δι᾽ αὐτήν F   124.9 αὑτὴν P: ἑαυτὴν F

| ἀνάλογον, εἰ τὸ κάλλος τὸ σωματικὸν δι' αὑτὸ αἱρετόν, καὶ τὸ τῆς ψυχῆς κάλλος εἴη ἂν δι' αὑτὸ αἱρετόν, κάλλος δὲ ψυχῆς ἐστὶν ἡ δικαιοσύνη· «τὸ» γὰρ «μηθὲν ἀδικεῖν καὶ καλοὺς ἡμᾶς ποιεῖ».

Sec. 6 Ts | Ὅτι τὰ τρία γένη τῶν ἀγαθῶν, τὰ περὶ σῶμα, τὰ περὶ ψυχήν, τὰ ἐκτός, ἀναλογίαν πρὸς ἄλληλα ἔχει καίτοι διαφέροντα.

Τὸν παραπλήσιον δ' εἶναι λόγον καὶ ἐπὶ τῶν ἀρετῶν διὰ τὸ δοκεῖν τὰ τρία γένη τῶν ἀγαθῶν ἐκ πλείστης | διαφορᾶς τῆς ἐν ἀλλήλοις ὅμως ἔχειν τινὰ πρὸς τὸν λόγον | ἀναλογίαν, ἣν καὶ δὴ πειράσομαι δηλῶσαι σαφῶς. Ὅπερ μὲν ἐν σώματί φαμεν ὑγείαν, τοῦτ' ἐν ψυχῇ καλεῖσθαι σωφροσύνην, ἐν δὲ τοῖς ἐκτὸς πλοῦτον· περιστέλλειν γὰρ τὰ πολλὰ τῶν ἁμαρτημάτων καὶ τοῦτον. | Ὅπερ δ', ἐν τῷ σώματι ἰσχύν, τοῦτ' ἐν ψυχῇ τὴν ἀνδρείαν, ἐν δὲ τοῖς ἐκτὸς τὴν ἀρχήν· ὅπερ δ' ἐν τῷ σώματι εὐαισθησίαν, τοῦτ' ἐν ψυχῇ φρόνησιν, ἐν δὲ τοῖς ἐκτὸς εὐτυχίαν· ὅ τι δ' ἐν σώματι κάλλος, τοῦτ' ἐν ψυχῇ δικαιοσύνην, ἐν δὲ τοῖς ἐκτὸς τὴν φιλίαν.

Sec. 7 Ts | Ὥστε τρία γένη τῶν ἀγαθῶν δι' αὕθ' αἱρετὰ ὑπάρχειν, τά τε περὶ ψυχὴν καὶ τὰ περὶ τὸ σῶμα καὶ τὰ ἐκτός· καὶ μακρῷ αἱρετώτερα τὰ περὶ ψυχὴν τῶν ἄλλων ἐπειδὴ καὶ ἡγεμονικώτερον καὶ αἱρετώτερον ψυχὴ σώματος. Δῆλον οὖν ὅτι τῶν τοῦ σώματος ἀρετῶν καὶ τῶν ἐκ- | τὸς αἱ τῆς ψυχῆς ὑπάρχουσιν αἱρετώτεραι. Ὑπεροχὴν ὁμοίως φερόμεναι στοχάζονται καὶ τῶν ἄλλων, πρῶτον μὲν ὡς δι' αὕθ' αἱρετῶν, ἔπειθ' ὡς χρησίμων πρός τε τὸν πολιτικὸν καὶ τὸν κοινωνικὸν βίον καὶ δὴ καὶ πρὸς τὸν θεωρητικόν. Παραμετρεῖσθαι γὰρ τὸν βίον ταῖς | πολιτικαῖς καὶ ταῖς κοινωνικαῖς πράξεσι καὶ ταῖς θεωρητικαῖς. Οὐ γὰρ φίλαυτον εἶναι τὴν ἀρετὴν κατὰ τὴν αἵρεσιν ταύτην, ἀλλὰ κοινωνικὴν καὶ πολιτικήν. Ἐπειδὴ γὰρ πρὸς ἑαυτὴν ᾠκειῶσθαι μάλιστα πάντων ἔφαμεν | τὴν ἀρετήν, δῆλον ὡς καὶ πρὸς τὴν

124.10
Sec. 14W
124.15
.20
125.1
.5
.10
.15
.20
126.1

124.12–13 Men. fr. 352 Kassel-Austin, S.E. PH 1.108

124.10 εἰ P: εἰς F   δι' αὐτὸ αἱρετόν P: δι' ἑαυτοῦτοαίρετόν F   124.15–17 *rubro scripta* F   124.15–16 περὶ σῶμα Meur.: περὶ σώματα FP   124.20 πρὸς τὸν λόγον *del.* Speng.   125.1–2 ἣν καὶ δὴ πειράσομαι δηλῶσαι σαφῶς. Ὅπερ μὲν ἐν σώματί φαμεν ὑγείαν: *om.* P   125.2 *ante* σώματί *add.* τῷ Mein.   125.3 ἐν P: εἰ F   125.4 περιστέλλειν P: περιστέλλει F   125.5 καὶ τοῦτον. Ὅπερ δ' Speng.: καὶ τοῦτο δ', ὅπερ FP   125.8 ὅ τι FP: ὅπερ Mein.   125.9 τὴν *om.* Heer.   125.10 δι' αὕθ'

→

own sake. Analogously, if bodily beauty is choiceworthy for its own sake, beauty of the soul would also be choiceworthy for its own sake, but beauty of the soul is justice; for "by not being unjust we become beautiful as well."

Sec. 6 Ts *That the three kinds of goods, those of the body, those of the soul and the external, are analogous to each other, although they are different.*

A similar argument applies to the virtues, because it seems that the three kinds of goods in spite of the great difference between them are nevertheless, according to the argument, analogous to each other, which I will attempt to show clearly. What we call health in the body in the soul is called temperance, and in external things wealth; for this too cloakes most defects. And what in the body we call strength, in the soul we call bravery and rule in external things. And what in the body we call soundness of the senses, in the soul we call practical wisdom and in external things good fortune; and the beauty of the body corresponds to justice in the soul, and to friendship in external things.

Sec. 7 Ts Therefore, there are three kinds of goods which are choiceworthy for their own sake, those belonging to the soul, those belonging to the body and the external ones; and the goods belonging to the soul are far more choiceworthy than the other ones, for the soul is more authoritative and choiceworthy than the body. It is clear, therefore, that the virtues of the soul are more choiceworthy than those of the body and the external (goods). Being superior to them in a similar way, the virtues of the soul aim at the others, first as being choiceworthy for their own sake, and then as being useful for the political and the social life and also for the contemplative one. For life is measured by political, social and contemplative actions. For according to this school, virtue is not selfish but social and political. Since we said that virtue is akin to itself more than to anything else, it is clear that it is necessarily also akin by nature to knowledge of the truth.

αἱρετὰ *Mein.*: δεῖ αὐθαίρετα *FP*: διαυθαίρετα *Heer.*   125.12 μακρῷ αἱρετώτερα *F*: μακροαιρετώτερα *P*   125.14 δῆλον οὖν ὅτι *Cant*: δῆλον οὖν τι *FP*   125.16 *post* στοχάζονται *suppl.* δὲ *Heer.*   125.17 δι' αὔθ' αἱρετῶν *Mein.*: διαυθαιρετῶν *F*   125.21 κατὰ *F*: καὶ *P*   125.22–126.2 ἐπειδή ... φυσικῶς αὐτήν *transp. Usen. post* πολιτικήν: *post* ἐναντίων *habent FP*   125.22–23 ἐπειδὴ γὰρ *FP*: ἐπειδὴ δὲ *Wachs.*: ἐπεὶ δὲ *Usen.*

τῆς ἀληθείας ἐπιστήμην ἀναγκαίως ᾠκειῶσθαι φυσικῶς αὐτήν. Τούτοις δ' ἀκολούθως καὶ τὰς μονὰς τὰς ἐν τῷ ζῆν παραμετρεῖσθαι ταῖς κοινωνικαῖς καὶ πολιτικαῖς καὶ θεωρητι | καῖς πράξεσι καὶ τὰς ἀφόδους ἐκ τῶν ἐναντίων. Ὥστε καὶ τοῖς σοφοῖς εὔλογον ἐξαγωγὴν ἐκ τοῦ ζῆν θεωρεῖσθαι καὶ τοῖς φαύλοις εὔλογον ἐν τῷ ζῆν μονήν· τοῖς γὰρ ἐκτελεῖν δυναμένοις τὰς κοινωνικὰς καὶ πολιτικὰς πράξεις καὶ θεωρητικὰς καὶ τῶν σπουδαίων καὶ τῶν φαύ | λων εὔλογον ἐν τῷ ζῆν εἶναι μονήν, τοῖς δὲ μὴ δυναμένοις εὔλογον ἐκ τοῦ ζῆν ἀπαλλαγήν.

Sec. 8 Ts Ἐπειδὴ μεγάλη τῆς ἀρετῆς ἐστιν ὑπεροχὴ κατά τε τὸ ποιητικὸν καὶ κατὰ τὸ δι' αὔθ' αἱρετὸν παρὰ τὰ σωματικὰ καὶ τὰ ἔξωθεν ἀγαθά, κατὰ τὸν λόγον οὐκ εἶναι | συμπλήρωμα τὸ τέλος ἐκ τῶν σωματικῶν καὶ ἐκ τῶν ἔξωθεν ἀγαθῶν οὐδὲ τὸ τυγχάνειν αὐτῶν, ἀλλὰ μᾶλλον τὸ κατ' ἀρετὴν ζῆν ἐν τοῖς περὶ σῶμα καὶ τοῖς ἔξωθεν ἀγαθοῖς ἢ πᾶσιν ἢ τοῖς πλείστοις καὶ κυριωτάτοις. Ὅθεν ἐνέργειαν εἶναι τὴν εὐδαιμονίαν κατ' ἀρετὴν ἐν πρά | ξεσι προηγουμέναις κατ' εὐχήν. Τὰ δὲ περὶ σῶμα καὶ τὰ ἔξωθεν ἀγαθὰ ποιητικὰ λέγεσθαι τῆς εὐδαιμονίας τῷ συμβάλλεσθαί τι παρόντα· τοὺς δὲ νομίζοντας αὐτὰ συμπληροῦν τὴν εὐδαιμονίαν ἀγνοεῖν ὅτι ἡ μὲν εὐδαιμονία βίος ἐστίν, ὁ δὲ βίος ἐκ πράξεως συμπεπλήρωται. Τῶν | δὲ σωματικῶν ἢ τῶν ἐκτὸς ἀγαθῶν οὐδὲν οὔτε πρᾶξιν εἶναι καθ' ἑαυτὸ οὔθ' ὅλως ἐνέργειαν.

Sec. 9 Ts Τούτων δὴ τοῦτον τὸν λόγον ἐχόντων, ἥ τε εὐεργεσία συστήσεται καὶ ἡ χάρις καὶ ἡ εὐχαριστία καὶ φιλανθρωπία | καὶ φιλοτεκνία καὶ φιλαδελφία καὶ πρὸς ταύταις, ὅ τε φιλόπατρις καὶ φιλοπάτωρ καὶ φιλοίκειος καὶ κατὰ τὸ προσῆκον ἥ τ' εὐκοινωνησία καὶ ἡ εὔνοια καὶ ἡ φιλία καὶ ἡ ἰσότης καὶ ἡ δικαιοσύνη καὶ πᾶς ὁ τῶν ἀρετῶν θεῖος χορός, οὗ τοὺς κατολιγωρήσαντας ἁμαρτάνειν φανερῶς | περί τε τὰς αἱρέσεις τῶν ἀγαθῶν καὶ τὰς φυγὰς τῶν κακῶν καὶ περὶ τὴν κτῆσιν καὶ περὶ τὴν χρῆσιν τῶν ἀγαθῶν, ὁμολογουμένως τε διασφάλλεσθαι περὶ μὲν τὴν αἵρεσιν παρὰ τὴν κρίσιν, περὶ

126.14–16 Didymus? ap. Stob. Eclog. 2, p. 46.10–13, Critol. fr. 19 Wehrli 126.19 Arist. EN 1.1098a16–17

126.2 ᾠκειῶσθαι FP: ᾠκείωται Usen.   αὐτήν FP: αὐτή Usen.   126.3 ἀκολούθως F: ἀκόλουθα P   μονὰς τὰς Heer.: μοναστὰς FP   126.5 τὰς ἀφόδους Heer.: ταῖς ἀφόδοις F: τὰς ἀφόδοις P   126.6 καὶ FP: κακῶς Wachs.   126.13 δι' αὔθ' αἱρετὸν Mein.: ἀεὶ αὐθαίρετον FP: διαυθαίρετον Gaisf.   126.16 αὐτῶν FP: ἁπάντων Usen.

→

In accordance with this, both remaining in life is measured by the social, political and contemplative actions, and the departure from it by the opposites. Therefore, both for wise individuals it is reasonable to consider departing from life, and for base individuals it is reasonable (to consider) remaining in life. For those—good and bad—who are able to accomplish social, political and contemplative actions, remaining in life is reasonable, while for those not able to accomplish such actions departure from life is reasonable.

126.5

.10

Sec. 8 Ts   Since virtue is far superior in respect to producing (happiness) and in respect to choiceworthiness for its own sake compared with bodily and external goods, in accordance with this, the final end is not jointly completed by bodily and external goods, nor is it the acquisition of them, but rather living in accordance with virtue surrounded by bodily and external goods, whether all of them or the majority and the most important of them. It follows that happiness is activity in accordance with virtue expressed in primary actions as one would wish. On the other hand, the goods belonging to the body and external goods are said to be productive of happiness by contributing something through their presence. Those who believe that they jointly complete happiness are unaware that happiness is a life, and life is completed by actions. None of the bodily and external goods is either an action in itself or an activity at all.

.15

.20

127.1

Sec. 9 Ts   For those who embrace this argument (as their own), doing good will be established and favour and gratitude and humanity and love for one's children and brothers and, besides these, people who love their country and their father and their relatives and, accordingly, good sociability and goodwill and friendship and equality and justice and the whole divine chorus of virtues. Those who neglect these are manifestly mistaken concerning the choices of goods and the avoidances of bad things and also the acquisition and the use of good things; as commonly agreed, people go wrong in choice because of their judgement,

.5

.10

126.18 ἢ πᾶσιν *F*: καὶ πᾶσιν *P*   126.20 προηγουμέναις *FP*: χορηγουμέναις *Wachs.*, *de verbo* προηγούμενος *vid. supra pp.* 7–9   127.1 πρᾶξιν *Cant.*: πρᾶξις *F*: πρᾶξεις *P*   127.3 τὸν λόγον ἐχόντων *P*: ἐχόντων τὸν λόγον *F*   127.5–6 ὅ τε φιλόπατρις καὶ φιλοπάτωρ καὶ φιλοικεῖος *FP*: τό τε φιλόπατρι καὶ φιλόπατορ καὶ φιλοίκειον *Wachs.* φιλοίκειος *Ts.*: φιλοικεῖος *FP*: φιλοίκειον*Wachs.*   127.9 οὐ *Heer.*: οὐ *FP post* κατολιγορῇ *lac.habet P*   127.10 περὶ *Heer.*: παρὰ *FP*   127.14 περὶ *Speng.*: παρὰ *FP*

δὲ τὴν κτῆσιν παρὰ τὸν τρόπον, περὶ δὲ τὴν χρῆσιν παρὰ τὴν ἀμαθίαν.

Περὶ | μὲν οὖν τὴν αἵρεσιν ἁμαρτάνειν, ὅταν τὸ μηδ' ὅλως ὂν ἀγαθὸν αἱρῶνται, ἢ τὸ ἧττον σφοδρότερον ἢ δεῖ. Τοῦτο δὲ περὶ τοὺς πλείστους ὑπάρχειν τὸ μὲν ἡδὺ τοῦ συμφέροντος, τὸ δὲ συμφέρον τοῦ καλοῦ προκρίνοντας καὶ τῆς ὁρμῆς ἀμέτρως προεκφοιτῶντας. Περὶ δὲ τὴν κτῆσιν, | ὅταν μήτε ὅθεν μήθ' ὅπως μήτε ἐφ' ὅσον χρὴ περιποιεῖσθαι ταῦτα προδιαλάβωσι. Περὶ δὲ τὴν χρῆσιν, ἐπεὶ πᾶσα χρῆσις ἢ πρὸς αὑτὴν ἔχει τὴν ἀναφορὰν ἢ πρὸς ἕτερον, ἐν μὲν <τῇ> πρὸς ἑαυτήν, ὅταν μὴ προσφέρωνται τοῖς πράγμασι συμμέτρως, ἐν δὲ τῇ πρὸς ἕτερον, | ὅταν τὸ κατ' ἀξίαν μὴ φυλάττωσι τοῦ πρέποντος. Εἰ δὲ περὶ ταῦτα ἁμαρτάνουσιν οἱ φαῦλοι, περὶ τὰ ἐναντία | πάντως κατορθοῦσιν οἱ σπουδαῖοι, καθηγεμόνα τῶν πράξεων ἔχοντες τὴν ἀρετήν.

Πάσαις γοῦν ὡς ἔοικε ταῖς ἀρεταῖς κοινὸν ὑπάρχειν τό τε κρίνειν καὶ τὸ προαιρεῖσθαι καὶ <τὸ> πράττειν. Οὔτε γὰρ ἄκριτον οὔτ' ἀπροαίρετον | οὔτ' ἄπρακτον εἶναι τὴν ἀρετήν, ἀλλὰ τὴν μὲν φρόνησιν ἐξάρχειν ὥσπερ ἡγεμονικὴν οὖσαν καὶ τῶν ὑφ' ἑαυτὴν καὶ τῶν ὑπὸ τὰς ἄλλας αἱρετῶν καὶ φευκτῶν καὶ πρακτῶν καὶ οὐ πρακτῶν καὶ τῶν μᾶλλον καὶ ἧττον· τῶν δ' ἄλλων <ἀρετῶν> ἑκάστην ἀποτέμνεσθαι μόνα τὰ καθ' ἑαυτήν.

| *Περὶ ἀρετῆς*

Ἀρετὴν δ' ὠνομάσθαι τὴν ἀρίστην διάθεσιν ἢ καθ' ἣν ἄριστα διάκειται τὸ ἔχον. Τοῦτο δ' ἐκ τῆς ἐπαγωγῆς δῆλον· σκυτοτόμου γὰρ ἀρετὴν λέγεσθαι καθ' ἣν ἀποτελεῖν ἄριστον ὑπόδημα δύναται, καὶ οἰκοδόμου καθ' ἣν | ἄριστα διάκειται πρὸς οἰκοδόμησιν οἰκίας καλῆς. Ὅτι μὲν τὸ ἄριστα διατιθέναι ἐστὶν ἀρετὴ ὁμολογούμενόν ἐστι.

Δύο δ' ὥσπερ ἀρχὰς τῶν ἀρετῶν ὑπάρχειν, τὸν λόγον καὶ τὸ πάθος. Ταῦτα δὲ ὁτὲ μὲν ἀλλήλοις ὁμονοητικῶς συμφωνεῖν,

---

128.10–15 *Arist. EE* 2.1218b37–1219a5, 1219a20–23   128.17–18 *MM* 2.1206b17–29

127.15 αἵρεσιν *Herr.*: χρῆσιν *FP*   127.16 ἧττον *P*: ἧττον *F*   ἢ δεῖ *Gaisf.*: ἤδει *FP*: ἤδη *Cant.*   127.18–19 τῆς ὁρμῆς *FP*: ταῖς ὁρμαῖς *Usen.*   127.19 περὶ *Speng.*: παρὰ *FP*   127.20–21 περιποιεῖσθαι *P*: περι ποιεῖσθαι *F*   127.21 περὶ *Speng.*: παρὰ *FP*   127.22 αὑτὴν *Heer.*: αὐτὸν *FP*   127.23 ἐν *P*: εἰ *F*   ante πρὸς suppl. τῇ *Heer.* ἑαυτήν *Heer.*: ἑαυτόν *FP*   127.26 ταῦτα *Speng.*: αὐτὰ *FP*   128.3 ante προαιρεῖσθαι om. τὸ *F*   προαιρεῖσθαι *F*: αἱρεῖσθαι *P*   128.4 ante πράττειν suppl. τὸ *Heer.*   128.8 post ἄλλων suppl. ἀρετῶν *Ts.*   128.9 καθ' ἑαυτήν *P*: καθ' αὑτήν *F*   128.10

in acquisition because of their character and in use because of their ignorance.

They fail in relation to choice when they choose something that is not good at all, or something less good with excessive eagerness. For the majority of people, this is the case when they prefer pleasant things rather than useful and useful rather than noble, and when they proceed impulsively without measure. They fail in relation to acquisition when they don't distinguish beforehand from where, how or to what extent they should accumulate such things. Regarding use, because of the fact that every use is referred to itself or to something else, when the use refers to itself, they fail when they don't refer to the things in due measure; when the use refers to something else, (they fail) when they don't preserve appropriateness according to merit. And if base people fail in these cases, excellent people invariably succeed concerning their opposites, having virtue as guide for their actions.

It seems at any rate that judging and choosing and acting are common to all virtues. For virtue is not lacking judgement, choice or action, but practical wisdom being as it were the leader among them, governs both the things subject to itself and those subject to the other virtues, namely the things to be sought and avoided, to be done or not, and which of them are more or less so (than others); each of the other virtues, on the contrary, picks out only the things that concern it.

Sec. 10 Ts *On Virtue* Sec. 15 W

Virtue is called the best disposition or that on account of which the possessor is best disposed. This is obvious from induction: for the virtue of the shoemaker is called that which enables him to make the best shoe, and (the virtue) of the builder that on account of which he is best disposed to build a fine house. That disposing things in the best way is virtue is agreed upon.

And there are two, as it were, principles of the virtues, reason and emotion; these two sometimes are concordant being in agreement with each other, and sometimes are discordant engaging in civil war, the reason for their opposition being

περὶ ἀρετῆς: *titulum in rubro mrg. F, de titulo vid. Fortenbaugh infra ch. 3 n. 4, 21* 128.11 ὠνομάσθαι *FP:* ὀνομάζεσθαι *Cant.* 128.16 *ante* τὸ ἄριστα *suppl.* οὖν *Cant.* τὸ *Speng.:* τὰ *FP* διατιθέναι *FP:* διατεθῆναι *Cant.:* διατιθὲν *Arn.(1926:14)* ἀρετὴ *FP:* ἀρετῆς *Speng.* 128.18 ὁμονοητικῶς *F:* ὁμονοηκῶς *P*

ὁτὲ δὲ στασιαστικῶς διαφωνεῖν· τὴν δ᾽ ἀντί- | ταξιν αὐτῶν .20
γίνεσθαι δι᾽ ἡδονὰς καὶ λύπας. Τὴν μὲν οὖν τοῦ λόγου νίκην
ἀπὸ τοῦ κράτους παρωνύμως ἐγκράτειαν ἐπωνυμίαν ἔχειν,
τὴν δὲ τοῦ ἀλόγου διὰ τὸ τῆς ὁρμῆς ἀπειθὲς ἀκρασίαν· τὴν δ᾽
ἀμφοῖν ἁρμονίαν καὶ συμφωνίαν ἀρετήν, τοῦ μὲν ἄγοντος ἐφ᾽
ὃ δεῖ, τοῦ δ᾽ | ἑπομένου πειθηνίως. .25

Sec. 11 Ts *Περὶ αἱρετῶν καὶ φευκτῶν* Sec. 16W

Αἱρετὸν δὲ λέγεσθαι τὸ ὁρμὴν ἐφ᾽ ἑαυτοῦ κινοῦν, | 129.1
φευκτὸν δὲ τὸ ἀφ᾽ αὑτοῦ, ὅταν ὁ λόγος σύμψηφος ᾖ. Καθάπερ
γὰρ τὸ βουλητὸν κατὰ τὴν βούλησιν ἔχειν τὴν ἐπωνυμίαν
ταύτην, οὕτως καὶ τὸ αἱρετὸν κατὰ τὴν αἵρεσιν. Τὸ δ᾽ αἱρετὸν
καὶ ἀγαθὸν ταὐτὸν ἐδόκει τοῖς ἀρχαίοις | εἶναι. Τὸ γοῦν .5
ἀγαθὸν ὑπογράφοντες οὕτως ἀφωρίζοντο· «ἀγαθόν ἐστιν οὗ
πάντ᾽ ἐφίεται».

Τῶν δ᾽ ἀγαθῶν ἔλεγον τὰ μὲν δι᾽ ἡμᾶς αἱρετὰ ὑπάρχειν,
τὰ δὲ διὰ τοὺς πλησίον· τῶν δὲ δι᾽ ἡμᾶς τὰ μὲν καλά, τὰ δ᾽
ἀναγκαῖα. Καλὰ μὲν τάς τε ἀρετὰς καὶ τὰς ἐνεργείας τὰς
| ἀπ᾽ αὐτῶν, φρόνησίν τε καὶ τὸ φρονεῖν καὶ δικαιοσύνην .10
καὶ τὸ δικαιοπραγεῖν καὶ κατὰ τὸ ἀνάλογον ἐπὶ τῶν ἄλλων·
ἀναγκαῖα δὲ τό τε ζῆν καὶ τὰ πρὸς τοῦτο συντείνοντα καὶ τὴν
τῶν ποιητικῶν ἔχοντα χώραν, οἷον τό τε σῶμα καὶ τὰ τούτου
μέρη καὶ τὰς αὐτῶν χρήσεις, καὶ τῶν ἐκτὸς | λεγομένων .15
εὐγένειαν, πλοῦτον, δόξαν, εἰρήνην, ἐλευθερίαν, φιλίαν, τούτων
γὰρ ἕκαστον συμβάλλεσθαί τι πρὸς τὴν τῆς ἀρετῆς χρῆσιν.

Sec. 12 Ts *Ἐκ τίνων ἡ εὐδαιμονία* Sec. 17W

Τὴν δ᾽ εὐδαιμονίαν ἐκ τῶν καλῶν γίνεσθαι καὶ |
προηγουμένων πράξεων· διὸ καὶ δι᾽ ὅλων εἶναι καλήν, καθάπερ .20
καὶ τὴν ἐν τοῖς αὐλοῖς ἐνέργειαν δι᾽ ὅλων ἔντεχνον. Οὐ γὰρ
ἐκβιβάζειν τὴν παράληψιν τῶν | ὑλικῶν τῆς εἰλικρινείας τοῦ 130.1
καλοῦ τὴν εὐδαιμονίαν, ὡς οὐδὲ τὴν τῆς ἰατρικῆς ἔντεχνον
δι᾽ ὅλων ἐνέργειαν τὴν τῶν ὀργάνων χρῆσιν. Πᾶσαν μὲν
γὰρ πρᾶξιν ἐνέργειαν εἶναί τινα ψυχῆς. Ἐπεὶ δ᾽ ὁ πράττων

129.1 *MM* 2.1206b25–26 129.6 Arist. *EN* 1.1094a2–3 129.19–130.12 iterat. in Stob. flor. 4.39.28

128.26 titulum in rubro. F de titulo vid. Fortenbaugh infra ch. 3 n. 29 128.27 ἑαυτοῦ F: ἑτοῦ P: ἑαυτὸ Cant. 129.1 ἦ Heer.: ἢ FP 129.4 ἐδόκει F: δοκεῖ P 129.5 ἀφωρίζοντο F: ἀφορίζοντο P 129.11 κατὰ τὸ ἀνάλογον F: κατὰ τὸν ἀνάλογον P 129.12 δὲ Heer.: τε FP 129.14 τὰς αὐτῶν χρήσεις Speng.: καὶ τὰς αὐτῶν καὶ τὰς →

pleasures and pains. The victory of reason gets its name from control (*kratos*) and that is why it is called self-control (*enkrateia*), whereas that of the irrational part because of the disobedience of the impulse (is called) lack of control (*akrasia*). The harmony and concordance of both is called virtue, the one of them (i.e., the rational part) leading to the right destination, the other (i.e., the irrational part) following obediently.

Sec. 11 Ts *On the Things to be Chosen and Avoided* Sec. 16W

That which sets in motion an impulse toward itself is said to be the object of choice, and (that which sets in motion an impulse) away from itself when reason agrees is said to be the object of avoidance. Just as that which is to be wished for, gets this name from wish, in the same way the thing to be chosen gets this name from choice. The choiceworthy and the good seemed to be the same thing to the ancients. At any rate, in describing the good in outline they used to give the following definition: "good is that which everything desires."

They used to say that among the goods some are to be chosen for our own sake, and some for the sake of our neighbours; and from the ones (chosen) for our own sake, some are noble and some necessary. Noble are the virtues and the activities deriving from them, practical wisdom and being prudent and justice and doing just deeds and analogously in the other cases. Necessary are living and the things that are directed toward that and belong among the things that are productive, like the body and its parts and their uses; and of the so-called external goods nobility, wealth, repute, peace, freedom, friendship, for each of these contributes something to the use of virtue.

Sec. 12 Ts *What brings about happiness* Sec. 17W

Happiness is brought about through noble and primary actions; that is why it is wholly noble in the same way that the activity of the flutes is wholly artistic. For the use of materials does not deprive happiness of the purity of nobility, just as the use of tools (does not deprive) medicine of its wholly artistic activity. For every action is a certain activity of soul. If the agent uses certain things for the fulfilment of his purpose, we shouldn't consider these parts of the activity, although each one

χρήσεις *FP*: καὶ τὰς αὐτῶν καλὰς χρήσεις *Heer.*: τὰς χρήσεις αὐτῶν *Wachs.* 129.18
titulum in rubro *F* 130.1 post ὑλικῶν add. ἀρχῶν *flor.*

συγχρῆταί τισι | πρὸς τὴν τελειότητα τῆς προθέσεως, μέρη 130.5
ταῦτα οὐ χρὴ νομίζειν τῆς ἐνεργείας, καίτοι γε ἐπιζητούσης
ἑκατέρας τῶν εἰρημένων <τεχνῶν> ἑκάτερον, οὐ μὴν ὡς μέρος,
ὡς δὲ ποιητικὸν τῆς τέχνης. Τὰ γὰρ ὧν ἄνευ πράττειν ὁτιοῦν
ἀδύνατον, μέρη τῆς ἐνεργείας λέγειν οὐκ ὀρθόν. Τὸ μὲν γὰρ
| μέρος ἐπινοεῖσθαι κατὰ τὸ συμπληρωτικὸν εἶναι τοῦ ὅλου, .10
τὰ δ' ὧν οὐκ ἄνευ κατὰ τὸ ποιητικὸν τῷ φέρειν καὶ συνεργεῖν
εἰς τὸ τέλος.

Sec. 13 Ts *Πόσα μέρη τοῦ ἀγαθοῦ· καὶ περὶ σκοποῦ* Sec. 18W

| Διαιρεῖσθαι δὲ τἀγαθὸν εἴς τε τὸ καλὸν καὶ εἰς τὸ .15
συμφέρον καὶ εἰς τὸ ἡδύ· καὶ τῶν μὲν κατὰ μέρος πράξεων
τούτους εἶναι σκοπούς· τὸ δ' ἐκ πάντων αὐτῶν εὐδαιμονίαν.
Εὐδαιμονίαν δ' εἶναι «χρῆσιν ἀρετῆς τελείας ἐν βίῳ τελείῳ
προηγουμένην» ἢ «ζωῆς τελείας ἐνέρ- | γειαν κατ' ἀρετήν» .20
ἢ «χρῆσιν ἀρετῆς ἐν τοῖς κατὰ φύσιν ἀνεμπόδιστον». Τὸ δ'
αὐτὸ καὶ τέλος ὑπάρχειν. Εἰ δὲ τὸ μὲν εὐδαιμονεῖν τέλος, ἡ
δ' εὐδαιμονία λέγεται σκοπὸς καὶ ὁ μὲν πλοῦτος ἀγαθόν, τὸ
δὲ πλουτεῖν | ὧν χρή, τοῖς μὲν οὕτω διορίζουσι τῆς ἀκριβείας 131.1
τῶν ὀνομάτων χάριν· ἀκολουθητέον μέντοι τῇ τῶν ἀρχαίων
συνηθείᾳ καὶ λεκτέον τέλος εἶναι «οὗ χάριν πάντα πράττομεν
αὐτὸ δὲ οὐδενός», ἢ «τὸ ἔσχατον τῶν ὀρεκτῶν», ἢ | «τὸ κατ' 5
ἀρετὴν ζῆν ἐν ἀγαθοῖς τοῖς περὶ σῶμα καὶ τοῖς ἔξωθεν ἢ πᾶσιν
ἢ τοῖς πλείστοις καὶ κυριωτάτοις».

Τοῦτο δὲ μέγιστον ὂν τῶν ἀγαθῶν καὶ τελειότατον ἐκ τῶν
ἄλλων ἁπάντων ὑπηρετεῖσθαι. Τὰ μὲν γὰρ συμβαλλόμενα
πρὸς αὐτὸ τῶν ἀγαθῶν ὁμολογουμένως χρὴ λέγειν, τὰ δ'
ἐναν- | τιούμενα <αὐτῷ τῶν κακῶν, τὰ δὲ μήτε συμβαλλόμενα .10
μήτε ἐναντιούμενα > τῶν οὔτ' ἀγαθῶν οὔτε κακῶν ἀλλὰ
τῶν ἀδιαφόρων. Οὐ πᾶσαν δὲ καλὴν πρᾶξιν εὐδαιμονικὴν
ὑπάρχειν.

«Τελείας» δ' εἶπον ἀρετῆς χρῆσιν τὴν εὐδαιμονίαν, | ὅτι .15
τῶν ἀρετῶν τὰς μὲν ἔλεγον εἶναι τελείας, τὰς δὲ ἀτελεῖς·
τελείας μὲν τὴν τε δικαιοσύνην καὶ τὴν καλοκαγαθίαν· ἀτελεῖς

130.15–16 *EN 2.1104b30–31* 130.18–19 *EN 1.1100a4–5, Cic. Fin. 2.19* 130.19–20 *Arist. EE 2.1219a38–39* 130.20–21 *Pol. 4.1295a36–37* 131.3–4 *Arist. EN 1.1094a18–19* 131.14 *Didym. ap. Stob. Eclog. 2.130.18–19 W.*

130.5 τελειότητα *FP*: τελείωσιν *Wachs.* ante χρὴ om. οὐ *flor.* 130.7 *post* εἰρημένων *suppl.* τεχνῶν *Speng.* οὐ μὴν *iterum* P ὡς δὲ *flor.*: οὐδὲ FP 130.10 εἶναι *om. Flor.*

→

of the crafts mentioned needs each thing, not however as a part but as productive of the craft. The things that are necessary for any kind of action shouldn't be called parts of the activity; for the part is thought of as completing the whole, whereas the necessary things (are thought of) as productive, because they conduce and contribute toward the end.

Sec. 13 Ts *How Many are the Parts of Good; and on the Goal* Sec. 18W

The good is divided into the noble and the useful and the pleasant; And these are the goals of the particular actions, whereas the composite of all of them is happiness. Happiness is "the primary use of complete virtue during a complete lifetime" or "the activity of a complete life according to virtue" or "the unimpeded use of virtue among things in accordance with nature." The same is also the end. If then being happy is the end, then happiness is called a goal of action, and if wealth is a good thing, then being wealthy is something "one should be," according to those who define in this way for the sake of the exactness of names; but we should follow the custom of the ancients and say that the end is "that for the sake of which we do everything but it for the sake of nothing" or "the ultimate object of desire" or "living virtuously surrounded by bodily and external goods, either all of them, or the majority and the most important among them."

This being the biggest and the most perfect among the goods, it is served by everything else. The things that contribute toward it must admittedly be called goods, those that oppose it evils, whereas those that neither contribute nor oppose it, neither goods nor evils, but indifferents. Again, not every noble action conduces to happiness.

They said that happiness is the use of complete virtue, because according to them some of the virtues are complete and some incomplete: complete are justice and noble-goodness,

---

130.13–14 *titulum in rubro* F   130.19 προηγουμένην *FP*: χορηγουμένην *Wachs.* 131.1 *post* χρή *lac. signavit Speng.*   131.6 ἔξωθεν *FP*: ἔξω *Heer.* κυριωτάτοις *P*: κυριοτάτοις *F*   131.10–11 *post* τὰ δ' ἐναντιούμενα *add.* αὐτῷ τῶν κακῶν, τὰ δὲ μήτε συμβαλλόμενα μήτε ἐναντιούμενα *Speng.*   131.11 τῶν οὔτ' ἀγαθῶν οὔτε *FP*: οὔτε τῶν ἀγαθῶν οὔτε τῶν *Rass.*   131.12 τῶν *del. Arn.* (1926:24)   131.14 εὐδαιμονίαν *F*: δαιμονίαν *P*

δὲ τὴν εὐφυΐαν καὶ τὴν προκοπήν· τῷ δὲ τελείῳ τὸ τέλειον ἁρμόττειν. Τέλος οὖν εἶναι τῆς τοιαύτης ἀρετῆς ἐνέργειαν ἧς οὐθὲν ἄπεστι μέρος. Καὶ | τὸ «ἐν βίῳ δὲ τελείῳ» προσέθεσαν 131.20 ἐνδείξασθαι βουληθέντες, ὅτι περὶ τοὺς ἤδη προήκοντας ἄνδρας ἡ εὐδαιμονία γίνεται· τὸ γὰρ μειράκιον ἀτελὲς καὶ ὁ τούτου βίος, διὸ οὐκ ἂν γενέσθαι περὶ τοῦτ' εὐδαιμονίαν, οὐδ' ὅλως ἐν | ἀτελεῖ χρόνῳ, ἀλλ' ἐν τῷ τελείῳ. Τέλειον δ' εἶναι 132.1 τοῦτον, ὅσον ὥρισεν ἡμῖν πλεῖστον ὁ θεός· ὥρισε δὲ κατὰ πλάτος καθάπερ καὶ τὸ τοῦ σώματος μέγεθος. Ὡς οὖν ἕνα στίχον μὴ ἂν συστήσειν ὑπόκρισιν μηδὲ μίαν χειρὸς | ἔκτασιν .5 ὄρχησιν, μηδὲ μίαν χελιδόνα ποιήσειν ἔαρ, οὕτως μηδὲ βραχὺν χρόνον εὐδαιμονίαν. Τελείαν γὰρ εἶναι δεῖν τὴν εὐδαιμονίαν ἐκ τελείου συνεστῶσαν ἀνδρὸς καὶ χρόνου καὶ δαίμονος.

«Προηγουμένην» δὲ τὴν τῆς ἀρετῆς ἐνέργειαν διὰ τὸ πάντως ἀναγκαῖον ἐν τοῖς κατὰ φύσιν ἀγα | θοῖς ὑπάρχειν, ἐπεὶ .10 καὶ ἐν κακοῖς ἀρετῇ χρήσαιτ' ἂν καλῶς ὁ σπουδαῖος, οὐ μὴν γε μακάριος ἔσται, καὶ ἐν αἰκίαις ἀποδείξαιτ' ἂν τὸ γενναῖον, οὐ μὴν εὐδαιμονήσει. Αἴτιον δ' ὅτι ἡ μὲν ἀρετὴ καλῶν μόνον ἐστὶν ἀπεργαστικὴ καθ' ἑαυτήν, ἡ δ' εὐδαιμονία καὶ καλῶν κἀγαθῶν. | Οὐ γὰρ ἐγκαρτερεῖν βούλεται τοῖς δεινοῖς, ἀλλὰ .15 τῶν ἀγαθῶν ἀπολαύειν πρὸς τῷ καὶ σῴζειν τὸ ἐν κοινωνίᾳ δίκαιον καὶ μήτε ἀποστερεῖν ἑαυτὴν τῶν ἐν τῇ θεωρίᾳ καλῶν μήτε τῶν κατὰ τὸν βίον ἀναγκαίων.

Sec. 14 Ts   Ἥδιστον γάρ τι καὶ κάλλιστον εἶναι τὴν εὐδαιμονίαν, | οὔτε δ' ἐπιτείνεσθαι καθάπερ τέχνην ὀργάνων πλήθει καὶ .20 παρασκευῇ· οὔτε τὴν αὐτὴν εἶναι θεοῦ καὶ ἀνθρώπου, οὔτε γὰρ τὴν ἀρετὴν ἀναπόβλητον ἔτι τῶν σπουδαίων | τὸ παράπαν, 133.1 δύνασθαι γὰρ ὑπὸ πλήθους καὶ μεγέθους ἀφαιρεθῆναι κακῶν· ὅθεν ἐνδοιάσειεν ἄν τις, μήποτ' οὐδὲ κυρίως εὐδαιμονιστέον τὸν ἔτι ζῶντα, διὰ τὸ τῆς τύχης ἄδηλον. Τὸ γὰρ τοῦ Σόλωνος

131.20 ibid. 130.19 W.   131.22–132.1 MM 1.1185a3–5   132.5 Arist. EN 1.1098a18–19   132.10–11 Pol. 7.1332a19–21   132.19 EN 1.1099a24–25   132.20 EN 1.1097b12–21   133.4–5 EN 1.1100a11

131.18–20 τὸ τέλειον ἁρμόττειν. Τέλος οὖν εἶναι τῆς τοιαύτης ἀρετῆς ἐνέργειαν. Καὶ τὸ «ἐν βίῳ δὲ τελείῳ» iter. F sine verbis ἧς οὐθὲν ἄπεστι μέρος   131.19 ἄπεστι F: ἄπεστη P   132.2 ante πλεῖστον add. τὸ Usen.   132.4 μὴ ἂν P²: μίαν FP¹   132.5 οὕτως F: οὕτω P   132.6 εἶναι om. P   132.8 προηγουμένην FP: χορηγουμένην Wachs., de verbo προηγούμενος vid. supra pp. 7–9   132.11 ἔσται Heer.: ἔστω FP   132.12 ἀποδείξαιτ' F: ὑποδείξαιτ' P   ante εὐδαιμονήσει add. γ' Mein.
→

incomplete are good natural endowment and moral progress; what is complete (*teleion*) is fitting for what is final (*teleiō*). So the end is the activity of such a virtue when no part is missing from it. And they added also "during a complete lifetime" because they wanted to indicate that happiness can be attained only by men of already advanced age; for a boy is not yet complete, and neither is his life, and for this reason he could not become happy and not at all during an incomplete period of time, but (only) in a complete one. Complete is the one which god has determined for us as the maximum; and it has been determined loosely, just like the size of the body. Just as one verse couldn't constitute a theatrical play, nor one extension of an arm a dance, nor will one swallow make spring, in the same way a short period of time will not make happiness. Happiness has to be complete, constituted by a complete man and period of time and destiny.

The activity of virtue is (in the definition called) "primary," as it is altogether necessary for it to be surrounded by goods which are in accordance with nature; for the morally good person could make a noble use of virtue even among evils but will not be blessed, and even tormented could show a high-born character, but will fail to attain happiness. The reason is that virtue in itself produces only noble things, whereas happiness both good and noble. For the latter does not want to endure terrible things but to enjoy good things in addition to preserving social justice and not depriving itself either of the fine things in contemplation or of the necessary things for living.

Sec. 14 Ts   For happiness is a most pleasant and noble thing and it is not made greater, as in the case of the crafts, through the number of instruments and equipment; and it is not the same for god as for human beings, for the virtue of morally good men is still not altogether secure, since they can be deprived of it by many and big evils. Hence someone could have doubts whether one still alive may properly be deemed happy, due to the uncertainty of fortune. For what Solon said is right: "look at the end of

εὐδαιμονήσει *Wachs.*: εὐδαιμόνως *FP*: εὐδαίμων ἔσται *Heer.*   132.13 μόνον *F*: μόνη *P*   132.14 εὐδαιμονία *P*: εὐνομία *F*   132.16 ἀπολαύειν *FP²*: ἀπολάβειν *P¹*   132.20 οὔτε *FP*: οὔτω *Cant.*   132.22 οὔτε *FP*: οὐδὲ *Wachs.* ἀναπόβλητον *P*: ἂν ἀπόβλητον *F* ἔτι *Usen*: ἐπὶ *FP*   133.4 τύχης *FP²*: ψυχῆς *P¹*

εὖ ἔχειν· «τέλος ὅρα | μακροῦ βίου». Μαρτυρεῖν δὲ τούτῳ καὶ τὸν βίον εὐδαιμονίζοντα τοὺς ἀνθρώπους ἡνίκ᾽ ἂν θνήσκωσι. Τὸν <δ᾽> ἀφαιρεθέντα τὴν εὐδαιμονίαν οὐκ εἶναι κακοδαίμονα, καθάπερ τὸν μηδ᾽ ὅλως ἔχοντα ταύτην, ἀλλ᾽ ἔσθ᾽ ὅτε μέσον. Βιοῦν γάρ ποτε καὶ σοφὸν καὶ μὴ σοφὸν τὸν | μέσον λεγόμενον βίον τὸν μήτε εὐδαίμονα μήτε κακοδαίμονα.

Περὶ δὲ τοὺς κοιμωμένους οὐκ εἶναι τὴν εὐδαιμονίαν ἢ οὐκ ἐντελεχείᾳ γε. Τὴν γὰρ ἐνέργειαν τῆς ψυχῆς περὶ τὴν ἐγρήγορσιν εἶναι, ταύτῃ δὲ προστίθεσθαι τὸ κατὰ φύσιν, διὰ τὸ μὴ πᾶσαν τὴν ἐγρήγορσιν | τῶν σπουδαίων τελείας εἶναι χρῆσιν ἀρετῆς, ἀλλὰ τὴν κατὰ φύσιν. Ταύτην δ᾽ εἶναι τὴν τοῦ μὴ μαινομένου μηδ᾽ ἐξεστηκότος· ἐπεὶ τήν γε μανίαν καὶ τὴν ἔκστασιν, ὡς τὸν ὕπνον, ἐξιστάνειν αὐτὸν ταύτης τῆς χρήσεως, τάχα δὲ καὶ τῆς τοῦ λόγου, καὶ ποιεῖν θηρίον. Οἷς γὰρ λογικόν | ἐστι τὸ ζῆν τούτοις καὶ τὸ εὐδαιμονεῖν ὑπάρχειν· οὐκ αἰεὶ δὲ οὐδὲ τούτοις, ἀλλ᾽ ὅτε προηγούμενον ἔχοιεν τὸ ζῆν.

Ὡς δὲ τὴν εὐδαιμονίαν λέγεσθαι χρῆσιν ἀρετῆς, οὕτως καὶ τὴν κακοδαιμονίαν χρῆσιν κακίας· οὐ μὴν ὡς τὴν κακίαν αὐτάρκη πρὸς κακοδαιμονίαν, οὕτως καὶ τὴν | ἀρετὴν πρὸς εὐδαιμονίαν. Ὡς δὲ τὸν σπουδαῖον τἀγαθὰ ἔχειν καὶ αὐτῷ συμφέρειν καὶ τοῖς ἄλλοις, <οὕτως τὸν κακὸν τἀγαθὰ ἔχειν καὶ αὐτὸν βλάπτειν καὶ τοὺς ἄλλους.> Φευκτὸν δὲ τὸν βίον γίνεσθαι τοῖς μὲν ἀγαθοῖς ἐν ταῖς ἄγαν ἀτυχίαις, τοῖς δὲ κακοῖς καὶ ἐν ταῖς ἄγαν εὐτυχίαις· πλεῖον | γὰρ ἁμαρτάνειν. Διὸ καὶ μηδὲ κυρίως εὐτυχεῖς εἶναι τοὺς φαύλους.

Sec. 15 Ts *Ποσαχῶς λέγεται τὸ ἀγαθόν* Sec. 19W

Ἐπεὶ δὴ μὲν εὐδαιμονία τὸ μέγιστον ἀγαθόν, διαιρετέον ποσαχῶς λέγεται τὸ ἀγαθόν. Τριχῶς δή φασι | λέγεσθαι τό τε γὰρ πᾶσι τοῖς οὖσι σωτηρίας αἴτιον καὶ τὸ κατηγορούμενον παντὸς ἀγαθοῦ καὶ τὸ δι᾽ αὕθ᾽ αἱρετόν· ὧν τὸ μὲν δεῖ θεὸν

133.5 τὸν βίον *FP*: τὸν Βίαντα *Heer.* 133.6 *ante* ἀφαιρεθέντα *suppl.* δ᾽ *Heer.* 133.8 τὸν μηδ᾽ ὅλως ἔχοντα *Wachs.*: μὴ δὲ τὸν ὅλως ἔχοντα *FP*: μηδὲ τὸν μηδ᾽ ὅλως σχόντα *Arn.* (1926:39) 133.12 ἐντελεχείᾳ *Rass.*: ἐντελέχειάν *FP* 133.13 ταύτῃ δε *Mein.*: ταύτῃ δε δεῖ *Heer.*: τοῦ τῇδε *FP* 133.16 ταύτην *Cant.*: ταύτῃ *FP* 133.17 ἔκστασιν *F*: ἔκτασιν *P* 133.18 ὡς *Wachs.*: καὶ *FP* ὕπνον *FP*: οἶνον *Mein.* 133.20 τούτοις *F*: ταύτοις *P* 133.21 ἀλλ᾽ ὅτε *Mein.*: ἀλλὰ τοῦτο *FP*: ἀλλὰ τοῦτο εἰ *Heer.*: ἀλλ᾽ ὁπότε *Usen.* προηγούμενον *FP*: χορηγούμενον *Wachs., de verbo* προηγούμενος *vid. supra pp.* 7–9 134.2 συμφέρειν *FP*: συμφέρον *Arn.* (1926:43) 134.2 *post* τοῖς ἄλλοις *suppl.* οὕτως τὸν κακὸν τἀγαθὰ ἔχειν καὶ αὐτὸν βλάπτειν καὶ τοὺς ἄλλους *Ts.* 134.3–4 ἀτυχίαις *F*: εὐτυχίαις *P¹*: δυστυχίαις *P²* 134.5

a long life." Public opinion also bears witness to this by judging people happy when they die. The one who is deprived of happiness is not wretched like the one who does not possess it at all, but is sometimes found between the two. For sometimes both the sage and the one who is not a sage live the so-called middle life which is neither happy nor wretched.

Happiness does not apply to those who are asleep, or at least not in actuality. For the activity of the soul belongs to the waking state, and to this is added "in accordance with nature," because not every waking state of the morally good men constitutes the use of perfect virtue but only the one which is in accordance with nature. This is the state of the person not driven mad or mentally deranged, for madness and derangement, like sleep, drive a person out of this use (of perfect virtue) and perhaps even of the use of reason and turn one into an animal. For happiness belongs to those who live a life according to reason; and this is not always the case even for them, but only when they live a life which is primary.

Just as happiness is called the use of virtue, in the same way misery is the use of vice; however, whereas badness is sufficient for misery, virtue is not similarly sufficient for happiness. And, as a morally good man who possesses goods is useful both to himself and to others, in the same way a vicious man who possesses goods harms both himself and others. For good men living their lives among great misfortunes is to be avoided, but for bad men also among very good fortune; for they go wrong more. That is why bad people are not properly speaking fortunate.

Sec. 15 Ts *How many senses of "good" there are* Sec. 19W

Now since happiness is the greatest good, we should distinguish in how many senses "good" is used. They say that it is used in three ways: as the cause of preservation for all beings, and as what is predicated of all good things and as what is choiceworthy for its own sake. Among these, the first one must be god,

---

εἶναι *Heer.*: εἶναι καὶ *FP*   134.7 *titulum in rubro F*   134.8 ἐπεὶ δὴ μὲν *F*: ἐπειδὴ δ' ἡ μὲν *P²*: ἐπεὶ δ' ἡμῖν *Usen.*   134.11 δι' αὕθ' αἱρετόν *Mein.*: διαυθαίρετον *FP*   134.12–13 *add.* τὸ δεύτερον *et* τρίτον τὸ *Usen.*   134.12 δεῖ θεὸν εἶναι τὸ πρῶτον *Heer.*: δεῖ θεὸν εἶναι τὸν πρῶτον *FP*: θεῖον εἶναι τὸ πρῶτον *Usen.*   134.14 δι' αὕθ' αἱρετόν *Mein.*: διαυθαίρετον *FP*

εἶναι τὸ πρῶτον, τὸ δὲ γένος τῶν ἀγαθῶν, τὸ δὲ τέλος ἐφ᾽ ὃ πάντα ἀναφέρομεν, ὅπέρ ἐστιν εὐδαιμονία.

Καὶ τὸ δι᾽ αὕθ᾽ αἱρετὸν | δὲ τριχῶς λέγεσθαι· ἢ οὗ χάριν τινὰ πράττομεν ὡς ἐσχάτου· ἢ οὗ χάριν πάντα· ἢ τρίτον ὃ μέρος γίνεται τούτων. Τῶν δὲ δι᾽ αὕθ᾽ αἱρετῶν τὰ μὲν εἶναι τελικά, τὰ δὲ ποιητικά. Τελικὰ μὲν τὰς κατ᾽ ἀρετὴν προηγουμένας πράξεις· ποιητικὰ δὲ τὰ ὑλικὰ τῶν ἀρετῶν. 134.15

| Τῶν δ᾽ ἀγαθῶν τὰ μὲν εἶναι τίμια, τὰ δὲ ἐπαινετά, τὰ δὲ δυνάμεις, τὰ δὲ ὠφέλιμα. Τίμια μὲν οἷον θεόν, ἄρχοντα, πατέρα· ἐπαινετὰ δὲ οἷον δικαιοσύνην, φρόνησιν· δυνάμεις δὲ οἷον πλοῦτον, ἀρχήν, ἐξουσίαν· ὠφέλιμα δὲ τὰ ποιητικὰ τούτων καὶ φυλακτικά, οἷον <γυμνάσια> ὑγιείας | καὶ εὐεξίας. .20 .25

| Ἔτι τῶν αἱρετῶν καὶ ἀγαθῶν τὰ μὲν καθ᾽ ἑαυτὰ εἶναι αἱρετά, τὰ δὲ δι᾽ ἕτερα. Τὰ μὲν γὰρ τίμια καὶ ἐπαινετὰ καὶ τὰς δυνάμεις καθ᾽ αὑτά· καὶ γὰρ τὰς δυνάμεις ὑπάρχειν τῶν καθ᾽ αὑτὰ ἀγαθῶν, οἷον πλοῦτον καὶ | ἀρχάς οἷς ἂν χρήσαιτο καὶ ἃς ζητήσειεν ὁ ἀγαθὸς ἀνήρ· καὶ οἷς δύναται εὖ χρῆσθαι ἀγαθὰ καὶ καθ᾽ αὑτὰ ἀγαθὰ πεφυκέναι, ὥσπερ ὑγιεινὰ ἃ καὶ ζητήσειεν ἂν ὁ ἰατρὸς καὶ δύναιτο χρῆσθαι· τὰ δὲ ὠφέλιμα δι᾽ ἕτερα· τῷ γὰρ ποιεῖν ἕτερα καὶ σῴζειν τῶν αἱρετῶν | ὑπάρχειν. 135.1 .5 .10

Ἄλλη διαίρεσις· τῶν καθ᾽ αὑτὰ ἀγαθῶν τὰ μὲν εἶναι τέλη, τὰ δὲ οὐ τέλη· οἷον δικαιοσύνην μὲν καὶ ἀρετὴν καὶ ὑγίειαν τέλη καὶ ἁπλῶς ὅσα ἐκ τῶν καθ᾽ ἕκαστα γενομένων κεκεφαλαιωμένα ὑπάρχειν ὥσπερ τὴν ὑγίειαν, | οὐ μὴν τό γε ὑγιεινὸν οὐδὲ τὴν θεραπείαν τοῦ κάμνοντος. Εὐφυΐαν δὲ καὶ ἀναμνήσεις καὶ μαθήσεις οὐ τέλη. .15

Ἄλλη διαίρεσις· τῶν τελῶν τὰ μὲν παντὶ ἀγαθὰ εἶναι, τὰ δ᾽ οὐ παντί. Τὴν μὲν ἀρετὴν καὶ φρόνησιν παντὶ ἀγαθά, ὅτῳ γὰρ ἂν παραγένηται ὠφελεῖν· πλοῦτον | δὲ καὶ ἀρχὰς καὶ 136.1

134.17–18 SVF 3.106–8   134.20–21 EN 1.1101b10–12, MM 1.1183b20–21
134.24–25 MM 1.1183b36–38   135.11–12 MM 1.1184a3–4

134.17 δι᾽ αὕθ᾽ αἱρετῶν Mein.: διαυθαιρετων FP   134.19 ἀρετῶν Meur.: αἱρετῶν FP   134.24–25 ὑγιείας καὶ εὐεξίας Wachs.: ὑγίειαν καὶ εὐεξίαν FP   ante ὑγιείας καὶ εὐεξίας add. γυμνάσια Ts. ex MM 1.1183b37; ibid. add. γυμνασίαν καὶ φάρμακα Wachs. dubitanter   135.1 αἱρετῶν καὶ del. Speng.   135.2 δι᾽ ἕτερα Speng.: δι᾽ ἑτέρων FP   135.5 ante ἂν χρήσαιτο add. εὖ Speng.   ἃς FP: ἂν Mein.: ἃ ... ἂν Speng. ὁ F: καὶ P   135.6 ἀγαθὸς Speng.: ἀγαθὰ FP   ante καθ᾽ αὑτὰ del καὶ Speng.   135.7 ὑγιεινά P: ὑγιεινά F   135.8–9 δι᾽ ἕτερα Speng.: δι᾽ ἑτέρων FP   135.9 αἱρετῶν Heer.: ἀρετῶν FP   135.14 κεκεφαλαιωμένα Speng.: καικεφαλαιωμένα FP   135.15 τό γε

→

(the second) the class of goods and (the third) the end to which we refer everything, namely happiness.

And the "choiceworthy for its own sake" is also used in three different ways: either as the ultimate thing for the sake of which we do something, or that for the sake of which we do everything, or in a third way as something which becomes a part of these. And of the things which are choiceworthy for their own sake, some are final, some productive; final are the primary actions which are in accordance with virtue, whereas productive are the materials of the virtues.

Of the goods some are held in honour, some are praiseworthy, some powers and some beneficial. Held in honour are such as god, the ruler, one's father; praiseworthy are things such as justice, practical wisdom; powers are things such as wealth, office, authority; beneficial are the ones that produce and preserve these, like gymnastic exercises of health and vigor.

And also of things that are choiceworthy and good some are in themselves choiceworthy and others on account of other things. For the honourable and praiseworthy and the powers are in themselves (choiceworthy); for the powers such as wealth and offices belong to the things which are goods in themselves as well, being things that the good man could use and seek for. And the ones he could use well are also by nature good in themselves, such as healthy things which the doctor would both seek for and be able to use. Beneficial things, on the other hand, are (chosen) for the sake of other things; for they are choiceworthy by producing and preserving other things.

Another division: some of the things which are goods in themselves are ends and some are not ends: for example justice and virtue and health are ends and, generally, in sum everything that results from individual actions, like health as opposed to what is healthy and the treatment of a sick person. Good natural endowment and recollections and learning do not constitute ends.

Another division: some of the ends are good for everyone and others not good for everyone. Virtue and practical wisdom are good for everyone, as they benefit whomever has them; wealth and offices and powers, on the other hand, are not

134.15

.20

.25

135.1

.5

.10

.15

136.1

Mein.: τό τε FP   ὑγιεινὸν Speng.: ὑγιαῖνον FP   135.17 τελῶν Speng.: τελέων FP: τελικῶν Usen.   135.18–19 παντὶ ... παντὶ FP: πάντῃ ... πάντῃ Mein.

δυνάμεις οὐ παντὶ ὁπωσοῦν ἀγαθά, καθ' ὅσον ἀφώρισται τὸ εἶναι ἀγαθὰ τῇ τοῦ ἀγαθοῦ ἀνδρὸς χρήσει· φαίνεσθαι δὲ ταῦτα καὶ ζητεῖν καὶ χρωμένοις ὠφελεῖν. Οἷς δὲ τὸν ἀγαθὸν εὖ χρῆσθαι, τούτοις τὸν | κακὸν κακῶς· ὥσπερ οἷς ἂν εὖ τὸν μουσικόν, τούτοις τὸν ἄμουσον κακῶς. Ἅμα δὲ κακῶς χρώμενον βλάπτεσθαι καθάπερ ἵππον ἀγαθὸν ὄντα τὸν μὲν ἱππικὸν ὠφελεῖν, βλάπτειν δὲ τὸν ἄφιππον οὐ μετρίως.

Ἔτι τῶν ἀγαθῶν τὰ μὲν εἶναι περὶ ψυχήν, τὰ | δὲ περὶ σῶμα, τὰ δ' ἐκτός. Περὶ ψυχὴν μέν οἷον εὐφυΐαν τε καὶ τέχνην καὶ ἀρετὴν καὶ σοφίαν καὶ φρόνησιν καὶ ἡδονήν· περὶ σῶμα δὲ ὑγίειαν καὶ εὐαισθησίαν καὶ κάλλος καὶ ἰσχὺν καὶ ἀρτιότητα καὶ πάντα τὰ μόρια σὺν ταῖς δυνάμεσι καὶ ἐνεργείαις· ἐκτὸς δὲ πλοῦτον καὶ δόξαν | καὶ εὐγένειαν καὶ δυναστείαν καὶ φίλους καὶ συγγενεῖς καὶ πατρίδα.

Τῶν δὲ περὶ ψυχὴν ἀγαθῶν τὰ μὲν αἰεὶ φύσει παρεῖναι καθάπερ γε ὀξύτητα καὶ μνήμην τό τε ὅλον εὐφυΐαν· τὰ δ' ἐξ ἐπιμελείας παραγίνεσθαι, ὡς τάς τε προπαιδεύσεις καὶ διαίτας ἐλευθερίους· τὰ δ' ἐκ τε- | λειότητος ὑπάρχειν, οἷον φρόνησιν, δικαιοσύνην, τελευταῖον δὲ σοφίαν.

Ἔτι δὲ τῶν ἀγαθῶν τὰ μὲν εἶναι καὶ κτήσασθαι καὶ ἀποβαλεῖν, ὡς πλοῦτον· τὰ δὲ κτήσασθαι μὲν ἀποβαλεῖν δ' οὔ, ὡς εὐτυχίαν, ἀθανασίαν· τὰ δὲ | ἀποβαλεῖν μὲν κτήσασθαι δ' οὔ, ὡς αἴσθησιν, ὡς τὸ ζῆν· τὰ δ' οὔτε κτήσασθαι οὔτ' ἀποβαλεῖν, ὡς εὐγένειαν.

Ἔτι τῶν ἀγαθῶν τὰ μὲν εἶναι δι' αὔθ' αἱρετὰ | μόνον ὡς ἡδονὴν καὶ ἀοχλησίαν· τὰ δὲ ποιητικὰ μόνον ὡς πλοῦτον· τὰ δὲ ποιητικὰ καὶ δι' αὔθ' αἱρετά, ὡς ἀρετήν, φίλους, ὑγίειαν.

Καὶ ἄλλως δὲ πολλαχῶς διαιρεῖσθαι τἀγαθὰ διὰ τὸ μὴ ἓν εἶναι γένος αὐτῶν ἀλλὰ κατὰ τὰς δέκα λέγεσθαι | κατηγορίας· ἐν ὁμωνυμίᾳ γὰρ ἐκφέρεσθαι τἀγαθόν, τά τε τοιαῦτα πάντα

136.9–10 *EN* 1.1098b12–14, *MM* 1.1184b2–5   137.8–10 *EN* 1.1096a23–29, *EE* 1.1217b27–28, *MM* 1.1183a9–10

136.1 ὁπωσοῦν *Usen.*: πῶς οὖν *FP*   136.3 χρωμένοις *FP*: χρωμένους *Speng.*   136.4 τὸν ... τὸν *P*: τὸ ... τὸ *F*   136.17 γε *Heer.*: γὰρ *FP*: del. *Speng.*   136.18 ἐξ *Speng.*: ἑξῆς *FP*   παραγίνεσθαι *Speng.*: περιγίνεσθαι *FP*   136.19 ἐλευθερίους *F*: ἐλευθέρους *P*   136.22 εἶναι *FP*: ἡμᾶς *Heer.*   136.24 εὐτυχίαν *FP*: εὐψυχίαν *Speng.*   ἀθανασίαν *FP*: ἀθαυμαστίαν *Usen.*   137.1–2 ὡς τὸ ζῆν *FP*: καὶ τὸ ζῆν *Speng.*   137.2 τὰ δ' *Heer.*: τὸ δ' *FP*   137.4 δι' αὔθ' αἱρετὰ *Mein.*: διαυθαίρετα *FP*   137.5 ἀοχλησίαν

→

unconditionally good for everybody, in so far as we have determined that they are good by the way the good man uses them; for (such people) appear to seek for them and are benefitted by their use. The things that the good person uses in a good way are used by the bad person in a bad way, just as the things that the musician uses in a good way are used in a bad way by the non-musical person. At the same time, (someone) is harmed by the bad use of things, just as a good horse benefits the one who is skilled in riding but damages a lot the one who is not.

Further, some of the goods belong to the soul, some are bodily and some external. Of the soul are such as good natural endowment and skill and virtue and wisdom and practical wisdom and pleasure; bodily goods are health and good function of the senses and beauty and strength and soundness of the body and all the bodily parts with their capacities and activities. External are wealth and reputation and good-birth and political power and friends and relatives and one's country.

And among the goods of the soul some are always present by nature like sharpness and memory, and generally a good natural endowment. Others are the result of care, such as preliminary studies and the way of life suited to a freeman; there are also the ones which result from perfection like practical wisdom, justice and, at last, wisdom.

Moreover, some of the goods can be acquired and lost like wealth; others can be acquired but not lost, like good fortune, immortality; some can only be lost and never acquired like perception and life; and some can neither be acquired nor lost, like good-birth.

Further, some of the goods are only choiceworthy for their own sake, such as pleasure and freedom from disturbance; some are only productive, such as wealth, and some are both productive and choiceworthy for their own sake, such as virtue, friends, health.

And the goods are divided in many other ways as well, because there is not a single genus of them but they are predicated according to the ten categories; for "good" is used homonymously and all such things have only a name in common,

Cant.: ὀχλησίαν FP   137.6 ante ποιητικὰ add. καὶ Mein.   137.6–7 δι' αὔθ' αίρετὰ Mein.: διαυθαίρετα FP

ὄνομα κοινὸν ἔχειν μόνον, τὸν δὲ κατὰ τοὔνομα λόγον ἕτερον.

Sec. 16 Ts *Περὶ τῆς ἠθικῆς ἀρετῆς, ὅτι μεσότητες* Sec. 20W

Τούτων δὲ δὴ διωρισμένων ἐπελθεῖν ἀκριβέστερον | ἀναγκαῖον τὰ περὶ τῆς ἠθικῆς ἀρετῆς λεγόμενα. Ταύτην γὰρ ὑπολαμβάνουσι περὶ τὸ ἄλογον μέρος γίνεσθαι τῆς ψυχῆς, ἐπειδὴ διμερῆ πρὸς τὴν παροῦσαν θεωρίαν ὑπέθεντο τὴν ψυχήν, τὸ μὲν λογικὸν ἔχουσαν, τὸ δ᾽ ἄλογον. Καὶ περὶ μὲν τὸ λογικόν, τὴν καλοκαγαθίαν γίνεσθαι | καὶ τὴν φρόνησιν καὶ τὴν ἀγχίνοιαν καὶ σοφίαν καὶ εὐμάθειαν καὶ μνήμην καὶ τὰς ὁμοίας· περὶ δὲ τὸ ἄλογον, σωφροσύνην καὶ δικαιοσύνην καὶ ἀνδρείαν καὶ τὰς ἄλλας τὰς ἠθικὰς καλουμένας ἀρετάς. 137.15 .20

Ταύτας δή φασιν ὑπ᾽ ἐνδείας καὶ ὑπερβολῆς | φθείρεσθαι. Πρὸς δὲ τὴν ἔνδειξιν τούτου τοῖς ἐκ τῶν αἰσθήσεων μαρτυρίοις χρῶνται, βουλόμενοι <περὶ> τῶν ἀφανῶν τὴν ἐκ τῶν φανερῶν παρέχεσθαι πίστιν. Αὐτίκα γὰρ ὑπὸ τῶν γυμνασίων πλειόνων τε γινομένων καὶ ἐλατ | τόνων φθείρεσθαι τὴν ἰσχὺν καὶ ἐπὶ τῶν ποτῶν καὶ σιτίων ὡσαύτως· πλειόνων γὰρ προσφερομένων ἢ ἐλαττόνων φθείρεσθαι τὴν ὑγίειαν, συμμέτρων δὲ τῶν εἰρημένων ὄντων σῴζεσθαι τήν τε ἰσχὺν καὶ τὴν ὑγίειαν. 138.1 .5

Παραπλησίως οὖν ἔχειν καὶ ἐπὶ τῆς σωφροσύνης καὶ ἀνδρείας καὶ τῶν | ἄλλων ἀρετῶν. Τὸν μὲν γὰρ τοιοῦτον ὄντα τὴν φύσιν ὥστε μηδὲ τὸν κεραυνὸν φοβεῖσθαι, μαινόμενον, ἀλλ᾽ οὐκ ἀνδρεῖον εἶναι· τὸν δ᾽ ἔμπαλιν πάντα φοβούμενον, ὥστε καὶ τὴν σκιάν, ἀγεννῆ καὶ δειλόν· ἀνδρεῖον δ᾽ ὁμολογουμένως τὸν μήτε πάντα μήτε μηδὲν φοβούμενον. | Ταῦτ᾽ ἄρα καὶ αὔξειν καὶ φθείρειν τὴν ἀρετήν, ὥστε τοὺς μὲν μετρίους φόβους αὔξειν τὴν ἀνδρείαν, τοὺς δὲ μείζονας ἢ ἐλάττονας φθείρειν. Ὁμοίως δὲ καὶ ἐπὶ τῶν ἄλλων ἀρετῶν τὰς μὲν οὔσας κατὰ ταύτας ὑπερβολὰς καὶ ἐλλείψεις φθείρειν αὐτάς, τὰς δὲ μετριότητας | αὔξειν. .10 .15 .20

Οὐ μόνον δὲ τούτοις ἀφορίζεσθαι τὴν ἀρετήν, ἀλλὰ καὶ ἡδονῇ καὶ λύπῃ. Διὰ γὰρ τὴν ἡδονὴν τὰ φαῦλα πράττειν ἡμᾶς,

---

137.24–138.26 MM 1.1185b1–27, EN 2.1104a11–19   138.15–26 MM 1.1185b27–38, EN 2.1104b8–11

137.12 τοὔνομα Speng.: τὄνομα FP   ἕτερον FP: δεύτερον Cant.   137.13 *titulum in rubro* F, *de titulo vid.* Fortenbaugh *infra* ch. 3 n. 43   137.18–19 λογικὸν FP: λόγον Gais.   137.24 φασιν F: φησιν P   138.2 *ante* τῶν ἀφανῶν *add.* περὶ Ts.: *add.* ὑπὲρ Speng.   138.4 πλειόνων F: πλεῖον P   138.6 πλειόνων Mull.: πολλῶν →

Didymus' Epitome of Peripatetic Ethics—An Edition with Translation

whereas the definition which corresponds to the name is different.

Sec. 16 Ts *On Moral Virtue; that they are means.*   Sec. 20W

Having determined these things, it is necessary to investigate in more detail what is said of moral virtue. For they understand this to belong to the irrational part of the soul, since they assumed, with a view to the present investigation, that the soul has two parts, a rational and an irrational one. And belonging to the rational part are noble-goodness and practical wisdom and shrewdness and theoretical wisdom and readiness in learning and memory and the like; belonging to the irrational part, on the other hand, are temperance and justice and bravery and the other so-called moral virtues.

They say that these are destroyed by deficiency and excess; in order to demonstrate this, they use the testimony of the senses, wanting to provide for non-apparent things the evidence of apparent ones. For, to begin with, strength is destroyed by excessive or insufficient bodily exercises. The same can be said of foods and drinks; when there is excessive or insufficient consumption health is destroyed, whereas when the things mentioned are in the right proportion strength and health are preserved.

The same goes for temperance and courage and the rest of the virtues. For the one who has such a nature as not to be afraid even of thunder is mad but not courageous; on the other hand, the one who is afraid of everything, even of (his own) shadow, is of low character and cowardly. Courageous is, by common consent, the one who is afraid neither of everything nor of nothing. The same things then promote and destroy virtue, so that moderate fears strengthen courage, whereas excessive or insufficient ones destroy it. Likewise regarding the other virtues, excesses and deficiencies relating to them destroy them, whereas moderation increases them.

Virtue is determined not only by these but also by pleasure and pain. For it is because of pleasure that we do bad acts, whereas because of pain we abstain from the noble ones; but we

---

FP   138.7 ὑγίειαν *F*: ὑγίαν *P* συμμέτρων *Mein.*: συμμέτρως *FP*   138.10 τὸν *Heer. ex cod. V*: τὸ *FP*   138.12 πάντα *P²*: πᾶν τὸ *FP¹*   138.13 ἀγεννῇ *F*: ἀγενῇ *P* 138.13–14 ὁμολογουμένως *Cant.*: ὁμολογοῦμεν ὡς *FP*   138.15: ταῦτ' *Rass.*: ταὔτ' *FP*   138.18 ταύτας *F*: πάντας *P*   138.23 πράττειν *FP²*: πλάττειν *P¹*

διὰ δὲ τὴν λύπην ἀπέχεσθαι τῶν καλῶν· οὐκ εἶναι δὲ λαβεῖν
οὔτ' ἀρετὴν οὔτε κακίαν ἄνευ λύπης | καὶ ἡδονῆς. Τὴν οὖν   138.25
ἀρετὴν περὶ ἡδονὰς καὶ λύπας ὑπάρχειν.

Sec. 17 | Πρὸς δὲ τὸ σαφῶς δηλῶσαι τὰ περὶ τούτων ἀναγκαῖον   139.1
Ts ἡγοῦντο τὰ περὶ ψυχὴν γινόμενα προσλαβεῖν τῷ λόγῳ. Ταῦτα
δή φασιν ὑπάρχειν ἐν ταῖς ψυχαῖς τῶν ἀνθρώπων· πάθη,
δυνάμεις, ἕξεις. Πάθη δ' εἶναι | ὀργήν, φόβον, μῖσος, πόθον,   .5
ζῆλον, ἔλεον, τὰ παραπλήσια τούτοις, οἷς καὶ παρακολουθεῖν
ἡδονὴν καὶ λύπην· δυνάμεις, καθ' ἃς παθητικοὶ τούτων εἶναι
λεγόμεθα, οἷον καθ' ἃς ὀργιζόμεθα, φοβούμεθα, ζηλοῦμεν,
τῶν τοιούτων ὁτιοῦν πεπόνθαμεν· ἕξεις δέ, καθ' ἃς πρὸς
ταῦτά | πως ἔχομεν καὶ ἀφ' ὧν ἡ τούτων ἐνέργεια εὖ ἢ   .10
κακῶς ἀποτελεῖται. Διὸ εἰ μὲν οὕτως τις ὀργίζοιτο ῥᾳδίως
ὥστε ἐπὶ παντὶ καὶ πάντως τὴν ἕξιν ἂν ἔχων φανείη τὴν τῆς
ὀργιλότητος· εἰ δὲ οὕτως ὥστε μηθὲν μήτε ἐφ' ὁτῳοῦν τὴν τῆς
ῥᾳθυμίας· ἀμφοτέρας δ' εἶναι ψεκτάς, ἐπαι- | νουμένην δὲ ἕξιν   .15
ὑπάρχειν τὴν πραότητα, καθ' ἣν ὅτε δεῖ καὶ ὡς δεῖ καὶ ᾧ δεῖ
ὀργιζόμεθα. Διόπερ ἕξεις εἶναι τὰς ἀρετάς, ἀφ' ὧν τὰς ἐν τοῖς
πάθεσιν ἐνεργείας ἐπαινεῖσθαι συμβέβηκεν.

Sec. 18 Ts Ἐπεὶ οὖν ἡ ἀρετὴ τῶν πρακτῶν, πᾶσαν δὲ πρᾶξιν | ἐν   .20
συνεχείᾳ θεωρεῖσθαι συμβέβηκε, παντὸς δὲ συνεχοῦς ὥσπερ
ἐν τοῖς μεγέθεσιν εἶναί τινα ὑπερβολὴν καὶ ἔλλειψιν καὶ
μεσότητα καὶ ταῦτα ἢ πρὸς ἄλληλα ὑπάρχειν ἢ πρὸς ἡμᾶς, ἐν
πᾶσι δὲ τὸ μέσον τὸ πρὸς ἡμᾶς βέλτιστον, τοῦτο γάρ ἐστιν ὡς
ἡ ἐπιστήμη κελεύει καὶ ὁ λόγος. | Τὸ γὰρ μέσον οὐ τὸν τοῦ   .25
ποσοῦ τόπον ὁρίζειν ἀλλὰ τὸν | <τοῦ> ποιοῦ, διὸ καὶ τέλειον   140.1
εἶναι τῷ οὕτω καὶ ἄκρως ἔχειν. Τὰ δ' ἐναντία πως καὶ ἀλλήλοις
ἀντικεῖσθαι καὶ τῷ μέσῳ· ἐναντία δ' εἶναι τήν τ' ἔλλειψιν καὶ
τὴν ὑπερβολήν, τὸ δὲ μέσον πρὸς ἑκάτερον ἔχειν, ὅπερ τὸ ἴσον
| πρὸς τὸ ἄνισον πέπονθε, τοῦ μὲν ἐλάττονος πλεῖον ὄν, τοῦ   .5
δὲ πλείονος ἔλαττον.

Τὸ οὖν πρὸς ἡμᾶς μέσον ἄριστον, οἷον, φησὶν ὁ Θεόφραστος, ἐν ταῖς ἐντυχίαις ὁδὶ μὲν πολλὰ διελθὼν καὶ μακρῶς

139.1–11 *MM* 1.1186a8–20, *EN* 2.1105b20–28   139.19–24 *EN* 2.1106a26–28, *EE*
2.1220b21–24   140.7–12 Theophrastus fr. 449A FHS&G

139.7 *post* δυνάμεις *add.* δὲ Heer.   139.8–9 τοιούτων Heer.: ποιούντων FP   139.11
ὀργίζοιτο P²: ὁρίζοιτο FP¹   139.13 μήτε FP: μηδὲ Speng.   139.19 πρακτῶν Speng.:
πρακτικῶν FP   139.23 δὲ FP: δὴ Mein.   139.25 τὸν τοῦ ποσοῦ P: τὸν το ποσοῦ
F   139.25–140.1 *ante* ποιοῦ *add.* τοῦ Usen.   140.1 τῷ οὕτω Heer.: τοῦ οὕτω FP

→

cannot acquire either virtue or vice without pain and pleasure. 138.25
So virtue is about pleasures and pains.

Sec. 17 Ts   In order to express those things clearly, they thought it was 139.1 necessary to add to their account things occurring in the soul. They say that the following are in the souls of humans: emotions, capacities, dispositions. Emotions are anger, fear, hate, .5 desire, emulation, pity and things similar to these which are followed by pleasure and pain. Capacities are that in respect of which we are said to be capable of these emotions, such as those in respect of which we are affected by anger, fear, emulation and anything of that sort. Dispositions are that in respect of which .10 we are in a certain condition toward these and as a result of which the emotional activity is performed in a good or bad way. For this reason, if someone were to grow angry easily and hence at everything and in every way, he would manifestly have the disposition of irascibility; if on the other hand, one were to be such as not (to get angry) at all and at nothing whatsoever, then that person would seem to have the disposition of indifference. Both of them are blameworthy, whereas the disposition that is .15 praised is mildness, according to which we become angry at the appropriate time, in the appropriate manner, and at the appropriate person. That is why the virtues are dispositions resulting in emotional activities that are praised.

Sec. 18 Ts   Since virtue concerns the domain of action and every action happens to be considered as continuous and of everything con- .20 tinuous, as in the case of magnitudes, there is an excess and a deficiency and a mean, and they are such either relatively to each other or to us, and in all things the mean relative to us is best, for this is what knowledge and reason dictate; for the mean .25 is not defined in terms of quantity but of quality, and that is why 140.1 it is also perfect by being in this extreme condition. Opposites on the other hand are opposed somehow both to each other and to the mean. Opposites are deficiency and excess, whereas the mean has such a relation to each of them as the equal to the unequal, being more than the less and less than the more. .5

Therefore the mean relative to us is best, like, (as) Theophrastus says, in social interactions one person goes through many things and chatters at length, another (says) little and

140.7 ἄριστον *F*: ἀόριστον *P*   140.8 ἐν ταῖς ἐντυχίαις *FP*: ἐν τοῖς περὶ εὐτυχίας Heer.

46   Georgia Tsouni

ἀδολεσχήσας, ὁδὶ δ᾽ ὀλίγα καὶ οὐδὲ τἀναγκαῖα, | οὗτος δὲ 140.10
αὐτὰ ἃ ἔδει μόνον τὸν καιρὸν ἔλαβεν. Αὕτη <ἡ> μεσότης πρὸς
ἡμᾶς <ἀρίστη>· αὕτη γὰρ ὑφ᾽ ἡμῶν ὥρισται τῷ λόγῳ. Διὸ
ἔστιν ἡ ἀρετὴ «ἕξις προαιρετική, ἐν μεσότητι οὖσα τῇ πρὸς
ἡμᾶς, ὡρισμένη λόγῳ καὶ ὡς ἂν ὁ φρόνιμος ὁρίσειεν».

Sec. 19 Ts | Εἶτα παραθέμενος τινὰς συζυγίας ἀκολούθως τῷ ὑφη- .15
γητῇ, σκοπῶν ἔπειτα καθ᾽ ἕκαστα ἐπάγειν ἐπειράθη τὸν
τρόπον τοῦτον· ἐλήφθησαν δὲ παραδειγμάτων χάριν αἵδε·
σωφροσύνη, ἀκολασία, ἀναισθησία· πραότης, ὀργιλότης,
ἀναλγησία· ἀνδρεία, θρασύ- | της, δειλία· δικαιοσύνη, <πλεο- .20
νεξία, μειονεξία>· ἐλευθεριότης, | ἀσωτία, ἀνελευθερία· 141.1
μεγαλοψυχία, μικροψυχία, χαυνότης· μεγαλοπρέπεια, μικρο-
πρέπεια, σαλακωνία.

Τούτων δὴ τῶν ἕξεων αἱ μὲν τῷ ὑπερβάλλειν ἢ ἐλλείπειν
περὶ πάθη φαῦλαί εἰσιν, αἱ δὲ σπουδαῖαι, τῷ μεσότητες |
εἶναι δηλονότι. Σώφρονά τε γὰρ εἶναι οὔτε τὸν καθάπαξ .5
ἀνεπιθύμητον οὔτε τὸν ἐπιθυμητικόν· τὸν μὲν γὰρ λίθου
δίκην μηδὲ τῶν κατὰ φύσιν ὀρέγεσθαι, τὸν δὲ τῷ ὑπερβάλλειν
ταῖς ἐπιθυμίαις ἀκόλαστον εἶναι· τὸν δὲ μέσον τούτων, ὧν
δεῖ καὶ ὁπότε καὶ ὁπόσον ἐπιθυμοῦντα | καὶ τῷ λόγῳ κατὰ τὸ .10
προσῆκον ὁρίζοντα καθάπερ κανόνι σώφρονα λέγεσθαί τε
καὶ κατὰ φύσιν εἶναι. Πρᾶόν τε <οὔτε τὸν ἀνάλγητον> οὔτε
τὸν ἐπὶ παντὶ ὀργιζόμενον, κἂν μικρότατον ᾖ, ἀλλὰ τὸν τὴν
μέσην ἔχοντα ἕξιν. Ἀνδρεῖόν τε οὔτε τὸν μηδὲν | φοβούμενον, .15
κἂν ᾖ θεὸς ὁ ἐπιών, οὔτε τὸν πάντα καὶ τὸ δὴ λεγόμενον τὴν
σκιάν. Δίκαιον δὲ οὔτε τὸν τὸ πλεῖον ἑαυτῷ νέμοντα οὔτε τὸν
τὸ ἔλαττον, ἀλλὰ τὸν τὸ ἴσον· τὸ δ᾽ ἴσον τὸ κατὰ τὸ ἀνάλογον, .20
οὐ κατ᾽ ἀριθμόν γε. <Ἐλευθέριόν τε> οὔτε τὸν προετικὸν
ὅπως ἔτυχεν οὔτε τὸν | ἀνελεύθερον. Μεγαλόψυχόν τε οὔτε

140.12–14 EN 2.1106b36–1107a2   140.15–142.5 Theophrastus Fr. 449A FHS&G.
141.6–7 EE 2.1221a22–23

140.10 μόνον Speng.: μόνα Wachs.: μέσον P²: μὴ FP¹: μὴ del. Madv.   140.11 post
ἡμᾶς add. ἀρίστη Meur.   140.13 ὡρισμένη Aspasius 48.13 ad Arist. EN 1107a1
et EN ed. Aldina maior (1497): ὡρισμένη FP et codd. Arist. EN καὶ ὡς ἂν Mein. ex
codd. Arist EN 1.1107a1: δὲ ὡς ἂν FP: καὶ ᾧ ἂν Aspasius 48.13 ad Arist. EN 1.1107a1
140.16 σκοπῶν Speng.: σκοπεῖν FP   ἔπειτα FP: ἐπὶ τὰ Speng.   140.17 ἐπάγειν
Speng.: ἐπάγων FP   140.20 post δικαιοσύνη suppl. πλεονεξία, μειονεξία Ts.: lac.
signavit Heer.   141.5–6 τὸν καθάπαξ F: τῶν καθάπαξ P   141.9 ὧν P²: ᾧ FP¹:
ὡς Speng.: οὗ Trend.: ὃ Mull.   141.12 post πρᾶόν τε add. οὔτε τὸν ἀνάλγητον
καὶ μηδενὶ μηδέποτε ὀργιζόμενον Speng.   141.13 ὀργιζόμενον F: ὁριζόμενον P
→

Didymus' Epitome of Peripatetic Ethics—An Edition with Translation 47

not even what is necessary, but a third acts appropriately to the occasion (by saying) only what is necessary. This is the mean relative to us, for it has been determined by us through reasoning. That is why virtue is "a disposition concerned with choice lying in the mean relative to us, this being determined by reason and as the practically wise person would determine it."

Sec. 19 Ts   Next, following the lead of his master, he displayed some pairings and attempted to draw inferences from the examination of individual cases in the following way. The following were chosen as examples: temperance, licentiousness, insensibility; mildness, irascibility, apathy; courage, over-boldness, cowardice; justice, taking more and less than one's due; liberality, wastefulness, stinginess; magnanimity, littleness of soul, vanity; magnificence, shabbiness, pretentiousness.

Of these dispositions, some are bad on account of excess or deficiency in relation to emotions and others morally good obviously by being mean dispositions. For temperate is neither the one who doesn't have any desires whatsoever, nor the one who is prone to desires; for the former is like a stone feeling no desire even for things which are according to nature, whereas the latter is licentious by indulging in excessive desires. The one who lies in the middle state between the two, desiring what is necessary in the appropriate time and measure and making decisions in a proper way using reason as a rule, is called temperate and is such according to nature. And mild is neither the insensible nor the one who gets angry at everything, even with the smallest things, but the one who has the mean disposition. And courageous is not the one who is not afraid of anything, not even when a god comes against him, nor the one (who is afraid) of everything and, as the saying goes, of one's own shadow. And just is neither the one who assigns the greater share to himself, nor the one (who assigns) the lesser, but the one (who assigns) the equal; equality is here understood proportionately and not numerically. Generous is the man who neither gives lavishly in a random way, nor the one who is a miser. And magnanimous is neither the one who considers oneself worthy of all great things,

---

141.16 post σκιάν lac. statuit Wachs.   141.18 γε P²: τε FP¹   141.18–19 ante οὔτε τὸν προετικὸν add. ἐλευθέριόν τε Heer. προετικὸν P: προαιρετικὸν F   141.20 ἀνελεύθερον Ts.: ἀπροαίρετον FP: ἀπρόετον Trend. post ἀπρόετον lac. statuit Wachs.   142.1 ὅλως P²: ὅμως FP¹

τὸν μεγάλων | πάντων ἀξιοῦντα ἑαυτὸν οὔτε τὸν μηθενὸς 142.1
ὅλως, ἀλλὰ τὸν τὸ δέον ἐφ᾽ ἑκάστου λαμβάνοντα καὶ εἰς
τὸ κατ᾽ ἀξίαν. Μεγαλοπρεπῆ τε οὔτε τὸν πάντοτε καὶ ἔνθα
μὴ δεῖ λαμπρὸν οὔτε τὸν μηδαμοῦ, ἀλλὰ τὸν κατὰ καιρὸν | .5
ἁρμόττοντα εἰς ἕκαστον.
    Τοιοῦτο μὲν τὸ τῶν ἠθικῶν ἀρετῶν εἶδος παθητικὸν καὶ
κατὰ μεσότητα θεωρούμενον ὃ δὴ καὶ τὴν ἀντακολουθίαν
ἔχει, πλὴν οὐχ ὁμοίως, ἀλλ᾽ ἡ μὲν φρόνησις ταῖς ἠθικαῖς κατὰ
τὸ ἴδιον, αὗται δ᾽ ἐκείνῃ | κατὰ συμβεβηκός. Ὁ μὲν γὰρ δίκαιος .10
ἐστι καὶ φρόνιμος· ὁ γὰρ τοιόσδε αὐτὸν λόγος εἰδοποιεῖ. Οὐ
μὴν ὁ φρόνιμος καὶ δίκαιος κατὰ τὸ ἴδιον, ἀλλ᾽ ὅτι τῶν καλῶν
κἀγαθῶν κοινῶς πρακτικός φαύλου δ᾽ οὐδενός.

Sec. 20 Ts *Περὶ παθῶν ψυχῆς*   Sec. 21W

| Τῶν δὲ παθῶν καὶ ὁρμῶν τὰ μὲν εἶναι ἀστεῖα, τὰ δὲ .15
φαῦλα, τὰ δὲ μέσα. Ἀστεῖα μὲν φιλίαν, χάριν, νέμεσιν, αἰδῶ,
θάρσος, ἔλεον· φαῦλα δὲ φθόνον, ἐπιχαιρεκακίαν, ὕβριν· μέσα
δὲ λύπην, φόβον, ὀργήν, ἡδονήν, ἐπιθυμίαν. Τούτων δὲ τὰ μὲν
αἱρετέον καθάπαξ, τὰ | δὲ ὁριστέον. Πᾶν δὲ πάθος περὶ ἡδονὴν .20
συνίστασθαι καὶ λύπην, διὸ καὶ περὶ ταύτας τὰς ἠθικὰς ἀρετὰς
ὑπάρχειν. Φιλαργυρίαν δὲ καὶ φιληδονίαν καὶ ἐρωτομανίαν
καὶ τὰ τοιαῦτα ἕξεις εἶναι ἀλλοίας περὶ τὰς κακίας. Ἔρωτα δ᾽
εἶναι τὸν μὲν φιλίας, τὸν δὲ συνουσίας, τὸν | δὲ | ἀμφοῖν· διὸ .25
καὶ τὸν μὲν σπουδαῖον, τὸν δὲ φαῦλον, τὸν δὲ μέσον.

Sec. 21 Ts *Περὶ φιλίας*   Sec. 22W

| Τῆς φιλίας δ᾽ εἶναι διαφορὰς τέσσαρας, ἑταιρικήν, 143.1
συγγενικήν, ξενικήν, ἐρωτικήν· εἰ δὲ καὶ τὴν εὐεργετικὴν καὶ
θαυμαστικὴν συγκαταριθμητέον λόγου δεῖ. | Ἀρχὴν δὲ τῆς 143.5
μὲν ἑταιρικῆς εἶναι τὴν συνήθειαν, τῆς δὲ συγγενικῆς τὴν
φύσιν, τῆς δὲ ξενικῆς τὴν χρείαν, τῆς δὲ ἐρωτικῆς τὸ πάθος,
τῆς δ᾽ εὐεργετικῆς τὴν χάριν, τῆς δὲ θαυμαστικῆς τὴν δύναμιν.

142.2 ἐφ᾽ ἑκάστου F: ἀφ᾽ ἑκάστου P   142.6 τοιοῦτο F: τοιοῦτον P   142.8 *post* ἀντακολουθίαν ἔχει *add.* τῇ φρονήσει *Zell.*   142.10 ὃ μὲν *Speng.*: ὅτι μὲν FP   142.11 οὐ μὴν ὁ *Speng.*: οὐ μὴν ὅτι FP   142.12 δίκαιος P: δίκαιον F κατὰ τὸ ἴδιον: *om.* P   142.13 κοινῶς *Heer.*: κοινὸς FP   142.14 *ante* ψυχῆς *habet* καὶ F   142.15 τῶν P: ὧν F   142.20 συνίστασθαι F: συνίσταται P   142.23 περὶ *Heer.*: παρὰ FP   143.2 τῆς P: ἧς F τέσσαρας P: τέτταρας F   143.5-6 τῆς δὲ συγγενικῆς F: τὴν δὲ συγγενικήν P

nor the one who doesn't deem oneself worthy of anything at all, but the one who takes what is appropriate in every situation and according to merit; and magnificent is neither the one who is dazzling on every occasion, even when one should not be, nor the one who is never, but the one who is adapted to every occasion properly.

Of this sort is the species of the moral virtues involving emotion and considered in relation to the mean; moral virtue also stands in a reciprocal relation (to practical wisdom), though not in the same way: practical wisdom follows the moral virtues in respect of their specific nature, whereas they follow it accidentally. For the just man is also practically wise, for this kind of reasoning gives him his specific character; but the practically wise man is not also just in respect of his specific character but because of the fact that, in common with (the just), he accomplishes noble and good deeds and nothing evil.

On the Emotions of the Soul

Of the emotions and impulses some are refined, some base and some are intermediate. Refined are friendship, gratitude, just resentment, sense of shame, boldness, compassion; base are envy, malignant joy, insolence; in the middle of these lie grief, fear, anger, pleasure, desire. Of these, some must be chosen at any time, whereas others must be limited. Every emotion involves pleasure and pain, and that is why the moral virtues are also concerned with these. Love of money and love of pleasure and mad sexual desire and the like are dispositions of another sort belonging to the vices. Erotic desire on the other hand is either for friendship, for sexual intercourse or for both; that is why one is noble, one is base and one is intermediate.

On Friendship

There are four different varieties of friendship: between companions, relatives, hosts and guests, and lovers; it is a matter for discussion whether we should include also the ones that involve benefaction and admiration. The starting point of the friendship between companions lies in familiarity, of the one between relatives in nature, in the case of hosts and guests in need, of the friendship between lovers in passion, of friendship involving beneficence in gratitude and of friendship involving

Πασῶν δὲ συλλήβδην εἶναι τέλη τρία, τὸ καλόν, τὸ συμφέρον, τὸ ἡδύ. Πάντα γὰρ τὸν ὁπωσ- | οῦν πρὸς φιλίαν ἰόντα διὰ τι 143.10 τούτων ἢ διὰ πάντα τὴν φιλίαν αἱρεῖσθαι.

Πρώτην μὲν οὖν, ὡς προέφην, εἶναι τὴν πρὸς ἑαυτὸν φιλίαν, δευτέραν δὲ τὴν πρὸς τοὺς γειναμένους· ἐφεξῆς δὲ τὰς πρὸς τοὺς ἄλλους οἰκείους καὶ ὀθνείους· διὸ καὶ ἐν μὲν τῇ πρὸς ἑαυτὸν εὐλαβεῖσθαι δεῖ | τὴν ὑπερβολήν, ἐν δὲ ταῖς .15 πρὸς τοὺς ἄλλους τὴν ἔλλειψιν· τὸ μὲν γὰρ φιλαυτίας, τὸ δὲ φειδωλίας ἔχει διαβολήν.

Sec. 22 Ts *Περὶ χάριτος* Sec. 23W

Χάριν δὲ λέγεσθαι τριχῶς, τὴν μὲν ὑπουργίαν ὠφελίμου αὐτοῦ ἐκείνου ἕνεκα, τὴν δ' ἄμειψιν ὑπουργίας | ὠφελίμου, .20 τὴν δὲ μνήμην ὑπουργίας τοιαύτης. Διὰ τοῦδε καὶ τὰς δαίμονας τρεῖς ὁ βίος κατεφήμισε. Λέγεσθαι δὲ χάριν καὶ τὴν ἐν ὄψει ἢ ἐν λόγοις, καθ' ἣν τὸν μὲν εὔχαριν ὀνομάζεσθαι, τὸν δ' ἐπίχαριν.

Sec. 23 Ts Βίον δ' αἱρήσεσθαι τὸν σπουδαῖον τὸν μετ' ἀρετῆς, Sec 24W | εἴτ' ἐφ' ἡγεμονίας ποτὲ γένοιτο τῶν καιρῶν αὐτὸν προ- .25 | αγαγόντων, εἴτ' ἐπὶ βασιλεῖ δέοι συμβιοῦν, εἴτε καὶ νομοθετεῖν 144.1 ἢ ἄλλως πολιτεύεσθαι. Τούτων δὲ μὴ τυγχάνοντα πρὸς τὸ δημοτικὸν τραπήσεσθαι σχῆμα διαγωγῆς ἢ τὸ θεωρητικὸν ἢ μέσον <τὸ> παιδευτικόν. Προαιρήσεσθαι μὲν | γὰρ καὶ πράττειν .5 καὶ θεωρεῖν τὰ καλά. Κωλυόμενον δε περὶ ἄμφω γίνεσθαι διὰ καιροὺς θατέρῳ χρήσεσθαι προτιμῶντα μὲν τὸν θεωρητικὸν βίον, διὰ δὲ τὸ κοινωνικὸν ἐπὶ τὰς πολιτικὰς ὁρμῶντα πράξεις. Διὸ καὶ γαμήσειν καὶ παιδοποιήσεσθαι καὶ πολιτεύσεσθαι καὶ ἐρασθήσεσθαι τὸν σώφρονα ἔρωτα καὶ μεθυσθήσεσθαι κατὰ συμπερι- | φοράς, κἂν εἰ μὴ προηγουμένως. Καὶ καθόλου .10 τὴν ἀρετὴν ἀσκοῦντα καὶ μενεῖν ἐν τῷ βίῳ καὶ πάλιν εἰ δέοι ποτὲ δι' ἀνάγκας ἀπαλλαγήσεσθαι ταφῆς προνοήσαντα

143.9–10 ὁπωσοῦν F: ὁποσοῦν P   143.10 διὰ τι τούτων F: διὰ τι τοῦ τούτων P: δι' ἔν τι τούτων Mein.   143.13–14 οἰκείους καὶ ὀθνείους P: ὀθνείους καὶ οἰκείους F   143.18 χάριν P: ἀριν F   143.19 ὠφελίμου F: ὠφέλιμον P   143.20 ὠφελίμου F: ὠφέλιμον P   143.20–21 διὰ τοῦδε FP: διὰ τοῦτο δὲ Gaisf.   143.21 δαίμονας Wilam.: τὰς δε μόνας FP: τάσδε μόνας Gaisf.: χάριτάς τε μόνας Heer.   ὁ βίος FP: ὁ Βίας Heer.   κατεφήμισε P: κατ'ευφήμισε F   143.22 δὲ F: γὰρ P   144.1 εἴτ'ἐπὶ FP: εἴτε τινὶ Usen.: εἴτε Speng.   144.4 τὸ add. Usen.   144.6 χρήσεσθαι Heer.: χρῆσθαι FP   144.7 προτιμῶντα Cant.: προτιμῶντας FP   τὸ κοινωνικὸν Heer.: τὸν κοινωνικὸν FP   144.9 παιδοποιήσεσθαι P: παιδοποιίσεσθαι F   144.10 →

admiration in authority. All these aim in short at three ends: the noble, the useful and the pleasant. For everyone who, in any way, enters a friendship chooses it for one or for all of the above reasons.

The first, as I said before, is the friendship toward oneself and second that toward one's parents. Next, come those toward other relatives and strangers. That is why one must be cautious on the one hand not to be excessive in one's feelings toward oneself, and on the other hand not to be deficient in those toward others; for in the first case one is accused of self-love, whereas in the second of meanness.

On Grace

Grace (*kharis*) is spoken of in three ways: first as rendering a beneficial service for its own sake, second as repaying a beneficial service and third as the remembrance of such a service. For this reason, also, popular myth announced three goddesses (sc. the three Graces). One also speaks of grace (*kharis*) in appearance or in words in respect of which we call one man graceful (*eukharin*) and the second charming (*epikharin*).

The virtuous person will choose a life that exhibits virtue whether as a ruler himself, if the circumstances promote him to that status, or if he has to live in the service of a king or legislate or in any other way be involved in politics. Obtaining none of the above, he will turn to the way of life of an ordinary citizen or the contemplative life or that of an educator, which lies in the middle. For he will choose both to accomplish and to contemplate noble things. In case he is hindered by circumstances from occupying himself with both, he will become engaged in one of the two, assigning on the one hand a greater value to the contemplative life, but on the other hand, because of his social nature inclining toward political actions. That is why he will get married and will have children and will take part in government and will experience temperate love and will enjoy heavy drinking in accordance with social gatherings, albeit not as a primary activity. And generally practicing virtue, he will remain alive or again, if it ever becomes necessary, he will depart (from life) having taken forethought for his burial according to the laws

---

μεθυσθήσεσθαι F: μεμυθήσεσθαι P   144.12 μενεῖν *Speng.*: μένειν FP   144.13
προνοήσαντα F: προνοήσαντας P

κατὰ νόμον καὶ τὸ πάτριον ἔθος καὶ τῶν ἄλλων ὅσα τοῖς κατ-
| οιχομένοις ἐπιτελεῖν ὅσιον. 144.15

Βίων δὲ τριττὰς ἰδέας εἶναι, πρακτικόν, θεωρητικόν, σύνθετον ἐξ ἀμφοῖν. Τὸν μὲν γὰρ ἀπολαυστικὸν ἥττονα ἢ κατ' ἄνθρωπον εἶναι, προκρίνεσθαι δὲ τῶν ἄλλων τὸν θεωρητικόν. Πολιτεύσεσθαί τε τὸν σπουδαῖον προηγου | μένως, μὴ κατὰ .20 περίστασιν· τὸν γὰρ πρακτικὸν βίον τὸν αὐτὸν εἶναι τῷ πολιτικῷ.

Βίον δὲ κράτιστον μὲν τὸν κατ' ἀρετὴν ἐν τοῖς κατὰ φύσιν· δεύτερον δὲ τὸν κατὰ τὴν μέσην ἕξιν τὰ πλεῖστα καὶ κυριώτατα τῶν κατὰ | φύσιν ἔχοντα· τούτους μὲν οὖν 145.1 αἱρετούς, φευκτὸν δὲ τὸν κατὰ κακίαν. Διαφέρειν δὲ τὸν εὐδαίμονα βίον τοῦ καλοῦ καθ' ὅσον ὃ μὲν ἐν τοῖς κατὰ φύσιν εἶναι βούλεται διὰ | παντός, ὃ δὲ καὶ ἐν τοῖς παρὰ φύσιν· καὶ .5 πρὸς ὃν μὲν οὐκ αὐτάρκης ἡ ἀρετή, πρὸς ὃν δὲ αὐτάρκης. Μέσον δέ τινα βίον εἶναι τὸν κατὰ τὴν μέσην ἕξιν ἐν ᾧ καὶ τὰ καθήκοντα ἀποδίδοσθαι· τὰ μὲν γὰρ κατορθώματα ἐν τῷ κατ' ἀρετὴν εἶναι βίῳ, τὰ δ' ἁμαρτήματα ἐν τῷ κατὰ | κακίαν, τὰ δὲ .10 καθήκοντα ἐν τῷ μέσῳ καλουμένῳ βίῳ.

Sec. 24 Ts   Τεθεωρημένων δὲ τούτων καὶ ταῦτα διαλάβωμεν· εἶναι μὲν   Sec. 25W
γὰρ τὴν ἠθικὴν ἀρετὴν κοινῶς ἕξιν προαιρετικὴν τῶν μέσων ἡδονῶν τε καὶ λυπῶν, στοχαστικὴν τοῦ καλοῦ ᾗ καλόν, τὴν δὲ κακίαν ὑπεναντίαν εἶναι ταύτῃ. | Κοινὴν δὲ δοξαστικοῦ καὶ .15 ἠθικοῦ ἕξιν <εἶναι τὴν ἀρετὴν>, θεωρητικὴν καὶ προαιρετικὴν καὶ πρακτικὴν τῶν ἐν ταῖς πράξεσι καλῶν.

Τοῦ δὲ διανοητικοῦ καὶ τοῦ ἐπιστημονικοῦ κοινὴν ἀκρότητα λογικῆς κατασκευῆς εἶναι, θεωρητικὴν καὶ πρακτικήν· σοφίαν δὲ ἐπιστήμην τῶν πρώτων αἰτίων· φρό- | νησιν .20 δὲ ἕξιν βουλευτικὴν καὶ πρακτικὴν ἀγαθῶν καὶ καλῶν ᾗ καλά.

145.12–13 EE 2.1227b8–9   145.13–14 MM 1.1190a9–11   145.15–21 EN 6.1144b14–21   145.21–146.14 MM 1.1190b9–1193a38, b25–26

144.13–14 κατὰ νόμον om. P   144.16 τριττὰς F: περιττὰς P   144.17 τὸν μὲν Cant.: τὸ μὲν FP   144.19 πολιτεύσεσθαί Meur.: πολιτεύεσθαί FP   144.21–22 τὸν κατ' ἀρετὴν F: τῶν κατ' ἀρετὴν P   144.22 τὸν κατὰ P: τῶν κατὰ F   145.1 φευκτὸν Speng.: φευκτέον FP   145.1–2 τὸν κατὰ κακίαν F: τῶν κατὰ κακίαν P   145.6 πρὸς ὃν δὲ P: πρὸς ὃ F   145.14 ᾗ P²: ἢ FP¹ ὑπεναντίαν Heer.: ὑπεναντίον FP   145.15 δοξαστικοῦ καὶ ἠθικοῦ coni. Wachs. in app. crit: δοξαστικῆς καὶ ἠθικῆς FP   145.17 τοῦ δὲ διανοητικοῦ Ts.: τὴν δὲ διανοητικὴν Usen.: τὴν δὲ κοινὴν FP: τὴν δὲ κοινὴ

→

and traditional customs and the rest (of the religious duties) that it is holy to offer to the dead.

There are three forms of life: the active, the contemplative and the one which combines both. The one devoted to pleasure is not worthy of human beings, whereas the contemplative one is deemed superior to the others. The virtuous agent will take part in politics as a primary activity and not only in special circumstances; for the active life is identical with the political one.

The best life is the virtuous one surrounded by the things which are according to nature; second best is the one which is according to the intermediate disposition in possession of the majority and the most important of the things which are according to nature; these (forms of life) are desirable, whereas the vicious one should be avoided. Now, the happy life differs from the noble one in that the former is meant to be surrounded constantly by things which are according to nature, whereas the latter one includes also things which are contrary to nature. And for the former virtue is not sufficient, whereas for the latter it is. An intermediate way of life is the one which is according to the intermediate disposition in which appropriate actions are exhibited; for right actions are found in the life which is according to virtue, wrong actions in the vicious life and appropriate actions in the so-called intermediate life.

Sec. 24 Ts   After having examined these matters, let us consider the following as well: moral virtue is, generally speaking, a disposition concerned with the choice of middling pleasures and pains, aiming at the noble in so far as it is noble, while vice is its opposite. Common to the judging and the ethical (parts of the soul) is a disposition concerned with contemplation and choice and doing noble things in actions.   Sec. 25W

Common to the discursive and knowledgeable parts of the soul is the acme of the rational constitution, which is both theoretical and practical; theoretical wisdom is the knowledge of first causes, whereas practical wisdom is a deliberative disposition resulting in good and noble actions, in so far as they are noble.

---

del. Mor. (1973: 392, n.245)   καὶ *F*: ἐκ *P post* ἐπιστημονικοῦ *lac. statuit Wachs.*
145.19 τῶν πρώτων *FP*: κατὰ πρώτων *Heer.*   αἰτίων *Speng.*: αἰτιῶν *FP*   145.21 ἢ *Heer.*: ἥ *FP*   *post* ἢ *add.* ἀγαθὰ καὶ *Speng.*

54   Georgia Tsouni

Ἀνδρείαν δὲ ἕξιν ἐν θάρρεσι | καὶ φόβοις τοῖς μέσοις 146.1
ἄμεμπτον· σωφροσύνην δὲ ἕξιν ἐν αἱρέσει καὶ φυγῇ <ἡδονῶν
καὶ λυπῶν> ἀμέμπτους ποιοῦσαν δι' αὐτὸ τὸ καλόν· πραότητα
δὲ ἕξιν μέσην ὀργιλότητος καὶ ἀναλγησίας· ἐλευθεριότητα
δὲ μεσότητα ἀσωτίας καὶ ἀνελευ- | θερίας· μεγαλοψυχίαν δὲ .5
μεσότητα χαυνότητος καὶ μικροψυχίας· μεγαλοπρέπειαν δὲ
<μεσότητα σαλακωνείας καὶ μικροπρεπείας· νέμεσιν δὲ> μεσ-
ότητα φθονερίας καὶ ἐπιχαιρεκακίας· σεμνότητα δὲ μεσότητα
αὐθαδείας καὶ ἀρεσκείας· αἰδῶ δὲ μεσότητα ἀναισχυντίας καὶ
| καταπλήξεως· εὐτραπελίαν δὲ <μεσότητα> βωμολοχίας καὶ .10
ἀγροικίας· φιλίαν δὲ μεσότητα κολακείας καὶ ἔχθρας· ἀλήθ-
ειαν δὲ μεσότητα εἰρωνείας καὶ ἀλαζονείας· δικαιοσύνην δὲ
μεσότητα ὑπεροχῆς καὶ ἐλλείψεως καὶ πολλοῦ καὶ ὀλίγου.

Sec. 25 Ts | Πολλῶν δὲ καὶ ἄλλων οὐσῶν ἀρετῶν τῶν μὲν καθ' αὑτὰς .15
τῶν δ' ἐν εἴδεσι τῶν εἰρημένων οἷον ὑπὸ μὲν τὴν δικαιοσύνην
εὐσεβείας, ὁσιότητος, χρηστότητος, εὐκοινωνησίας, εὐσυ-
ναλλαξίας· ὑπὸ δὲ τὴν σωφροσύνην εὐκοσμίας, εὐταξίας,
αὐταρκείας· <ὑπὸ δὲ τὴν ἀνδρείαν | εὐψυχίας, φιλοπονίας>, .20
ἐπιδραμεῖν οὐκ ἄτοπον καὶ τοὺς | τούτων ὅρους. 147.1

Εὐσέβειαν μὲν οὖν εἶναι ἕξιν θεῶν καὶ δαιμόνων θερα-
πευτικὴν μεταξὺ οὖσαν ἀθεότητος καὶ δεισιδαιμονίας· ὁσιό-
τητα δὲ ἕξιν δικαίων τῶν πρὸς τοὺς θεοὺς καὶ κατοιχομένους
τηρητικὴν μεταξὺ ἀνοσιότητος | οὖσαν καὶ ἀνωνύμου .5
τινός· χρηστότητα δὲ ἕξιν ἑκουσίως εὐποιητικὴν ἀνθρώπων
αὐτῶν ἐκείνων χάριν μεταξὺ πονηρίας οὖσαν καὶ ἀνωνύμου·
εὐκοινωνησίαν δὲ ἕξιν ἀμέμπτους ἐν κοινωνίᾳ παρεχομένην,
μεταξὺ ἀκοινωνησίας οὖσαν καὶ ἀνωνύμου· εὐσυναλλαξίαν δὲ
ἕξιν εὐλα- | βητικὴν τῆς ἐν τοῖς συμβολαίοις ἀδικίας, μεταξὺ .10
ἀσυναλλαξίας οὖσαν καὶ ἀνωνύμου· τὴν δὲ ἀνώνυμον κατὰ
τὸ ἀκριβοδίκαιον εἶναί πως· εὐκοσμίαν δὲ ἕξιν περί τε κινήσεις
καὶ σχέσεις τηρητικὴν τοῦ πρέποντος μεταξὺ οὖσαν ἀκοσμίας

146.7–12 EE 3.1233b18–1234a23, EN 2.1108a19–b6   146.17 Virt. et Vit. 1250b21–23

145.21 θάρρεσι Mein.: θάρσεσι Speng.: θαρρήσει F: θάρσει P   146.2 post φυγῇ
add. ἡδονῶν καὶ λυπῶν Ts.   δι' αὐτὸ τὸ F: διὰ τὸ τὸ P   146.3–4 ἀναλγησίας F:
ἀναλογησίας P   146.6–7 post μεγαλοπρέπειαν δὲ suppl. μεσότητα σαλακωνείας καὶ
μικροπρεπείας· νέμεσιν δὲ Heer.   146.8–9 σεμνότητα ... ἀρεσκείας om. F   146.10
post εὐτραπελίαν δὲ add. μεσότητα Heer.   146.11 κολακείας Heer.: καλοκαγαθίας
FP   146.18 σωφροσύνην F: σοφροσύνην P   146.19–20 ante ἐπιδραμεῖν add.
ὑπὸ δὲ τὴν ἀνδρείαν εὐψυχίας, φιλοπονίας Meur.   147.4 κατοιχομένους Heer.:
→

Didymus' Epitome of Peripatetic Ethics—An Edition with Translation 55

Courage is a blameless disposition in middling boldness and fears; temperance a disposition concerned with the choice and avoidance of pleasures and pains which makes people blameless for the sake of the noble itself; mildness a mean disposition between irascibility and apathy; generosity a mean between wastefulness and lack of generosity; greatness of soul a mean between vanity and littleness of soul; magnificence a mean between showiness and shabbiness; just resentment a mean between envy and malignant joy; dignity a mean between wilfulness and obsequiousness; shame a mean between shamelessness and extreme shyness; wittiness a mean between buffoonery and boorishness; friendliness a mean between flattery and hostility; truthfulness a mean between mock-modesty and boastfulness; justice a mean between excess and deficiency and much and little.

Sec. 25 Ts As there are many other virtues, either in their own right, or as species of those already mentioned, for example under justice are reverence toward the gods, piety, goodness of heart, good fellowship, fair dealing; under temperance decency, orderliness, self-sufficiency and under courage stoutness of heart and tenacity, it wouldn't be inappropriate to examine also the definitions of these.

Reverence is a disposition concerned with the worship of gods and spirits being between godlessness and superstition; piety a disposition which ensures just behavior toward the gods and the dead being between impiety and an anonymous vice; goodness of heart a disposition willingly to benefit people for their own sake being between baseness and an anonymous vice; good fellowship a disposition which makes people blameless in social interactions being between unsociability and an anonymous vice; fair dealing a disposition which takes care to avoid injustice among people making deals being between the refusal to make contracts and an anonymous vice —the nameless disposition having something to do with being a stickler for justice; decency a disposition which guards propriety in movements

κατοιχομένων *FP* 147.6 ἐκείνων *Cant.*: οἰκείων *FP* 147.8 ἐν *Heer.*: ὅθεν *FP* 147.9 ἀνωνύμου *F*: ἀκοινωνύμου *P* 147.10 συμβολαίοις *Usen.*: συμβαλλομένοις *FP* 147.10–11ἀσυναλλαξίας *F*: συναλλαξίας *P* 147.11 ἀνώνυμον *F*: ἀνωνύμου *P* 147.12 ἀκριβοδίκαιον *Trend.*: ἀκροδίκαιον *FP* 147.12–14 εὐκοσμίαν … εὐταξίαν *om. P*

καὶ ἀνωνύμου· εὐταξίαν δὲ ἕξιν στο- | χαστικὴν τοῦ περὶ τάξιν 147.15
καλοῦ μεταξὺ ἀταξίας οὖσαν καὶ ἀνωνύμου· αὐτάρκειαν δὲ
ἕξιν ἀρκουμένην τοῖς τυχοῦσι μετὰ ἐλευθεριότητος μεταξὺ
πτωχείας οὖσαν καὶ πολυτελείας· εὐψυχίαν δὲ ἕξιν ἀήττητον
ἐν δεινῶν ὑπομοναῖς μεταξὺ ἀψυχίας καὶ ἀρειμανιότητος·
φιλοπονίαν | δὲ ἕξιν ἀνένδοτον πόνοις ἐξεργαστικὴν τοῦ .20
καλοῦ μεταξὺ μαλακίας τε καὶ ματαιοπονίας.

Τὴν δὲ ἐκ πασῶν τῶν ἠθικῶν ἀρετὴν συνεστηκυῖαν
λέγεσθαι μὲν καλοκαγαθίαν, τελείαν δ᾽ ἀρετὴν εἶναι, τά
τε ἀγαθὰ ὠφέλιμα καὶ καλὰ ποιοῦσαν τά τε καλὰ δι᾽ | αὐτὰ 25
αἱρουμένην.

Sec. 26 Ts   Διωρισμένων δ᾽ ἱκανῶς τῶν περὶ τὰς ἀρετὰς καὶ | σχεδὸν Sec. 26W
τῶν πλείστων ἀνειλημμένων κεφαλαίων τοῦ ἠθικοῦ τόπου,
ἀναγκαῖον ἐφεξῆς καὶ περὶ τοῦ οἰκονομικοῦ τε καὶ πολιτικοῦ
διελθεῖν ἐπειδὴ φύσει πολιτικὸν ζῷον ἄνθρωπος.

| Πολιτεία δὲ πρώτη σύνοδος ἀνδρὸς καὶ γυναικὸς 148.5
κατὰ νόμον ἐπὶ τέκνων γενέσει καὶ βίου κοινωνία. Τοῦτο δὲ
προσονομάζεται μὲν οἶκος, ἀρχὴ δὲ πόλεώς ἐστι· περὶ οὗ δὴ καὶ
λεκτέον. Μικρὰ γάρ τις ἔοικεν εἶναι πόλις ὁ οἶκος, εἴ γε κατ᾽
εὐχὴν αὐξομένου τοῦ γάμου καὶ τῶν παί- | δων ἐπιδιδόντων .10
καὶ συνδυαζομένων ἀλλήλοις, ἕτερος οἶκος ὑφίσταται καὶ
τρίτος οὕτω καὶ τέταρτος ἐκ δὲ τούτων κώμη καὶ πόλις.
Πλειόνων γὰρ γενομένων κωμῶν πόλις ἀπετελέσθη. Διὸ καὶ τὰ
σπέρματα καθάπερ τῆς γενέσεως τῇ πόλει παρέσχεν ὁ οἶκος,
οὕτω καὶ τῆς πολι- | τείας· καὶ γὰρ βασιλείας ὑπογραφὴν εἶναι .15
περὶ τὸν οἶκον καὶ ἀριστοκρατίας καὶ δημοκρατίας. Γονέων
μὲν γὰρ πρὸς τέκνα κοινωνίας τὸ σχῆμα βασιλικόν· ἀνδρῶν
δὲ πρὸς γυναῖκας ἀριστοκρατικόν· παίδων δὲ πρὸς ἀλλήλους
δημοκρατικόν.

Συνέρχεσθαι γὰρ τῷ θήλει τὸ ἄρρεν κατὰ πόθον | τεκν- .20
ώσεως καὶ τῆς τοῦ γένους διαμονῆς· ἐφίεσθαι γὰρ ἑκάτερον
γεννήσεως. Συνελθόντων δὲ καὶ συνεργὸν τῆς | κοινωνίας 149.1

147.23 *EE* 8.1249a18   148.3–4 *EN* 1.1097b11, *Pol.* 1.1253a3   148.12–13 *Pol.*
1.1252b27–28   148.13–15 *Cic. Off.* 1.54   148.16–17 *EN* 8.1160b24–25   148.19–
20 *Pol.* 1.1252a26–28   148.21–149.5 *Pol.* 1.1253b14–1255b15

147.17 πτωχείας P: πτωχίας F   147.19 ἀρειμανιότητος *Gaisf.*: ἀριμανιότητος FP
147.20 ἀνένδοτον F: ἀνένδοπον P   147.26 διωρισμένων P: δι᾽ ὡρισμένων F   148.3
ζῷον F: ζώων P   148.4 ἄνθρωπος Ts.: ἄνθρωπος FP   148.6 γενέσει FP: γεννήσει
Speng.   148.11 ὑφίσταται FP²: ἀφίσταται P¹   148.13–14 γενέσεως F: γνώσεως P

→

and postures being between indecency and an anonymous vice; orderliness a disposition aiming at noble order being between lack of order and an anonymous vice; self-sufficiency a disposition which contents itself with chance things in a generous way being between beggary and luxury; stoutness of heart a disposition unyielding in enduring terrible things being between faint-heartedness and warlike frenzy; tenacity a disposition which does not give in to pain when accomplishing the noble being between softness and vain labour.

And the virtue which is composed of all the moral virtues is called noble-goodness and constitutes complete virtue making the good things useful and noble and choosing the noble ones for their own sake.

Having defined sufficiently the things pertaining to the virtues and having taken up nearly most of the chief points of the ethical domain of philosophy it is necessary, in the following, to examine the topics of household management and politics, since humans are by nature political animals.

The first political association is the coming together of man and woman according to law for the purposes of the procreation of children and partnership in life. This is called a household but is also the starting-point of the city; so we must comment on it. For the household seems to be a small city, if, of course, marriage brings the increase that is wished for and the children grow up and, coming together in pairs, another household comes into being and so a third and a fourth, and from these a village and a city; for from multiple villages results a city. That is why the household offers, as it were, the seeds for the generation of the city, and so of the political constitution. For the household manifests an outline of kingship, as also of aristocracy and democracy; for the association of parents toward their children has the form of kingship, that of husbands toward their wives (the form of) aristocracy, and that of children toward one another (the form of) democracy.

Now, the male comes together with the female driven by a desire for procreation and the preservation of the family; for each desires procreation. Having come together and taken in addition a co-worker for their association, either a slave by

148.14 οὕτω P: οὕτως F   148.18 δὲ Heer.: τὲ FP   148.19 συνέρχεσθαι Wachs.: συνέρχεται FP   τῷ θήλει F: τῷ θῆλυ P   148.20 τεκνώσεως F: τεκνόσεως P

προσλαβομένων εἴτε φύσει δοῦλον—ἰσχυρὸν μὲν τῷ σώματι πρὸς ὑπηρεσίαν νωθῆ δὲ καὶ καθ᾽ ἑαυτὸν ἀδύνατον διαζῆν, ᾧ τὸ ἄρχεσθαι συμφέρειν—εἴτε καὶ νόμῳ δοῦλον, ἐκ τῆς ἐπὶ τὸ αὐτὸ συνόδου καὶ τῆς πάντων πρὸς | ἓν συμφέρον προμηθείας 149.5 οἶκον συνίστασθαι.

Τούτου δὲ τὴν ἀρχὴν κατὰ φύσιν ἔχειν τὸν ἄνδρα. Τὸ γὰρ βουλευτικὸν ἐν γυναικὶ μὲν χεῖρον, ἐν παισὶ δ᾽ οὐδέπω, περὶ δούλους οὐδ᾽ ὅλως· τὴν δ᾽ οἰκονομικὴν φρόνησιν διοικητικὴν οὖσαν αὐτοῦ τε καὶ τῶν κατ᾽ οἶκον | οἰκείαν ἀνδρὸς ὑπάρχειν. .10 Ταύτης δὲ τὸ μὲν εἶναι πατρικόν, τὸ δὲ γαμικόν, τὸ δὲ δεσποτικόν, τὸ δὲ χρηματιστικόν. Δεῖν γὰρ ὥσπερ στρατιᾷ μὲν παρασκευῆς, πόλει δὲ προσόδων, τέχνῃ δ᾽ ὀργάνων, οὕτω καὶ οἴκῳ τῶν ἀναγκαίων.

Διττὰ δὲ ταῦτα πρός τε τὸ κοινότερον ζῆν καὶ πρὸς τὸ | εὖ. Τούτων γὰρ πρῶτον ἔχειν δεῖν πρόνοιαν τὸν οἰκονομικόν .15 ἢ τὰς προσόδους αὔξοντα διὰ πορισμῶν ἐλευθερίων ἢ τὰ δαπανήματα συστέλλοντα· μέγιστον γὰρ τοῦτο τὸ κεφάλαιον τῆς οἰκονομικῆς. Διὸ καὶ πολλῶν ἔμπειρον <δεῖν> εἶναι τὸν οἰκονομικόν, γεωργίας, προβατείας, μεταλ- | λείας, ἵνα τοὺς .20 λυσιτελεστάτους καρποὺς ἅμα καὶ δικαιοτάτους διαγινώσκῃ.

Τῆς δὲ χρηματιστικῆς τὴν μὲν εἶναι κρείττω, τὴν δὲ χείρω· κρείττω μὲν τὴν φύσει γιγνομένην, χείρω δὲ τὴν διὰ καπηλικῆς. <Περὶ οἰκονομικῆς> ἀπόχρη.

Sec. 27 Ts | Περὶ δὲ πολιτικῆς ταῦτ᾽ ἂν εἴη κεφάλαια· πρῶτον μέν ὅτι 150.1 συνέστησαν αἱ πόλεις τῇ μὲν διὰ τὸ φύσει κοινωνικὸν εἶναι τὸν ἄνθρωπον τῇ δὲ διὰ τὸ συμφέρον. Εἶτα ὅτι ἡ τελειοτάτη κοινωνία πόλις ἐστὶ καὶ ὅτι πολίτης | ἐστὶν ᾧ μέτεστι πολιτικῆς 150.5 ἀρχῆς. Πόλις δὲ τὸ ἐκ τῶν τοιούτων πλῆθος ἱκανὸν πρὸς αὐτάρκειαν ζωῆς. Τοῦ δὲ πλήθους ὅρον εἶναι τοιοῦτον ὥστε μήτε τὴν πόλιν ἀσυμπαθῆ μήτ᾽ εὐκαταφρόνητον ὑπάρχειν, παρασκευάσθαι δὲ καὶ τὰ πρὸς τὴν ζωὴν ἀνενδεῶς καὶ τὰ πρὸς τοὺς ἔξωθεν | ἐπιόντας ἱκανῶς. Εἶναι γὰρ τῆς φρονήσεως 150.10

149.6–8 Pol. 1.1260a12–14   150.4–5 Pol. 3.1275a22–23   150.5–6 Pol. 3.1275b20–21

149.8 post δούλους add. δ᾽ Mein.   149.9 post αὐτοῦ τε add. οἴκου Henk.   149.10 οἰκείαν F: οἰκίαν P   149.15 δεῖν Wachs.: δεῖ FP   149.17 post γὰρ habet δὴ P   149.19 post ἔμπειρον add. δεῖν Wachs. προβατείας F: προβατίας P   149.23 καπηλικῆς F: καπηλικοῖς P   149.23–24 περὶ οἰκονομικῆς om. FP: καὶ ταῦτα μὲν περὶ οἰκονομικῆς suppl. Cant.   150.5 ᾧ Heer.: ὧν FP   150.6 αὐτάρκειαν F: αὐτάρκιαν P   150.7 μήτε om. P   150.8 παρασκευάσθαι P: παρεσκευάσθαι F   150.9 τὴν om. P

nature—someone who has a strong body for service but is slow and unable to survive on his own and who is benefitted by being ruled—or else a slave by convention, the household comes to be from the coming-together for a single purpose and the forethought of everyone toward a single advantage. 149.5

The man is the ruler of the household according to nature; for the deliberative faculty is worse in a female, it does not yet exist in children, and is altogether absent in slaves. (Thus), the wisdom pertaining to the household being concerned with the administration of the house and the persons within it properly belongs to a man. This encompasses the role of the father, the .10 husband, the master (of slaves) and the acquisition of resources; for the household needs necessities in the same way as an army needs equipment, a city revenues, and a craft tools.

And these (necessities) are of two sorts: for the more communal life and for the good life. The administrator of the house- .15 hold needs first to take care of these, either by increasing the income through money-getting activities which pertain to a free person, or else by reducing the expenses; for this is the chief point of household management. That is why the administrator of the household needs to be experienced in many things: in agriculture, keeping of sheep, mining, in order to discern the .20 most profitable and, at the same time, most just resources.

Of acquiring resources, there is the better and the worse way; better is that which is according to nature, worse that which involves retail trade. Let this suffice on household management.

Sec. 27 Ts   The following are the chief points on politics: first, that cit- 150.1 ies were established, on the one hand, because humans are by nature social, and, on the other hand, for the sake of advantage. Next, that the most complete association is a city and a citizen is someone who participates in political rule. A city consists of 150.5 a number of such persons which is adequate for a self-sufficient life. There is a limit in the number (of citizens), such that the city is neither wanting in fellow-feeling nor readily despised, and is provided with the things necessary for life without shortage and also adequate for defending itself against foreign invaders. For these are species of practical wisdom: household management, 150.10

τὸ μὲν οἰκονομικόν, τὸ δὲ νομοθετικόν, τὸ δὲ πολιτικόν, τὸ δὲ στρατηγικόν. Οἰκονομικὸν μέν, ὡς εἶπον, τὸ διοικητικὸν αὐτοῦ τε καὶ τῶν περὶ οἶκον, νομοθετικὸν δὲ…, <στρατηγικὸν δὲ> τὸ | περὶ τὴν θεωρίαν καὶ διοίκησιν τῶν στρατοπέδῳ συμφερόντων. .15

Ἄρχειν δ' ἀναγκαῖον τῶν πόλεων ἢ ἕνα ἢ ὀλίγους ἢ πάντας. Τούτων δ' ἕκαστον ὀρθῶς ἢ φαύλως ἔχειν. Ὀρθῶς μέν, ὅταν οἱ ἄρχοντες τοῦ κοινῇ συμφέροντος | στοχάζωνται· .20 φαύλως δέ ὅταν τοῦ ἰδίου. Τὸ δὲ φαῦλον παρέκβασιν εἶναι τοῦ ὀρθοῦ. Βασιλείαν μὲν οὖν καὶ ἀριστοκρατίαν καὶ δημοκρατίαν ἐφίεσθαι τοῦ ὀρθοῦ· τυραννίδα δὲ καὶ ὀλιγαρχίαν καὶ ὀχλοκρατίαν τοῦ φαύλου. Γί- | νεσθαι δέ τινα καὶ μικτὴν ἐκ τῶν 151.1 ὀρθῶν πολιτειῶν ἀρχήν. Μεταβάλλειν δὲ τὰς πολιτείας πολλάκις πρὸς τὸ ἄμεινον καὶ τὸ χεῖρον. Καθόλου δ' ἀρίστην εἶναι πολιτείαν τὴν κατ' ἀρετὴν διακεκοσμημένην, χειρίστην δὲ τὴν κατὰ | κακίαν. Ἄρχειν δὲ καὶ βουλεύειν καὶ δικάζειν ἐν .5 μὲν ταῖς δημοκρατίαις ἐκ πάντων, ἢ αἱρέσει ἢ κλήρῳ· ἐν δὲ ταῖς ὀλιγαρχίαις ἐκ τῶν εὐπόρων· ἐν δὲ ταῖς ἀριστοκρατίαις ἐκ τῶν ἀρίστων.

Στάσεις δ' ἐν ταῖς πόλεσι γίνεσθαι τὰς μὲν κατὰ | λόγον, .10 τὰς δὲ κατὰ πάθος. Κατὰ λόγον μὲν ὅταν οἱ ἴσοι ὄντες ἄνισα ἔχειν ἀναγκάζωνται· κατὰ πάθος δὲ διὰ τιμὴν ἢ φιλαρχίαν ἢ κέρδος ἢ εὐπορίαν. Καταλύεσθαι δὲ τὰς πολιτείας διὰ δύο αἰτίας, ἢ βίᾳ ἢ ἀπάτῃ. Μονιμωτέρας δὲ γίνεσθαι τοῦ | κοινῇ .15 συμφέροντος ἐπιμελουμένας.

Δικαστήρια δὲ καὶ βουλευτήρια καὶ ἐκκλησίας καὶ ἀρχὰς διωρίσθαι ταῖς πολιτείαις οἰκείως. Κοινοτάτας δ' ἀρχὰς εἶναι ἱερωσύνην θεῶν, στρατηγίαν, ναυαρχίαν, ἀγορανομίαν, γυμνασιαρχίαν, γυναικονομίαν, παιδονομίαν, | ἀστυνομίαν, .20 ταμιείαν, νομοφυλακίαν, πρακτορείαν. Τούτων δ' εἶναι τὰς μὲν κατὰ πόλεις, τὰς δὲ κατὰ πόλεμον, τὰς δὲ περὶ τοὺς λιμένας καὶ τὰς ἐμπορίας.

150.19–20 *Pol.* 3.1279a28–31   151.13–14 *Pol.* 5.1304b7–8

150.13 post αὐτοῦ τε add. οἴκου Henk.   150.14 post νομοθετικὸν δὲ lac. statuit Heer. ante τὸ περὶ τὴν θεωρίαν suppl. πολιτικὸν δὲ … στρατηγικὸν δὲ Mein.   150.15 στρατοπέδῳ Heer.: στρατοπέδων FP   150.21 παρέκβασιν Speng.: παράβασιν FP   150.22–23 τυραννίδα F: τυραννία P   151.1 πολιτειῶν ἀρχὴν P: πολιτιῶν ἀρχὴν F: πολιτείαν ἀρίστην Usen.   151.7 ὀλιγαρχίαις Heer.: ὀλιγαρκίαις FP   151.11 ἄνισα ἔχειν Ts.: ἴσα ἔχειν FP   ante ἴσα ἔχειν suppl. ἄνισα, οἱ δὲ ἄνισοι ὄντες Speng.

→

legislation, politics and military strategy. The one concerned with household management is, as I said, the one occupied with the administration of the house and the persons within it, the legislative one…, whereas <the one concerned with military strategy> is about the investigation and administration of what is beneficial for the army.

It is necessary for a city to be ruled either by one person, or by a few, or by all. And each of these is correct or bad. (A city is ruled) correctly when the rulers aim at the common advantage and badly when (they aim) at their own. The bad is a deviation from the correct. Kinsgship and aristocracy and democracy aim at what is correct, whereas tyranny and oligarchy and mob-rule at what is bad. There is also a mixed rule which is a combination of the correct constitutions. Political constitutions often change for the better or worse. In general, the best constitution is the one arranged according to virtue, whereas the worst the one (arranged) according to vice. In democracies ruling, deliberating and passing judgement are carried out by all, (selected) either by election or by lot; in oligarchies by the wealthy; in aristocracies by the best.

Civil strife happens in cities either in accordance with reason, or in accordance with emotion: in accordance with reason, when those who are equal are forced to have unequal shares; and in accordance with emotion, because of honor or love of power or gain or easy procurement of advantages. Political constitutions are undone by two causes, either violence or deceit; those which exhibit concern for the common advantage become more stable.

Law courts and councils and assemblies and offices are properly determined in accordance with the constitutions. Especially common offices are those of a priest, general, commander of a fleet, overseer of the market place, superintendent of the gymnasia, overseer of women, overseer of education, overseer of the city, treasurer, guardian of the laws, tax collector. Of these some concern the cities, some war, some the ports and some (the regulation of) trade.

151.13 *post* κέρδος *habet* ἢ φυγαρχίαν F: φιλαρχίαν *iter*. P   151.17 κοινοτάτας P: κοινωτάτας F   151.19 ἀγορανομίαν *Mein. ex. cod. Aug.*: ἀγορονομίαν FP   151.21 τὰς δὲ κατὰ πόλεμον *om*. P

Πολιτικοῦ δ' ἀνδρὸς ἔργον εἶναι καὶ τὸ διορθῶσαι πολιτείαν, ὃ πολὺ χαλεπώτερον φαίνεσθαι τοῦ κτίσαι· | καὶ τὸ διανεῖμαι τὸ πλῆθος τῶν ἀνθρώπων τὸ μὲν πρὸς τἀναγκαῖα, τὸ δὲ πρὸς τὰ σπουδαῖα. Δημιουργοὺς μὲν γὰρ καὶ θῆτας καὶ γεωργοὺς καὶ ἐμπόρους πρὸς τὸ ἀναγκαῖον, ὑπηρέτας γὰρ εἶναι τοῖς πολιτικοῖς τούτους· τὸ | δὲ μάχιμον πᾶν καὶ βουλευτικὸν κυριώτερον εἶναι διὰ τὸ ἀρετῆς ἐπιμελεῖσθαι καὶ περὶ τὰ καλὰ σπουδάζειν. Τούτων δὲ τὸ μὲν πρεσβύτερον προβουλεύειν, τὸ δὲ γεραρώτερον θεραπεύειν τὸ θεῖον, τὸ δὲ νέον ἅπαν προπολεμεῖν. Ταύτην δ' ἀρχαίαν εἶναι πάνυ τὴν διάταξιν, Αἰγυπτίων πρώ- | των καταστησαμένων.

Πολιτικῶν δὲ καὶ τῶν ἄλλων οὐχ ἧττον καὶ τὸ τὰ ἱερὰ τῶν θεῶν ἐν τοῖς ἐπιφανεστάτοις ἱδρῦσθαι τόποις· καὶ τὸ τῆς τῶν ἰδιωτῶν χώρας τὸ μὲν ἕτερον πρὸς ταῖς ἐσχατιαῖς διατετάχθαι, τὸ δ' ἕτερον πρὸς τῇ πόλει ἵνα | δύο κλήρων ἑνὶ ἑκάστῳ νεμηθέντων ἀμφότερα τὰ μέρη τῆς χώρας εὐσύνοπτα ὑπάρχῃ. Χρήσιμον δὲ καὶ τὸ νομοθετεῖν συσσίτια ποιεῖσθαι καὶ τὸ περὶ τῆς κοινῆς παιδείας τῶν τέκνων σπουδάζειν· καὶ τὸ πρὸς τὴν ῥώμην τῶν σωμάτων καὶ τελειότητα δεῖν μήτε νεωτέρων ἄγαν | μήτε πρεσβυτέρων τοὺς γάμους ποιεῖσθαι, ἀτελῆ γὰρ γίνεσθαι κατ' ἀμφοτέρας τὰς ἡλικίας καὶ τελείως ἀσθενῆ τὰ ἔκγονα. Καὶ τὸ νομοθετεῖν δὲ μηθὲν ἐκτρέφειν πεπηρωμένον, μηδ' ἐκτιθέναι τέλειον, μηδ' ἐξαμβλοῦν συμφορώτατον δήπου. Καὶ τῶν μὲν πολιτικῶν τὰ κεφάλαια | ταῦτα.

152.8–10 *Pol. 7.1329b31–32*   152.13–16 *Pol. 7.1330a14–16*   152.19–22 *Pol. 7.1335a11–13*   152.22–23 *Pol. 7.1335b20–22*

151.24 φαίνεσθαι Usen.: φαίνεται FP   152.1 τὸ πλῆθος Usen.: τοῦ πλήθους FP   152.3 θῆτας Gaisf.: θέτας FP   152.6 ante ἀρετῆς habet καὶ P   152.7 τὸ μὲν πρεσβύτερον Heer.: τὸν μὲν πρεσβύτερον FP   152.7 τὸ δὲ γεραρώτερον Heer: τὸν δὲ γεραρώτερον FP   152.8 ἅπαν FP: ἁπάντων Mein.   152.9 ἀρχαίαν F: ἀρχαίων P   152.11 πολιτικῶν FP: πολιτικὸν Madv.   152.15 ἑνὶ ἑκάστῳ Mein.: ἐν ἑκάστῳ FP

It is a task of the statesman to correct a constitution, something which seems to be much more difficult than to establish one; and also to distribute the number of people, on the one hand, with a view to what is necessary, and, on the other, with a view to what is morally good. Craftsmen and hired labourers and farmers and merchants (are distributed) with a view to what is necessary, for they serve the statesmen. The entire fighting force and the deliberative (councils) are more authoritative by taking care of virtue and being concerned with the noble things. Of these, the more senior are concerned with deliberation, the more aged with worshipping the gods, whereas the young as a whole with defending the city. This arrangement is quite ancient having been first laid down by the Egyptians.

Not less than other matters, it is the task of the statesmen to set up temples of the gods on the most prominent places; and to arrange the territories belonging to private citizens, one (part) near the farthest (boundary), the other near the city, in order that both parts of the territory, through the distribution of two lots to each (citizen), be well considered together. It is also useful to establish through law common meals and to care for the common education of children; and in order to ensure bodily strength and perfection, marriages need to be avoided among very young or very old people, as in both age groups offspring are born imperfect and utterly feeble. (It is also necessary to) establish through law that it is not advantageous at all to raise a disabled child, nor to expose a perfect one, nor to perform an abortion. These are the chief matters relating to the polis.

INDEX NOMINUM ET POTIORUM VERBORUM

ἀγαθά 118.17, 119.6, 119.10-11, 124.19, 127.10, 127.12, 127.16, 129.4-6, 130.13, 130.15, 130.23, 131.5, 131.7, 131.9, 131.11, 132.15-16, 134.1, 134.7, 134.9, 134.11-12, 135.1, 135.17, 135.19, 136.1-2, 136.16, 136.22, 137.8, 137.10, 145.20, 147.19 κατὰ φύσιν 118.14, 118.17, 119.16, 123.24, 124.5-7, 130.20, 132.9-10, 141.7, 144.22-145.1, 145.4 παρὰ φύσιν 118.14, 119.17, 145.5 ἔξωθεν, ἐκτός 122.8, 123.22, 124.16, 125.3, 125.6, 125.8-9, 125.11-12, 125.14-15, 126.14, 126.16-17, 126.21, 127.1, 129.14, 131.6, 136.10, 136.14 σωματικά 123.17, 123.22, 126.13-15, 127.1 ποιητικά 126.21, 129.13, 134.18-19, 134.24, 137.5-6 ἀναγκαῖα 129.8-9, 129.12 καλὰ κἀγαθά 132.14, 142.12 τελικά 134.17-18 τίμια 134.20-21, 135.2 ἐπαινετά 134.20-22, 135.3 ὠφέλιμα 134.21, 134.24, 135.8 καθ' αὑτὰ 135.4, 135.6-7, 135.11

ἀδιάφορα 131.12

αἰδώς 142.17, 146.9

αἵρεσις 119.5, 119.9, 119.20, 127.10, 127.13, 127.15, 129.3 αἱρετόν 122.20, 125.12-13, 125.15, 125.22, 128.7, 128.26-27, 129.3-4, 135.2, 135.9, 145.1, 146.2 <δι'> αὕθ' αἱρετόν 118.17, 119.22-23, 120.9, 120.16-18, 121.2, 121.17, 121.23, 121.24, 122.3, 122.4-5, 122.8, 122.11-12, 122.14-18, 122.20, 123.7, 123.13, 123.17-19, 123.25, 124.3, 124.6, 124.9-11, 125.10, 125.17, 126.13, 134.11, 134.14, 134.17, 137.4, 137.6-7

ἀκρασία 128.23

ἀλήθεια 126.1, 146.12

ἄλογον 117.7-8, 117.11-12, 117.16, 118.1, 137.16, 137.18, 137.21

ἁμαρτία 119.19 ἁμάρτημα 125.4, 145.9

ἀνδρεία 124.7, 124.9, 125.5-6, 137.22, 138.9, 138.16, 140.19, 145.21 ἀνδρεῖος 138.12-13, 141.14, 146.19

ἀντακολουθία 142.7-8

ἀξία 121.2, 127.25, 142.3

ἀρετή 117.9-10, 118.5, 119.4, 119.13-14, 122.19, 123.1, 123.20-21, 123.24-27, 124.18, 125.14, 125.21, 126.1, 126.12, 127.8, 128.2-3, 128.5, 128.10-11, 128.13, 128.16-17, 128.24, 129.9, 129.17, 132.10, 132.13, 132.22, 133.15, 133.22, 134.1, 134.19, 135.12, 135.18, 136.11, 137.7, 138.10, 138.15, 138.18, 138.21, 138.24-25, 139.17, 139.19, 140.12, 143.24, 144.11, 145.6, 146.15, 147.22, 147.26, 151.4, 152.6 ἠθική 118.2, 137.13, 137.15, 137.23, 142.6, 142.9, 142.21, 145.12 τελεία 130.18-19, 131.14-16, 147.23 ἀτελής 131.16-17 κοινωνικὴ καὶ πολιτική 125.22 εἶδος ἀρετῶν 117.18 λογικόν 118.1 ἄλογον 118.1 παθητικόν 142.6

ἀριστοκρατία 150.21-22, 151.7

Ἀριστοτέλης 116.19

ἀρχή 119.17 ἐκ φύσεως 116.22, τῶν ἀρετῶν 128.17 τῆς ὁρμῆς καὶ τοῦ καθήκοντος καὶ τῆς ἀρετῆς 119.3

βασιλεία 150.21

βίος 121.8, 122.1, 125.19, 126.24, 131.22, 132.18, 133.5, 134.1, 143.24, 148.6 πολιτικός 125.18, 144.21 κοινωνικός 125.18 θεωρητικός

125.19, 144.7, 144.16, 144.19
πρακτικός 144.16, 144.20 σύνθετος
144.17 ἀπολαυστικός 144.17
τέλειος 130.19, 131.20 μέσος
133.10, 145.6-7, 145.10 κατ' ἀρετήν
144.21-22, 145.9 κατα κακίαν
145.9-10 εὐδαίμων 145.3 καλός
145.3
βούλησις 129.2 βουλητόν 129.2

δημοκρατία 150.22, 151.6
διαίρεσις 135.11, 135.17 διαιρεῖσθαι
(τἀγαθὸν) 130.15, 137.8 (ποσαχῶς
λέγεται τὸ ἀγαθόν) 134.8-9
δικαιοσύνη 124.12, 125.9, 127.8,
129.10, 131.16, 134.22, 135.12,
136.20, 137.22, 140.20, 146.12-13,
146.17 δίκαιος 141.16, 142.10,
142.12, 147.3
δοῦλος 149.8

ἐγκράτεια 128.21-22
ἔθος 116.22, 117.1, 118. 6 ἐθικὴν 117.2
ἐθισμός 117.6
ἐκλογή 119.8, 119.16 ἀπεκλογή 119.16
ἐλευθεριότης 140.20, 146.4 ἐλευθέριος
141.18-19
ἐνέργεια 119.2, 119.13, 127.2, 129.9,
129.21, 130.2-3, 130.6, 130.9,
133.12, 136.14, 139.10, 139.17 κατ'
ἀρετὴν 126.19, 130.19-20, 131.19,
προηγούμενη 132.8
ἕξις 139.4, 139.9, 139.12, 139.15-16,
141.3, 142.23, 146.1, 146.3, 147.1,
147.3, 147.5, 147.7, 147.9, 147.12,
147.14, 147.16, 147.18, 147.20
προαιρετική 118.3, 140.12, 145.12-
13, 145.16 μέση 141.14, 144.23,
145.7 θεωρητική 145.15 πρακτική
145.16, 145.20 βουλευτική 145.20
ἄμεμπτος 145.21-146.1
ἐπιστήμη 118.3, 139.24, 145.19
εὐδαιμονία 126.19, 126.21, 126.23,
129.18-19, 130.1, 130.18, 130.22,
131.14, 131.21, 131.23, 132.6-7,
132.14, 132.19, 133.7, 133.12,
133.22, 134.1, 134.8, 134.14
εὐδαιμονεῖν 120.2, 130.22, 132.12,
133.3, 133.5-6, 133.20 εὐδαίμων
133.10, 145.3
εὐσέβεια 146.17, 147.1
εὐτραπελία 146.10
εὐτυχία 125.8, 134.4, 136.24

ζῆν 129.12, 133.20, 137.2, 149.14
κατ' ἀρετὴν ζῆν 126.17, 131.5
μονή ἐν τῷ ζῆν 126.3, 126.7,
126.10 ἐξαγωγή ἐκ τοῦ ζῆν 126.6
ἀπαλλαγή ἐκ τοῦ ζῆν 126.11
προηγούμενον 133.21-22 ζωή
τέλεια 130.19

ἡδονή 118.16, 128.20, 137.5, 138.22,
138.25, 139.6, 142.18, 142.20,
145.13 ἡδὺ 127.17, 130.16, 136.12,
143.9
ἦθος 116.21, ἠθικὴν 117.2

Θεόφραστος 140.8
θεωρία 118.2, 132.17

καθῆκον 119.4, 119.18, 145.8, 145.10
κακόν 118.20, 119.7, 119.10, 123.18,
127.11, 131.10-11, 132.10, 133.2
κακία 138.24, 142.23, 145.2, 145.14
καλοκαγαθία 137.19, 147.23
καλόν 118.3, 127.18, 129.8-9, 129.21,
130.1, 130.15, 131.12, 132.13,
132.17-18, 138.23, 143.9, 144.5,
145.14, 145.16, 145.21, 146.2-3,
147.15, 147.20, 147.19, 152.6
κατόρθωμα 145.8 κατόρθωσις 119.18
κατορθοῦν 128.1
κοινωνία 118.8, 132.16, 147.8, 148.6,
148.17, 149.1, 150.4 κοινωνικός
120.14, 125.18, 125.20, 125.22,
126.4, 126.8, 144.7, 150.3

λόγος 118.6, 121.9, 123.14, 124.18, 124.20, 127.3, 128.17, 128.21. 129.1, 137.12, 137.18, 139.3, 139.24, 142.11 λόγῳ 117.4, 117.5, 117.9, 133.19, 140.12-13, 141.10 κατὰ λόγον 117.7, 118.11, 121.17-18, 123.12, 126.14, 151.9-10 εὔλογον 123.5, 126.6-7, 126.10-11 ἀνάλογον 124.10, 129.11 ἀναλογία 124.16, 125.1

μακάριος 132.11
μεγαλοπρέπεια 141.2, 146.6 μεγαλοπρεπής 142.3
μεγαλοψυχία 141.1, 146.5 μεγαλόψυχος 141.20
μεσότης 137.13, 139.22, 140.11-13, 141.4, 142.7, 146.4-13 μέσος 139.23, 139.25, 140.3-4, 140.7, 141.9, 145.13, 146.1, 146.3

νέμεσις 142.17, 146.7
νόμος 149.4

οἰκειοῦσθαι (πρὸς ἑαυτόν) 118.12-13, 123.25, 125.23 (πρὸς τοὺς ἐπαινοῦντας) 122.3 (τοῖς καλοῖς) 123.9 (πρὸς τὴν τῆς ἀληθείας ἐπιστήμην) 126.2 οἰκειότης 120.13
οἰκονομικός 148.2, 14915-16, 149.18-19, 149.24, 150.10-12
οἶκος 148.7, 148.9-10, 148.14-15, 149.5, 149.9, 149.13, 150.13
ὀρεκτικόν 117.16 ὀρεκτόν 131.4
ὁρμή 119.3, 127.19, 128.23, 128.27, 142.15 ὁρμητικόν 117.12

πάθος 124.5, 128.18, 139.4, 139.17, 141.4, 142.14, 142.20, 143.7, 151.10, 151.12 ἀστεῖον 142.15-16 φαῦλον 142.16-17 μέσον 142.16, 142.18
Περιπατητικός 116.19-20

ποιητικόν 126.13, 126.21, 129.13, 130.7, 130.11, 134.18-19, 134.24, 137.5-6
πόλις 148.7-8, 148.12-14, 149.12, 150.2, 150.4-5, 150.7, 150.17, 151.9, 151.21, 152.14
πολιτεία 148.5, 148.14-15, 151.1-3, 151.13, 151.17, 151.24
πολιτικός 125.18, 125.20, 125.22, 126.4, 126.8, 144.8, 144.21, 148.3, 150.1, 150.5, 151.23, 152.4, 152.11, 152.24
πρᾶξις 118.2, 119.15, 125.20, 126.5, 126.9, 126.24. 127.1, 130.3, 130.17, 131.12, 139.19, 144.8, 145.16 προηγούμενη 126.20, 129.20, 134.18-19
πρᾳότης 140.19, 146.3 πρᾷος 141.11
προαιρεῖσθαι 128.3 προαιρετικός 118.3, 140.12, 145.12-13, 145.16
προηγούμενος 126.20, 129.20, 130.19, 132.8, 133.21-22, 134.18-19 προηγουμένως 144.10, 144.19
προκοπή 131.17

σεμνότης 146.8
σκοπός 130.13-14, 130.17, 130.23
Σόλων 133.4
σοφία 137.20 σοφός 126.6, 133.9
σπέρμα 116.22, 148.13
σπουδαῖος 126.9, 128.1, 132.11, 132.22, 133.15, 134.1, 142.25, 143.24, 144.19
συμπλήρωμα 126.15 συμπληροῦν 126.24 συμπληρωτικόν 130.11
σωφροσύνη 124.4, 125.3, 137.22, 138.9, 140.18, 146.1, 146.18

τέλος 126.15, 130.12, 130.21-22, 131.3, 131.18, 134.13, 135.12-13, 135.16-17, 143.8
τέχνη 130.7-8, 132.20, 136.11, 149.13

φαῦλος 126.7, 126.9-10, 127.26, 134.6

Didymus' Epitome of Peripatetic Ethics—An Edition with Translation 67

φιλανθρωπία 121.22, 127.4
φιλαυτία 143.16 φίλαυτος 125.21
φιλία 120.12, 120.15, 120.18, 121.17,
    121.24, 125.9, 127.7, 129.16, 142.16,
    143.2, 143.10, 143.12, 146.11 φίλος
    118.20, 119.1, 121.23, 121.24,
    136.15, 137.7, 142.24
φιλοστοργία 120.3
φρόνησις 125.7, 128.5, 129.10,
    134.23, 135.18, 136.11, 136.20,
    137.20, 142.9, 145.19-20, 150.10
    οἰκονομική 149.8, 149.18, 149.24
    χρηματιστική 149.21 φρόνιμος
    142.10-11
φυγή 119.5, 119.9, 123.5, 127.10,
    146.2 φευκτόν 128.7, 129.1, 145.1
    δι' αὑτὸν φευκτὸν 118.20, 123.6,
    123.14, 123.18
φύσις 118.6, 119.13, 120.1, 121.11,
    121.21, 138.10, 143.6, 150.2 ἐκ
    φύσεως 116.22, 120.13 φύσει
    118.12, 136.16, 148.3, 149.1, 149.22

φυσικός 121.16 φυσικῶς 123.9,
    126.2

χρεία 119.23, 120.17, 123.7, 123.10,
    143.6

ψυχή 118.10, 122.10, 122.13, 123.20,
    124.3, 124.7-8, 124.11-12, 124.16,
    125.3, 125.5, 125.7, 125.9, 125.11-
    13, 125.15, 130.4, 136.9-10, 136.16,
    137.18, 139.2-3 μέρος ψυχῆς 117.6,
    123.19 λογικόν 117.11, 117.12-13,
    137.19 ἄλογον 117.7-8, 117.11-
    12, 117.16, 137.16, 137.18, 137.21
    παθητικόν 117.9 κριτικόν 117.12
    ὁρμητικόν 117.12 θεωρητικὸν
    117.13-14 ἐπιστημονικὸν 117.14,
    145.17 βουλευτικόν 117.15, 149.6-7
    ὀρεκτικὸν 117.16 ἐπιθυμητικόν
    117.16-17 ἀμυντικὸν 117.17
    θυμικόν 117.17-18 θεῖον 118.10
    δοξαστικόν 145.15 ἠθικόν 145.15
    διανοητικόν 145.17

2

The Quest for an Author

David E. Hahm

The quest for the original author of Stobaeus' Peripatetic epitome (*Doxography C*) was launched by Hermann Diels in 1879 on the basis of a suggestion of August Meineke and has continued to be tested and refined down to the present day.[1] This search to discover an author took its point of departure from Stobaeus' text and pursued the source or sources of his text in the hope of discovering the original author or compiler.[2] By a happy coincidence Stobaeus quoted from this same Peripatetic doxography in another book and there identified his immediate source as "Didymus." It seemed highly probable, therefore, that the source of the entire *Doxography C* was from this "Didymus." Then, since Stobaeus' Peripatetic doxography followed immediately after another doxography, similar in form and in the type of information it contained, but devoted to Stoic ethical philosophy

---

[1] The approach was suggested by Meineke (1859) and fully developed by Diels (1879) 69–88. For its current status see Moraux (1973) 259–60; Kahn (1983); Hahm (1990) 2975–3048; and Göransson (1995) esp. 203–26.

[2] The evidence in favor of Diel's hypothesis was reviewed again by Hahm (1990). Since then additional questions have been raised that cast further doubt on the hypothesis.

(*Doxography B*), it seemed reasonable to conjecture that both these doxographies were derived from the same author. If that author was Didymus and this Didymus compiled summaries of both Peripatetic and Stoic ethics, it seemed plausible to identify this author with the author of the doxography that Eusebius quoted for Stoic teaching under the title "The Epitomes of Arius Didymus."[3]

Finally, since Stobaeus placed the Stoic and Peripatetic ethical doxographies immediately after a set of excerpts from still another ethical doxography (*Doxography A*), it seemed worth considering whether *Doxography A* came from the same source as the two subsequent doxographies. This third Stobaean doxography was arranged in a different format, viz., as a series of topics, each with one or more opinions of different philosophers. The difference in arrangement suggested it came from a different book; but since it dealt with a third Late Hellenistic philosophical school, the Academy, and could be construed as compatible with the other two in its doxographic function, Diels and some, but not all, other scholars after him conjectured that it derived from the same author, Arius Didymus, either from a topically arranged introduction or from a completely different book of his.[4]

Who this hypothetical "Arius Didymus" was raised a more difficult question. The *termini post quem* for the three doxographies ranged from the end of the second century BC (Peripatetic) and the beginning of the first century (Stoic) to the middle or second half of the first century BC (*Doxography A*).[5] If all were from the same author, he would have had to have composed them in the second half of the first century BC at the earliest. This led scholars to speculate that the author might have been an

---

[3] The evidence with specific references is discussed by Hahm (1990) 3012-31.

[4] Diels (1879) 69-88 and Moraux (1973) 259-60. Hahm (1990) 2975-3048 reviews the evidence and marshals it to make the strongest possible case for attributing *Doxography A* to the same author as *Doxographies B* and *C*. This attribution is generally acknowledged as less persuasive than the common authorship of *Doxographies B* and *C*, and is now less widely accepted than formerly; cf. Göransson (1995) 203-26. Hahm (1983) explored the methodological parallels shared by the three texts, though these are not sufficient grounds for inferring common authorship.

[5] The dating is reviewed by Hahm (1990) 2079-82. *Doxography A* is the hardest to date. It refers to Philo of Larissa, head of the Academy from ca. 110 BC to ca. 84 BC and to Eudorus of Alexandria. Eudorus cannot be precisely dated. Strabo (64 BC-24 AD) refers to him as *kath' hēmas*, which probably means "in our time"; but how close in time remains an open question. It could refer to a contemporary or to someone older or younger, but it seems to date him no earlier than the middle of the first century BC and probably later.

advisor of Augustus and member of his court, who had the name "Arius."[6] There are a few other references to an Arius with philosophical connections, including one at the end of the list of Stoics originally found at the end of Diogenes Laertius' *Lives of the Philosophers,* book 7.[7] In the absence of positive ancient testimony that there was more than one writer named "Arius," it was conjectured, as the simplest hypothesis, that all refer to the same Arius, the Arius Didymus who authored Stobaeus' doxographies. If this conjecture is correct, then we have some welcome biographical evidence for Arius Didymus as a Stoic and a friend of Augustus.[8] In this way "Arius Didymus" was brought to light by classical scholars as an Augustan era philosopher and author of the three doxographies found in Stobaeus, book 2. The conjectural attribution of all three Stobaean texts to Arius Didymus and the speculative, but not impossible, identification with the friend of Augustus, has now obtained wide currency, not because it is persuasive, but because no plausible alternative theory has been proposed for the composition and arrangement of the three texts.[9]

Attractive as we might find the chain of conjectures, first, for the construction of the ancient text containing a comprehensive doxography of Hellenistic philosophy, and then, for putting a name and a human face on it, the resulting hypothetical construct is of dubious value as basis for historical or philosophical interpretation of the actual texts. For it rests on three unprovable assumptions: (1) there was only one author named "Didymus" who wrote doxographies of Hellenistic philosophers; (2) there was only one "Arius" interested in philosophy in the period; and (3) this single individual must therefore be (a) the Stoic philosopher known to Diogenes Laertius and Tertullian by the name of "Arius," (b) the doxographer known to Eusebius by the double name "Arius Didymus," and (c) the advisor to Augustus. Ultimately we are left with the historiographical dilemma of choosing between (a) the Law of Parsimony that explanatory factors (in this case, authors) ought not be multiplied beyond necessity, and (b) coming to grips with the possibility that the friend of Augustus, the doxographer quoted by Stobaeus, and the Stoic known to Diogenes Laertius were several different individuals.

[6] Hahm (1990) 3035–47.
[7] Hahm (1990) 2980–81.
[8] See Moraux (1973) 260–62.
[9] The problems with the speculative identification of all these references and texts are detailed and stressed by Göransson (1995) 202–18.

In the face of the paucity of historical data from this period and the difficulties that arise when we try to make all the evidence fit a single individual, skepticism regarding the Meinecke-Diels hypothesis is in order. It is not implausible to postulate more than one Didymus or Arius. "Didymus" was not an uncommon name; several are known, including a prolific Alexandrian grammarian and antiquarian contemporary with Augustus, Didymus Chalcenterus (PW 8).[10] "Arius," though not as common as "Didymus," was not unknown either; there was an Athenian archon named "Arius" (PW 6) in the last quarter of the first century BC.[11] Furthermore, the common authorship of two or more of the three Stobaean doxographies (as postulated by Diels' hypothesis) depends on a subjective judgment of their degree of similarity. Then, too, even if we think we can see enough similarity between *Doxography C* and *Doxography B* to infer that they came from the same intellectual milieu, they need not necessarily have been composed by the same author; a common cultural and literary tradition is another plausible explanation for their formal similarities. Furthermore, the fact that *Doxography A* is arranged in an entirely different format makes common authorship even less likely. In the light of such doubts we would be well advised to consider alternatives to the hypothesis of a single author by the name of "Arius Didymus" for all three of Stobaeus' doxographies.[12]

If the three doxographies were not composed by the same author or cannot be attributed to a contemporary and friend of Augustus, we have no external grounds to date them in or after the second half of the first century BC, as is routinely done when they are attributed to a conjectural doxographer named "Arius Didymus." A datable external allusion in the Peripatetic doxography, specifically a criticism of a conception of happiness known to have been defended by Critolaus, secures a *terminus post quem* of the late second century BC, that is, after Critolaus had assumed headship of Aristotle's school and after his conception of the Peripatetic good had become known and had come in for criticism and revision; but to assign *Doxography C* to any particular date after the middle of the second century BC, we shall have to resort to some other basis for dating.

---

[10] PW lists a dozen people named "Didymus." At least two were philosophers and more were grammarians. Four or five lived in the Augustan period, contemporaries of Arius, the friend of Augustus.

[11] PW lists seven besides the friend of Augustus and the author of the epitomes known to Eusebius, both of which PW treats as a single individual under the name of "Arius Didymus."

[12] See, e.g., Inwood (2014) in his insightful survey of Aristotelian ethical thinking in the Hellenistic and post-Hellenistic period.

Furthermore, even if we could confidently date *Doxography C* to the Augustan age and identify its author with the friend of Augustus, we still cannot answer the question of who formulated the individual ideas, arguments, or component parts, contained in it or when.[13] Getting behind the text of *Doxography C* to its original Peripatetic source or sources has proven to be as intractable a challenge as identifying the doxographer who transmitted it to Stobaeus. Speculative attempts to trace all or most of the material back to a single particular source, for example, Theophrastus, Antiochus of Ascalon, Xenarchus, or Aristo (student of Antiochus) have all been proposed, but have found little support; the material is simply too diverse in point of view and underlying assumptions.[14] The quest for Stobaeus' ultimate source or sources seems to have reached a dead end with the text itself.

There can, of course, be little doubt that Stobaeus used a preexisting text, but the time-honored methodology of source criticism has yielded no sure answer to the questions of the original author or compiler or what earlier sources were used in composing it. We can recognize references to various Peripatetics, ranging from Aristotle and Theophrastus in the fourth century down to Critolaus in the second century BC; but the number and diverse dates of the recognizable references, together with evidence of discontinuity in the exposition, suggest that the doxography incorporated material from multiple sources of different eras. Charles Kahn aptly described it as a "multilayered collage, built up over a period of three centuries."[15] It is hardly surprising, then, that it has become conventional to refer to the author of the Peripatetic doxography as "Arius or his source," at least among those who still regard the Peripatetic doxography as one of the set of three Stobaean doxographies derived from a single source named "Arius Didymus." The alternative is to acknowledge that each of the Stobaean doxographies almost certainly had an independent existence at some time and that the Peripatetic doxography was found in a book ascribed to a man named "Didymus," whether as author or as editor; but who he was or when he wrote remains a mystery.

---

[13] Some of the component parts are so different (e.g., the opening argument containing the concept of *oikeiôsis* [116.21–119.21] vs. the concluding summary of Aristotle's *Politics* [148.5–152.25]) that we may at least assume different motives and contexts for the original production of each text.

[14] The proposals are discussed by Moraux (1973) 271–76. The proposal that Antiochus was the source is discussed and dismissed by Moraux later in his discussion of *oikeiôsis* (333–38).

[15] Kahn (1983) 7.

Works Cited

Diels, H. 1879. *Doxographi Graeci*. Berlin: Reimer.

Fortenbaugh, W. W. (ed.). 1983. *On Stoic and Peripatetic Ethics: The Work of Arius Didymus*. Rutgers University Studies in Classical Humanities 1. New Brunswick, N.J.: Transaction.

Göransson, T. 1995. *Albinus, Alcinous, Arius Didymus*. Göteborg: Acta Universitatis Gothoburgensis.

Hahm, D. E. 1983. "The Diaeretic Method and the Purpose of Arius' Doxography." In Fortenbaugh (1983) 15–37.

———. 1990. "The Ethical Doxography of Arius Didymus." *ANRW* II.36.4. Berlin: De Gruyter, 2935–3055; index, 3234–43.

Inwood, B. 2014. *Ethics after Aristotle*. Cambridge, Mass.: Harvard University Press.

Kahn, C. 1983. "Arius as a Doxographer." In Fortenbaugh (1983) 3–13.

Meinecke, A. 1859. "Zu Stobaeus, Socrates." (Mützells) *Zeitschrift für das Gymnasialwesen* 13: 563–65.

Moraux, P. 1973. *Der Aristotelismus bei den Griechen von Andronikos bes Alexander von Aphrodisias*. Vol. 1: *Die Renaissance des Aristotelismus im I. Jh v. Chr*. Berlin: De Gruyter.

3

Moral Virtue in Didymus' Epitome of Peripatetic Ethics

William W. Fortenbaugh

The epitome of Peripatetic ethics by (Arius?) Arius Didymus[1] is part of a larger work entitled "On the Ethical Branch of Philosophy." The work is tripartite, beginning with a general introduction to ethics, followed by a survey of Stoic and Peripatetic ethics. The three parts are conventionally marked off by the letters A, B and C. The last carries the heading "The (teachings/views[2]) of Aristotle and the other Peripatetics on Ethics" (116.19–20) and has much to say about virtue. It begins by mentioning character and virtue, *êthos*, and *aretê* (116.21, 117.9–10) and closes with a reference to perfect virtue, *teleia aretê* (147.23), after which we are told that enough has been said concerning virtue and most of the topics belonging

---

[1] The identity and hence the full name of Didymus is problematic. See above, Tsouni's introduction pp. 1–3 and Hahm's article, chap. 2.

[2] The title lacks a noun. *Dogmata* may be supplied from the title that announces Didymus' account of Stoic ethics (57.13–14 W). That account precedes the epitome of Peripatetic ethics. Its conclusion is announced by Didymus who says that he has covered everything that he intended to cover (116.15–18 W).

to ethics (147.26–148.2).[3] In between there are subheadings[4] that announce discussions of virtue (128.10, 137.13) as well as sections in which virtue figures as a primary or secondary topic. In what follows, I shall not attempt a full discussion of all references to virtue; rather, I shall focus on a selection of sections within the work: (1) sections 1–2 Ts, in which we are not only introduced to the psychic dichotomy that is fundamental to Peripatetic discussions of virtue, but also told that the perfection which is virtue depends on three things: nature, habit and reason; (2) sections 10 and 11, in which virtue is elucidated by reference to crafts and by a division of goods into those that are necessary and those that are noble; (3) sections 16–19, in which moral virtue *qua* mean-disposition is discussed, Theophrastus' example of saying only what is necessary is introduced, and an explanation is given of the relationship between moral virtue and practical wisdom; (4) sections 24–25, in which three different definitions of virtue are discussed; attention is focused on thirteen mean-dispositions, none of which is referred to as a virtue and six of which are refused that label in the *Eudemian Ethics*; noble-goodness *qua* complete/perfect virtue brings discussion to an end. An appendix on temperament follows.

(1) Sec. 1–2 Ts = p. 116.21–119.21 W

Section 1 of Didymus' summary begins, "He says[5] that character, *êthos*, takes its name from habituation, *ethos*, for we possess from nature, *ek physeôs*, beginnings and seeds, *spermata*, whose perfections, *teleiotêtes*, are achieved by habituation and correct training." And that, we are told,

---

[3] The statement begins the transition from ethics to a much briefer account of Peripatetic politics (147.26–152.25).

[4] Wachsmuth prints the subheadings in brackets, thereby indicating that they postdate Arius. In his translation, Sharples (2010) follows Wachsmuth, replacing brackets with braces. Simpson (2014) 104 n. 2 calls attention to Wachsmuth's judgment concerning the subheadings, but he does not introduce brackets into his translation. Tsouni follows Simpson in not bracketing the subheadings. I am inclined to see the subheadings as additions to the original text, but prefer to leave the issue open. See below, nn. 21, 29 and 43.

[5] The Greek text has the verb *phêsi* with the subject left unexpressed (116.21). It seems reasonable to understand Aristotle from the immediately preceding heading, which has "of Aristotle and the other Peripatetics" (116.19–20). To be sure, that can be questioned. See, e.g., Sharples (2010) 111 n. 2, who queries, "Aristotle? Or the author whom Stobaeus—or his source—is excerpting?" Nevertheless, we may compare, the opening of the epitome of Stoic ethics, where the heading begins "of Zeno and the other Stoics" (57.13), and text that follows has *phêsin* with the subject expressed, namely, Zeno (57.18). More important, what follows in the Peripatetic epitome—the remarks concerning nature, habituation and the alogical part of the soul (116.22–117.10)—are demonstrably Aristotelian.

involves the use of reason, *logos*, and not force as is the case with other living creatures (116.21–117.6). We may compare Aristotle's *Nicomachean Ethics*, in which a similar etymology of *êthos* is given (2.1 1103a17–18) and the importance of nature and seed is recognized (10.9 1179b20, 26). In addition, perfection is attributed to training (2.1 1103a25–26), which is said to involve teaching and not force such as one uses in training animals (10.9 1179b21, 1180a12).

In what follows, Didymus tells us that the habituation under consideration is that of the alogical part of the soul (117.6). Here, too, Didymus is reporting the teaching of Aristotle, who explains moral virtue, *êthikê aretê*, in terms of a bipartite psychology that divides the (human) soul into an alogical and a logical part: *to alogon* and *to logon echon* (*EN* 1.13 1102a27–28).[6] The former is the sphere of the moral virtues: for example, courage and good-temper. The latter is the sphere of the intellectual virtues: for example, practical and theoretical wisdom. In regard to the alogical part of the soul, Didymus is careful to add "not entirely," *ou kathapax* (117.8), for without it a reader unfamiliar with Aristotelian doctrine might think that the alogical part of the soul is completely closed to *logos* or reason, that is, that it is limited to sensation in the way that animals are.[7] Were that the case, moral training would proceed through compulsion or necessity and not reason (117.4). But in fact reason has a prominent role in moral training/education. Young people are taught moral principles, and as they grow older they are provided with the reasons that underlie and explain what they have learned. In time, the principles become action-guiding, determining the emotional responses that make up much of youthful behavior.

What comes next adds further clarification. Didymus characterizes the alogical part as emotional, *pathêtikon* (117.9).[8] It is, as it were, the seat of

---

[6] Basing a conception of virtue on a division of the soul is not original with Aristotle. In the *Republic*, Plato had advanced a tripartite psychology that divided the soul into rational, spirited and appetitive parts, each of which was the seat of particular emotions and particular virtues. In the *Laws*, Plato adopted a bipartite psychology, which is illustrated by a puppet, whose actions are determined by a soft, golden cord and hard, iron cords. The former represents calculation and the latter pleasure and pain, confidence and fear, two emotions that are explicitly tied to opinion (644C–E). We have here a dichotomy, which looks forward to Aristotle's distinction between logical and alogical parts of the soul. See Fortenbaugh (1975a, repr. 2002) 24–25.

[7] Cf. Aristotle, *EN* 1.13 1102b13–14, where the alogical part is said to partake in some way of reason, *metechein pêi logou*; also 1102b24–25 without *pêi*.

[8] In Aristotle's *Metaphsics*, the adjecive *pathêtikon* is used in combination with *poiêtikon* to characterize things that are relative in virtue of their potentialities: e.g., what can be heated is said to be relative to what can heat and what can be cut is relative to what

pathê and in particular emotional responses like anger and fear, which are cognitive phenomena.[9] That is the view of Aristotle, whose treatment of emotions in book 2 of the *Rhetoric* is well known. Take anger as an example. Aristotle recognizes that anger is painful, but also makes clear that anger is caused by thought: namely, the belief that a slight has occurred and that the slight is unjustified (2.2 1378a30–32).[10] In other words, anger involves factual apprehension (someone has done or said something that harms another person either physically or in regard to reputation) and an evaluation of what has occurred (the harm is unjustified, so that revenge is appropriate). Young people and generally those who lack a good upbringing are prone to error, especially in regard to evaluation. They are apt to think the harm unjustified when it is entirely appropriate. Or they might over-respond to a minor slight, thinking that their self-worth has been outrageously diminished. Training in such matters is central to moral education, and when the training is successful the alogical part of the soul is said to be "disposed according to reason" (117.7): that is, a person's emotional responses are reasonable.

Didymus tells us that perfection in those things, of which we have the beginnings and seeds from nature, is achieved by habit and correct training (116.22–117.2). Since what follows is primarily concerned with the alogical part of the soul, to which emotions are assigned, it is natural to understand perfection with special reference to the alogical part, that is, to the moral virtues like good temper and courage, which are perfected dispositions in regard to anger and fear, respectively. That would not be wrong. An early musical education combined with a heavy dose of paraenetic literature and practical experience in situations that arouse emotional response can be and often is successful in establishing good habits. These habits may

---

can cut (4.15 1021a14–19). In the *Nicomachean Ethics*, the adjective is used specifically of man's capacity for emotional response. We are told that there are three things in the soul emotions, capacities and dispositions, *pathê*, *dunameis* and *hexeis*. Capacities are explained as that in virtue of which human beings are said to be capable of emotion, *pathêtikoi*, e.g., that in virtue of which a person is able to respond to his particular situation in anger or with pity. Cf. Didymus 139.4–9, on which, see below p. 93.

[9] In have written "in particular," because *pathê* can be used inclusively to include psychic phenomena other than emotional responses. See, e.g., Aristotle, *On Soul* 1.1 403a3 with Hicks (1907) 177, 198, 474. But in the present context, picking out emotional response is correct. Indeed, it was Aristotle's work on emotional response that led to the development of a bipartite psychology, in which emotional response and deliberative capacity are assigned to different parts.

[10] On belief as the efficient cause of emotion, see *Topics* 6.13 151a14–19 with Fortenbaugh (1970) 57–58, (repr. 2006) 25–26 and (1975a, repr. 2002) 11–12.

be spoken of as perfections of a person's emotional side, but it should be underlined that in a different context "perfection" may refer not only to the alogical part of the soul but also to the logical part, whose perfection is exhibited both in action, practical wisdom, and in scientific reflection, philosophic wisdom (cf. 118.5–11).

I have said that Didymus is reporting the teaching of Aristotle, who explains moral virtue in terms of a bipartite psychology: one that divides the soul into alogical and logical parts. I do not want to withdraw that assertion, but variation in terminology merits brief mention. In the *Nicomachean Ethics*, when Aristotle introduces the bipartite soul, he speaks of *to alogon* and *to logon echon* (1.13 1102a28). In the *Eudemian Ethics*, Aristotle introduces the same two parts, saying that both partake of reason, *logou metechein*, but not in the same way: the one gives orders, while the other obeys and listens, *peithesthai kai akouein* (2.1 1219b28–31). Later the *Eudemian Ethics* agrees with the *Nicomachean Ethics* in using *to alogon* and *to logon echon* (2.1 1220a10–11). The latter phrase, *to logon echon*, is not used by Didymus when he first introduces bipartition,[11] and when he refers to the alogical part, he agrees with the *Eudemian Ethics* by using the verb "to obey," *peithesthai* (117.8). It would be rash to see here a special connection between the epitome and the *Eudemian Ethics*. For the *Nicomachean Ethics* subsequently uses *peithesthai* in describing the relationship between the alogical and logical parts of the soul. Indeed, the *Nicomachean Ethics*, like the *Eudemian*, speaks of the alogical part "obeying and listening" to the logical part (*EN* 1.13 1102b26–27, 33, 1103a3; *EE* 2.1 1219b31).

After the soul has been divided into logical and alogical parts: *to logikon* and *to alogon*. (117.11–12), the former is glossed as *to kritikon* and the latter as *to hormêtikon* (117.11–12). The variation in terminology is noticeable, but it introduces no significant difficulty. In regard to *to logikon* and *to kritikon*, we can say that *logikon* emphasizes the capacity to reason (reflect, deliberate) and that *kritikon* stresses the capacity to reach a reasoned judgment.[12] In regard to *to alogon* and *to hormêtikon*, we can say that the former highlights the fundamental division of the bipartite soul: the alogical part is emotional, *pathêtikon* (117.9), and not deliberative/calculative as is the logical part. The latter calls attention to the impulsive aspect of emotional response: central cases of emotion like anger and fright motivate a person to act. And when the emotion is strong, an angry man may be

---

[11] But see below, n. 44 on the opening of sec. 16.
[12] Both adjectives are used by Aristotle in his ethical treatises: *logikos EN* 2.7 1108b9; *kritikos EN* 6.9 = *EE* 5.9 1143a10 and *EN* 6.11= *EE* 5.11 1143a23, 30.

driven to lash out and a frightened man may be impelled to flee. That does not mean that emotions are thoughtless. As stated above, they are caused by belief, and should the emotions be controlled, they become the occasion for deliberation and reflection.[13]

In what follows, Didymus tells us that the logical part is itself bipartite: there is a scientific part that contemplates eternal and divine things and a deliberative part that is concerned with action relating to things human (117.3–15). That too is in line with what Aristotle says in the *Ethics*. There he divides the logical part in two, saying that with one of the parts we consider things whose principles are invariable, and with the other we consider things that admit variation (*EN* 6.1 = *EE* 5.1 1139a5–8, cf. 6.11 = 5.11 1143b16, 6.12). More interesting may be the subsequent division of the alogical part into an appetitive part, *epithumêtikon*, which desires things that depend on us, and a spirited part, *thumikon*, which prompts a person to defend himself against his neighbors, *pros tous plêsion amuntikon* (117.16–18). It is hard not to think of Plato's tripartite soul, of which the two lower parts are referred to as *thumoeides* and *epithumêtikon*. Indeed, in his work *On Soul*, Aristotle uses *thumikon* for *thumoeides* (3.9 432b25), and in the *Ethics* he uses *thumoeideis* of persons, whose temperament makes them prone to engage danger (*EN* 3.8 1116b26). Like the persons whom Plato believes suitable for his guardian class, so Aristotle recognizes the value of an innate temperament that makes men ready to confront danger. In itself, such a temperament is not courage, for courage involves standing up to threatening situations because it is noble to do so, *dia to kalon*,[14] but it

---

[13] In the apparatus to his text, Wachsmuth cites *hormêtikon* (117.12) and comments *non est vox Aristotelica*. Sharples (2010) 111 with n. 5 translates *hormêtikon* with "impulsive" and comments that "the terminology is Stoic, though the thought is Aristotelian." It is true that the adjective *hormêtikos* is not found in Aristotle's *Ethics*, but it does occur in the *History of Animals*, where animals are said to be most driven, *hormêtikôtata*, to engage in sexual intercourse during the spring (6.18 573a27). Moreover, Didymus may be drawing on a source that has no special commitment to reproducing Aristotelian usage. Our concern is whether Didymus' text fairly represents Aristotelian/early Peripatetic doctrine. That it does is supported by, e.g., *EN* 1.1 1102b30, where Aristotle characterizes the alogical part of the soul as the seat of appetite and impluse in general, *epithumêtikon kai holôs orektikon*. Cf. *EE* 1221b31–32, where the alogical part is said to possess *orexis*, for not any part whatever of the soul, *ou gar hotioun meros tês psuchês*, assuming the soul to be divisible, possesses *orexis*.

[14] The Greek adjective *kalos*, when used in regard to virtue and virtuous action, is frequently translated by "noble." That is sensible, for in this usage *kalos* introduces an ethical perspective. Well known is Tyrtaeus (7th c.) fr. 10, vv. 1 and 30 West. In the first verse, falling and dying while fighting in the vanguard for one's native land is called *kalon*. In the later verse, a person who falls fighting while in the bloom of youth is said to be *kalos*. Here a

can be said to support, *sunergein*, courageous action (3.8 1116b30–31). Be that as it may, the adjective *amuntikos*, which Didymus uses to characterize the spirited part of the alogical soul (117.17), occurs in the *Nicomachean Ethics* but not within the discussion of courage. Rather, it occurs within the discussion of anger and with reference to the apathetic person, who is said to be *ouk amuntikos*, someone who fails to respond in anger when treated badly (4.5 1126a7). A corresponding use of *amuntikos* is not found in the *Eudemian Ethics*.[15]

In the preceding paragraph, I said that for Aristotle a virtuous action like confronting danger courageously involves doing so because it is noble to do so. Didymus recognizes the tie between virtue and noble action when he says that moral virtue is a disposition to choose noble things, *proairêtikê tôn kalôn* (118.3). After that comes the statement that virtue is perfected from three things, *ek triôn*: from nature, habit and reason: *phusis, ethos* and *logos* (118.5–6). Wachsmuth makes that statement the beginning of a new paragraph. Sharples makes it the beginning of a new section (his no. 3). Tsouni prefers to begin a new section (her no. 2) some five lines later (at 118.11). Görgemanns suggests that the statement is a join between texts that were drawn from separate sources.[16] Wherever one chooses to mark a new beginning, it is true that the statement in question refers to virtue being perfected, *teleiousthai* (118.5), and that invites comparison with Didymus' previous assertion that from nature we have beginnings and seeds, of which the perfections, *teleiotêtes*, are achieved through habit and training (116.22–117.2).[17] It is also true that the statement looks forward

---

translation like "fair" might be preferred, for nobility and beauty seem combined. (Cf. West [1993] 24, who translates "he is lovely yet," and Fowler [1992] 77, who prefers "fair"; West [2011] 230 has "fair"). That said, I am not suggesting that within fr. 10 *kalos* should have two different translations, vv. 1 and 30. Rather, I am calling attention to an ambiguity in the use of *kalos*: it can be used to describe what is noble, what is beautiful, and what is well-made so as to be useful. See below, pp. 87–91, end of part 2.

[15] Cf. *Hist. an.* 1.1 488b8–10, where Aristotle distinguishes between animals that are *amuntika* and *phulaktika*, and then divides the former into those that attack and those that fight back when ill-treated. In the pseudo-Aristotelian *Economics* 1.3 1344a1–2, male and female are said to differ in that the former is *amuntikôteron* and the latter *phulaktikôteron*.

[16] Görgemanns (1983) 174.

[17] It might objected that the two passages, 116.22–117.2 and 118.5–6, are not entirely comparable in that the latter but not the former errs in regard to perfection. Seeds are imperfect in that they are by nature beginnings, which develop into mature plants and animals. In contrast virtue is a perfection of a preexisting disposition and *qua* perfection cannot be perfected. Fair enough, but in regard to 118.5 that is no more than a quibble. The Peripatetics understood the logic of apical terms like perfection, but were also prepared to

to Didymus' assertion that a human being differs from all other living creatures in body and soul and reasonably desires the perfection of both, *amphoin teleiotês* (118.11).

What especially interests me is the way in which the mention of nature as a source of virtue (118.5–6) relates to the earlier reference to beginnings and seeds that human beings possess from nature (116.21). If I understand correctly, in both sections "nature" is used with reference to innate attributes. In the earlier passage, the focus is on man's innate predisposition to experience emotional response, that is, the beginnings and seeds, which can be improved and perfected through habituation and correct training (117.1–2). If the plural, beginnings and seeds, can be pressed, Didymus' wording recognizes that emotions differ in kind and that an individual may be predisposed differently in regard to different emotions. A person given to strong outbursts of anger may be quite deficient in regard to shame. Later when Didymus lists nature along side habit and reason (118.5–6), the focus is still on innate dispositions, but the reference to the rational, *ta logika* (118.9) and earlier remarks concerning the logical part of the soul (117.11–15) encourage a more inclusive understanding of nature. We are to think not only of a person's innate capacity to experience various emotions but also to engage in deliberation and reflection.

Habit, *ethos* (118.6), is not an innate predisposition and therefore not to be included among beginnings and seeds, which are described as "from nature" (116.22). To be sure, it is listed as one of three sources: *ek triôn* (118.5), but it is not a preexisting source. Rather, it is a mode of training that is brought to what is an innate capacity in order to habituate the capacity, so that it is obedient to reason. In contrast, reason, *logos* (118.6), may be viewed as both an innate capacity and an external mode of training. Intellectual capacity varies, and the person who is born a fool will fail in dealing with particular situations and never acquire an adequate understanding of how the several virtues relate to each other. But when a person/youth has the requisite intellectual capacity, then he can be taught. Unlike an animal, whose master employs necessity, *anagkê*, a young person can be instructed by an educator, who brings reason, *logos*, to his student (117.4–7), both in planning his lessons and in conveying them to the student.

---

use ordinary language and to speak of a person being more or less virtuous (see below, my essay on "Lives," chap. 7 with n. 64). Similarly, they could speak of virtue being perfected, *teleiousthai*, where it is understood that they are speaking of a disposition being improved through habituation/training to the point of perfection.

The sections that follow (2-5 118.11-124.13) are of considerable interest in that they involve the doctrine of appropriation, *oikeiôsis*, which is generally regarded as Stoic and different from relatedness, *oikeiotês*, which Theophrastus is reported to have embraced, in order to extend justice to animals and in this way to oppose animal sacrifice. At least that is what Porphyry would have us believe (*On Abstinence from Eating Animals* 3.25.1-4 = 531 FHS&G).[18] I leave the larger topic of *oikeiôsis* as it appears in Didymus to Stephen White who discusses it in chapter 4 of this volume. Here I want to call attention to section 2, in which emphasis is placed on likes and dislikes that are naturally present in human beings.[19] We are told that a person is eager to obtain health, desires pleasure and clings to life, because they are according to nature, worthy of choice in themselves and good. In contrast, a person rejects and avoids illness, pain and destruction, because these are contrary to nature, in themselves objects of avoidance and evil. For our body is dear to us as is our soul and their parts and capacities and their activities (118.15-119.2). Take avoiding destruction. That is a natural response to imminent danger, and as such it manifests a predisposition to experience fright when threatened. But that is not all. Depending on the situation, a particular response may be deemed excessive, while another may be labeled deficient. Such responses are mistaken actions, *hamartiai*, and differ from responses that suit the situation. The latter are correct actions, *katorthôseis* (119.18-19), which moral education aims to promote by instilling moral virtue. In the example concerning fright, that means instilling courage.

(2) Sec. 10-11 Ts = p. 128.10-129.17 W

I turn now to sections 10-11,[20] of which the first is preceded by the subheading: "On Virtue" (128.10). The section itself opens with an explanation

---

[18] See Fortenbaugh (2011) 553-70.

[19] See, e.g., *asmenizein* and *duscherainein*, "to be pleased" and "to be displeased" (118.13-14) and *peripoieisthai spoudazein* and *diakrouesthai*, "to be eager to obtain" and "to reject" (118.15, 19).

[20] Section 10 begins what Moraux (1973) 316-17, 350-53 regards as the second part of Didymus' epitome (128.10-147.25). In contrast to the first part, which is said to be a unified whole which proceeds systematically, the second part is characterized as a collection of definitions and divisions, which are placed next to each other without consideration of thematic relevance. He is, however, careful to recognize 137.13-142.13 on moral virtue *qua* mean as an exception (see below, part 3). Indeed, he subsequently lists that portion of text along with 129.18-134.6 on happiness, 134.7-137.12 on divisions of goods, 143.24-145.10 on forms of life (see below, chap. 7), and 145.11-147.25 on ethical virtues (see below, part 4) as segments that exhibit a certain thematic unity. See below, n. 31.

of the word *aretê*.[21] We read that it is used of the best disposition or of that according to which the possessor is best disposed (128.11–12). That statement is immediately clarified by an inductive argument: the *aretê* of a shoemaker is said to be that by which he is able to produce the best shoe, *ariston hupodêma*, and the *aretê* of a builder is that by which he is best disposed in regard to the building of a fine house, *oikia kalê*. In conclusion, it is said to be agreed (*homologoumenon* 128.16) that putting something in the best disposition belongs to *aretê* (128.12–16).[22] Argument on the basis of arts/crafts, *technai*, is familiar from Plato and Aristotle,[23] and will have been readily understood by Didymus' reader.

Problematic is how to translate *aretê* in section 10. Sharples chooses "excellence," which is appealing, for "virtue" might seem forced when used of a builder's skill. But to adopt a translation like "excellence" runs the risk of confusing the Greekless reader, who may not realize that the subheading speaks of *aretê* and that the first word of the opening sentence is *aretê* (128.10–11). In the epitome *aretê* is used frequently in reference to moral virtue but also inclusively, so that it covers bodily excellence and here the excellence of a craftsman.[24] Hence, Sharples translates the subheading "On excellence/virtue" and adds a footnote pointing out that in Greek *aretê* can mean "excellence" in general.[25]

Still within section 10, a further clarification of *aretê* is offered. It begins with the statement that there are two, as it were, beginnings, *archai*, of the virtues: namely, reason and emotion, *logos* and *pathos* (128.17–18). The use of *archai* recalls section 1 of the epitome, in which we read that from

---

[21] The subheading runs "On Virtue," and the first word of the first sentence is "virtue." That suggests that the subtitle is a late addition based on the incipit, but it falls short of certainty. See above n. 4 and below nn. 29 and 43.

[22] Cf. *Eudemian Ethics* 2.1 1218b37–1219a5, where a similar but not identical inductive argument occurs. In both works, *aretê* is the best disposition or state of things that have some use or function. But in the the *EE* the things introduced as examples are not persons; rather, they are material things that have a use, e.g., a house (1219a4). In Didymus' epitomê, the possessor is a person who has some work or activity, e.g., a housebuilder (128.14).

[23] Regarding Plato, see, e.g., *Republic* 1.7 332C–333D; and regarding Aristotle, see, e.g., *EN* 1.7 1098a7–18.

[24] Cf. sections 4–5 122.9–123.27, where *aretê* occurs seven times (once as a supplement at 123.1). We are told that the parts of the body and their *aretai* are objects of choice on their own account. And if that is true, then the parts of the soul and their *aretai* must be objects of choice on their own account. Sharples (2010) 114–15 translates *aretê* six times with "excellence" and once with "virtue" (123.21). Tsouni prefers "virtue" throughout. The latter seems preferable, perhaps with a footnote. Or would a note be unnecessarily helpful?

[25] Sharples (2010) 118 n. 24.

nature there are in us *archai* and *spermata*, whose perfections are achieved by habituation and correct training.[26] In addition, section 1 introduces the bipartite soul: there is explicit reference to the alogical part, which is said to be emotional, *pathêtikon*, capable of obeying reason, *logos*, and receptive of virtue (117.7–10). If I understand correctly, the reference in section 10 to two *archai* of the virtues is to be interpreted in a similar way. The reference to *logos* (128.17) should be understood in terms of the logical part of soul,[27] and the reference to emotion (128.18) takes us to the alogical part (117.6–10). In addition, the references to harmony and obedience (128.18–19, 25) may be said to pick up the earlier reference to the ability of the alogical part to obey reason (117.8–9).

It may be helpful to compare *Magna Moralia* 2.7, for there emotion is opposed to reason, *pathos* to *logos*, as it is in section 10.[28] We are told that the beginning, *archê*, of virtue is not reason but rather emotion. In children there arise first alogical impulses of emotion toward what is noble; later reason supervenes and casting a vote of approval brings about noble action. Both reason and emotion are necessary for noble action, so that both may be regarded as *archai*, which occur naturally in human beings (cf. sec. 1 116.22), but emotion has the greater claim to be the *archê*, the original impulse toward virtue (1206b17–29). To be sure, nature is not perfect. Some people, a few, are born with impulses that are misdirected. But in most children, there are good impulses, albeit differing in degree. And these impulses can be developed/improved by a proper moral education, a training in emotional response, to which later is added a training in reason.

Sections 1 and 10 also share an interest in etymology. The former, apparently citing Aristotle, says that character, *êthos*, has its name from habit, *ethos* (116.21–22). The latter focuses on moral strength, *egkrateia* and moral weakness *akrasia*. After mentioning reason and emotion as the *archai* of the virtues and after recognizing that they may be in harmony or in conflict brought on by pleasure and pain, Didymus says that the victory of reason is called moral strength, *egkrateia*, from strength/power

---

[26] Sharples (2010) 111, 118 translates *archai* at 116.22 with "beginnings" and at 128.17 with "principles." Tsouni does the same. To be sure, "principle" can be used of an original faculty or endowment (so Webster), but it may suggest a settled rule or law that is learned. Moreover, to vary the translation obscures a connection that I find helpful for understanding the two passages.

[27] The logical part of the soul is explictly mentioned first in sec. 1 117.11.

[28] As *logos* and *pathos* at 128.17–18 are to be interpreted in terms of the logical and alogical parts of the soul, so too, at *Magna Moralia* 2.7 1206b20–22. Cf. *MM* 2.11 1121a34–36, where explicit mention is made of parts of the soul.

over, *kratos*. Similarly the victory of the irrational is called *akrasia*, lack of strength. (128.20–23). The derivations are obvious and implicitly recognized by Aristotle when he says that moral strength, *egkrateia*, consists in being strong/having power over, *kratein* (*EN* 7.7 = *EE* 6.7 1150a34–35).

Section 11 begins with the subheading "On Objects of Choice and Avoidance" (128.26),[29] after which we read, "That which causes an impulse[30] toward itself is said to be an object of choice, *haireton*, and that (which causes an impulse) away from itself (is said to be) an object of avoidance, *pheukton*, (in both cases) when reason is in agreement (with emotion). For just as the object of wish, *boulêton*, has this name in accordance with wish, *boulêsis*, so too the object of choice, *haireton*, (has its name) in accordance with choice, *hairesis*" (128.27–129.3). The concern with etymology relates section 11 to both section 1 and section 10. Regarding the clause "when reason is in agreement," we may compare the middle and the end of section 10, where Didymus directs our attention to the virtuous soul, whose parts are in a harmonious relationship: the one leads to what it should and the other follows obediently (128.17–19, 23–25). That focus is continued in section 11. Didymus is concerned not with any and every object of choice. Rather he is concerned with that which is choiceworthy, that is, that which moves, *kinoun*, a virtuous soul, in that it arouses impulse toward itself. *Mutatis mutandis*, the same holds in regard to objects of avoidance. The virtuous soul is moved to choose avoidance on the right occasions.[31]

In what follows, Didymus reports that to the ancients, *archaioi*, the object of choice and the good seemed to be the same. At least in describing the good in outline,[32] they defined it this way: "Good is what all things long for/aim at" (129.6). The definition is found at the very beginning of the *Nicomachean Ethics*, where we read, "Every art and every investigation, and similarly action and choice seem to aim at some good. Men, therefore,

---

[29] As with section 10, so here in section 11 the first word of the text, *haireton* (128.27), repeats a word occurring in the subheading (128.26). Once again that suggests but does not prove that the subheading is a late addition based on the text that follows (here the incipit). See above nn. 4 and 21, and below n. 43.

[30] On impulse, *hormê* (128.27), see above, pp. 3–4 with n. 13 on 117.12.

[31] I do not want to claim an altogether seamless relationship between sections 10 and 11, but equally I am reluctant to embrace wholeheartedly the idea that beginning with section 10 Didymus proceeds without consideration of thematic unity. See above n. 20.

[32] The phrase "describing in outline" is Tsouni's translation of *hupographontes* (129.5). "Sketching out" is that of Sharples (2010) 118. The ancients are unlikely to have been Didymus' immediate source. The noun *hupographê* occurs in the phrase *kata tên hypographên* "according to the outline" (122.6). Cf. *tên holên tês haireseôs hupogrphên*, "the whole outline of the school" (119.20).

have correctly declared the good to be that at which all things aim" (1.1 1094a1–3). Here Aristotle offers a brief inductive argument in support of a definition, which others have advanced. The definition recurs later in the *Ethics* where it is part of an argument advanced by Eudoxus, who regarded pleasure as the good. He thought it an observable fact that all things, rational and irrational, aim at pleasure. And what is good for all and what all things aim at is the good (10.2 1172b9–15). But that does not tell us who first defined the good as that at which all things aim. Eudoxus (c. 390–340 BC) was only slightly older than Aristotle (384–322 BC), and the plural verb (*apephênanto*, "they declared") in the earlier Aristotelian passage (1094a2–3) suggests that not a few predecessors accepted the definition.[33]

The ancients' understanding of the good as what all things long for (129.6) is followed by a division of goods into objects of choice on account of ourselves and on account of our neighbors, and those on account of ourselves into those which are noble and those which are necessary, *ta men kala, ta d' anagkaia* (129.6–9). An editor might be tempted to create a new paragraph, but that would be a mistake, for not only is the focus still on things good but also the ancients continue to be the subject. The third person plural *elegon*, "they said" agrees in tense and number with the preceding *aphôrizonto*, "they defined," and in context both verbs have as their subject "the ancients" (129.3–6).

Of special interest is the division of goods that are choiceworthy on account of ourselves into those that are *kala*, and those that are *anagkaia* (129.8–9). To the former belong the virtues, *aretai*, and the activities that derive from them: for example, practical wisdom and exercises of wisdom and justice and just action. To the necessary belong being alive and things that contribute to being alive and have their place among the productive: the body, its parts and their uses as well as the external goods such as good ancestry, wealth, reputation, peace, freedom, friendship, for each of these contributes something to the use/exercise of virtue (129.9–17). In earlier sections of the epitome, Didymus has already told us that people strive to exist and cling to life. That is said to be natural; life/existence belongs among things that are good and objects of choice on their own account (sec. 2 118.11–17). But in this respect, virtues and their exercise are far superior: they are much more objects of choice, *polu mallon haireta*, than mere existence, even life involving health and bodily strength (sec. 5

---

[33] According to Trapp (2007) 147 n. 52, Didymus' reference to the ancients is in the style of Antiochus of Ascalon.

124.2–7).³⁴ For it is virtue that disposes a person to choose things/actions that are noble, *proairetikê tôn kalôn* (sec. 1 118.3–4).³⁵

Here a word concerning the adjective *kalos* and the noun *kallos* is in order. The adjective is used in reference to moral and nonmoral qualities. It can describe what is aesthetically beautiful, what is of fine quality/useful, and what is morally good (LSJ *s.v.* I, II, III).³⁶ In the case of a house, an *oikia kalê*, built by a skilled craftsman (128.14–15), the reference might be aesthetic (the house is visually attractive), or it might concern utility (the house satisfies everyday needs), or it might be to both. In the case of virtues like practical wisdom and justice (129.10), the reference is moral, so that the translation "noble" is appropriate.³⁷ Nevertheless, there are passages, where a different translation seems desirable. I think especially of section 5, where bodily excellences are compared with moral virtues.³⁸ The comparison begins with health and temperance, moves to strength and courage, and concludes with beauty and justice. To introduce bodily beauty, the noun *kallos* (double lambda) is used.³⁹ The same noun is then used twice in reference to justice, which is said to be an object of choice on its own

---

³⁴ Cf. sec. 7, where we read that there are three kinds of goods that are choiceworthy in themselves: those of the soul, those of the body and those that are external. And of these three, the goods of the soul, namely the virtues, are far more choice worthy, *makrôi hairetôtera* (125.12).

³⁵ Recognizing that virtue and virtuous action are far superior to mere existence is compatible with and even paves the way for accepting suicide in particular situations. On Aristotle's alleged opposition to suicide and Peripatetic interest in circumstances that prompt the morally good man to take his own life, see below, my paper on "Lives," chap. 7.

³⁶ Similarly in English, the adjective "beautiful" has a wide range of uses. See, e.g., *Webster's Third International Dictionary* (1966) *s.v.* 1–3. The same is true of the noun "beauty."

³⁷ Cf. Arist. *Rhet.* 1.9 1366a33–36: "*Kalon* is that which, being an object choice for its own sake, is an object of praise, or that which, being good, is pleasant because good. Indeed, if that is the noble, necessarily virtue is noble (*anagkê tên aretên kalon einai*), for being good, it is an object of praise." N.b.: while virtue is an object of praise (139.14–18, see p. 93), praise extends to dispositions that are not considered virtues. See below pp. 106–8 on *EE* 3.7 1233b16–1234a34, where Aristotle discusses six praiseworthy mean-dispositions that are said not to be virtues.

³⁸ Cf. Plato, *Republic* 4 444D–E.

³⁹ Konstan (2014) 31–61 argues that the noun *kallos* and the adjective *kalos* are etymologically related, yet they differ in their range. Whereas *kallos* refers primarily to corporal beauty, *kalos* is broader in its signification. That is correct, especially in regard to early Greek literature (Homer and the archaicc poets). Konstan (35) is careful to add that the usage of *kallos* evolved over time. Inclusive usage is well illustrated by the passages in Aristotle, Isocrates, Plato and Xenophon, cited in what follows.

account (124.10–12). After that Menander is cited: "Doing no wrong makes us *kalous*" (single lambda, 124.13). Since the noun *kallos* is commonly used of physical beauty, it is not surprising that Sharples, Simpson and Tsouni all translate the first occurrence of the noun with "beauty" and then repeat the translation in reference to the soul. That achieves consistency. But only Simpson and Tsouoni maintain consistency in translating the words of Menander: *kalous ... poiei*. The former chooses the verb "to beautify," and the latter uses the phrase "makes beautiful." Sharples differs in that he translates "makes fine." That is not wrong,[40] but here I prefer consistency. The noun *kallos* and the adjective *kalos* are cognate, and like the adjective the noun can be used not only of the body but also of the mind, action and life: for example, Aristotle, who speaks of the beauty of the soul and of the body, *to tês psychês kallos kai to tou sômatos* (*Politics* 1.5 1255a1); Isocrates, who speaks of deeds surpassing in magnitude and beauty, *tôi megethei kai tôi kallei* (*Panathenaicus* 12.36; cf. Plato, *Laws* 12 964A–B); and Xenophon, who writes of a life aimed at beauty, *eis kallos* (*Agesilaus* 8.9.1; cf. *Education of Cyrus* 8.1.33). Moreover, physical beauty may be said to share an important feature with moral virtue: the two are chosen for their own sake (122.22–21, 123.6–7, 17.124.13). Both are attractive and both evoke a positive response. It is obvious, we are told, that beauty possesses something that summons/attracts people, *prosklêtikon ti* (123.8);[41] at any rate, everyone has a natural affinity to those who are beautiful, *phusikôs oikeiousthai tois kalois*, apart from any utility (123.9);[42] everyone is ready to benefit them, so that beauty seems to be capable of generating goodwill, *eunoias paraskeuastikon* (123.11–12). In much the same, way we are to think of a beautiful soul—one characterized by moral virtue and practical

---

[40] On "fine" as a translation of *kalos*, see above n. 14.

[41] Manuscript F and the first hand in P read *proklêtikon*. The second hand in P reads *prosklêtikon*, which is to be preferred. See LSJ s.v. *prosklêtikos*, where Philo Mechanicus 2.496 is cited. He uses the adjective in regard to *to kallos*, saying that beauty has the capacity to call/attract men to itself. That does not mean that beauty is not an object of choice on account of utility. Arius is clear that beauty is an object of choice both for utility and on its own account (123.6–7).

[42] How best to translate *phusikôs oikeiousthai* at 123.9 is puzzling. Sharples chooses "has a natural affinity," Simpson offers "is naturally akin," and Tsouni "has by nature an affinity." At first reading I wanted to construe *oikeiousthai* as the middle voice and to translate "naturally feels akin." But the occurence of *ôikeiôthê* at 123.25 speaks for understanding *oikeiousthai* as a passive infinitive. Translating with the verb "to feel" would take account of the fact that a positive aesthetic response can be compared with a positive emotional response like gratitude: both typically involve being pleased, which may involve a pleasant sensation/feeling. But that might be deemed overtranslating and therefore best left aside.

wisdom—not only exhibiting itself in virtuous acts but also arousing a positive response. Among peers, courage in one person inspires emulation in another (Arist. *Rhet.* 2.11 1388b10–11, 15–17). And acts of beneficence typically evoke a well-meant response (*Rhet.* 1.13 1374a23–24), if not a return in kind, then a word of thanks or praise (*EN* 1.12 1101b14–16, 31–32, *Rhet.* 1366a33–36.

Nor surprisingly ugliness has an opposite effect. As Didymus observes, no right thinking individual would welcome being deformed and mutilated in appearance, even if no disadvantage would result from such an appearance; in itself ugliness is an object of avoidance, which causes an impulse away from itself (123.1–7, 128.27–129.1). That ugliness is repulsive is a matter of experience, but today young people are often taught to overlook an ugly face or body; they are told that beauty is in the eye of the beholder. That is not Peripatetic and certainly not the view of Aristotle, who on occasion indicates what constitutes beauty. In *Topics* 3.1 116b21–22, we read, "Beauty is thought to be a certain symmetry of the limbs"; in *Metaphysics* 13.3 1078a36–b1: "The main species of beauty are order, symmetry and definiteness"; and in *Poetics* 7 1450b36–37: "Beauty consists in magnitude and order." That does not mean that Aristotle or any other Peripatetic would endorse removing or otherwise mistreating a deformed person simply because he is ugly. The Peripatetics knew their Homer and could point to Thersites. He was the ugliest of the Achaeans, but it was his abusive behavior that prompted Odysseus to strike him (*Iliad* 2.211–77). A rather different case is Socrates. Physically he was no beauty, but his beautiful mind made him a welcome discussant, at least most of the time. Indeed, as Didymus makes clear, the Peripatetics recognized that the virtues of soul, both moral and intellectual, are far more worthy of choice than those that belong to the body: comeliness, strength and the like (123.24–27, 124.3, 6 and 125.12–16).

Here a caveat seems appropriate. The Aristotelian passages cited above mention symmetry and order. That might suggest understanding beauty as balanced arrangement. That is not entirely wrong but it could be misleading in that it makes no explicit reference to size or magnitude (*Poet.* 7). In the *Nicomachean Ethics* we are told that beauty implies stature; small people may have charm and proportion but not beauty (4.3 1123b7–8). In the *Rhetoric*, size is mentioned alongside beauty (1.5 1361a2, 6). Whether one understands stature to be an essential part of beauty or a closely related attribute, it is clear that stature does work an effect on the beholder. It may be attractive as in the case of a statuesque woman, or it may inspire awe as in the case of a male warrior (*Rhet.* 1.5 1361a6, b12–13). In addition,

Aristotle tells us that what counts as beauty varies according to age. In a young man, beauty is the possession of a body fit to endure physical activities/contests involving speed and strength (1361b7–11); in a man in his prime, it is a condition fit for the exertions of warfare together with a pleasant yet forbidding appearance (1361b11–13); in an old man, it is a condition sufficient for necessary exertions and free from deformities that cause pain to the beholder (1361b13–14). If I understand correctly, we are being told that when a human being appreciates the beauty of another individual, his response is apt to be twofold; he is not only pleased by symmetry, order and size but also associates that shape with age related activities. That is a cognitive response that goes beyond the purely visual.

(3) Sec. 16–19 Ts = p. 137.13–142.13 W

Section 16 is preceded by the subheading "On Moral Virtue: that (it consists of) means, *hoti mesotêtes*."[43] The text that follows states that a more accurate investigation of moral virtue is necessary, for they (*sc.* the Peripatetics), with a view to the present investigation, divide the soul in two: into a logical[44] and an alogical part (137.13–18). That takes us back to the beginning of the epitome, section 1, where the bipartite soul is introduced.[45] Moreover, the reference to the present investigation (137.17) is, as it were, a reminder that bipartition is a peculiarly human psychology, tailored for use in ethics. Indeed, in section 1, the alogical part is said to be not entirely, *ou kathapax*, alogical (117.8), thereby indicating that the alogical part is

---

[43] The subheading is bracketed by Wachsmuth (see above nn. 4, 21 and 29) and might be deemed a late addition, which was inspired in part by the opening sentence: "These things having been distinguished, it is necessary to consider in greater detail the things said concerning moral virtue" (137.14–15). But that cannot be the whole story, for reference to moral virtue as a mean does not occur straightway. Indeed, the noun *mesotês* occurs first in section 18, where it is used in reference to actions (139.22) and subsequently applied to moral virtue (140.11, 12–13). Whoever wrote the subheading had read beyond the incipit.

[44] The Greek here is *to men logikon echousan* (137.18). That is the manuscript text, which is printed by Tsouni. Wachsmuth, following Gaisford and Trendelenburg, prints *to men logon echousan*. That seems awkward at best. The participle *echousan* is feminine singular in agreement with the preceding *psychên*. The definite article *to* is neuter, so that one might understand or supply *echon* and then understand *meros* from the preceding *dimerê*. That would give *to men logon (echon meros) echousan*. But that is too complicated and also unnecessary. In section 1, the phrase *to logikon* has been used to refer to the part that possesses the capacity to reason (117.11, 13) and it recurs in that sense in the problematic passage (137.18).

[45] See above, p. 77.

not totally cut off from reason. Like the logical part it is cognitive, albeit in a different way.

Section 16 continues by assigning virtues to the two parts of the soul. We are told that noble-goodness, practical wisdom, mental acuteness, wisdom, readiness to learn, memory and the like belong to the logical part, while temperance, justice, courage and the others belong to the alogical part (147.19–23). At first reading that may seem straightforward, but if we compare *Magna Moralia* 1.5 a difficulty arises, for there the same two lists of virtues occur with a single exception. Noble-goodness, *kalokagathia*, is omitted from the list of virtues of the logical part (1185b6–7). Indeed, its inclusion by Didymus among the logical virtues becomes more puzzling, when one realizes that later at the end of the discussion of Peripatetic ethics, noble-goodness is said to be composed of all the moral virtues (147.22). I shall postpone further discussion of noble-goodness until the end of this paper, where I take account of its relationship to practical reason and the idea that it is perfect virtue.[46] For the moment, I want to focus on the remainder of section 16.

The conclusion of section 16 (137.24–138.26) is closely related to both the *Nicomachean Ethics* 2.2-3 1104a11–b11 and to the *Magna Moralia* 1.5-6 1185b13–38. All three texts accept the principle that moral virtue being a mean disposition is destroyed by excess and deficiency, and both appeal to the evidence of the senses.[47] We are told that excessive and deficient exercise undermines a person's strength and that the same is true of health. Eating and drinking too much harms one's health. In contrast, moderation preserves both strength and health. The same is said to hold in regard to the moral virtues. Temperance and courage are introduced as examples. The person who fears and flees everything becomes a coward, and the man who is never frightened and endures all dangers becomes rash. In contrast, the man who experiences the right amount of fear at the right moment preserves his virtuous disposition. Indeed, confronting dangers properly not only preserves courage but also generates and increases it. The latter is important to moral education: for example, to habituating the young to endure the threats of war.[48] *Mutatis mutandis*, the same holds for temperance. Finally both texts emphasize the importance of pleasure and pain. They are said to be not only signs or determinants of a person's

---

[46] See pp. 112–14 on Didymus 147.22–25.
[47] Didymus 138.1–3; *EN* 2.2 1104a13–14; *MM* 1.5 1185b15–16.
[48] Cf. *auxein* at Didymus 138.15 and *MM* 1185b26, 29, 30 with *geneseis kai auxêseis* and *ethizomenoi* at *EN* 1104a27.

moral character but also important to early training and the acquisition of moral virtue.[49]

Moving on to section 17, we again find a reminder that ethics is focused on human beings. We are told that they (the Peripatetics) found it necessary to take into account things in the soul. In particular, they say that emotions, capacities, and dispositions, *pathê*, *dunameis* and *hexeis*, are present in the souls of human beings, *en tais psuchais tôn anthrôpôn*. Emotions are anger, fear, hate, longing, emulation, pity and the like. Capacities make us capable of experiencing emotions, and dispositions are those (states) according to which our emotions are good or bad (139.3–11).[50] That is a different division of psychic phenomena from that of bipartition, but the two are compatible. Indeed, as presented in section 17, the tripartite division relates to the alogical part of the bipartite soul, which is the seat of emotional response. Each person (aberrations excluded) has an innate capacity for emotional response and that capacity is central to the alogical part of the soul. An apparent slight arouses the emotion of anger, and in a person who is well disposed—neither irascible nor overly mild, but good-tempered—the response is measured in that it suits the situation. The concluding sentence of section 17 makes the point in general terms: "Therefore the virtues are dispositions resulting in emotional activities that are praised" (139.11–18).

Section 18 develops what has been said by focusing on action, *praxis*. We are told that virtue is concerned with matters of action, and that every action is considered as continuous. And in everything continuous, there is a certain excess and deficiency and mean, *mesotês*, which relate either to each other or to us. The mean in relation to us is best, for this is what knowledge and reason demands (139.19–24). Here Didymus (or his source) is following closely the *Eudemian Ethics*, in which Aristotle tells us that everywhere the mean produces the best state/disposition and that moral virtue is concerned with certain means and is itself a certain mean (2.3 1220b21–35). To this Didymus adds that the mean is defined not in terms of quantity but of quality (139.25–140.1). If I understand correctly, the epitomist is taking account of the fact that correct emotional response involves several factors, not all of which are obviously quantitative. To be sure, we may speak of a person harboring excessive anger for too long. But if asked to explain ourselves, we are apt to introduce factors that resist

---

[49] Cf. Didymus 138.21–26 with *EN* 1104b3–13 and *MM* 1185b33–38.
[50] Cf. Arist. *EN* 2.5 1105b19–28 and *EE* 2.2 1220b7–20. On emotional capacity qua relative capacity, see above n. 8, and on *pathos* and *pathêma*, see below n. 85.

quantification: for example, the anger is that of a son toward his father; it finds expression in inappropriate circumstances like a family reunion and involves unacceptable crudities. In Peripatetic jargon, an evaluation of emotional response takes into account the particular moment including persons, occasion and manner: *hois, hote* and *hôs* (*EE* 2.3 1221a17).[51]

The mean in relation to us is said to be the best (*ariston* 140.7, picking up *beltiston* 139.23–4) and then illustrated by an example (*hoion* 140.7) drawn from Theophrastus. According to Didymus, Theophrastus said, "During meetings one man goes through many things and chatters at length, another says little and not what is essential, but a third says only what is necessary and so lays hold upon due measure. This is the mean relative to us, for it is determined by us by means of reason" (140.8–12). That is my translation[52] based on Wachsmuth's text, which introduces a correction: where the manuscripts read *mê*, "not," Wachsmuth prints *mona*, "only" (140.10). The negative *mê* is certainly an error[53] and *mona* (neuter plural) agrees with the preceding *auta ha edei*, "the things that are/were necessary." Spengel prefers *monon* (used as an adverb), which might be considered better style.[54]

More interesting is the translation of *en tais entuchiais* (140.8). Sharples translates, "When we meet people," which is compatible with all kinds of meetings including everyday social intercourse. Tsouni translates "in social interactions," which points to everyday encounters that involve conversations. Different is Dirlmeier, who compares the use of *entugchanein* in Theophrastus' *Characters* 1.3, where the verb is used of seeking a meeting urgently. He also compares Plutarch, *How to Tell a Flatterer from a Friend* 26 67C, where we read that Plato, involved in suspicions and disagreements

---

[51] The importance of taking account of persons in assessing behavior is made abundantly clear in two fragments of Theophrastus (He is mentioned by name in section 18 [140.8]). One fragment occurs in Plutarch's *Life of Sertorius*, where Theophrastus is cited for saying that a general should die the death of a general and not that of an ordinary soldier (13.6 = fr. 622 FHS&G). The other fragment is found in Plutarch's *Life of Lysander*, where Theophrastus is named as the source of a report concerning the death of the general Philocles: After bathing and putting on a rich robe, he went first, leading his soldiers to execution (13.1–2 = fr. 623).

[52] Fortenbaugh (1983) 203. "Goes through" translates *dielthôn* (140.8). In Theophrastus *Characters*, the chatterer is said "to go through completely," *diexelthein* (3.2) what he had eaten for dinner. The fuller form suits the Theophrastean sketch in that it adds punch by underlining the foolishness of excessive chatter.

[53] *Pace* Zeller (1879) 860–61, n. 1. See Fortenbaugh (2011) 305–6.

[54] Tsouni prints *monon* and translates "only." Sharples' translation has "only," which suggests that he reads *mona* or *monon*.

with Dionysius, requested time for a meeting, *kairon entuchias*. That suggests construing *entuchiai* in Didymus' text as business meetings, in which focusing on the issues is desirable and extraneous pleasantries unnecessary and even unwelcome.[55] And that would fit what Didymus attributes to Theophrastus: neither chattering at length nor saying too little but rather saying what is necessary and only that (140.8–10).

My inclination is to follow Dirlmeier, but whether we think of a business meeting or a casual meeting, the mention of chattering at length, *adoleschein makrôs* (140.9), is important for it calls attention to a mode of behavior—we might say a behavioral regularity—that is not normally referred to an emotion. But it is a mode of behavior that can be criticized as failing to observe the mean that is relative to us and determined by reason. Loquacity is funny on the comic stage; it arouses laughter in the audience.[56] But in real life loquacious speech is annoying, so that people are acting reasonably, when they seek to avoid a person who is known to be a chatterer. We may compare the *Gnomologium Vaticanum* in which fifteen sayings are attributed to Theophrastus. The tenth runs as follows, "The same man (Theophrastus) encountering a babbler said, 'Tomorrow, where will it be possible not to see you?'"[57]

In section 19 Didymus again refers to Theophrastus albeit obliquely: "following his teacher" (140.15) refers to Theophrastus *qua* pupil of Aristotle, whose definition of moral virtue is given at the end of section 18 (140.12–14 = *EN* 2.6 1106b36–1107a2). Theophrastus, we are told, offered by way of example a list of coordinate dispositions (140.17–141.2).[58] The text is faulty, but it is clear that seven virtues were listed beginning with temperance and in combination with coordinate vices. The latter, being deficiencies and excesses, are said to be concerned with emotions, *pathê*, and to be base. The former are described as good through being mean-dispositions, *mesotêtes* (141.3–5). There follows a list of the persons, who exhibit the same seven virtues and vices. The list offers little detail: only the

---

[55] Dirlmeier (1937) 6 with n. 6, where *entuchia* is explained as bureaucratic language of the court of a Hellenistic king.

[56] Paradigmatic is the cook, a minor character, whose chatter is stock humor in New Comedy. See Fortenbaugh (1981) 247–48; repr. (2003) 296–97.

[57] *Gnom. Vat.* no. 331 (p. 259 Sternbach) = 452 FHS&G. See also the spurious epilogue to Theophrastus' sketch of the *adoleschês* (*Char.* 3.5). Irritation with unwanted chatter can be traced back to the very beginning of Greek literature. See Homer's *Iliad* 2.212, where Thersites is introduced as a person of unmeasured speech, *ametroepês*.

[58] The mention of examples followed by a list of coordinate dispositions invites comparison with *EE* 2.3 1220b34–1221a12.

first entry goes beyond the bare minimum. We are told that the temperate individual is neither the person who totally lacks appetite nor the person given to appetite. For the former is like a stone[59] and the latter is wanton. The temperate individual is in middle. He is said to desire what he should, when he should, and to the extent he should. These he determines by reason according to the appropriate, as by a rule.[60] He is said to be in accord with nature (141.5–11).

The fact that the list of coordinate dispositions begins with temperance (140.18) and the list of persons begins with the temperate individual (141.5) is noteworthy, for temperance does not have pride of place in the corresponding portions of the *Nicomachean* and *Eudemian Ethics*. A possible explanation for this difference is suggested by the Theophrastean title *On Education* or *On Virtues* or *On Temperance*. That is the title as reported in the catalogue of Theophrastean works found in Diogenes Laertius' *Life of Theophrastus* (5.50 = fr. 1.283 FHS&G). It is tripartite, joining three alternative titles by the conjunction "or." The first is found by itself in an Arabic source (Ibn-an-Nadim, *The Index* 7.1, chap. on Theophrastus, p. 252.8 Flügel) and the third by itself in a papyrus of the third century AD (pap. Petersburgiensis Gr. 13, fr. 1.10). The ordering of the titles is sensible: Mention of education comes first followed by virtues. That tells us that the education in question is moral education. Last comes temperance, which is of especial importance in educating young people, for they are given to indulging themselves in bodily pleasures. That will not have escaped Theophrastus, who in writing a work on education may well have given temperance pride of place among the virtues That priority will have given rise to the third title; it may also be reflected in the lists of coordinates in section 19. That is a guess but not unreasonable.[61]

What must strike the reader is that loquacity, *adoleschia*, does not appear among the coordinates in section 19. In the preceding section,

---

[59] Cf. *EE* 2.3 1221a23.

[60] Here at 141.10, "rule" translates *kanôn*. The translation is not wrong, but to the English-speaker it is apt to suggest a ruler or straight-edge. In some contexts that would not be misleading, but when a virtuous man determines what to do, he considers the circumstances, which may vary greatly from one occasion to the next. Hence, we should keep in mind *Nicomachean Ethics* 5.10 1137b30–32, where Aristotle refers to the leaden rule, *molibdinos kanôn*, which was used in Lesbian construction work. It is not rigid but adapts its shape to a given stone. What's right for Milo is not the same as what's right for the beginner (2.6 1106b3–4).

[61] Section 19 is not the only place in the epitome where temperance enjoys pride of place. see also 5.124.4, 6.125.3, 16.137.22 and 16.138.2. For fuller discussion of the Theophrastean title, see Fortenbaugh (2011) 152–56.

Theophrastus was cited to illustrate the mean in relation to us. The illustration opposes chattering at length to saying not enough and to saying only what is necessary. In section 19 Theophrastus is again cited and the opposition between two extremes and a mean continues, but without loquacity and related coordinates. To be sure, section 19 gives names to all the dispositions and persons that are listed. That is not true of section 18, in which only the excess has a name and only in the form of a participle, *adoleschêsas* (140.9). But that difference seems inadequate to explain the omission. Loquacity might be opposed to reticence, *siôpê*,[62] and an unnamed mean-disposition might be recognized as such. Indeed, both the *Nicomachean* and the *Eudemian Ethics* recognize unnamed dispositions.[63]

Perhaps Theophrastus recognized that loquacity and reticence and the coordinate mean disposition are not normally referred to emotions and therefore do not belong among coordinate dispositions that are concerned with emotion. That does not mean that Theophrastus was disinterested in run-on chatter. In the *Characters*, he offers sketches of both *adoleschia* and *lalia*: we might say "loquacity and garrulity." No attempt is made to relate these traits to particular emotions; rather, they are presented as behavioral regularities that can be explained in more than one way (*Char.* 3 and 7).[64]

A different possibility is suggested by the fact that loquacity, reticence and moderation in speech can be understood as behavioral regularities like friendliness and punctuality and their coordinates. Such regularities are important to human society in that the mean-dispositions facilitate interaction, while the extremes are impediments. The person who has a friendly manner finds it easy to join with others in conversation/discussion, while both the person who is unfriendly and the person who appears fawning

---

[62] In a young person, reticence may be considered a safe adornment (Plutarch, *On Listening to Lectures* 4 39B); it gives the appearance of temperance (Demosthenes 61, *The Erotic Essay* 21). But in an educated person, depending on the circumstances, silence can be foolish (cf. D.L., *Lives* 5.40 = Theophrastus fr. 1 FHS&G).

[63] *EN* 2.7 1107b30, 1108a5; *EE* 2.3 1221a3.

[64] The Theophrastean sketch of *lalia* is instructive in that it gives the impression that run-on talkers may be motivated by the desire to establish one's own importance. But it does not rule out other motives and leaves open the possibility that on occasion a bodily condition like too much hot black bile may play a decisive role. See ps.-Arist. *Problems* 30.1 954a34 with Fortenbaugh (1975b) 64–65, repr. (2003) 132–33; and (1981) 246–47, repr. (2003) 296–97. Theophrastus' irritation with the run-on chatterer is captured in a humorous saying: "The same man (Theophrastus), encountering a babbler, said 'Tomorrow where will it be possible not to see you?'" (fr. 452 FHS&G). Hostility to excessive talk finds expression at the beginning of Greek literature in Homer's *Iliad*, where Thersites is said to be unmeasured in words, *ametroepês* (2.212).

create difficulties for themselves. And in business, punctuality is important in that it enables the persons involved to finish their work in a timely manner. Too early and too late have a negative effect. I want to believe that Theophrastus understood the importance of such regularities, and that he resisted including them among the moral virtues, not only because they lack an essential tie to emotion, but also because the Peripatetics conceived of moral virtue as a disposition to choose what is noble (118.3, 124.13, 129.9).[65] In contrast, behavioral regularities like friendliness, punctuality and moderation in speech were recognized as good, but they were valued as means and not as noble ends in themselves. We might say that they are productive of conditions necessary for the exercise of virtue, both moral and intellectual, within in the city-state. Here I am influenced by what is said earlier in sections 11 and 12 (128.26–130.12), but there the focus is on bodily and external goods, not on mean-dispositions that are psychic and manifest themselves in behavioral regularities. Nevertheless, regularities like friendliness, punctuality and moderation in speech are similar to bodily and external goods in that they are functionally related to the exercise of virtue. Each can be said to contribute to the employment of virtue (cf. 129.16–17). They are necessary/not without which, *hôn ouk aneu* (130.11), and can be conceived of as productive, *kata to poiêtikon* (130.11–12), by contributing to and assisting toward virtuous interaction.

At the end of section 19, we read "Such is the form, *eidos*, of the moral virtues, being concerned with emotion and considered according to the mean" (142.6–7). What follows is introduced by the relative pronoun *ho*. Being neuter singular, it picks up *eidos* and introduces a conceptual point: namely, that reciprocal implication exists between the moral virtues and practical wisdom, only not in the same way. Whereas practical wisdom follows on the moral virtues as a characteristic property, *idion*, the moral virtues follow on practical wisdom accidentally, *kata sumbebêkos* (142.7–10). We understand that practical wisdom is essentially tied to the moral virtues, being included in the definition of moral virtue (cf. the Aristotelian definition of moral virtue at 140.12–14). In contrast, the definition of practical wisdom does not make reference to moral virtue. Nevertheless, since practical wisdom is a disposition according to which men do what is noble (cf. 145.19–21) and since moral virtue is tied to choosing what is noble (118.3), a man of practical wisdom is in fact a man of virtue.

---

[65] Aristotle repeatedly ties virtue to what is noble, saying that the actions of a virtuous man are for the sake of the noble. See, e.g., *EN* 1.8 1099a22; 3.7 1115b12, 22; 4.1 1120a12, 24; 4.2 1122b6.

Didymus illustrates the point by reference to the just man. He is said to be also practically wise, for it is reason of this sort (i.e., practical wisdom), which gives him his form. But the practically wise man is not also just as a characteristic property, but because in common with (the just man)[66] he does noble and good deeds and nothing base (142.10–13).

Arnim thinks that the concluding portion of section 19 (142.6–13) continues to report Theophrastean material. The idea is not foolish. Not only is the opening sentence backward looking (142.6–7), but also earlier in section 19 Theophrastus is referred to (without being named): he is reported to have offered the list of moral virtues and vices and that of persons who possess these virtues and vices (140.15). Moreover, in section 18, Theophrastus is cited by name and Aristotle's definition of moral virtue is quoted (140.7–14).[67] That definition mentions the man of practical wisdom, which opens the door to a discussion of the relationship between moral virtue and practical wisdom. That is what section 19 provides, and it is reasonable to believe that in one of his writings Theophrastus addressed the topic. But it does not follow that what we read in the concluding portion of section 19 is drawn from a work of Theophrastus. The sentence with which the portion begins is transitional and as such may introduce material from a new source. And that is suggested by the shift from indirect discourse in what precedes (the list of virtuous and vicious persons) to direct discourse in the concluding portion.[68] In addition, the fact that the concluding portion includes Stoic vocabulary—in particular, *antakoluthia*, "reciprocal implication," and *eidopoiein*, "to give a form/specific character" (142.7–8 and 11)[69]—might indicate a change in source.

Moraux suggests that the concluding portion represents a relatively late Peripatetic response to the Stoic doctrine of reciprocal implication

---

[66] In translating *koinôs* (142.13) with "in common with (the just man)," I am agreeing with Tsouni against Sharples (2010) 126, who translates *koinôs* with "generally." To be sure, "generally" is a possible meaning of *koinôs* (LSJ s.v. *koinos* B.4), but in context it seems that "in common with" (LSJ B.1) is to be preferred. For while "generally" might be construed as "usually," "in common with" underlines that being practically wise is also to be just.

[67] As mentioned above on p. 95, the Aristotelian definition of moral virtue is found in *EN* 2.6 1106b39–1107a2. Moraux (1973) 388 thinks it unlikely that the occurence of the definition at 140.12–14 is attributable to Theophrastus. Rather, it has been shoved in by the compiler. Moraux may well be correct, but there is no reason to believe that Theophrastus was critical of his teacher's definition. See Fortenbaugh (2011) 304–5.

[68] Arnim (1926) 68 takes the occurrence of direct dialogue to be a sign that Didymus is reporting Theophrastus' own words. In my judgment, it tells the other way.

[69] See Adler's Index, *SVF* vol. 4 p. 18 s.v. *antakoloutheô, -ia* and p. 45 s.v. *eidopoieô*.

between all virtues.[70] The suggestion is attractive, when one considers that Didymus' account of the relationship between moral virtue and practical wisdom does not do justice to what Aristotle says in his *Ethics*. To be sure, if one begins from Aristotle's initial characterization of practical wisdom in *EN* 6 = *EE* 5, Didymus' account may seem satisfactory. For Aristotle makes no mention of moral virtue: he says that practical wisdom is a truthful disposition to act with reason in matters good and bad for man (*EN* 6.5 = *EE* 5.5 1140b5–6). In contrast, when he tells us how to construe moral virtue, he refers to reason and the person who possesses practical wisdom (EN 2.6 1107a1). That does fit Didymus' account, for it is not one of unqualified reciprocal implication. In fact, the implication, understood as a conceptual relationship, goes only in one direction: from moral virtue to practical wisdom. To move from practical wisdom to moral virtue, Didymus relies on an appeal to what can be observed to happen: the practically wise person and the morally virtuous person both respond to situations in the same way, that is, in a morally correct way.

That is true, but it fails to consider that practical wisdom without moral virtue, or rather the ability to reason well unaccompanied by moral virtue is apt to become an exercise in cleverness. Aristotle makes the point when he marks off practical reason from cleverness, *deinotês*, and tells us that practical wisdom does not occur without virtue, *ouk aneu aretês* (*EN* 6.12 = *EE* 5.12 1144a30). For practical syllogisms/deliberations have a beginning/goal, *archê/telos* (1144b32), which only a good person clearly grasps (1144a34). It is moral virtue that makes the target correct, *skopos orthos* (1144a8). Wickedness distorts and produces error concerning the beginnings of practical syllogisms/deliberations (1144a34–36). If that is correct, practical wisdom needs moral virtue. Being a truthful disposition to act correctly with reason, it needs to get the end right and that requires moral virtue. Aristotle might have made that clearer, had he added "not without moral virtue" or some equivalent to his initial characterization of practical wisdom (1140b5–6). But his subsequent discussion of the relationship between moral virtue and practical wisdom makes up for the omission. He tells us that moral virtue does not occur without, *ouk aneu*, practical wisdom (1144b17, b31) and that practical wisdom does not occur without, *ouk aneu*, moral virtue (1144a30, b32). "Not without" could be understood factually: lacking either practical wisdom or moral virtue a person is apt to make a bad choice (1145a4–5). But "not without" can be and in my judgment is better understood conceptually. Indeed, Aristotle's discussion is

---

[70] See Moraux (1973) 386.

informed by certain people who say that all the virtues are kinds of practical wisdom. Socrates is named: he is said to have erred in thinking that all the moral virtues are kinds of practical wisdom. Reference is also made to contemporaries, who in defining, *horizein*, moral virtue add "according to correct reason," that is, according to practical wisdom (1144b17–24). Aristotle agrees with these contemporaries, only his use of *ouk aneu* strongly suggests that the relationship between moral virtue and practical wisdom is reciprocal: not without, *ouk aneu*, moral virtue is just as true as not without, *ouk aneu*, practical wisdom.[71] In saying that, I am following Alexander of Aphrodisias (fl. c. 200 AD), who interpreted the relationship between moral virtue and practical wisdom as one of reciprocal implication. He did so both in his *Supplement to the Book* On the Soul 18 (CAG suppl. 2.1 p. 155.13–156.27 Bruns) and in his *Ethical Questions* 22 (CAG suppl. 2.2 p. 142.23–143.8 Bruns). In the latter text, *ouk aneu ... oud' aneu* (142.30) may be said to echo Aristotle's use of *ouk aneu ... ouk aneu*. And if that is correct, then Didymus' account of the relationship between moral virtue and practical wisdom is not that of Aristotle. Most likely the epitomist is drawing on a relatively late source.[72]

---

[71] Cf. *EN* 6.12 = *EE* 5.12 1144a36–b1: Not being good, it is impossible, *adunaton*, to be practically wise. See also *MM* 1.34 1197b36–1198a9.

[72] To avoid possible confusion concerning the phrase *ouk aneu*, further comment on section 12 (129.18–130.12) may be helpful (see above pp. 98–99). The section carries the subheading "What brings about Happiness," after which we read, "Happiness comes from noble and primary actions, and for this reason is noble throughout, just as the activity of pipe-playing is artful throughout. For the involvement/employment of material things does not cause happiness to depart from pure nobility, just as the use of tools (does not alter) the artful activity of medicine throughout" (129.18–22). In what follows, we are told that every action is an activity of the soul, and that when a person acts and makes use of things with view to accomplishing some purpose, these things are not to be considered parts of the activity: "Things without which, *hôn aneu*, a particular action is impossible are not correctly spoken of as parts of the activity. For the part is thought of as completing the whole, but things not without which, *hôn ouk aneu*, (are thought of) as productive by conducing and contributing toward the end" (130.8–12). Here we have the phrase *ouk aneu* twice, and as in the Aristotlelian passages cited above it is properly translated "not without," referring to something that is necessary. But there is an important difference. While Didymus' text refers to material things, in Aristotle the focus is on virtues of the soul. And in Didymus the relationship of necessity is between an intended accomplishment and a material means to that end, while in Aristotle the relationship is within the soul: between two virtues that together constitute complete or perfect virtue, *teleia aretê*.

(4) Sec. 24–25 Ts = p. 145.11–147.25 W

Following a discussion of forms of life, Didymus returns to the topic of virtue. He begins with three definitions of virtue, of which the first runs: "Moral virtue is, generally speaking, a disposition that chooses middling pleasures and pains, while aiming at the noble *qua* noble, *tou kalou hêi kalon*; vice is the opposite of it" (145.12–14). The idea of aiming at the noble recalls the definition of moral virtue found in section 1 (118.2–4). It also invites comparison with *Magna Moralia* 1.18, where the author puts the question, "At what does virtue aim?" and then answers by telling us that the end at which virtue aims is the noble (1190a8–28). The idea of choosing middling pleasures and pains may be compared with *Eudemian Ethics* 2.10, where we read that moral virtue is said to be a disposition to choose the mean in relation to us in pleasures and pains (1227b8–9). So Moraux, who observes that Aristotle repeatedly takes note of the fact that pleasure and pain divert us from the good *qua* goal according to nature.[73] Here I add only that the pleasures of food and drink and the prospect of painful physical exertion are not the only pleasures and pains that can cause a person to act badly. The pleasures and pains involved in an emotion like anger can have the same effect. The person who has been insulted may be so pleased by the prospect of revenge and so pained by what has occurred that he takes revenge in a way that is quite out of proportion to the provocation.[74]

More important is that the first definition fails to mention either *logos* or practical wisdom. Different is Aristotle's definition at *Nicomachean Ethics* 2.6 1106b36–1107a2, where we are told that the mean in relation to us is determined by reason, *logos*, and as the man of practical wisdom, the *phronimos*, would determine it. That definition has already been reported by Didymus at 140.12–14. As I understand the present passage, Didymus has not forgotten what he reported earlier. Rather, in omitting any mention of *logos* and the *phronimos*, he offers a first, minimal definition of moral virtue, which focuses on the alogical part of the soul. In what follows, that is, in the second definition, the omission is made good, at least by implication. In translation, the received text reads, "Common to (virtue) based on opinion and moral (virtue) is a disposition that considers and chooses and brings to action, *praktikê*, things that are noble in actions, *tôn en tais*

---

[73] Moraux (1973) 390–91, to whom I am indebted throughout this part of my essay. On pleasure and pain being the cause of base action, see, e.g., *EN* 2.3 1104b9–11, 21–24; 3.4 1113a33–b2; *EE* 2.4 1222a1–3; and *MM* 1.6 1185b34–35; also Didymus 127.17–18, 128.19–20, 138.22–23.

[74] On the pleasure and pain involved in anger, see Arist. *Rhet.* 2.2 1378a30–b10.

praxesi kalôn" (145.15–16).⁷⁵ As in the first definition, so here reference is made to what is noble, but now the emphasis is on action. And that calls not only for moral virtue but also for practical wisdom, which is a virtue of the logical part of the soul and important not only for accomplishing what one chooses to do, means-end deliberation, but also for dealing with a complex situation, that is, for reflecting on and getting right the particular situation.

Problematic are the words with which the second definition begins. The received text reads *koinên de doxastikês kai êthikês*, "common to (virtue) based on opinion and moral (virtue)" (145.15). In his apparatus to the text, Wachsmuth suggests reading *koinên de doxastikou kai êthikou*.⁷⁶ Tsouni accepts the emendation and translates: "common to the judging and ethical (parts of the soul)." The emendation finds precedent in Aristotle's *Ethics*, where reference is made to the part of the soul that forms opinions, *to doxastikon*—in context, the calculative part—and to the part that is moral, *to êthikon*. Cleverness and practical wisdom are assigned to the former, while natural virtue and virtue in the strict/full sense are assigned to the latter. In addition, we are told that virtue in the strict sense does not occur without practical wisdom (6.13 1144b14–17). That fits well with the words that begin the second definition. For it takes account of the fact that noble action often involves calculation/deliberation.⁷⁷ Moral virtue makes the end correct, and practical wisdom makes the means correct. But nothing here strikes me as incompatible with reading the received text. The

---

⁷⁵ Aside from a slight change in wording, the translation is that of Sharples (2010) 129. The phrase "that considers" translates *theôrêtikên* (145.15). The Greek might suggest a translation like "that contemplates," for *theôria* and its cognates are used in reference to the contemplation of a philosopher. Nevertheless, *theôria* and its cognates can be used quite widely. See, e.g., Arist. *EN* 6, where it covers reflections concerning both fundamental realites that do not admit change and contingent matters that do (1139a7). Among the latter belong technical matters that fall under productive arts (1140a11–12) and those that are practical and the focus of *phronêsis*. For an exmple in Didymus, I cite his discussion of political matters. There military strategy is treated as a species of *phronêsis*, practical wisdom, and *theôria* is used together with *dioikêsis* in regard to observing and administering what is advantageous to the army of a city state (150.10, 15). For an example of wide usage in Didymus, see 117.13–15, where *theorêtikon* bridges the division of the logical part of the soul: it is used to introduce the capacity for scientific reflection, *to epistêmonikon*, and then understood with the capacity for practical deliberation, *to bouleutikon*.

⁷⁶ The feminine genitive singular has has been replaced by the neuter genitive singular. The noun *merous* is understood, or the fuller phrase *merous tês psuchês*.

⁷⁷ I have written "often" to allow for exceptions: e.g., Aristotle's more courageous man who responds to sudden alarms straightway. He does not have time to deliberate, but he does act courageously (*EN* 3.8 1117a18–22). See Fortenbaugh (1975a) 78.

phrase *koinên de doxastikês kai êthikês* makes clear that the second definition is not concerned with a narrow, minimal definition that ignores the calculative part of the soul. On the contrary, we understand that the second definition is focused on moral virtue in combination with practical wisdom and therefore with a disposition that bridges the divide of bipartition. I leave the issue open, except to say that I prefer a conservative text that gives preference to the manuscript readings.

At the beginning, the third definition is seriously corrupt but not so hopelessly corrupt that we cannot pick out the central points. The opening phrase *tên de dianoêtikên* refers to intellectual virtue (*EN* 1.13 1103a3–7; *EE* 2.1 1220a4–6, 2.4 1221b27–30), which divides in two according to the division of the logical part of the bipartite soul. The mention of the *epistêmonikon* refers to the knowledgeable half of the logical part, which in section 1 had been explained as that which contemplates things eternal and divine (117.13–14). The other half of the logical part is not named in the corrupt portion of the epitome, but we can guess that it was referred to as *to logistikon*, which is the name assigned by Aristotle to that half of the logical part that deliberates and calculates concerning things that can be different from what they are (*EN* 6.2/*EE* 5.2 1139a12–15). In the subsequent portion, which is not corrupt, the virtues of the two halves of the logical part receive names: *sophia*, which is said to be knowledge, *episteme*, of the first causes, and practical wisdom, *phronêsis*, which is said to be a disposition, *hexis*, that is deliberative and practical, *bouleutikê* and *praktikê*, of the things good and noble *qua* good and noble, *agathôn kai kalôn <hêi agatha> kai kala* (145.19–21).

Section 24 continues with a list of thirteen mean-dispositions, beginning with courage and ending with justice. In between come temperance, good temper, liberality, greatness of soul, magnificence, righteous indignation, dignity, modesty/shame, wittiness, friendliness and truthfulness (145.21–146.14). The list invites comparison with *Magna Moralia* 1.20–33, where the same mean-dispositions are listed in the same order but discussed more fully. Indeed, what the epitome offers is brief in the extreme. Ten of the entries, the third through the twelfth, do nothing more than identify the disposition as a mean between two coordinate dispositions, each of which is named (146.3–12).[78] The last entry, that concerning justice, is different in that the coordinate dispositions are not named. Instead we read of excess and deficiency, much and little (146.12–14). The first entry

---

[78] In writing "each of which is named," I am accepting Heeren's supplements to the text at 146.6–7. They are printed by Wachsmuth and by Tsouni.

identifies courage as a faultless disposition involving middling[79] confidence and fear; no reference is made to coordinate dispositions (145.21–146.1). The second entry concerning temperance speaks generally of a disposition in choice and avoidance that makes people blameless on account of what is noble itself, *di auto to kalon* (146.1–3). Unlike courage whose sphere is limited by reference to the emotions of confidence and fear (145.21–146.1) and other dispositions whose sphere is delimited through the mention of coordinate dispositions, for example, good temper by the mention of irascibility[80] and truthfulness by the mention of irony and boasting (146.1, 3–4, 11–12), the definition of temperance includes no explicit or implicit limitation to its sphere. That is striking when one considers the beginning of the discussion of temperance in *EN* 3.10, for there Aristotle associates temperance with pleasures, which are progressively delimited: bodily pleasures, those humans share with animals, those of touch and taste, in particular eating and drinking and sex (1117b23–1118b8). Tsouni chooses to introduce limit by supplying "of pleasures and pains" to the definition of temperance at 146.2. The supplement is certainly intelligible, but if printed as part of the text as against in the *apparatus criticus*, an interesting connection with what is said concerning temperance in section 25 is obscured.[81] Moraux compares Stoic definitions of temperance that are similarly without limitation and suggests Stoic influence.[82] That may well be correct; certainly Stoic influence can be detected elsewhere in the epitome. But it is worth noting that Moraux's suggestion would be stronger had knowledge, *epistêmê*, occurred in the definition instead of disposition, *hexis* (146.1).[83] Moreover, mentioning choice together with avoidance, *hairesis* with *phugê* (146.2), is Peripatetic (e.g., *EN* 2.2 1104b30; *EE* 8.31249b1–2; *MM* 1.35 1197a2), and in Didymus' epitome, in a passage that exhibits no obvious Stoic influence, we find a similar pairing: the object of choice is mentioned together with the object of avoidance, *haireton* and *pheukton* (sec. 11 128.27–129.1).

---

[79] Here "middling" translates the adjective *mesos*, which is used of two opposed emotions, confidence and fear. Cf. the earlier definition of moral virtue, in which *mesos* qualifies pleasures and pains (145.13).

[80] I have omitted insensitivity, *analgêsia* (146.3–4), because like insensitiviy in English *analgêsia* in Greek can be used widely, not only of the pain caused by insult/outrage but also, e.g., of the pain caused by misfortune/bad luck, and so used it may be contrasted with greatness of soul (*EN* 1.10 1100b32).

[81] See below, p. 109 on 147.12–13.

[82] Moraux (1973) 393–94 with n. 252, citing *inter alia* Didymus B *ap*. Stobaeus 2.59.8–9.

[83] Contrast 146.1 (Peripatetic) with 59.2 (Stoic). See below, pp. 108–9 on the use of *hexis* in sec. 25.

In the preceding paragraph, I have avoided speaking of virtues and vices in favor of mean-dispositions and coordinate dispositions, for the text itself runs from beginning to end without using the terms "virtue" and "vice," *arête* and *kakia*. That may be nothing more than variation in vocabulary, but it does raise the question whether there might be substantive reasons for not using *aretê* and *kakia*. In this regard Aristotle's *Eudemian Ethics* 3.7 may be instructive. For there Aristotle discusses praiseworthy and blameworthy states of character, six sets in all (1233b16–1234a34), each of which appears in Didymus' list: namely, righteous indignation, shame, friendliness, dignity, truthfulness, wittiness and their coordinates (146.7–12). According to Aristotle, the six sets are not virtues and vices, for they do not involve choice. All are said to be in the classifications of emotions, *en tais tôn pathêmatôn diairesesin*, for each is an emotion, *pathos*. And because they are natural, they contribute to the natural virtues (1234a23–27). If I understand Aristotle correctly, when he refers to the classifications of *pathêmata*, he is referring to his own *Classifications/Divisions, Diaireseis*, which he will have drawn upon as needed, for example, in composing his discussion of emotions in the *Rhetoric* 2.2–11 (1378a29–1388b30).[84] These classifications are likely to have been inclusive, covering not only innate likes and dislikes, such as those surveyed by Didymus in sections 2–5 (118.11–123.27), but also variations in, for example, temperament and manner.[85] That is speculation, but if it is not far

---

[84] That Aristotle drew upon his *Diaireseis*, when composing the account of emotion found in the Rhetoric—that is suggested by the use of *diairein* in *Rhet.* 2.1 1378a22, 28—seems to me a reasonable conjecture, but exactly how the two works related to each other is problematic. Indeed, *Rhet.* 2.1 presents problems of its own: e.g., the statement that emotions are accompanied by pain and pleasure (1378a19–21) seems out of line with the later assertion that hate, *misos*, occurs without pain (2.4 1382a12–13). See Fortenbaugh (1996) 174–75, (repr. 2006) 398. Didymus at 139.4–6 lists hate as an emotion accompanied by pleasure and pain.

[85] It is well known that *pathos* can be used widely of all psychic phenomena; see above n. 9. Moreover, *pathêma* and *pathos* can be used interchangeably: cf. Bonitz' Index *s.v. pathêma* with *EE* 2.2 1220b10–14, where Aristotle refers to the division made elsewhere between *pathêmata, dunameis* and *hexeis* and then explains, "by *pathê* I mean the likes of anger, fear shame and generally the phenomena that are in themselves accompanied by sensory pleasure and pain." How the reference in 2.2 to the division made elsewhere between between emotions and capacities and dispositions relates to the reference in 3.7 to divisions of emotions (3.7 1234a26) is not immediately clear. The later reference might be an abbreviated version of the earlier. What we can say is that collections of divisions taken together will have cast a wide net. Indeed, a single collection of divisions might be quite long and diverse. Striking is Ptolemy's catalogue of Aristotelian writings, in which a work on divisions is reported to have run for twenty-six books and to have included *inter*

off the mark, we can understand why Aristotle refuses the labels "virtue" and "vice," and Didymus avoids the labels. Two of the six sets, righteous indignation, shame and their coordinates, are better viewed as emotions or emotional dispositions in that they are tied to emotions and not to particular modes of action whose end is noble or ignoble. Three, friendliness, dignity, truthfulness and their coordinates are not tied to particular emotions; they are stylistic traits or manners that are manifested throughout a man's behavior.[86] Wittiness is more complicated in that Aristotle ties it to both making jests and responding to them (1234a14–17). The latter

---

alia divisions of the soul, the passions, good and bad qualities. See Düring (1957) 226 and Dietze-Mager (2015) 107, 110.

[86] Caveat: Aristotle does not say that a behavioral regularity like friendliness is necessarily indifferent to moral considerations. In the *Eudemian Ethics*, he says that the friendly individual falls in with what seems best (1233b33–34), and in the *Nicomachean Ethics*, he tells us that the friendly man aims to provide pleasure and to avoid causing pain, and in doing so takes into account what is noble and useful (4.6 1126b28–30). Should providing pleasure contribute to unacceptable behavior, the friendly person will prefer to cause pain. That is an important qualification. For Aristotle friendliness is an expression of character (*EN* 4.6 1126b22–25) in that it manifests care and consideration when interacting with others. Unlike grouchy individuals who care not at all, *oud' hotioun phrontizontes* (1126b15–16), for the people with whom they interact, friendly individuals exhibit concern, *phrontizein*, for others. In particular, they vary their behavior depending upon whether they are interacting with familiar or unfamiliar persons (1126b25–28). Much the same can be said concerning the truthful person: he cares about the truth and on whole speaks the truth, but on the right occasion he will boast or depreciate himself (4.7 1127b26). So too, the dignified person is concerned to maintain socially approved norms, but not in a way that ignores the particular circumstance. Regarding care and concern, see Roberts and Wood (2007) 40, 60, whose remarks I find quite helpful, though I do not want to suggest that either Aristotle or Didymus recognized care and concern—*phrontis, epimeleia, spoudê*—as a special, well-defined category of behavior. I offer two reasons. First, conceptually care and concern are incomplete. They call for objects: e.g., a father cares for his children, and a citizen soldier concerns himself with the defense the state. In both cases, the concern is commendable but very different. Indeed, we might say that while care and concern are integral to all forms of good character, they are manifesed in ways that differ significantly and therefore discourage recognizing care and concern as an independent character trait. Second, care and concern can be both passionate and dispassionate. By way of illustration, I cite Didymus: when a father nears death and takes care, *spoudazein/phrontizein*, to provide for his children, his concern is an expression of strong love, *philostorgia* (120.1–7), but when he or a legislator takes care, *ex epimeleias/spoudazein*, to provide young people with a sound educuation (136.18–19, 152.17–18), such concern need not be driven by emotion. Rather it manifests prudent forethought concerning the future of the family and the city state. That means that care and concern cannot be pigeonholed as phenomena found either in the alogical part of the soul *qua* locus of emotional response or in the logical part. In itself that is not a fault: perfect virtue and noble-goodness are dualizers (see below pp. 113–14),

108 William W. Fortenbaugh

may be viewed as an emotional response (laughing), but the former need not involve a response (though some people laugh at their own jokes). A witty person may aim at arousing a favorable response in someone else, but equally a manifestation of wit may be only loosely tied to intention, for jesting can become a manner that manifests itself throughout a person's behavior.

Above in discussing section 18,[87] I had occasion to cite Theophrastus' *Characters*, in which loquacity is described (1) along with other traits that may be viewed as behavioral regularities. Examples are obsequiousness, *areskeia*, and self-will, *authadeia*, both of which are sketched in the *Characters* (5, 15) and listed by Didymus in section 24 (146.8–9).[88] To be sure, the *Characters* is a light-hearted work, so that it might be challenged as a credible witness to Theophrastean interest in behavior regularities. Perhaps, but a popular teacher like Theophrastus might choose to enliven his teaching by drawing on the *Characters* during lecture.[89] And if one insists on a serious school text, then we might look to *On Dispositions* and *Varieties of Virtue* (436 no. 1 and no. 7 FHS&G). In any case, I like to think that Didymus' treatment of dispositions in section 24 relates not only to Aristotle but also to Theophrastus.

Section 25 focuses on virtue and turns our attention to subordinate species: in particular, the species of justice, temperance and courage (146.15–147.21). The treatment is quite similar to the treatment of subordinate species that Didymus preserves in the Stoic portion of his work (5^{b2} 60.9–62.6). There are, however, differences. Here are four: (1) The Stoic text includes species of practical wisdom and gives them pride of place. They are omitted in the Peripatetic text. (2) There is variation in the order of treatment. In the Peripatetic text, the subordinate species of justice precede those of temperance and courage; in the Stoic text they come last. (3) The Stoic text omits two subordinate species that are found in the Peripatetic text: namely, holiness, *hosiotês*, a species of justice and self-sufficiency, *autarkeia*, a species of temperance (146.17, 19).[90] (4) Whereas the Stoic version refers to each of the subordinate species as knowledge, *epistêmê*, the

---

and care and concern might be recognized as such. But in an ethical system that bases itself on bipartition, it would be uneconomical to consider all possible forms of dualizing.

[87] See above pp. 94–95.

[88] See Fortenbaugh (1975) 71–76, repr. (2003) 137–41.

[89] On Theophrastus' popularity and lively manner in lecture, see Diogenes Laertius 5.37 and Athenaeus 1.38 21A–B (fr. 1.16 and 12 FHS&G).

[90] *Kosmiotês*, decency, as a species of temperance in the Stoic text (5^{b2} 61.9) is a variation for *eukosmia* in the Peripatetic text (146.19).

Peripatetic version characterizes each of the species as a disposition, *hexis*. These differences are real, but even taken together they do not obscure the obvious similarity between the two texts. According to Moraux, the two treatments are not independent of each other. The Stoic treatment is the earlier, but the Peripatetic version is not a mindless borrowing. It has been adapted in accordance with Peripatetic doctrine. In particular, *hexis* has replaced *episteme*.[91]

The three subordinate species of temperance listed in section 25 are of special interest, for taken together they suggest an inclusive notion of temperance: decency/decorum, *eukosmia*, is said to preserve what is appropriate in movements and poses/postures; orderliness, *eutaxia*, aims at what is *kalon* in regard to order; self-sufficiency, *autarkeia*, is adequate for what happens in combination with liberality (147.12–18). To be sure the three species may be said to point to certain areas in which temperance is exhibited, but decency and self-sufficiency seem quite different from each other, and much the same can be said of orderliness: at very least it seems remote from self-sufficiency. That inclusiveness recalls section 24, in which temperance is said to be a disposition in choice and avoidance that makes people blameless on account of what is noble itself, *di auto to kalon* (146.1–3). Understood as a definition, the statement is remarkable, for it provides no clear limits. It is general enough to cover decorum, orderliness and self-sufficiency, and as Moraux observes, it suggests Stoic influence.[92] Nevertheless, what we are told concerning decency, *eukosmia*—it concerns motions and poses/postures—gives pause. For it is tempting to construe motions and poses, *kinêseis* and *scheseis* (147.13), as manners, modes of social interaction, which may be described as fine[93] or decorous[94]

---

[91] Moraux (1973) 442. In the Stoic portion prior to the treatment of the subordinate species, the so-called primary virtues (5^{b2} 60.9), practical wisdom, temperance, courage and justice, have been recognized as forms of *episteme* (5^b 58.11–12, 5^{b1} 59.4–11). Regarding Peripatetic terminology, see, e.g., *hexis* in Aristotle's definition of moral virtue (*EN* 2.2 1106b36–1107a2), which recurs in Didymus 140.12–14. See also 118.4 (supplied); 141.3, 14; 145.12, 15, 20, 21; 146.1, 3.

[92] See above, n. 82.

[93] In English we might speak of "refined" manners or even "beautiful" manners, but among ordinary Americans it would be odd to speak of "noble" maners, though one might speak of the manners of an English nobleman.

[94] Hence, Simpson (2014) 101 translates *eukosmia* (147.12) as "decorum." Pomeroy (1999) 107 n. 20, in his comment on *kosmiotês* in the Stoic portion of Didymus' epitome (61.9–10), writes, "This would include correct deportment and appropriately masculine gesture for males (females also being expected to conduct themselves as appropriate to their sex), which were regarded as matters of a general societal interest in the ancient

or beautiful,[95] but are not noble in themselves. Aristotle's great-souled individual, the *megalopsuchos*, is instructive. He is someone who deems himself worthy of great things and is actually worthy of great things, especially the greatest: namely honor. That is his essential character: being properly disposed to honor and dishonor (*EN* 4.3 1123b2, 15–22). But he is also thought to move slowly, for he cares little about other things. A slow gait is his manner as is his tendency to speak with a deep voice (1125a12–16). We might say that these are behavioral traits, which are frequently exhibited by the great-souled individual but are not to be confused with what makes him great-souled: namely, his attitude toward honor. That seems to me correct, and might be applied to decency and orderliness. To be sure, they are commendable mean-dispositions, which a virtuous/well-educated person may be expected to exhibit, but that does not mean that they are to be viewed as moral virtues on a par with courage and good temper. We should keep in mind that the *Eudemian Ethics* recognizes the importance of mean-dispositions like dignity, friendliness and modesty. They are said to be praiseworthy, but not to be virtues (3.1 1234a23–24). It might be objected that mentioning the *kalon* in regard to orderliness (147.14–15) connects that disposition with moral virtue, for in the opening portion of section 24 moral virtue is associated with the *kalon* (145.14, 16). True, but the objection can be countered by observing that the opening portion of section 24 (145.11–21) is only loosely connected with what follows (145.21–146.14). Indeed, the absence of any mention of moral virtue in the subsequent portion creates a clear divide. Moreover, *kalon* itself is not univocal. As observed above,[96] it can be used of moral virtue, of useful things and of beauty. All are goods and all are desirable in individuals. A native speaker would have little trouble discerning how *kalon* is being used on a particular occasion. The difficulty is to determine which mean-dispositions are to be labeled moral virtues and which are not. Apparently

---

world." Taking a cue from an earlier passage in the Peripatetic epitome, we might think of decency as an acquired disposition, which is a good of the soul and is instilled through careful training, *ex epimeleias*. It has a place in preliminary studies, *propaideuseis*, and is manifested in the lives of free men, *diaitas eleutherias* (136.18–19). But it does not follow that appropriate motions and gestures are in themselves noble *qua* manifestations of virtue. Similarly, failure to exhibit propriety in movement invites disapproval—think of Hippoclides, whose unrestrained dancing cost him a marriage (Herodotus 6.129)—but in itself inappropriate motion need not be condemned as vicious.

[95] At 147.14–15, we read that orderliness is a disposition *stochastikên tou peri taxin kalou*. Simpson translates "aiming at beauty in order."

[96] See p. 88.

Aristotle left the issue undecided. The *Eudemian* and *Nicomachean Ethics* disagree, and the *Magna Moralia* takes no stand. We are referred to another discussion (1.32 1193a37–38).[97]

Also of interest in section 25 are the species subordinate to justice (147.1–12), for they invite comparison with a fragment of Theophrastus that is preserved in the *Anthology* of Stobaeus (3.3.42 p. 207–8 Hense = 523 FHS&G). First, the text of Didymus. It begins with piety, *eusebeia*, and holiness, *hosiotês*. The former is said to be a disposition to serve/worship gods and *daimones*. The latter is characterized as a disposition to maintain a just relationship with the gods and the departed, that is, one's ancestors. The mention of *daimones* and of the departed serves to distinguish the two dispositions, but the two are closely related, and in his work *On Piety*, Theophrastus seems not to have drawn a distinction between piety and holiness. As the text of Didymus continues, living humans become the focus. Goodness, *chrêstotês*, is said to be a disposition that treats people well voluntarily and for their sake. Easy to deal with, *eukoinôsia*, is a disposition whereby one remains faultless in his common dealings. And fair commerce, *eusunallaxia*, protects one against injustice in dealings (147.5–10). As defined fair commerce is a defensive disposition, which may seem far removed from piety, but if we keep in mind that Didymus is listing dispositions that are subordinate to justice, the jump is not so great. Moreover, there is the Theophrastean fragment, which exhibits a similar jump. We are first told that the man who is going to be admired for his relationship to the divinity must be one who likes to sacrifice frequently. After that we are told that a person must take good care of his parents, wife and children, for not to do so is to be disdainful of the laws of nature and of the city and to transgress both kinds of justice. Moreover, if it is necessary to loan money to someone, one should try to do so on a solid basis and to regain it on friendly terms, rather than to contract with benevolence and to recover it with hostility (fr. 523 FHS&G). Here the move from family to business dealings is an undeniable jump and editors mark a lacuna before the reference to lending money. Fair enough, but a lacuna indicates no more than omission, and if we keep in mind the earlier reference to justice, *dikaiosunê* (523.6), and take a cue from Didymus, then the jump is not unintelligible. In both texts the overriding concern is justice and in both there is a move

---

[97] To avoid possible confusion, I note that the order, *taxis*, to which Didymus refers in section 25 (147.15) is different from the order, *taxis*, that Aristotle mentions in the *Metaph.* 13.3 1078b1 and the *Poet.* 7 1450b37 (see above, p. 90). In the former the order is exhibited in a person's behavior, and in the latter it is exhibited by an object that has parts.

from the gods to the world of humans and the need to protect oneself when doing business.

The ethical part of Didymus' compendium ends with a brief comment concerning noble-goodness, *kalokagathia* (147.22–25). Combining all the moral virtues, it is said to be perfect virtue, *teleia aretê*, making good things useful and noble, and choosing noble things for their own sake (147.22–25). As a conclusion to the ethical part, the focus on perfect virtue seems appropriately upbeat. It also returns us to the beginning of the ethical part, where we were told of beginnings and seeds whose perfections, *teleiotêtes*, are achieved by habituation and correct training (116.21–117.2). I would like to think that this return is deliberate and a mark of careful editing, but it is not. The several treatments of moral virtue and their separation tell otherwise.[98]

Didymus also makes reference to noble-goodness in discussing happiness. He reports several definitions of happiness, one of which is "the primary employment of complete virtue in a complete life" (130.18–19). Subsequently he explains the mention of complete virtue by citing a distinction between incomplete and complete virtues. The former are good natural endowment and moral progress; the latter are justice and noble-goodness (131.14–16). What interests me here is not the distinction between incomplete and complete virtue. It marks off what is innate and partially developed[99] from what has been fully developed or trained. Rather, my interest is in the pairing of justice and noble-goodness (131.16–17). For Aristotle recognizes two kinds of justice. There is justice *qua* fairness in the distribution of goods and justice *qua* law-abiding. In regard to the latter, Aristotle is thinking of codes of law that are properly enacted: they make pronouncements about everything and aim at the common advantage. It follows that the person who is just *qua* law-abiding possesses complete or perfect virtue, but not in an unqualified sense. Rather, he possesses complete virtue

---

[98] Usener (1973) 395 compares the *Eudemian Ethics*, where noble-goodness is discussed in the last chapter and compared with health of the body, which requires that all the parts of body, or the greatest number or the most important of them, be healthy (8.3 1248b8–16). Allowing for exceptions is typical of Aristotle and suits health, but it is not to be pushed in regard to noble-goodness. Aristotle ends his discussion by saying that noble-goodness is perfect/complete virtue, *aretê teleios* (1249a16–17). Unlike Didymus who ends the ethical part of his epitome with a comment on noble-goodness, Aristotle's remarks on noble-goodness do not come last in the final chapter. That position is taken by the contemplation of God, though noble-goodness is mentioned in a final summary sentence (1249b9–25).

[99] Here the Greek is *prokopê*, virtue in progress. See D.L., *Lives* 7.127 and below, chap. 7 on "Types of Life," 18 nn. 51–53.

in regard to the community, that is, to other people. Hence, justice in this sense is like noble-goodness, in that both are inclusive dispositions, but noble-goodness is entirely without qualification: it is not limited by reference to law and other people.[100]

Finally, I return to a promise made earlier toward the beginning of part 3 of this paper. There I called attention to the fact that Didymus introduces a discussion of moral virtue by recognizing that the soul is bipartite: it has a logical and an alogical part. Assigned to the logical part are noble-goodness, practical wisdom, mental acuteness, wisdom, readiness to learn, memory and the like. Assigned to the alogical part are justice, temperance, courage and the other so-called moral virtues (137.14–23). Striking is the assignation of noble-goodness to logical part of the soul. For in a parallel passage in the *Magna Moralia*, the same two lists occur, but with a single exception. Noble-goodness is not mentioned: either in the list of virtues of the logical part, as it is in Didymus, or in the list of virtues of the alogical part (1185b5–8). Moreover, later in the *Magna Moralia* we read that the name "noble-goodness" is applied to the man who is perfectly good. It is in respect to virtue that men speak of the noble and good individual: for example, the just, the courageous, the temperate individual; speaking generally in respect to the virtues (2.9 1207b23–27). That might suggest assigning noble-goodness to the alogical part. But to do so would be a mistake, and the *Magna Moralia* does well to resist the assignation. For noble-goodness not only brings together the several moral virtues but also includes practical wisdom. Indeed, it could not be perfect/complete virtue without practical wisdom. For virtuous action demands both moral virtue and practical reason. I have already called attention to the way in which moral virtue and practical wisdom combine in choosing a proper response to a particular situation.[101] For example, the good-tempered man, when insulted, is moved to take revenge, but how best to take revenge is a matter for deliberation and so for practical wisdom. Here I add that the good-tempered man may also want to consider, indeed is likely to consider, whether the insult is exactly as perceived. Here too practical wisdom plays

---

[100] For Aristotle, noble-goodness is also closely related to greatness of soul, *megalopsuchia*, in that the man who possesses greatness of soul possess all the virtues, for otherwise his claims to deserve great things, especially honor, would be unjustified. At one point, Aristotle says that "greatness of soul is, as it were, the crown of the virtues, for it makes them greater and would not exist without them. Therefore, it is truly difficult to be great of soul, for it is not possible without noble-goodness" (*EN* 4.3 1124a1–4).

[101] Above, pp. 100–101.

a role: it is essential to reviewing and assessing what has occurred.[102] Such considerations make clear that practical wisdom belongs to the logical part of the soul and is of special importance in regard to virtuous action,[103] but they do not adequately explain assigning noble-goodness pride of place in front of practical wisdom in a list of virtues assigned to the logical part. Indeed, the assignation is misleading, for as Didymus himself recognizes, noble-goodness is perfect/complete virtue and as such brings together all the moral virtues (146.22–23). I conclude that in the earlier passage (137.19) Didymus has expressed himself incautiously, but in his concluding remarks on Peripatetic ethics (147.22–25), he is clearer, at least to the extent that he speaks of noble-goodness as perfect virtue, which makes good things beneficial and noble. Without practical reason, noble-goodness could not accomplish that. And the same holds regarding moral virtue. Noble-goodness bridges the divide of the bipartite soul.

An Appendix on Temperament

In discussing moral virtue, I have twice made reference to temperament. First, within a discussion of the bipartite soul I called attention to the fact that Didymus divides the alogical half into an appetitive and a spirited part, *epithumêtikon* and *thumikon*, and describes the latter as confrontational, *amuntikon*, tha*t* is, that part which makes a person ready to defend himself against his neighbors (117.17). Citing Plato's *Republic* and Aristotle's *Ethics*, I suggested understanding this description in terms of temperament. The person who is *amuntikos* is innately disposed to respond vigorously in the face of danger.[104] The second reference to temperament occurs within a discussion of praiseworthy and blameworthy states of character. There I made reference to Aristotle's *Classifications/Divsions* of *pathêmata* and said that these writings are likely to have taken account not only of paradigm emotions like anger and fright but also of variations in temperament and manner.[105] No other reference occurs. Given the importance of temperament in determining both individual and group behavior that may surprise and disappoint, but unlike Aristotle, Didymus largely ignores the

---

[102] We might say reflecting on what has in fact occurred as against means-end deliberation concerning how best to accomplish the goal of revenge,

[103] Cf. 145.19–21, where Didymus characterizes practical wisdom as a disposition that is deliberative and practical resulting in good and noble actions, *bouleutikê kai praktikê agathôn kai kalôn*.

[104] See p. 80.

[105] See p. 106.

topic. In regard to individual behavior, Aristotle discusses moral weakness at length (*EN* 7.7–10 1150a9–1152a36), and in the course of that discussion he makes clear that temperament—acuteness, swiftness and intensity—contribute to moral weakness,[106] that is, the kind of weakness that Aristotle calls impetuosity *propeteia* (*EN* 7.7 1150b19). Didymus does otherwise: he only touches on moral weakness and makes no mention of the way swiftness, impetuosity and the like, dispose a person to sudden, strong emotional response (128.18–23).[107] In regard to group behavior, Aristotle tells us that people in colder places and those of Europe are naturally full of spirit, *thumos*, but deficient in intelligence, *dianoia*. The result is that they live comparatively free but lack political organization. In contrast, the peoples of Asia are intelligent, but lacking in spirit they are in continuous subjection and slavery. Different from both these people are the Greeks. They possess both spirit and intelligence and therefore continue to enjoy freedom, to be well organized politically, and to be capable of ruling over all people, were they to obtain political unity (1327b19–33).[108] Didymus offers nothing similar. In what follows, I shall not try to counter the obvious: Didymus' epitome, as it comes to us through Stobaeus, has little to say about temperament. But I shall call attention to Didymus' remarks concerning the household (148.5–149.24), for there the epitomist seems not only to take notice of temperament but also to do so in a way that highlights his readiness to join material drawn from different sources.

At the outset, Didymus tells us that a man and a woman come together for the sake of children and companionship in life. That union is said to be a household, *oikos* and the beginning of the city-state, *polis* (148.5–7). We are also told that the relationship between a man and a woman is aristocratic, that of parents to children kingly and that of children to each other democratic (148.16–19). Didymus repeats the idea that a man and a woman are brought together by the desire for children (148.19–20) and then tells us that once united a man and woman acquire a fellow-worker, who is either

---

[106] Cf. *oxus*, *tachutês* and *sphodrotês* at *EN* 7.7 1150b25–27.

[107] For an example of swift, impetuous temperament, I cite the *Perikeiromene*, a comedy written by Menander, who is reported to have been a pupil of Theophrastus. The play is set in motion by an impetuous act—Polemon cuts off the hair of his mistress, whom he erroneously believes to be unfaithful—and ends with Polemon impetuously promising never again to find fault with his mistress. The promise is quite absurd, for Polemon's actions are all too often determined by a natural/innate temperament, which manifests itself throughout his behavior, See Fortenbaugh (1974) 441–43.

[108] Aristotle does, of course, recognize that not all Greeks exhibit a perfect mix of spirit and intelligence: some are said to be onesided (1327b33–36).

a slave by nature—one who is strong of body, slow, *nôthês*, and unable to live on his own—or a slave by law. After that, common advantage is said to motivate the establishment of the household (148.21–149.5). Finally Didymus tells us that by nature the man holds rule over a household, for the deliberative element in a woman is worse, in children it is not yet developed, and in slaves it is wholly absent (149.5–8).

As I understand this passage, its roots are diverse. The final portion concerning the deliberative element in men women, children and slaves has its roots in Aristotle's *Politics* 1.13, but what precedes concerning the slave has its roots in Plato's *Statesman*, where the Eleatic Stranger is made to advance a doctrine of competing dispositions.[109] On the one hand, there are swiftness, intensity and acuteness,[110] which are exhibited in many kinds of action including mental, bodily and vocal performances. They are often admired and when praised they are called courage or vigor, *andriea* (306C10–E12). On the other hand, there are restraint, gentleness and quietness, which when praised are spoken of as decorum or moderation, *kosmiotês* (307A1–B3).[111] It is clear that the Stranger is not thinking of *andreia* and *kosmiotês* as moral virtues in the sense of habituated dispositions acquired through a system of moral education. Such virtues are not opposed to one another (cf. 306A8–C1). It is also clear that the Stranger is not focusing on different emotional capacities, which manifest themselves from time to time depending on the particular situation. Rather the Stranger is interested in opposed temperaments that manifest themselves throughout a person's behavior: in the way a person thinks, in the motions of his body and in the tempo of his voice (306C10–D1, E3–5, 307A8–9). Such dispositions, being innate, are attributable to genetic factors and are open to legislative controls such as those proposed at the end of the *Statesman* (310A7–311C7): marriages between men and women of the same temperament are to be disallowed, for they result in extremes of

---

[109] In the *Statesman*, temperament is discussed within the framework of a bipartite soul: one that divides into an eternal part and a zoogenetic part (309C1–3). This psychic dichotomy is not to be confused with either the bipartite psychology that underlies Aristotle's ethical writings or the incipient form of bipartition found in Plato's *Laws*. See Fortenbaugh (1975c) 283–305.

[110] *Oxutês, tachos* and *sphodrotês* (306C10, E4–5). Cf. *EN* 7.7 1150b25–7 above n. 106.

[111] The Stranger is careful to note that vigor and decorum are praiseworthy only when they are suitable. Sharpness and swiftness in excess of what is suitable are called insolent and maniacal, while unsuitable slowness and softness are labeled cowardly and indolent (307B5–C2).

temperament. Vigor morphs into madnesss and moderation into sluggishness and slavery (309A6, 310D6–E3).[112]

Noteable is the Eleatic Stranger's use of *nôthês*. He tells us that a string of marriages between persons whose soul is full of modesty with no alloy of boldness has negative consequences: the soul becomes more sluggish, *nôthestera*, and completely crippled (310E2–3). Indeed, the kingly art places those persons who wallow in humility under the yoke of slavery, *eis to doulikon hupozeugnusi genos* (309A). Here we have the natural slave, whom Didymus describes as sluggish, *nôthês*, and unable to live on his own. And if that is correct, then I think it misleading to refer to Didymus' remarks on slavery as a single, unbroken segment (148.21–149.8). Rather, it divides into two parts, of which the first relates closely to Plato's *Statesman* (149.2 recalling 310E2)[113] and is focused on temperament, while the second relates to Aristotle's *Politics* (149.5–8 recalling 1.13 1260a12–14) and is focused on deliberative capacity. In other words, there is a decided shift of focus when Didymus says, "Of this, the man has by nature the rule" (149.5–6). In itself the shift is not disturbing—"this" picks up "household" from the previous sentence—but such a transition is a matter of style. It eases without undoing the substantive shift from temperament to deliberative capacity.

It might be objected that too much weight is being attributed to the adjective *nôthês*. Perhaps, but in Aristotle the adjective is extremely rare: it does not occur in Aristotle's discussion of the household or anywhere else in the *Politics*. Indeed, it occurs only in *Research on Animals*, where it is used once of the chamaeleon, whose motion is said to be slow or sluggish like that of the tortoise (2.11 503b8). The cognate noun *nôtheia* is not found. That does not mean that *nôthês*, as it occurs in Didymus, is limited to physical/bodily motion. On the contrary, a survey of the passages listed in LSJ makes clear that the adjective can be used widely of both physical and mental mobility. And that fits well with innate temperament as characterized by the Eleatic Stranger: slowness and its opposite quickness are

---

[112] A similar concern with temperament is found in the *Laws*, only there marriage between persons alike in temperament is not prohibited by legislation. Rather the issue is addressed in a preamble stating that quick and hasty individuals should form a union with slow and moderate partners (6 772E7–773E4).

[113] Being closely related to Plato's *Statesman* is also true of the what Didymus says some fifteen lines earlier, where he tells us that the household seems to be a small city-state (148.8–9). The statement is striking, for it is contradicted by Aristotle, who indirectly but unmistakeably criticizes Plato's words at *Statesman* 259B.

exhibited in actions of all kinds, both mental and physical,[114] and when they are excessive they are destructive and end in slavery (306C–308A).[115]

To avoid confusion, I want to state clearly that I am not suggesting that everything said by Didymus concerning the slave *qua* fellow-worker within the household should be referred to the *Statesman*. When the epitomist introduces the distinction between the natural slave and the slave by law (149.1–4) he is most likely drawing on Aristotle's *Politics* 1.2 (1253b21). Moreover and more importantly, the introduction of the slave by law jars with what follows (149.5–8). For there the focus is on the rule of the male within the household. His rule is said to be according to nature, *kata phusin* (149.6), for the deliberative capacity in a women is worse, in children it is not yet developed, and in slaves it is wholly absent, *holôs* (149.8). The characterization of the slave is faithful to Aristotle, who refers to nature and characterizes the slave as wholly, *holôs*, lacking deliberative capacity (*Pol.* 1260a8, 12), but that does not eliminate awkwardness. One wonders what has happened to the slave by law. He has been mentioned in what precedes (149.3–4) and is not to be confused with a slave wholly lacking in deliberative capacity. For slaves by law are typically persons who have been captured in battle and have some measure of deliberative capacity. Indeed, they must be able to think ahead and improvise, if they are to perform useful tasks within the household and the larger community. My guess is that what we have here is not a single passage that builds on itself, but rather two passages. At first reading, the join at 149.5 appears seamless (*toutou* picking up *oikon*), but on reflection it is clear that the grammatical join only masks a substantive difficulty.

A further difficulty is created by a change in wording. Didymus says that the deliberative capacity of a woman is worse, *cheiron* (149.7), than that of a man. In the *Politics*, Aristotle said that it lacks authority, *akuron* (1260a13). The change to *cheiron* may be a simple attempt at variation or

---

[114] Sharples translates *nôthês* with stupid" and Simpson with "dull." These translations are not altogether wrong, but I prefer to follow Tsouni, who translates with "slow," which is more inclusive and therefore better suited to a temperament that is exhibited throughout a person's behavior. When slowness becomes extreme and hence harmful, we might emphasize that by translating *nôthês* with "sluggish."

[115] The variant form *nôthrotês* occurs in Aristotle's *Rhetoric* (2.15 1390b30), and the adjective *nôthros* is found in the zoological works (see Bonitz' *Index s.v.*). The *Rhetoric* passage tells us that well-born families; i.e., those of good stock, deteriorate. In particular, those that are steady or stable degenerate toward fatuousness and sluggishness, *abelteria* and *nôthrotês*. That suggests a change that affects whatever a person does in the way that a change in temperament does.

simplification in wording, but if the change is taken at face value, then it too has substantive consequences. For in the *Politics*, Aristotle accepts the Platonic principle that virtue is tied to work or function, that work is tied to natural ability, and that difference in degree of natural ability does not justify the assignation of different roles (*Rep.* 5 456A–B; *Pol.* 1.13 1259b32–38). In Didymus the difference between the deliberative capacity of a women and that of a man has become one of degree ("worse"), so that it is wrong to assign all women indiscriminately a subordinate role that is fundamentally different from that of men. Perhaps Didymus himself did not notice that, but earlier in the *Politics*, Aristotle himself introduces difference in degree and ties it to a difference in role: the male is said to be naturally superior and the female worse, *cheiron*; the one rules and the other is ruled (1.5 1254b13–14). It is possible that Didymus or an intermediary was influenced by the earlier passage when he replaced *akuron* with *cheiron* in the later passage (149.7). But however that replacement is explained, Aristotle created difficulties for himself: he needed to choose between the comparative adjective *cheiron* and the positive adjective *akuron*.[116] If he accepted the Platonic principle (1259b32–38), then he could not invoke difference in degree to justify the unqualified subordination of the female to the male (1254b13–14). Rather, he needed to characterize the female intellect as *akuron*, as he does later toward the end of book 1 (1260a13).

Since I have recently discussed in fuller detail Aristotle's characterization of women in *Politics* 1.13,[117] I shall go no further except to say that the two problems just mentioned in regard to Didymus' text—that concerning the slave by law and that concerning difference in degree—do not affect the preceding lines (148.21–149.5), which seem to have roots in the Eleatic Stranger's characterization of the natural slave as someone who is by temperament sluggish and best brought under the yoke of slavery.

Works Cited

Arnim, H. von. 1926. *Arius Didymus' Abriss der peripatetischen Ethik*. SB Wein 204, 3. Wien: Hölder-Pichler-Tempsky.

Dietze-Mager, G. 2015. "*Die Pinakes* des Andronikos im Licht der Vorrede in der Aristoteles-Schrift des Ptolemaios." *Aevum* 89: 93–123.

---

[116] *Cheiron* is the comparative adjective coordinate with *ameinôn*, "better." *Akuron* is a positive adjective (neither a comparative nor a superlative) beginning with an alpha privative.

[117] Fortenbaugh (2015) 395–404.

Düring, I. 1957. *Aristotle in the Ancient Biographical Tradition.* Göteborg: Elanders.

Fortenbaugh, W. 1970. "Aristotle's *Rhetoric* on Emotions." *Archiv für die Geschichte der Philosophie* 52: 40–70; repr. 2006: 9–37.

———. 1974. "Menander's *Perikeiromene*: Misfortune, Vehemence and Polemon." *Phoenix* 28: 430–43.

———. 1975a. *Aristotle on Emotion.* London: Duckworth; repr. with epilogue, 2002.

———. 1975b. "Die *Charaktere* Theophrasts: Verhaltensregelmässigkeiten und aristotelische Laster." *Rheinisches Museum* 118: 62–82; repr. in English: "The Characters of Theophrastus: Behavioral Regularities and Aristotelian Vices." In *Theophrastean Studies.* Stuttgart: Steiner, 2003, 131–45.

———. 1975c. "Plato: Temperament and Eugenic Policy." *Arethusa* 8: 283–305.

———. 1981. "Theophrast über den komischen Charakter." *Rheinisches Museum* 124: 245–69; repr. in English: "Theophrastus on Comic Character." In *Theophrastean Studies.* Stuttgart: Steiner, 2003: 295–306.

———. (ed.). 1983. *On Stoic and Peripatetic Ethics: The Work of Arius Didymus.* Rutgers University Studies in Classical Humanities 1. New Brunswick, N.J.: Transaction.

———. 1983. "Arius, Theophrastus and the Eudemian Ethics." In Fortenbaugh (1983) 203–23.

———. 1996. "On the Composition of Aristotle's *Rhetoric*: Arguing the Issue, Emotional Appeal, Persuasion through Character, and Characters Tied to Age and Fortune." In *Lênaika: Festschrift für Carl Werner Müller*, ed. Chr. Mueller-Goldingen and K. Sier = Beiträge zur Altertumskunde 89. Stuttgart: Teubner, 165–88; repr. in *Aristotle's Practical Side: On His Psychology, Ethics, Politics and Rhetoric.* Brill: Leiden, 389–412.

———. 2003. *Theophrastean Studies.* Philosophie der Antike 17. Stuttgart: Steiner.

———. 2006. *Aristotle's Practical Side: On His Psychology, Ethics, Politics and Rhetoric.* Leiden: Brill.

———. 2011. *Theophrastus of Eresus Commentary.* Vol. 6.1: *Sources on Ethics.* Leiden: Brill, 203–23.

———. 2015. "Aristotle on Women: *Politics* 1.13 1260a13." *Ancient Philosophy* 35: 395–404.

———. 2016. "Aristotle on Bipartition and the Questionable Meaning-Dispositions." In *For a Skeptical Peripatetic: Studies in Greek Philosophy in Honour of John Glucker*, ed. P. Destrée, Chr. Horn, and M. Zingano. Studies on Ancient Moral and Political Philosophy. Bonn: Academia Verlag.

Fowler, B. H. 1992. *Archaic Greek Poetry*. Madison: University of Wisconsin Press.

Görgemanns, H. 1983. "*Oikeiôsis* in Arius Didymus." In Fortenbaugh (1983) 165–89.

Hicks, R. 1907. *Aristotle, De Anima*. Cambridge: Cambridge University Press.

Konstan, D. 2014. *Beauty: The Fortunes of an Ancient Greek Idea*. Oxford: Oxford University Press.

Moraux, P. 1973. *Der Aristotelismus bei den Griechen: von Andronikos bis Alexander von Aphrodisias*. Berlin: De Gruyter.

Pomeroy, A. 1999. *Arius Didymus, Epitome of Stoic Ethics*. Atlanta: Society of Biblical Literature.

Roberts, R., and W. J. Wood. 2007. *Intellectual Virtues: An Essay in Regulative Epistemology*. Oxford: Clarendon.

Sharples, R. 2010. *Peripatetic Philosophy 200 BC to AD 200*. Cambridge: Cambridge University Press.

Simpson, P. 2014. *The Great Ethics of Aristotle*. New Brunswick, N.J.: Transaction.

Trapp, M. 2007. *Philosophy in the Roman Empire*. Aldershot: Ashgate.

West, M. L. 1993. *Greek Lyic Poetry*. Oxford: Oxford University Press.

―――. 2011. *Hellenica*. Vol. 1. Oxford: Oxford University Press.

Zeller, E. 1879. *Die Philosophie der Griechen in ihrer geschichtlichen Entwicklung*. Vol. 2.2. 3rd ed. Leipzig: Reisland.

4

Intrinsic Worth of Others in the Peripatetic *Epitome* (Doxography C)

Stephen A. White

Doxography as a whole does not enjoy a very high reputation for argumentation, and deservedly so. Ancient "collections of briefly formulated tenets from a systematic point of view" (to adopt a handy definition) rarely bother to record any reasons or basis for the tenets they retail.[1] Some varieties do more than others in this regard, notably those focused on a single figure or school: summary accounts of the doctrines of a particular philosophical tradition or "stance" (αἵρεσις or Latin *secta*). Yet even this form of doxography, sometimes called "haeresiography," rarely offers any sustained argumentation, anything more than an occasional brief rationale. On this count, then, the summaries of Stoic and Peripatetic ethics widely ascribed to Arius Didymus stand near the upper end of the spectrum for "tenet-writing" as a whole. Both, and especially the Peripatetic summary, are thick with inferential and explanatory particles; both give considerable space to explaining and supporting the various views and positions they

---

[1] Mansfeld (1999) 17. My characterization applies only to doxography in this "narrow" sense, not the critical or polemical use of its materials in other contexts, as, for example, in Aristotle, Cicero, or Sextus; cf. Mansfeld (2012).

report, and the claims they paraphrase or occasionally quote. Attention to argument reaches a peak in the early pages of the Peripatetic summary, where an authorial voice enters in the first-person singular to announce that "nearly the whole synopsis of the *hairesis* derives its impulse from those things, precisely as I shall show very briefly" (119.20–21). This attempt to show or "display" (ἐπιδείξω) the motivating "impulse" (ὡρμῆσθαι) behind the school's stance in ethics, condensed though it is, continues for the next several pages (secs. 3–9 Tsouni: 4–12 Sharples), occupying roughly a quarter of the entire work as we have it. Its avowed brevity (διὰ βραχυτάτων), in short, is neither absolute nor proportional but simply relative to the complexity of its topic, which the author implies calls for fuller treatment than he will provide. As we shall see, this portion of the work stands out on other counts too, not only the scale and detail of its argument but also its format, style, and tone. The entire passage would repay close analysis, but its length and complexity preclude more than partial treatment here.

Beginning is half the whole: Hesiod's maxim fits our text to a T, and so I shall focus on the opening stage of its argument, which at points rises to striking rhetorical heights in the service of showing that (as our author puts it in conclusion) "external goods are inherently [πέφυκεν] worth choosing on their own account" (122.7–9).[2] This initial passage (sec. 3 Tsouni: 4–5 Sharples) records a series of puzzling arguments about a single sort of external good, though a very special one, namely, the well being of other people, and it does so in terms that evoke Stoic accounts of "social *oikeiôsis*"—roughly the ostensibly natural affinity and attraction we all have to other people by virtue of our familial or social relationships and shared humanity more generally. Its argument, though elliptical, is developed more fully and vigorously than anything else in the entire work, and its aim, I shall argue, is to isolate a common denominator in ordinary human sentiments both familiar and widely shared on one hand and a distinctive factor in Aristotelian accounts of virtuous motivation on the other. Underlying its edifying rhetoric is a carefully structured argument for two fundamental Peripatetic tenets: first, that interpersonal relationships have or involve intrinsic worth (they are what our author calls δι' αὐτὰ αἱρετά, literally

---

[2] Moraux (1973) 316–17 cites sec. 3 (n. 2) to exemplify how "sein Stil ist stellenweise sehr lebhaft und hat eine gewisse rhetorische Brillanz"; cf. Görgemanns (1983) 181 on its "rhetorical, almost passionate presentation" and Kahn (1983) 11 on its account "developed at great length and with great ardor." Contrast the author's own language of "headings" (κεφάλαια: 148.1, 150.1, 152.24; cf. 57.16, 116.16 for the Stoic summary) and "survey" (ἐπιδραμεῖν, 146.20) for the much more abridged format of later sections; cf. "compendium" (ὑπομνηματισμόν) for the Stoic summary as a whole (57.15, 116.18).

"worth choosing for themselves" or "on their own account"), and not only relations among the virtuous but the full spectrum of human interactions ranging from closest friends to total strangers; and second, that the recognition of intrinsic worth which these relations typically involve establishes a basic congruence and continuity in ethical motivation among the virtuous and others alike.

This passage is only the first stage in a larger argument about the wellsprings of Peripatetic ethics—its motivating "impulse"—that purports to show how and why these and other factors figure in Peripatetic accounts of eudaimonia as an inclusive end comprising a broad array of goods, not only friends and other external goods but various physical and psychic capacities and activities, including rational virtues foremost, all combined in notoriously problematic ways. In order to see how our passage contributes to this larger argument, we shall begin by surveying its full course (secs. 1–9), even more briefly than our author does. But first a few words about the author and his work as a whole.

An authorial voice speaks in the first person seven times in the Peripatetic summary, always editorially to address the progress of his exposition or the meaning of its terms.[3] The identity of this voice is a notoriously vexed question, problematic on multiple counts. Foremost is the author's name, which our text of Stobaeus fails to provide but can be plausibly identified on the basis of a short passage (sec. 12) quoted again later in the *Anthology* under the heading "from the Epitome of Didymus" (4.39.28; cf. 2.1.17); and so I shall call the work and its author, if only for the sake of convenience, leaving aside the related question whether Didymus is to be identified with the Arius of Alexandria close to Augustus.[4] Additional questions about the unity of this voice arise from the text itself, which exhibits distinct strata or layers throughout, not only by explicit quotation and citation—most prominently some Aristotelian formulas for eudaimonia in section 13 and material on virtue from Theophrastus in sections 18–19—but also by wider borrowing and paraphrasing evident in the pervasive use of indirect discourse. Much of this material echoes passages in the Aristotelian corpus;

---

[3] A total of eighteen first-person verbs, only twice after sec. 9: eight authorial uses, four singular (119.21, 122.10, 125.1, 143.11), four plural (122.6, 123.21, 125.23, 145.11), and another ten generic plurals (116.22, 119.7–15 [8×], 125.2: all broadly for "we human beings"); εἶπον in 131.14 is third person, as προσέθεσαν in 131.20 shows.

[4] The link with Didymus goes back to Meineke (1859); for discussion, see Diels (1879) 69–88; Moraux (1973) 259–71; Kahn (1983); Hahm (1990); Göranssen (1995) 182–226; Mansfeld and Runia (1997) 238–44; and Hahm (in this volume). Inwood (2014a) neatly sidesteps the question by dubbing the author "Harry" (77–78).

still more of it presumably draws on any number of lost works by later figures, however well digested by the immediate author. The opening sections are a case in point. Similarities to material explicitly ascribed to Antiochus of Ascalon by Cicero in book 5 of *De finibus* have led many to suspect him lurking behind much of the work and especially the opening sections that will be our focus here. Be that as it may, frequent shifts from direct to indirect discourse and back again indicate the presence of at least two distinct voices or strata throughout the opening sequence; and bumps or wrinkles in the train of argument have led some to suspect still more.[5]

It is not my aim here to examine, much less to resolve these issues of *Quellenforschung*. I mention them only to caution against two common but potentially misleading assumptions. One is simply that our text speaks throughout with a single voice. For the passage under discussion here (sec. 3) and the larger argument in which it figures (secs. 1–9), it is enough for present purposes to recognize the presence of a single first-personal voice directing or orchestrating the entire segment, however many "sources" he may have drawn on in presenting or compiling his case. Naming this voice Didymus or "Twin" is thus doubly apt as a reminder that additional voices may at any point lie behind his text. Nor does it matter here whether the same voice directs the rest of the *Epitome*, as it seems to do, let alone whether it belongs to the author of either of the two preceding excerpts in Stobaeus, either the immediately preceding summary of Stoic ethics (Doxography B) or the introductory material (Doxography A) preceding it in turn. The other common assumption I want to caution against is that Didymus as the directing voice at any point endorses the positions he records or reports. Detail, rigor, even ardor in presentation are virtues for expositors generally, partisan or not, whether advocating, criticizing, or simply expounding and explaining. The views on offer here are plainly Aristotelian in a broad sense, but given the doxographic purpose of their presentation, the expositor may not be.[6]

---

[5] So Kahn (1983) 7–8 calls this and the preceding summaries "a multi-layered collage" and "heterogeneous scrapbook"; cf. Görgemanns (1983) and Inwood (1983). For Stobaeus' own practice, which effectively rules out any paraphrasing on his part, see Hahm (1990) 2938–75; Piccione (1994); and Mansfeld and Runia (1997) 204–8. On Antiochus' possible influence, see Moraux (1973) 316 n. 1; and Kahn (1983) for synopses of earlier discussion; cf. Schofield (2012) 182–84; Inwood (2014a) 77–78; and Gill (2016).

[6] Annas, in two seminal studies (1990) and (1993) 279–90, reads the use of Stoic vocabulary here as primarily dialectical, designed to show how Aristotelian positions can be recast in ways that neutralize Stoic challenges; cf. Inwood (2014a) 88; Gill (2016) 226–33. An alternative, which I can only sketch here, is that Didymus (or his source for secs.

1. Introducing Peripatetic Ethics

The *Epitome* as we have it begins abruptly with Didymus reporting, "Character [ἦθος], then, he says, takes its name from habit [ἔθους]" (116.21–22). The failure to identify *who* made this point suggests, and the use of resumptive particles (μὲν οὖν) confirms, that our text is an extract taken from a larger work now deprived of its opening, presumably by Stobaeus in the course of his anthologizing. We can identify Aristotle as the likely designee behind the vague "he says" here (cf. *EN* 2.1 and *EE* 2.2), though Didymus might have known him as Nicomachus or Eudemus.[7] But what or how much is missing before this first remark is impossible to say. Be that as it may, the opening sentence typifies the format of the bulk of what follows. Didymus reports views of "Aristotle and the rest of the Peripatetics" (as a heading in one manuscript labels the extract) for the most part in indirect discourse, which he occasionally introduces in his own voice but otherwise rarely intervenes.[8]

In that respect the opening segment (secs. 2–9) differs dramatically from the rest of the work, which consists almost entirely of concise summary supported by little or no argument. Here by contrast, Didymus, whether in his own voice or paraphrasing another work, intervenes repeatedly and decisively at pivotal points in the argument. His directing role as indicated in the first instance by first-person remarks and sustained direct discourse is most prominent in the opening and closing parts of the sequence (119 and 127). Recall the expositor's promise I quoted at the outset: "nearly the whole synopsis of the *hairesis* derives its impulse from those things, precisely as I shall show very briefly" (119.20–21). The mention of *hairesis* here refers in the first instance specifically to the distinctive Peripatetic "stance" in ethics (cf. 125.22). But together with the mention of

---

2–9) speaks as a Stoic himself, using school language simply to indicate how Aristotelian positions correspond to Stoic views, in effect translating a rival account into his own terms, much as Cicero does with his Greek models or as we still do today. That might explain more effectively why the Stoic language is limited to the opening and closing sections (secs. 2–3 and 9) that frame the sequence, and absent from both the intervening account of Peripatetic views and the rest of the *Epitome*. It would also better suit the hypothesis that Didymus is identical with the Arius (of Alexandria) listed as a Stoic in the so-called "larger index" to Diogenes Laertius; cf. Dorandi (1992). Cf. pp. 139–50 and n. 31 below.

[7] Unlikely but possible; cf. Cicero *Fin.* 5.12 and Aspasius *In EN* 151.24–26.

[8] Cf. n. 3 above. The use of direct discourse in the explanation that follows here is exceptional: "for *we have* [i.e., humankind generally has] starting points and seeds of them [sc. character traits] from nature" (116.22–117.2); nowhere in the latter part of the *Epitome* (secs. 10–27) is any such gloss or explanation presented in direct discourse.

its motivating "impulse" the term also highlights a fundamental issue in Peripatetic ethics as outlined in the opening section: the relation between two distinct factors in human motivation distinguished in section 1, the drives or "impulses" (ὁρμαί) originating in the nonrational or "hormetic" capacity of the human soul (117.11–12) on one hand, and the corresponding "choices" (αἱρέσεις) made by the "deliberative" or "deciding" (προαιρετικήν) side of its "reasoning" or "critical" (κριτικόν) capacities on the other (117.11–118.4).[9] The double meaning here, more wordplay than ambiguity, thus serves to flag an important point about the Peripatetic theory by indicating its connection to the underlying rationale for ethical theory in the first place. For as Didymus proceeds to argue, adopting the Stoic language of *oikeiôsis*, our "first desire" as humans is for our own being, including our health, pleasure, and being alive generally, since everyone "has a natural affinity and attraction to oneself" (118.11–20). Then recasting the explanation in terms of self-concern, he explains: "for our body is dear to us [φίλον ἡμῖν], our soul dear to us, and so are their parts, capacities, and activities" (118.20–119.2). It is from "our forethought about the preservation of these" (sc. our body and soul and their attributes), he concludes, that ethical theory arises: our concern for our own well-being provides "the original basis [ἀρχή] for impulse, duty, and virtue" (119.2–4).

To explain this preliminary thesis, Didymus now shifts to direct discourse, using collective first-person plurals for humankind generally. In a remarkable thought experiment, he imagines a world in which everyone achieved full well-being in accordance with their natural impulses without the help of theory or informed deliberation: "for if there were never any error at all in our choices and avoidances and we continually attained only the good things and none of the bad," he contends, "we would never have sought out the correct and unfaltering selection in these matters" (viz. pursuit and avoidance of "natural" and "unnatural" things; 119.4–8). But given that, on the contrary, the world is in fact much messier and "in our ignorance we were often deceived in our choices and avoidances … , we were compelled to seek out secure knowledge for assessing" what to choose and avoid; and this practical insight is precisely what came to be called "virtue" (119.8–15). To conclude, he reiterates his preliminary thesis (quoted above): "for it turns out that our actions have their starting points [ἀρχαί] from the *selection* of natural things and the *rejection* of unnatural things,

---

[9] Reading τὰ πρακτικά with the manuscripts, or τὰ πρακτά with Tsouni, rather than Spengel's emendation τὰ <φθαρτὰ> πρακτικόν, adopted by Wachsmuth. On this synopsis of Aristotelian moral psychology, see Fortenbaugh (in this volume).

and so do what are called *duties*; and that is why both *right actions* [i.e., virtuous ones] and mistaken ones also involve these things and deal with them [sc. natural and unnatural things]" (119.15–18; italics indicate parallels to the triad of terms in 119.2–4 introducing the thought experiment).

In focusing on "choice and avoidance" of what is good and bad, or in comparable Stoic terms on "selection and rejection" of natural and unnatural things, and the moral psychology behind normative ethics, Didymus sets the stage for his exposition of Peripatetic theory. For by characterizing the rationale for ethics as a search for *sustained and consistent* correctness in choice or selection, he also declares his own rationale for showing or "displaying" (ἐπιδείξω), as he now promises to do, how "nearly the whole synopsis of the *hairesis* derives its impulse from those things" (119.20–21). Our main passage (sec. 3), then, is the first step in that project, as he reaffirms at its conclusion in terms that echo his opening promise (122.7–10):

> [§3] As a result, in this first way [ταύτῃ μὲν] it has been shown clearly [ἐπιδεδεῖχθαι σαφῶς] that the good things arising from outside are of a sort to be worth choosing *on their own account*. [§4] How, then, are goods involving us and within us not much more so [sc. worth choosing on their own account]? I mean of course those involving the body and soul.

"This first way" refers to the focus in section 3 on what Didymus now characterizes for the first time as "external" goods (cf. 136.9–16). His reference to things "from outside" also serves to introduce the next two steps of his exposition, which takes up the complementary class of goods "within us": first bodily goods (122.11–123.16: sec. 4), then those of the soul (123.21–124.14: sec. 5). To mark the transition from the first of those to the second, he intervenes again to announce in similar terms his preliminary conclusion for bodily goods specifically (123.17–20):

> [§5] As a result, if also the bodily goods have been shown [δέδεικται] (to be) worth choosing *on their own account*, and the bad things opposed to them worth avoiding *on their own account*, then necessarily [ἀναγκαῖον] also the parts of the soul are worth choosing *on their own account*, and also their virtues and those of the whole soul.

First external goods and now bodily goods, Didymus claims, "have been shown" to be "worth choosing on their own account"; and turning now to the third and final class, he makes the same claim for goods of the soul. Providing little in the way of argument this time, he briefly recaps his introductory synopsis before simply stating the Peripatetic conclusion that virtues of the soul rank far above anything else (123.21–27):

[§5] For after virtue makes its entry precisely the way we indicated [καθάπερ ὑπεδείξαμεν][10] and turns away from bodily and external goods toward itself and observes why it too is one of the natural things much more than the body's virtues are, it develops an affinity toward itself as worth choosing *on its own account*, and much more so toward itself than toward the body's virtues. As a result the soul's virtues are far more highly esteemed [sc. than the body's].

To "corroborate" (ἐπιλογίσαιτο) this result on the basis of "the points previously examined" (ἀπὸ τῶν προεφωδευμένων), Didymus next draws an analogy (κατὰ τὸ ἀνάλογον) between bodily excellences and ethical virtues, correlating physical health, strength, and beauty in turn with temperance, courage, and justice (124.1–14).[11] Having now introduced the traditional Peripatetic classification of "three kinds of goods" (as he labels them in the immediate sequel, again in indirect discourse),[12] Didymus briefly elaborates the analogy he has just introduced, again in programmatic terms (124.18–125.1):

[§6] [They hold that] a very similar account applies also to the virtues, because it is [their] view that the three kinds of goods, despite their very great difference from one another, still have a certain analogy relevant to the argument,[13] which of course I shall also try to make perfectly clear [δηλῶσαι σαφῶς].

After extending the analogy to include external goods and a fourth virtue of "intelligence" (φρόνησις) as well, Didymus reiterates the Peripatetic conclusion in similar terms (125.14–19):

[§7] So it is clear [δῆλον οὖν] that the soul's virtues are *more worth choosing* than the body's virtues and external things, inasmuch as they bear a similar superiority [sc. over the others]; <and> they [sc. the virtues] take as their target [στοχάζονται] also the others [sc. external and bodily goods] primarily as worth choosing *on their own account*, and then as useful for social and political life and of course also for a life of study.

---

[10] The reference is to sec. 2; cf. Moraux (1973) 324; Görgemanns (1983) 177.

[11] "Previously examined" in the preceding sec. 4; the term προεφωδευμένων recalls the use of διεξωδευμένη and περιωδευμένη ("thoroughly examined") in reports of Carneades' critique of the criterion of truth for perception; cf. Sextus *M* 7.182–89 with Bett (1989) esp. 73. For the role of "critical comparison" in "appraisal" (ἐπιλογισμός), see Schofield (1996) esp. 233.

[12] Cf. sec. 6; for the significance of this distinctively Peripatetic classification of goods see Inwood (2014b) and Hatzimichali (in this volume).

[13] "Relevant to the argument" for πρὸς τὸν λόγον, which Sharples (2010) 116 omits following Görgemanns (1983) 172; Tsouni (in this volume) has "according to the argument"; cf. οὐδὲν πρὸς ἔπος for "irrelevant" (120.16) at the end of the passage quoted below as [3A].

Having previously discussed each of the three kinds of goods individually, Didymus here indicates how they are related on Peripatetic theory—external and bodily goods are "targets" of virtuous choice and action "worth choosing on their own account" (cf. 145.12–14)—before going on to present a preliminary account of their combination and coordination in an inclusive model of eudaimonia (125.19–127.2), all in indirect discourse aside from a single cross-reference (at 125.23 to 123.25). He then brings the entire sequence to a close, returning to direct discourse and elaborate phrasing that echoes both the rationale for ethical theory presented at the outset in section 2 and the catalogue of interpersonal relations presented in section 3. Opening with a bold image of "the entire divine chorus of virtues" (127.8–9), he frames his conclusion around the same basic triad of desire, conduct, and virtue (cf. 119.3–4), now cast in largely Peripatetic terms as "choices of good things and avoidances of bad things" (127.10–11 and *passim*, cf. 119.5–7), though not without some distinctly Stoic terminology that echoes the introduction too, notably "impulse" (127.19; cf. 119.3) and "correct action" (128.1; cf. 119.18). Finally, to emphasize the critical importance of sound "decision" and "choice" in achieving consistently correct conduct, he ends by assigning intelligence the "initiating" role as a "directive" capacity (ἐξάρχειν ὥσπερ ἡγεμονικὴν οὖσαν) governing both its own aims and those of the other virtues (128.2–9).[14]

So concludes the opening sequence of the *Epitome*, which stands out from the rest of the work not only in its relatively detailed argumentation but also in format, style, and tone. Unlike virtually all that follows, it makes heavy use of direct discourse, especially in the frequent use of signposting surveyed above, which is plainly self-conscious and explicitly characterizes the epistemic status of successive claims. By contrast, what follows shifts immediately to the cataloguing format typical of doxographic summaries, including the preceding epitome of Stoic ethics: mainly indirect discourse marked now and again by third-person verbs referring to the proponents of the views summarized.[15] In style as well, the opening sequence employs more vivid and varied diction, including Stoic terminology, more complex constructions, and more polished phrasing, including flourishes like

---

[14] The phrase borrows a Stoic label for the reasoning capacity or "commanding factor" (τὸ ἡγεμονικόν) common to humans and gods, including the cosmic mind. The "chorus of virtues" enumerated here includes labels for most of the interpersonal relations discussed in sec. 3: at least eight and arguably all of the first twelve (out of fourteen) terms listed here.

[15] So here ἐδόκει, ἀφωρίζοντο, ἔλεγον (129.4–6); εἶπον and προσέθεσαν (131.14, 20); φασιν (134.9); ὑπολαμβάνουσι and φασιν (137.15, 24); χρῶνται (138.2); and ἡγοῦντο and φασιν (139.2–3), mainly at transitional points introducing a new topic (secs. 11, 15, 16, 17).

parallelism, rhetorical questions, vivid examples, and poetic embellishment—all virtually absent from all that follows. And as we shall see, its magisterial tone exhibits at the outset a remarkable ardor that smacks of genuine conviction and has led many to assume partisan commitment—even though nothing quite like it appears anywhere else in the rest of the *Epitome*.

2. Introducing Intrinsic Worth: Concern for Children and Others

Turning to section 3, which presents the first step in his progression from external goods to virtue and eudaimonia, Didymus focuses exclusively on a single class of external goods: the well being of other people across the entire gamut of social and personal interactions. His discussion has two parts. The first (3A and 3B below), presented in indirect discourse but in elaborate and vivid language capped with two lines of verse, focuses directly on our concern for other people and our actions on their behalf. The second (3C), all direct discourse thick with simple conditionals, focuses instead on other people's attitudes towards us and our conduct. The first part begins with the concern parents have for their own children and moves outward to concern for complete strangers; the second follows a similar outward movement but from an external perspective, proceeding from friendship to impersonal approbation. It will be helpful to take each part in turn, starting with the first half of the first (119.22–120.17).

> [3A] [1] For it is well known from their actual behavior that parents hold their children worth choosing not only for their usefulness but also *on their own account*.[16] At any rate, no one is so savage and brutish in his nature that he would not seriously care [σπουδάζοι] about his children being happy after his death and continuing to lead honorable lives rather than the opposite. At any rate it is from this affectionate concern [φιλοστοργίας] that people on the verge of dying compose a will and worry about offspring still in the womb, appointing protectors and guardians, and entrusting their children to those most dear to them [τοῖς φιλτάτοις] and urging them to look after them, some even dying when their children do. [2] Given that children are cherished [ἀγαπωμένων] this way as worth choosing *on their own account*, necessarily our parents, siblings, bedmate, relatives, and other kin and fellow citizens also have our friendly concern [φιλίας] *on their own account*. For we have by nature various sorts of kinship [τινὰς οἰκειότητας] toward these people too, since humans are animals with a

---

[16] Reading ἐκ τῆς ἐνεργείας with the mss. (lit. "from their activity"; cf. 119.2, 127.2, etc.) rather than ἐκ τῆς ἐναργείας with Wachsmuth (following Usener; roughly "from the evidence"), a term otherwise not found in either the *Epitome* or Doxographies A or B.

propensity for mutual concern and community [φιλάλληλον καὶ κοινωνικόν]. It is irrelevant that some friendly relations [τῶν φιλιῶν] are distant and others close, since every form is worth choosing *on its own account* and not only for its usefulness.

The initial claim, which the rest of (1) seeks to support and (2) then exploits to advance further claims of wider scope, resembles a truism invoked in Stoic accounts of social *oikeiôsis*, that parental love reflects a "natural affinity and attraction" adults have towards at least some other people.[17] But Didymus cites parental behavior to support a related but distinct point, distinguishing two different and often competing reasons or motives for parental concern. The key claim, introduced as "well known" (γνώριμον) in the first sentence, taken as given at the beginning of (2), and reiterated at the end, is the stronger thesis that children are "worth choosing not only for their usefulness but also on their own account" (119.22–23). The evidence adduced in (1) (marked by γοῦν) thus serves not to corroborate the Stoic truism; Didymus does not simply deny any parents are "so savage and brutish" as to have no concern for their children. Rather, he advances the considerably stronger thesis that parents care for their children specifically "on their own account." This phrase, which appears repeatedly in section 3 and throughout the larger argument it launches, thus seems to be presented as the linchpin in the Peripatetic theory.[18] But what exactly does it signify, and what is its force here?

The point may be in part dialectical, marking a contrast with rival schools. On the standard Epicurean line, for example, other people often count as "worth choosing" but solely for reasons of utility, for their contribution to our pleasure (be it kinetic or katastematic), not "on their own account"; the value of interpersonal relations, on that view, is at bottom purely instrumental, grounded in each person's own pleasure and self-interest.[19] For Stoics conversely, interpersonal relations often have value "on their own account" but are never "worth choosing" in the strict sense unless and insofar as virtue is involved, since they count only the virtues and their various embodiments and expressions in virtuous states,

---

[17] See Plutarch, *Sto. Rep.* 1038B (LS 57E) for Chrysippus, with Whitlock Blundell (1990); Annas (1993) 265–76; Algra (2003); Brennan (2005) 154–68; McCabe (2005); Inwood (2016).

[18] So Moraux (1973) 322, though he conflates it with the narrower notion of "naturally good"; cf. 118.17. The similar term αὐθαιρετόν, found in the mss. at points (118.17, 120.9, 121.17, etc.), is plainly a corruption of δι' αὐτὸ αἱρετόν, and editors emend accordingly.

[19] The rationale for friendship was actually a matter of debate among Epicureans; see Frede (2016) with O'Keefe (2001) and Algra (2003) 278–83.

attitudes, and activities as having the distinctive kind of goodness that warrants being "chosen"; anything else counts at best as "worth getting" (ληπτά or *sumenda*, etc.) or selecting. Thus both terms of the thesis were contested. But that still leaves open the key question: what does the phrase add here?

A closer look at the examples tendered as evidence for the initial claim points to an answer. Didymus first cites the aspirations parents typically harbor for their children even after their own death eliminates any possibility of "usefulness" on their children's part, and presumably even any awareness or interest in them at all, let alone joy or sorrow in how they fare. Death, after all, marks the end of self-interest along with the self itself.[20] A parent's concern beyond the grave therefore cries out for explanation, which the appeal here to children being "worth choosing on their own account" is apparently meant to supply. This notion of intrinsic worth, as I shall call it, thus contrasts in the first instance with the utility or instrumental value marked by "usefulness": any ways in which children might serve or promote their parents' own interests.[21] But intrinsic worth seems to involve something more. Immediately following his use of Stoic terminology in section 2, Didymus here speaks pointedly of children being "worth choosing" rather than simply having the "value" Stoic theory ascribes to

---

[20] Or so the argument seems to assume, ignoring traditional beliefs in an afterlife where souls still worry about the lives of those they once held dear; Aristotle weighs a different perspective on this question in *EN* 1.11. As for wills and bequests, Champlin (1989) demonstrates their importance for the Roman elite among whom Arius, hence possibly Didymus, moved: "The Roman will was indeed an expression of deepest emotion, particularly of affection in the form of concern for the future happiness or security of family and friends. But it was also a solemn evaluation of the surrounding world, one prompted by a deep sense of duty and of reciprocity. ... At all points the testator's motives intersected with the needs or expectations of other people, from those benefited explicitly in the will to the community interested in the proper fulfillment of the testator's duty to it."

[21] I adopt the anomalous term "intrinsic worth" mainly for two reasons: to avoid confusion with the distinctive (and distinct) Stoic notion of "value" (ἀξία), and to avoid prejudging whether it is equivalent to modern notions of "intrinsic value" understood simply as noninstrumental value. It is worth emphasizing in this connection that the notion of "choice" (αἵρεσις) at issue here is a distinctly rational and reason-based form of desire. Didymus in sec. 10 characterizes what is "worth choosing" [αἱρετόν] according to Peripatetics as "what stimulates an impulse for itself ... when reason endorses [σύμψηφος ᾖ]" the impulse, and "choice" itself accordingly (128.27–129.3); the Stoic summary does much the same in counting choice a form of eupathic "volition" (and arguably therefore invariably correct), specifically "a volition (arising) out of (comparative?) reasoning [ἐξ ἀναλογισμοῦ]" (87.14–22), and it equates what is "worth choosing" with what evokes "a reasonable choice [εὔλογον αἵρεσιν]," hence only what is genuinely good (72.14–22); cf. Doxography A 42.15–20 and Inwood (1985) 238–40.

the "preferred indifferents" that are the proper objects of natural drives and "selection" (cf. 119.3–4 and 15–18, with pp. 128–29 above). To be sure, the aspirations he ascribes to parents involve two emphatically positive factors: their eudaimonia and "honorable conduct" (120.2). Parents, he claims, want their children not only to fare well by conventional standards but also to lead good and happy lives. But the point of invoking such conduct here is not to provide a basis or justification for parental concern by contending that parents consider their children worth choosing *because* they want them to lead good lives. On the contrary, his point is that parents want their children to live well because they consider them "worth choosing" in the first place, and what is more, "on their own account" or "for themselves." So we are again left wondering: what does this peculiar phrase add?

Julia Annas, in her influential studies of the *Epitome* (cf. n. 6 above), takes the phrase to designate specifically impartial concern. The thrust of our passage, as she reads it, is to neutralize Stoic challenges by embracing their demand for impartial concern for others as central to virtue—part of what she calls "the moral point of view"—and showing how Peripatetic positions can accommodate it. But while the key clause "for themselves" does not rule out such a reading—as does "for their usefulness," which hinges on the parents' own interests—the choice of examples seems decidedly ill suited to make that point. Parental concern, after all, restricted as it is to each parent's *own* children, is hardly impartial.[22] Still, Annas points us in the right direction.

By focusing on how children fare after the death of their parents, Didymus isolates room for intrinsic worth over and above any personal interest. Parents, he proposes, care especially about their own children; and so their concern is not impartial. But caring about them "for themselves" or "on their own account"—over and above any care based on "their usefulness"—implies something besides personal interest: parental concern *of this sort* is devoid of self-interest. That is not to say it is impartial; on the

---

[22] Cf. Brennan (2005) 163 on the force of οἰκεῖον or "akin" generally for "things whose welfare gives [us] reasons to act" but always "*qua* our own" and never wholly impartially; related reservations in Algra (2003) 289–91. On the other hand, Annas rightly highlights the added force of the formula "for itself" (δι' αὑτό), which has a sound Aristotelian pedigree, not only generally (cf. *EN* 1.7) but also in his analysis of *philia*; there, along with "for his sake" (αὑτοῦ ἕνεκα)—a locution the *Epitome* uses only once (143.29 for "favors"), though it occurs nine times in the Stoic summary and three in Arius' doxographic reports on physics—it may serve to indicate something like treating friends as ends in themselves. Even if it does, however, the question here, which I address further below, is whether this sort of attitude is compatible with the kind of partiality implicit in anything being οἰκεῖον.

contrary, it is always limited to each parent's own children. But concern *of this sort* is independent of any possible impact or consequences on the parents' own affairs, which death of course curtails. Moreover, such concern need not depend on any prior familiarity or contact with the children either: Didymus claims it extends even to unborn children "still in the womb" (120.4–5). According to his final example, in fact, this kind of concern in some parents trumps even their "first desire" for life itself invoked at the outset (118.11–20), when the death of their children overwhelms their very will to go on living (120.7–8).[23]

What are we supposed to make of such extreme behavior? I see no sign here that either Didymus or the Peripatetic authorities he is expounding meant to condone such devastating grief, much less recommend it.[24] Exposition, again, does not imply endorsement. Moreover, taking his series of examples as models of how parents *should* behave would undercut their logical role here as evidence for the initial claim about how people in fact do behave and the attitudes they in fact do have towards their own children, all plainly meant to indicate at least some recognition of intrinsic worth in at least some others. Everyone in the first case (οὐδένα … ὅς οὐκ, 119.24), only "some" (τινας 120.7) in the last case, but allegedly a great number in the other cases show *some* concern for the welfare of *some* others after their own death. What larger point this serves will become clearer if we return to the continuation of the passage.

With the initial thesis in hand, Didymus proceeds to draw a surprising inference in (2): given the role of intrinsic worth in parental concern, "necessarily" it also has a place in many other interpersonal relations, first within the immediate family, then the extended family and fellow citizens generally (120.8–12). In every case, he reports (all in indirect discourse), people consider the well-being of others "worth choosing not only for their usefulness … but also on their own account" (119.22–3; cf. 120.16–17). At first sight, the talk of necessity here looks purely cosmetic, claiming a logical connection that is far from obvious.[25] But the following sentence promptly explains in two steps (each introduced by γάρ). Human nature

---

[23] "Dying together" presumably refers to parents succumbing to grief at their children's death, not taking their own lives by suicide; cf. Aristotle *EN* 9.8 1169a18–29 on dying *on behalf of* friends (ὑπεραποθνῄσκειν).

[24] Cf. sec. 7, where Didymus takes the trouble to explain why, on a Peripatetic account, everyone, wise and foolish alike, should persevere in the face of adversity (126.2–11).

[25] The genitive absolute here is evidently causal with the logical force of "since" in what Stoic logic calls a "paraconditional": *given* the antecedent, the consequent is supposed to follow.

gives us all a natural "propensity for mutual concern and community"; and that is the basis for "various sorts of kinship" among members of the same household or wider community, which are then the basis for people attributing intrinsic worth to their partners in each of these relationships (120.12–14). Unfortunately, Didymus or his source leaves the nature of these kinds of kinship unspecified. A similar account of "natural kinship" among members of the same family or lineage or community, which Porphyry ascribes to Theophrastus (*Abst.* 2.25: fr. 531 FHSG), appeals to birth, lineage, social interaction, cultural heritage, and ultimately physical and psychological similarity to ground these ties. That makes it tempting, given the use Didymus makes of Theophrastus later in the *Epitome* (secs. 18–19), to draw on his account of natural kinship to fill the gap left here.[26] Even without pursuing that path, however, it is clear that the *Epitome*, in appealing to human nature, bases its account on similarly universal factors, and in particular on a natural human propensity for interpersonal relations, and for relations spanning a wide range of concern for others, from the most intimate (immediate family and dearest friends) to largely notional forms of solely civic ties, all conventionally subsumed under the highly elastic category of *philia* (120.12 and 15). Then, on the further premise, endorsed by all the major Hellenistic schools of thought, that anything natural is in principle valuable or good, it does follow that interpersonal relations are so too.[27] The two-step explanation Didymus supplies then does support, at least on shared Hellenistic premises, the inference that the other familial and communal relations listed in (2) are also "worth choosing" just as the welfare of children is for their parents. That does not yet show, however, that all of these relations are specifically "worth choosing *on their own account*"—that they all have or involve some sort of intrinsic worth—as the concluding sentence of our passage insists (120.12–14), reiterating its opening claim (119.22–23). To see how that too is supposed to follow here, we need to return to the path Annas pursues: the special role and status of friendly concern as a basic natural impulse for humans, as the argument here claims.

In the preamble to the larger argument launched by [3A], Didymus specifies the primary or basic object of all human desire as our own being,[28]

---

[26] On the Theophrastus report and its relation to sec. 3 here, see Brink (1956) and Fortenbaugh (2011) 553–70.

[27] For this shared commitment to some form of ethical naturalism, see Annas (1993) 214–20 and Inwood (2016).

[28] For "first" (πρῶτον) having logical as well as chronological force in this context, see Inwood (1985) 187–90. The "being" (τοῦ εἶναι) here given as the object of our "first desire"

and he explains this desire by claiming that everyone "has a natural affinity and attraction to oneself" (ᾠκειῶσθαι πρὸς ἑαυτόν, 118.11–13). Although the wording echoes Stoic accounts of personal *oikeiôsis*, the way Didymus elaborates the claim in the following lines takes a sharp turn away from Stoic positions and in Aristotelian directions, as Annas (1990) has shown. For he goes on to explicate this self-centered concern—or at least to illustrate it (γάρ again, 118.15)—by attributing our interest in our own health, pleasure, and life itself to their being not only natural but "also worth choosing on their own account and good" and their contraries conversely both "unnatural and also worth avoiding on their own account and bad" (118.13–20), both claims that the Stoics reject emphatically because they sharply distinguish what is merely natural or unnatural from what is good or bad and hence worth choosing or avoiding, all titles they reserve in the strict sense exclusively for virtue and vice (and their various embodiments).[29] Unlike the Stoics, moreover, Didymus goes on to specify a further basis for our interest in these and other objects of natural desire, namely, a kind of concern characterized as liking or loving or holding dear (118.20–119.4).

> [§2] For [they hold that] our body is dear to us [φίλον ἡμῖν], so is our soul, and so are their parts, capacities, and activities; and it is from forethought about the preservation of these that the original basis for impulse, duty, and virtue arises.

Behind our interest in natural things like health (and conversely our aversion to unnatural things like sickness), on this account, is a special concern for ourselves, and if holding something "dear" is a form of love for it, then it is fair to call this concern a form of self-love, inasmuch as the three natural things (and their unnatural contraries) Didymus lists in the preceding lines—health, pleasure, and the rest—are all personal attributes, either bodily or psychic states or activities. This self-love is apparently then meant to explain (γάρ again, 118.20) why we consider them "natural and

---

is widely construed baldly as "existence" and hence life itself. But given that the immediate sequel uses τοῦ ζῆν to specify simply being alive (118.16), it may be better to take "being" as an incomplete predicate here, and one whose proper complement is given in the immediate context, which specifies "the full realization of both" (ἀμφοῖν τῆς τελειότητος) sides of human nature, both body and soul, nonrational and rational capacities, mortal and divine factors (118.6–11); that would also be more in keeping with the elaboration of this account that follows (118.11–119. 4).

[29] The divergence is widest in the case of pleasure, which our two main reports of the early Stoic account of personal *oikeiôsis* reject emphatically: D.L. 7.85–86 and Cicero *Fin.* 3.17.

also worth choosing on their own account and good" (or the contrary). But the initial appeal to a natural affinity and attraction we all ostensibly have toward ourselves has already provided an explanation for these things being natural (δι' ὅ, 118.13). Hence, either self-love is essentially equivalent to this self-affinity and logically redundant, or it is invoked to support a further claim: either to explain self-affinity in turn, or to explain the one new factor introduced in the previous step of the argument, namely, why the several factors listed are not only natural—which the appeal to affinity has already explained—but also "worth choosing on their own account and good" (and their contraries the converse), in short, why they have intrinsic worth.[30]

Both the first and second options are compatible with the train of argument here, and the latter—that self-love underpins our self-affinity—has been vigorously supported by Annas.[31] The third nonetheless has distinct advantages, both locally and for the *Epitome* as a whole. For one, it provides precisely the connection we found missing from the opening stage of section 3, where our liking or loving others is apparently supposed to entail their having intrinsic worth (120.8–12). In treating "worth choosing" and "good" as virtually equivalent, the third option also corresponds exactly to a view Didymus later ascribes to "the ancients" generally (sec. 11: 129.4–5, invoking the opening lines of *EN* 1.1). In the same vein, that equivalence aligns neatly with the first two in a series of divisions he reports in section 15 to distinguish "how many ways (the predicate) good is said" (134.8–9). The first of the two isolates the term's primary force in Aristotelian ethics by equating "the good" with "what is worth choosing on its own account," which is then specified as "the end to which we refer everything, namely

---

[30] On this third reading, the two trios of contraries in the preceding pair of claims (118.15–20) each form two, not three groups, the first in each case ("natural" and its contrary) reiterating what the previous lines claim, and the latter two in each ("worth choosing on their own account and good" and their contraries) introducing a new point; the position of ὑπάρχειν in 118.20 accordingly separates the latter pair from the first.

[31] Cf. n. 6 above. For support Annas (1990) 88–90 points to three features of the *Epitome*: (1) its "shriveled remnant" of Aristotle's own accounts of *philia* (in *EN* 8–9 and *EE* 7) in sec. 21, which refers back to sec. 2 as counting self-love as the "first" (or primary) form of *philia* (143.11–13); (2) an abundance of *philia* terminology in secs. 2–9; and (3) its denial that virtue is "self-loving" (125.21–126.2) despite the "refined sense of self-love" Aristotle approves in *EN* 9.8. But the omission and simplification on which the first and third points turn are not peculiar to this topic but pervasive features of the *Epitome* and its condensed summary style (excepting sec. 3); and the second rests entirely on terms in sec. 3 and its recapitulation in sec. 9 (cf. n. 26 above).

eudaimonia" (134.10–14);[32] and the second then distinguishes three kinds of ends: the end or goal of any particular action or endeavor ("the last thing for the sake of which we do *something*"), the ultimate end of all we do (apparently either eudaimonia itself again or one's conception of it), and any "part" of either of the other two (134.14–16). The upshot of this pair of divisions is to make intrinsic worth the primary and basic form of ethical goodness, which subsequent divisions then elaborate and extend. However, this initial equation of intrinsic worth and goodness as an end (whether the "most final end" or particular final ends; cf. *EN* 1.7) not only favors the third construal of our passage in section 2 (118.15–20); it also goes some way (though perhaps not very far) towards explaining the otherwise surprising absence in section 21 of any mention of two central factors in Aristotle's own analysis of *philia*, namely, "wanting good things *for someone*" (τινι) or "for that person's *sake*" (ἐκείνου ἕνεκα). For if choosing something "on its *own account*" either implies or is a special case of choosing it "for its *own sake*" (as the second division in sec. 15 implies), then the Aristotelian formula for *philia* could be loosely paraphrased in those terms: "wanting good things for people for their own sake" would imply viewing them as at least partial ends of one's own, hence people considered worth choosing "on their own account" in the language of the *Epitome* (and Aristotle's, too).[33]

Turning back to the discussion of self-affinity in section 2, we can now see one way its claim that our bodies and souls "and their parts, capacities, and activities" are "dear to us" could serve to support the preceding claim that natural conditions like health and pleasure have intrinsic worth (and their contraries the contrary), namely, because anything "dear" to us—anything we like or love—has intrinsic worth for us as something "worth choosing on its own account."[34] The same connection might also help to fill

---

[32] The two others are identified as god and "the genus of goods" (a universal "predicated of all goods"); *EE* 1.8 is organized around the same or very similar trichotomy. For the whole series of divisions in sec. 15, see Sharples (1983).

[33] Cf. *EN* 8.3 1156b9–11, for example. On the other hand the absence of the formula here may be simply a case of abbreviation, given that sec. 21 does echo Aristotle's related threefold division of the reasons or rationales behind any *philia*: advantage, pleasure, or the honorable, all characterized here both as "ends" and factors "because of" or "on account of" which (διά again) people "choose *philia*" (143.8–11). On the differences between the three *formal* factors involved here—a constitutive attitude ("wanting good things *for someone*"), its aim or purpose (doing so "*for the sake of* someone"), and its underlying reasons or rationale ("*because of* who or what they are": helpful, pleasant, honorable, etc.)—and their interplay in Aristotle's own analysis, see Riesbeck (2016) 60–80.

[34] Schematically, then, this third reading of the argument runs like this (omitting

the gap in the move from (1) to (2) in the opening stage of section 3 (3A) that extends intrinsic worth from anyone's own children to various others in one's family or wider community. For if any form of *philia* typically involves each partner being "worth choosing on their own account" for the other, then on the assumption that parents, siblings, spouses, relatives, and fellow citizens (120.10–12) all count as "dear"—as *philoi*—then they too all have intrinsic worth, just as one's own children do, and "necessarily" so given those premises.[35] As for the unstated assumption about the wide scope of *philia*, it was part of standard Greek usage, Aristotle's included, that not only friends and immediate family members but also members of the extended family and wider community counted as "dear" to some degree, whether any of these relations involved what we would call love or friendship or something much weaker.[36] For Didymus or his source simply to assume that *philia* has such a wide extension, then, is perfectly reasonable, especially in a condensed and rhetorical context like this. But if this much of the argument has a firm basis in Aristotelian doctrine and conventional Greek attitudes alike, it is not yet clear why the wider extension for the kind of concern involved in any form of *philia*, be it liking or loving or something else, should involve, much less "necessarily" entail (120.9), the key factor at stake here, specifically *intrinsic* worth: other people being not only "worth choosing" but being so "on their own account." Nor have we yet seen any basis for extending this kind of concern still further to include people beyond one's own family, friends, and community, as the next stage of the argument in section 3 proceeds to do.

---

the converse attitudes toward the contraries for clarity's sake, and supplying the unstated principles behind its explicit premises):
1. If A likes or loves B (and B is dear to A), then A values B on its own account.
2. If A values B on its own account, then A values B's welfare on its own account.
3. If A values B's welfare, A pursues and welcomes B's welfare.
4. But we each love our own body and soul. (119.1–2: §2 above)
5. And their welfare includes health, pleasure, and more (118.15–16)
6. So we each value those conditions on their own account. (118.16–17)
7. And we each pursue and welcome those conditions. (118.11–16).

[35] The first premise follows Aristotle's account in assuming mutuality and reciprocity of some sort (what he calls proportional if not exactly equal terms) as an essential feature of *philia* (cf. *EN* 8.2), though it may be worth noting that this is another point missing from Didymus' summary in sec. 21. Cf. nn. 31 and 33 above.

[36] See Whitlock Blundell (1989) 31–49 for a rich synopsis of classical usage; cf. Konstan (1997) 53–92 on the special status of friendship within this range.

3. Extending Intrinsic Worth: From Community to Humanity

The argument Didymus reports in section 3 starts in (1) with parental concern for children in order to isolate a special kind of concern based on a recognition of internal worth in a very narrowly defined set of people, namely, each parent's own offspring. It then in (2) extends this kind of concern to successively wider groups, first to others within the same immediate family, then to the extended family, and finally to everyone within the same civic community. The sequel extends this concern to encompass first entire regions and past generations, then all of humankind, past, present, and future alike (120.17–121.21).

> [3B] [3] If friendship toward fellow citizens is worth choosing *on its own account*, then necessarily so too is friendship toward people of the same region or ancestry, and as a result also toward all humans. [4] In fact, all who act to save others are so disposed towards those nearby that they act for the most part not by usefulness but for something worth choosing *on its own account*.[37] For who, if he could, would not rescue someone he sees under assault by a wild beast? Who would not show the way to someone who has lost his way? Who would not help out someone perishing from need? Who, if he happened upon a spring in the desert, would not post signs for others traveling the same way? [5] Who does not put a premium on being well spoken of after death? Who does not despise remarks like these for being contrary to human nature:
>
>> After I die, let earth be wracked with fire!
>> I could care less, since all that's mine is fine![38]
>
> [6] So it is clear that we have a natural goodwill and friendly concern toward everyone, which exhibits something worth choosing *on its own account* and rationality. For "One is the lineage of men and gods, and we breathe both from one mother" [Pindar, *Nemean* 6.1–2], namely, nature.

Lofty rhetoric, to be sure, but what does it show? Is there anything more here than eloquent moralizing of the sort for which Cicero disparages leading Hellenistic Peripatetics (*Fin.* 5.13–14)?[39] The passage draws two explicit conclusions in (6). First, the examples of kindness to strangers are supposed to establish the pervasive presence of "natural goodwill

---

[37] "By usefulness": reading κατὰ χρήσεις (Heeren) for τὰς πράξεις in the mss. instead of πρὸς ἀξίαν or "relative to merit" (Wachsmuth, from Usener), as in Annas (1993) 283 and Tsouni in this volume; cf. Schofield (2012) 183.

[38] *TGF* Anon. fr. 513; Cicero has Cato quote the same lines (translated) in *Fin.* 3.64 in a very similar Stoic argument.

[39] The disparaging assessment, though enormously influential, is very likely misleading, as I argue in White (2002); cf. Russell (2010); Inwood (2014a) 30–72.

and friendly concern" (φιλία) for everyone. That in turn is supposed to imply (ἐμφαίνουσα) in each case the presence of intrinsic worth: something "worth choosing on its own account and rationality" (τὸ δι' αὔθ' αἱρετὸν ... καὶ τὸ κατὰ λόγον).[40] Here again the point of the argument may be in part dialectical. The Stoics, for example, accept the first inference; they too appeal to *oikeiôsis* to show that sympathy or benevolence is a natural human sentiment and should ideally extend universally to all of humankind. Although they restrict friendship and goodwill in the strict sense to sages, what they dispute are not the phenomena here described, but whether the phenomena satisfy their demanding standard for genuine friendship or goodwill.[41] The second inference, however, they reject on the grounds that only virtuous people, states, and actions have intrinsic worth; ordinary friendship and goodwill are only "preferred," never "worth choosing," much less "on their own account." Our passage, in stark contrast, infers that *all* such concern, even in its "natural" forms, involves a recognition of intrinsic worth in others.

Intrinsic worth, as introduced in section 2 and deployed in 3A, involves a special kind of value or goodness comparable to intrinsic value that calls for a special kind of concern responsive to things *on their own account*, independently of (but not necessarily incompatible with) any further benefit or advantage it might afford either us or anything else. To consider anything (or anyone) "worth choosing for itself"—as having intrinsic worth—thus involves adopting it as a distinctive kind of end, namely, one whose own well-being warrants support and action on its behalf (whether by us or others) regardless of any effect its well-being or very being itself might have on our own interests or endeavors. Many such things—be it health, pleasure, knowledge, or any number of other bodily or psychic capacities, states, and activities—we value and desire in the first instance for ourselves, as things to have, cultivate, and enjoy in our own lives.[42] But many of them we

---

[40] The received text, in assigning each prepositional phrase a definite article of its own, treats them as two distinct factors, rather than a single factor characterized by two attributes; cf. Sharples (2010) 114. For the point of the latter phrase here, singling out what humans and gods have in common, cf. Moraux (1973) 322 n. 14.

[41] See Doxography B (Stobaeus 2.7.5–12) 101.24–102.4 and 108.5–25 with D.L. 7.116 and 124.

[42] Cf. Schofield (2012) 183 comparing the end of 3A and the examples in 3B with Cicero's Antiochean account of Peripatetic positions in *Fin.* 5.67–69 (emphasis in original): friendship, for example, "counts as desirable *in itself* because we want it not (or not solely) because friends give scope to the exercise of virtue or are a useful resource in one's own enterprises, but because ... we want to have them for ourselves. A friend is an intrinsically attractive thing *to have and enjoy*."

also value independently of our own interests and affairs, simply as things whose presence in the world we value, approve, and appreciate, whether or not they have any impact on us, whether or not we ever encounter them (think of remote peoples, lands, species), in some cases even without any awareness of them or how they fare (likewise any varieties or instances of such groups or kinds). The world is simply better off, we suppose, when populated by such things and they fare well, or at least as we wish them to do, however near or remote they may be.[43] This seems to be the same kind of concern as the series of examples in (4) envisions: concern for complete strangers, independent of any personal stake beforehand or any prospect of personal benefit later, in every case without any prior encounter, in the first case even at some risk or cost to oneself, and in the last case without ever meeting at all, without even learning whether one's efforts ever have any effect at all. The following two examples in (5) go still further to include matters after we die: in the first case caring what others will think of us thereafter, in the second caring how they themselves will fare then.

As the initial stage of the argument in 3A singles out examples of parental concern in (1) that highlight intrinsic worth by minimizing or eliminating any role or even any room for self-interest or self-love, so here the examples in (4) of helping strangers go still further in the same direction by removing any obvious prior basis for this concern for others, any residual self-interest or personal connection at all. And yet people do these things, even the great majority of us (or at least the work's intended audience), the argument implies by its rhetorical questions in hectoring anaphora: "who would *not*" (it asks all of six times) do these and similar things? Their actions therefore demand explanation, which the conclusion in (6) confidently supplies, pronouncing it now "clear"—even "obvious" (φανερόν)—that we all have a "natural goodwill and friendly concern" that extends universally to everyone and "exhibits (a recognition of) intrinsic worth" in others as a driving force on which people act (121.16–17), the sole driver in these cases but a contributing factor in many others. None of this precludes, of course, caring about the outcome of our efforts; taking

---

[43] Williams (1973) draws a contrast between what he calls "I-desires" with "non-I desires" to make a similar point: the former are any desires in which I (or any desirer) figure in the content of the desire, the latter any in which I do not. So on one hand, when I want to drink, what I want is for *me* to drink; but if I desire your speedy recovery, or the survival of a species, what I want is for *you* to get well, or for *its reproduction* to continue. To show that the latter can and often do occur on their own, independent of any self-interest or I-desires, he elaborates some of the same kinds of cases Didymus invokes: wills and helping strangers; cf. n. 50 below.

the welfare of anyone or anything to be worth choosing on its own account involves wanting them to fare well, at least in some way or other. The crucial point is simply that this form of concern is *independent* of self-interest, not that it is incompatible with self-interest, or that it precludes our acting on mixed motives, *both* "for ourselves" (out of self-concern) *and also* for the intrinsic worth of someone or something else. Conversely, the claim in (5) that we "despise" a misanthrope's disregard for the entire world singles out a *total* absence of this kind of concern, which thereby serves to indicate that most people do care enough to wish the world well after their death, even when death rules out any possibility of personal benefit.

What light, we might wonder, do these strange, even outlandish cases of altruism (or its total absence) shed on the conduct and decisions of daily life? Few may spurn the desperate or curse the world entire, as imagined in (4) and (5), but what does that have to do with the everyday challenges of balancing our own interests or well-being against those of others—our self-concern and concern for others, as we are directed to do in section 21, where Didymus cautions against too much of the former and too little of the latter (143.14–16)? Nowhere in 3B is there any mention of obligation. Conceding that our commitment to the intrinsic worth of others has its limits, the argument concedes in (4) that we help strangers "if we can"—when it poses no significant risk or cost to our own interests.[44] After all, the stakes vary widely here from case to case: it is easy enough to give strangers directions, but rescuing them from the clutches of a wild beast puts one's own life and limbs in play. Instead of claiming any of this altruism is required, the argument simply contends in (5) that most people find it *inhuman* (παρὰ τὴν ἀνθρωπίνην ... φύσιν) to have *no regard* for others in such situations. And provided the preceding cases involve helping others without any prospect of gain, the conduct they illustrate calls for explanation. There is no suggestion here that anyone should actively seek out ways to help strangers, much less that anyone is obliged to do so. The point is simpler: to indicate that most people value altruism of this sort on its own account. It is enough that many *do* help strangers, and that most of us *approve* of them doing so. That is enough to show both that disinterested action occurs and that it is widely valued on its own account, by

---

[44] Brink (1956) 136–37, citing Cicero, *De off.* 1.51 (with Ennius, *Trag.* frr. 313–15) and 3.54, calls all four examples of kindness in (4) "injunctions" and "duties toward strangers" and observes that the second "was considered a crime prohibited at Athens on pain of public execration." Even so, they are presented here only as pervasive expectations and conventional standards, not as obligations, either moral or legal, and only to illustrate how most people are inclined by "natural goodwill" to help others; cf. Annas (1989) 162.

those who so act and others alike. What the examples of helping strangers establish, then, is not that anyone *must* be helpful, only that it is something people tend to value not for any self-interested reasons but purely on its own account—as having intrinsic worth. Leaving duty aside, in short, the argument here simply isolates a distinctive kind of motive and attitude.

4. Extending Intrinsic Worth: From People to Attitudes

The argument so far has focused mainly on conduct, presenting two series of peculiar scenarios designed to isolate a special kind of concern for others, especially offspring and strangers, that is supposed to hinge on a recognition of their intrinsic worth. Linking those scenarios to the full gamut of interpersonal relations, on this account, is a distinctive form of this concern, occurring in widely varying degrees, that is an essential factor in every relationship that merits the title of *philia*. The continuation of the argument now extends the range of this concern to a series of related attitudes, arguing that those in turn are "worth choosing on their own account"—that those too have intrinsic worth along with the people at whom they are directed (121.22–122.12).

> [3C] [7] Since we share a shared concern for humanity [κοινή τις φιλανθρωπία], it is more readily apparent that there is something worth choosing *on its own account* much more in relation to our familiar friends. [8] But if a friend is something worth choosing *on his own account*, so too are friendship and goodwill, both from all who share in one's life and from most people.[45] [9] As a result, approbation is also worth choosing *on its own account*, since we have a natural affinity and attraction [οἰκειοῦσθαι] to those who show approbation. [10] But if approbation is worth choosing *on its own account*, so too is a good reputation; for we follow the delineation in construing good reputation as nothing else than approbation from many people.[46] [11] As a result, in this first way it has been

---

[45] The translation follows the Paris ms. (P), which has no definite article before either of the last two prepositional phrases; Sharples (2010) 114 and Tsouni (in this volume) follow Wachsmuth, who supplies one before the second to match the ἡ before the first in the Farnesinus (F). But a singular would call for punctuating differently, after φιλία: "if a friend and friendship are ... , so too is goodwill ..."; and the train of argument shifts here from people themselves to their attitudes toward one another, in line with Wachsmuth's punctuation as above.

[46] A "delineation" (ὑπογραφή), in this case one "taken over" (παρειλήφαμεν) or adopted from some (presumably standard) authority, is in Stoic logic (D.L.7.60) something like a definite description, not a formal definition but an instructive basis for developing one; cf. 129.5 for its use in this sense (ὑπογράφοντες οὕτως ἀφωρίζοντο), and see Crivelli (2010) 394–95, who calls it a "sketch." Didymus uses the same term, apparently in a broader but related sense, in sec. 2 to describe the "synopsis" of Peripatetic ethics

shown clearly that the good things arising from outside are of a sort to be worth choosing *on their own account*. [§4] How, then, are goods involving us and within us not much more so? I mean, of course, those involving the body and soul. For if people are worth choosing *on their own account*, their parts must be so, too.

The first step here (7) looks like a straightforward argument *a fortiori*: if we have concern for all of humanity on their own account, including total strangers and future generations as argued in 3B, then surely we have such concern for our friends too, indeed far more so. The inference is nonetheless puzzling, and on multiple counts. First, why infer any concern for friends from concern for strangers? Surely the reverse is more plausible, deriving attenuated forms of concern for others from its primary or central forms, as 3A and 3B have just done, and as similar Stoic accounts do, starting from the pervasive and more intense concern everyone has for themselves and their closest friends.[47] Further, if intrinsic worth here contrasts with *usefulness* as in 3A, then the inference breaks down: helping strangers exemplifies intrinsic worth precisely because the absence of any personal relationship minimizes expectations or motives of further gain; friendship involves the very opposite. Conversely, if intrinsic worth here is supposed to involve *selfless* concern, the inference is again problematic because friendship always involves the *personal* ties absent from chance encounter with strangers. Why then would Didymus appeal to casual acts of altruism toward strangers as a basis for *friendship*, least of all close friends (τοὺς ἐν συνηθείᾳ φίλους)?[48]

The solution, I suggest, is that he does not do so, that the argument is not so straightforward or *a fortiori* at all. The point is a subtler one, and the crux is again intrinsic worth. If the aim were simply to show that friendship is a good thing, Didymus could call it "worth choosing" and be done. But his insistent refrain that every relationship or attitude considered here is "worth choosing *on its own account*" shows that the argument remains focused on *how and why* we care about other people, using that special kind of concern now to show why we also care about what other people

---

presented in secs. 3–9.

[47] Cf. Cicero, *Fin.* 5.65 in a developmental account (*serpit sensim foras*) ostensibly endebted to Antiochus; cf. similar Stoic accounts in *Fin.* 3.62–63 and Hierocles, *Elements* col. 9–11 and *How to Treat Our Relatives* in Stobaeus 4.671–73, with McCabe (2005) 419–24.

[48] Didymus, when classifying types of *philia* in sec. 21, makes "familiarity" the basis for its closest form, lit. "companionate" (ἑταιρικήν) friendship (143.5); cf. *EN* 8.5 1157b19–24, 8.11 1161a25–27. Not all "familiar" friendships are based on character (those based on pleasure and advantage often lead to familiarity, too), but a correlation is enough for the argument here.

think about us. The aim in (7), then, is not to show that we care about our close friends *because* we care about strangers, nor in (8) to show that we care about friendship *because* we care about friends, which in either case hardly needs argument. It is rather to establish a narrower and stronger thesis—that we care about friends and friendship not merely for ourselves, as something worth cultivating and sustaining for our own good, but also *independently* of any self-centered interests. Similarly, as the end of 3C announces in section 4, the following sections will go on to argue that we each care about our own body and soul "on their own account" because we care about external goods *in that way*. If the point were only that we care about our own physical and mental well-being, as expressions of inborn self-love, then the argument would again be trying to derive the obvious from the controversial.[49] Here too the direction of the inference shows that the argument is designed to establish a narrower and stronger claim, that people care about their own well being *on its own account*, not simply as promoting their own interests but as having intrinsic worth in the same way as the well being of other people does, strangers included. In none of these cases does Didymus rule out self-interest. What the argument he reports aims to show is rather that there is a place in every case for intrinsic worth as well. It thus exploits the kind of concern introduced in 3A and extended in 3B to argue in (7) that the same kind of concern figures also in closer relationships, that "familiar" friendships involve *both* self-interest and intrinsic worth. What motivates selfless acts of helping strangers, in short, has a place in these relationships too, in fact "far more" there than in more remote relations.[50]

Lest this point seem too obvious to call for argument, we might recall that some denied friendship has any basis other than pleasure or utility.[51] Aristotle likewise, as Didymus reports in section 21, recognizes the leading

---

[49] Moraux (1973) 323 poses a related objection: wealth and power would then be more compelling examples of external goods we want for ourselves than goodwill and a good reputation.

[50] It would therefore be misguided to *equate* this type of concern with altruism, since it figures also in our self-concern, and in precisely the areas (each person's own body and soul) singled out as central to the self-love on which Didymus bases his preliminary argument in sec. 2 (cf. pp. 138–40 and §2 above). The upshot of secs. 3–5 is rather that this kind of concern—caring for things "on their own account"—is a common denominator in *both* self-love and altruism. Williams (1973) 262–65 makes the same point about his "non-I desires"(cf. n. 43 above) by sketching examples of wills that do not serve the good of anyone else.

[51] For Epicureans, cf. n. 17 above; some Cyrenaics held still dimmer views: see D.L. 2.91, 93, 98.

role those factors play in many or even most friendships (esp. *EN* 8.3–4; *EE* 7.2). That, as we saw earlier, explains why the argument of section 3 appeals to peculiar scenarios involving wills and helping strangers in (1) and (4): to isolate the kind of concern responsive to intrinsic worth alone. Consider again the examples of helping strangers. Anyone whose aim in such situations is only to win gratitude or reward, or to enhance his or her own reputation or self-esteem acts from self-interest. But it begs the question simply to assume that our conduct is invariably and exclusively self-interested in some such way. Even if we expect some gain, altruistic acts of that sort typically express at least some degree of concern for others "on their own account" too, which by the lights of the argument reported in section 3 expresses a recognition of their intrinsic worth, and ultimately the intrinsic worth of any and every human being in (6)—what Didymus characterizes as "a shared concern for humanity" in (7). That kind of concern, of course, does not ensure right action or correct conduct; its application may often be misguided or misplaced. All that the cases in 3A and 3B are designed to show, however, is that much of our conduct engaging with others is motivated by more than self-interest alone, namely, some form or degree of concern for them as having intrinsic worth. That done, the argument now goes on in (7) to return to close friends as a paradigm locus of this concern, then to extend the scope of this concern to include first friendship and goodwill (εὔνοια) generally in (8), and then two attitudes widely associated with virtues and other kinds of excellence in (9) and (10), first praise or approbation (ἔπαινος), then good reputation (εὐδοξία).[52] To see how this argument is supposed to work, it will be helpful to begin with a schematic outline of the passage as it stands (8–11 in 3C), then consider how its inferences either are or might reasonably be supported.

> P1. If close friends have intrinsic worth, so do friendship and goodwill generally.
> P2. But friends of all sorts do have intrinsic worth. (cf. 3A–B)
> C1. So friendship and goodwill have intrinsic worth. (by P1 and P2)
> P3. People have an affinity toward those who approve (of them).

---

[52] In calling these four factors "attitudes" I mean to highlight the underlying motivation in each case, not to exclude the various expressions in language or conduct associated with them. Just as goodwill is essentially an attitude that can result in certain kinds of behavior, and *philia* consists in similar kinds of concern that generate active expressions (or so 3A and 3B imply), so praise is simply a verbal expression of an underlying approbation, and as (10) here observes, "good reputation" simply shorthand for widespread approbation, lit. the "positive opinion" many people have of someone. See further below on (9) and P3.

P4. If goodwill has intrinsic worth, so does approbation.
C2. So approbation has intrinsic worth. (by C1 and P4)
P5. Good reputation is approbation from many. (from "the delineation")
C3. So good reputation has intrinsic worth. (by C2 and P5)
P6. But friendship etc. are external goods.
C4. So some external goods (viz. friendship etc.) have intrinsic worth. (by C1–3)

The passage is telegraphic, and at least some of its obscurity is probably due to epitomizing. Only two steps (P4 and C3) receive any explicit support (from P3 and P5, each marked by γάρ); and in the first case (P3–4), the nature of the alleged support is not at all obvious: what bearing does affinity have on approbation, or vice versa? We might also wonder why goodwill joins friendship in P1 and C1 only to disappear without making any apparent contribution to the argument. Rather than address these questions directly, however, or others lurking around them, it may be more instructive to consider each inference in order, starting with the initial premise P1 for the first inference C1. Why should we suppose, as P1 evidently does, that intrinsic worth in any pair of friends extends to their friendship as well? Transitivity of that sort clearly does not hold either for every kind of relationship or for every attribute involved. For two people who each have intrinsic worth to live far apart—or nearby—has no implications for the worth of their distance from one another, unless of course one or both also have some sort of concern for (or against) the other. Nor does the friendship of people who are short or tall, funny or smart, young or old, or any number of other things, itself share any of those features, unless they play a significant part in the friendship in the first place. Why then should intrinsic worth be any different?

The difference evidently hinges on the kind of concern at issue here, and specifically its desiderative dimension, or what in particular either party likes or cares about. As the opening stage of the argument claims and the preceding sentence (7) reaffirms, any two "familiar friends" each consider the other "worth choosing on the other's own account"—and especially so. If their friendship affords them adequate opportunity to express that concern actively by promoting the other's good, as the frequent association of "familiar" friendship does "much more" than most other relationships, then they have good reason to consider it worth choosing in turn. But that does not yet answer the further question, why friendship should be worth choosing *on its own account*, why it has *intrinsic* worth. Worse, it might seem to yield the wrong answer by reducing friendship to a purely instrumental role, simply an effective context for friends to promote the primary object of their concern, the good of their friend. Appearances, however, are misleading, and the worry here ill founded. Intrinsic worth, after all, is not exclusive. All it requires is some degree of independent worth in some respect, not the absence of any other kind of value; and that, as we saw, is broadly compatible with serving self-interested ends as well. Moreover, the independence at issue here is only from any contribution to the self-interest of either partner in the friendship, or so the examples in 3A and 3B are designed to show. Friendships based on the good traits or virtues of each friend, for example, are typically also pleasant and useful for each of them in any number of ways; but that does not preclude such a friendship having intrinsic worth itself any more than it undercuts the intrinsic worth of the friends themselves. The same holds, though typically to less extent, for friendships based on pleasure or usefulness; there too the interaction of the friends itself has intrinsic worth to the extent it expresses or embodies their rational and social nature as human beings (cf. sec. 2). Or to put the key point in the argument's own terms, when friends choose to do something with or for one another "on the other's own account" (as sec. 3 repeatedly puts it), they do so because they view the other as having intrinsic worth, and not only at the most general level as human beings, but in some more or less specific respects: for being who or what each of them is, someone who does certain things or acts certain ways, be those genuinely good or simply enjoyable or useful. In that way, then, their friendship in turn has intrinsic worth—is "worth choosing on its own account"—as an expression and enactment of each friend's character and nature; and the more fully and widely the specific reasons underlying their friendship also align with our human nature as rational creatures, the greater the worth of those activities and the friendship they constitute.

So much might reasonably be said, if only by extrapolation from 3A and 3B, to support the connection P1 draws between friends and friendship. But that leaves unexplained the further link P1 makes with goodwill and its role here. For that, Didymus can appeal first to the end of 3B, which draws the same link in (6) when it concludes from the series of examples in (4) and (5) that "we have a natural goodwill and friendly concern toward everyone" (121.16–17). One aspect of the link is also reflected in the rider appended to P1 in (8): "both from all who share in one's life [τῶν τοῦ βίου κοινωνούντων] and from most people" (122.1–2; cf. n. 45 above). Here the first group encompasses all the forms of "friendship" considered in 3A, from family to fellow citizens, in line with what is characterized in

(2) as our native human "propensity for mutual concern and community [κοινωνικόν]" (120.14); and the second covers the still wider range of concern considered in 3B, regional, ancestral, and ultimately universal, which extends beyond any personal or communal ties. That is not to say that these two groups correspond exactly to the two attitudes, only that the pairing in all three instances—in (2) and (6) and now here in (8)—better reflects conventional usage, which tends to limit "friendly concern" to relations within a community and characterizes any wider concern for others as "goodwill," than does the markedly revisionist argument in 3B for extending such concern, and the language of "friendship" accordingly, well beyond its conventional limits to embrace all of humanity.

Behind standard usage, however, lies a deeper connection between the two terms, and one that was common ground for Aristotle and Stoicism alike, that goodwill is nothing other than wishing people well, or more precisely "wanting good things for someone."[53] My good will for you, in short, is simply my wanting things to go well for you. Aristotle, in fact, counts goodwill so understood as an essential feature of friendship (*EN* 8.3 1156b7–11); and although he rejects the idea, which he cites as a "reputable view," that friendship is *equivalent* to mutual goodwill (8.2 1155b33–34), he does so precisely because he thinks friendship in its primary or paradigmatic form requires considerably more, not least the kind of sustained association implicit in the "familiarity" (1156b25–32) singled out in (7) here. So too in (8), then, the appeal to goodwill is probably best understood in the first instance as highlighting a factor recognizably common to *all the kinds* of concern for others considered in 3A and 3B, namely, wishing others well, in some way or other and to some degree or other. As the sequel shows, however, it also provides the crucial link to two more attitudes introduced in the remainder of the argument, approbation and good reputation.

One other feature of (8) calls for emphasis before proceeding, and that is the explicit shift in focus it introduces from what people do for others and the motivation underlying their conduct on one hand, to the attitudes other people have towards them and the value of those attitudes in turn on the other hand. This double shift is marked in part grammatically, by a return to direct discourse and a change both in subjects (from people to abstract nouns) and in prepositions (from how we respond "towards" [πρός] others to the responses we receive "from" [παρά] them), but also

---

[53] See *EN* 9.5; *EE* 7.7; *MM* 2.12 1212a1–13; D.L. 5.31; for Stoics, cf. ps.-Andronicus, *On Emotions* 6 with D.L. 7.116 (*SVF* 3.431–32).

logically by a shift from a rhetorical style of argument heavily reliant on examples to a terse string of syllogisms virtually devoid of ornamentation. By isolating this shift, P1 also reveals the logical connection between the first steps in 3C and what precedes: given its antecedent as established in 3A–B and as supplied above in P2, the conclusion C1 follows directly, and with it the extension of intrinsic worth from other people as beneficiaries of our conduct to the corresponding attitudes people have towards the conduct of others in turn.

The rest of the argument now extends intrinsic worth to similar attitudes in impersonal contexts more generally. In its next step in (9), the conclusion formulated in C2 would follow directly from P4 by way of C1. But P4 is curiously missing, or at least not explicitly stated. What the argument offers instead is only a puzzling appeal to *oikeiôsis* in P3: an alleged "affinity and attraction" people have to those who praise or approve of them. A preliminary question here is whether this affinity is supposed to be directed only towards those who express their approval in some way, for example by voicing it in praise, or more broadly to everyone who approves of someone, whether or not they express it. On the face of it, both the verbal association of approbation with praise on one hand and the motivational implications of *oikeiôsis* on the other appear to favor the narrower reading. In that case, however, P3 reverts to the perspective of 3A and 3B in appealing again to people's responses to the approval of them expressed by others: we welcome and are motivated by their praise. Not only is that claiming more than C1 can support; there goodwill, which often remains unexpressed, has no implications for any attraction of that sort. Worse, it also removes the basis for the conclusion in C2 that approbation has *intrinsic* worth as something worth choosing specifically "on its own account" and independently of its impact on our own interests, whether its usefulness in other pursuits or simply the pleasure in receiving praise. On a broader reading, by contrast, only the attitude of approbation is at issue, whether expressed or not, and a convergence of values is enough for "affinity" and any attendant attraction. In that case, the focus remains squarely on intrinsic worth, and P3 aligns more securely with C1 and its appeal to goodwill, expressed or not.

The continued focus on *intrinsic* worth is crucial. If the point of C1 were only that goodwill is worth choosing, it could readily be supported simply by observing that having the goodwill of others is often useful.[54] But that would be an appeal to self-interest and its instrumental value, and the

---

[54] Cf. *EN* 8.8; *EE* 7.4; *MM* 2.11 1210b3–22.

argument here plainly seeks to establish the narrower and stronger claims that first goodwill in C1, and now approbation in C2 have intrinsic worth. On a broader reading, then, the role of P3 in this sequence falls into place. Goodwill, to draw on Aristotle again as an index of conventional views, rests on judgments of character: "in general, goodwill occurs because of some virtue or probity [ἐπιείκειαν], when someone appears honorable, brave, or the like to another" (*EN* 1167a18–20). When the judgments are accurate and the others actually have such qualities, then just as both those traits and those who possess them clearly have intrinsic worth, and considerably more than any external goods as Didymus goes on to argue in sections 5–8, so too it could be argued that an accurate recognition of their intrinsic worth by others would have some too. In any case, the recognition of excellent traits in others is enough to establish a convergence of values for both those who approve and those approved, and one that, by virtue of the shared appreciation of the relevant excellence it implies, has intrinsic worth independent of any effect on anyone's other interests. On a broader reading, then, which does not require any expression of approval in praise of other forms, that recognition is nothing short of approbation. The inference in (9) from goodwill to approbation thus relies again on a conventional understanding of approbation as a recognition and appreciation of specifically ethical traits.[55]

The remainder of the argument is straightforward. First, in (10), a direct appeal to standard usage extends the reach of intrinsic worth finally to "good reputation" by equating it in P5 with widespread approval, literally "approbation from many people" (122.5–7). From that, together with C2 in the previous step, the third conclusion C3 follows directly. The argument then draws a final conclusion in C4 by collecting the first three (C1–3) together in (11) under the conventional rubric of "external goods" in P6: the four attitudes of others canvassed in 3C have been shown to have intrinsic worth.

We can now see the role of 3C in the larger argument of sections 1–9 more clearly. After a brief summary of Peripatetic views of character and capacities of soul in section 1, Didymus presents a condensed account of *oikeiôsis* in section 2 to indicate a natural origin and basis for intrinsic worth. Both that preliminary argument and its elaboration in sections 3–9 differ importantly from Stoic accounts. In those, *oikeiôsis* is essentially

---

[55] Cf. *EN* 1.12 and *Rhet.* 1.9. For a related Stoic chain of syllogisms meant to establish the extensional equivalence of what is good and what is honorable by way of approbation, see Plutarch, *SR* 1039C with *SVF* 3.37 (all from Cicero) and Graver (2016).

developmental: we seek survival and our own good from birth, and only over time do we develop concerns for others, starting with childhood concern for our parents, then extending our concern progressively outward from the family to embrace neighbors, friends, community, and ultimately, if all goes as it should, to rational virtue itself and thereby all of humanity as key parts in the rational governance of the cosmos as a whole and in its every part. That diachronic story, echoed as well by the account Cicero presents in Antiochus' name in *De finibus* 5 (esp. 5.61–65), is here replaced by an entirely synchronic picture focused squarely on mature adults (cf. *Fin.* 5.67). The argument Didymus reports in section 3 first invokes parents' love for their children in (1). It then infers that "necessarily" everyone—parents included—also cares for their own parents, siblings, spouses, relatives, and even fellow citizens, "since we have a kinship toward these people too" (2). From there it goes on to infer in (3) that "necessarily" we have some care for everyone. Yet rather than stopping there, where the Stoic story ends, the Peripatetic argument goes on to single out strangers in (4) and future generations in (5), before returning to friends in (7), then moving outward again to impersonal concern in (8)–(11) and finally ending where both it and the Stoic story begin, with concern for ourselves: our "body and soul" in the sections following section 3. One reason for continuing beyond Stoic accounts in this way, we have seen, is to emphasize something they reject: the presence of intrinsic worth—of independent concern for other people and their attitudes "on their own account"—throughout, hence a fundamental continuity and congruence in the kind of concern people have for others whether either they themselves or those others are virtuous or not.

The initial outward sequence parallels Stoic accounts of social *oikeiôsis*, which picture a gradual extension of concern outward from ourselves at the center across a series of concentric circles representing degrees of affinity and concern for other people. The goal on the Stoic model is centripetal: to pull all these circles inward and increase our concern for everyone, even those most remote from us, in effect to expand or extend the scope of our inborn self-centered impulses.[56] That process is entirely absent here. But it would be misguided to fault Didymus or his Peripatetic source(s) for assuming the process comes easily. Issues of moral development are simply irrelevant here, where the aim is instead to show that distinctly ethical forms of concern are present in many relations Stoics consider ethically

---

[56] See McCabe (2005) on this Stoic model of "extending" self-interest: "a Mrs. Bennett kind of altruism" which she dubs "parlour altruism" (414).

"indifferent": radically distinct from "the moral point of view" uniquely achieved by the wise as the sole embodiments of perfect rational virtue. The strategy, in that respect, has a dialectical edge: exploiting notions of natural kinship and affinity to support Aristotelian conceptions of moral psychology and value. Highlighting the most remote relations, which appear last in Stoic accounts, the Peripatetic argument tries to show in 3B how kindness to total strangers involves concern for their welfare "on its own account" or for their intrinsic worth. It then inverts the perspective in 3C, turning from why people act on behalf of others to the attitudes their conduct elicits in others, including disinterested observers, to argue that goodwill, approbation, and good reputation have intrinsic worth too. Like favors and gratitude in section 22, these attitudes typically reflect assessments that depend on more than self-interest alone; but unlike those, they typically depend on evaluations of character. Concern for intrinsic worth thus turns out to be remarkably pervasive, part of goodwill, approbation, and good reputation wherever those occur.[57] That implies in turn that the ethical point of view is remarkably widespread too, shared by the virtuous and others alike, simply to different degrees. A major implication of the argument, then, is that intrinsic worth plays a significant role in many of our personal and impersonal relations. The sequence of steps is evidently designed to show not simply that people naturally care about others, which is hardly controversial, but that their natural concern typically includes a distinctively ethical dimension, a responsiveness—an "affinity and attraction"—to the *intrinsic* worth of others, as section 3 emphasizes at every step.

In so doing, the argument fastens on one of the three factors Aristotle specifies as necessary conditions for virtuous action: acting knowingly, from a settled disposition, and choosing our actions on their own account (*EN* 2.4 1105a28–33). The first two factors figure prominently in Stoic accounts too. But whereas those put most weight on the first, the Peripatetic argument emphasizes the third, the one factor Stoics reserve for the virtuous exclusively (cf. n. 21 above). The differences are connected. Stoic accounts maintain that systematic ethical understanding is essential for virtue because only it affords the impartial perspective necessary to assess

---

[57] The ethical status of εὐδοξία was controversial: early Stoics evidently considered it wholly indifferent, but some after Carneades deemed it "preferred in its own right" (Cicero, *Fin.* 3.57). Part of the issue here is the reliability of popular opinion: Cicero renders εὐδοξία as *bona fama* when worried about its basis, but as *gloria* when arguing for its value (*Off.* 2.30–51); cf. Long (1995) 231–33 and Graver (2016) 128–29 and 136–38.

accurately what is genuinely good—not merely "preferred" or "worth getting" but "worth choosing" as an expression of fully rational virtue—about any action. The argument in section 3 contends rather that most of us often recognize both what to do and at least some factor "worth choosing on its own account"—at least something of intrinsic worth—even without fully understanding why our choice is correct; and to support that claim, it singles out clear-cut cases of altruism that highlight selfless concern in the conduct of ordinary people. That is not to deny that understanding matters, but rather to claim that commonplace attitudes correspond more closely to virtuous ones than the Stoics allow. Virtuous conduct thus differs less radically from ordinary good conduct than on Stoic accounts. Only the virtuous act *regularly* on correct assessments of intrinsic worth. But if their motives are an expression of natural human impulses, as the argument Didymus recounts here tries to show they are, then natural goodness and virtue are essentially connected on a continuum. The advance to virtue, on the Peripatetic account, is less a transformation in perspective, as Stoic theory envisions, than a gradual process of habituation to the accurate recognition and correct assessment of intrinsic worth, in short the development of good character, which is precisely the topic with which the *Epitome* as we have it begins, and a fundamental feature of Aristotelian approaches to ethical theory.

Works Cited

Algra, K. 2003. "The Mechanism of Social Appropriation and Its Role in Hellenistic Ethics." *Oxford Studies in Ancient Philosophy* 25: 265–96.

Annas, J. 1989. "Cicero on Stoics and Private Property." In *Philosophia Togata*, ed. M. Griffin and J. Barnes. Oxford: Oxford University Press, 151–73.

———. 1990. "The Hellenistic Version of Aristotle's Ethics." *Monist* 73: 80–96.

———. 1993. *The Morality of Happiness*. Oxford: Oxford University Press.

Annas, J. and G. Betegh (eds.). 2016. *Cicero's De Finibus: Philosophical Approaches*. Cambridge: Cambridge University Press.

Bett, R. 1989. "Carneades' *Pithanon*: A Reappraisal of Its Role and Status." *Oxford Studies in Anient Philosophy* 7: 59–94.

Brennan, T. 2005. *The Stoic Life: Emotions, Duties, and Fate*. Oxford: Clarendon.

Brink, C. O. 1956. "*Oikeiôsis* and *Oikeiotês*: Theophrastus and Zeno on Nature in Moral Theory." *Phronesis* 1: 123–45.

———. 1989. "*Creditur vulgo testamenta hominum speculum esse morum*: Why the Romans Made Wills." *Classical Philology* 84: 198–215.
Crivelli, P. 2010. "The Stoics on Definition." In *Definition in Greek Philosophy*, ed. D. Charles. Oxford: Oxford University Press, 359–423.
Diels, H. 1879. *Doxographi Graeci*. Berlin: Reimer.
Dorandi, T. 1992. "Considerazioni sull' *index locupletior* di Diogene Laertio." *Prometheus* 18: 121–26.
Fortenbaugh, W. W. (ed.). 1983. *On Stoic and Peripatetic Ethics: The Work of Arius Didymus*. Rutgers University Studies in Classical Humanities 1. New Brunswick, N.J.: Transaction.
———. 2011. *Theophrastus of Eresus: Sources on Ethics, Commentary*. Vol. 6.1. Leiden: Brill.
Frede, D. 2016. "Epicurus on the Importance of Friendship in the Good Life (*De Finibus* 1.65–70; 2.78–85)." In Annas and Betegh (2016) 96–117.
Gill, C. 2016. "Antiochus' Theory of *Oikeiôsis*." In Annas and Betegh (2016) 221–47.
Göranssen, T. 1995. *Albinus, Alcinous, Arius Didymus*. Studia Graeca et Latina Gothoburgensia 61. Gothenburg: University of Gothenburg.
Görgemanns, H. 1983. "*Oikeiôsis* in Arius Didymus." In Fortenbaugh (1983) 165–89.
Graver, M. 2016. "Honor and the Honorable: Cato's Discourse in *De Finibus* 3." In Annas and Betegh (2016) 118–46.
Hahm, D. 1990. "The Ethical Doxography of Arius Didymus." In *ANRW* II.36.4. Berlin: De Gruyter, 2935–3055.
Inwood, B. 1983. "Comments on Professor Görgemanns' Paper: The Two Forms of *Oikeiôsis* in Arius and the Stoa." In Fortenbaugh (1983) 190–201.
———. 1985. *Ethics and Human Action in Early Stoicism*. Oxford: Clarendon.
———. 2014a. *Ethics After Aristotle*. Cambridge, Mass.: Harvard University Press.
———. 2014b. "*Tria Genera Bonorum*." In *Strategies of Argument: Essays in Ancient Ethics, Epistemology and Logic in Honor of Gisela Striker*, ed. M. Lee and M. Schiefsky. Oxford: Oxford University Press, 255–80.
———. 2016. "The Voice of Nature." In Annas and Betegh (2016) 147–66.
Kahn, C. 1983. "Arius as a Doxographer." In Fortenbaugh (1983) 3–13.
Konstan, D. 1997. *Friendship in the Classical World*. Cambridge: Cambridge University Press.

Long, A. A. 1995. "Cicero's Politics in *De Officiis.*" In *Justice and Generosity: Studies in Hellenistic Social and Political Philosophy*, ed. A. Laks and M. Schofield. Cambridge: Cambridge University Press, 213–40.
McCabe, M. M. 2005. "Extend or Identify: Two Stoic Accounts of Altruism." In *Metaphysics, Soul, and Ethics in Ancient Thought: Themes from the Work of Richard Sorabji*, ed. R. Salles. Oxford: Clarendon, 413–43.
Mansfeld, J. 1999. "Sources." In *The Cambridge History of Hellenistic Philosophy*, ed. K. Algra, J. Barnes, J. Mansfeld, and M. Schofield. Cambridge: Cambridge University Press, 3–30.
———. 2012. "Doxography of Ancient Philosophy." In *Stanford Encyclopedia of Philosophy*. http://plato.stanford.edu/entries/doxography-ancient/.
Mansfeld, J. and D. Runia. 1997. *Aëtiana*. Vol. 1: *The Method and Intellectual Context of a Doxographer*. Leiden: Brill.
Meineke, A. 1859. "Zu Stobaeus." *Zeitschrift für das Gymnasialwesen* 13: 563–65.
Moraux, P. 1973. *Der Aristotelismus bei den Griechen*. Vol. 1. Berlin: De Gruyter.
O'Keefe, T. 2001. "Is Epicurean Friendship Altruistic?" *Apeiron* 34: 269–305.
Piccione, R. M. 1994. "Sulle fonti e le metodologie compilative di Stobaeo." *Eikasmos* 5: 281–317.
Riesbeck, D. 2016. *Aristotle on Political Community*. Cambridge: Cambridge University Press.
Russell, D. 2010. "Virtue and Happiness in the Lyceum and Beyond." *Oxford Studies in Ancient Philosophy* 38: 143–85.
Schofield, M. 1996. "*Epilogismos*: An Appraisal." In *Rationality in Greek Thought*, ed. M. Frede and G. Striker. Oxford: Clarendon, 221–37.
———. 2012. "Antiochus on Social Virtue." In Sedley (2012) 173–87.
Sedley, D. (ed.). 2012. *The Philosophy of Antiochus*. Cambridge: Cambridge University Press.
Sharples, R. 1983. "The Peripatetic Classification of Goods." In Fortenbaugh (1983) 139–59.
———. 2010. *Peripatetic Philosophy 200 BC to 200 AD*. Cambridge: Cambridge University Press.
White, S. 2002. "Happiness in the Hellenistic Lyceum." In *Eudaimonia and Well-Being: Ancient and Modern Conceptions*, ed. L. Jost and R. Shiner. *Apeiron* 35 suppl., 69–93.
Whitlock Blundell, M. 1989. *Helping Friends and Harming Enemies: A Study in Sophocles and Greek Ethics*. Cambridge: Cambridge University Press.

———. 1990. "Parental Nature and Stoic Οἰκείωσις." *Ancient Philosophy* 10: 221–42.
Williams, B. 1973. "Egoism and Altruism." In his *Problems of the Self*. Cambridge: Cambridge University Press, 250–65.

5

Two Conceptions of "Primary Acts of Virtue" in Doxography C

Jan Szaif

My aim in this essay is to investigate the Peripatetic conception of "primary (προηγούμεναι) actions," or "primary acts of virtue," as it is laid out in some passages of Doxography C (a text commonly attributed to Arius Didymus and excerpted in Stobaeus, *Ecl.* II.7 116.19ff.). In the first section of my essay, I will comment briefly on the composition and sources of Doxography C in order to justify my methodology. Sections 2 and 3 will be dedicated to the analysis of the argument in a key segment of this text (quoted as T-2 below) and of the concept of "primary actions" presented in this segment and some parallel passages. I will discuss the reasons why a subset of virtuous activities is singled out as primary. To this end, both their role as constituent parts of a eudaimonic life and as acts that fulfill the inherent teleology of human virtue will have to be scrutinized. In section 4, I will analyze yet another passage (quoted as T-8), which offers comments on the notion of primary acts of virtue. I am going to argue that T-8 articulates a different understanding of "primary" activity and thus reflects a different strand of Peripatetic reasoning on the question of the human *telos*. Whereas T-2 responds to Stoic challenges by formulating a conception of human happiness that reduces all somatic and external goods to a strictly instrumental role for the sake of "noble activities," T-8 articulates a more inclusive view of happiness, a view that gives room for the "enjoyment of natural goods" separate from, and in addition to, "noble activities."[1]

1

My methodological approach to this text is, in a certain way, a rather traditional one; yet it agrees, I think, with the specific nature of this text and its history of transmission. Let me state the main points, albeit rather dogmatically. A detailed argument would require another essay.

Doxography C (like Doxography B, a text dedicated to Stoic ethics and preserved in the same chapter of Stobaeus' anthology) exemplifies a type of doxographic literature that seeks to give an overview of the doctrines of a philosophical school, based on some kind of thematic arrangement. Although it draws its material from different sources, this type of doxography refrains from pointing out disagreements *within* the school. Its aim is, rather, to highlight positions that distinguish this from other schools (cf. Gottschalk [1987] 1129). Doxography B, for instance, covers views of Stoic authors ranging from Zeno of Citium to Panaetius and Posidonius (cf. Hahm [1990] 2980)—views that clearly include some considerable doctrinal developments and controversies, yet the existence of such controversy within the school is never explicitly acknowledged in this text. We have to expect a similar pattern for the account of Peripatetic ethics in Doxography C: a superficially harmonizing compilation of Peripatetic material drawn from different sources and arranged in a thematic order, which, because of the disparity among the sources, cannot fully erase the tensions and inconsistencies of the doxographical content (cf. Moraux [1973] 438).

There is, to be sure, one significant exception in Doxography C to the rule that differences within the school are not highlighted: C criticizes, without naming him, the approach of Critolaus and his followers (dubbed the "younger Peripatetics" in Doxography A).[2] Thus it seems that C is taking

---

[1] I first formulated this thesis in chapters II-C and II-D of my German habilitation dissertation (Bonn, 2001), which appeared in print as Szaif (2012). This chapter develops my interpretation further and (as I hope) strengthens my argument concerning the two different conceptions of "primary activities" in Doxography C. I want to thank the participants in the Arius Didymus conference at Rutgers for their feedback during discussion, and Bill Fortenbaugh, Margaret Graver, and Steve White for comments on my paper draft.

[2] While Critolaus is mentioned by name only in Doxography A (46.11), it is now generally agreed that his position is a target of criticism in C (esp. 126.12–127.2 and 130.4–12); cf. Philippson (1932) 464; Annas (1993) 415; Hahm (2007) 69f.; Sharples (2007)

sides in an inner-Peripatetic debate about how to formulate and defend a Peripatetic account of the human *telos*, a debate that pitted certain modernizers (as one might call them), who made ample use of Stoic technical terminology, against a more orthodox Peripatetic approach.[3] However, these orthodox (or classicist) preferences of Doxography C have not precluded the incorporation of topics and argumentations that very obviously presuppose, or react to, Hellenistic and especially Stoic theories, the most prominent example being the long sequence containing an adaptation of the Stoic theory of *oikeiôsis*. And even material in this doxography that clearly harks back to Aristotelian and early Peripatetic sources is often presented in ways that seem to indicate familiarity with Stoic concepts and the desire to contrast central tenets of the Peripatetic school with their Stoic counterparts (Moraux [1973] 364f.). Since its approach also clearly differs from the practice of the later Peripatetic tradition of commentary and analysis based on close scrutiny of the original Aristotelian treatises—a tradition that seems to have started with Andronicus of Rhodes—we have very good reason to believe that Doxography C is rooted in the late Hellenistic period, combining material from old Peripatetic school texts with more recent material.

Although C is not truncated in such a blatant manner as A, we have to assume that it too has been heavily epitomized.[4] Various awkward transitions in C are quite likely the result of manipulations of the text by late epitomizers. Surprising gaps, such as the absence of chapters on pleasure or on deliberation (core elements of an Aristotelian account of ethics), might also be due to loss. A (for us) particularly unfortunate feature of C in its current state is that it does not name its Peripatetic sources (with the sole exception of a long explicit quotation, or epitomized paraphrase, from Theophrastus[5]). Thus we have to try to track those different sources solely on the basis of discrepancies and incompatibilities of doctrinal content and terminology.

I do not need to take a stand here on the question of authorship.[6] Rather, I would like to add a comment as to why the very category of authorship

---

629f. (My quotations from Doxographies A and B, like those from C, use the page and line numbers of the Wachsmuth edition of Stobaeus, *Ecl.* 2.7).

[3] Cf. Szaif (2016) for more background.
[4] Hahm (1990) has used scholia on Lucan to prove epitomization for Doxography B.
[5] 140.7–142.5 (or 142.13?); cf. Theophrastus fr. 449A Fortenbaugh.
[6] I agree, though, that it is plausible to localize the doxographer, at least tentatively, in the classicist and eclectic philosophical milieu of Alexandria during, roughly, the transitional period between the Hellenistic and Imperial eras (cf. Hatzimichali [2011]

is of comparatively little relevance in connection with this text. First, the authorial contribution in the case of this type of doxographical literature seems to revolve around the ways in which the author selects, epitomizes, and arranges the material. Thus it is not the doxographer's role to articulate, or defend, his own views.[7] Second, the text that we find in chapter II.7 of Stobaeus' *Eclogae* is not, in any clear sense of the word, an "original text," not even an original *doxographical* text. What we are presented with is a text that has an unknown number of historical layers, starting from its original sources through stages of compilation—which at some point, presumably in the first century BC or early first century AD, resulted in the comprehensive doxographical summary that we ideally refer to when speaking of Doxography C—yet which was then further subjected to rearrangement, epitomization, and accidental loss. On account of these facts, the idea of an author becomes rather ephemeral.[8] I am going to relate to Doxography C as a *text* that presents us with a collage of different Peripatetic voices—voices that we can try to trace through a veil of distortions caused by doxographic simplification and subsequent rearrangement and epitomization.[9]

Since the subdivision and titles given in the manuscripts are of little use, I am using my own breakdown. Here is how I divide the first three parts of C.

I (116.21–118.4): Introductory remarks about the designations "ethics" and "ethical virtue"
II (118.5–128.9): The human *telos* derived from an account of natural attachments (*oikeiôsis*)[10]
III (128.11–134.6): On *eudaimonia*

25–66 for a description of this milieu). It cannot be proved that the Arius Didymus, who we know was responsible for (at least) some part or version of Doxography C, is identical with the Alexandrian philosopher Arius associated with Augustus. But at least the time and milieu seem right.

[7] This means that the method behind this type of doxography is very different from the ways in which Aristotle shaped his doxographic reports. Compare the remarks at the beginning and end of Doxography B, 57.15–17 and 116.15–18.

[8] I am saying this in response to, for instance, Brad Inwood's recent discussion of "Harry," the putative Peripatetic author of Doxography C (Inwood [2014] 78–88). Note that the doxographer's own philosophical affiliation is neither certain nor important. One does not have to be a Peripatetic in order to compose a report of the views of the Peripatos.

[9] See also Kahn (1983) 7f., who speaks of a "multilayered collage."

[10] It is part of my overall thesis that the original sources for this account of *oikeiôsis* (cf. Görgemanns [1983])—or at least one of its two main sources—, with the exception of

The focus of my discussion will be on part III. I am dividing III into two smaller parts, III-a (128.11–130.12) and III-b (130.15–134.6), based on an argument concerning sources, since I believe that III-a and III-b (or, at least, some part of III-b) represent different Peripatetic viewpoints and thus must originate (directly or indirectly) from different sources. However, I am not going to focus here on the question of "sources," strictly speaking, but rather on the difference of ideas expressed in different parts of the text.

2

We need to look at the argumentative structure of III-a as a whole since it represents a coherent piece of reasoning leading up to what is the most relevant piece for our purposes, quotation T-2 below.[11] III-a sets out with two suggestions for a nominal definition of *aretê*[12] in general: "best disposition" (ἀρίστη διάθεσις) or "that thanks to which the thing having it is best disposed" (128.11f.). Both formulations seem to amount to the same idea. As a justification, the text adduces an (incompletely reported) epagogic argument that links *aretê*, qua "best" disposition, to "best" performance (128.12–16).[13] Turning then to the case of human virtues, it states that these are anchored in reason (λόγος) and passion (πάθος) (128.17f.)—a distinction that harks back to the division of the soul into a rational and a passionate (or irrational) part, and a corresponding division among virtues, introduced in part I (117.4–118.4). The text goes on to state that these two parts of the soul can be in a state of harmonious agreement (ὁμονοητικῶς

---

a passage that includes T-5 quoted below, belong to the tradition of Critolaus and that the conception of virtue and of good or choiceworthy things underlying the argument of Part II is at odds with the accounts provided in I and III-a. But this is not something I am going to discuss in this paper.

[11] My discussion of the segments leading up to T-2 can be usefully compared with Bill Fortenbaugh's comments on 128.10–129.17 in his chapter "Moral Virtue in Didymus' Epitome of Peripatetic Ethics" included in this volume.

[12] I am leaving certain key terms of ancient ethics untranslated, terms that are notoriously hard to translate into contemporary English, such as *aretê* (excellence, "virtue"), *eudaimonia* (the blessed or happy condition of a life), *telos* (goal, completion).

[13] In line 128.16, the manuscripts have τὰ ἄριστα διατιθέναι ἐστὶν ἀρετή, which is odd since ἀρετή, qua ἕξις, cannot be equated with an activity. If the active and transitive διατιθέναι is kept, ἀρετή should be emended to ἀρετῆς (Spengel e.a., followed by Wachsmuth). Yet I prefer emending διατιθέναι, replacing it with the aorist passive participle διατεθέν (rather than von Arnim's διατιθέν [1926] 14, which is a present active participle). The ἄριστα διατεθέν of 128.16 would correspond to the ἄριστα διάκειται in 128.12. On either proposal, the τὰ in 128.16 should probably be corrected to τὸ (Spengel, Wachsmuth, Tsouni).

συμφωνεῖν) or of internal strife (στασιαστικῶς διαφωνεῖν) (128.18f.). The condition of internal harmony requires that the irrational part, also described as the seat of ὁρμή (impulse, desire), obey reason (128.25). If, due to the influence of pleasures and pains on our ὁρμή, the irrational part is in a state of conflict with reason, the resulting condition is either ἐγκράτεια or ἀκρασία (self-control or lack of self-control), depending on whether or not reason succeeds in subjugating the inordinate impulse (τὸ τῆς ὁρμῆς ἀπειθές) (128.18–23). If, on the other hand, the two parts are in harmonious agreement (ἁρμονία καὶ συμφωνία), the resulting condition is virtue (128.23–25) (or, more precisely, virtue taken as a complete whole rather than as some particular virtue[14]).[15] All this can be traced back to material in Aristotle or, even more so, in the *MM*,[16] which most scholars today take to be a school text produced in the context of the old Peripatos.

The next segment (128.27–129.3) introduces definitions for the terms "choiceworthy" (αἱρετόν) and "worthy of avoidance" (φευκτόν). The definition of αἱρετόν will then serve as a basis for explicating the notion "good" (ἀγαθόν). This thematic progression is sensible:[17] *aretê* has been defined with the help of the superlative form of "good" (ἄριστον); therefore we should now expect an account of "good."

The text states that something is a αἱρετόν (or a φευκτόν), if and only if it has the ability to turn desire/impulse (ὁρμή) toward itself (or away from itself) such that this orientation *also* receives the approval of reason. In other words, the αἱρετόν is not just a factual object of desire or choice but one that, from the perspective of reason, is worthy to be desired and chosen.

The text then goes on to claim that the "ancients" (ἀρχαῖοι)—presumably philosophers in the era before the Stoics, especially from the old Academy and old Peripatos—identified the notions "good" (ἀγαθόν) and "choiceworthy/desirable" (αἱρετόν) (129.4f.). This is to be understood as contrasting with Stoic practice. Stoics, known for the subtlety of their terminological distinctions (and often criticized for it), stipulated a conceptual difference between these two notions while ascribing the same extension to them.[18] In order to prove the claim that the "ancients," unlike the Stoics,

---

[14] We know from a piece of Peripatetic doxography in Doxography A (51.2–8) that this was one of several senses in which Peripatetics could understand the notion of τελεία ἀρετή.

[15] Note the absence of an account of ethical κακία. The text could not have defined κακία as lack of inner harmony since this was already covered by ἐγκράτεια/ἀκρασία.

[16] Cf. von Arnim (1926) 15–17. The notion of ὁρμή is prominent in Stoicism, yet increasingly replaces the term ὄρεξις already in the *MM* (cf. Inwood [1985] 243–49).

[17] *Contra* Moraux (1973) 352, who sees here only disconnected pieces of doxography.

[18] For the Stoics, good things are also αἱρετά, and vice versa. An example for how

identified the two notions, the text cites a famous assertion mentioned at the beginning of Aristotle's *EN* (1094a2f.): "Good is what all things strive at," calling it a "rough (or preliminary) definition" (ὑπογραφή) of the concept "good" (129.5f.). We know from another passage in the *EN* (1172b9f.) that this statement was also attributed to Eudoxus of Cnidus. But the doxography neither quotes it from Aristotle specifically nor mentions Eudoxus. A generic attribution to "the ancients" suffices for its purposes.[19]

Since the two notions αἱρετόν and "good" (ἀγαθόν) have been equated, and the subsequent divisions of the notion "good" use the term αἱρετόν, I surmise that the leading idea here is that the definition of αἱρετόν can also be used as an explication of the term "good," and that "good" should, hence, be understood as denoting something that can move our impulse/desire with the (added) approval of reason. This account does not reduce goodness to rational approvability, since it includes subrational impulse as a nonreducible element.[20] It is built on the dichotomy between reason and passion (πάθος), or impulse (ὁρμή), and thus aligns itself very well with the definition of *aretê* in the preceding segment and with the general psychology of part I.[21]

Now that a general account of "good" has been provided, the text introduces a series of dichotomous divisions of this notion: First, "good" is divided into what is "choiceworthy because of ourselves" (δι' ἡμᾶς αἱρετά) and what is "choiceworthy because of our fellow-humans"[22] (διὰ τοὺς

Stoics could distinguish *conceptually* between these two notions (with αἱρετόν adding an additional conceptual element) can be found in Doxography B, 72.19–25 (= *SVF* III.88).

[19] It is not clear, though, if this formula is really compatible with the definition of *haireton* just given, since it does not include reference to reason. Cf. Doxography A, 53.23, which restricts the application of this formula to rational beings (a possibility also mentioned in Aristotle, *Rhet.* 1362a23f.).

[20] For this reason, the definition of αἱρετόν (and, implicitly, of "good") in III-a should not simply be equated with the Chrysippean(?) definition of this term (τὸ ὁρμῆς αὐτοτελοῦς κινητικόν, *SVF* III.131), although both formulae connect the term αἱρετόν with the idea of something that "moves" the ὁρμή. Cf. Moraux (1973) 366, who demonstrates the connections with formulations in the *MM*, yet also (wrongly, I think) claims that there is no difference in content between the account of αἱρετόν in III-a and the Stoic definition (ibid, n. 160).

[21] Other features shared by I and III-a are a predilection for political metaphors in describing psychological facts and for brief accounts of word-formation (cf. n. 37 below).

[22] On the use of the expression οἵ πλησίον in Doxography C; cf. 117.17f., 120.17–121.3, 122.14–18. Of these passages, the first two in particular show quite clearly that this expression, by the time when this text, or its Hellenistic sources, were formulated (and possibly even earlier), had acquired a more abstract meaning in the sense of "other people," or "fellow humans," rather than just "people near to you," let alone "neighbors." This is also confirmed by the use of the term in the Eudorus fragment in Doxography A (44.20–24) and

πλησίον [αἱρετά]) (129.6–8). This division has no exact precedent in Aristotle. The text also offers no further explanation, but this certainly appears to be a distinction between self-regarding and altruistic goals.[23]

The next dichotomous step divides the self-regarding goals into those which are καλά (noble/fine/beautiful) and others that are ἀναγκαῖα (necessary). The contrasting use of these two terms can also be found in Aristotle (at least six examples in the *EN*, for instance).[24] In this context, καλόν denotes something that we can appreciate and choose for its own sake. It has inherent desirability. The ἀναγκαῖον, on the other hand, is something we are constrained to do, or use, for the sake of some other goal. We would not opt for it just for its own sake. The notion of "necessary goods" could relate to the necessities of life in the sense of what we need simply to survive, but the examples given below, in T-1, and the explicit connection there with "the use of *aretê*"—which is a key conceptual component in the account of *eudaimonia*[25]—point more specifically to *eudaimonia* as the point of reference for deciding what is *needed*. It is, moreover, clear that we are dealing here with *hypothetical* necessity.

---

by some passages in Doxography B (93.19–94.1, 111.10–13).

[23] Strache (1909) 46 and others have pointed out that the same distinction can be found in Varro's account of the *divisio Carneadea* as reported by Augustine (*Civ.* XIX.1, 658.71–79 CCSL). Varro, in turn, depends on Antiochus (but may have added thoughts of his own). Compare also the Eudorus fragment in Doxography A (44.20–24) for a corresponding division of "fitting" actions (καθήκοντα) and "right" actions (κατορθώματα) into those that concern our relation to others and those that do not. (N.b.: the notion of δι' ἡμᾶς αἱρετά should not be confused with that of δι' αὑτὰ αἱρετά, developed in part II of Doxography C.)

[24] *EN* 1116b2f., 1120b1, 1155a29, 1164b29f., 1165a4, 1171a2f.; cf. Plato *Rep.* 493C. However, Aristotle tends to use the term ἀναγκαῖα more narrowly in his ethics, dividing things chosen on account of their utility into ἀναγκαῖα and χρήσιμα (i.e., things that are indispensable for life versus things can be foregone but are still useful), cf. *EN* 1099b25–28 (see also 1177a27–34, 1178a23–35); *Pol.* 1333a30–b5; and Aspasius' remark in 159.4–6 (CAG XIX.1).

[25] Cf. T-7 (1) below: the "use of (complete) *aretê*," if supported by the right kinds of productive goods in a complete life, is nothing other than *eudaimonia*. The reference to *eudaimonia* is also confirmed by the fact that T-1 equates the "necessary goods" (other than life) with "productive goods." For the notion of "productive goods," as it is commonly used in the debates between Stoics and Peripatetics, bears on the question of which kinds of things contribute to *eudaimonia*; cf. *SVF* III.106–9 concerning the Stoic understanding of the term ποιητικὸν ἀγαθόν.

Two Conceptions of "Primary Acts of Virtue" in Doxography C 169

While the καλά are subdivided into virtues and virtuous activities (129.9–11),[26] the following sentence divides the ἀναγκαῖα and also gives us some examples:

T-1 Both life and things that relate to it and assume the place of productive[27] [goods][28] (ποιητικά) are necessary [goods] (ἀναγκαῖα), for instance the body, its parts, and their uses, and among the so-called externals respectable birth, wealth, reputation, peace, freedom, friendship. For each of them makes a contribution (συμβάλλεσθαί τι) to the use of *aretê*. (129.12–17)

This sentence contains a third step in the downward dichotomy (marked by a τε ... καὶ ...), dividing the necessary goods into, first, life itself, and second, things that relate to life in the manner of "productive" goods (ποιητικά). (The second "and" is epexegetic.) The productive goods are then further divided into somatic and external goods.

T-1 thus clearly implies an anti-Stoic stance on the question of what is to count as a good and what is required for human *eudaimonia*. Unlike the Stoics, it includes bodily advantages, such as health, and external assets, such as wealth and a good reputation, among the goods, and it presents them as contributing to *eudaimonia*. The next paragraph (T-2 below) is going to address a *Stoic objection* that relates to exactly this point, the inclusion of nonpsychic goods among the prerequisites of *eudaimonia*:

T-2 *Eudaimonia* arises from noble (καλαί) and primary (προηγούμεναι) actions.[29] Therefore it is altogether noble, just as the activity (ἐνέργεια) on

---

[26] Was the division of goods into καλά and ἀναγκαῖα originally meant to intersect with that between self-regarding and other-regarding goals such that the other-regarding goals would also have been divided into καλά and ἀναγκαῖα? Or was the idea that good things provided to others for their sakes are always only ἀναγκαῖα ἀγαθά (viz. hypothetical necessities relative to the other person's well-being), whereas the καλόν is something an agent can convey only to himself or herself, through freely choosing to perform virtuous actions? (This latter claim could be based on the argument in Aristotle's *EN* IX.8; cf. 1169a18–32.)

[27] "Life" should not be construed as the object of ποιητικά (such that the ποιητικά are said to "produce life"; cf. Simpson [2014]). The ποιητικά are supportive goods whose use goes beyond securing mere survival (cf. n. 25 above). When the text calls the body and its parts ποιητικά, they are understood as tools of human practice, not as biological causes of life. Cf. Sharples' 2010 translation of the same passage.

[28] I use square brackets in my translations to include words that are not in the Greek text but are implied.

[29] As the remainder of the passage shows, the γίγνεται ἐκ (translated as "arises from") is to be understood in the sense of "being composed of." T-2 talks about "noble and primary actions" as constituent parts of *eudaimonia*.

(ἐν) the pipes is altogether artful. For the addition of the material[30] [aspects of action][31] does not make *eudaimonia* depart from the purity of [its] nobility (τῆς εἰλικρινείας τοῦ καλοῦ), just as the use of tools does not [make] the altogether artful activity of medicine [depart from the purity of its artistry].[32] For every action (πρᾶξις) is an activity (ἐνέργειά τις) of the soul; yet one should not, just because an agent's action is coupled with the use of certain things [that help] toward the completion[33] of the task, consider these things *parts* of the activity; [one should not do so] despite the fact that either [activity][34] [i.e., *pipe-playing and medical treatment, JSz*] seeks to add either [kind of tool], yet not as a part, but as a productive thing (ποιητικόν) [used by] the art.[35] For it is

---

[30] This specific usage of the term ὑλικά seems to be influenced by its use in Stoic ethics. Cf. Cicero, *Fin*. III.61: *prima autem illa naturae ... sub iudicium sapientis et dilectum cadunt, estque illa* subiecta quasi materia sapientiae; Plutarch, *Comm. not.* 1071B (= *SVF* III, 195); see also *SVF* III.114, 115, and Alexander of Aphrodisias, *Mant.* (CAG suppl. II.1) 160.4–7. (According to *SVF* III.491, this terminology goes back at least as far as Chrysippus.) The Stoics seem to use this terminology because they view the so-called "primary natural advantages (πρῶτα κατὰ φύσιν)" (i.e., the things that are the natural objects of human desire before the full self-realization of wisdom as the only foundational good) as the subject-"matter" of the correct selection carried out by *aretê*. Yet while for the Stoics the quality of this subject-"matter" is indifferent with respect to a person's *eudaimonia*, the Peripatetics view them as supporting goods that are indispensible for the fulfillment of the goals of virtuous practice, analogously to how the quality of the materials and tools used by a skilled craftsman affects the quality of his or her work.

[31] The text of T-2 is also recorded in chapter IV.39.28 of Stobaeus' *Anthologium* (= book II of the *Florilegia*). The text in IV.39.28 has τὴν παράληψιν τῶν ὑλικῶν ἀρχῶν, while the same clause in II.7 lacks ἀρχῶν. Since ἀρχῶν does not give a good sense in the context of this sentence, it should be either athecised or emended to ἀγαθῶν, as Wachsmuth in his apparatus for II.7 points out. There is something to be said in favor of retaining ἀγαθῶν since the "material" aspects of an action are not always good, but the argument of T-2 talks about the addition of material aspects that *support* the action and are, hence, instrumental goods. However, this textual uncertainty does not really affect our analysis of the argument since, with or without ἀγαθῶν, it is clear from the context that the reference is to material aspects that are supportive goods. (Note that we find the term ὑλικά also in one of the divisions of goods, in 134.17–19, where it is explicitly equated with the class of τὰ ποιητικά.)

[32] Huby's (1983) interpretation of this passage gets off the right track because of a misleading (though grammatically possible) translation of this and the next sentence: the genitive τῆς εἰλικρινείας should be related to ἐκβιβάζειν, not to τῶν ὑλικῶν; and τισι (translated here as "certain things") harks back to "tools," not to "action" (127). Compare the translations by Sharples (2010) 119 and Gigon (1961) 272.

[33] Accepting Wachsmuth's conjecture τελείωσιν for τελειότητα.

[34] I am rejecting Spengel's unnecessary and slightly misleading conjecture τεχνῶν, adopted by Wachsmuth and Tsouni. Cf. Strache (1909) 114–16 on the text. The pronoun ἑκατέρας harks back to the preceding ἐνεργείας.

[35] Taking the genitive τῆς τέχνης as a *genitivus subiectivus*. (The ποιητικόν is "of the τέχνη" not because it "produces the τέχνη"—this would not make sense—but because the τέχνη uses it to produce something.)

not correct to call the things *without which it is impossible* to carry out some action *parts* of that activity. For a part is thought of as being *symplerotic* of a whole, while *that without which* [something cannot be done] is thought of as being *productive*, because it carries, in a collaborative way (φέρειν καὶ συνεργεῖν),[36] toward the goal (εἰς τὸ τέλος). (129.19–130.12)

Doctrinally, this passage is fully compatible with the other segments of III-a and the psychological account in I. We notice, to be sure, a certain change of tone. While the previous segments of III-a contained bare-bone definitions and divisions, paired with linguistic explanations of how some of these terms were formed,[37] T-2 pursues an apologetic agenda (cf. von Arnim [1926] 22). Here is what seems to be the vulnerable point causing the need for a defense: since the Peripatetic account makes human happiness depend not just on virtue but also on the availability of external goods, it can be portrayed as lacking moral rigor compared to the Stoics' uncompromising commitment to virtue. It stands to reason that this kind of objection was raised in Stoic quarters.

As part of its defensive strategy, T-2 also criticizes a rival Peripatetic approach associated with the name of Critolaus. Critolaus argued that the highest fulfillment of a human life required the addition of nonpsychic goods; virtue and virtuous activities alone were not sufficient to guarantee "full completion" resulting in a eudaimonic "flow of life."[38] From a Stoic perspective, this did invite the objection that the Peripatetic account diluted the nobility of the human *telos*. Critolaus seems to have had his own strategy for responding to this charge.[39] Our source here uses a dif-

---

[36] The verb συνεργεῖν is used by Aristotle, but it is also related to a Stoic technical term for auxiliary causes (cf. Long and Sedley [1987] I.342). The καί might be epexegetic. With the text as it is, the idea seems to be that it is thanks to productive goods that someone is "carried" toward the goal (*telos*); i.e., toward eudaimonic practice. Usener's conjecture <συμ>φέρειν would simplify the interpretation, yet the usage of this terminology in connection with nonpsychic goods that help the virtuous agent achieve eudaimonic practice is also documented in another Peripatetic source: Alexander of Aphrodisias, *Mant.* (CAG suppl. II.1) 167.13–17 (cf. 167.28, 165.10). It uses a cognate of φέρειν, the adjective φορόν, in tandem with συνεργεῖν. (See also Strache [1909] 116, who cites a passage from Aspasius to defend φέρειν.)

[37] Cf. 128.11f: implicit derivation of ἀρετή from ἀρίστη; 128.20-23: "paronymic" derivation of ἐγκράτεια and ἀκρασία from κράτος; 129.2f: the derivation of αἱρετόν from αἵρεσις confirmed by an argument from analogy.

[38] Cf. Critolaus fr. 20 Wehrli (= Clemens Alexandrinus, *Strom.* II.xxi.129.10). I cannot discuss my understanding of Critolaus' account of the human *telos* here; but compare my remarks on fr. 20 in part 2 of Szaif (2016).

[39] The simile of the scales attributed to Critolaus (frr. 21–22 Wehrli) was probably

ferent strategy, part of which is to claim that Critolaus was, indeed, guilty of the mistake in question, thus setting up Critolaus as a kind of scapegoat and deflecting the Stoic charge onto the followers of Critolaus.[40]

The crucial elements of its defensive strategy are to argue, first, that the "correct" Peripatetic account does not conceive of *eudaimonia* as an aggregate of virtuous acts and other (nonpsychic) goods, but as something that is made up of virtuous acts alone; yet, second, that there is still a difference between the life of virtue, as such, and a life of virtue which is also eudaimonic,[41] a difference that can be captured by the notion of "primary acts (of virtue)." The argument clearly assumes that *all* "primary acts" are also noble/fine (καλαί), but not vice versa. For, on the one hand, if all noble (i.e., virtuous) acts were also primary, then the addition of "primary" would be redundant, and the whole thesis would turn out to be identical with Stoicism. If, on the other, primary actions did not have to be noble, then *eudaimonia* could turn out to be composed of actions of which some are just noble, others noble and primary, and others again just primary (but not noble). As a consequence, *eudaimonia* would loose the purity of its noble or fine character. Accordingly, the notion of "primary actions" (προηγούμεναι πράξεις) is here reserved for a subset of the acts of virtue.

The success of this defense against Stoic criticism depends on whether or not it is possible to show that the restriction of *eudaimonia* to those "primary acts" does not, in some surreptitious way, dilute the ethical purity of the eudaimonic life. To this end, the argument uses analogies taken from the field of technical skills, namely pipe-playing and medicine. We may flesh out the example of pipe-playing as follows: For a piper to produce an optimal result, i.e., an optimal performance of a certain piece of music, he or she needs, aside from mastery of the art, a well-made pipe, health, the

---

part of an argument addressing the worry that the *symplêrôma*-account could have the consequence that someone would be justified in forgoing virtue for the sake of a greater amount of nonpsychic goods (cf. White [2002] 89; Hahm [2007] 66f.).

[40] I do not think the criticism directed at Critolaus relates primarily to his alleged confusion between constitutive and instrumental goods (Hahm [2007] 70). This is, rather, a corollary of the argument, whose main charge is that Critolaus fails to preserve the pure nobility of the eudaimonic life.

[41] See also 131.12f., which states that not every fine/noble activity is eudaimonic (οὐ πᾶσαν δὲ καλὴν πρᾶξιν εὐδαιμονικὴν ὑπάρχειν); 145.3–6, which emphasizes that the difference between the eudaimonic life and the virtuous life (καλὸς βίος) lies in the fact that the former requires a persistent endowment with natural goods (τὰ κατὰ φύσιν), whereas the former can be maintained also under circumstances that conflict with our nature (τὰ παρὰ φύσιν); 132.8–19 (= T-8 below), a text that I am going to interpret in part 4 of this essay.

absence of interfering noise etc.[42] The optimal performance in the case of pipe-playing is the analogon of the "primary" acts in the domain of virtue. Since optimal performance is a goal inherent to a τέχνη (art/skill) such as pipe-playing, the analogy suggests that the orientation toward "primary acts of virtue" is *not* the result of interests foreign to virtue but corresponds to goals inherent to virtue itself.

The argument also stresses that even under worse conditions and with inferior instruments, the player's art will be on display since he or she will still produce the *relatively* best result; but the outcome/performance will not be optimal as such. "Productive goods" do, hence, contribute to the success of the performance, yet they do not do so as *parts* of the performance (unlike playing a short sequence of notes, which is a *part* of playing the whole piece). Similarly, the nonpsychic goods that contribute to virtuous *praxis* so as to render it "primary" do not do so as parts of the activity but only in the manner of "productive goods," externally supporting the optimal, and hence eudaimonic, manifestation of virtue.

Our interpretation of this argument receives further support from a passage in a short dialectical treatise by Alexander of Aphrodisias (or a follower) (CAG suppl. II.1: 160.31–161.3).[43] It uses the example of pipe-playing in order to justify the following two observations: First, there are two different levels of performance by a skilled piper (or, analogously, by a virtuous agent), one that counts as primary since it has optimal results

---

[42] I am following here the way in which Alexander of Aphrodisias (or a follower) fleshes out this example in *Mant.* (CAG suppl. II.1) 160.31–161.3.

[43] This passage is part of a treatise (listed as sec. 20 of the *Mantissa* in Sharples [2008]) which collects dialectical arguments representing a Peripatetic critique of the Stoic self-sufficiency thesis. The collection belongs, of course, to the late (post-Hellenistic) Peripatos, but it contains a lot of argumentative material that harks back to the Hellenistic debates. (Cf., for instance, the way in which Striker [1986] makes use of this text for the reconstruction of second-century BC debates). In line with the dialectical nature of this treatise, the argument cited relies on the Stoic premise that virtue itself *is* a τέχνη, namely the art (τέχνη) of living (whereas Aristotle would allow only for a limited analogy between virtuous action and the practice of a τέχνη). As good Aristotelians, Alexander and his school do not share this Stoic assumption. Yet the other key features of this argument are fully in line with the Peripatetic stance: first, the distinction between two levels of performance, one of which is activity supported by the requisite goods (ἐν προηγουμένοις), while the other is activity with inferior tools and under inferior circumstances; second, the connection between the primary, or desirable, mode of activity and the inherent *telos* of a virtue. On the conceptual link between the phrases ἐνέργεια ἐν προηγουμένοις and προηγουμένη ἐνέργεια compare my brief remarks above and in Szaif 2012: 205–8. (There is a textual issue in line 161.2; cf. Giusta [1961/62] 254, n. 1; Huby [1983] 126; and the text and critical apparatus in Sharples [2008] 243; it does not affect the main point of the argument.)

thanks to the availability of the *requisite* tools and circumstances, and another with suboptimal results owing to *deficient* tools and circumstances.[44] Second, the inherent goal (*telos*) of a τέχνη such as pipe-playing (or, analogously, of a virtue) is optimal performance, supported by the requisite tools and circumstances. Since virtue shapes the agents' intentions, the fact that something is an inherent goal of a virtue entails that this goal also informs the intentions of a virtuous agent. The reasoning of this passage does, hence, support the idea that the difference between primary and secondary acts of virtue is grounded in the ways in which virtue directs our desires toward certain optimal performances.[45]

T-2 also provides some more information regarding other value terms, information that we should compare with the divisions of "good" in the previous segments. In connection with its criticism of Critolaus, T-2 distinguishes between *parts* of a life's activity, which are themselves activities, and the external necessary conditions (ὧν ἄνευ ἀδύνατον) that need to be fulfilled if such a life is to be not just virtuous but also happy (130.8–12). There is an obvious correlation between the modal import of the term ἀναγκαῖον ("necessary"), used in the previous set of divisions, and the phrase ὧν ἄνευ ἀδύνατον (lit., "without which it is impossible"). As mentioned before, it is clear that we are dealing here with *hypothetical* necessity.

The "parts" are also said to be "symplerotic" (συμπληρωτικόν). This technical term, which I left untranslated, is used by the Stoics and Critolaus alike.[46] It designates *parts* that *jointly make up (or "fill") a whole*. According to Critolaus' theory (which I am calling the "*symplêrôma*-account"), the human *telos* is made up of goods from all three classes of goods, including somatic and external goods (in addition to the goods of the soul). Yet, according to the argument in T-2, somatic and external goods function only as external enabling conditions. Their contribution to *eudaimonia* must therefore be of the type of merely "productive" goods (ποιητικά), as opposed to symplerotic goods.

Although the term ποιητικά can also be found in Aristotle's ethics and in the *MM*, the contrasting use of the terms ποιητικά and συμπληρωτικά seems to be characteristic of later Hellenistic debates.[47] However, the cru-

---

[44] See also CAG suppl. II.1: 167.9-13.

[45] See also Aspasius (CAG XIX.1) 24.3–7, commenting on *EN* 1099a31–33. Aspasius uses the same examples as T-2, pipe-playing and medicine.

[46] On the meaning of the term, cf. Moraux [1973] 329, n. 29; Szaif [2012] 155–60 and n. 9 (p. 154f.).

[47] *SVF* 107 documents the contrasting use of ποιητικά and τελικά (which also found its way into Doxography C; cf. 134.17–19) and the link between the notions τελικά and

cial underlying idea, the conceptual contrast between a constitutive part (μέρος) of *eudaimonia* and an external necessary condition, is already articulated in *EE* I.2, 1214b11–27 and thus has a good Aristotelian pedigree.[48]

Another noteworthy feature of the argument in T-2 concerns the term καλόν ("noble"), used to characterize an action as virtuous. The argument suggests that the activity of a virtuous agent is no less virtuous under unfavorable circumstances than under favorable ones, just as the actions of a skilled craftsperson are always equally manifestations of his or her skill, even if the results are not optimal owing to the deficiency of the tools, materials, etc. In other words, detrimental circumstances do not diminish the character of the action, or performance, as noble (καλή) or artful respectively. This tenet seems to be a concession (if we want to call it that) to the Stoic principle that virtuousness does not come in degrees. Yet since only virtuous practice supported by the requisite "productive goods" is eudaimonic according to T-2, we are faced with a sharp distinction between ethical correctness (expressed as "nobility") and eudaimonic quality. There are, to be sure, Aristotelian precedents that gesture in this direction, but it would be hard to pinpoint a similarly clear-cut conceptual distinction in Aristotle between an action's nobility or moral beauty (καλὴ πρᾶξις) and its eudaimonic quality.[49] I suspect the tendency in Aristotle is to view the

___

συμπληρωτικά. (Cf. also *SVF* 146 and Cicero *Fin.* III.41.) The Stoics acknowledge goods that are both symplerotic and productive, viz. the virtues. There is no trace of this mixed class in Doxography C.

[48] See also *Pol.* 1328a21–37. *EE* I.2 calls the external necessary conditions "ὧν ἄνευ οὐχ᾽ οἷόν τε [or οὐκ ἐνδέχεται]" (1214b11–15, 24–27). This differs only verbally from the "ὧν ἄνευ ἀδύνατον" in T-2. The same distinction between parts of *eudaimonia* and external necessary requirements was also defended by Xenocrates (cf. Clemens Alexandrinus, *Strom.* II.22.133.5–6). Inwood 2014 (137f., n. 19), in a comment on Szaif (2012), suggests that this way of connecting the terminology of symplerotic parts with Aristotle's use of the term "part" in *EE* I.2 is problematic (a "conflation"), but he does not elaborate his reasons. I would, of course, also emphasize that this is a new terminologocial tool. Yet in both cases, the key idea seems to be that of a contrast between constitutive parts and external enabling, or supporting, factors.

[49] Aristotle's usage of this terminology is not easy to reduce to a common denominator, and since this is not an essay on Aristotle, I can only gesture at some of Aristotle's own statements. There are passages in Aristotle that use καλῶς ζῆν as equivalent to *eudaimonia* or εὖ ζῆν, as pointed out in Bonitz' *Index Aristotelicus* (e.g., *EE* 1214b6–17, 1215a9–11; *Pol.* 1278b21–23). However, these passages do not preempt the Stoic self-sufficiency view. In an Aristotelian context, this equivalence implies, rather, that the beauty/nobility of one's life-style depends, at least to some extent, also on favorable external circumstances. The related idea that the moral beauty of the virtuous agent's conduct is a matter of degrees, rather than just a matter of correct versus incorrect behavior, is clearly implied in his

desirable actions that contribute to a virtuous agent's *eudaimonia* as *more* "beautiful" (καλαί) than perseverance in the face of misfortune.

3

Having completed my perusal of III-a, I would now like to return to the topic of primary actions. The crucial question to be addressed is why acts of virtue that sustain the agent's *eudaimonia* are called "primary." It cannot simply be the fact that they sustain *eudaimonia*, as this would lead into a circle of reasoning: *eudaimonia* would be defined as something composed of primary acts of virtue, while the primary acts of virtue would be defined as those acts of virtue that make up *eudaimonia*. We need an independent reason for singling out a subset of virtuous actions as sustaining *eudaimonia*. (Our discussion of the analogy with the piper already pointed in the right direction.) We should also still wonder what the precise meaning of the term προηγούμενον is when applied to actions. My translation as "primary" is, for the time being, only tentative.

The term προηγούμενον is derived from the verb προηγέομαι (and is, hence, unrelated to the somewhat similar sounding Stoic term προηγμένον,

---

argument for why virtuous *political* activity is "more noble" (κάλλιον), and thus ranks higher, than virtuous activity in one's private domain (*EN* 1094b7-11; cf. 1177b16f.). Compare also his notion of a "beautiful death" in his discussion of courage (*EN* 1115a32-b6): In quintessential acts of courage, the agent is willing to risk death, knowing that the circumstances and goals of his action would render his death "noble/beautiful." However, in certain other life-threatening situations, such as shipwreck, the agent's conduct would still reflect his courageous character disposition but lack this kind of ethical beauty or nobility. In passages that specifically address the question of the virtuous agent's conduct in the face of great misfortune (especially in *EN* I.8-10), Aristotle's position is quite nuanced and not easy to pin down. In 1099a32f., he states that it is "impossible, or [at least] not easy," to act "beautifully" (τὰ καλὰ πράττειν) without the requisite tools and circumstances. Yet shortly afterwards, he also emphasizes that the nobility of a person's character will "shine through" even in distressing situations (1100b30-33). The virtuous agent will always make the best out of the given circumstances (ἐκ τῶν ὑπαρχόντων ἀεὶ τὰ κάλλιστα πράττειν, *EN* 1100b35-1101a6; cf. 1100b20-22) and thus avoid a failed life. Yet his life will still fall short of *eudaimonia* if struck by great misfortune (1100b33-35, 1101a6-13). The good person will deal with a *bad* situation in a correct/noble manner (καλῶς), although *such* an action (as opposed to the virtuous agent's use of good circumstances) will count as fine/noble (καλαί) not *simpliciter* (ἁπλῶς), but only *relative to the circumstances* (implied in *Pol*. VII.13 1332a19-25). While these statements in *EN* I.8-10 and *Pol*. VII.13 assure us that virtue can prove itself in the face of misfortune, they are also compatible with what seems to be Aristotle's general stance, namely the view that the beauty of virtuous conduct can fully and properly manifest itself only when not obstructed, or marred, by detrimental circumstances (*EN* 1099a33-b6, 1100b25-30; cf. Szaif [2012] 147-54, Annas [1993] 382f.).

Two Conceptions of "Primary Acts of Virtue" in Doxography C 177

"preferred"). The basic literal meaning of the verb is something like "to go first and lead the way" (as stated in LSJ), and from there we get to usages of the participle προηγούμενον and the adverb προηγουμένως in the sense of "primary" or "primarily" (as opposed to "secondary," "derivative," "accidental," etc.).[50] When used as an attribute of actions, one might translate this term as "first-rate" (Fortenbaugh [1983] 212f.), for instance, or just stick to the basic meaning "primary," as I have been doing here, following Sharples (2010).[51] The term as such is nowhere defined in Doxography C, although it does offer an account of what kinds of virtue-governed activity can count as "primary" (132.8–19, cited as T-8 below). Since T-8 does not define the *meaning* of this expression, and since, moreover, I believe that it implies a different theory of "primary activity" than the one articulated in T-2, I am going to disregard this passage until we have surveyed some of the other available evidence.

In 144.19–20, we find the following statement:

T-3   The virtuous person (ὁ σπουδαῖος) will engage in political activity (πολιτεύεσθαί) in a primary manner (προηγουμένως), [i.e.] not [just] because of particular circumstances (μὴ κατὰ περίστασιν).

The passage to which T-3 belongs talks about the virtuous agent's choices that enter into his life-plan. Circumstances permitting, political activity is going to be included in such a life-plan. It will not be chosen only on account of certain particular circumstances necessitating such a choice (as, for instance, seeing a doctor is a merely circumstantial choice in reaction to illness). Rather, it is a "first choice" for a virtuous agent, and in that sense something chosen and done προηγουμένως ("in a primary manner").

For further confirmation, we can look at how the activity of getting yourself drunk, mentioned at the end of the following quotation, is described as *not* being "primary":

T-4   For [the virtuous person] will prefer to engage in both noble actions and the study (θεωρεῖν) of noble things (τὰ καλά); yet if the opportunities of life (οἱ καιροί) prevent his engagement with both [kinds of activity], he will commit himself to only one of them; he will grant greater worth to the activity of

---

[50] The use of the adverb προηγουμένως in opposition to κατὰ συμβεβηκός can be documented already for Theophrastus (*De igne* 14; cf. Dirlmeier [1937] 19). For examples from later Peripatetic literature, compare, for instance, Aspasius (CAG XIX.1) 81.21, 96.35, 145.7; Alexander of Aphrodisias, *Mant.* (CAG suppl. II.1) 150.11, 166.18, 177.8; idem, *Eth. Qu.* (CAG suppl. II.2) 119.11; Anonymus, *In II–V EN* (CAG XX) 125.24, 170.17. Cf. also Alcinous 4.1, 30.3, 32.7; Sextus Empiricus, *Math.* I.169.

[51] Similarly von Arnim [1926] 31.

study, yet, because of [his] social nature (τὸ κοινωνικόν), strive to perform political actions. For this reason [*i.e., because of his social nature*, JSz], he will also marry, beget children, engage in politics, fall in love in the manner of temperate love, and [even] get himself drunk during social gatherings—although he will not do so in a primary way (μὴ προηγουμένως). (144.4–11)

The idea behind the comment on getting drunk is that participation in certain social functions that require getting drunk (celebrations, *symposia*, and the like) is a vital aspect of an excellent social life-style grounded in the social nature of human beings. Yet virtuous people do not get drunk because drunkenness attracts them, but because this is a concomitant of something else they hold desirable, viz. involvement in those important manifestations of a social life.[52]

T-3 and T-4 together give us an idea of what the key point of this terminology in the context of Doxography C might be: There are certain activities a virtuous person finds desirable in themselves, which is why he or she chooses them προηγουμένως, or as προηγούμενα, and not just compelled by the circumstances or because of certain hypothetical necessities (as in the case of heavy drinking during a *symposium*).[53] Note that texts that belong to the Stoic and Platonist traditions also document the terminological use of προηγουμένως and προηγούμενον in connection with activities that would be the virtuous person's first choice. Hierocles and Doxography B can be cited for the Stoic tradition, Alcinous for the Platonist tradition.[54] This was, hence, an established usage.

There is another passage in Doxography C that corroborates the connection specifically between primary activity and *desirability*, 126.12–127.2. (In my breakdown, it belongs to part II, the exposition of a Peripatetic version of the theory of *oikeiôsis*.) The passage in question formulates a refutation of the *symplêrôma*-account of the human *telos* associated with Critolaus. Its main argument against Critolaus is essentially the same as the one that was included in the reasoning of T-2. Since criticism of Critolaus is not my topic here, I am going to focus on the part of the argument that bears directly on the notion of "primary actions":

---

[52] I take it that the clause κἂν εἰ μὴ προηγουμένως refers back only to μεθυσθήσεσθαι κατὰ συμπεριφοράς, not to the earlier items in the list. The item mentioned second to last, viz. ἐρασθήσεσθαι τὸν σώφρονα ἔρωτα, is a primary activity since it exercises a *virtuous* kind of *erôs*.

[53] On T-3 and T-4 see also Hirzel (1882) II: 815f.; Giusta (1961/62) 251; Sharples (2007) 633.

[54] Cf. Hierocles *apud* Stobaeus IV.22a.22 (p. 502.9–14 Hense); Doxography B, 109.10–18, 111.5–9; Alcinous 2.3, 3.2; see also Moraux (1973) 416, n. 310.

T-5 [...] but [the *telos* is,] rather, (i) to live virtuously surrounded by (ἐν)[55] somatic and external goods, either all or most and the most significant ones; which is why (ii) happiness (*eudaimonia*) is virtuous activity in primary (προηγούμεναι) actions as one would wish (κατ' εὐχήν). (iii) Bodily and external goods are called things "productive" (ποιητικά) of happiness since they, if present, make some contribution (συμβάλλεσθαί τι) to happiness. (126.16–22)

The clause immediately preceding T-5 contains a statement against the idea that the *telos* is a *symplêrôma* inclusive of nonpsychic goods. T-5 then offers a correct formulation, (i), of what the *telos* is and links it, in the next clause (ii), to a definition of *eudaimonia*. The latter formulation includes a reference to the wishes of the virtuous agent and thus renders explicit what we merely stipulated in light of T-3 and T-4, namely that there is a connection between the desirability of a virtuous action and its status as "primary."

Since T-5 claims that formulation (ii) can be justified with reference to formulation (i), we should compare the two. Note that for the Peripatetics, unlike the Stoics, talk of the "human *telos*" and talk of "human *eudaimonia*" amount to the same thing.[56] The *definientia* in formulations (i) and (ii) should, hence, be interchangeable, and we might also expect some correspondence between their components. It is not difficult to see how "living virtuously" (κατ' ἀρετὴν ζῆν) and "virtuous activity in ... actions" (ἐνέργεια κατ' ἀρετὴν ἐν πράξεσι ...) are interchangeable. But how about the added qualifications? In (i), we get (a) "surrounded by somatic and external goods" (ἐν τοῖς περὶ σῶμα καὶ τοῖς ἔξωθεν ἀγαθοῖς), which is then further qualified by (b) "either all or most and the most significant ones" (ἢ πᾶσιν ἢ τοῖς πλείστοις καὶ κυριωτάτοις). There is nothing in (ii) that would correspond to the differentiation between the two levels of supply

---

[55] The (somewhat odd) formulation that eudaimonic virtuous activity takes place, lit., "in" (i.e., among, or surrounded by) such goods has several parallels in Doxography C: 130.20f., 131.5f., 132.8–12, 144.21f., 145.3–5; see also 118.13f., 119.19, 134.2–4. In each case, the idea seems to be that the things "in which" virtuous and eudaimonic activity unfolds are the goods external to the soul, or the good circumstances that support the agent's activity. The same idea also underlies the later Peripatetic practice of characterizing *eudaimonia* as virtuous activity ἐν προηγουμένοις (cf. n. 59 below). An Aristotelian precedent for this use of ἐν can be found in *Pol.* 1332a21 (cf. Schütrumpf [2005] 453 on this passage).

[56] The Stoics draw an ontological und conceptual distinction between the human τέλος (=εὐδαιμονεῖν) and the human σκοπός (=εὐδαιμονία) (cf. *SVF* III.16). A passage in Doxography C signals awareness of this distinction, only to dismiss it in favor of the simpler terminological practices of the "old" philosophers (130.21–131.3). We can assume that T-5 is also written with the assumption that the human *telos* and *eudaimonia* amount to the same thing.

mentioned in (b). Clause (a), on the other hand, has a counterpart in (ii), viz. (c): the qualification of the "actions" in question as "primary, as one would wish" (πράξεις προηγούμεναι κατ' εὐχήν).⁵⁷ The correspondence between (a) and (c) confirms that the status of an action as "primary" and its endowment with nonpsychic goods go hand in hand. Yet, as T-5 also emphasizes, these nonpsychic goods are desired only as ποιητικά, that is, in view of their instrumental function, not in their own right.

All this is still fully in line with what we learned from the discussion of the example of pipe-playing: The virtuous agent, qua virtuous, desires to act in an optimal way, which also requires certain nonpsychic instrumental goods. In this connection, however, we should also note that the focus on *nonpsychic* goods as the (apparently) only "productive," or instrumental, goods is a simplification; certain natural goods of the *soul* also have a "productive" rather than "symplerotic" function, for instance, good memory. Yet this is an aspect we can neglect here, as it is often neglected in the ancient discussions. The bone of contention is the status of the somatic and external assets.

Returning to the first sentence of T-2, we can now formulate the following interim result: Our review of some parallel passages has confirmed that the "primary actions" referred to in T-2 are actions that represent a virtuous agent's first choice. They stand in contrast with actions that such an agent would choose in response to adverse circumstances or because of certain necessities. This result also provides a justification for translating προηγούμενον as "primary" (in conformity with its basic meaning), with the understanding that, in this case, the implied contrast between "primary" and "secondary" hinges on a distinction between first choices and merely circumstantial choices.⁵⁸

The later Peripatetic commentators often speak of the favorable nonpsychic factors that support *eudaimonia* as προηγούμενα.⁵⁹ One might

---

⁵⁷ It is not entirely certain what the grammatical referent of the qualifying phrase κατ' εὐχήν is (ἐνέργειαν … κατ' ἀρετὴν or πράξεσι προηγουμέναις?); but even if we relate κατ' εὐχήν to virtuous activity, we are certainly meant to understand that the virtuous activity that fulfills the agent's wishes is not just virtuous but also primary.

⁵⁸ Giusta (1961/62) recognizes the connection between the status of an action as primary and the fact that virtuous agents choose such actions freely and in an unconstrained manner; but he goes too far when he claims that this term, in its philosophical use, actually came to mean "free" when applied to actions (cf. n. 67 below). His attempt to ground this alleged meaning also in the etymology of the word προηγέομαι (247f., 255) is unconvincing.

⁵⁹ Aspasius (CAG XIX.1) repeatedly states that eudaimonic activity takes place ἐν προηγουμένοις (26.14f., 112.18f., 173.31f., 151.10–13). Alexander of Aphrodisias, *Eth. Qu.* (CAG suppl. II.2) 148.31–33, affirms that the προηγούμενα "in" which eudaimonic action

therefore think that this concept revolves around the idea of a class of "primary goods" (other than virtue)—either "goods desirable in themselves" or, more generally, "(*prima facie*) preferable things"—and that the term προηγούμενον, when applied to activities, simply *means* "equipped with goods that are προηγούμενα."[60] Yet, first, Doxography C never calls the supportive goods προηγούμενα (which, however, could also be due to accidental loss or epitomization). Secondly, and more importantly, our discussion has already produced sufficient evidence to prove that the priority in question, at least from the point of view articulated in part III-a, is that of certain kinds of virtuous activity. The external (nonpsychic) supporting factors are merely "necessary goods," in the sense of hypothetical necessity. For this reason, the prioritizing among certain nonpsychic goods will depend on how the virtuous agent prioritizes among virtuous activities, and not *vice versa*.[61]

So, in order to explain the kind of priority indicated by the term προηγούνενος, our analysis has to start from the actions. There must be

---

unfolds are instrumental goods. In Doxography C, this phrase is definitely absent—*pace* Huby (1983) 127, who claims that the formulation in 130.18f. (her Bi1, my T-7 (1), quoted below) contains the phrase ἐν προηγουμένοις, thereby contradicting her own quotation of the same sentence on p. 123. This inadvertent error seems to have misled Russell (2010) 166, who, citing Huby, claims that Doxography C identifies *eudaimonia* as activity ἐν προηγουμένοις. There is an example of the phrase ἐν προηγουμένοις in the received text of Doxography A (50.11f.), as part of a doxographic report on the Peripatetics. Yet I am inclined to accept Wachsmuth's (and Hirzel's) emendation "... ἐν <βίῳ τελείῳ>," to be followed by προηγουμένην. This brings 50.11f. in line with the subsequent comments in 50.12–51.15. The segment 51.8–12 very clumsily interrupts the ongoing comments and repeats, in the third place, what probably was the original formulation in 50.11f. It is out of place also in view of the fact that the entire discussion from 48.12 until the transition in line 51.16 purports to be on the notion of the human *telos*, while the inserted bit purports to define *eudaimonia*. Cf. Hirzel (1882) 811–13, n. 1; Moraux (1973) 309, n. 17.

[60] Cf. Hirzel (1882) 820f.; see Giusta (1961/62) 234–40 for a critique of this kind of approach.

[61] This order of priority receives further confirmation through Alexander of Aphrodisias, *Eth. Qu.* (CAG suppl. II.2) 148.29-33: ὥστε εἴη ἂν ἡ εὐδαιμονία [...] ἐνέργεια κατ' ἀρετὴν ψυχῆς λογικῆς, προσκειμένου τοῦ γε "ἐν βίῳ τελείῳ" [...] καὶ ἔτι τοῦ "ἐν προηγουμένοις" διὰ τὸ δεῖσθαι ὀργάνων τὰς προηγουμένας τε καὶ βουλητὰς ἐνεργείας ("... which is the reason why *eudaimonia* ... is 'virtuous activity of the rational soul,' with the addition of 'in a complete life' ... and, furthermore, 'surrounded by primary [assets],' since the activities which are primary and such as one would wish require tools"). This quote shows that the supporting items or assets are understood as primary in virtue of the fact that the activities they support are primary and such as a virtuous agent wishes them to be. (On the received βουλητὰς, wrongly emended by Bruns, cf. Giusta [1961/62] 229: n. 1; Cooper [1985] 187, n. 18; Sharples [1990] 65, n. 221.)

something in the actions themselves that explains why they are called primary. This cannot be their virtuous character as such, as this would only constitute "nobility" (καλὴ πρᾶξις), nor can it be their role in constituting *eudaimonia*, since this, as we have seen, would lead into a circle of reasoning. Take the example in T-3 (also mentioned in T-4): the virtuous agent's preference for "political" activities, i.e., for activities through which a virtuous person could truly serve the community as a whole in a leadership role. It suggests that the "primary" status of such an activity presupposes, first of all, certain facts about human nature—in this case our social nature, which is the root for the agents' natural attachment to their socio-political community. Yet if the political activity is to involve a true commitment to the common good, it also presupposes a character formed through certain virtues, such as practical wisdom (φρόνησις) and justice. The fact that political activity belongs among a virtuous agent's first choices is, hence, not simply the result of a natural predisposition, but rather a result of the way in which the agent's natural social predisposition has been shaped and perfected by the acquired virtues.[62] All this is, I think, good Aristotelian doctrine that can be traced back to Aristotle's own ethical and political writings.[63]

Putting together a life-plan that contains one's preferred activities (such as political engagement or *theôria*) is clearly one of the tasks of practical wisdom (φρόνησις). Yet the choices of practical wisdom are also informed, at least in part, by values grounded in the agents' particular character virtues. The values of liberality, for instance, or of justice, are going to shape the virtuous agents' conception of their social interaction, and this will bear on how they conceive of the "primary activities" through which they hope to achieve a eudaimonic life.

Doxography C (at least in its preserved state) does not tell us anything about the connection between primary activities and particular virtues. We may therefore include, at least tentatively, some additional evidence

---

[62] There is (at least) one text in the Peripatetic corpus that uses the notion of προηγούμεναι ἐνέργειαι also outside the domain of virtuous acts. The anonymous scholia *In EN II–V* (CAG XX), which are believed to include material from the second-century AD Peripatetic Adrastus of Aphrodisias, mention προηγούμεναι ἐνέργειαι of both ἀρετή and κακία (230.27–32). Both kinds of "primary activity" are rendered possible by the agent's endowment with the requisite external goods. Yet also in the case of the vicious person, the term προηγούμεναι ἐνέργειαι does not simply mean "well-equipped acts"; it designates, rather, acts that are "primary" because they are full, unrestrained realizations of the bad intentional dispositions rooted in this person's character.

[63] I cannot argue for this claim here; it is one of the main themes of Szaif (2012).

Two Conceptions of "Primary Acts of Virtue" in Doxography C

from the Peripatetic commentator Aspasius. The extant parts of Aspasius' paraphrase commentary provide us with examples of the use of the notion of "primary activities" in connection with two *particular* virtues, liberality (ἐλευθεριότης) and courage. The crucial idea in these passages seems to be that the primary activities are those that really "typify" a certain virtue or, in other words, give us a correct idea of what this virtue is really about. It is, moreover, only through those quintessential applications of a virtue that the virtuous person can find full satisfaction.

Let us first look at the case of courage (ἀνδρεία, lit., "manliness"). Important as a background to Aspasius' discussion is the fact that Aristotle's treatise on courage does not search for an account that would apply equally to the entire broad range of phenomena that could be called instances of courage. Rather, he seeks to understand what the main point (or *telos*) of this virtue is by zooming in on certain exemplary situations for courageous action. The most exemplary situations for such a virtue are those in which it can achieve the most significant kind of καλόν (i.e., the most significant kind of noble deed). In the case of courage, according to Aristotle, these are situations of war in which a person risks his life for the sake of his country and his loved ones, thus (potentially) reaping a "beautiful death" (*EN* 1115a24–b6; cf. 1169a18–25). Aspasius (81.18–82.2), following Aristotle's explanations closely, observes that the courageous person would not want to face the risk of a pointless death that serves no higher purpose, such as death in a shipwreck. The agent's courage would show also in a situation like that, yet the essence of courage has to do with risking one's life in a noble manner for a noble cause. The situation of a shipwreck has nothing of the sort to offer. Accordingly, actions that might reap a "beautiful death" are the primary manner (προηγουμένως) of courageous conduct, whereas the agent's collectedness during situations such as a shipwreck will only be a *consequence* (ἕπεται) of his courageous disposition, not its fulfillment (81.28–30).

Liberality is defined by Aristotle as a correct attitude with regard to material wealth (money and things with monetary value), observing the right mean in acts of giving and taking (*EN* 1119b22–27). Yet giving rather than correct taking (or foregoing incorrect taking) is the main function of liberality (*EN* 1119b25f.; cf. 1120a4–21)—or, as Aspasius puts it, its "primary" activity and function (προηγουμένη ἐνέργεια/προηγούμενον ἔργον, 52.32–36, 97.27–32, 98.5–9). Although *taking correctly* is also a function of this virtue, encompassed by its definition, it is not the kind of activity that "typifies" liberality (98.5–9 καθ᾽ ὃ εἰδοποιεῖται; cf. 96.9–15). Accordingly, an instance of correct taking (for instance, collecting money that is owed to you when you are running short of money), although virtuous, is not chosen by the virtuous person strictly on its own merit, but (in Aspasius' words, 52.32–35) only ἐξ ὑποθέσεως,[64] i.e., on account of certain special circumstances. Thus we see Aspasius distinguish between acts that fall under the purview of a virtue according to its definition, and a subset of these acts that are not just applications of this virtue but "typify" it. In order to justify the primacy of certain applications of liberality over others, he rehearses reasons indicated by Aristotle—reasons such as the primacy of the good use of assets over mere acquisition and of doing good over accepting good deeds (97.18–27). Yet the general idea in the background seems to be, again, that not all applications of a virtue are also a fulfillment of this virtue. Only its primary applications represent a free and unhindered choice and can give joy or satisfaction to a virtuous agent (cf. Aspasius 151.32–152.8). Accordingly, applications of liberality which are not primary are chosen under *constraint* and do not please the agent.[65] They are mere *reactions* to certain circumstances,[66] unable to fulfill this virtue's inherent teleology.

As a general point emerging from the passages surveyed so far, we may retain that virtues, according to the Aristotelian and Peripatetic approach, do not just aim at *reacting* to given circumstances in the most correct manner, but seek after significant noble achievements generated by the agent's own choices. Such activity, being more than just a correct adaptation to the circumstances, requires the availability of appropriate tools and contexts of action; and this cannot be guaranteed by the agent's own efforts alone but is also a matter of luck.

These results still fall short of giving us a full theory of "primary activities," but they certainly give us a better understanding of what this terminology is about. They also confirm our thesis that the notion of "προηγούμεναι activities" does not simply *mean* "well-equipped activities,"[67] but designates

---

[64] On this terminology, cf. Aristotle *Pol.* 1332a7–11, which connects this phrase with actions that are necessitated by undesirable circumstances.

[65] Cf. Anonymus, *In EN II–V* (CAG XX), 181.14–19: οὐ γὰρ προηγουμένως λήψεται ὁ ἐλευθέριος, ἀλλ' ἀναγκαίως, [...] ὡς ἂν ἔχοι διδόναι. [...] διὸ καὶ ἐλλείπει κατὰ τὴν λῆψιν, καὶ οὐχ ἡδέως λαμβάνει (cf. *EN* IV.1, 1119b25f., 1120a26f., 1120a31–b2).

[66] Cf. Anonymus, *In EN II–V* (CAG XX) 230.32–35. (This passage probably requires a change of punctuation to restore the μέν ... δέ link, and perhaps also an emendation of ταῖς αἱρετωτέραις to τοῖς αἱρετωτέροις.)

[67] Very much to the point is Sharples' comment ([1990] 65, n. 220) that we need to distinguish between the meaning of a term and its implications relative to certain specific contexts of application; for instance, the primary acts of virtue are *free* in the sense that they are not chosen under constraint but on their own merit (as we also said above), but

acts of virtue that are *primary* because they fulfill the teleology of the virtue in question, or of virtue as a whole, yet need certain supporting goods in order to be carried out successfully.[68]

Before concluding this part of our discussion, we should also note that this theory entails that virtue (or the virtuous agent qua virtuous) pursues two materially different ends, which are ranked relative to each other as the minimal and the maximal goal of virtuous activity. The minimal goal is to act correctly in reference to the given (favorable or unfavorable) circumstances. T-2 uses the traditional term of ethical praise, καλὴ πρᾶξις, as a label for this minimal goal. Yet virtuous agents also have a maximal goal that goes beyond maintaining the correctness, or "nobility," of their conduct. This maximal goal is for their virtuous activity to unfold and flourish under favorable circumstances—for instance, to make plentiful generous gifts to worthy recipients rather than to share the last crumb of bread with a fellow inmate on death row.[69] The maximal goal pursued through virtuous activity coincides with the agent's natural overarching interest in

---

that does not show that the term προηγούμενος *means* "free" when applied to acts of virtue (*contra* Giusta [1961/62]). Likewise, just because acts of virtue can be προηγούμεναι only if the requisite tools and circumstances are available, it does not follow that προηγούμενος *means* "well-equipped" when applied to acts of virtue.

[68] Huby (1983) 126f. makes a tentative suggestion that points in the right direction, stating (with reference to Aspasius 52.32-35) that "the *prohêgoumenê* activity [...] is the *proper* and *special activity* of the liberal man." However, this does not yet explain why taking money under appropriate circumstances is not a *prohêgoumenê* activity, given that Aristotle defines the virtue of liberality as a mean with respect to both giving and taking (*EN* 1107b8f., 1119b22–26; cf. *EE* 1231b28f.). Sharples (1990) 65, n. 220 states that "in the case of a human agent simply *qua* human [primary activities] will be activities characteristic of human virtue *as such*, or [activities] that are primarily conducive to or constitutive of virtue." He also mentions that these are to be contrasted with activities that are "called for in particular and special circumstances, especially those that are less than favorable." This seems right, but still does not provide us with clear reasons for why a subset of virtuous activities is singled out as primary, or as most characteristic of virtue, such that the circumstances enabling them count as favorable. Von Arnim (1926) 31 declares that "primary activities" are activities that take place under conditions that agree with human nature ("nature" understood in its teleological sense of completed, or fully developed, nature). This, too, seems right, but does not answer the question just raised. My thesis here has been that a full answer to this question would require an analysis of the teleology of each particular virtue and of virtue as a whole.

[69] In this connection, we have to bear in mind that these are assertions about what kind of life is "happy" or desirable. We also have to abstract from certain moral intuitions we may have, intuitions that put particular emphasis on the value of suffering and compassion and that are rooted in certain religious traditions (e.g., the Judeo-Christian tradition, Buddhism).

leading a good and happy life (*eudaimonia*), since, for a virtuous agent, the goal of *eudaimonia* would have no content without an understanding of what the kinds of excellent performances are through which the excellent disposition of a soul (=*aretê*) can fully realize itself. The agent's notion of *eudaimonia* needs, hence, to be filled out with a conception of the "primary acts of virtue."

While the maximal goal determines the content of *eudaimonia*, the minimal goal must, accordingly, represent a lower achievement than *eudaimonia*. The distinction between a minimal and a maximal goal of virtuous activity thus correlates with the distinction in Doxography C between two levels of living that rank above a miserable (or "damned") life (κακοδαιμονία): Even under adverse circumstances, the constancy of the virtuous agent's noble conduct will guarantee that such a life does not deserve to be called miserable, as it does not completely miss the human *telos*. Yet it will also not be blessed (or eudaimonic). Such a "middling life"[70] would, hence, only be second best compared to the optimal life performance characterized by primary acts of virtue.

4

I am now going to look at some passages in the second half of part III, which I have labeled III-b (130.15–134.6). My goal is to show that these passages imply a significantly different view concerning the human *telos* and the notion of "primary activity" than what we find in III-a. We do not need to discuss III-b in its entirety. Yet a brief overview of its structure will help.

Superficially at least, III-b is simply a continuation of the discussion in III-a concerning the notion "good," its divisions, and the ways in which the different kinds of good things contribute to *eudaimonia*. III-b begins by adding another classification of things that are good, now also called "targets of action" (T-6 below). This is followed by a list of three alternate definitions of *eudaimonia* (T-7 below), the first of which is then going to be commented on (131.14–132.19). Contiguous with these comments, the text formulates answers to a number of standard questions in Hellenistic

---

[70] On the μέσος βίος, cf. 132.22–133.11, accepting von Arnim's conjecture ([1926] 33) for line 132.22: <οὔτ'> ἀναπόβλητον ἐπὶ τῶν σπουδαίων κτλ (with τὴν εὐδαιμονίαν as the implied subject of the implied infinitive εἶναι in the mode of indirect speech). See also 144.21–145.2 (yet this text is problematic since it seems to merge two different and independent(!) causes for why a life may be less than eudaimonic: the agent's own ἕξις and the level of supply with natural goods—cf. the comments on 144.21–145.2 in Bill Fortenbaugh's contribution to this volume, "Didymus on Types of Life").

ethics concerning *eudaimonia* such as: Is *eudaimonia* a matter of degree?, Can it be lost?, Is there an intermediate state between *eudaimonia* and misery?, etc. (132.20–134.6).

Sandwiched between the list of alternate definitions of *eudaimonia* and the comments, the text presents some remarks on conceptual differentiations affecting the notion *telos*, together with a list of three alternate definitions of *telos*,[71] followed by a distinction between goods, evils, and indifferent things on account of their different relations to the *telos*. Despite the very close thematic connections between discussions of the *telos* and of *eudaimonia*, this segment (130.21 till 131.12 or 13) seems out of place here as it not only interrupts the natural progression from the citation of the three definitions of *eudaimonia* to the comments on the first definition, but also does not contribute anything to these comments.

Let us look first at the new division of "good things" or "targets of action" introduced in 130.15–18:

> T-6 (1) "Good" is divided into what is noble/fine (καλὸν), what is beneficial (συμφέρον), and what is pleasant (ἡδύ);
> (2) and the particular actions (τῶν κατὰ μέρος πράξεων), on the one hand, have these as their targets (σκοποί),
> (3) while that which is composed of all of them (τὸ δ' ἐκ πάντων αὐτῶν), on the other, is *eudaimonia*.

First, we should note that this division of "good" does not harmonize with the preceding set of divisions. The earlier classification (129.6–17) included, to be sure, the class of noble things (καλά), while the category of beneficial goods (τὸ συμφέρον) in T-6 can be equated with the necessary goods in the earlier divisions, since "necessity" is there understood as hypothetical necessity and linked to the function of a "productive" and "contributive" good. Yet there is no room for pleasure as a good in the earlier divisions. Pleasure cannot, without further qualification, be subsumed under the category of τὸ καλόν, and it is also not a "necessary" good (in the sense of hypothetical necessity). Since the text in III-a defined "good," via the term "choiceworthy" (αἱρετόν), as that which can elicit our desire in a rationally approved way, it could also have listed pleasure—or, more

---

[71] The first two formulations provide formal definitions of the concept *telos*. The third is a real (or material) definition of the human *telos* that could also be used as a formula for *eudaimonia* (cf. von Arnim [1926] 26f.). It is identical with the definition of the human *telos* used in T-5. In my view, this segment might be a continuation of the argument in III-a and got to its current position as a result of the compilation of two sources accompanied by some reordering. For the purposes of this essay, we can disregard it.

precisely, certain kinds of pleasure—as one of the potential objects of rationally approved desire. But it did not.

The classification in T-6 has an important precedent in Aristotle's theory of the grounds of motivation. *EN* 1104b29–1105a1 presents it as a classification of objects of choice/desire (αἵρεσις). From Aristotle's perspective, however, it cannot function as a division of what is good, for the obvious reason that many pleasant things are merely *apparent* goods.[72] T-6 fails to acknowledge this. We might say, though, that this mistake is somewhat mitigated by the fact that the division is also presented as being of the *targets of action*, which would include all *de facto* motivating grounds and, as such, be in line with the Aristotelian precedent.

Essentially the same distinction also underlies the opening statement of the *EE* (1214a1–8; cf. *EN* 1099a7–31), which introduces the claim that the three grounds of motivation, designated by the notions "fine/noble" (καλόν), "good" (here, as so often, used in the sense of "beneficial/useful"), and "pleasant," are realized to the highest degree by *eudaimonia*. In the course of Aristotle's discussion of eudaimonic activities, it becomes clear that this *union* of the three motivating qualities is meant to be realized not just by the eudaimonic life as a whole but also by the particular actions that characterize a eudaimonic lifestyle (cf. *EE* 1248b16–37, 1249a17–21; cf. *EN* 1099a29).[73] Yet looking closely at how clause (2) of T-6 is formulated, we have to record that it suggests that particular actions have different targets such that some of them pursue pleasure (or pursue it primarily), others a useful outcome, while others again are motivated by their inherent nobility or the fineness of their objects.

In clause (3), the grammar of the sentence does not determine the antecedent of "them." Does it refer back to the three kinds of action or to the three kinds of incentives? It is more likely that "actions" is the antecedent, since we have repeatedly been told that the eudaimonic life is composed of

---

[72] In the Aristotelian perspective, there is, hence, a subtle distinction between objects of αἵρεσις and αἱρετά: while the former comprise all *de facto* objects of human choice/desire, including merely apparent goods, the latter include only things *worthy* to be desired.

[73] A similar idea also underlies Aristotle's taxonomy of kinds of friendship (*EN* 1155b17–19; *EE* 1236a7–16) on the basis of a division of three types of φιλητά, with the one difference that the category labeled καλόν is now labeled ἀγαθόν. This terminological switch has to do with the contingent linguistic fact that καλόν is the term of moral praise with respect to *actions*, while ἀγαθός/ἀγαθή is used to characterize a *person* as virtuous. In either case, the intended meaning is that something or somebody is appraised with respect to virtuousness. The claim associated with this division is that the best type of friendship (ethical friendship) unites all three characteristics (similarly to how *eudaimonia* comprises all three motivational stimuli).

actions. Note, moreover, the μὲν ... δὲ construction that specifically highlights the contrast between the particular actions and what is composed of "them." Hence, according to what I take to be the most likely reading, this clause expresses the claim that *eudaimonia* is a composite of the three different kinds of action specified by the three different kinds of motivational incentives. If this is the intended meaning, we would have departed from the original Aristotelian idea, which was to show that the typical activities of a eudaimonic life respond to all three kinds of incentive simultaneously. We would, moreover, also have moved away from the central claim of T-2, which asserted that the actions that make up the eudaimonic life are noble (καλαί) *throughout*. I am formulating this result hypothetically since it might be the unintended outcome of insufficient precision in the doxographer's phrasing.

The text continues with a list of three alternate definitions of *eudaimonia*:

> T-7 (1) *Eudaimonia* is "the primary (προηγουμένη) use (χρῆσις) of complete/perfect *aretê* in a complete life," or
> (2) "the virtuous activity of a complete life," or
> (3) "the unhindered use (χρῆσις ἀνεμπόδιστος) of *aretê* surrounded by (ἐν) the things that accord with nature." (130.18–21)

These formulations are presumably inherited from older Peripatetic sources and listed here in the manner of a doxographical collection.[74] Formulation (1) uses the new technical term προηγούμενος, which is not used in the *MM* but might still go back to the third century BC. It substitutes for the Aristotelian expression κεχορηγημένος ("well-equipped"; e.g., *EN* 1101a14–16). Although the two expressions are not synonymous (as we have seen), they both point to the role of nonpsychic factors in enabling eudaimonic practice (the latter directly, the former indirectly).

---

[74] Cf. Huby (1983) 131. Editors and commentators usually link formulation (2) to *EE* 1219a38f.; yet compared to the *EE* passage, (2) misses the τελείαν after ἀρετήν, which is essential in the context of the argument of the *EE* passage. (It might have been lost in the textual transmission of Doxography C.) As to (3), there is a good Aristotelian precedent for the use of the term "unhindered" (ἀνεμπόδιστος) in connection with eudaimonic activity (*EN* 1153b7-25, cf. *Pol.* 1295a36f). Aristotle also speaks, in this context, of the availability of somatic and external goods as that which allows for "unhindered activity." The terminology of "natural goods" (φύσει ἀγαθά) is also not foreign to Aristotle (cf. *EN* 1170a14–16, 1148a29f.; *EE* 1237b30–32, 1238a16–19, 1248b26–30, b39–1249a7, a24–b3, b16–21; cf. Szaif [2012] 62–67), yet he does not assemble these elements into one formula as we find it in (3).

Notwithstanding this terminological innovation, formulation (1) is certainly very close in spirit to what we find in Aristotle and in the *MM*. Regarding the phrase "use (χρῆσις) of *aretê*" (i.e., making use of one's *aretê*) instead of (the more typically Aristotelian) "activity (ἐνέργεια) in accordance with *aretê*," we can point to precedents in Aristotle's own works.[75] The two phrases are here meant to be interchangeable, as we can tell from the fact that the text of the comments on formulation (1) moves from one expression to the other without hesitation (130.18f., 132.8f., 10f.).

Of the three definitional formulae, (1) is the most complete, which might explain why it is singled out for further comments. It is obvious that the minimalist formulation (2) lacks some crucial elements.[76] As for definition (3), it fails to mention that the virtue in question has to be complete, or perfect, and that the life, too, should be complete. Yet one might object that (3) contains at least one element not present in (1), viz. reference to natural goods. But according to the comments on definition (1), the notion of "primary" activity entails the idea of an endowment with natural goods (132.9f.). By the same token, the notion of an "unhindered" activity is also implied, since adverse circumstances represent external evils (or things that *do not* accord with human nature).

The comments in 131.14–132.19 address three of the five elements of definition (1).[77] I will skip directly to what, for our purposes, is the most relevant piece, the discussion of the qualifying expression προηγουμένη:

T-8 (1) [They say that][78] the activity of *aretê* [*required for eudaimonia; JSz*] is "primary" (προηγουμένη), since it is entirely necessary that it take place (ὑπάρχειν) among natural goods (ἐν τοῖς κατὰ φύσιν ἀγαθοῖς);
(2) for the virtuous person (ὁ σπουδαῖος) would make right use (χρήσαιτ' ἂν καλῶς) of his *aretê* also among bad things (ἐν κακοῖς) [*i.e., under bad circumstances, deprived of natural goods; JSz*], yet not so as to be blest (*makarios*),

---

[75] Compare the use of the term χρῆσις in the argument of *EE* 1218b37–1219a39 (esp. 1218b37–1219a1, 1219a13–18, 24) and 1219b1f. See also *EN* 1098b31–1099a7, 1129b31–1130a1, 1130b18-20; *Pol.* 1328a37f., 1332a9; *MM* 1184b9–17, 31–36.

[76] It misses the qualification of the required *aretê* as complete (or perfect) and fails to mention that the use, or activity, should be "primary" (or "unhindered").

[77] The elements *not* commented on are the notions of "use" (χρῆσις) and *aretê*. I suspect that the compiler of Doxography C, or a later epitomizer, thought that it was not necessary at this point to include comments on the facts that *eudaimonia* is based on *aretê* and that it involves use rather than mere possession (κτῆσις) of *aretê*. These points have already been addressed in other passages. Compare the parallel text in Doxography A, 50.11–51.15, which distinguishes, and comments on, all five elements of the same formula, yet with different comments than C (cf. n. 59 above on this passage).

[78] Cf. εἶπον in 131.14.

and he would prove the nobility [of his character] (τὸ γενναῖον) [even] in tormenting situations,[79] yet not do so happily (εὐδαιμόνως).[80]
(3) This is due to fact (αἴτιον δ') that *aretê*, by itself, brings about (ἀπεργαστικὴ καθ' ἑαυτήν) noble things only (καλῶν μόνον), but *eudaimonia* both noble things and good things (καὶ καλῶν κἀγαθῶν).
(4) For (i) it [i.e., *eudaimonia*][81] does not wish (βούλεται)[82] to persevere through dreadful circumstances, but [wishes], rather, to enjoy the good things (τῶν ἀγαθῶν ἀπολαύειν),
in addition both to (ii) preserving justice in the community, and to (iii) neither depriving itself (ἀποστερεῖν ἑαυτήν) of the noble objects (καλά) in scientific study nor (iv) of the necessities of life.[83]
(5)[84] For *eudaimonia* is something most pleasant and most noble (κάλλιστον). (132.8–19)

Let us first look at segments (1)-(3) of T-8. We can summarize the train of thought by the following three claims, bearing in mind that the whole

---

[79] The meaning here could also be "under torture." Either way we have to think of situations causing great pain and distress.

[80] I see no compelling reason for changing the received εὐδαιμόνως (which contrasts with the καλῶς in the preceding clause) into εὐδαιμονήσει (Wachsmuth, Tsouni). The adverb is well formed, and the sentence in its received form gives a good sense. It does not, at any rate, make a difference for the interpretation whether or not we adopt Wachsmuth's emendation.

[81] The reflexive pronoun in "μήτε ἀποστερεῖν ἑαυτὴν …" in (4-iii) requires a feminine noun as the implied subject. The preceding sentence has two feminine nouns that could provide the subject, viz. *aretê* and *eudaimonia*. Since the description in (4) talks about the contents of *eudaimonia*, not of *aretê*, the former must be the implied subject of (4).

[82] Note the switch from the infinitive of indirect speech (quite consistently maintained throughout this text) to a finite verb in a main clause. This could be a sign that (4) is a literal quotation from some Peripatetic work. Yet I think it is more likely that it is the effect of an assimilation to the finite verb-form in the preceding ὅτι-clause: the γάρ-clause in (4) is meant to be read as a continuation of the explanation (αἴτιον δ') that begins with the ὅτι-clause in (3). (5) slides back into usual mode of indirect speech.

[83] von Arnim (1926) 30f. provides a short description of certain rhetorical features of clause (4). He surmises (quite plausibly) that a verb at the end of (4-iv) has been lost in the doxographic transmission that would have balanced the ἀποστερεῖν ἑαυτήν of (4-iii) and replicated the chiastic structure of (4-i). This could be a verb like ἐλλείπειν. Yet nothing essential for our interpretation depends on this.

[84] Editors of the Greek text have traditionally put a full stop, or even a paragraph break, before clause (5), "ἥδιστον γάρ τι …," and a comma at its end. It would thus represent the beginning of a new thought (so also in Sharples' 2010 translation and in Tsouni's text). Yet I agree with Hirzel (1882) II: 710, n. 2; von Arnim (1926) 31; and Moraux (1973) 356 that this γάρ-clause should be connected with the preceding argument (requiring only a change of punctuation). Clause (5) provides an important premise for this argument, which would not be complete without it (as I will try to show).

argument is meant to explain why a virtuous activity has to be primary in order to qualify as a constituent part of *eudaimonia*.

Supplementing an implicit premise, the reasoning of segment (1) can be paraphrased as follows:

> Claim 1: The virtue-governed activity that defines the happy life has to be primary, since (a) it has to be endowed with *natural goods* and (b) virtuous activity endowed with the requisite natural goods is of the *primary* sort.

As we noticed, the third definition of *eudaimonia* in T-7 also refers to the availability of natural goods (130.20f.). Claim 1 establishes a link between "primary" virtuous activity and the availability of certain goods that are "natural" (or, in other words, agree with human nature).[85] As we know from other contexts (e.g., 126.14-20), such supplementary goods tend to be identified with somatic and external goods.

Segment (2) of T-8 further elaborates on the connection between *eudaimonia*, *aretê*, and natural goods, providing a reason (ἐπεί) for why eudaimonic virtuous activities require an endowment with natural goods (cf. premise (a) in claim 1). It can be summarized as follows:

> Claim 2: While a virtuous person will act nobly even when deprived of natural goods, this will not suffice for a happy life.

Claim 2 obviously implies premise (a), since it is, in part, just its negative complement in the *modus tollens*. It allows to infer that the eudaimonic life requires the presence of certain nonpsychic ("natural") goods, since detrimental circumstances that deprive us of them, or cause the opposite evils, prevent *eudaimonia*. In addition, claim 2 also points out that, even under adverse circumstances, virtue will manifest itself in the form of noble conduct. This is in line with an idea expressed in T-2 and elsewhere in Doxography C (e.g., 131.122f., 145.3–6): virtue as such is sufficient for the nobility of one's actions, but not for *eudaimonia*.

Segment (3) purports to explain (αἴτιον δ') the facts expressed in (2). Yet the sentence causes some problems for the translation and interpretation. First, how are we to understand the connection that relates *eudaimonia* to noble and good things according to this passage? The text says

---

[85] In a later section of Doxography C, on the topic of life-styles, we find two more passages that affirm the correlation between a virtuous life lived happily and endowment with natural goods: 144.21–145.2 and 145.3–6. These two passages speak just of τὰ κατὰ φύσιν, not of τὰ κατὰ φύσιν ἀγαθά. But in the context of Peripatetic value theory these two expressions can be used interchangeably.

about *aretê* that it "brings about" noble things (i.e., noble actions), using an expression that can evoke the idea of a craft-like operation (ἀπεργαστική). Such language seems justifiable in light of the fact that *aretê* is the key causal factor shaping our actions. *Eudaimonia*, on the other hand, is a result, or outcome, rather than a cause. It is therefore odd that the expression ἀπεργαστική seems to carry over to the comment on *eudaimonia*, as if *eudaimonia* were something that "brings about" noble things and good things (rather than presupposing them). This strange manner of speaking might be due to a certain rhetorical impetus noticeable in this passage, which talks about *eudaimonia* in a quasi-personifying mode.[86] Yet it could also be the case that a word serving as the counterpart of ἀπεργαστική for the case of *eudaimonia* has been lost in the transmission.[87] However that may be, the basic idea is clear enough: we are, again, presented with the claim that virtue as such correlates with nobility, while *eudaimonia* includes good things in addition to just nobility.

The phrase "καὶ καλῶν κἀγαθῶν" ("both noble things and good things")[88] also causes problems. In light of the remarks in segment (4) of T-8, the term καλά should be taken to include both morally praiseworthy actions and noble activities of scientific and philosophical study, yet with an emphasis on moral praiseworthiness since we have just been invited to think of situations of noble conduct under tormenting circumstances. The term "good" (ἀγαθά), on the other hand, has to be taken in a nonmoral meaning (as is so often the case). In fact, it should be related to the notion

---

[86] Cf. the use of βούλεται in the subsequent clause; see also n. 83 above.

[87] An alternative solution can be found in Simpson (2014), whose translation construes the clause "ἡ δ' εὐδαιμονία καὶ καλῶν κἀγαθῶν" as an elliptical sentence with a genitive in the sense of "belonging to." This would yield the statement that *eudaimonia* "belongs to good and noble things." While grammatically viable, I hesitate to adopt this suggestion since it seems to me that it is much more natural to read the predicative "ἐστὶν ἀπεργαστική" as carrying over to the "δὲ …"-clause of this periodic "μὲν … δὲ …"-sentence. Fortunately, this difficulty does not affect the overall interpretation of this passage.

[88] The contrast with "καλῶν μόνον," I think, clearly requires that the "καὶ … καὶ …"-construction be translated as "both … and …" (rather than as "also … and …," which would result in the odd claim that *eudaimonia* has good-and-noble things *in addition to* noble things). This fact is perhaps somewhat obscured by the spelling of the phrase καὶ καλῶν κἀγαθῶν in the received text—with *crasis* of καὶ and ἀγαθῶν—which, in this particular case at least, may be nothing but the result of scribal conventions. However, once it has been agreed that the "καὶ … καὶ …" should here be translated as "both … and …," it still is an open question whether or not the καλά and the ἀγαθά mentioned in this sentence are identical ("things that are both noble and good") or belong to different sets ("both noble things and good things"). The Greek wording allows for both interpretations. I am opting for the latter alternative in light of how the words ἀγαθόν and καλόν are used in the other parts of T-8.

of "natural goods" mentioned in (1) and taken up in (4-i) if we want to preserve the coherence of the argument as a whole. Accordingly, the statement in (3) basically just reiterates that *eudaimonia* requires the availability of the requisite nonpsychic "natural" goods.

So far, so good. Yet there is still another worry relating to the phrase καὶ καλῶν κἀγαθῶν: Since T-8 distinguishes, as we have just seen, between noble activities on the one hand and natural goods on the other, we are entitled to assume that this phrase refers to two nonoverlapping sets of items (i.e., noble activities and natural goods). Yet Aristotle's own viewpoint would be more fittingly described as the claim that, in the case of *eudaimonia*, each of the activities, and also their supporting goods, are both good/beneficial and καλά—beneficial because both virtuous actions and supportive goods contribute to the agent's *eudaimonia*; καλά because they either are, or support and agree with, virtuous activities. However, this is not the strategy pursued in T-8, as will become more obvious when we look at segment (4) of T-8.[89]

Although segment (3) purports to explain what is said in (2), it more or less only reiterates, or summarizes, what was implied in (1) and (2). We can paraphrase the argument expressed in (3) as follows:

> Claim 3: Virtuous activity in bad circumstances does not yield a happy life (cf. claim 2), because virtue, just by itself, only guarantees that one's conduct is noble (i.e., ethically correct or praiseworthy), whereas happiness involves, in addition

---

[89] When the expressions καλόν and ἀγαθόν are used in conjunction, this typically serves to denote persons or things that are both good and noble. As has often been observed, the phrase οἱ καλοὶ καὶ ἀγαθοί, in its original application, articulates the traditional self-image of the Greek aristocratic class. Socratic authors, on the other hand, tend to detach this notion from its class associations in order to give it a new sense informed by a rationalist approach to ethics. The corresponding virtue can be called καλοκαγαθία (also mentioned in some passages of Doxography C, including part III-b, 131.16f.; cf. n. 93 below). Aristotle formulates his own understanding of καλοκαγαθία in *EE* VIII.3, and a key element in his explication of this virtue is the claim that, for those who embody it, all good things are also noble things (καλά), and vice versa. This is how we get to the idea that, from the perspective of an accomplished human being, the καλά and the ἀγαθά form two identical sets (see esp. *EE* 1248b37–1249a16). I am arguing that this is not what we find in T-8, since the goods are here understood as natural nonpsychic goods, and those are no longer included among the καλά. In this connection, we should bear in mind that these late Hellenistic sources are not, in general, beholden to the *precise* ways in which Aristotle argues his position; rather, they try to formulate a (broadly defined) Aristotelian standpoint for the dialectical purposes of the debates in the second and first centuries BC (cf. Szaif [2016])—which involves varying degrees of adjustment to argumentative strategies and terminological practices characteristic of the late Hellenistic period (see also n. 97 below).

Two Conceptions of "Primary Acts of Virtue" in Doxography C 195

to the nobility of one's conduct, also the presence of what is good (i.e., the presence of the natural goods mentioned in claim 1).

Up to this point, the formulations in T-8 can still be considered compatible with T-2. We would have to equate the natural goods of T-8 with the good "material" circumstances of T-2. But this would not be illegitimate. Yet the picture will change once we include the rest of T-8 in our analysis. Let us look first at the statements in (4).[90]

The implied subject of sentence in (4) (until "necessities of life") is *eudaimonia*.[91] The passage lists several basic intentions inherent in, and satisfied by, the eudaimonic life. I count the pair of complementary requirements mentioned in (4-i) as the *first* intention: The eudaimonic life "wishes" or "wants" to enjoy good things rather than to persevere in the face of "dreadful" things (i.e., situations or objects that can induce fear and pain). Since T-8 sets out with a reference to good things in the sense of "natural goods," and since this class was primarily meant to include certain somatic and external goods, this is also how we should understand the "good things" mentioned in this line. This reading is also supported by the fact that the dreadful things (δεινά) with which the good things are contrasted clearly mean external or somatic evils.

The intention of enjoying natural goods (and avoiding the opposite evils) is said to come in addition to (πρὸς τῷ) three other intentions listed in the subsequent clauses: intention (ii), which aims at the preservation of justice in the community; intention (iii), opportunities for studying the "noble" objects of theoretical science; and intention (iv), procurement of the necessities of life.[92] Justice functions here as a communal virtue and as

---

[90] This part of T-8 is rarely mentioned, let alone analyzed, in the secondary literature on Doxography C. Annas (1993) 417, for instance, cites and discusses only the first two segments of T-8.

[91] Cf. n. 81 above.

[92] There is some uncertainty regarding the scope of the πρὸς τῷ. Like most of the other translators (Sharples [2010]; Simpson [2014]; and Tsouni in this volume), I take it to include all three intentions (ii)–(iv). Gigon (1961) takes it to include only (ii), while (iii) and (iv), though still governed by the finite verb βούλεται, are not included in the scope of the πρὸς τῷ. This is certainly possible grammatically. If we follow Gigon, the καί in (ii) (= 132.16) should be translated as "also." If we follow the majority of translators, we should identify a καὶ ... καὶ ...-construction in (ii) and (iii). The subsequent μήτε ... μήτε (iii and iv) would then be subordinate to the second καί. I am opting for this latter construal, while acknowledging the viability of the other alternative. My overall interpretation would also stand if we adopted Gigon's construal, since the crucial point for my interpretation is the observation that the *enjoyment* of natural (nonpsychic) goods is here added as a distinct component of *eudaimonia*. It has to be a distinct component, since (iii) and (iv) cannot just

an exemplary ethical achievement.[93] Mentioning justice right after "enjoyment of goods" is very fitting, since these natural goods are also very often "contested goods"[94] whose acquisition and distribution has to be regulated by the norms of justice according to standard Aristotelian analysis. The noble things contemplated in *theôria* are contrasted with the necessities of life. This coupling may be rhetorical, the author wishing to contrast the most elevated ingredient of a good life, i.e., *theôria*, with its most basic prerequisites (for instance, the availability of sufficient food). Or it might hark back to the Aristotelian claim that the performance of *theôria*, as such, does not require more than the basic level of external and somatic goods.[95]

Since the absence of dreadful circumstances and fulfillment of our basic needs are mere preconditions of happiness, we are left with three types of activity that together lift a life to the level of *eudaimonia*: scientific study/contemplation, practicing justice in the community, and enjoyment of natural goods. This outcome partially agrees with the ideal of a "combined" life-style (βίος σύνθετος) endorsed elsewhere in Doxography C.[96] Yet while the βίος σύνθετος, as it is usually described, integrates the political (or social) with the philosophical life-style, T-8 goes further in that it also includes the activity of enjoying natural goods as a distinct component of the eudaimonic life. In this connection, we need to emphasize that the Greek term translated as "enjoyment" (ἀπολαύειν) does not just mean acquisition or possession of such goods. We are talking here about activities such as enjoying a good and healthy meal or enjoying nice companionship, which correspond to natural human needs that go beyond the

---

be a fleshing out of the point about enjoying natural goods, as those do not include the καλά contemplated in pure science (*theôria*) and go beyond the necessities that merely satisfy our basic needs.

[93] Cf. 131.16f., which also belongs to the comments on T-7 (1). I take it that in 131.16f. justice functions as the highest ethical virtue, while καλοκἀγαθία is the highest rational virtue, as it is in 137.14-23. (The more orthodox understanding of καλοκἀγαθία, in line with *EE* VIII.3, can be found in 147.22–25.)

[94] Cf. *EN* 1168b19, 1169a21; *EE* 1248b27.

[95] Cf. *EN* 1177a27–34, 1178a23–35. The κατὰ τὸν βίον ἀναγκαῖα mentioned in this passage of T-8 should be distinguished from the much more inclusive sense of the term ἀναγκαῖα in part III-a, 129.8-17, of Doxography C, which I discussed in section 2 of this chapter. The latter, more inclusive, use comprises all goods that are conducive to living and living well (*eudaimonia*), while the former seems to follow the common practice in Aristotle's ethics of calling ἀναγκαῖα all those goods that only serve our basic needs (cf. n. 24 above). In T-8, the ἀναγκαῖα are distinguished both from the καλά contemplated in *theôria* and from the goods that are a source of enjoyment and thus an aspect of living well.

[96] Cf. 144.4–8 together with 144.16f.

necessities for mere survival. At first blush, one might think that the source of T-8 wants to supplement the "combined life" with a third life-style mentioned by Aristotle, the βίος ἀπολαυστικός ("life of gratification"), identified by the same Greek verb ἀπολαύειν. Aristotle famously dismisses this life-style as a life for brutes, beneath the dignity of a rational living being (*EN* 1095b14-22, cf. 1178b24-32). For this reason, T-8's vindication of ἀπολαύειν seems surprising in an Aristotelian context (cf. Hirzel [1882] 710f.). Yet we have to take into account that in T-8 this form of enjoyment or gratification is understood as an aspect of primary virtuous activity (cf. 132.8f.) or of the primary use of *aretê* (cf. 130.18f., 132.10f.). What Aristotle had in mind when he rejected the apolaustic life-style was a form of enjoyment or gratification not moderated and coordinated by virtue and prudence. This is clearly not what T-8 is talking about.

In interpreting segment (4) of T-8, we have to bear in mind that it has an explanatory or justificatory role, signaled by the particle γάρ. What (4) aims to explain is why, according to claim (3), *eudaimonia* requires that the nobility of virtuous activities be complemented with natural goods. The answer is: because *eudaimonia* includes the *enjoyment* of such goods. Leaving out the reference to satisfaction of basic needs (since this, as we said, is only a precondition and does not directly contribute to *eudaimonia*), we can summarize the argument in (4) as follows:

> Claim 4: Happiness requires the availability of natural goods, because the requirements of happiness include, in addition to maintaining ethical standards (esp. justice) and engaging with noble objects of *theôria*, also the enjoyment of natural goods (and avoidance of opposite natural evils).

The key element of claim 4 is the assertion that the enjoyment of natural goods has to be included in the account of *eudaimonia*. This assertion, in turn, is justified by yet another γάρ-clause, (5) of T-8 (which is why it should not be detached from T-8 as in the existing editions and translations). (5) tries to justify the key assertion in (4) by pointing out that *eudaimonia* is both most pleasant and most noble/fine. The underlying argument seems to be that virtuous practice could not qualify as most pleasant (in addition to being most noble) if it did not include the enjoyment of natural goods. Hence, without this added feature, it could not be eudaimonic, given that *eudaimonia* is something most noble and most pleasant. We may paraphrase this claim as follows:

> Claim 5: Happiness requires the enjoyment of natural goods (alongside noble ethical and scientific activities), because happiness is something most pleasant

and most noble, but could not be most pleasant if the enjoyment of natural goods were not included.

Yet what justifies the premise that *eudaimonia* is something most pleasant? This leads us back to the statement with which the reasoning of part III-b began (quote T-6 above). It contained the claim that the eudaimonic life is a composition of particular actions pursuing the goals of nobility, utility, and pleasure. According to the most likely literal translation, this seemed to amount to the claim that the happy life is an aggregate of actions, some of which are directed primarily toward pleasure, others toward nobility, and again others toward utility. Yet we had qualms since the sentence could also be construed in a different way, and Aristotle's own view is that the eudaimonic life is constituted by actions that (at least in the most typical instances) realize all three kinds of value simultaneously. However, in light of T-8 (4), it is now much more likely that the guiding idea in T-6 is that of a composite life-style in which actions separately defined by three different kinds of value come together. For the list of actions in T-8 (4) is easily matched to the three targets of action listed in T-6: Just conduct and *theôria* (ii & iii) correspond to the value καλόν, while the procurement of the necessities of life (iv) correlates with mere utility, and enjoyment of natural goods (unaffected by dreaded evils) with the target of pleasure. In Greek, the connection between "enjoyment" (ἀπολαύειν) and pleasure/joy (ἡδονή) is less tautological than in English; yet there is still a clear conceptual link between the two notions.

We can now also see what distinguishes the view contained in T-8 from the one expressed in T-2: The latter assumes, as we might say, a high moral ground in which every action is dedicated to being a noble expression of virtue. Among these acts of virtue, there are, to be sure, primary acts that stand out and are to be discerned from merely circumstantial acts of virtue. Yet they are still primary acts *of virtue*, pursuing the καλόν. Moreover, the dichotomies of the "good" that the argument in T-2 was based on are clearly incompatible with the view articulated in T-8: Natural nonpsychic human goods were reduced to the status of mere necessary goods (ἀναγκαῖα ἀγαθά) and "material aspects" (ὑλικά) of eudaimonic actions. There was no place for the idea of enjoying such goods just for the sake of enjoying them, separately from the noble exploits that they can also support, since admitting such an element into *eudaimonia* would have diluted the "purity" of the nobility of a eudaimonic life stipulated in T-2. T-8, by contrast, presents us with a more down-to-earth conception of the

Two Conceptions of "Primary Acts of Virtue" in Doxography C 199

eudaimonic life which provides room for activities not primarily directed toward something noble.[97]

There is an objection that might be raised against this interpretation: T-8 comments on a conception of *eudaimonia* as a qualified form of "using *aretê*" (χρῆσις ἀρετῆς, T-7 (1)); and this, one could argue, entails that the author of these comments cannot mean to introduce enjoyment of natural nonpsychic goods as an independent factor of *eudaimonia*, as this would imply that there would be one component of *eudaimonia* disconnected from the use of *aretê*. This possible objection would, however, overlook the role of an assumption shared by all ethicists since Plato, namely that any form of *benefiting* from nonpsychic goods has to be based on sensible choice and sensible use, because otherwise harmful outcomes cannot be avoided. In light of this assumption, there is no incompatibility between the inclusion of the "enjoyment of natural goods" and the idea that all eudaimonic activity is based on the use of *aretê* (which comprises, of course, the use of φρόνησις). The position of T-8 does, however, advocate a more inclusive understanding of the teleology of virtue than T-2, allowing for

---

[97] I suspect that the inclusion of the "enjoyment of natural goods" in the account of eudaimonic activities is also influenced by Carneades. There is some evidence that the position Carneades defended for dialectical purposes in his debate with the Stoics made use of this terminology. The crucial point of dissent between Carneades and his Stoic opponents was whether or not the obtaining of the correctly selected (ἐκλογή) natural assets—the πρῶτα κατὰ φύσιν—matters for the eudaimonic quality of a life (cf. Long [1967]; Striker [1986]). The key Greek term for "obtaining" was probably τυγχάνω (*c. gen.*). While Carneades (like the later Peripatetics) argued for the relevancy of the obtaining, he also had to give an answer to the question of what agents were supposed to do with these assets once they had obtained them, in order to formulate a complete account of *eudaimonia*. Just *having* them does not suffice. He could not simply resort to the term "use," or "using well," since that would have elicited the question of what they are used for. In order to stop the potential regress, he could say that what we do with these assets is to enjoy them (ἀπολαύειν). That this was actually his strategy seems to be indicated by Cicero's language in his report of the *Divisio Carneadea* in *Fin.* V.16–23 (drawing on Antiochus as his main source). He uses expressions for "attaining," "obtaining," etc. (V.19: *consequi, assequi, adipisci, obtinere*) in order to record the difference between views that put the emphasis on actual acquisition (which includes Carneades' assumed position) and the Stoic approach that focuses on correct preferences and choices, as opposed to the actual obtaining. Yet when Cicero then gives a general list of all conceivable "simple" accounts of the highest good, he uses the term *frui* (which would be the Latin equivalent of ἀπολαύειν) to describe Carneades' dialectical standpoint (V.20: *fruendi rebus iis quas primas secundum natura esse diximus, Carneades ... defensor disserendi causa fuit*). Cf. Szaif (2012) 186–90 for some more discussion.

the prudent enjoyment of natural goods *for the sake of enjoyment* as one type of primary activity.

In sum, segment T-8 (in conjunction with T-6) broadens the conception of a virtuous and happy life so that it now also includes the enjoyment of somatic and external goods independently of their (equally important) function as tools used toward strictly moral ends or to enable *theôria*.[98] In practical terms, the position of T-8 and the *symplêrôma*-account defended by Critolaus seem to be of a kindred spirit. Technically, however, T-8 represents a different position, since it identifies the several components of the *telos* as *activities* and thus becomes immune to the standard objection against Critolaus contained in T-2. On behalf of the view expressed in T-8, we could point out that enjoying a bottle of good wine, for instance, does not come from just owning it, nor from gulping it down straight from the bottle, but from consuming it in a certain conscious and measured way. This corresponds to the idea expressed in T-8 that natural nonpsychic goods are not, strictly speaking, constituent parts of *eudaimonia*, only the sensible ways of enjoying them are. But, to stay with our example, it is still the wine that we enjoy, not our intelligent way of going about enjoying it.

What does this result mean for the notion of a "primary action" or a "primary act of virtue" in T-8? The attribute "primary" still serves to single out the kind of activity regulated by virtue that also supports a happy life and thus goes beyond a merely virtuous life-performance. We should therefore also expect roughly the same duplication of ends as I described it for T-2 at the end of section 3 of this essay: a minimal goal of maintaining standards of ethical conduct, and a maximal goal that defines the content of *eudaimonia*. This hypothesis receives some support by the way in which the enjoyment of natural goods is included in the list of partial goals in segment (4) of T-8, namely as something that is to be *added* (πρὸς τῷ) to the goals of

---

[98] Strache ([1909] 44–54) is the only author I am currently aware of who postulates two different sources for roughly the same textual segments as the ones I am calling parts III-a and III-b. Yet he does so for the wrong reasons. He acknowledges that the remarks on *eudaimonia* in 131.14–134.6 (which includes T-8) are incompatible with Antiochus (in light of Antiochus' commitment to the self-sufficiency of virtue relative to a base-level of *eudaimonia*), but argues that T-2 belongs to the tradition of Antiochus. In this connection, he suggests that the ποιητικά mentioned in T-2 are *not* necessary requirements for base-level *eudaimonia* (which is similar to how Hirzel [1882] 711 reads 126.12–127.2, of which T-5 is a part). But this is a wrong interpretation of T-2 (and T-5, for that matter). As we have seen, the point of the distinction between καλὴ πρᾶξις and προηγουμένη πρᾶξις in T-2 is to allow for virtuous activity that is not eudaimonic. καλὴ πρᾶξις is, hence, not a label for base-level happiness in the sense of Antiochus, and the ποιητικά are required for eudaimonic activity. Strache also does not mention the role of *apolausis* in T-8.

justice and of not depriving oneself of the study of noble things. Both unjust behavior toward others, and missing out on *theôria* through one's own fault ("depriving *yourself* of it[99]), would represent instances of ethically incorrect choices. While correctness thus understood is the minimal goal, the *added* enjoyment of natural goods completes the maximal goal.

Ultimately, the different viewpoints underlying T-2 and T-8 have to be connected with different conceptions of what it means to fulfill *human nature*. For Hellenistic philosophers in general, the task of virtue was typically linked to the ideal of living in accordance with nature. For the Peripatetics, this meant living in accordance specifically with human nature, supported by the kinds of goods that agree with human nature. But as we can see from the examples discussed here, this shared assumption left room for significantly different views on what agreement with human nature entails.

Works Cited

Annas, Julia. 1993. *The Morality of Happiness*. Oxford: Oxford University Press.

Arnim, Hans von. 1926. *Arius Didymus' Abriß der peripatetischen Ethik*. Wien: Akademie der Wissenschaften.

Cooper, J. M. 1985. "Aristotle on the Goods of Fortune." *Philosophical Review* 94: 173–96.

Dirlmeier, Franz. 1937. *Die Oikeiosis-Lehre Theophrasts*. Philologus, suppl. 30.1. Leipzig: Dieterich'sche Verlagsbuchhandlung.

Fortenbaugh, W. W. (ed.). 1983. *On Stoic and Peripatetic Ethics: The Work of Arius Didymus*. Rutgers University Studies in Classical Humanities 1. New Brunswick, N.J.: Transaction.

———. 1983. "*Arius, Theophrastus, and the* Eudemian Ethics." In Fortenbaugh (1983) 203–23.

Gigon, Olof. 1961. *Aristoteles: Einführungsschriften*. Zürich: Artemis.

Giusta, Michelangelo. 1961/62. "Sul significato filosofico del termine *proêgoumenos*." *Atti dell' Accademia delle Scienze di Torino. Classe di scienze morali, storiche e filologia* 96: 228–71.

---

[99] The text uses the phrase "depriving itself" (ἀποστερεῖν ἑαυτήν) with reference to a quasi personified *eudaimonia*. Yet, translated into a less metaphorical manner of speaking, this amounts to saying that the person who is (or tries to be) in a eudaimonic state does not want to deprive himself or herself of opportunities for the study of noble things. (The unusual reflexive formulation ἀποστερεῖν ἑαυτήν was first highlighted by von Arnim [1926] 30f.)

Görgemanns, Herwig. 1983. "*Oikeiosis* in Arius Didymus." In Fortenbaugh (1983) 165–89.
Gottschalk, H. B. 1987. "Aristotelian Philosophy in the Roman World from the Time of Cicero to the End of the Second Century AD." In *ANRW* II.36.2, ed. W. Haase. Berlin: De Gruyter, 1079–1174.
Hahm, David E. 1990. "The Ethical Doxography of Arius Didymus." In *ANRW* II.36.4, ed. W. Haase. Berlin: de Gruyter, 2935–3055.
———. 2007. "Critolaus and Late Hellenistic Peripatetic Philosophy." In *Pyrrhonists, Patricians, Platonizers (Tenth Symposium Helenisticum)*, ed. A. M. Ioppolo and D. N. Sedley. Naples: Bibliopolis, 47–101.
Hatzimichali, Myrto. 2011. *Potamo of Alexandria and the Emergence of Eclecticism in Late Hellenistic Philosophy*. Cambridge: Cambridge University Press.
Hirzel, Rudolf. 1882. *Untersuchungen zu Cicero's Philosophischen Schriften*. Vol. 2: *De finibus. De officiis*. Leipzig: Verlag von S. Hirzel.
Huby, P. M. 1983. "Peripatetic Definitions of Happiness." In Fortenbaugh (1983) 121–38.
Inwood, Brad. 1985. *Ethics and Human Action in Early Stoicism*. Oxford: Oxford University Press.
———. 2014. *Ethics After Aristotle*. Cambridge, Mass.: Harvard University Press.
Kahn, Charles H. 1983. "Arius as a Doxographer." In Fortenbaugh (1983) 1–13.
Long, A. A. 1967. "Carneades and the Stoic Telos," *Phronesis* 12: 59–90.
Long, A. A. and D. Sedley. 1987. *The Hellenistic Philosophers*, 2 vols. Cambridge: Cambridge University Press.
Moraux, Paul. 1973. *Der Aristotelismus bei den Griechen von Andronikos bis Alexander von Aprodisias*. Vol. 1: *Die Renaissance des Aristotelismus im 1. Jh. v. Chr.* Berlin: De Gruyter.
Philippson, Robert. 1932. "Das 'Erste Naturgemäße.'" *Philologus* 87: 445–66.
Russell, Daniel. 2010. "Virtue and Happiness in the Lyceum and Beyond." *Oxford Studies in Ancient Philosophy* 38: 143–85.
Schütrumpf, Eckart. 2005. *Aristoteles: Politik. Buch VII/VIII*, übers. und erl. (= Aristoteles. *Werke in deutscher Übersetzung*, ed. H. Flashar, Vol. 9.4). Berlin: Akademie Verlag.
Sharples, R. W. 1990. *Alexander of Aprhodisias: Ethical Problems*. Translation with introduction and notes. London: Duckworth.
———. 2007. "Peripatetics on Happiness." In *Greek and Roman Philosophy 100BC–200AD*. Vol. 2, ed. R. W. Sharples and R. Sorabji. London: Institute of Classical Studies, University of London, 627–37.

———. 2008. *Alexander Aphrodisiensis:* De anima libri mantissa. With introduction and commentary. Berlin: De Gruyter.

———. 2010. *Peripatetic Philosophy 200 BC to AD 200: An Introduction and Collection of Sources in Translation.* Cambridge: Cambridge University Press.

Simpson, Peter L. P. 2014. "*Epitome of Peripatetic Ethics* by Arius Didymus." In Simpson, *The Great Ethics of Aristotle.* New Brunswick, N.J.: Transaction, 87–107.

Strache, Hans. 1909. *De Arii Didymi in morali philosophia auctoribus.* Ph.D. Diss. Berlin.

Striker, Gisela. 1986. "*Antipater, or the Art of Living.*" In *The Norms of Nature*, ed. M. Schofield and G. Striker. Cambridge: Cambridge University Press, 185–204.

Szaif, Jan. 2012. *Gut des Menschen: Problematik und Entwicklung der Glücksethik bei Aristoteles und in der Tradition des Peripatos.* Berlin: De Gruyter.

———. 2016. "Disagreement and Reception. Peripatetics Responding to the Stoic Challenge." In *Reading the Past Across Space and Time: Receptions and World Literature*, ed. R. Hexter and B. Schildgen. London: Palgrave Macmillan, 121–47.

White, Stephen A. 2002. "Happiness in the Hellenistic Lyceum." *Apeiron*, suppl. 35: 69–93.

6

Bodily and External Goods in Relation to Happiness

Myrto Hatzimichali

The division of good things into those belonging to the soul, those belonging to the body and external ones is at least as old as Plato, who says in the *Laws* (3.697a–b): "it is right that the goods of the soul should be highest in honour and come first, provided that the soul possesses temperance; second come the good and fair things of the body; and third the so-called (*legomena*) goods of property and money."[1] As Inwood (2014b, 255) points out, Plato recognised in this division "a common-sense starting point for substantial ethical theorising," and Aristotle too made use of the classification as a point of received wisdom, an *endoxon*: "given that the goods have been divided into three, and some are said to be external, others to relate to the soul and body respectively" (*EN* 1.8.1098b12–15; cf. *Pol.* 7.1.1323a24–27). But this tripartition never played a central role in the ethical philosophy of either of the two fourth-century pioneers.[2] By contrast, it was formalised and became, according to our sources, a central point of contention in the Hellenistic debate between Stoics and Peripatetics over

---

[1] Cf. *Grg.* 467e; 477c; *Alc.* 132b–c.
[2] Cf. Bett (1997) 83.

the pursuit of happiness.[3] The controversy over whether all three types are indeed goods and contribute to happiness is given great prominence by Cicero, especially in *Tusculans* 5 and *On Ends* 3–5, which expound the 'tremendous clash' between Stoics and Peripatetics on this very issue:

> There is a dispute between the Stoics and the Peripatetics. The Stoics argue that there is nothing good except what is moral, the Peripatetics claim that there are certain bodily and external goods as well, even while attributing far and away the greatest value to morality. Here we have a truly honourable contest, a tremendous clash. (Cic. *Fin.* 2.68; transl. Woolf)

This passage stresses the central role of virtue for both schools (and goes on to contrast it with the Epicureans' failure to give virtue its due, which makes them far inferior), and thus suggests that any points of controversy between Stoics and Peripatetics in the field of ethics will centre around what are called here "bodily and external goods." For the Stoics, these items do not even merit the characterisation 'good' because that applies exclusively to virtue, and their presence or absence has no bearing on the achievement of happiness (see, e.g., D.L. 7.101–3). The Peripatetics, on the other hand, treated all three classes as goods and made use of the tripartition when seeking to establish a role for all of them in the happy life. In the context of this Peripatetic position and its various versions and developments, the aim of the present chapter is to examine what the composer of the Peripatetic ethical doxography preserved by Stobaeus, "Doxography C," (henceforth Didymus) has to say about the role played by items that are not virtues (such as health, beauty, speed, wealth, good birth, fame, etc.) in the achievement of one's end in life, namely happiness.

For a doxographical account of Peripatetic ethics, such as the one that concerns us here, cross-school differences and confrontations with the Stoics are arguably of less importance than the presentation of a full picture of the Peripatetic position. More relevant are the internal problems that, as we shall see, were created within the school in articulating the role of bodily and external goods for the happy life. Pressure from the Stoics would certainly have contributed toward forcing modifications and clarifications, and Stoic ideas could indeed be constructively appropriated. But this did not make the internal problem any less pressing: Aristotle did not provide a fully worked-out view of the importance of virtue and nonmoral goods for the happy life: he states that virtue is not sufficient for happiness ("those who assert that the person tortured on the wheel and falling into great

---

[3] This development is discussed in Inwood (2014b).

misfortunes is happy, if only he is good, are, whether willingly or unwillingly, talking nonsense," *EN* 7.13 1153b19–22). He acknowledges that external goods[4] have a role to play in the happy life and that not obtaining them or losing them undermines one's happiness (*EN* 1.8 1099a31–33; 1099b2–6). And yet, he stops short of saying that a virtuous person who lacks external goods is miserable ("For the truly good and wise person, we believe, bears all the fortunes of life with dignity and always does the finest thing with what is available [...] If this is so, the happy person could never become wretched, though he will not be blessed if he meets with luck like that of Priam," *EN* 1.10 1101a 1–7[5]). Thus even the attempt to remain faithful to Aristotle's own views could lead the Peripatetics in different directions.

Annas has drawn attention to the pitfalls of Aristotle's position that tries to do justice both to the "intuitive requirement" that the happy life must be pleasant and include the basic ingredients of prosperity, and to the "theoretical pull" of the definition of happiness as complete, self-sufficient and within the agent's control. The incompatibility between the two, Annas argues, leaves Aristotle with an "unstable view," and his followers inherit the task of clarifying how external goods can contribute to happiness (thus retaining some intrinsic value), but without making it incomplete and subject to the vicissitudes of chance.[6] Inwood also speaks of "a struggle within Aristotelian ethics over the conditions of happiness, a hesitancy between the highest aspirations we can have for human reason and the sometimes deflationary view, rooted in more careful and naturalistic observation of human affairs, of how human beings actually live."[7]

In addition to Stoic critique and internal interpretative issues, Peripatetics in the late Hellenistic period also had to face the challenge of Carneades, who demanded that both the Stoics and the Peripatetics show that their differences are more than merely verbal. He struck a chord because the two theories were not really all that distant and each contained elements of its counterpart. The Peripatetics maintained that the importance of virtue for the good life far outweighs that of the other goods, while the Stoics attached some kind of value even to bodily and external advantages, which

---

[4] Aristotle does sometimes speak of "external goods" (*ektos agatha*) in a more general sense, lumping bodily and external goods together, cf. Annas (1993) 377; Cooper (1985).

[5] *EN* 1.10 is characteristic of the ambiguity inherent in Aristotle's account, as it introduces a potential distinction between "happy" (*eudaimôn*) and "blessed" (*makarios*); cf. Sharples (2007) 627–28.

[6] Annas (1993) 364–84.

[7] Inwood (2014a) 37.

they called "preferred indifferents." Cicero's Stoic spokesman Cato tries to answer the challenge on behalf of the Stoics, indicating that what matters is not whether something is called 'good' but its role in the happy life:

> Carneades […] would tirelessly contend that on the whole issue known as "the problem of good and evil" there was no dispute between the Stoics and the Peripatetics other than a verbal one. To my mind nothing could be more obvious than that the dispute between these schools is substantial rather than verbal. The difference, I assert, between Stoics and Peripatetics is far more a matter of ideas than language. After all, the Peripatetics claim that the whole range of things which, as far as they are concerned, are to be called good, contribute to a happy life; whereas we Stoics deny that a thing's having some value makes it constitutive of such a life. (Cic. *Fin*. 3.41; transl. Woolf)

For a successful defence both against the Stoics and against Carneades, our Peripatetics need to show that bodily and external advantages are indeed goods in their own right, and they also need an account of the sense in which they are necessary for happiness. Given that much of the debate concerns the relative contributions to happiness of virtue and bodily/external goods respectively, Didymus' discussion is also preoccupied with clarifying the disparity of value that places virtue so far apart from the other goods.

We may now turn to look at how these issues are raised and dealt with in specific passages of the doxography.

Establishing the *Trigeneia*

The summary of Peripatetic ethics opens with a bipartition of the soul into rational and irrational, with their respective virtues (116.20–118.4). This approach, along with the remark that virtue is perfected through nature, habituation and reason (118.5–6), is quickly abandoned in favour of an alternative bipartition between body and soul. This time the irrational is not associated with a part of the human soul, but with the body, which is what humans share with other mortal animals, as opposed to the divine element of the soul that connects humans to rational immortal beings. The second bipartition then serves as the basis for a double account of human motivation,[8] where the vocabulary of *oikeiôsis* first makes its appearance: "and first of all, they desire existence, for they have an affinity (*ôikeiôsthai*) toward themselves by nature;[9] that is why they experience a suitable enjoy-

---

[8] "Accordingly, they desire (*ephiesthai*) the perfection of both (i.e., body and soul)," 118.11.

[9] As Inwood (2014a) 85 notes, there is no cradle argument here; the desire to exist is not connected specifically with newborns.

ment among things according to nature and are annoyed by things which are contrary to nature"[10] (118.11–14).

It is here that we find the first reference to items termed "goods" (*agatha*), alongside the other two key terms that come into play when assessing the value of various things for the happy life, namely "according to nature" (*kata phusin*) and "choiceworthy for their own sake" (*di' hauta haireta*). These terms are not always interchangeable,[11] but they are important criteria introduced early on, accompanied by their neatly symmetrical counterparts, "contrary to nature," "in themselves to be avoided," "evils" (118.19–20). Scholars have puzzled over the use of the more characteristically Stoic concept of *oikeiôsis*[12] in a Peripatetic doxography, especially since Didymus does not make use of it in the Stoic section (Doxography B), and some have suggested a Peripatetic origin for the whole theory.[13] Whatever the ultimate origins of the theory, in these pages of Didymus' doxography it is set to work for Peripatetic purposes, as is clear from the first examples of 'goods', which would never have been acknowledged as such by the Stoics, namely health, life, even pleasure (118.15–16).[14]

Furthermore, the Stoic account of *oikeiôsis* is characterised by its developmental approach, whereby the initial drive toward self-preservation leads to selection of what is in accordance with nature and rejection of its opposite. This process of correct selection, once it has become stable and continuous, leads to realisation of what is truly good, and the reasoning and "consistency" of action comes to be valued much more highly than the selected items themselves (Cic. *Fin.* 3.20–21).[15] Didymus is in agreement with the Stoics in connecting virtue (what is truly good) with the correct selection of natural things, but his intellectualist approach here (cf. "secure knowledge," 119.12) presents virtue more like a prerequisite for rather than a natural outcome of correct selection.[16] The opening appeal

---

[10] All translations from Didymus are Tsouni's, unless otherwise indicated.

[11] Cf. Görgemanns (1983) 174.

[12] See the parallels at, e.g., D.L. 7.85–86; Cic. *Fin.* 3.16.

[13] See Görgemanns (1983) 166–68; Annas (1993) 279–81. For fresh arguments on the Peripatetic origin, see Tsouni (2010).

[14] Stoic accounts make a special point of excluding pleasure from primary natural attachments, probably in response to Epicurean cradle arguments, cf. D.L. 7.85–86; Cic. *Fin.* 3.16–17. Cicero's Antiochean spokesman is exercised by the issue, but leaves it open (*Fin.* 5.45).

[15] This constitutes a "radical shift of motivation" for which the Stoics do not provide adequate explanation, cf. Gill (2015) 230.

[16] "But, since frequently out of ignorance we are deceived in relation to the choices and avoidances and we dismiss good things while we approach bad ones as though they

to *oikeiôsis* (118.5–119.21) is rounded off with the claim that the whole outline of Peripatetic ethics is based around selection of things that are in accordance with nature and rejection of their opposites, couched in the Stoic vocabulary of "appropriate actions" (*kathêkonta*) and "right actions" (*katorthôseis*, 119.18).[17]

Its difficulties notwithstanding, this section has established the key concepts that will play an important role in the discussion of bodily and external goods, namely "accordance with nature" and "choiceworthiness for their own sake."[18] A further discrepancy between this first section and what follows lies in the binary body/soul distinction, which appears to leave no room for the third category of external goods, whereas the argument starting at 119.22 begins precisely from externals.[19] The argument contains elements that are reminiscent of the accounts of "social *oikeiôsis*" offered both by the Stoics (Cic. *Fin*. 3.62–68) and by Antiochus of Ascalon, presented as a consensus among "the Ancients," Academics and Peripatetics alike (*Fin*. 5.65–66). Didymus first shows that children are choiceworthy for their parents not only because they are useful but "for their own sake" (*di' heauta*, 119.23). The basis for this argument is self-evidence ("manifest facts," *enargeia*, 199.24), in that, as everyone can see, parents are concerned with the welfare of their children even after their own death.[20] Children's choiceworthiness for their own sake makes it "necessary" that "parents and brothers and one's wife and relatives and other close persons and fellow-citizens are befriended for their own sake." It is not at all clear why this

---

were good, we necessarily had to seek for a secure knowledge for our judgment; since we found it to be consonant with nature, on account of the magnificence of its activity, we named it virtue and admiring it as unique, we valued it above all other things," 119.8–15. Cf. 127.3–128.9 on virtue as a guard against error.

[17] It is not entirely clear what the *apo toutôn hôrmêsthai* ("derives from these") at 119.20–21 refers to; I take the claim to be that Peripatetic ethics starts from actions of selection and rejection of natural and unnatural items respectively, which must involve virtue. Inwood (1983) 193 takes "these" to refer to "personal *oikeiôsis* and associated concepts."

[18] Szaif (2012) 242–43 argues that a particular sense of *di' hauto haireton* is deployed here, such that can include instrumental goods.

[19] Görgemanns (1983) 179 suggests tentatively that the omission of external goods from the section ending at 119.21 may be due to the way in which different source texts have been combined—if the first source ended with a reference to external goods our author may have omitted it on purpose to avoid repetition given that the next section begins with them. Inwood (1983) 192 places more emphasis on the body/soul duality, which he traces back to Antiochus of Ascalon.

[20] The Stoic account of *oikeiôsis* offers further justification based on natural teleology and providence, Cic. *Fin*. 3.62; cf. Inwood (2015) 151–55.

should follow necessarily, but further support (*gar*) is offered through the natural kinship (*oikeiotêtas*, 120.13) among human beings and their nature as "social beings with affection for one another." This affection is expanded to the entire human race (as in the Antiochean account, *Fin.* 5.65) in an argument supported by further observable facts of human behaviour and embellished with a number of rhetorical questions: "for who wouldn't rescue, if one could, someone who is seen being overpowered by a beast? Who wouldn't indicate the way to someone who is lost? Who wouldn't assist someone who is dying through lack of means? And who, if he came upon a spring in the middle of a waterless desert, wouldn't use signs to reveal its whereabouts to those who travel the same route?" (121.3–8). From this *consensus omnium*[21] on documented types of behaviour Didymus feels entitled to conclude that there is a natural goodwill, friendship and affection for all other human beings. From the fact that friends are choiceworthy for their own sake he infers that friendship and goodwill are so too, and so are praise (because "we have an affinity, *oikeiousthai*, toward those who praise us," 122.3–4) and good reputation.

No real support has been offered for these final transitions, other than the natural status and intuitive self-evidence of certain behavioural traits that pertain to the earliest stages of the series of inferences that resulted in friendship, goodwill, praise and good reputation being established as choiceworthy for their own sake. Wealth, the most typical example of an external good in the traditional tripartition, is omitted here.[22] It is significant, though, that the tripartition of goods is explicitly applied at the conclusion of this argument on external goods for the first time in the doxography, leading to the way to the *a fortiori* establishment of the goods of the body and the soul as even more choiceworthy for their own sake:

> So in this way, it has been clearly shown that the so-called external goods are by nature choiceworthy for their own sake. Aren't therefore the goods which relate to us and are inside us much more choiceworthy? I mean the goods related to our body and soul. If human beings are choiceworthy for their own sake, so also would their parts be choiceworthy. The most general parts of a human being are body and soul. (122.7–13)

---

[21] A similar line of thought is pursued in the Stoic account at *Fin.* 3.64, where there is reference to "a familiar Greek verse," quoted by Didymus at 121.12: "When I die, let the earth mix with fire."

[22] Görgemanns (1983) 177 remarked that the focus is on social relations as external goods. This has to be connected to the reliance on the social *oikeiôsis* theory, but most lists of external goods, other than their inclusion of wealth, consist in social goods such as good family, friendship, reputation, etc.

In addition to the *a fortiori* arguments that purport to establish the value of bodily goods such as health, power, beauty, swiftness of foot, vigour and soundness of the senses (122.21–22), Didymus offers another demonstration through *consensus omnium* and self-evidence (here there is reference to the obvious, *emphanes*, 123.8—the argument is very close to the Antiochean one at *Fin.* 5.46). This time he shows the choiceworthiness of beauty via its opposite, by pointing out that no one would choose to be ugly and mutilated, even if this led to no disadvantage. Moreover, everyone naturally "has an affinity toward" (*oikeiousthai*, 123.9) beautiful people irrespective of any utility, hence beauty is choiceworthy for its own sake, and the same applies to the other bodily goods listed above.

Having established the value of external and bodily goods in this way, Didymus proceeds again *a fortiori* to the soul and to virtue:

> Therefore, if the bodily goods have been shown to be for their own sake choiceworthy and their opposite evils to be avoided for their own sake, it is necessary also that the parts of the soul are to be chosen for their own sake and their virtues and those of the whole soul. For after virtue was introduced, as we showed, by the bodily *and external goods* and turned to view itself, because it too belongs to the things which are according to nature much more than the bodily virtues, it became akin to itself as to something choiceworthy for its own sake and more so to itself than toward the bodily virtues; therefore, the virtues of the soul are much more valuable (than the virtues of the body). (123.17–27)

The reference to a prior discussion of how virtue makes its entrance from bodily and external goods is thought to be pointing to 118.4–21, where it was the knowledge guiding the correct selection and deselection of natural and unnatural things respectively. The developmental element is more prominent here, and is closer to the Stoic version described above, whereby virtue follows from rather than being presupposed by the correct selection of things according to nature.[23] Another difference is that in the earlier passage there was no reference to external goods, as it was operating only with the soul/body bipartition. In fact, even in the current section (123.21–124.14) the body/soul dichotomy is much more pertinent as there is no reference to externals other than the single one at 123.22 italicized above. Other than that, the passage goes on to develop the *a fortiori* argument by creating analogies between virtues of the body (health, strength, beauty) and virtues of the soul (temperance as health of the soul; bravery and endurance as strength of the soul; justice as beauty of the soul) at 124.1–14.

---

[23] However, the presentation of virtue as a reflexive power turning back toward itself remains a distinctive feature of Didymus' account, as noted by Szaif (2012) 238.

This gives an indication of the problems and tensions of these opening sections of the doxography that employ the concept of *oikeiôsis*. They stem to a large extent from the interweaving of passages that apply the body/soul duality and focus on the developmental link between nonmoral goods and virtue with passages that introduce external goods on a comparative scale where virtue occupies the highest position. It is highly possible that different sources have been used.[24] The problematic interweaving can be explained to a certain extent if we consider that our text is aimed at demonstrating the intrinsic value of the three types of goods. The tripartition is taken for granted when first introduced at 122.7–10, and we have seen how Didymus uses selected elements of the *oikeiôsis* theory, which was not developed in connection with the tripartition, in support of his main aim. He is not offering so much an account of *oikeiôsis*, but an account of the *trigeneia*, which is why we find this material in the Peripatetic rather than the Stoic doxography.

In other accounts of *oikeiôsis* that are not preoccupied with arguing for the *trigeneia* of goods, the social aspect is quite separate from the developmental account that culminates with virtue, but here an attempt has been made to link all three types of goods with the *a fortiori* sequence. It was never an attempt to show how "personal" and "social" *oikeiôsis* fit together, which is why it will disappoint anyone looking for a coherent link.[25] Further evidence for the deliberate attempt to link all three types of goods in a systematic, if contrived, scheme is provided by the expansion of the analogies between virtues of the soul and virtues of the body to cover external goods too, at 124.15–125.9. Scholars have understandably suspected the authenticity of this section,[26] because it is highly artificial, claiming, for example, that as health is to the body and temperance is to the soul, wealth is in externals.[27] Its conclusion, however, reveals the overall purpose of the doxography thus far: "therefore, there are three kinds of goods which are

---

[24] Görgemanns (1983) 177–79; Inwood (1983) 193.

[25] Inwood (1983) 194–95. Annas (1993) 285–87 interprets Didymus' moves as "a sustained attempt to develop Aristotle's ethics from a starting-point of self-love, as indicated in *Nicomachean Ethics* IX 8" (285). She comments on how "social *oikeiôsis* has been inserted into the process of personal *oikeiôsis*" (285) and how this is effected "by interpreting other-concern as concern for one of the kinds of good that self-concern focuses on" (286).

[26] Moraux (1973) 325–27; Görgemanns (1983) 180 proposes the ps.-Aristotelian *Divisions* as a possible source, but Inwood (1983) 191 suggests it was rather a text of the same type, because there are important discrepancies.

[27] Similarly, strength–bravery–rule; beauty–justice–friendship.

choiceworthy for their own sake, those belonging to the soul, those belonging to the body and the external ones" (125.10–11).

The Goods and the *Telos*

Apart from establishing that all three types of goods included in the *trigeneia* are choiceworthy for their own sake and thus intrinsically valuable, the passages discussed above were also aimed at showing the inequality among the three types, with goods of the soul being far superior. Indeed, the passage just quoted continues as follows: "and the goods belonging to the soul are far more choiceworthy than the other ones, for the soul is more authoritative and choiceworthy than the body. It is clear, therefore, that the virtues of the soul are more choiceworthy than those of the body and the external (goods)" (125.12–16). This insistence can be interpreted as a reaction to the pressure from the theoretically robust, if less intuitive, Stoic view on virtue's sufficiency for happiness, but the preponderance of virtue is seen already in Aristotle's efforts to establish that happiness must not be subject to fortune (*EN* 1.9–10, and see Annas' remarks about the "theoretical pull," discussed above).

Still, Peripatetics were not inclined to relinquish the status of bodily and external advantages as goods,[28] so the main challenge was to explain how they can contribute to happiness without undermining the far superior role of virtue. The surviving evidence for Hellenistic debate on the *telos* of human life indicates that much of it was taking place internally within the Peripatetic school.[29] Following some proposals that promoted joy and freedom from disturbance,[30] the debate came to focus on the three kinds of goods with Critolaus in the second century: "by the younger Peripatetics from [the school of] Critolaus [the end is said to be] what is completed (*sumpeplêrômenon*) from all the goods"—that is, from the three kinds', (Doxography A, 46.10–12 = Fr. 19 Wehrli). This report on Critolaus is confirmed by Clement:

> Critolaus, himself too a Peripatetic, said that the [the end is] perfection of a well-flowing life according to nature, indicating the triple perfection completed

---

[28] Cf. 133.23–134.1: "whereas badness is sufficient for misery, virtue is not similarly sufficient for happiness."

[29] Peripatetics may have occupied up to four out of the six possible positions in the *Carneadea divisio*, cf. Hahm (2007) 74–75.

[30] By Lycon and Hieronymus respectively, see White (2002) 75–84; Inwood (2014a) 38–46.

(*sumplêroumenên*) from the three kinds [of goods]. (Clem. *Strom.* 2.21.129.10 = fr. 20 W)

This account must have enjoyed a degree of success within the Peripatetic school and the sources that reported on it from a doxographic point of view, because it is presented as the "official" Aristotelian position in Diogenes Laertius:

> He set forth one [ethical] end, the employment of virtue in a complete (*teleiôi*) life. He said that happiness was a completion (*sumplêrôma*) made up of three [types of] goods: those concerning the soul, which indeed he calls first in power; secondly those concerning the body health and strength and beauty and the like; thirdly external [goods], wealth and good family and reputation and things like these. Virtue is not sufficient for happiness; for there is also need of bodily and external goods, since the wise man will be unhappy in pains, poverty and the like. But wickedness is sufficient for unhappiness, even if it possesses external and bodily goods to the greatest extent possible. (D.L. 5.30; transl. Sharples 2010)

That virtue is "first in power" was indeed part of Critolaus' position (cf. Cic. *Tusc.* 5.51), but he still treated all three kinds of goods as commensurable: in the *Tusculans* passage Cicero criticises his image of virtue outweighing the other goods, because it remains on the same scale. Critolaus' insistence that virtue 'will weigh more to such an extent that it will outweigh the earth and the seas' and similar claims bring the Peripatetics closer to the Stoic position, and it is the best they can do against the objection that their view allows for a wicked man to be happy.[31] But it still does not provide a failsafe against the possibility of luck and life's circumstances overwhelming the power of virtue.[32]

Other than this issue, which was faced by all Peripatetics, Critolaus came under fire for his main original contribution to the ethical debate, namely his notion of the happy life as "filled out" or "completed" by the three types of goods, which is recognisable in our sources, even when Critolaus' name is not mentioned, by the verb *sumplêroun* ("to complete") and its derivatives. As Inwood has shown, this conception emphasises the *possession* of goods at the expense of the fundamental Aristotelian insight that the *telos* is an *activity* in accordance with virtue.[33] It is precisely on

---

[31] Hahm (2007) 66–67.

[32] Inwood (2014a) 58–61. Cf. Cic. *Tusc.* 5.25.

[33] Inwood (2014a) 55–66. Inwood rightly puzzles about the motivation behind this move by Critolaus. He rejects an easy attribution to ignorance of Aristotle's works on Critolaus' part, in favour of the impact of the philosophical environment, where debate was constrained by the terms of the *Carneadea divisio*.

this point that Didymus' doxography takes Critolaus' view to task, and it is primarily as a response to issues raised by the *sumplêrôma* thesis that he presents his account (or accounts) of how bodily and external goods fit into the happy life.[34]

The first reference to the *telos* comes at 126.15, presented as a consequence of the arguments from *oikeiôsis*:

> Since virtue is far superior in respect to producing (happiness) and in respect to choiceworthiness for its own sake compared with bodily and external goods, in accordance with this, the final end is not jointly completed by bodily and external goods,[35] nor is it the acquisition of them, but rather living in accordance with virtue *surrounded by* bodily and external goods, whether all of them or the majority and the most important of them. It follows that happiness is activity in accordance with virtue expressed in primary actions as one would wish. On the other hand, the goods belonging to the body and external goods are said to be *productive of happiness by contributing something through their presence*. Those who believe that they jointly complete happiness are unaware that happiness is a life, and life is completed by actions. None of the bodily and external goods is either an action in itself or an activity at all. (126.12–127.2)

Critolaus' name is not mentioned here, but the view that is being criticised is clearly associated with him in the extracts discussed above.[36] Didymus initially presents the rejection of the aggregate account as following from virtue's superiority, which in turn is taken as established in the *a fortiori* sequence and the culmination of the developmental process where it turns to and values itself for itself (123.21–27). But this issue had been addressed by Critolaus in his metaphor of the scales, and a more effective response in this regard would be to stress, as the Stoics did, that virtue is incommensurable with the other advantages, indeed on a different scale.[37] The criticism advanced in the last few lines is more successful, returning to

---

[34] As Szaif (2012) 166–76 has shown, the later Peripatetic development of a position on the moral end, as seen in the pages of Didymus, was closely connected with the critique of the "completion" thesis.

[35] Our other evidence on the aggregate view makes clear that all three kinds of goods are included. We can put it down to Didymus' critical haste here that he seems to attribute a radical exclusion of psychic goods to the proponents of the aggregate view.

[36] The critique here is fuller than the one in Doxography A, which names Critolaus, but the main objections are the same (see also below on parts vs. conditions for happiness): 'not all good things are part of the end; bodily goods are not, nor are those derived from outside, but the activities of virtue in the soul alone. So it would have been better to say, instead of "completed," "activated, so that it might be apparent that virtue employs (these things)," 46.13–17.

[37] Hahm (2007) 66.

the authentically Aristotelian insight about happiness as a particular kind of *activity* (cf. *EN* 1.8 1098b31–99a7), that had been conspicuously absent from Critolaus' theory, as we saw above.[38]

A further related criticism of the aggregate view on bodily and external goods occurs a few pages later, albeit with a reference generally to 'materials' (*hulika*) rather than explicitly to these types of goods (129.19–130.12). In this section we find articulated the distinction between constituent parts and necessary conditions, which had been brought to the fore already by Aristotle, most clearly in the following passage of the *Eudemian Ethics*:

> It is therefore most necessary first to decide within oneself, neither hastily nor carelessly, in which of the things that belong to us the good life consists, and what are the necessary conditions (*tinôn aneu ouk*) for men's possessing it. For there is a distinction between health and the things that are necessary conditions (*hôn aneu ouk*) of health, and this is similarly the case with many other things; consequently also to live finely is not the same as the things without which living finely is impossible. [...] for some people regard the things that are necessary conditions of being happy as actual parts (*merê*) of happiness. (*EE* 1.2 1214b12–27)

Didymus' point at 130.4–12 is that proponents of the aggregate view mistakenly treat the instruments or materials that the agent uses toward his/her purpose as *parts* of the activity: "the things without which (*hôn aneu*) it is impossible to perform[39] any kind of action shouldn't be called parts of the activity; for the part is thought of as completing (*sumplêrôtikon*) the whole" (130.8–9). He employs an analogy with crafts (flute-playing and medicine) to highlight that, just as the use of instruments does not detract from the craftsman's skill, in the same way material things do not deprive happiness of the purity of its connection with "the noble" (*to kalon*), because they are necessary conditions (129.19–130.12). There is a defensive tone here, as Didymus tries to ward off any suggestion, presumably coming from Stoic quarters, that use (*paralêpsis*) of materials compromises the noble character of happiness. The craft analogy is reprised at 132.19–21, where the point should be that neither happiness nor the

---

[38] The emphasis on activity is also evident in the definitions of the end that are given at 130.18–131.6 with references to "activity" and "use" of virtue. Cf. Huby (1983); Szaif (2012) 170. Inwood (2014a) 68–72 shows that the emphasis on activity also plays a big part in the 'Antiochean' account of *De finibus* 5, along with a systematic naturalism that is also characteristically Aristotelian. Inwood doubts whether Antiochus is solely responsible for this move, and detects the hand of Cicero himself, but developments in the Peripatetic circles that are behind Didymus' critique here must also be part of the story.

[39] "The things that are necessary for," Tsouni.

skill involved in craft is intensified by the addition of resources or tools.[40] This type of craft analogy, along with the view treating bodily and external goods as necessary conditions and instruments for virtue's activity proved successful in the Peripatetic tradition,[41] as it is found again in Aspasius, coupled once more with the rejection of the aggregate view:

> Happiness needs external goods not as parts or as things that complete it (*anaplêrôtikôn*) but as instruments, just as pipe-playing needs instruments for its own end, in order to achieve its particular end. For it is impossible, (Aristotle) says, to do noble things without provision; it is not possible to practise medicine if one is not provided with medical instruments and drugs. Then he reckons up the external goods, at the same time showing how virtue uses them as instruments for happiness. (Aspasius, *On Aristotle's Ethics* 24.3–9; transl. Sharples 2010)

The other notable feature of this section of our doxography (129.19–130.12) is the use of "the noble" as a counterpart to material advantages. Indeed there is here a strong claim that happiness consists only in noble actions, realised in favourable circumstances, in what Szaif has identified as the 'stricter' version of the Peripatetic end.[42] An alternative, and more moderate, appeal to the noble occurs in the discussion of types of life (145.3–6), where Didymus introduces a separate category, that of the noble life, distinct from the happy life.[43] Natural advantages (bodily and external goods) are necessary for the latter, but not for the noble life:

> Now, the happy life differs from the noble one in that the former is meant to be surrounded constantly by things which are according to nature, whereas the latter one includes also things which are contrary to nature. And for the former

---

[40] This is supported more by the parallel operation of the analogy at 129–30 than by the Greek itself, which is quite ambiguous, and has been translated as: "For happiness is a most pleasant and noble thing and it is not made greater, as in the case of the crafts, through the number of instruments and equipment" (Tsouni); "Happiness is a thing that is most pleasant and most noble, and it is not, like a craft, intensified by a plurality of instruments and equipment" (Sharples 2010, 120).

[41] For the Aristotelian background of non-virtue goods as necessary conditions and instruments cf. *EN* 1.9 1099b25–30. The prominence of the instrumental account among Peripatetics around the first century BC–first century AD is suggested also by the fact that it becomes a target for Seneca, who points out that there is no similarity between crafts, where the result is what counts, and virtuous action, where doing things rightly matters more than the result (Sen. *Ep.* 85.30–32).

[42] Szaif (2012) 190–92. He contrasts this with the "soft" view, according to which the enjoyment (*apolauein*) of bodily and external goods belongs to happiness, as seen at 132.8–19; Szaif (2012) 168, 177–82.

[43] This is incompatible with 129.21, where happiness is said to be "wholly noble."

virtue is not sufficient, whereas for the latter it is. An intermediate way of life is the one which is according to the intermediate disposition in which appropriate actions are exhibited. (145.3–9)

We see here a tactic for accommodating the theoretical demand for virtue's preeminence with the intuitive requirement for natural advantages, by introducing a new sort of life we may aspire to, which is distinct from happiness. This brings to mind Antiochus of Ascalon and his introduction of the "happiest life" (Cic. *Ac.* 1.22; *Fin.* 5.71, 81), but the difference is that in his case virtue was sufficient for happiness whereas in this Peripatetic move virtue is sufficient only for the newly introduced type of life, that is the noble life. Moreover, the relative status of Didymus' happy and noble lives is not as clearly situated in an evaluative scale as the two lives in Antiochus' "degrees of happiness" view.

In any case, the "intermediate way of life" in the passage quoted above cannot be intermediate between the two. The "intermediate disposition" is a state between virtue and vice associated with the performance of appropriate actions, but not right actions, which are the province of virtue only. Despite this, Didymus' preoccupation with the role of bodily and external goods led him to include degrees of possession of natural advantages where they really do not belong, in his distinction between the "best" life (governed by virtue, possessing all (?) natural advantages) and the "second best" life (governed by the intermediate disposition, possessing the most and most important natural advantages, 144.21–145.1).[44]

In terms of Didymus' specification of the moral end, thus far we have seen that he reflects a strand of Peripatetic thought that was critical of Critolaus' aggregate view on the grounds that (a) it treats happiness as an aggregate of three kinds of good things whereas in fact it is made up of actions; and (b) it fails to distinguish between parts and necessary conditions. We may now turn to see what constructive proposals Didymus has to offer as an improvement. As we have already mentioned, the substantive point on which an answer was required was the sense in which bodily and external goods are necessary for happiness, since on the view adopted by Didymus they do not complete it in the way that parts complete a whole. The solution that Didymus opts for is that of bodily and external goods as necessary conditions or prerequisites for happiness. This answers to the

---

[44] Effectively this is a split into two of what was earlier a unified specification in definitions of the end: "whether all of them or the majority and the most important of them" (126.18, 131.6). For a discussion of this awkward pairing of lives and goods, see Fortenbaugh, "Didymus on Types of Life" in this volume, pp. 243–46.

intuitive point that without a basic provision of these goods one cannot be happy (if tortured on the rack, if one's fatherland has been overrun, if one's children become evil etc.), but it stops short of making them integral and constitutive parts of happiness, thus safeguarding the preeminence of virtue. Question marks remain over what precise amount of bodily and external goods is required, and this will always be a weakness of this type of view vis-à-vis the Stoic one. Didymus shows some awareness of this problem at 126.18, where he remarks that the goods needed are 'whether all of them or the majority and the most important of them', but this is still very vague, and remained a continuing source of debate for the Peripatetics.[45]

A remarkable feature of Didymus' text is the variety of different formulations articulating the prerequisites view. Some linguistic and terminological subtlety is deployed here, because the doxography is trying to convey that bodily and external goods are not parts of the end, and yet are somehow very intimately connected with it. We find the following expressions used to capture the role of bodily and external goods: (i) "living in accordance with virtue *surrounded by* (prepositional phrase with *en*) bodily and external goods" (126.16–18, repeated at 131.5–6); (ii) "the goods belonging to the body and external goods are said to be productive (*poiêtika*) of happiness by contributing something[46] through their presence (*tôi sumballesthai ti paronta*)" (126.20–22); "the necessary things (*hôn ouk aneu*) (are thought of) as productive (*poiêtika*)[47] because they conduce and contribute (*pherein kai sunergein*) toward the end" (130. 11–12).

The prepositional phrase *hôn ouk aneu* (lit. "not without which," *sine qua non*), found already in Aristotle, became formulaic for referring to necessary conditions, as a tool for articulating relationships where some things are essential and necessary, but not as constituent parts. The formula is adopted in the *Magna Moralia*, to address the same issue that is at stake for Didymus: "since happiness is not without (*ouk aneu*) external goods, and these result from good fortune, as we just said, then good fortune would be a contributor to happiness" (*MM* 2.8 1207b16). It was also the way in which the only self-identified Eclectic philosopher from Antiquity, Potamo of Alexandria, chose to articulate the moral end, selecting on

---

[45] See Aspasius, *On Aristotle's Ethics* 16.32–17.17.

[46] This again leaves vague the nature of their actual contribution, whether we translate the *ti* as 'something' or we opt for "to a certain extent," "somewhat." Sharples (2010) 117 translates "make a contribution").

[47] "Productive" here is contrasted with "part" (*meros*), which is in turn conceived of as "completing" (*sumplêrôtikon*), 130.7–12.

this occasion from a particular strand of the Peripatetic tradition:[48] "the end is that to which all things are referred, a life perfect with respect to all virtue, not without (*ouk aneu*) the things pertaining to the body by nature and external things" (D.L. 1.21). The most 'baroque' version of this type of classification through prepositions occurs in a passage attributed to Xenocrates, which is generally agreed not to go back to him in this form:

> Xenocrates of Chalcedon defines happiness as the possession of one's proper virtue and the ability which serves this virtue. Then he clearly specifies the soul as that in which (*en hôi*) it comes about; as regards those things by whose agency (*hyph' hôn*) [it comes about, he specifies] the virtues; as for the things from which (*ex hôn*) [it is constituted] as parts, he specifies noble actions and excellent states, dispositions, movements and relationships [of the soul]; as regards the necessary conditions (*hôn ouk aneu*), these are the bodily and external things. (Clem. Strom. 2.22.133 = Xenocrates fr. 232 Parente)

It is quite likely that the shaping of Xenocrates' position in this form dates from the period of our doxography,[49] although Didymus did not avail himself of the possibilities of the richer prepositional scheme.

We have thus seen that Didymus' account of the role of bodily and external goods in the happy life consists mainly of a critique of the aggregate view of Critolaus, which would make them constituent parts of happiness. Instead Didymus favors the necessary conditions view and articulates the contribution made by these goods in the "production" of happiness through a series of subtle verbal nuances. This propensity for subtle and often complex distinctions and classifications surfaces again in the series of divisions of goods that occupy pages 134–37.

Classifications of Goods

It is clear that the section does not form a single coherent whole—it lists possible ways of distinguishing and dividing goods without much interest in how the divisions are related either to each other or to the rest of the doxography. The exhaustiveness of the classification seems to be the main preoccupation. Nevertheless, as Sharples noted, some of the consecutive divisions are linked in "chains," whereby one product of a division is further subdivided in the subsequent division.[50]

---

[48] On Potamo's ethics, see Hatzimichali (2011) 124–39.

[49] Dillon (2003) 141 with n. 152 proposes that the prepositional scheme should be attributed to "late Hellenistic scholasticism."

[50] Sharples (1983) 143.

The first such chain starts from the three senses of the word "good" (*posachôs legetai to agathon*, 134.9), one of which is the "choiceworthy for its own sake," specified as the "end" and "happiness" (134.11–14). The subdivision of the "choiceworthy for its own sake" is of interest in connection with Didymus' earlier accounts of the end:

> And the "choiceworthy for its own sake" is also used in three different ways: either as the (1) ultimate thing for the sake of which we do something, or (2) that for the sake of which we do everything, or in a third way as (3) something which becomes a part of these. And of the things which are choiceworthy for their own sake, some are final, some productive; final are the primary actions which are in accordance with virtue, whereas productive are the materials of the virtues. (134.14–19)

This passage passes from a semantic distinction of senses to a classification of actual things that are choiceworthy for their own sake. It raises the legitimate question as to which of the listed senses we should apply to the items in the classification—for our purposes we are particularly interested in the 'materials of the virtues', which are none other than the bodily and external goods, and which were also termed "productive" at 130.7–11. Sharples argued that the sense in question must be (3) above. This would create a conflict with the earlier passages where Didymus was at pains to show, against Critolaus, that material goods are *not* "parts" of happiness (here identified with [2] in the classification). As possible solutions Sharples suggested that the distinction of senses may not be exhaustive and thus the classification into "final" and "productive" may operate with a wider range of meanings for "choiceworthy for its own sake." Alternatively, according to Sharples, these divisions may be independent from the critique of Critolaus and we should not be looking for consistency across the doxography because a range of different sources may be in play.[51] Sharples does not consider the possibility that "productive" goods may constitute the aim of *some* (but not all) of our actions, as in (1) above, for example freedom of their fatherland is that for the sake of which people have entered armed conflict, and health is that for the sake of which we visit the dentist. This would place 'productive' goods clearly under one of the three distinguished senses, but without making them parts of the overall ultimate aim.

This reference to productive materials of the virtues juxtaposed with "final" virtuous actions is one manifestation of the bipartite division of

---

[51] See Sharples (1983) 145–46.

goods that groups all nonmoral goods together. The traditional *trigeneia* appears at 136.9–16 as another one among many possible divisions of goods (cf. "here is another division" at 135. 11 and 17). Those other divisions do not always map onto the *trigeneia*, nor do they depend on it in any way (e.g., the division at 135.11–16 groups virtues together with health).

Of particular interest is the division into "ends that are good for everyone and others not good for everyone" (135.17–18), where the latter emphatically *do not* lose their status as goods, as they do for the Stoics, due to the fact that they can be used badly. It is clearly stated that their use by the good man is what counts: "we have determined that they are good by the way the good man uses them" (136.2–3).[52] The same point is also made at 135.4–8, where the doxographer needs an argument to show that what he classified as "capacities" (wealth, political office, power) are in fact good in themselves (*kath' hauta*).[53] A puzzle has arisen as to status of wealth, because the division at 137.4–7 gives wealth as an example of a good that is not choiceworthy for its own sake but only productive.[54] But it is the latter division that is the 'odd one out': it is wholly inconsistent (not just on the issue of wealth) with 134.17–18 (quoted above) where productive goods are a subcategory of things choiceworthy for their own sake. In addition, its only examples of things choiceworthy for their own sake are the Epicurean pair of pleasure and freedom from disturbance, which are completely outside the spirit of the rest of the doxography.

On the whole, then, these divisions indicate a preoccupation with the role of bodily and external (or "material") goods, which are given a "productive" or "capacity" role. Their status as goods is not questioned but, on the contrary, is reinforced by appeal to the Peripatetic specification of the good man's use as a criterion. Nevertheless, the main preoccupation in this section remains the classification project itself, and the lengths to which it is taken have attracted criticism both in Antiquity and in modern scholarship. The "Middle" Platonist Atticus (fr. 2, ch. 17 Des Places, late 2nd century AD) is highly critical of a series of classifications that are identical, including their sequence but without the examples and subdivisions, with those found at 134.20–136.10. This suggests that the Peripatetic division sequence had met with some success, whether through Didymus or some

---

[52] This approach is paralleled in the *Magna Moralia* (1.2 1183b31), in a text that has a lot in common with this section of Didymus. See Sharples (1983) 143–45 and Furley (1983).

[53] On goods classified as capacities see Szaif (2012) 212–25.

[54] See Sharples (1983) 146–49.

other text (his source?) where it appeared in a similar form, to the extent that it needed to be addressed and neutralised in a Platonist context.[55]

Conclusions

A study of Didymus' summary of Peripatetic ethics reveals that the status of bodily and external goods in relation to happiness was a major preoccupation in the Peripatetic sources he accessed and used. This reflects the dialectical context, both vis-à-vis the Stoics and the Carneadean challenge, and internally as the school reacted to the aggregate view put forward by Critolaus. Several tensions and oddities in the doxography may find an explanation if we treat them as deriving from an effort to apply the tripartite division of goods and their relative contributions to happiness even to doctrines that were not conceived in these terms. In particular, we saw that the theory of *oikeiôsis* was awkwardly marshalled to support the intrinsic choiceworthiness of all three types of goods, producing an arbitrary *a fortiori* connection between social and personal *oikeiôsis*. In addition, the provision of natural advantages was clumsily inserted into the distinction between the "best" and the "intermediate" life. Didymus' treatment of the role of bodily and external goods was also characterised by the occasional classificatory zeal, as we saw in the divisions criticised by Atticus for their scholasticism. These criticisms should not, however, detract from the value of Didymus' doxography for tracing important developments in Peripatetic thought, especially in terms of the way in which the school settled on the view of bodily and external goods as necessary conditions / instruments. Thanks to Didymus we can see that this process involved a reaction to Critolaus, but also, crucially, that it made the most of Aristotelian ideas such as the distinction between conditions and constituent parts and especially the very important insight that happiness is an activity: it belongs to those who *act* correctly, just as Olympic prizes are only awarded to those who take part.

Works Cited

Annas, J. 1993. *The Morality of Happiness*. Oxford: Oxford University Press.
Annas J. and G. Betegh (eds.). 2015. *Cicero's* De Finibus: *Philosophical Approaches*. Cambridge: Cambridge University Press.

---

[55] Atticus' point is that such elaborate classifications bring us no closer to the truth of Plato. Especially in the order in which he lists the divisions, Atticus is much closer to Didymus than to *MM* 1.2. Cf. Inwood (2014b) 256–59.

Bett, R. 1997. *Sextus Empiricus, Against the Ethicists (Adversus Mathematicos XI)*. Oxford: Oxford University Press.
Cooper, J. 1985. "Aristotle and the Goods of Fortune." *Philosophical Review* 94: 173–97.
Dillon, J. 2003. *The Heirs of Plato: A Study of the Old Academy*. Oxford: Oxford University Press.
Fortenbaugh, W. W. (ed.). 1983. *On Stoic and Peripatetic Ethics: The Work of Arius Didymus*. Rutgers University Studies in Classical Humanities, vol. 1. New Brunswick, N.J.: Transaction.
Furley, D. 1983. "Comments on Dr. Sharples' Paper: A Note on Arius and *Magna Moralia* 1.1–2." In Fortenbaugh (1983) 160–64.
Gill, C. 2015. "Antiochus' Theory of *Oikeiōsis*." In Annas and Betegh (2015) 221–47.
Görgemanns, H. 1983. "*Oikeiōsis* in Arius Didymus." In Fortenbaugh (1983) 165–89.
Hahm, D. 2007. "Critolaus and Late Hellenistic Peripatetic Philosophy." In *Pyrronists, Patricians, Platonizers: Hellenistic Philosophy in the Period 155–86 BC*, ed. A.-M. Ioppolo and D. Sedley. Proceedings of the Tenth Symposium Hellenisticum. Naples: Bibliopolis, 49–101.
Hatzimichali, M. 2011. *Potamo of Alexandria and the Emergence of Eclecticism in Late Hellenistic Philosophy*. Cambridge: Cambridge University Press.
Huby, P. 1983. "Peripatetic Definitions of Happiness." In Fortenbaugh (1983) 121–34.
Inwood, B. 1983. "Comments on Professor Görgemanns' Paper: The Two Forms of *Oikeiōsis* in Arius and the Stoa." In Fortenbaugh (1983) 190–201.
———. 2014a. *Ethics after Aristotle*. Cambridge, Mass.: Harvard University Press.
———. 2014b. "Ancient Goods: The *Tria Genera Bonorum* in Ethical Theory." In *Strategies of Argument: Essays in Ancient Ethics, Epistemology and Logic*, ed. M.-K. Lee. Oxford: Oxford University Press, 255–80.
———. 2015. "The Voice of Nature." In Annas and Betegh (2015) 147–66.
Moraux, P. 1973. *Der Aristotelismus bei den Griechen von Andronikos bis Alexander von Aphrodisias* I. Berlin: De Gruyter.
Sharples, R. W. 1983. "The Peripatetic Classification of Goods." In Fortenbaugh (1983) 139–59.
———. 2007. "Peripatetics on Happiness." In *Greek and Roman Philosophy 100 BC–200 AD*, ed. R. W. Sharples and R. Sorabji. London: Institute of Classical Studies, University of London, 627–37.

———. 2010. *Peripatetic Philosophy 200 BC to AD 200: An Introduction and Collection of Sources in Translation.* Cambridge: Cambridge University Press.

Szaif, J. 2012. *Gut des Menschen: Untersuchungeh zur Problematik und Entwicklung der Glücksethik bei Aristoteles und in der Tradition des Peripatos.* Berlin: De Gruyter.

Tsouni , G. 2010. "Antiochus and Peripatetic Ethics." Ph.D. Diss., University of Cambridge.

White, S. 2002. "Happiness in the Hellenistic Lyceum." *Apeiron* 35: 69–92.

7

Didymus on Types of Life

William W. Fortenbaugh

Toward the end of his account of Peripatetic ethics and before turning to politics, (Arius?) Didymus takes up different kinds or types of life (p. 143.24–145.10 W). Preceding are brief discussions of emotion, friendship and favor (142.14–143.23) and following is a somewhat longer discussion of moral and intellectual virtue (145.11–147.25). These topics have already received attention earlier in the epitome,[1] so that the discussions give the appearance of poorly placed afterthoughts: they record/summarize what Didymus found in several unused sources. The discussion of types of life gives a similar impression. It is treated briefly and might be deemed an unimportant after-thought based on sources that Didymus wanted to include before turning to politics. That might be correct, at least in regard to placement within the epitome, but the topic is not to be ignored as

---

[1] In close proximity, see 139.1–18 on emotion and 137.14–138.26, 140.19–142.13 on moral and intellectual virtue. But emotion and virtue are in play much earlier, indeed, at the very beginning of the epitome (the emotional part of the soul is said to be receptive of virtue [117.9–10]), which is hardly surprising.

unimportant, for it received significant attention in the early Peripatos, in the Platonic Academy and in Greek literature of a still earlier date.[2]

(1a) 143.24–28

Whereas the manuscripts of Didymus' epitome often mark a change in topic with a heading, the beginning of the discussion of types of lives (143.24) lacks a heading.[3] Instead, the discussion begins with an assertion, of which the first part runs as follow:

> The morally good man will choose the life with/involving virtue.

Moraux calls the assertion *Unsinn*, "nonsense,"[4] which strikes me as more than a bit harsh. In the absence of a heading, the assertion functions as an announcement of a new topic. To be sure, the assertion is tautological: the morally good man, the *spoudaios*, is a man of virtue and as such will choose/has already chosen to lead a virtuous life.[5] But the assertion also indicates what will be discussed: the types of life that will be chosen by a morally good man.

The opening assertion is completed with a list of the ways in which the morally good man might live according to virtue (143.25–144.2):

> Whether he is at some time in a position of leadership, circumstances advancing him, or he must live in the service of a king, or engage in legislation, or be politically active in some other way.

---

[2] For an overview of early discussions of the best life see, e.g., Joly (1955) 12–139 and Fortenbaugh, "Clearchus, *On Lives*," forthcoming in RUSCH 21.

[3] *Re vera*: a subheading under the heading with which the Peripatetic section of the *Epitome* begins (116.19–20). See above, chap. 3, p. 76 n. 4. The end of the discussion of lives is signaled by the phrase: "These things having been considered" (145.11). Similar wording occurs elsewhere: e.g., "these distinctions having been made" (137.14). In both passages, the phrase takes the form of a genitive absolute and is attributable to Didymus. But it is not found at the end of the discussion of favor, which precedes that of lives (143.23). Hence, the addition of a heading at the beginning of the discussion of lives would be helpful. A heading like "On Types of Life" is suggested by the opening sentence.

[4] Moraux (1973) 405.

[5] Sharples (2010) 127 translates *spoudaios* with "good." That is economical. I have preferred "morally good" in order to emphasize that the goodness in question is ethical. Tsouni prefers "virtuous," which is not wrong, but in the sentence under consideration, it turns the sentence into a glaring tautology, which using "morally good" avoids. Throughout this paper, I shall translate *spoudaios* with "morally good."

The list invites comparison with two passages in Didymus' account of Stoic ethics. In the earlier passage, we read that the wise man engages in politics especially in political systems/under constitutions that are progressing toward completeness/perfection; he also engages in legislation and in education (94.8–12). In the later passage we are told that the man possessing intelligence will sometimes act as king and will live with a king who exhibits natural ability and a love of learning. But he will not engage in politics, if there will be no benefit for the fatherland and great dangers will arise (111.3–9). According to Moraux, not only are the ideas expressed in these two passages closely related to what Didymus attributes to the Peripatetics, but also it was the Stoics, who made these ideas a central matter of discussion within the Hellenistic schools of philosophy. For the ideas are directly related to the Stoic notion of the wise man/sage, who alone is fully qualified to claim the title of king. In regard to the Peripatetics, Moraux cites Critolaus (mid-2nd c. BC), who is said to have discussed these ideas,[6] and concludes that the position attributed to the Peripatetics is hardly to be dated before the second century, that is, it is significantly later than Aristotle, Theophrastus and the other early Peripatetics.

The date has an initial plausibility, for Didymus' immediate source may well belong to the late Hellenistic period. But that does not mean that the Stoics played a special/unique role in giving prominence to the ideas expressed in the three passages, and even if they did, it is well to keep in mind that the ideas have their roots in an earlier period. I think of Plato (perhaps not perfect like the Stoic sage, but a man of wisdom nonetheless) who attempted to realize the philosopher-king in Dionysius II and in doing so involved himself in dangers, which were ultimately fatal to Dion.[7] In addition, Aristotle tried his hand at working with Hermias of Atarneus

---

[6] Moraux (1973) 413 refers to Critolaus, fr. 35 Wehrli, in which the Peripatetic is said to forbid a philosopher's participation in the foundation of a city and to acknowledge that philosophers who do not engage in politics assist their fatherland greatly by teaching young people always to obey the laws. The text is polemical and as such needs to be interpreted with caution. But even taken at face value, it is not clear how and to what extent the passage supports Moraux's claim that the position attributed to the Peripatetics by Didymus cannot be dated before the second century BC. Certainly the importance of educating the young was of special concern to the early Peripatetics. E.g., Theophrastus wrote a work *On Education* (D.L. 5.50 = Theophr. 436 no. 9) and addressed the issue whether one must always obey the law (Gellius, *Attic Nights* 1.3.8–14, 21–29 = Theophr. 534 and *Digest* 1.3.3, 1.3.6 = Theophr. 629, 630). That Critolaus would have accepted an unqualified "always" (*aiei*; Crit. fr. 35.14) is doubtful.

[7] Plato, *Letters* 7 350B–E.

and Philip of Macedon,[8] and Theophrastus is said to have played a role in removing tyranny from Eresos.[9]

Moreover, the two Stoic passages are not alone in recognizing the importance of particular circumstances (94.9–10 and 111.6–9). They are also mentioned by Didymus in the Peripatetic passage, where reference is made to the *kairoi* (143.25). The importance of the *kairoi* in a political context was well known to the early Peripatetics and received special attention from Theophrastus, who wrote works entitled *Politica pros tous kairous, Politics regarding Crises* (5.45 = 589 no. 4 FHS&G) and *Peri kairôn, On Crises* (5.50 = 589 no. 5).[10] Finally, the earlier of the two Stoic passages refers to political arrangements showing progress, *prokopê*, toward perfection. That certainly has a Stoic ring, but the Peripatetics appear not only to have used the term *prokopê*[11] but also to have recognized a distinction between perfect and imperfect constitutions,[12] the latter being constitutions that may be thought of as either progressing toward or falling away from completeness/perfection.[13]

After the list of ways in which the morally good man may be politically active, we are told (144.2–4):

---

[8] D.L., *Lives* 5.3, with Düring (1957) 272–94.

[9] Plutarch, *A Pleasant Life Is Impossible* 15 1097B and *Against Colotes* 33 1126F = Theophr. fr. 33A–B FHS&G. In *Against Colotes*, Theophrastus is said to have twice delivered his fatherland from tyrants. The first occasion is likely to have been in 343 BC when the three brothers, Apollodorus, Hermon and Heraius were removed and the second will have occurred a decade later when Agonippus and Eurysilaus were removed. On the first occasion, Theophrastus will have been at Mytilene with Aristotle before the two went to Macedonia. Returning to Eresus and playing a hands-on role in the removal of the tyrants is not difficult to imagine. On the second occasion, Theophrastus will have been in Athens with Aristotle. He could have returned to Eresus, but equally he may have played a role at a distance. For completeness' sake, I add that Plutarch, in *A Pleasant Life*, tells us that Phainias participated with Theophrastus in driving out tyrants from Eresus. For brief discussion of Phainias, see Fortenbaugh (2015) 107–10 and for fuller discussion of tyranny in Eresus, see Teegarden (2014) 115–41.

[10] A third work listed by Diogenes, *Kairoi, Crises* (5.50 = 589 no. 6 = Pausanias the Atticist, *Collection of Attic Words*, on *archê Skyria* [no. 159, *ADAW* (1949) 2.1661.1 Erbse]) may refer to one of the other two works listed by Diogenes. I return to the *kairoi* below.

[11] See below, p. 249 on D.L. 7.127.

[12] On perfect and imperfect constitutions, see Fortenbaugh (1976) 125–37.

[13] To be thorough, I call attention to a difference. Whereas the later of the Stoic passages refers to the man who possesses intelligence actually taking on the role of king, *basileuein* (111.3), the corresponding Peripatetic passage does not speak explicitly of taking on the role of king but rather of playing a leadership role, *hêgemonia* (143.25). That may or may not be significant.

> Should he fail to obtain (one of) these, he will turn to the ordinary form of life (i.e., the life of the common citizen) or to the life of contemplation, or to that of a teacher, which is in between.

At first reading, it might seem that the three lives listed here, including that of contemplation, are second best. The morally good person will turn, *trapêsesthai* (144.3), to them, (only) when a life of political action is not an option. But as I understand the text that follows (144.5–8), that is not correct.

> For he will choose to do and to contemplate things noble. And should he be prevented by circumstances from being concerned with both, he will engage in one or the other, giving precedence to the contemplative life, but desiring political activity on account of his sense of community.

Now we are told that the morally good man is not one sided: not either a doer or a contemplator, but both. If he must choose between action and contemplation, he will prefer the latter, but he does not lose the urge/desire to be politically active.[14] If that is correct, and I think it is, the epitomist has not made comprehension easy. By beginning with political involvement and by speaking of "turning to" other modes of life, the reader might think that the political life is rated higher than all other forms, but that turns out not to be the case. In the end, the life that mixes political and nonpolitical activities, including contemplation, takes precedence.

To explain what is patently an awkward text, Moraux suggests the following. The epitomist believed that the Peripatetics viewed the ideal life as one that mixed theoretical and practical activity. The Peripatetics also held that this life is best achieved by a ruler, his advisor, a legislator or the like. These two views motivated the epitomist to combine awkwardly two different notions of the best life: that which gives precedence to political activity

---

[14] At 144.6 *amphô*, "both," refers to the two major areas: political activity (being a leader, an advisor, legislator etc.) and private life (everyday/ordinary business, contemplation, teaching). Caveat: Although the focus here is on the morally good man, the *spoudaios* (143.24), and sense of community is introduced to explain his desire to be politically active, *dia to koinônikon* (144.7), it would be a mistake to think that sense of community is peculiar to the morally good man. Rather it is a natural characteristic of human beings generally, defective individuals aside. See 120.13–14 and 150.2–3. Much the same is true of the desire to engage in contemplation. As Didymus puts it, we are by nature inclined toward contemplation (118.1–2). We may compare the opening sentence of Aristotle's *Metaphysics*, "All men naturally desire to know" (1.1 980a22). In quite young children, that desire manifests itself in curiosity; in philosophers it becomes their passion. See Fortenbaugh (2016), "Aristotle on Bipartition," end section with n. 30.

and that which combines contemplation with practical pursuits. Moraux's suggestion is certainly possible, but there are other possibilities. The opening sentence (143.24), which Moraux criticizes, may have taken the place of omitted material that will have oriented the reader in regard to what the epitomist has chosen to print. In addition, the printed text itself may have been abbreviated before or after the assertion that the morally good man will choose both to do and to contemplate things noble (144.4–5). I leave the matter undecided.

It might be suggested that the above remarks overlook an important and frequently mentioned text: namely, Cicero's letter to Atticus 2.16.3, in which we read of a great controversy, *tanta controversia*, between two prominent Peripatetics. Dicaearchus is said to rate the active life far above all other lives, while Theophrastus is said to prefer the contemplative life (fr. 33 M; Theoph., fr. 481 FHS&G). By "active life" we are to understand one that involves political/civic engagement and by "contemplative life" that of the philosopher. If that is correct, we may want to say that the remarks of the epitomist reflect a real division among Peripatetics. The opening sentence, which tells us that the morally good man will choose a life involving virtue and then goes on to list several modes of political activity, reflects the position of Dicaearchus. The subsequent reference to an alternative form of life outside the political arena, one involving everyday business, contemplation and teaching, is essentially that of Theophrastus, who rated contemplation highly, taught students and was concerned with everyday issues of household management, economics, including the business of the School. The trouble here is that the great controversy between the two Peripatetics is the creation of Cicero.[15] When the fragments of the two Peripatetics are taken into account, it seems clear that any difference between the two was a matter of emphasis. Both will have endorsed a mixed life that makes room for both doing and contemplating things noble (144.5). Indeed, Dicaearchus, the alleged champion of the active life, spent much time in research, when he will not have been engaged in the politics of his native city Messana.[16] And as already mentioned, Theophrastus, the proponent of quiet contemplation, is reported to have played a role in the removal of tyranny from his native city Eresus.[17]

---

[15] See Fortenbaugh (2013) 483–86.

[16] See the titles of Dicaearchus' works in the edition of Mirhady (2001) 6–11. Included are works not only on music and poetry (fr. 1 no. 14–18) but also on geography (no. 19–21) and psychology (no. 1).

[17] See above, n. 9.

In the segment of text under consideration, the noun *kairos* occurs twice in the plural, *kairoi*, where it has been translated with "circumstances." The first occurrence has already been mentioned above. It concerns circumstances that advance a morally good man to a position of leadership, for example, to be a monarch or king (143.25–144.1). The second occurrence concerns circumstances that prevent the morally good man from both doing and contemplating things noble, so that he chooses one or the other (144.5–6). The idea being expressed is common enough. What a sensible person chooses to do often depends upon circumstances. And for the Peripatetics, the morally good man, the *spoudaios* (143.24), is sensible. He is the man who combines moral virtue with practical wisdom, so that he assesses his situation correctly and does what is possible as well as morally correct. It might be objected that the possible and the morally correct often come apart, but a Peripatetic would have a ready reply: ethical behavior involves choosing and choice is of the possible or at least of what appears possible (Arist. *EN* 3.2 1111b20–26). The morally good man recognizes that there are situations in which it is not immediately clear what action is to be chosen, but pausing for reflection will result in sound choice. To be sure, there are sudden situations that rule out reflection/deliberation concerning the possible: for example, when a soldier is confronted by an unexpected danger that demands immediate response (cf. *EN* 3.8 1117a17–23). In such a situation, a cowardly soldier might flee, but the more courageous soldier gets it right. He confronts the danger, understanding that it is noble to defend the city-state even if he dies doing so.[18]

(1b) 144.8–15

Having said that the morally good man desires political activity on account of his sense of community (144.7–8), the epitomist continues:

> For this reason he will marry and will beget children and will engage in politics and will experience love in moderation and will drink in accordance with social gatherings, even if not as a primary activity.

The phrase *di'ho*, "for this reason" (144.8), picks up the reference to the morally good man's sense of community, which explains the introduction of marriage and children. The nuclear family is the basic community and natural to human beings (Arist. *Pol.* 1.2 1252a24–31). The reference to political involvement, *politeuesthai*, which follows (144.9), might be

---

[18] On the phrase "more courageous" at *EN* 3.8 1117a18, see below p. 250 with n. 66.

deemed unnecessary, given the preceding references to political involvement (144.2), but it also comes naturally after the mention of family: marriage, children, involvement in the civic life of the larger community.

Moraux is less forgiving.[19] He recognizes that the preceding reference to sense of community (144.7) brings on, *zieht nach sich*, the remarks concerning marriage, children and political involvement, but he argues that in regard to content these remarks do not belong to what precedes. For they apply to the morally good man whatever his mode of life might be. In contrast, the preceding remarks are tied to particular modes of life. Circumstances determine how a person participates in politics, and in some cases circumstances force a person to turn to an ordinary life or one of contemplation or teaching (143.25–144.4). In what follows, circumstances are ignored in favor of a general statement: the morally good man will participate in politics (144.9). Fair enough, but the transition between passages remains intelligible. We understand that the morally good man *qua* human being has a natural drive to be politically active (144.8) and that generally he will act upon it. I do not want to defend the transition between segments as seamless, but I do not find it disturbing.

If one keeps in mind that the focus is on the morally good man, extending the list of marrying, begetting children and political involvement to include engaging in erotic love and in drinking might seem odd. But that may be only a first impression, for the reference to erotic love is qualified as *sophrôn*, "moderate," and drinking is qualified by *kata sumperiphoras*, "in accordance with social gatherings" (144.9–11). Neither the serial adulterer nor the closet-alcoholic is under consideration. Rather, the focus remains on the morally good man and his behavior. In regard to drinking, we are being told that he enjoys imbibing, but he regulates his drinking in accordance with, *kata*, the particular gathering; that is, according to social norms. Hence, Simpson translates "in accord with the company he is with."[20]

---

[19] Moraux (1973) 406.

[20] Sharples translates with "drink socially." That may be a succinct way of saying in conformity with social standards, but it might mean no more than doing one's drinking with others. Hence, I prefer a fuller translation that makes clear that *kata sumperiphoras* qualifies *methusthêsesthai* much as *ton sôphrona erôta* qualifies *erasthêsesthai* (144.9–10). In both cases, the virtuous individual observes limits. He is not obsessed with sex; i.e., he is not marked by *erôtomania* (142.22–3), and in regard to imbibing, his drinking is in accordance with social norms. On this use of the preposition *kata*, see Goodwin and Gulick 1218.b.4. For the moment, I am ignoring the phrase "even if not as a primary activity" (144.11). See below, p. 241 on 144.19–20.

Moraux sees in the passage a Peripatetic reaction to those Stoics who held that the wise man would never get drunk. He cites Seneca, who tells us that Zeno, the founder of the School, held such a view, arguing that no one entrusts a secret to a drunken man, but rather to a good man (*Epist.* 83.9). Also cited is Didymus' epitome of Stoic ethics, in which we are told that the person possessing intelligence cannot become drunk, for that makes one capable of doing wrong[21] (109.5–6).[22] Moraux is certainly correct to see disagreement between the Peripatetics and Stoics in regard to drunkenness, but it is well to underline that Peripatetic interest in drunkenness is qualified and did not arise along with Stoicism. The topic was of general interest and one that Plato famously addressed in the *Laws* with special reference to alleviating the despondency that comes with age (2 666B). Moreover, both heavy drinking/drunkenness and *eros* were discussed at length by the early Peripatetics. Indeed, separate works concerning drunkenness are attributed to Aristotle, Theophrastus, Hieronymus and Chamaeleon, while works on *eros* are attributed to Aristotle, Theophrastus, Clearchus, Demetrius of Phalerum and Aristo of Ceus.[23]

In what follows (144.11–15), the possibility of suicide is considered.

> And in general (the morally good man) practicing virtue will remain in life, and again, if ever it should be necessary, he will depart (from life), having given thought beforehand to his burial in accordance with law and ancestral custom and whatever else it is pious to perform for the departed.

This is not the first mention of suicide in Didymus' epitome of Peripatetic ethics. Two earlier passages address the issue. In the first, we are told that life is measured by actions in the city-state and in the community and in contemplation, and that remaining and departing from life is measured by these activities (125.19–126.5).[24] In the second, we are told that good

---

[21] The phrase "capable of doing wrong" translates *harmatêtikon* (109.6). Didymus tells us that for the Stoics every inappropriate act occurring in a rational creature is a mistaken act, *hamartêma* (86.10–11). See below pp. 247–49 on 145.9–10.

[22] Moraux (1973) 413–14 is careful to note that the Stoic position concerning the wise man and drunkenness admitted variation.

[23] Concerning works on drunkenness, see Fortenbaugh (2011) 222–26 and (2012b) 372–85. For works on *eros*, see Fortenbaugh (2011) 212–18, (2012a) 11–23 and for a possible work by Phainias, (2015) 122 with n. 66.

[24] Caveat: in the immediately following sentence (126.5–7) Wachsmuth changes *kai* to *kakôs*. In their translations, Sharples and Simpson accept the change and translate: "So it is wrong to consider that departure from life can be reasonable for the wise" and "so that to exit from life is reasonably a bad thing for the wise to contemplate." That contradicts what

people should flee life in excessive misfortunes, and bad people should do the same in excessive good fortunes (134.2–4). The three passages taken together are of interest, for in the *Nicomachean Ethics* Aristotle twice expresses himself in a way that might be thought to rule out suicide as an option for the morally good person, no matter what the circumstances. In book 3, Aristotle characterizes courage as a mean disposition on account of which a man chooses to endure the fearsome because it is noble to do so and shameful not to do so. To die fleeing poverty or love or something painful is what a coward does and not a courageous individual. It is softness to flee things that are toilsome and not to endure because it is noble (3.7 1116a12–15). In book 5, Aristotle tells us that what the law does not enjoin it forbids. And when a man is angry and strikes himself he acts voluntarily and in violation of right reason, which the law does not permit. He acts unjustly not toward himself but toward the city-state. And that is why the state exacts a penalty and imposes dishonor on the person who commits suicide (5.11 1138a3–14).

We may think that the first part of the argument in book 5 involves an unacceptable premise: what the law does not enjoin it forbids (1138a7),[25] but the second part of the argument finds support in Athenian practice. At least, Aeschines says that the hand involved in committing suicide was buried apart from the body (*Against Ctesiphon* 244). Be that as it may, Moraux tells us that the Nicomachean passages present a view of suicide that is fundamentally different from that recorded in the three passages of Didymus cited above. We are also told that it is different from that of the Stoics, who explicitly accepted suicide under certain conditions.[26] Apparently the text of Didymus represents a view held by later Peripatetics, who were influenced by the Stoics. In addition, Moraux refers to the Epicurean notion of the wise man, which rules out concern for one's own burial (D.L., *Lives* 10.118). Since the third/last of the three texts of Didymus treats such

---

the received text says, "for wise individuals it is reasonable to consider departing from life." To be sure, the occasions will be few, when a wise person deems it best to depart from life, but that does mean that reflecting on the present situation and the possibility of taking one's own life is wrongheaded/a bad thing.

[25] Ostwald 143 n. 75, following Stuart (1892) 1.533–34, suggests that here "law," *nomos*, should not be understood as positive law but rather as law and custom. Perhaps that is correct, but it may only shift the problem. Is it true, as Stuart suggests, that "Custom (fashion, public opinion) forbids the most innocent actions, if it does not enjoin them"? And is it true that custom does not admit exceptions, or is custom for the most part?

[26] Concerning the Stoics, see, e.g., Epictetus, *Discourses* 1.25.18–20 and Marcus Aurelius, *Meditations* 5.29 on leaving a room that is filled with smoke.

a concern as a preliminary to committing suicide (144.13), Moraux suggests that it represents the thinking of later Peripatetics who were not only influenced by the Stoics but also critical of the Epicureans.[27]

Consistent with Moraux's view is Didymus' concern with the critical moment. Although the word *kairos* is not used by Didymus in the three passages dealing with suicide, taken together they leave no doubt that circumstances can be decisive in deciding to take one's own life.[28] In the first passage, we are told that suicide is reasonable for people who are unable to accomplish communal, political and theoretical activities (126.10-11).[29] In the second passage, we read that good people should flee life in excessive misfortune, *en tais agan atuchiais*, and bad people should do the same in excessive good fortune, *en tais agan eutuchiais* (134.2-4).[30] In the third passage, we are told that generally the morally good man[31] remains in life, but there are occasions when he should depart on account of necessities,

---

[27] Moraux (1973) 414, 441-2; cf. Joly (1956) 153.

[28] Concerning *kairos*, see above p. 230.

[29] Being unable to accomplish a variety of activities (some of which are quite ordinary, like those of community) strongly suggests overwhelming circumstances. In the other two passages, the notion of adverse circumstances is clear.

[30] In order to explain why a bad person should flee life in excessive good fortune, Didymus tells us that bad persons go wrong more, and for this reason they are not fortunate in the strict sense (134.4-6). Later we are told that goods like wealth, rule and power are not good for everyone. The good individual uses them well and the bad individual uses them badly. For clarity's sake, Didymus compares music and horses. The things that the musical individual uses well, the nonmusical individual uses badly and at the same time hurts himself. Similarly, a good horse benefits a skilled rider, but harms considerably the person who is unskilled (135.19-136.8). Here I am following Tsouni and Simpson against Sharples, who has the skilled rider benefiting the good horse and the unskilled rider harming the horse (136.7-8). Sharples seems to confuse subject and object, which is easy to do when both are in the accusative case. Moreover, the paragraph begins by distinguishing between things that are good for everyone and things that are not good for everyone (135.17-136.3). The good horse belongs to the latter group. It can harm the unskilled rider who is unaccustomed to a swift moving, high jumping mount and therefore likely to take a tumble and crack his head open.

[31] The morally good man, the *spoudaios*, was mentioned at 143.24 and is explicitly referred to in what follows. It seems reasonable to hold that he is the subject in 144.8-15. In regard to committing suicide, the reference to practicing virtue (144.11-12) and being concerned with burial rites including ancestral custom (144.13-15) point to the *spoudaios*. Of the two earlier passages that mention suicide, the first refers explicitly to the *spoudaios* (126.9). The second refers to good men, *agathoi* (134.3), but since the *spoudaios* is mentioned in the immediately preceding sentence (134.1), it is reasonable to understand the good men as morally good men, *spoudaioi*.

di' anagkas (144.13).[32] Fair enough, Didymus recognizes the importance of the *kairos*. But are we to believe that Aristotle ignored the *kairos*, that he banned suicide no matter what the circumstances might be? I am doubtful and offer four considerations. First, Aristotle was an active member of the Platonic Academy when Plato wrote the *Laws*. In that dialogue, the Athenian Stranger is made to discuss suicide. He says *inter alia* that a penalty is to be imposed if the person who takes his own life is not acting in obedience to a legal decision, is not forced by severe and unavoidable misfortune,[33] or has not fallen into irremediable disgrace (9.873C). The Stranger expresses himself negatively, thereby implying that suicide is acceptable when a sentence of death has been imposed, when misfortune is unbearable or when disgrace cannot be undone.[34] Aristotle will have known the passage and understood the implication of the Stranger's words. Second, the way Aristotle expresses himself in book 3 of the *Nicomachean Ethics* is suggestive. When he writes that seeking death to avoid poverty, love or some other painful experience is cowardly, and to run away from troubles is softness (1116a12–15), he seems to imply that there are other circumstances in which taking one's own life is acceptable. That is how John Rist understands the text and I am inclined to agree.[35] Third, the *Nicomachean Ethics* is an esoteric work, which Aristotle will have used in the School when lecturing to students. In writing such a work he might express himself succinctly, and then during lecture or afterwards in discussion he could flesh out his remarks adding clarification. In regard to suicide, he could spell out the circumstances in which suicide is acceptable.[36] Fourth, in Diogenes' catalogue of Aristotelian writings, there are listed four titles that refer to certain theses. One of these, *Argumentative Theses*, is reported to have been twenty-five books in length. It is easy to imagine that this work made room for argument *pro* and *contra* concerning the morality of suicide. And since

---

[32] We should be careful not to confuse the necessities that justify taking one's own life (144.13) with the necessities required for life (132.18). In the former, we have the plural noun *anagkai* referring, e.g., to extreme sickness and unbearable torture and in general whatever might compel a person to commit suicide. In the later we have the plural adjective *anagkaia* referring, e.g., to food and sleep and whatever might be basic to maintaining life. The noun and the adjective are cognates. Context determines the difference in reference.

[33] Here at *Laws* 873C "forced" translates the participle *anagkastheis*. Cf. the use of the noun in Plato's *Phaedo* 62C and in Arius at 144.13, cited above.

[34] Schöpsdau (2011) 336.

[35] Rist (1969) 235–36.

[36] The idea is not new: see, e.g., Heath (2008) 247 who observes that regarding natural slaves Aristotle was content to express himself succinctly, omitting qualifications which in context are deemed obvious. Also Fortenbaugh (2015) 402–3.

Aristotle made theses part of his instructional program not only with a view to teaching persuasive argument but also to appropriate style, the topic of suicide may well have found a place in classroom debate.[37] For example, a clever student might defend the proposition "In excessive misfortunes, *en tais agan atuchiais*, men ought to flee life" (134.3–4) by citing the Delphic maxim "Nothing in excess," *mêden agan*. Or the suicide of Ajax might be cited as an acceptable way to deal with irremediable disgrace. Or Socrates' drinking hemlock might be explained as acting in obedience to a legal decision. That is, of course, speculation. But it is not unreasonable, so that I am willing to believe that Aristotle did not close the door on suicide. Rather he saw it as a complex issue that merited serious debate within the Peripatos.[38]

Before leaving this portion of the epitome, a word concerning style may be of interest. I am thinking of the repeated use of *kai*, "and," four times in order to mark off five different activities: marrying, begetting children, being political, erotic love and drinking (144.8–11). That is striking and might give the impression that all five activities are on a par. But they are not as the qualifying phrases added to the last two make clear. Perhaps we should explain this use of polysyndeton as stylistic and taken over from the epitomist's source. The very next sentence seems to support such an interpretation, for *kai* occurs five times with the last four occurrences forming two short but noticeable lists: first, the pairing of remaining in and departing from life (hence the translation "both … and"), and second, the

---

[37] Aristotle was interested in appropriate style, but Cicero engages in overstatement when he tells us that Aristotle trained his students in theses not for the sake of the subtle argumentation of philosophers but for the abundance of rhetoricians (*Orator* 46).

[38] According to Athenaeus, Clearchus of Soli, who was a student of Aristotle, wrote a work *On Lives*, in which the Pythagorean Euxitheus is made to describe human souls as bound to the body as a form of punishment. The person who does not accept this punishment but seeks his own release is forced to suffer a still greater punishment. For this reason, people avoid committing suicide and welcome the death that comes with old age (*Sophists at Dinner* 4.157C–D = Clearchus fr. 38 Dorandi). As reported, Euxitheus presents an argument against taking one's own life, no matter how intolerable the circumstances might be. But that does not tell us how Clearchus used the report in his work *On Lives*, which is likely is have been an exoteric work aimed at an audience larger and more inclusive than that of students within the Peripatos. Moreover, we cannot simply assume that Clearchus, *qua* student of Aristotle, will have adopted his teacher's view of suicide. See Plutarch, *On the Face of the Moon*, where Lamprias is made to say that Clearchus, who was an intimate associate of Aristotle, perverted many doctrines of the School: *polla tou Peripatou paretrepsen* (2.920F = fr. 116). Perhaps one of the perverted doctrines concerned suicide, but that is neither asserted nor implied in what Lamprias says.

tripartite list: law and ancestral custom and whatever else is called for by piety (144.12–14).

(2a) 144.16–21

In what follows, Didymus presents a view of the best life that is in line with what precedes but adds a new perspective. The text runs as follows:

> There are three forms of life: practical, theoretical, combining both. The apolaustic life is less than human, and the theoretical is deemed superior to the others. The morally good man will engage in politics as a primary activity, not (just) according to circumstances, for the practical life is the same as the political.

Given the occurrence of polysyndeton in what precedes, the absence of a conjunction in the list "practical, theoretical, combining both" (144.16–17) is notable and might be taken to signal a change in source, but I do not press the matter. More important is the reference to a *synthetos bios*, a "mixed/combined" life (144.16–17), which unites the practical and the theoretical. The idea has already been introduced in the opening segment of the discussion of types of lives: the morally good man was said to choose "both to do and to contemplate" what is noble (144.4–5).

Whereas the opening sentence of the present passage begins by referring to three kinds of lives, one of which combines the other two (144.16), a fourth kind is mentioned in the sentence that follows—namely, the apolaustic life, which is characterized as less than human. That recalls the first book of the *Nicomachean Ethics*, in which Aristotle says that ordinary men, drawing on their own lives, identify the good and happiness with pleasure, and for this reason they welcome the apolaustic life. After that Aristotle speaks of three prominent lives: the apolaustic, the political and the theoretical, and then says that the apolaustic life resembles that of cattle (1.5 1095b14–22). The mention of three lives and the denigration of the apolaustic life as that of an animal invites comparison with what we read in Didymus. Only Didymus anticipates the diminished status of the apolaustic life and does not include it in the opening list of three lives. Nor does Didymus follow Aristotle, who argues at length against those people who see the good life in political activity whose end is honor (1095b23). Rather he asserts the primacy of contemplation and then acknowledges that the morally good man will engage in politics as a primary activity and not just in special circumstances.[39] Didymus adds that the practical life is the same

---

[39] "Not just in special circumstances" is Sharples' (2010) 127 translation of *mê kata peristasin* (144.20). I have preferred "not (just) according to circumstances." Both

as that of politics (144.20–21). That is not everyone's notion of the practical life,[40] but it is in line with or at least suggested by Aristotle's argument in book 1 of the *Ethics*, for there Aristotle presents the political life as that of active men, *praktikoi* (1095b22).

When Didymus says that the morally good man will engage in politics as a primary activity, *proêgoumenôs* (144.19–20), he is using an adverb, which is not found in either the corpus Aristotelicum or in the fragments of Theophrastus. In Didymus' epitome, the same adverbial form occurs some eight lines earlier, where we are told that the morally good man will drink heavily, albeit not as a primary activity, *mê proêgoumenôs* (144.11). If I understand correctly, these occurrences reflect Hellenistic usage[41] and are not incompatible with Peripatetic doctrine. *Proêgoumenôs* is used of an activity that is proper to the agent,[42] who in this case is the morally good man. In the earlier occurrence, heavy drinking is not proper to the morally good man, but certain circumstances permit/require it, that is, being in a convivial social context. In the later passage, engaging in politics is proper to the morally good man, and not just a response to special circumstances, *mê kata peristasin* (144.20).

The mention of circumstances invites comparison with an earlier passage which opens the discussion of types of lives. There the first sentence

---

translations are taking account of the fact that the Greek phrase by itself might be translated "not according to circumstances," which might be construed to mean that circumstances do not count. That is clearly false. See above where we are told that the person who fails to obtain a role in politics will turn to an ordinary life (144.2–3) and below where we read that necessities may cause a man to commit suicide (144.12–13). To understand correctly, we need to focus on the immediately preceding adverb *proêgoumenôs*, "as a primary activity" (144.19–20). What follows concerning circumstances introduces a secondary consideration. See below with n. 41.

[40] A soldier leads a life of action, which need not and most often does not include politics (though in Athens the office of a general was elective). Nevertheless what Arius is saying is clear enough. Earlier we have been told that the morally good man will chose to be active and to contemplate, *prattein* and *theôrein* (144.5). Now we are told that the morally good man will engage in politics, *politeusesthai*, as a primary aim (144.19). The two passages are brought into line with each other by the saying that the practical life is the same as the political (144.20–21). Moreover, the political life may be identified with (treated as representative of) the active life as its finest form.

[41] There are four occurrences of *proêgoumenôs* in Arius' epitome of Stoic ethics. All occur within a section dealing with the main functions of the several virtues. E.g., we are told that the function of temperance, *sôphrosunê*, is "primarily to provide balanced impulses and to view them" and the function of courage, *andreia*, is "primarily to endure everything one must" (63.15–17 and 63.20–21; transl. Pomeroy [1999] 19).

[42] See Huby (1983) 126–27 and Sharples (1990) 65 n. 220.

mentions the morally good man and states that he acts as a leader or monarch, when circumstances take him in that direction, or he serves a king or legislates or takes on some other political role (143.24–144.2). To be sure, this sentence refers to the *kairoi* and not to *peristaseis*, as does the present passage, but that is a variation in terminology. Both passages are concerned with circumstances: the earlier tells us that circumstances determine the role that a good man chooses to play in politics, and the later that playing a role in politics is proper to being a morally good man and not (just) an accident of circumstances.

Toward the end of the discussion of three lives in book 1 of the *Ethics*, Aristotle refers to the life of contemplation and defers comment until later (1096a4–5). He then closes the discussion by adding a fourth life, that of the money-maker. This life is quickly dismissed. It is said to involve constraint and to have as its goal wealth, which is a means to something else (1096a5–10). Didymus' failure to mention this fourth mode of life may be taken not only as an endorsement of Aristotle's position but also as sensible. No need to mention a form of life that has been adequately discredited. Nevertheless, it should be noted that the life of money-making was early on recognized as a prominent form of life. We may recall the comparison between the lives people lead and the intentions of people who attend the Olympic Games. Persons whose life is oriented toward the accumulation of wealth are likened to the merchants who attend the games in order to make money; those who strive for honor in civic life are likened to the competitors at the games; and those who enjoy a life of contemplation are like the spectators. The comparison is reported by Cicero in his *Tusculan Disputations*. Cicero cites Heraclides of Pontus as his source and tells us that Heraclides attributed the comparison to Pythagoras (5.3.8–9). The attribution has been challenged by scholars,[43] but that need not concern us here. Rather we should take note of the fact that Plato in his *Republic*, when comparing the lives people lead with constitutions, recognizes the life of money-making as a discrete way of life (550C–555B), but later when he divides lives on the basis of his tripartite soul, he argues that money is not loved for its own sake but as a means to satisfying the desires of the appetitive part of the soul. That enables him to recognize three kinds of men who live three kinds of lives: those who aim at wisdom, those who strive for victory and those whose desire to make money is driven by appetite (580D–581A,

---

[43] See Jaeger (1948) 432; Gigon (1951) 553–54; Joly (1956) 33–35; and Düring (1961) 212.

581C). It should, then, be no surprise that Aristotle rejects money-making as an end in itself, and that Didymus passes over it in silence.[44]

(2b) 144.21–145.2

The text that follows distinguishes between three types of life.

> The best life is that according to virtue in things according to nature; second is that according to the intermediate disposition possessing the most and especially important of things according to nature. These (lives), therefore, are to be chosen; that according to vice is to be fled.

In his edition of Stobaeus book 2, Wachsmuth prints as a single paragraph both the present text (144.21–145.2) and the immediately preceding text, which is focused on the political and theoretical forms of life (144.16–21). A reason for doing so is that both sections are concerned with different forms of life (both begin with the word *bios*[45]) and which form is to be preferred. That reason may be sufficient, but we should not overlook the fact that there is a difference in orientation. Whereas the preceding segment is concerned with the theoretical and political, that which follows is concerned with the presence and absence of virtue.[46] The best life is said to be that according to virtue in things according to nature. Second is that according to the intermediate disposition (between virtue and vice) and possessing most things according to nature. These two lives are worthy of choice, but the third life—that according to vice—is not.[47]

---

[44] More precisely, Didymus passes over both the apolaustic life and that of the money-maker. When the former is rejected from consideration, the latter is too.

[45] *Bios* in the plural occurs at 144.16 and in the singular at 144.21.

[46] So Moraux (1973) 407.

[47] Adopting modern terminology, we might say that the later passage (144.21–145.2) offers an analysis in terms of polar opposites. I.e., not opposites like odd and even which admit nothing in between (cf. Arist. *Cat.* 10 11b38–12a9, 12b27–32), but rather opposites like full and empty, which do not exclude half full and half empty. The best life, the *bios kratiston*, occupies one end of a scale in that it contains everything that makes for happiness: namely virtue and a full complement of goods according to nature. Opposed at the other end of the scale is the life of vice which is the worst of lives. It is marked by vice, which nullifies any benefits that goods according to nature might bring. In between is a life marked by an intermediate disposition (cf. Arist. *Cat.* 8 10b26–11a5, 10 12a9–25) and the possession of most goods according to nature. This in between life is called second and said to be worthy of choice (145.1). We are to think of it as occupying a middle position as long as we recognize that the position is not a fixed point that admits no gradation. Like the glass that falls short of being full, the life that falls short of perfection may fall short by only a little

The phrase "things according to nature" refers to good things (cf. 132.9–10) and covers both bodily and external goods (cf. 131.5–6).[48] In regard to the two acceptable forms of life, a difference is recognized in the possession of these goods. Regarding the best life, that according to virtue, the possession is unqualified (144.22). Regarding the second life, that according to the intermediate disposition, the possession is qualified by "most and especially important" (144.23–145.1). Are we to understand that the best life has all things that are according to nature? The issue is already present in an earlier passage concerned with happiness *qua* goal of everything a person does (130.13–131.2). After telling us that we should follow the ancients (131.2), Didymus lists three views of the end: "It is that for the sake of which we do everything, but it for nothing else, or the ultimate of things desired, or living according to virtue in bodily and external goods, either all or the most and especially important" (131.3–6). The third view relates closely to the present passage in that both include the words "the most and especially important" (131.6; 144.23–145.1). But there is a difference: the earlier passage reads "either all or the most and especially important." Here we have a disjunction ("either-or," ê-ê [131.6]) concerning the happy life, which in the later passage morphs into two lives. The best life contains without qualification—understand "all" from the earlier passage (131.6)—things according to nature, while the second best life contains most and those that are especially important (144.21–145.1).

At first reading, that might seem absurd. No human life involves all good things according to nature. And if it did, the sheer number of external goods would be an impossible burden. We may compare 132.20–21, where we are told that unlike an art/craft, happiness is not increased/intensified by many instruments and equipment. Adding more does not produce an increase in happiness. Also relevant is book 1 of Aristotle's *Politics*, in which acquisition as part of household management is discussed. We are told that the art must gather supplies that are necessary for life and useful for the community. Such a supply is labeled "true wealth" and said not to be unlimited, *ouk apeiros*. In what follows, Solon is criticized for saying that wealth knows no boundary, and limited acquisition is recognized as according to nature, *kata phusin* (1.3 1256b27–39). That may be unfair to

---

or by a noticeable amount. If it gets too close to the life of vice or to a life overwhelmed by bad fortune or both, then it ceases to be worthy of choice.

[48] The early Peripatetics held that happiness requires both goods of the body and external goods (as well as goods of the soul). That is well known; see, e.g., Cicero, *Lucullus* 134 and *Tusculan Disputations* 5.23–25 = Theophrastus, fr. 492 and 493 FHS&G with *Commentary* 6.1 (2011) 431–32.

Solon, assuming he is focused on greed *qua* vicious disposition that knows no limit to the accumulation of riches. But fair or unfair, Aristotle presents a clearly favorable view of Solon toward the end of the *Nicomachean Ethics*, where he tells us that Solon well described men who are happy: they are moderately supplied with external goods, have performed what Solon considered most noble actions, and lived a temperate life (10.8 1179a9–12).[49] Be that as it may, some limitation to the accumulation of wealth is necessary, and that holds for the best life as well as the second. Yet Didymus fails to say so. Or is the limitation to be found in the references to virtue and to nature (144.22)? The best life is said to be "according to virtue," which is a mean-disposition that recognizes limit. A virtuous person understands that happiness is not intensified by piling up ever more good/useful things (cf. 132.19–21). If he is exceptionally fortunate, he may be able to pick and choose without constraint, but even if he is not so blessed, he can make sensible choices and lead what can be described as a happy life. In any case, the virtuous individual will observe limits in the accumulation of riches, and in doing so he will follow Aristotle and act according to nature.[50]

Even if the preceding is correct, I am uncomfortable with the pairing of lives and goods—that is, filling out a distinction between lives based on character, virtue and the intermediate disposition, by adding a distinction in terms of goods according to nature. For there is no necessary connection between virtue and the unqualified possession of goods, and the same holds between the intermediate disposition and the most and especially important goods. Consider the second life. What is it about an intermediate disposition that ties it to the most and especially important of things according to nature? And cannot the man who lives according to virtue find himself in less than perfect conditions? There is no simple explanation, so that I am tempted to suggest that the distinction in terms of circumstances (unqualified vs. qualified possession of things according to nature) has been imported from the earlier passage to the later, where it does not belong. But in saying "imported from," I do not want to suggest that Didymus must have recalled the earlier passage when composing the second and deliberately drew on the earlier passage to fill out the later. The responsible individual may have been an earlier compiler, upon whom Didymus drew.[51]

---

[49] See Schütrumpf (1991) 318–19.

[50] As so often the difficulty may be the result of abbreviation. A fuller text might remove difficulties and the need to speculate.

[51] In the case of an epitome it is natural to attribute lack of clarity to abbreviation (see

The rejection of the vicious life is unqualified and emphasized by the use of *pheugein*, "to flee," or more precisely, the verbal adjective *pheukton*, "to be fled." Sharples translates it as "an object of avoidance."[52] That is not wrong, but here it strikes me as too weak. "To be fled" adds an urgency that is missing in "avoidance" and expanding the translation with "object of" makes better English but at the expense of punch. We may compare the use of *pheukton* in an earlier passage, already referred to above (134.2–4).[53] In both places the verbal comes first,[54] which gives emphasis. In the earlier passage, suicide is being recommended. Good men, who find themselves in excessive misfortunes, should flee life, and bad men should do the same in excessively fortunate circumstances, for they will do wrong all the more. That suggests that *pheukton* at 145.1 is recommending fleeing life itself, when changing one's vicious style of life proves impossible. But that is not quite said, and the immediate context offers no support. Nevertheless, we should not forget the earlier passage, where we are told that the employment of vice is misery, and that while virtue is not sufficient for happiness, vice is sufficient for misery (133.22–134.1). Apparently a vicious man's particular circumstances are irrelevant and could be ignored in the later passage.

(3) 145.3–6

Reference to things according to nature also occurs in the passage that follows (145.3–6):

> The happy life differs from the noble life to the extent that the former calls for the presence of things according to nature throughout, while the latter also (occurs) in things contrary to nature. And virtue is not sufficient for the former, but it is for the latter.

Moraux suggests that the present passage has been placed immediately after that which precedes, because both passages mention things according to nature.[55] He also points out that the possibility of a virtuous life without things according to nature is entirely overlooked in the preceding passage. He concludes that the two passages present *doxai*, which were originally independent of each other. That may well be correct, but it need

---

the preceding note), but here addition could be in play.
[52] Sharples (2010) 127. Tsouni offers a similar translation: "should be avoided."
[53] See above, p. 237 on suicide.
[54] At 145.1 placing the verbal adjective first involves the introduction of chiasmus.
[55] Moraux (1973) 408.

not mean that the epitomist proceeded in an entirely mindless manner. He may have understood his ordering of texts as a progression involving clarification. After characterizing the best life as one according to virtue in things according to nature, he thought it necessary to distinguish between the truly happy life and that which is noble, *kalos* (145.3). Both involve virtue, but the noble life can be lived in things contrary to nature. That is not true of the happy life. It is lived in things according to nature *dia pantos*, "throughout" (145.4–5).

The qualifier "throughout" is important, for it takes account of Solon's injunction to look to the end of a man's life as well as a particular case like that of Priam, who met disaster at the end of his life. We may compare the *Nicomachean Ethics*, in which Aristotle says that happiness requires complete virtue and a complete lifetime. He then remarks that many changes for the worse can occur in the course of a person's life and that a prosperous person can suffer serious reversal in old age. Mention is then made of Priam's fate and Solon's injunction to look to the end (1.9–10 1100a4–12). In Didymus' epitome, earlier within the discussion of happiness *qua* goal or end of life, Solon has already been referred to.[56] After telling us that not every noble action brings happiness (131.12–13) and that nobility differs from happiness (132.10–12), Didymus cites Solon, "Look to the end of a long life" (133.4–5).[57] I would like to think that Didymus chose to express himself with greater brevity in the present passage, because the difference between acting nobly and being happy had already been made clear, but more likely the two blocks of text were composed/abridged independently of each other.

(4) 145.6–10

The discussion of different types of life ends with a brief segment focused on the intermediate life.[58] It runs as follows:

> There is a certain intermediate life according to an intermediate disposition, in which appropriate actions are exhibited/performed. For there are correct actions in the life according to virtue and mistaken actions in the life according to vice, and appropriate actions in the so-called intermediate life.

---

[56] This earlier discussion has been referred to in the preceding section on p. 244.

[57] On what counts as a complete, long life, see 132.2–3, where Arius speaks of the maximum time that god has laid down for us, allowing some latitude as with bodily size.

[58] That the discussion of types of lives ends at 145.10 is made clear by the sentence that follows. See above, n. 3.

The text opens by referring to a certain intermediate life, *mesos tis bios*, and ends with the phrase "the so-called intermediate life" (145.6–7, 10). That creates a kind of mini-ring-composition, in which a connection is asserted between an intermediate life and appropriate actions. The phrase "so-called" suggests that "intermediate life" is to be understood as jargon, a quasi–*terminus technicus*.

In addition to the intermediate life, which is said to be in accordance with an intermediate disposition, *mesê hexis* (145.7), mention is made of the life according to virtue and the life according to vice (145.9–10). That takes us back to an earlier passage in which the same three lives are mentioned (144.21–145.2). But there is a difference in that the earlier passage introduces things according to nature, which are possessed to a different degree by the life according to virtue and the life according to the intermediate disposition. That difference in degree involved difficulties,[59] which are not involved in the present passage. For now the focus is on character and the actions associated with virtue, vice and the so-called intermediate disposition.

The phrase "intermediate life" (145.6–7, 10) occurs still earlier within the discussion of happiness *qua* goal of life (133.10). There we read, "The person deprived of happiness is not miserable like the person who does not possess it at all. Rather, he is sometimes in an intermediate state. For both the wise and the not wise live the so-called intermediate life, which is neither happy nor miserable" (133.6–11). If I understand, the not wise person is neither the utter fool nor someone entirely vicious. He is the decent individual, perhaps better than average, who falls short of wisdom but can live a moderately happy life, assuming he has an adequate supply of things that are according to nature. He turns up later as the person who is capable of living the second best life (144.22–145.1).[60]

Further explanation of the difference between the three lives is provided by distinguishing between the actions associated with each of the lives. The life according to virtue is marked by correct actions, *katorthômata*, that according to vice by mistaken actions, *hamartêmata*, and that according to the intermediate disposition by appropriate actions, *kathêkonta* (145.8–10). The Greek terms are established Stoic terminology,[61] but that does not

---

[59] See above, p. 244.

[60] I have not hesitated to write "moderately happy," for the Peripatetics did not treat "happiness" as an apical term, such that there is no more or less. See Fortenbaugh (2011) 434–35, 451 and above n. 47.

[61] See Didymus' epitome of Stoic ethics, 85.12–86.16.

rule out their use by members of the Peripatos. Indeed, *kathêkonta* occurs early in Didymus' epitome of Peripatetic ethics, where we read: "Actions have their beginnings in the selection of things according to nature and the rejection of things contrary to nature, and (that includes those actions) that are called appropriate, *ta legomena kathêkonta*. And for that reason correct actions and mistaken ones occur in these things and concern these things" (119.15–19). Here things according to nature include health and one's own existence, so that people are eager for health and cling to life (118.11–17). Such behavior is called appropriate, but there are occasions when putting one's own health and existence first is not acceptable but rather vicious or cowardly. That does not prove that such a use of *kathêkonta* goes back to a member of the early Peripatos, but Theophrastus is a possibility. So Dirlmeier, who cites Aulus Gellius, *Attic Nights* 1.3.28 = Theophr., fr. 534 FHS&G, where *officia* translates *kathêkonta*.[62]

Moraux suggests that the notion of an intermediate disposition, a *mesê hexis*, was developed in the Peripatos in opposition to the Stoics.[63] That makes sense, for according to the Stoics, a man must be either virtuous or vicious. Just as a stick must be either straight or crooked, so in regard to virtue and vice there is nothing in between.[64] Moreover, Diogenes Laertius tells us that the Peripatetics disagreed: they held that between virtue and vice there is *prokopê*, progress in the direction of virtue (7.127). Nevertheless, the early Peripatetics, on their own, would have had no trouble picking out a disposition that is intermediate between virtue and vice and leads to appropriate action. I am thinking of the disposition of the person who has enjoyed a sound musical/moral education but has yet to acquire practical reason. His early training has focused on emotional response and proper manners, but his reasoning capacity still needs perfecting, so that he cannot fully explain the moral principles that he has acquired and may err in means-end deliberations. Alternatively, a person may have made

---

[62] See Dirlmeier [1937] 82–83 and cf. Moraux [1973] 408–9. In both the *EN* and the *Rhet.*, Aristotle uses *hamartêma* with reference to mistaken action, but in both these works the mistake is dissociated from vice (5.8 1135b17–18; 1.13 1374b8–9). That differs from the Didymus passage where a connection is made with the life according to vice (145.9–10). In the *Magna Moralia*, the author uses *katorthôma* in regard to success that is due to luck or good fortune (1.17 1199a13). That too differs from the Didymus passage, where connection is made with the life according to virtue 145.8–9.

[63] Moraux (1973) 409.

[64] We might say that the Stoics treated "virtue" and "vice" as opposites like "odd" and "even," which admit nothing in between. On opposites that do admit intermediaries marked by more or less, see n. 66 and above n. 47.

progress in controlling his emotions, but not enough. He has learned that facing danger is noble, and normally he is able to steel himself, whatever danger might be on the horizon. But sudden alarms are another matter. The person who has not gained full control over his emotions has no time to steel himself and might run when he should hold his ground. We can say that he has made progress but needs more training.[65]

In addition, the Peripatetics had a healthy respect for ordinary language. They will have recognized that virtue is a good of the soul and "good" regularly admits degrees: *agathos, ameinôn, aristos*, "good, better. best."[66] Similarly with individual virtues: they will have seen no reason to ban an everyday phrase like "more courageous" (Arist. *EN* 3.8 1117a18). Indeed, the phrase is useful in that it can be used to mark off the person whose moral education is well advanced in comparison with the person who is still in the early stages and might run at the sound of the war trumpet.[67] But it does not entail complete virtue, so that the more courageous man, who has steeled himself against sudden alarms, might still need to improve his reasoning capacity, so that he can both explain why courage is important and determine how best to confront danger.

(5) In Conclusion

The preceding discussion has wound its way through a series of passages that sometimes seem disorderly. On occasion, I have tried to mitigate that impression, pointing out connections and suggesting that Didymus may be thinking for himself when organizing his material.[68] In addition, I have followed scholars in recognizing that certain passages reflect Peripatetic reaction to positions taken by the Stoics. But equally I have suggested that recognizing Stoic connections should not obscure roots that are Peripatetic and even predate the Stoa.[69] Furthermore, Peripatetic concern with

---

[65] See Fortenbaugh (1975) 70–79.

[66] I.e., the Peripatetics recognized virtue and vice, good and bad as polar opposites, which make room for an intermediate condition. See Arist. *Cat.* 10 12a13–25, 13a22–31 with Fortenbaugh (2011) 300–302.

[67] In referring to "war trumpet," I am thinking of the *salpinx*, the sound of which could terrify a person. See Apollonius, *Amazing Stories* 49.1–3 = Theophr. 726A.1–3 FHS&G = Aristoxenus, fr. 6 Wehrli

[68] See p. 228 on 143.24 (opening sentence), p. 234 on 148.8 (intelligible transition) and p. 247 on 145.3–6 (progression involving clarification).

[69] See pp. 229–30 on 143.25–144.8 (Hellenistic discussion of political involvement), p. 235 on 144.10–11 (heavy drinking), pp. 235–39 on 144.11–15 (suicide).

circumstances, the *kairos*, has been noticed,[70] and stylistic observations have been included.[71] Now I want to close by turning back to what was said in the opening paragraph of this paper: namely, that types of life received significant attention in the early Peripatos. Mention has already been made of the opening book of Aristotle's *Nicomachean Ethics*, in which three lives are picked out as prominent: apolaustic, political and theoretical.[72] In addition, reference has been made to an alleged great controversy between Dicaearchus and Theophrastus concerning the active and the contemplative life.[73] What needs to be added is reference to the several Peripatetic writings that carried the title *On Lives*. These works are lost, but it seems certain that they were not biographies but rather discussions of different types of life. Diogenes Laertius in his catalogue of Theophrastean works lists *On Lives* in three books (5.42), and in his catalogue of Strato's writings, Diogenes includes *On Lives*, but the number of books is not reported (5.59). Diogenes also refers to the first book of Dicaearchus' *On Lives* when discussing Plato's participation in the Isthmian Games (3.4). That tells us that the work was at least two books long, but whether it ran for two or three books or more remains unknowable.

Finally there is Clearchus, whose work *On Lives* was at least eight books long. He appears to have composed a dialogue and not a treatise, but we are left guessing whom he chose as speakers. Also problematic is the content of the work taken as whole. To be sure, Athenaeus in his work *The Sophists at Dinner* preserves a goodly number of fragments, some thirty-two or thirty-three, many of which exhibit an interest in the life devoted to excessive luxury and the disastrous consequences that follow. But these fragments constitute only a small sampling of what will have been included in a work that ran for eight books or longer. Moreover, Athanaeus' selection of fragments will have been determined by his own interest in eating, drinking and luxurious living. Half the surviving fragments are found in book 12 of *The Sophists at Dinner*, in which Athenaeus is focused on luxury. My guess is that the Clearchan work not only had much to say about the life of the politician and that of the philosopher, but also made room for issues not

---

[70] See p. 230 on 143.24–144.1 (being a leader), pp. 231–32 on 144.5–6 (doing and contemplating), pp. 235–39 on 144.12–13 (suicide), pp. 234–35 on 144.10–11 (drinking heavily) and pp. 243–45 on 144.21–145.1 (possessing most things according to nature).

[71] See pp. 239–40 on 144.8–11 (polysyndeton), pp. 234–35 on 145.1 (the use of the verbal and chiasmus), p. 246 on 145.3–6 (brevity) and pp. 247–48 on 145.6–10 (ring-composition).

[72] See p. 240.

[73] See p. 232.

closely tied to morality: for example, lexical matters, firsts or beginnings and proverbs.[74] In any case, the work will have been very different from what we find in Didymus: not just longer but varied in interest and full of examples, some titillating and others not so.

Works Cited

Arnim, H. v. 1926. *Arius Didymus' Abriss der peripatetischen Ethik*. SB Wien 204, 3. Wien: Hölder-Pichler-Tempsky.

Dirlmeier, F. 1937. *Die Oikeiosis-Lehre Theophrasts*. Philologus suppl. 33. Leipzig: Dieterich.

Fortenbaugh, W. 1975 (repr. with epilogue 2002). *Aristotle on Emotion*. London: Duckworth.

———. 1976. "Aristotle on Prior and Posterior, Correct and Mistaken Constitutions." *Transactions of the American Philological Association* 106: 125–37.

———. 2011. *Theophrastus of Eresus, Commentary*, Vol. 6.1: *Sources on Ethics*. Leiden: Brill.

———. 2012a. "Aristo of Ceos: the Fragments concerning Eros." In *Islamic Philosophy, Science, Culture, and Religion*, ed. F. Opwis and D. Reisman. Leiden: Brill, 11–23.

———. 2012b. "Chamaeleon on Pleasure on Drunkenness." In *Praxiphanes of Mytilene and Chamaeleon of Heracla: Text, Translation and Discussion*, ed. A. Martano, E. Matelli and D. Mirhady. Rutgers University Studies in Classical Humanities 18. New Brunswick, N.J.: Transaction, 372–85.

———. 2013. "Cicero's Letter to Atticus 2.16: A Great Controversy." *Classical World* 106: 483–86.

———. 2015. "Two Eresians: Phainias and Theophrastus." In *Phaenias of Eresus: Text, Translation and Discussion*, ed. O. Hellmann. Rutgers University Studies in Classical Humanities 19. New Brunswick, N.J.: Transaction, 101–31.

———. 2015. "Aristotle on Women: *Politics* 1.13 1260a13." *Ancient Philosophy* 35: 395–404.

———. 2016. "Aristotle on Bipartition and the Questionable Mean-Dispositions." In *For a Skeptical Peripatetic: Studies in Greek Philosophy*

---

[74] See Fortenbaugh, "Clearchus, *On Lives*" (forthcoming in RUSCH 21). I disagree with Tsitsiridis (2008) 70–71, who sees the work as an extended attack on the life of excessive luxury.

in Honour of John Glücker. Edited by P. Destrée, Chr. Horn, and M. Zingano. Studies on Ancient Moral and Political Philosophy.

———. forthcoming. "Clearchus, *On Lives*." In *Clearchus of Soli: Text, Translation and Discussion*, ed. D. Mirhady. Rutgers University Studies in Classical Humanities 21. New Brunswick, N.J.: Transaction.

Gigon, O. 1951. *Marcus Tullius Cicero. Gespräche in Tusculum*. München: Heimeran.

Huby, P. "Peripatetic Definitions of Happiness." In *On Stoic and Peripatetic Ethics: The Work of Arius Didymu*, ed. W. Fortenbaugh. Rutgers University Studies in Classical Humanities 1. New Brunswick, N.J.: Transaction, 121–34.

Heath, M. "Aristotle on Natural Slavery." *Phronesis* 53: 243–70.

Jaeger, W. 1948. "On the Origin and Cycle of the Philosophic Life." Translated by Richard Robinson from the German (1928) and published in *Aristotle: Fundamentals of the History of His Development*. 2nd ed. Oxford: Clarendon, 426–61.

Joly, R. 1956. *Le Thème Philosophique des Genres de Vie dans l' Antiquité Classique*. Bruxelles: Palais des Académies.

Moraux, P. 1973. *Der Aristotelismus bei den Griechen*. Berlin: De Gruyter.

Ostwald, M. 1962. *Aristotle, Nicomachean Ethics*. Indianapolis: Bobbs Merrill.

Pomeroy, A. 1999. *Arius Didymus, Epitome of Stoic Ethics*. Atlanta: Society of Biblical Literature.

Rist, J. 1969. *Stoic Philosophy*. Cambridge: Cambridge University Press.

Schöpsdau, K. 2011. *Platon,* Nomoi *Buch VIII–XII*. Göttingen: Vandenhoeck & Ruprecht.

Schütrumpf, E. 1991. *Aristoteles,* Politik, *Buch I*. Berlin: Akademie Verlag.

Sharples, R. 1990. *Alexander of Aphrodisias, Ethical Problems*. London: Duckworth.

———. 2010. *Peripatetic Philosophy 200 BC to 200 AD*. Cambridge: Cambridge University Press.

Stewart, J. 1892. *Notes on the Nicomachean Ethics*. Oxford: Clarendon.

Teegarden, D. 2014. *Death to the Tyrannts! Ancient Greek Democracy and the Struggle against Tyranny*. Princeton: Princeton University Press.

Tsitsiridis, S. 2008. "Die Schrift *Peri Biôn* des Klearchos von Soloi." *Philologus* 152: 65–76.

Tsouni, G. 2016. "*Didymus' Outline of Peripatetic Ethics*." In this volume.

Wehrli, F. 1969. *Die Schule des Aristoteles: Texte und Kommentar*. Basel: Schwabe.

8

Arius Didymus' Epitome of the Economic and Political Topic

Eckart Schütrumpf

The Endeavor

In the main part of this paper, I shall attempt both to identify the source of the individual statements found in Arius Didymus' (in future: Didymus) excerpt of "the economic and political topic" that is preserved in Stobaeus *Anthologium* (2.7.26 W) and to assess the success of Didymus' endeavor. In doing so, I will simply refer to and speak of Aristotle—and not for instance of a "summary of Peripatetic politics" or "the doctrine of the Theophrastean Peripatos."[1] And for brevity's sake, instead of saying "in Stobaeus' account of Didymus' excerpt" I will say "in Didymus."

It is not indicated that the section on "the economic and political topic" is still a summary of Aristotle's views. At 2.7.13 116.19f.,[2] Didymus had announced an "account of the ethics of Aristotle and the other Peripatetics" (Ἀριστοτέλους καὶ τῶν λοιπῶν Περιπατητικῶν περὶ τῶν ἠθικῶν), and

---

[1] Regenbogen, *RE* Suppl. VII, 1517.22f.; 1518.62–1519.11, cited below, n. 120.
[2] The citations by page and line refer to vol. 2 of C. Wachsmuth's edition of Stobaeus' *Anthologium*.

at 2.7.26 147.26–148.3 he introduces "the economic and political topic" after he considered the preceding explanations of the main points of the ethical topic as being "sufficient."[3] The section on "the economic and political topic" is here linked to the previous one on ethics as an unannounced supplement or postscript. We do not learn why it "must" follow "next" (ἀναγκαῖον ἐφεξῆς …) after the "account of the ethics."

For this section of the *Anthologium*, we are in the enviable position of being able to compare the late text, the epitome, with the original. Already the introductory remarks to this section reveal the different approach the excerptor has from that of the author of the work he condenses. We read in Didymus that after most of the main points of ethics had been explained, one has to deal next with "the economic and political topic." Aristotle did not use the term "topic" but *methodos*.[4] What for Aristotle is an enquiry that has to be pursued, a task still ahead of the writer—the imagery invoked in *methodos* comes close to that of "investigation"—has become for Didymus a topic one needs "to go through" (*dielthein*). He has a completed treatise in front of him which can be summarized and whose subjects are distinguished according to the different places (*topos*) they are assigned to in a system of philosophy through which one can move (*dielthein*).

When assessing an excerpt, there are several issues to consider: how well did the excerptor understand the original text? How accurate is the reproduction of the argument? Did the excerptor make a judicious selection from the many issues covered in the original, and what interest does the selection of the views excerpted—or omitted—reveal? And finally, does he offer an adequate impression of the original?

In making at the very beginning the distinction between *oikonomikos* (οἰκονομικός) and *politikos* (πολιτικός) in order to describe the topics to be covered and accordingly in making the distinction between the respective disciplines *oikonomikē* (οἰκονομική)[5] and *politikē* (πολιτική) (149.24–150.1), Didymus does not correctly present the Aristotelian concept, since Aristotle does not deal in *Pol.* 1 with a discipline *oikonomikē* distinguished from *politikē* which is covered in the rest of *Pol.* In *Pol.* 1.1 he outlines a

---

[3] 147.26–148.3: Διωρισμένων δ' ἱκανῶς τῶν περὶ τὰς ἀρετὰς καὶ σχεδὸν τῶν πλείστων ἀνειλημμένων κεφαλαίων τοῦ ἠθικοῦ τόπου, ἀναγκαῖον ἐφεξῆς καὶ περὶ τοῦ οἰκονομικοῦ τε καὶ πολιτικοῦ διελθεῖν. After preceding τοῦ ἠθικοῦ τόπου one needs to understand οἰκονομικοῦ and πολιτικοῦ as adjectives agreeing still with the preceding noun τόπου.

[4] *Pol.* 4.8 1293b30f. ἡμῖν δὲ τὴν μέθοδον εἶναι περὶ πολιτείας; 2.1 1260b35f. ταύτην … ἐπιβαλέσθαι τὴν μέθοδον, cf. 7.2 1324a20f.

[5] 149.24 περὶ οἰκονομικῆς is conjecture.

general method[6] that provides the understanding of the issue under investigation. This method consists in splitting up the subject matter into its smallest parts. From the very beginning of *Pol.* 1.1 the *polis* is the subject matter of the analysis,[7] and thus after having described the development of associations which starts with the smallest parts, the household and the various relationships within the house, and ends with the *polis* as the final stage (1.2 1252b27ff.), he can summarize in 1.3 the result reached so far: "Since it is clear out of which parts the *polis* consists. …" The household and its master, the *oikonomos*, are not topics of investigation in their own right belonging to a discipline *oikonomikē*, but are a subordinate aspect of the investigation of the *polis*[8] so that some of the results of the study of *oikonomikē* not only apply to the *polis*[9] but advance its understanding. A distinction between *oikonomikē* and *politikē* exists in Aristotle's *Pol.*, but is used only for a subordinate aspect: forms of rule.[10]

The difference between Aristotle and Didymus becomes obvious if one compares the transition from ethics to the next subject both authors make: according to Aristotle *EN* 10.10 1181b12ff. the subject that needs to follow ethics is "legislation" and "constitution", and indeed *Pol.* 1.1 begins with the *polis*. However, in Didymus the first subject that needs to be dealt with after ethics is the *oikonomikos topos*, and accordingly he starts with the union of man[11] and wife which, as he says, is called *oikos* (148.5ff.).

The reason given by Didymus for his dealing with the *two* topics, the economic and the political, is: "because man is by nature a creature that belongs to the *polis*" (ἐπειδὴ φύσει πολιτικὸν ζῷον ἄνθρωπος, 148.3). However, this is not a satisfactory explanation of his treatment of the *two* issues. That man belongs to the *polis* can justify only the topic *polis* but not the topic household. Didymus' statement contains a *non sequitur*.

---

[6] *Pol.* 1.1 1252a17–19 ἐπισκοποῦσι κατὰ τὴν ὑφηγημένην μέθοδον. ὥσπερ γὰρ ἐν τοῖς ἄλλοις τὸ σύνθετον μέχρι τῶν ἀσυνθέτων ἀνάγκη διαιρεῖν … . See Schütrumpf (1989) 2009, 57f.

[7] 1.1 1252a1; a6; a13; a20.

[8] See Schütrumpf 1991, vol. 1. p. 227f.; 230 n. on 14.38 (b6).

[9] *Pol.* 1.11 1259a33–36; cf. 8 1256b30; b36f.; 7 1255b16ff.

[10] 1.7 1255b16–20; 3.6 1278b37f.–1279a8. Political or economic offices respectively have their own specific tasks, and in this sense they are different: 4.15 1299a20-23; however, one can ask whether both, the man responsible for the household (*oikonomikos*) and the statesman (*politikos*), do not have to deal with the same issue of providing necessary goods: 1.10 1258a19ff.

[11] While Didymus ignores the programmatic remarks from *Pol.* 1.1, he refers at 148.8 (μικρὰ γάρ τις ἔοικεν εἶναι πόλις ὁ οἶκος) to Aristotle *Pol.* 1.1 1252a13, however, out of the original context and against the sense of the Aristotelian passage, see below, p. 263; 286.

Furthermore, the justifications of Aristotle for his investigation of the *polis* and that of the excerptor are not identical. Aristotle does not deal with the *polis* because men are by nature its members but because it is the highest association which pursues the highest good (*Pol.* 1.1 1252a1ff.). It seems that Didymus, because of his intention to deal with the political topic, *peri tou politikou* (148.3, cf. 153.24), seized the first mention of *politikon* that could be found in Aristotle's *Pol.* after the introductory section 1.1, that is, the *zōion politikon* of *Pol.* 1.2, and used it as justification for the investigation of the *polis*.

After this introduction Didymus turns to the content of *Pol.*[12] Of the 118 lines of the excerpt 41 lines (148.5; 148.7–149.22; 150.4) summarize parts of *Pol.* 1:

13 lines (150.1–3; 4–7 καὶ ὅτι πολίτης ...; 17–23) summarize *Pol.* 3
14 lines (151.1; 3–8; 16–20; 23–24) summarize *Pol.* 4
9 lines (151.2–3; 9–15) summarize *Pol.* 5
3 lines (151.18–20) summarize specifics of *Pol.* 6
28 lines (150.8–10; 152.1–25) summarize *Pol.* 7/8
7 lines (148.6; 150.10–14; 151.14–15) summarize views found in *EN*
7 lines (150.9–16) cannot be identified—do they summarize *EN*?

[12]
Didymus	Source in Aristotle
148.3–5	*Pol.* 1
6	*EN* 8.12
7–149.23	*Pol.* 1
150.1–3	*Pol.* 3
4	*Pol.* 1
4–6	*Pol.* 3
6–8	difficult to identify
8–10	*Pol.* 7
10–12	*EN* 6
12–16	n.t.d.
17–23	*Pol.* 3
23–151.1	*Pol.* 4
151.2–3	*Pol.* 5
3–8	*Pol.* 4
9–14	*Pol.* 5
14–15	*EN*
16–17	*Pol.* 4
18–20	*Pol.* 4 and 6
20–22	difficult to identify
23	*Pol.* 4
152.1–24	*Pol.* 7–8.

In the excerpt, Didymus' primary focus is the first book of Aristotle's *Pol.* which accounts for almost 35 percent of the whole summary,[13] with the two last books *Pol.* 7/8 trailing as a distant second (23%), followed by *Pol.* 4 (12%), *Pol.* 3 (10%), and *Pol.* 5 (8%). Of *Pol.* 6, only names of specific offices mentioned in ch. 8 make it into the excerpt (see below, p. 282f.); however, since this book is presented by Aristotle as an addition to previous explanations (6.1 1326b36ff.) the absence of a summary of its content is not something one would miss. It is surprising that *Pol.* 2 which deals with Aristotle's criticism first of Plato and other authors of best states and then of historical constitutions, Sparta, Crete, and Carthage, is completely ignored by Didymus.[14] Was the reason for this omission that the various ideas expressed in the detailed criticism of *Pol.* 2 could not be reduced to a few main points (κεφάλαια, 150.1; 152.24) that would give a fair impression of the complexity of the whole book? Or did Didymus not want to mention that Plato was criticized so extensively and severely? There is no explanation for the absence of a whole book from the excerpt.

It was pointed out that *Pol.* 1 covers almost 35 perent of the whole of Didymus' excerpt. The difference in length of the excerpts of *Pol.* 1 on the one hand and the other six books (considering that book 2 is ignored) on the other cannot be explained from the lesser importance of the content of these six books. Could it be that Didymus had planned a more detailed summary of *Pol.* but changed his mind after the summary of *Pol.* 1? Did he originally intend to deal with all parts of *Pol.* in the same detail as he had described the content of book 1 but then felt that this would become too long? Did he start his project on a larger scale than he was willing or able to carry through? Or was the subject matter of *Pol.* 3-8 too complex to lend itself to an account that would do justice to the complexity of the topics discussed, or would the mass of information found there offer a confusing array of views? None of this is likely. Given the erratic nature of the selection of topics chosen, or ignored, for inclusion in the summary, it

---

[13] The following percentage figures do not add up to 100 since 147.26; 148.1–3; and 152.24-25 are not counted, 150.6–8, 12-16; 151.20–22 are difficult to identify, and the different sections distinguished here do not start at the beginning of a line or end at the end of a line.

[14] Πόλις δὲ τὸ ἐκ τῶν τοιούτων πλῆθος ἱκανὸν πρὸς αὐτάρκειαν ζωῆς, 150.5f. is neither the summary of *Pol.* 2.2 1261b12f.: βούλεταί γ' ἤδη τότε εἶναι πόλις ὅταν αὐτάρκη συμβαίνῃ τὴν κοινωνίαν εἶναι τοῦ πλήθους nor of 7.4 1326b8 πρώτην μὲν εἶναι πόλιν ἀναγκαῖον τὴν ἐκ τοσούτου πλήθους ὃ πρῶτον πλῆθος αὔταρκες πρὸς τὸ εὖ ζῆν, but of 3.1 1275b21: πόλιν δὲ τὸ τῶν τοιούτων πλῆθος ἱκανὸν πρὸς αὐτάρκειαν ζωῆς ... because of the common τῶν τοιούτων.

would have been possible to reproduce any concept of the original. I offer a different answer: since Didymus set out to discuss after the "economic topic" the "political topic" and both topics had been introduced as being of equal importance they received almost the same attention regardless of the fact that the first was dealt with by Aristotle in one book and the second in seven books. One difference should be noted: except for *Pol.* 1 whose content is presented in one block, the summaries of the rest of *Pol.* are not given as independent, clearly separated accounts of each book but are interrupted and supplemented by summaries of other sections of *Pol.* or even *EN*.

Oikonomikos topos

By marking in his edition at 148.5 the beginning of a new paragraph Wachsmuth[15] obscured that Didymus might have wanted to establish a link between his initial quote that man is *by nature* a political creature and the following remark that man and wife form a constitution *by law*: the contrast *physei–kata nomon* seems intentional. If an internal connection between these arguments was intended, Didymus distinguished two aspects: on the one hand the existence of man as member of the *polis by nature* and on the other, within the species man, the *legally established* relationship between the two sexes—it is hierarchically ordered since a *constitution*, which is formed by them according to Didymus, is defined by Aristotle as a an order that determines who wields the power (*Pol.* 3.7 1279b25ff.; 4.3 1290a7ff.).

Didymus writes: "the first union of man and wife is a constitution" (Πολιτεία δὲ πρώτη σύνοδος ἀνδρὸς καὶ γυναικὸς). It should be noted that in the passage Didymus reproduces Aristotle[16] does not speak of man and woman but of female and male (θῆλυ, ἄρρεν), not focusing from the start on humans as Didymus does when he adds that this relationship exists "according to law" (*kata nomon*). Aristotle by contrast places their union into the widest context of procreation which is based on a universal desire of all living creatures, of animals and plants, to leave behind something of their kind (*Pol.* 1.2 1252b29f.), and thus among humans the union of the sexes is the work of nature, not regulated by *nomos*. The distinction between nature and law is used by Aristotle in *Pol.* 1 under the topic household in the context of *slavery* (3 1253b20–22; 5 1255a1–6 1255a5ff.), whereas the *union of man and wife* for the begetting of children is here

---

[15] Not Meineke II 91.24.
[16] *Pol.* 1.2 1252a26f., differently at *EN* 8. 12 1160b32, see below, n. 20 and n. 28.

not an institution sanctioned by law. However, at 7.16 1334b29ff. Aristotle discusses the responsibility of the *lawgiver* to secure the best bodily constitution of the children raised in the best state: the *lawgiver* issues orders for physical activity of pregnant women (1335b14), and a *law* makes stipulations about exposure or bringing up of those who are new-born (1335b20). Didymus might have had the specific arrangements of Aristotle's best state in mind[17] when he describes marriage as a bond secured by law. However, Didymus gives the account of marriage a twist that did not interest Aristotle in *Pol.* 1.2.

Which noun is modified by "first" (πρώτη)? Does Didymus talk here about marriage as "the first constitution" or about "the first union of man and woman" as a constitution? The latter does not seem to make sense since male and female did not live for a longer period apart before they formed "the first union" so that there is no need to mark this first coming together. It is hardly introduced as a counterpart to the following stage, the *first* emergence of a village which is formed out of a greater number of households[18]—here this new phase needed to be emphasized since men had lived before in associations which were not villages. The other option, in Tsouni's translation: "The first political association is the coming together of man and woman," makes this remark a statement about politics, not the household, and its substance is contradicted by the chapter Didymus summarizes.[19] The rule over women is referred to in the line quoted at *Pol.* 1.2 1252b22f. from Hom. *Od.* 9.114f.: "each (of the Cyclopes) rules over children and wives," however, these Cyclopes are "lawless" (*Od.* 9.105), and their marriage cannot be a constitution since constitutions exist for Aristotle only where there is the rule of law (*Pol.* 4.4 1292a32).

None of the two alternatives makes great sense. It seems that Didymus had the phrase of Aristotle: "it is necessary that *first* male and female unite ..." (ἀνάγκη δὴ πρῶτον συνδυάζεσθαι ...) in mind, and because of

---

[17] Didymus refers to this legislation at 152.22; see below, p. 286.

[18] *Pol.* 1.2 1252b15f. ἡ δ᾽ ἐκ πλειόνων οἰκιῶν κοινωνία πρώτη χρήσεως ἕνεκεν μὴ ἐφημέρου κώμη. Cf. the next stage, the forming of a *polis* by one man: 1253a30 ὁ δὲ πρῶτος συστήσας μεγίστων ἀγαθῶν αἴτιος.

[19] One cannot defend the understanding "the first constitution" by reference to 7.4 1326b7 where Aristotle defines "the first polis" as the association "of a number of men which is the first to be sufficient for the good life in the political association. ..." This particular concept in which a development reaches a certain threshold where certain conditions, an increase in quality, results in the formation of a new entity which is in terms of quality a more advanced form of association, the polis, is not comparable to that of marriage as the "first constitution" since for that union no previous stages are assumed.

this Aristotelian model one should assume that Didymus' πρώτη modifies σύνοδος and not πολιτεία: among the associations considered for a household to exist stands *first* and foremost the need for sexual union of male and female; this necessity exists before the second association which provides help from slaves needed to be formed. The process of condensing the text resulted in the awkward "the first union of male and female was a constitution" where there are, as a matter of fact, two ideas: "the first union was that of male and female" and "this union was as constitution." Didymus' summary suffers at times from brevity, and as a result it is overfraught with information to the detriment of clarity and accuracy, cf. 149.21–150.5.

As for the second thought: "this union was a constitution," it was pointed out above (p. 261) that this statement is wrong for the earliest past for which Aristotle refers to the conditions among the lawless Cyclopes. However, Aristotle assumes in *EN* 8 that relationships within the household, which include the institution of marriage, are *counterparts, homoiōmata,* of constitutions (8.12 1160b22).[20] However, he does not elevate them to constitutional forms. Nevertheless, I assume that Didymus had this passage of *EN* 8.12, and not a later one in *Pol.* 1.12 1259b1f., in mind because at 1.12 he does not use the category of constitution in order to describe what the equivalent of relationships within the household would be in the political sphere. Rather, in *Pol.* 1.12 he uses the wider term "kind of rule," for example, in a political or kingly fashion.[21] Furthermore, at 148.6 Didymus adds as the purpose of the union between husband and wife: "for the procreation of children and for sharing life" which comes close to the description of marriage at *EN* 8.14: "not only for the sake of producing children, but of things that contribute to life"[22] whereas this latter part is missing in *Pol.* 1.2. Didymus combines here, as elsewhere, statements from two different works, adding a detail that was missing in the main source he summarized.

When at 148.6 Didymus claims that marriage is called *oikos*[23] he is plainly wrong since for Aristotle an *oikos* consists of at least the *two*

---

[20] Between husband and wife it is aristocratic (1160b32ff.).

[21] *Pol.* 1.12 1259a40f.: οὐ τὸν αὐτὸν δὲ τρόπον τῆς ἀρχῆς, ἀλλὰ γυναικὸς μὲν πολιτικῶς τέκνων δὲ βασιλικῶς.

[22] Didymus 148, 5f. ἐπὶ τέκνων γεννήσει καὶ βίου κοινωνίᾳ, *EN* 8.14 1162a20: οἱ δ' ἄνθρωποι οὐ μόνον τῆς τεκνοποιίας χάριν συνοικοῦσιν, ἀλλὰ καὶ τῶν εἰς τὸν βίον. Didymus' βίου κοινωνίᾳ is good Aristotelian, cf. *Pol.* 4.11 1295a29f.: βίον τε τὸν τοῖς πλείστοις κοινωνῆσαι δυνατόν.

[23] It needs to be stressed that the term Didymus uses, *oikos*, occurs in Aristotle *Pol.* 1.1–2 only twice: 1252b11 (a quote from Hesiod) and 1252b14 (in a reference to expressions used by Charondas and Epimenides), and only twice more in the rest of *Pol.*: 1.7 1255b19;

relationships husband–wife *and* master–slave (*Pol.* 1.2 1252b9f.) or three relationships: in addition to the two mentioned that of father–son (1.3 1253b5ff.). Didymus reveals at 148.21–149.5 that he knows better when he explains the formation of the household from the coming together of the *two* unions, husband–wife and the slave. Some erroneous statements are not due to ignorance.

Didymus' claim that the marriage is the "beginning of the *polis*" (*archē poleōs*, 148.7) had not been made by Aristotle. That expression could, however, simply be imprecise, and one could think that Didymus wanted the *oikos*, not marriage, to be the "beginning of the *polis*." Such a statement can be related to the terms Aristotle used when he described his method of inquiry as "viewing how things grow from their beginning" (*ex archēs … phyomena, Pol.* 1.2 1252a24, see above, p. 257), and by this approach the smallest parts out which the polis consists are identified—the part out of which the *polis* is formed is the household (1.3 1253b1ff.), and this thought could be condensed to "beginning of the *polis*" (*archē poleōs*).

Didymus considers it necessary to give a reason for the statement that the union of man and wife which constitutes the household is "the beginning of the *polis*", and the reason he mentions is that "the household seems to be a small *polis*" (148.8). This contradicts flatly what Aristotle wrote since he criticized at the beginning of *Pol.* 1.1 Plato who had identified the ruler of household and *polis* "as if there were *no* difference between a large household and a small *polis*."[24] This kind of thinking as proposed by Plato in *Polit.* 258e–259a reduces the difference between the associations at best to one of quantity whereas it is for Aristotle one of kind (*eidei, Pol.* 1.1 1252a10). Didymus reproduces the phrase of Aristotle that a household is perceived as "a small *polis*," ignoring that for Aristotle it was a statement of the absurd consequence to which the Platonic position leads.

For Didymus the remark "the household seems to be a small *polis*" anticipates the result of a marriage that is blessed with children[25] who in turn marry among one another so that new houses are formed out of which first the village and then the *polis* develop (148.8–13). This part of the account reproduces Aristotle (*Pol.* 1.2 1252b15ff.) who, however, did not elaborate on the notion of procreation and did not remark that "as

---

2.6 1265b14, but otherwise always *oikia* is used: 1252a13; b10; b15; b17; b20; b34; 1253a18; a19; b3 (2×); b4; b6; b23 and passim.

[24] 1.1 1252a12: ὡς οὐδὲν διαφέρουσαν μεγάλην οἰκίαν ἢ μικρὰν πόλιν.

[25] Didymus 148.9: κατ' εὐχὴν αὐξομένου τοῦ γάμου—the term αὐξομένου τοῦ γάμου seems unusual. Could it be an echo of *OT Moses* I 9.7: Αὐξάνεσθε, καὶ πληθύνεσθε, καὶ πληρώσατε τὴν γῆν? This refers to procreation in marriage.

the house provided seeds (*spermata*) of the procreation for the *polis* so (it provided seeds) for the constitution as well" (Didymus 148.13–15). And whereas in *EN* 8 Aristotle considered relationships within the household to be *counterparts, homoiōmata*, of constitutions (see above, p. 262) which suggests the notion of analogy and not of physical source, as Didymus' metaphor "seeds of the procreation of the constitution" seems to imply.

The account given by Aristotle and the excerpt by Didymus differ here since Aristotle added to the union of male-female immediately that of master–slave[26] which necessitates explaining the difference in the status of those ruled: that of wife and slave respectively (1252a34ff.). This subject is then picked up by Aristotle in the clarification of the rule that is practiced in a village which consists of many households: since "every household was ruled by the oldest one as a king" this form of rule was then adopted by the new separate settlements, villages and by *poleis* "in olden times" (*to archaion*) (1252b19–27). Didymus by contrast leaves out here the relationship master-slave, and in his continued focus on the household he refers first to the form of rule over the members of the *oikos* as that of a king – Didymus remarks incorrectly that it is exercised "by the parents (*goneōn*) over their children" where Aristotle writes "by the father over his sons"[27] excluding the mother and mentioning of the children only the sons. With his less specific and inaccurate terminology Didymus reveals that he did not grasp that in Aristotle's concept of *rule* the ruler is male and exercises his rule in different roles as male over female or father over son (1.13 1260a10f.)[28] while only for the assessment of the *quality* of the *polis* that of females counts (1260b16-18; 2.9 1269b17-23). Only later Didymus makes the correct statement: "The man exercises by nature the rule over the household" (149.5f.). The excerptor who is only superficially familiar with Aristotle's political theory is likely not to observe in his excerpt the strict terminology of his philosophical source.

Furthermore, Didymus expands on this aspect of rule within the household by identifying in addition to that of the father over sons the form of rule between husband and wife—he calls it aristocratic—and that between children (148.15–19), something Aristotle does not do in the context of *Pol.* 1.2–3. Only at *Pol.* 1.12 1259a37ff. does he distinguish forms

---

[26] 1.2 1252a30–34: "what rules by nature or is ruled" is still apposition to the subject of "who cannot exist without one another."

[27] *EN* 8.12 1160b24f.; cf. *Pol.* 1.12 1259a38: "of the father" (*patrikē*).

[28] *EN* 8.12 1160b34 does not explicitly assign to the wife a rule over persons although she might control the daughters and some slaves.

of relationships within the household in terms of different kinds of *political* rule (see above, p. 262), however, here the relationship of husband–wife is not aristocratic as for Didymus but political, a form which grants to women a more equal share than the identification as aristocratic. This determination of the form of rule among spouses as aristocratic is found in *EN* 8.12 1160b32–35. And there—not at *Pol.* 1.12—the relationship among brothers is addressed. However, it is identified as timocratic,[29] not as democratic[30] as in Didymus. Again (see above, p. 262) *EN* is used to provide additional information not given by Aristotle in the context summarized by Didymus. This passage is typical for Didymus' approach: a statement by Aristotle about the form of rule in the household in *Pol.* provides Didymus with the cue to elaborate on other forms of rule in other relationships within the house, and for the information needed Didymus turns to the less complicated explanation of this matter in *EN*.

Why Didymus returns at 148.19–21 to the union of man and wife for the purpose of procreation which he had mentioned already at the beginning of this section (148.5f.) is not clear to me. Here Didymus' source is not *EN* 8.12 but *Pol.* 1.2 1252a27–30. Does the arrangement of arguments suffer because Didymus followed different Aristotelian texts and did not completely succeed in integrating them into a coherent whole? As in Aristotle *Pol.* 1.2 1252a30ff., so in Didymus (148.21–149.4) the relationship master–slave follows as the second association in the household after that of husband–wife. Didymus establishes a closer connection between slaves and the preceding union of husband–wife by saying that *they* add the slave as someone who contributes with his work (*synergon*) *to their association,* thereby assigning to slaves a role that supports the married couple not given to slaves by Aristotle. His justification of slavery by nature starts with the need of "tools" for the business of providing the necessary things for the *household* (*Pol.* 1.4 1253b25ff.), not just the *married couple*.

Among these "helpers" there are in Didymus on the one hand slaves by nature who possess bodily strength for their service[31] but are intellectu-

---

[29] *EN* 8.12 1161a3; 13 1161a27ff.

[30] This identification is in Didymus consistent since he considers democracy not a mistaken form but a good constitution, see below, p.276; 290.

[31] Didymus 149.1 ἰσχυρὸν μὲν τῷ σώματι πρὸς ὑπηρεσίαν seems to go back to Aristotle *Pol.* 1.5 1254b28.

ally inferior,[32] unable to live by themselves,[33] and for whom being ruled is advantageous.[34] On the other hand there are slaves by law. And that law is according to Aristotle the agreement that men defeated in war belong to the victors.[35] Didymus is not interested in any specifics about this sort of slavery as was Aristotle who first referred to a controversy on this issue at *Pol.* 1.3 (1253b20–23) and later rejected in a detailed argument slavery according to law (6 1255b14), something Didymus does not do.

Didymus ends this section by tracing the formation of the *oikos* back to forethought (*promētheia*)—I understand: of the master of the household— for the purpose of "one single advantage of all"—the juxtaposition of "all" and "one single" must be intentional and goes in its rhetorical antithesis beyond Aristotle who simply stated that "the same thing benefits master and slave."[36] Didymus shows at times interest in careful stylistic wording. Here it stresses the idealistic view of the mutual benefit of the relationship master–slave and more so, it assigns to the foresight (*promētheia*) of the master of the household the decisive role for the *creation* of the *oikos*, a view not found in Aristotle who limits himself in this context to describing the intellectual ability (τῇ διανοίᾳ[37] προορᾶν) of the master which destines him to be the *ruler* over slaves.

---

[32] Didymus 149.2 νωθῇ, implied by Aristotle *Pol.* 1.2 1252a31f., elaborated at 5 1254b22: ὁ κοινωνῶν λόγου τοσοῦτον ὅσον αἰσθάνεσθαι ἀλλὰ μὴ ἔχειν; cf. 13 1260a12 ὁ μὲν γὰρ δοῦλος ὅλως οὐκ ἔχει τὸ βουλευτικόν, cited by Didymus 149.6–8.

[33] Didymus seems to exaggerate Aristotle's remark about the slave as someone "who is able to belong to another person," *Pol.* 1.5 1254b20f. (Didymus 150.5–10), cf. *EN* 4.9 1124b31f.

[34] Didymus 149.3 ᾧ τὸ ἄρχεσθαι συμφέρειν; cf. Aristotle *Pol.* 1.5 1254b6ff., in particular b19f.

[35] Aristotle *Pol.* 1.6 1255a6f.; see above, p. 260.

[36] Didymus 149.4f. τῆς πάντων πρὸς ἓν συμφέρον προμηθείας is very likely based partially on Aristotle *Pol.* 1.2 1252a34: διὸ δεσπότῃ καὶ δούλῳ ταὐτὸ συμφέρει. I do not believe that πάντων should be considered as depending on προμηθείας ("forethought of everyone," Tsouni) but should be connected with συμφέρον: There is *one* advantage for *all*. The other model for Didymus' phrase is Aristotle *Pol.* 1.2 1252a31: τὸ μὲν γὰρ δυνάμενον τῇ διανοίᾳ προορᾶν ἄρχον φύσει ... with προορᾶν inspiring Didymus' προμηθείας. "Forethought of everyone" seems to be excluded by the following remark in Didymus: "the man exercises by nature the rule over the household." If only the man rules over the house, can *everybody* possess this gift of forethought? At 149.15 Didymus reserves the forethought (πρόνοια) to the master of the household. In the Aristotelian passage the two items: the subject; i.e., the person who cares, and the ruler are linked: they are the same.

[37] Aristotle seems to follow Plat. *Rep.* 2 371d5f., see Schütrumpf (2003) 2009, 68f. with nn. 15 and 17.

For Aristotle the master of slaves is defined by foresight (*Pol.* 1.2 1252a31f., see n. 36). Naturally Didymus moves at this juncture (149.5ff.) to the man who rules over the household, comparing different levels of inferiority in the deliberative faculty (τὸ βουλευτικόν) of those ruled: of women, children, and slaves. Here Didymus follows Aristotle *Pol.* 1.13 1260a12ff., omitting only that the man possesses ethical *arête*—and its prerequisite deliberative faculty—in its complete form (1260b17ff.). Instead Didymus inserts a remark about the intellectual faculty required in the master of the household, which he calls *oikonomikē phronēsis* (149.8ff.). The counterpart to this subject in Aristotle *Pol.* 1 is the quality the master of slaves should possess, which is, however, *not* knowledge (*epistēmē*) but a specific quality (*toiosd' einai*, 1.7 1255b20ff.), and this is an ethical quality.[38] In *Pol.* 1, apart from the remark at 2 1252a31 (cited above, n. 36) and 13 1260a16–19, the intellectual faculty required in masters of the household is not dealt with.[39] However, at *EN* 6.5 1140b10 accomplished household managers are listed among those men who are considered to possess reason (*phronimoi*) because they know what is useful for themselves and for men.[40] This passage seems to be the source for Didymus, who again at 149.8ff. supplements arguments used by Aristotle in *Pol.* by those of *EN*. However, Didymus' explanation of this *oikonomikē phronēsis* as the "faculty to administer the household and the things belonging to the household"[41] is a truism or tautology since the verb (*dioikētikēn ousan*) and the object (*oikou* ...) of the explanation use the stem of the term to be explained, *oikos*.[42] The definition is probably so weak since Didymus had nothing in Aristotle he could follow and makes it up himself rather unsuccessfully.

When Didymus goes on to subdivide the *oikonomikē phronēsis* into four categories—as he will later at 150.10-12 distinguish four categories of *phronēsis*—referring to the role as father, husband, master of slaves and provider,[43] he grossly simplifies matters. Whereas the first three roles are

---

[38] Schütrumpf 1991, vol. 1, 294 n. 20,27 on 1255b21.

[39] Nor is it dealt with at 3.6 1278b37f., pace Wachsmuth 149 ap. crit. on ll. 8–10.

[40] Cf. 6.8 1141b31 on *oikonomia*, legislation, and politics as parts of *phronēsis*; 9 1142a9f.

[41] 149.9: διοικητικὴν οὖσαν αὐτοῦ τε <οἴκου> καὶ τῶν κατ' οἶκον. Aristotle never uses the adjective διοικητικός.

[42] The same is true for the definition of the general 150.14–16.

[43] 149.10f.: Ταύτης δὲ τὸ μὲν εἶναι πατρικόν, τὸ δὲ γαμικόν, τὸ δὲ δεσποτικόν, τὸ δὲ χρηματιστικόν. Because of the addition of *chrēmatistikon* I consider as source *Pol.* 1.3, and not 1.12 1259a37, contra Wachsmuth 149 ap. crit. on ll. 10.11.

for Aristotle in *Pol.* 1.3 "parts of *oikonomikē*" (scil. *technē*), not *phronēsis*, he raises the question whether this is true as well for the art of providing the household with necessary goods[44]. Clearly, the master of the household has some responsibility for the material well-being of the household which, however, consists not in *providing* the goods needed but in *using* them. Therefore, for Aristotle the *oikonomikē* is not identical with every sort of *chrēmatistikē* (*Pol.* 1.8 1256a10ff.), but only with its natural form, the "true wealth" (b26ff.). Strictly speaking, it is nature's task to provide man with the goods he needs, and for this reason providing these things is not the responsibility of the master of the household (1.10 1258a19ff.) as Didymus implies who states as reason for the existence of the *chrēmatistikon* within the *oikonomikē phronēsis* the household's need for necessary things: "As an army needs equipment, a city revenues, a technē tools, in the same way a household needs necessary goods."[45] Here the part of the sentence "a craft (*technē*) needs tools" cites Aristotle, but not his arguments about *oikonomikē* or *chrēmatistikē*. Rather, the introduction to the justification of slavery by nature is cited,[46] and this statement of Didymus does not prove what it is supposed to prove since the need of certain things in the household does not make it the task of the household master's *oikonomikē phronēsis* to provide them. Aristotle argues differently: because there is a need for certain things, slaves serve their masters (1.3 1253b14–16). The part of Didymus' statement: "a city needs revenues" (149.12f.) could be an echo of Aristotle's later remark about the practical side of *chrēmatistikē*.[47] Aristotelian arguments have been rearranged, abbreviated, and condensed to a degree that as they stand in Didymus they do not give a fair impression of the complexity and subtlety of the thought of the model.

Didymus presents a double purpose of the necessary goods that are provided by the *chrēmatistikē*: living a life of a rather common quality and living well,[48] and he clearly follows Aristotle *Pol.* 1.4 1253b24f.,[49] who, however, does not qualify the first alternative by "of a rather common quality"

---

[44] 1.3 1253b3–14.

[45] 149.12f. Δεῖν γάρ, ὥσπερ στρατιᾷ μὲν παρασκευῆς, πόλει δὲ προσόδων, τέχνῃ δ' ὀργάνων, οὕτω καὶ οἴκῳ τῶν ἀναγκαίων.

[46] *Pol.* 1.4 1253b25f.: ὥσπερ δὴ ταῖς ὡρισμέναις τέχναις ἀναγκαῖον ἂν εἴη ὑπάρχειν τὰ οἰκεῖα ὄργανα, εἰ μέλλει ἀποτελεσθήσεσθαι τὸ ἔργον, οὕτω καὶ τῷ οἰκονομικῷ.

[47] *Pol.* 1.11 1259a34f.:πολλαῖς γὰρ πόλεσι δεῖ χρηματισμοῦ καὶ τοιούτων πόρων, ὥσπερ οἰκίᾳ.

[48] 149.14f.: Διττὰ δὲ ταῦτα, πρός τε τὸ κοινότερον ζῆν καὶ πρὸς τὸ εὖ.

[49] ἄνευ γὰρ τῶν ἀναγκαίων ἀδύνατον καὶ ζῆν καὶ εὖ ζῆ. Differently Wachsmuth 149 ap. crit. on ll. 14.15 who refers to 1.8 1256b26–32.

(*koinoteron*). Didymus seems to have wanted to emphasize the privileged status of the "good life," opposed to what is "commonly" within reach, and this reminds of the distinction between the best life and "a life which the greatest number of people can share."[50] That the master of the household has the obligation to increase revenues (Didymus 149.15-17) is not mentioned by Aristotle in *Pol.* 1, but found in contemporary authors, for example, Xen. *Oec.* 1.5; 16; 2.1; 11.13. The wife's task is to preserve the goods brought in (7.25). In Didymus the alternative to increasing revenues is reducing expenses.[51]

The last subject of Aristotle *Pol.* 1 addressed by Didymus concerns the practical experience needed by the master of the household. Didymus lists agriculture, keeping of sheep, and mining of minerals 149.18-23). With this short list he gives only a small part of the sources of income the art concerned with this task (*chrēmatistikē*) could pursue according to Aristotle *Pol.* 1.11 1258b12ff. Aristotle is careful not to state that the master of the household needs this experience but leaves unexpressed the subject of "to be experienced,"[52] since he considers the household chores a sort of nuisance which the master of the household avoids if he can hire someone to do them so that the master can devote himself to politics or philosophy (1.7 1255b35-37).

Didymus concludes this section by stating that among the kinds of providing income (*chrēmatistikē*) the natural one is superior while that through trade is inferior (149.21-24). Not only is Aristotle's account more detailed since he deals as well with income from lending money as the worst kind of earning (9 1257b20ff.; 11 1258b25), but also the reader of Didymus' account did not also learn *what* the natural form of providing necessary things is, and this is what matters for Aristotle. Didymus is probably at his worst when he tries to summarize an Aristotelian argument that is very specific and nuanced in its many distinctions which the excerpt cannot reproduce. Furthermore, Didymus misses the conceptual aspect Aristotle addresses at *Pol.* 1.11: after the theoretical considerations have been completed Aristotle turns to issues of practical use.

---

[50] *Pol.* 4.11 1295a29f., cited above, n. 22; cf. 1 1288b38.
[51] This is a recommendation given by Aristotle at *Rhet.* 1.4 1359b23 for the revenues of the *polis*.
[52] *Pol.* 1.11 1258b12f.: τὸ περὶ τὰ κτήματα ἔμπειρον εἶναι ...; b15 δεῖ γὰρ ἔμπειρον εἶναι ...

Politikos topos

When Didymus turns (150.1ff.) to *politikē*[53] he paraphrases a remark from Aristotle *Pol.* 3.6 (1278b19ff.) about the causes of founding states; however, in starting the topic *politikē* with this subject Didymus omits Aristotle's preceding theoretical explanations, in particular the conceptual link between constitution (*politeia*), city (*polis*), and its part, that is, the citizen (*politēs*) (3.1–5). Rather, he mentions briefly only the cause for the forming of cities: the social nature of man and the common benefit enjoyed in living together. When choosing this starting point for *politikē*, Didymus might have wanted to establish a closer connection with the beginning of *Pol.* 1 which he had summarized (148.7ff.). As for the social nature of man, he avoids at 150.2f. the term *politikon* which he had used himself at the start (148.3) in the same context, following Aristotle (see above, p. 258). Didymus now uses *koinōnikon* instead which is not found as a modifier of people in Aristotle's *Pol.*[54] With this terminology Didymus cuts the etymological and conceptual connection with *polis* and does no longer view man as "part of the *polis*" as Aristotle had stressed in this context in *Pol.* 1.2 1253a26–29. Didymus' choice of the term *koinōnikon* instead of *politikon* does not do justice to *Pol.*, and Didymus seems to cite here *koinōnikon anthrōpos zōion* from *EE* 7.10 1242a25f.[55] This choice shows the randomness of his citations which at times reveal an attempt at reaching beyond the source he summarizes; however, in doing so he does not recognize the coherence of the subjects discussed by Aristotle and the consistency of the philosophical terminology applied in his source.

Didymus adds to these reasons for forming a *polis* the claim that the city is "the most perfect association," a remark found not at Aristotle *Pol.* 3.6 which Didymus was summarizing but at the beginning of *Pol.* 1, and there not in the superlative[56] and not in the context of the formation of cities. The last reason added by Didymus as a cause for forming a *polis* (150.4),

---

[53] For *politikē* as discipline, see Aristotle *EN* 1.1 1094a27, in *Pol.* with the addition *philosophia* 3.12 1282b23 or *dianoia kai theōria* 7.2 1324a19f.

[54] *Koinōnikos* is used by Aristotle only at *Pol.* 3.13 1283a38 to qualify *aretē*, and *EN* 8.12 1161b14 to qualify forms of friendship, *philia*. *Koinōnikon zōion anthrōpos* as well Didymus 120.14.

[55] *Pol.* 3.9 1280b39f. to which Wachsmuth 150 ap. crit. on l. 3 refers does not deal with the quality of man but the efforts of cities to foster friendship among its citizens. For the concept of *koinōnia politikē*, see Schütrumpf (1981; now 2009) 47–54.

[56] 1.2 1252b28: ἡ δ' ἐκ πλειόνων κωμῶν κοινωνία τέλειος πόλις. 3.9 1280b40ff. referred to by Wachsmuth 150 ap. crit. on l. 4 does not deal with the perfect nature of the *polis*, but with the perfect life for which it exists.

namely that a citizen is defined by access to political office, reproduces the definition of the citizen from *Pol.* 3.1[57] which, however, has nothing to do with origin of the *polis*. Could it be that Didymus understood already Aristotle's phrase *phusei politikon zōion*, which in *Pol.* 1.2 characterizes a man who enjoys the final stage of the development of associations, the polis, as "having a natural claim to exercising political rights," as one reads today at times? In a cut and paste technique Didymus combines freely statements that are more or less close to those of the original but outside the context they were used in. This observation shows again that Didymus was not simply an excerptor but intended to accomplish more. Here he considers the subject: "the cause of the forming of cities" most important and buttresses it with additional arguments which Aristotle had not used for that purpose.

After having presented the reasons for the formation of the *polis* Didymus proceeds to give a definition of the *polis* (150.5f.) which echoes *Pol.* 3.1 1275b21 (see above, n. 14). While this sequence of arguments reverses that of the original it makes sense: once we have reached the stage of the *polis* it serves well to know what a *polis* is; however, this interest in a definition reproduces Aristotle's reasoning neither at 1.2 where, after having outlined its coming into existence, he dwells on the *polis* as association in which justice rules (1253a1ff.; a14–18; a31-39)—this has no counterpart in Didymus—nor at 3.6 where after having referred to the earlier account of the origin of the *polis* he moves on to develop a first taxonomy of constitutions.

Pol. 3 argues at the beginning that an explanation of what the *polis* is must precede the investigation of the concept of constitution (*politeia*). This leads to a definition of what a *citizen* (*politēs*) is. On the basis of that, the definition of the *polis* is: "a number (*plēthos*) (of citizens) of the sort that is adequate for self-sufficiency of life."[58] This remark is quoted verbally by Didymus 150.5f. who goes on to determine the limit of the number (*plēthos*) of citizens. This topic Aristotle investigates in *Pol.* 7.4.[59] Here we find *horos* and *plēthos*, terms used by Didymus as well, in the context of the self-suffiency of the *polis*, which Aristotle had addressed in *Pol.* 3.1. Didymus seems to have recognized that the definition of the *polis* at *Pol.* 3.1 and a first indication of the number (*plēthos*) of citizens needed additional

---

[57] 150.4f.: καὶ ὅτι πολίτης ἐστὶν ᾧ μέτεστι πολιτικῆς ἀρχῆς; cf. Aristotle *Pol.* 3.1 1275b18f.: ᾧ γὰρ ἐξουσία κοινωνεῖν ἀρχῆς βουλευτικῆς καὶ κριτικῆς. Didymus' choice "political office" is good Aristotelian usage, cf. *Pol.* 1.12 1259b4; 3.6 1279a8.

[58] 3.1 1275b20f.: πόλιν δὲ τὸ τῶν τοιούτων πλῆθος ἱκανὸν πρὸς αὐτάρκειαν ζωῆς.

[59] 7.4 1326b23f.: οὗτός ἐστι πόλεως ὅρος ἄριστος, ἡ μεγίστη τοῦ πλήθους ὑπερβολὴ πρὸς αὐτάρκειαν ζωῆς εὐσύνοπτος.

clarification which he provides by paraphrasing a passage from a different book that addresses the issue. He must have had an idea of the complete work when he was summarizing its earliest arguments (see above, p. 261; below p. 287).

There is another reason why Didymus, when turning after the *definition* of citizen as it had been presented by Aristotle at *Pol.* 3.1f. to the *number* of citizens (150.5–10), could have been following Aristotle. At *Pol.* 3.3 Aristotle deals with the question under which conditions one can consider a polis as being "one". This condition is not met if the *polis* possesses the size of Babylon (3.3 1276a29f.). Didymus' arrangement of arguments at 150.4-7 is in line with Aristotle *Pol.* 3.1–3 even if Didymus supplemented Aristotle's brief reference to the problems of a megacity with a summary of his more fundamental discussion of the size of the population from 7.4. Didymus provides a fair account of the Aristotelian concept of the *polis* and accomplished this by piecing together statements from different books of *Pol.*

Didymus departs more from Aristotle's text when he explains what goals the determination of the number of citizens should accomplish. While Didymus uses the genuine Aristotelian approach of teleology, contrasting two results that should be avoided with two goals that should be reached, not all these arguments use Aristotelian terms, and some are actually difficult to trace to *Pol.* Didymus writes at 150.6–10:

"The number of citizens should be fixed in such a way that the city is neither without feeling (for one another) nor easily regarded with contempt, but equipped both for the (necessities of) life without needs and for (actions) towards attackers from outside adequately."[60]

I do not know in Aristotle's *Pol.* of any remark of the sort "that the city is not without feeling for one another", or "without fellow-feeling (ἀσυμπαθής)."[61] Could Didymus be thinking of Aristotle's reference to the size of Babylon that came closer to that of a tribe than a city, where "for three days a part of it had not realized (οὐκ αἰσθέσθαι) that it had been captured" (3.3 1276a29f.; see above)? Does Didymus express an ideal of a city of such a size that citizens are *aware* of what happens to *all* of them, so that the part that is under attack can receive the support of the rest, based on compassion? This understanding is supported by the fact that both authors, Aristotle and Didymus, have a condition of a city in mind

---

[60] ὥστε μήτε τὴν πόλιν ἀσυμπαθῆ μήτ' εὐκαταφρόνητον ὑπάρχειν, παρεσκευάσθαι δὲ καὶ τὰ πρὸς τὴν ζωὴν ἀνενδεῶς καὶ τὰ πρὸς τοὺς ἔξωθεν ἐπιόντας ἱκανῶς.

[61] The latter version is Liddell-Scott-Jones' translation of ἀσυμπαθής, s.v. I.

where size is not an obstacle to the interaction of citizens. If this was Didymus' concern he understood Aristotle quite well. In *Pol.* 7, Aristotle sets the limit of the *number of citizens* of the best state in such a way that it allows citizens to know one another. This he considers a precondition for choosing men for offices and juries whose quality the other citizens know (7.4 1326b16f.). Didymus would favor this concept of a face-to-face society because it does not allow indifference of citizens towards one another.

It should, however, be stressed that this particular goal "not without feeling for others" is not a prominent concern of Aristotle's *Pol.*, but it is one emphasized by Plato in *Rep.* 5 where Socrates considers that behavior the greatest good for a city which creates greatest unity, and this is explained as the sharing of pleasure and pain by all citizens. The requirement for a city: "not without feeling for others" (μήτε ἀσυμπαθῆ) in Didymus had been described by Plato: "If one citizen experiences something good or suffers something bad, such a city will most of any declare that this experience (πάσχον) belongs to it and will as a whole either share the joy or share the pain."[62] Didymus' "not without feeling for others" has a strong Platonic ring to it.

The second condition to be avoided regarding the number of citizens according to Didymus is that a city is easily regarded with contempt (εὐκαταφρόνητον), which must refer to the reputation it enjoys among other cities, very likely regarding the impression it makes as a military power that is not considered so weak as to invite attackers. While the security of the best state receives considerable attention in Aristotle's *Pol.* from the perspective of the conditions of the territory,[63] for the aspect of size of the population there are only a few passages to which one could refer. Aristotle criticizes at *Pol.* 4.4 1291a6ff. Plato's sketch of the earliest stage of a *polis* as outlined in *Rep.* 2 where among its very few ("four or whatever their number") first members soldiers are missing. Aristotle considers them as necessary "if they don't want to be doomed to serve as slaves to their attackers. It is impossible to call a city that is enslaved by nature a city." Such a city would have lost its status as a free *polis* due to its failure to build a strong army and deserves contempt. It was imprinted in the consciousness of ancient Greeks since Tyrtaeus that it is *honorable* (*kalon*) to fight, and die, for one's fatherland (F 10.1 *IEG* II), and Aristotle considers all

---

[62] *Rep.* 5 462d8: Ἑνὸς δὴ οἶμαι πάσχοντος τῶν πολιτῶν ὁτιοῦν ἢ ἀγαθὸν ἢ κακὸν ἡ τοιαύτη πόλις μάλιστά τε φήσει ἑαυτῆς εἶναι τὸ πάσχον, καὶ ἢ συνησθήσεται ἅπασα ἢ συλλυπήσεται.

[63] *Pol.* 7.5 1326b39ff.

preparations for war as being *honorable* or noble (*kalos*, 7.2 1325af.). Easily despised is a city that is defeated because of the small numbers of citizens who could defend it.[64]

There are other comments that could be referred to here. At *Pol.* 7.2 (1324a25ff.) Aristotle discusses the ambition of some states to dominate their neighbors. Such a focus on and preference for war and domination of others as practiced by Sparta was *praised* by many (7.14 1333b5ff.). In the opinion of many, the Spartan state would not be "easily despised" because its constitution and education aim at military strength which gives it prestige. However, Aristotle finds fault with Sparta since it did not realize the potential of its territory to sustain 1,500 horsemen and 30,000 hoplites but suffered scarcity of citizens (*oliganthrōpia*) and did not survive one military defeat[65] so that he considered Sparta as "finished," "dead" (*apōleto*, 2.9 1269b29-34). Here the dwindling number of citizens ended a glorious history of a *polis*. Rare must be the opposite scenario of a city that is too large to which Aristotle responds with the rhetorical question: "Who will be general of an exceedingly large crowd?" (4 1326b5f.)—the large number of citizens would hamper an effective leadership.

The first of the two positive requirements regarding the number of citizens in Didymus states that a city be "equipped for the (necessities of) life without needs" (150.8f.). Aristotle addresses similar concerns in different contexts. Very close comes 7.5 1326b29 where he discusses the quality of the territory surrounding the city and starts with its productivity. Everybody would praise a land that is most self-sufficient, and he explains self-sufficient as "that all things are available and one does not need anything."[66] However, Aristotle not only considers natural resources required for the needs of life as means which secure self-sufficiency but also includes men: a self-sufficient society must possess the professionals who master necessary tasks in order to meet the needs of a city.[67] While Didymus left out this dimension of autarky he recognized its importance in Aristotle's political theory[68] when including it in his summary.

The final requirement Didymus makes here concerns the (actions) toward attackers from outside. The need for a military was stressed by Aristotle in his criticism of the earliest stage of *polis* in *Rep.* book 2 which

[64] Cf. 7.4 1326a22–25; see below, p. 275.
[65] In the battle at Leuctra in Boeotia 371 BC.
[66] 7.5 1326b29 δεῖσθαι μηθενὸς αὔταρκες corresponds closely to Didymus παρεσκευάσθαι δὲ καὶ τὰ πρὸς τὴν ζωὴν ἀνενδεῶς, 150.4f.
[67] 7.8 1328b17: ἡ γὰρ πόλις πλῆθός ἐστιν οὐ τὸ τυχὸν ἀλλὰ πρὸς ζωὴν αὔταρκες.
[68] For autarky, see Schütrumpf 1991, vol. 1, pp. 203–7, n. 13,12 on 1252b29.

did not possess soldiers (4.4 1291a6ff.; see above, p. 273). Suggesting that an association of men without a military was a *polis* is a radical, truly utopian proposal of Plato. Less radical but equally mistaken is the possibility in contemporary politics that a state possesses many laborers but few hoplites; this condition does not result in a "great city" (7.4 1326a22–25). Among the six necessary "parts" of a city, Aristotle lists men who possess heavy arms "against those who try to inflict injustice from outside" (7.8 1328b8–10)—at 4.4. 1291a8 they are called attackers (ἐπιοῦσιν) exactly as in Didymus 150.9f. (ἐπιόντας). However, the larger and more comprehensive scope of this topic as indicated by Aristotle at *Pol.* 7.4 1327b4–6 and 2.6 1265a20 where he points out that the strength of the military power of a city has to match its political ambitions, is missing in Didymus, together with all aspects of political theory contained in *Pol.* 2.

All in all, one can trace these four expectations for the size of the citizenry to a lesser or greater extent to Aristotle's *Pol.*; however, not all can count as a summary of his political concepts, and one might well determine that Didymus deviates here from Aristotle, for whom the size of the *polis* was a subordinate issue.[69] There is no other case of Didymus himself assembling arguments of more or less Aristotelian provenance in order to support a concept Aristotle had alluded to. Moreover, this one instance cannot support the assumption of an intermediate source, which was responsible for the insertion of a topic which was not of particular interest for Aristotle. At times Didymus puts emphasis on aspects that we might consider less important than they appear in his summary, for example, the formation of the city (see above, p. 263; 270f.), and given his penchant for bringing together arguments from different contexts in Aristotle to support a claim, the possibility that things were misrepresented did arise.

Didymus goes on to offer in the next sentence (150.10f.) a reason (γὰρ) for these requirements for the size of the citizenry. However, how a distinction between four kinds of *phronēsis*: economic, legislative, political, military leadership,[70] can meet this objective is not clear. Here he follows closely the distinctions made by Aristotle at *EN* 6.8 1141b23ff. where the first three mentioned by Didymus can be found—and only these three. He omits Aristotle's ranking of these activities, with legislative knowledge

---

[69] Cf. Regenbogen, *RE* Suppl. VII, 1517.23–25: "das Referat (ist), von wenigen Abweichungen abgesehen, ganz auf der Politik des Ar. aufgebaut."

[70] When listing them, Didymus does not use the feminine gender, which would agree with *phronēsis*, but shows preference for using the neuter where something like *eidos* must be understood as the noun governing the adjectives.

(*nomothetikē*) leading as the architectonic form, whereas *politikē* is inferior since it deals with particulars. Didymus adds as fourth "fit for military leadership" (στρατηγικόν) which is missing in Aristotle *EN* 6.8., and also in *Pol*. There, as far as the defense of the country is concerned, the focus is on the existence of hoplites (see above, p. 274f.), but little is said about military leadership. This becomes important for him in a different context. Because of the extraordinary powers generals wield and the impact this power has on the political order and its stability[71] Aristotle discusses at *Pol*. 5.9, in the larger context of the qualification of officials, the one required from generals. Here he calls it *empeiria* (1309b4f.), not *phronēsis* as Didymus did.[72] Was Didymus influenced by Aristotle *EN* 1.1[73] where he lists the art of military leadership (*stratēgikē*) besides that of managing a household (*oikonomikē*) and rhetoric as the most highly regarded forms of knowledge (*epistēmē*) which are subordinate to political knowledge (1094b3)?

Turning next to the content of *Pol*. 3, Didymus begins immediately (see above, p. 270) with the taxonomy of constitutions (150.17ff.) which Aristotle developed in *Pol*. 3.6–7, skipping the preceding systematic inquiry. Didymus distinguishes the rule (ἄρχειν) of "either one man or few or all" whereas in Aristotle *Pol*. 3.7 1279a27 the last alternative is not "all" but "the many." However, in his very detailed account of the decision-making process under various constitutions in *Pol*. 4.14, democracy is defined by the arrangement that "*all* decide on all issues" (1298a9ff.). Didymus omits in his account the general principle behind this taxonomy, namely that the constitution is the sovereign (*to kyrion*) of the cities, and this, and not the word "to rule" (ἄρχειν), is the terminology usually employed by Aristotle.[74]

Here Didymus distinguishes between correct and mistaken constitutions—expressed again in the indefinite neuter (*hekaston*)—using the Aristotelian criterion of whether they pursue the common well-being or the advantage of the rulers and employing Aristotle's term *parekbasis* for the latter group. However, when listing the individual constitutions, he counts democracy among the correct ones: in Aristotle the rule of the many for the common good is the *polity* (3.7 1279a37–b4), whereas democracy is one of the mistaken forms.[75] The place of democracy in Aristotle's system as the

---

[71] 3.11 1282a31; 14 1285a7; a15; b22; b27; b38f.; 16 1287a5; 5.5 1305a8; a11; 7 1307a4; b7ff.

[72] Cf. *EN* 1.4 1096a31–33; *epistēmē*, 1097a9f.; 1.5 1097a17; a 19 *technē*.

[73] Thus Wachsmuth 150 ap. crit. on ll. 10–12.

[74] *To kyrion*: 3.6 1278b10ff. ἄρχειν is commonly used in a more restricted sense for the activities of men who hold an office, cf. 3.11 1281b34; 6.4 1318b33–1319a2.

[75] Aristotle at *Pol*. 4.2 1289b6–11 insists on this point against the ambiguous use of

rule of the great number for their own advantage is taken in Didymus by *ochlokratia*, a term Aristotle never used (see below, p. 290). Didymus omits that for Aristotle, after this basic scheme, a more philosophical investigation which reveals "the truth" about constitutions has to be conducted (3.8 1279b12ff.). Didymus moves directly to the mixed constitution which is discussed by Aristotle in the following book of *Pol.* 4, chs. 7–9. Here Didymus omits as well, as he had omitted an account of *Pol.* 3.1–5, Aristotle's remarks on the principles of constitutional theory presented at *Pol.* 4.1–2 in a program that outlines the content of *Pol.* books 4–6.

Didymus claims that a constitution which mixes the correct constitutions is the best (150.23–151.1). Again, he is unaware of the detailed argument in *Pol.* 2.6 1265b31ff. that discusses exactly this question and argues against Plato's ranking of constitutions in the *Laws*. Here Aristotle dismissed Plato's view that the best constitution should be mixed of democracy and tyranny, objecting that they are either not constitutions at all or the worst ones–a position which agrees very much with Didymus' statement that the best constitution is a mixture of the correct ones. However, Aristotle goes on to discuss the opinion of "some" that the best constitution should be a mixture of all constitutions, and he leans in that direction since "the constitution that consists of a greater number of constitutions is better" (1266a4f.). Here he does not insist that all specific constitutions out of which the best one is mixed must themselves be good, and this is generally his view: in his extensive treatment of mixed constitutions in *Pol.* 4.7–9 he allows the designation of aristocratic for mixed constitutions that consist of oligarchic, democratic and aristocratic elements (1293b10ff.)— oligarchic and democratic constitutions are mistaken forms, but still are included in a mixed constitution of aristocratic character.[76] Didymus' strategy of condensing a complex subject to an one line statement is bound to cause inaccuracies. I will return to this at the end.

Why Didymus at this juncture, before completing his account of the content of *Pol.* 4—he returns to it at 151.3–8 and 23ff.—moves to the subject matter of book 5, change of constitutions, is not clear. He starts abruptly at 151.2f. with "constitutions change often to the better and the worse," and with this statement he was most likely thinking of Aristotle's response in the last chapter of *Pol.* 5 to Plato's account of the change of constitutions in the *Rep.* which are replaced by the next worse one. Aristotle points out

---

democracy in Plato.

[76] The mixture only of extreme oligarchy and democracy, without the aristocratic element, is tyranny and the worst constitution: *Pol.* 5.10 1310b3–7.

that the direction of change can be the opposite: a tyranny can change into an aristocracy (12 1316a29–33), although this is just one possibility among the many Aristotle lists.[77]

Didymus now seems to return to *Pol.* 4[78] where in ch. 2 1289a30–b3 Aristotle identified the best constitutions, kingship and aristocracy, which are both based on *aretē*—very similar to Didymus' description[79]—and are contrasted by Aristotle with tyranny as the worst constitution. For Didymus tyranny rules according to depravity (*kakia*). Aristotle did not say this explicitly in *Pol.* 4.2; however, he does so at *EN* 8.13 1160b7–12.[80] Again *EN* seems to have provided Didymus with the key term "badness" which at *Pol.* 4.2 is only implied.[81]

After having touched upon an issue addressed by Aristotle in *Pol.* 4.2, Didymus moves next (151.5) to the last topics discussed by Aristotle in *Pol.* 4: deliberation, offices, and judicial decisions (4.4–16),[82] however, Didymus switches the order of the first two, starting with offices and mentioning deliberation next. And while Aristotle addresses three fundamental aspects: *who* appoints these men, *from which group* and *in which manner* (4.15 1300a1ff.) they are appointed, and devotes additional attention to the *issues* over which one deliberates, the *tasks* for which one assigns offices, or the *issues* and *disputes* over which judicial decisions are made under different constitutions, Didymus limits himself here (he returns to the subject at 151.16–22) mainly to the groups *from* which these three bodies are filled: all, the wealthy, the best.[83] His language is extremely abbreviated: Aristotle

---

[77] Cf. *Pol.* 5.1 1301b9: from democracy or oligarchy a change to polity or aristocracy is possible. The reference by Wachsmuth 151 ap. crit. on ll. 2.3 to *Pol.* 5.1 1302a4–15 does not provide the source for Didymus' remark.

[78] The source for this remark cannot be *Pol.* 3.13 or 3.18 referred to by Wachsmuth 151 ap. crit. on ll. 3.4 since at *Pol.* 3 Aristotle does not contrast the best and worst constitution.

[79] Arist. *Pol.* 4.2 1289a32f.: βούλεται γὰρ ἑκατέρα κατ' ἀρετὴν συνεστάναι κεχορηγημένην; Didymus 151.3f.:ἀρίστην εἶναι πολιτείαν τὴν κατ' ἀρετὴν διακεκοσμημένην. Did Didymus misunderstand κεχορηγημένην, which refers to the existence of external means and not embellishment?

[80] κάκιστον δὲ τὸ ἐναντίον τῷ βελτίστῳ. μεταβαίνει δ' ἐκ βασιλείας εἰς τυραννίδα· φαυλότης γάρ ἐστι μοναρχίας ἡ τυραννίς, ὁ δὲ μοχθηρὸς βασιλεὺς τύραννος γίνεται.

[81] The advice given to the tyrant at 5.11 1315b9f. "not to be bad but only half-bad" suggests that tyrants preferred to be bad, and 1314a1–5 shows the bad company they attracted.

[82] This does not anticipate the distinction of the three branches of government: legislature, executive, judiciary, cf. Schütrumpf 1980, 240 n. 4.

[83] Only for democracy he adds the manner of appointing officials "either by election or by lot" (151.6), correctly, cf. *Pol.* 4.15 1300a32f.

does not say that "some rule out of this or that class" (ἄρχειν ... ἐκ πάντων, 151.5f.) as Didymus expresses himself, but that one appoints (*kathistanai*) those who hold offices from this or that class (1300a12ff.).[84]

Didymus next (151.9-15) moves back (see above, p. 278) to the content of Aristotle *Pol.* 5 abbreviating the wide range of topics of the investigation listed by Aristotle in the introduction to this book[85] to just two: civil war or struggle for power (*stasis*) and the overthrow of constitutions.[86] Within the former Didymus describes two categories, obviously causes, of civil war, first *kata logon*, which consists in the fact that equals are forced to have an unequal (share) or vice versa, and second *kata pathos*, that is because of honor (*timē*), political ambition (*philarchia*), gain or wealth.

The distinction between *kata logon* and *kata pathos* as universal explanations of civil unrest has no counterpart in Aristotle. And while (in-)equality of (un)equals is the first cause of *stasis* which Aristotle mentions in *Pol.* 5.1 1301a37ff., it is not a condition citizens are "forced" to live under (ἀναγκάζωνται, Didymus 151.11f.), but which they "perceive" to endure, for example, "if those who strive for equality *believe* that they possess less while they are equal with those who have more."[87] Aristotle does not speak of objective conditions one is "forced" to live under but the way citizens perceive their situation.[88]

Furthermore, Didymus would have been closer to the Aristotelian view if he had presented the reaction to (in-)equality not as *kata logon* but *kata pathos*. After all, the perception of being treated as unequal while one believes to be equal or the perception of being treated as equal while one

---

[84] Aristotle and Didymus seem to approach this subject from opposite ends: Aristotle identifies the various theoretically possible options and assigns them to constitutions (e.g., 4.14 1298a14ff.) whereas Didymus starts with the constitutions and explains out of which group they fill offices.

[85] 5.1 1301a20–25. cf. 4.2 1289b22–26.

[86] *Katalyesthai*, 151.13; cf. Aristotle *Pol.* 5.1 1301b20 and elsewhere.

[87] 1302a24–26; cf. 1301a37: καὶ διὰ ταύτην τὴν αἰτίαν, ὅταν μὴ κατὰ τὴν ὑπόληψιν ἣν ἑκάτεροι τυγχάνουσιν ἔχοντες μετέχωσι τῆς πολιτείας, στασιάζουσιν; 2 1302a25–29: στασιάζουσιν ἂν νομίζωσιν ἔλαττον ἔχειν ὄντες ἴσοι τοῖς πλεονεκτοῦσιν, οἱ δὲ τῆς ἀνισότητος καὶ τῆς ὑπεροχῆς ἂν ὑπολαμβάνωσιν ὄντες ἄνισοι μὴ πλέον ἔχειν ἀλλ' ἴσον ἢ ἔλαττον (τούτων δ' ἔστι μὲν ὀρέγεσθαι δικαίως, ἔστι δὲ καὶ ἀδίκως). By adding that they can strive after (in)equality rightly or wrongly he elaborates on the subjective nature of the response.

[88] The perception of a condition does not necessarily accord with logos, *kata logon*, but can for Aristotle result from an emotional state; e.g., fear is a pain or upheaval resulting from a perception (*phantasia*) of a serious threat, that is, if something threatening *appears* to be close (*Rhet.* 2.5 1382a21ff.).

believes to be superior is not very different from the feeling to be slighted which is one cause of *anger* according to *Rhet.* 2.2 (1378b10ff.). This assessment that Didymus uses here the wrong categories is supported by *Pol.* 5 where Aristotle actually introduces the distinction between calculation (*logismos*) and emotion (*pathos*), in order to describe the serious nature of attacks against a tyrant if the attackers act out of anger because this emotion makes the attacker set aside reasoning (*logismos*, 5.10 1312b25–34). Aristotle identifies "in a certain way seven, and in another way more causes why men (who are engaged in civil war) are in such a state of mind" (5.2 1302a34ff.); however, in his explanation at *Pol.* 5.2 the two causes mentioned by Didymus are not found nor could they be considered a correct summary of what Aristotle explains.

Ambition (*philarchia*) as the first of the four causes of *stasis kata pathos* in Didymus is not used by Aristotle in *Pol.*, and the term that comes closest to this concept, *spoudarchiaō* (4.11 1295b12; 5.5 1305a31), is not given by Aristotle as a cause of political unrest. Honor (*timē*) and gain which are mentioned next by Didymus as causes of *stasis kata pathos* are listed by Aristotle prominently (5.2 1302a32; a 38; b7-14). According to *EN* 4.10 1125b1ff. there is a right *attitude* in the pursuit of honor (*philotimia*) and gain (*kerdos*). The right practiced in distribution (*dianemētikon dikaion*, 5.7 1131b27f.; cf. 5 1130b31) regulates the appropriate conduct. Trying to secure for oneself more than one deserves violates specific principles of equality, that is justice (4 1130a14ff.), and Aristotle refers to these concepts in *Pol.* 5, starting with the introductory chapter 1 (1301a25ff.). When Didymus focuses on the aspect *kata pathos* he must have the underlying *desire* for honor and material goods in mind; however, he ignores the conceptual framework in which they were placed in Aristotle for whom virtues and vices are stable attitudes towards emotions (*EN* 2.4 1105b25f.), and this would include desire for honor or gain. All in all, the contrast *kata logon* and *kata pathos* is not used by Aristotle for a general explanation of civil war and is not an adequate description of the Aristotelian classification of causes of *stasis*.

Of the first two causes of *stasis kata pathos* mentioned by Didymus, honor (*timē*)[89] and political ambition (*philarchia*), the second could be

---

[89] Stobaeus is more specific at 4.4 21.5–8 where he quotes Aristotle's view that most civil wars break out because of love of honor, adding that not everybody but the most powerful men fight (over honor)"—this could be inspired by Aristotle *Pol.* 2.7 1266b38ff.: Αἱ πλεῖσται στάσεις διὰ φιλοτιμίαν ἐν ταῖς πόλεσι γίγνονται· περὶ τιμῆς γὰρ οὐχ οἱ τυχόντες, ἀλλ' οἱ δυνατώτατοι διαμφισβητοῦσι.

understood as a more specific form of the first; in the same way, the last cause mentioned, wealth (*euporia*), seems the specific form of gain (*kerdos*). Should Didymus have distinguished only two causes[90] and given two alternatives within each?

At 151.12f. Didymus reproduces correctly Aristotle's view for whom *gain* becomes a cause of political troubles if political offices enrich (*kerdainein*) the officeholders.[91] As for *wealth* (*euporia*): in Didymus it is a very abbreviated expression by which several things could be meant, for example, that the wealthy cause the overthrow of oligarchies: (*Pol.* 5.6 1305b2ff.), that a constitution gives predominance to the wealthy who then abuse their position which leads to discord among citizens (5.7 1307a19f.); or the destabilizing contrast between rich and poor.[92]

Next Didymus claims as Aristotle's view "that constitutions are dissolved by two causes (*aitias*), violence or deceit" (151.13f.). Aristotle mentions indeed these two factors (5.4 1304b7), but not as *causes* of the dissolution of constitutions—he had just finished that account with the remark that "the *origins* and *causes* (*archai kai aitiai*) of civil wars and changes of constitutions occur in the described way" (4 1304b7)—but as the *manner* in which these political crises are initiated: "by violence or deceit" (1304b8), and these *strategies* can be used in almost all cases regardless of the *causes* that bring about civil wars and constitutional changes. Due to the close proximity of the statements about causes and strategies in Aristotle, Didymus might have overlooked the difference in subject matter and understood the second (on "manner") as belonging to the first (on "causes").

In his last statement referring to an aspect of the content of *Pol.* 5, the conditions that make a constitution stable,[93] Didymus claims that constitutions that strive after the common well-being last longer. The goal "common well-being," as opposed to the advantage for the rulers, serves in Aristotle *Pol.* 3.6–7 as the criterion that distinguishes correct from mistaken constitutions (see above, p. 276). However, it is not referred to in *Pol.* 5 as a factor

---

[90] 5.2 1302a31f.: περὶ ὧν δὲ στασιάζουσιν ἐστὶ κέρδος καὶ τιμὴ καὶ τἀναντία τούτοις.

[91] 5.3 1302b5ff.; 8 1308a31–33; cf. Schütrumpf 1996, vol. 3, n. 52.40, p. 441f.

[92] Cf. 4.11 1296a9ff. Hostility toward the wealthy supports the bid for tyranny: 5.5 1305a22ff. Cf. *EN* 8.12 1160b12ff., the explanation of the change of an aristocracy into an oligarchy "because of the corruption of the rulers who value highest to be rich"; see below. Cf. *EN* 8.12 1160b12ff. (see below); cf. in private relationships, *Pol.* 5.4 1303b33ff.

[93] Didymus 151.14f.: μονιμωτέρας δὲ γίνεσθαι τοῦ κοινῇ συμφέροντος ἐπιμελουμένας. *Pol.* 1 1302b13–15 referred to by Wachsmuth 151 ap. crit. on ll. 14. 15 explains the stability of a constitution that is based on the middle class and its vicinity to democracy not on the quality of its rule.

that contributes to their stability—in fact, the term "common well-being" (κοινῇ συμφέρον)[94] is not used at all in this book. The claim Didymus made contradicts some statements in Aristotle *Pol.* 5, for example, when he refers to the old oligarchy in Erythrae which was overthrown "although those who possessed full citizen rights took good care;" nevertheless, the demos resented being ruled by a few (6 1305b18ff.). Good policies of a government alone do not guarantee that it will last. Didymus simplifies Aristotle's more nuanced and complicated reasoning.[95]

Closer to the statement by Didymus comes *EN* 8.12 1160b12ff.: the explanation of the change of an aristocracy into an oligarchy "because of the corruption of the rulers who distribute ... all or most of the goods to themselves ... valuing highest to be rich." Generally in *EN* 8.12 1160b10f. Aristotle not only contrasts good and bad constitutions as in *Pol.* 3.6–7 but considers the latter the result of bad policies of the former. Again in Didymus' summary, the political theory of *Pol.* is complemented by a remark in *EN*, and in this case the reason for turning to *EN* might be that it presents a simpler account of the changes of constitutions than the complex and detailed explanations of *Pol.* 5 which defy a correct summary in a few words.

Why the next section 151.16–22 returns to the discussion of various institutions under different constitutions, which was started at 151.5–8 (see above p. 278), is not clear. In Aristotle, such an inquiry is part of a more comprehensive study of the three most important political functions or bodies of political and judicial decision making and offices (*archai*) in *Pol.* 4.14–16. The introductory remark in Didymus according to which courts, bodies of decision making, and offices (*archai*) are set up specifically in a way fitting to the constitutions (151.17) echoes the announcement in *Pol.* 4.14 1297b41ff.[96] Didymus, however, then limits himself to one subject only, offices (*archai*). These are dealt with by Aristotle in *Pol.* 4.15 and 6.8. Some offices listed by Didymus are mentioned in both chapters of Aristotle's treatment: generalship (4.15 1299a21; 1300b21; 6.8 1322a39), supervision of the market (ἀγορανομία, 4.15 1299b17; 6.8 1322a14),

---

[94] Didymus, see previous note; Aristotle *Pol.* 3.3 1276a13; 6 1278b22 and more often in book 3.

[95] See Schütrumpf, "Little to do with justice. Aristotle on distributing political power," in Th. Lockwood, Th. Samaras (eds.), *A Critical Guide to Aristotle's Politics* (Cambridge 2015).

[96] The order in which the three topics are mentioned is different in Aristotle from that in Didymus, see above, p. 278. "Fitting to the constitutions," ταῖς πολιτείαις οἰκείως; cf. Arist. *Pol.* 4.15 1299a13f.

supervision of women (γυναικονομία, 4.15 1299a22; 1300a4; 6.8 1322b39; 1323a4), or of children (παιδονομία, 4.15 1299a23, 1300a4; 6.8 1322b39; 1300a4). Others are mentioned only in 6.8: priests (ἱερωσύνη θεῶν, 1322b24), command of the fleet (ναυαρχία 6.4 1322b3), supervision of the gymnasia (γυμνασιαρχίαν, 1323a1) and of the city (ἀστυνομία, 1321b23; 1322a14), guarding of the laws (νομοφυλακία, 1322b39; 1323a7f.),[97] treasurer (ταμιεία, 1321b33), exchequer (πρακτορεία—in Aristotle πράξεις 1321b41f.; 1322b35). This is not only an excellent example of the synthesizing strategy of Didymus, but it reveals his intimate knowledge of Aristotle's *Pol.*, even of very technical details of specific institutions.[98]

Why Didymus turns from a topic discussed by Aristotle in *Pol.* 4.14–16 and 6.8 to a remark made in 4.1: "it is no lesser task to resurrect a constitution than to establish it from the beginning" (1289a3f.),[99] is not clear. Aristotle's expression "no lesser task" could be a litotes for "a more important task," and Didymus understands it this way by writing "far more difficult." He is not aware that the political and social order he describes at 152.1ff. is that of a state to be founded, and in fact, in an anticlimax, he moves from the discussion of the more important task of helping a constitution to the treatment of the lesser task, that of founding a state, Nevertheless, this movement to the lesser task is balanced by the fact that the state with whose foundation he now deals with is the best state.

Here Didymus skips again[100] the introductory chapters, the discussion about the best life both for individuals and states (*Pol.* 7.1–3) and about the external conditions of the best constitution (7.4–7) but starts with its social

[97] This office is mentioned as well in *Pol.* 4, but not the chapter on *archai*, but the deliberative bodies (*bouleuomenon*): 4.14 1298b29.

[98] Whether in the remark that summarizes the areas in which these offices function: "some of them deal with the cities, others with wars, others with harbors and activities of trade" (151.91f. Τούτων δ' εἶναι τὰς μὲν κατὰ πόλεις, τὰς δὲ κατὰ πόλεμον, τὰς δὲ περὶ τοὺς λιμένας καὶ τὰς ἐμπορίας). The first area "about cities" (τὰς μὲν κατὰ πόλεις) refers to the *task* that has to be performed, this is "affecting the city, its administration," or refers to the *locale* for which they are responsible (in *Pol.* 6.8 for this part of administration *asty* is used: 1321b18; 1322b33) is by no means clear. I prefer the latter option since everything somehow affects the city and such a description of the tasks of offices would be too vague to have any meaning. The expression περὶ … τὰς ἐμπορίας can be found in Aristotle *Pol.* 4.4 1291a5.

[99] ἔστιν οὐκ ἔλαττον ἔργον τὸ ἐπανορθῶσαι πολιτείαν ἢ κατασκευάζειν ἐξ ἀρχῆς, Didymus: Πολιτικοῦ δ' ἀνδρὸς ἔργον εἶναι καὶ τὸ διορθῶσαι πολιτείαν, ὃ πολὺ χαλεπώτερον φαίνεσθαι τοῦ κτίσαι. Didymus' διορθῶσαι gets rid of the notion of a constitution that has fallen to the ground and needs to be resurrected (ἐπανορθῶσαι), however, his choice is good Aristotelian usage, cf. *Pol.* 6.1 1317a34f.

[100] Cf. above p. 270; 276 on *Pol.* 3, and p. 277 on *Pol.* 4.

structure, the hierarchy of people who fulfill conditions without which the state cannot exist on the one hand and three groups which belong to the citizen body on the other (152.1–10). While this description contains elements of the Aristotelian argument of *Pol.* 7.8–9 it does not reproduce it accurately. First, in Aristotle this structure is not the work of the statesman whom one has to understand as the subject of "to assign to, allocate" (διανεῖμαι) in Didymus[101] but is an explanation of a general structural principle which is valid in entities which are organized according to nature. There is in Didymus a stress on the statesman (πολιτικός) or "fitting to a polis" (πολιτικόν, 152.11; see below, p. 285) which goes beyond Aristotle.

Secondly, whereas Didymus distinguishes the *tasks* to be performed by the inhabitants of the *polis* in terms of being either necessary or good/noble (152.2) Aristotle considers all six groups as necessary and distinguishes between them in terms of whether they are either "parts" (*merē*) or conditions "without which the whole cannot exist."[102] The terminology of Didymus reminds more of a different account of the necessary groups a polis needs as we find it in in *Pol.* 4.4—clearly a doublet of *Pol.* 7.8, and of 3.4 (1277a5–12) for that matter, and a reminder that *Pol.* is not a work "aus einem Guss," completed in one piece, as the unitarian school keeps saying. At 4.4 all groups distinguished are necessary (cf. 1290b26ff.; 1291a7); however, the *accomplishments* of the different groups are described as being either necessary or noble,[103] and it is this latter goal for which the state was formed (1291a17). Didymus' account at 152.1f. comes closer to Aristotle's description of society in *Pol.* 4.4 than that in 7.8. This assessment is supported by the fact that two of the four terms used by Didymus for specific groups are found only in Aristotle *Pol.* 4.4 and not in 7.8.[104] This section in Didymus combines the concepts of these two passages of *Pol.*: the distinction of the *tasks* performed as either necessary or good of 4.4 and the distinction of the *population* into two groups, one that executes the necessary tasks and the other that benefits from the work of the lower group and

---

[101] Aristotle uses at *Pol.* 7.9 1329a16 the passive νενεμῆσθαι without the subject expressed, he qualifies the specific arrangement as just and refers to his concept of the right practiced in distribution.

[102] 7.8 1328a21ff.; 9 1329a34ff.

[103] 1291a17; a 33; a 36; b1. Some, like technical crafts, might serve both purposes, 1291a3f.

[104] Δημιουργούς Didymus 152.2—Aristotle 4.4 1291a35 (otherwise Aristotle uses *banousoi*, 1291a1; 1328b39); ἐμπόρους Didymus 152.3—Aristotle 1291a16 (otherwise *agoraios*,1291a4; 1328b39).—θῆτας Didymus 152.3 is used by Aristotle both at 4.4 1291a6 and 7.8 1328a36.

serves as hoplites or is responsible for judicial or political decisions, of 7.8f. The function of the inferior group is expressed clearly in Didymus: "they are servants".[105] One has to conclude from other remarks, in particular that they are "living parts of property,"[106] that in Aristotle *Pol.* 7.8 they are in the position of slaves. However he does not say that they exist in order to serve the *politikoi* as Didymus does (152.4); the correct term would be *politai*, citizens.[107]

Didymus distinguishes correctly within the higher class those who serve with arms[108] and make decisions.[109] And he explains accurately the elevated position warriors and those who make political and judicial decisions enjoy by the fact that they possess *aretē* (152.5f.). This reproduces Aristotle's argument from *Pol.* 7.9 1328b33ff. Didymus describes them as being *kyriōteron*, that is possessing more authority, which seems to pick up on Aristotle's discussion at 7.9 1329a11ff. Didymus follows Aristotle (7.9) in assigning these two groups to different age brackets to which in both authors the very old are added as a third group who are to be priests (1329a31-34; Didymus 152.7f.). Like Aristotle Didymus finishes the treatment of the social structure of the best state by pointing out its old age, tracing it back to Egypt (*Pol.* 7.10; Didymus 152.9f.).

Aristotle moves then to city planning (*Pol.* 7.11-12). Of the many recommendations he makes regarding the location of the city, the need for fortifications and other issues, Didymus who follows the sequence of Aristotle's argument cites only the one that affects the location of sacred buildings which are to be erected on highly visible places (Aristotle *Pol.* 7.12 1331a28; Didymus 152.11f.). Why Didymus calls this regulation *politikon* is not clear, and there is in Aristotle no statement that corresponds to it.[110] However, Didymus' account aims at covering the "main points of the political topics" (*kephalaia tōn politikōn*, 152.24), and city planning is one of them.[111]

---

[105] 152.4: ὑπηρέτας γὰρ εἶναι τοῖς πολιτικοῖς τούτους.

[106] 7.8 1328a 35: πολλὰ δ' ἔμψυχα μέρη τῆς κτήσεώς ἐστιν; cf. 1.4 1253b28; 1254a17. For the status of the inferior group in *Pol.* 7, cf. as well 1328a22ff.: necessary conditions are not part of the whole; there is no community between the two levels; a28ff.: the lower exist for the purpose of the others; the former produce, the latter receive.

[107] *Pol.* 7.9 1328b40.

[108] 152.5 *to machimon,* the term used by Aristotle *Pol.* 7.8 1328b22; 9 1329b1.

[109] *To bouleutikon,* used by Aristotle *Pol.* 7.9 1329a31; a38.

[110] Unless one assumes that Didymus referred to the establishment of a "free market" as the Thessalians called it which has to be kept free from merchandise and to which non-citizens had no access: 7.12 1331a30ff.

[111] On *politikos* as a favorite topic of Didymus, see above, p. 284.

The stipulation that follows in Didymus (152.13–16) that citizens should possess two properties seems to fit into this context of city planning, however, in Aristotle it is discussed at *Pol.* 7.10 as part of the privileges citizens enjoy, and one of these is ownership of land. Aristotle justifies his recommendation that citizens own land in two areas, both close to the borders and in the city, by the expectation that this arrangement will make citizens concerned about attacks from enemies against any of these areas instead of worrying only about the part of the territory, the one in which they own land and houses (10 1330a14ff.). Didymus' explanation of the rationale for this stipulation, namely that both parts can be easily overseen (εὐσύνοπτα, 108) has no basis in Aristotle. However, in a related context Aristotle described the desirable number of citizens as "easily overseen" (*eusynoptos,* 7.4 1326b23f, cited above, n. 59) and a territory that can be "easily overseen" (*eusynoptos*) as "easy to defend" (7.5 1327a2f.). Didymus might refer to these remarks although the reader who does not have Aristotle's complete text in front of him cannot understand the peculiar meaning of "easily overseen" which Aristotle himself considers as needing an explanation. Next (152.16f.) Didymus repeats from Aristotle (7.10 1330a3ff.[112]) the statement that it is useful to establish common meals. Didymus jumps then to the organization of public education (152.17f.) addressed by Aristotle in *Pol.* 8.1.[113]

The last topic Didymus discusses (152.18–24) covers issues dealt with by Aristotle in *Pol.* 7.16, first the age when a couple should marry in order to have strong and healthy children,[114] then legislation[115] that forbids bringing up a disabled child, exposing a healthy child, and performing an abortion at a certain stage in the development of the fetus (1335b19-26). Here Didymus' summary is at odds with Aristotle who actually *permits* abortion as long as the fetus does not possess "sense perception and life." At this point the account of the "main topics" (*kephalaia*) of the political issues ends.

Assessment of the Excerpt

How accurate is Didymus' excerpt? Lapses can be found as that concerning the best mixed constitution (see above, p. 277), but no scholar is completely immune against this kind of mistake. There are more serious

---

[112] The reference in Wachsmuth 152 ap. crit. on ll. 16. 17. to 1330a34 must be a misprint.
[113] Not *Pol.* 7.17 as Wachsmuth 152 ap. crit. on ll. 17–19 claims.
[114] *Pol.* 7.16 1335a7ff.
[115] See above, p. 261.

misrepresentations like that concerning *phronēsis* as a qualification of generals (see above, p. 275f.). However, that might be a well-intended extension of an otherwise genuine Aristotelian view. And there is the distinction between *logos* and *pathos* as causes of *stasis* for which there is no basis in Aristotle, at least in the general validity which Didymus claimed. Here Didymus substitutes *force* through which inequality is imposed on parts of the citizens for Aristotelian *perception* of inequality (see above, p. 279). I do not believe that we find here a conscious modification of Aristotle's political philosophy, rather the excerptor tried to place what he incorporated into a system, although it was not always that of Aristotle. However, Didymus' claim that the *oikos* is a small *polis* (see above, p. 263) is a serious misunderstanding. Taking words almost verbally over from the source does not prevent Didymus from offering a wrong summary of the original.

Does the summary give a fair impression of the "main topics" (κεφάλαια, 150.1; 152.24) of Aristotle's political theory as Didymus intends to? If one understands "main topics" in the sense of the items listed in a table of content of a modern book then Didymus is quite successful, because he mentions so many specifics of the Aristotelian theory, and from this perspective he compares favorably with some modern "introductions" to Aristotle's *Pol.*[116] which reduce Aristotle's political theory to one or a few central concepts, like *eudaimonia*, justice, nature, common good, to which everything else is subordinated,[117] if the many other things Aristotle deals with are mentioned at all. It is refreshing how Didymus is interested in giving an impression of the variety of issues dealt with by Aristotle.

A related virtue of Didymus' approach is his aspiration to give a comprehensive account of the individual issues he addresses. He does what almost everybody does who teaches about a philosophical text: instead of following it as it is written one refers often to other sections of the work, or other works of the same author, in order to present and explain the topic in question in its larger context, and Didymus proceeds this way. There seems to be a specific principle behind Didymus' jumping around between passages from different books: He seems to follow the line of argument of his source but "improves" on it by filling in well suited explanations from other contexts. His interest is in the main points (κεφάλαια, 150.1; 152.24) of the

---

[116] E.g., compared with Aristotle, *The Politics and the Constitution of Athens*, edited by Stephen Everson, Cambridge Texts in the History of Political Thought (Cambridge 1996), ix–xxxvii.

[117] Cf. E. Schütrumpf 2015, see above n. 95.

system of Aristotle's *Pol.*,[118] not a summary of the arguments of the work as we have it. Therefore it is not left to the reader of the excerpt to recognize, or fail to recognize, related concepts of the original. Rather, Didymus presents them as they belong together, and thus his summary conveys at times a more unified account than the original.[119]

From the very beginning of the summary it is obvious that Didymus was not a superficial excerptor; he does not simply reproduce individual statements; he also knew Aristotle's *Pol.* and Ethics well enough to complement remarks he found in one context by others from a different context (cf. p.264f.). He does not simply follow the text he condenses and select specific issues for inclusion in his summary as he comes across them but already in his excerpt of the earlier books of *Pol.* he reveals knowledge of the content of the later books of *Pol.*, or of *EN*, which he cites for specific issues (see above, p. 260f.; 272). This shows that he aspires to completeness in a systematic manner that goes far beyond what one expects from an excerpt. It might have been the recognition that the format of an excerpt which follows the original would prevent him from presenting all aspects of a subject as a reader should learn them which made Didymus rearrange the material. This strategy gives his text a coherence which a simple excerpt could not provide.

Is Didymus' comprehensiveness comprehensive enough? We answered this question in the affirmative for the variety of the topics included. From a philosophical point of view the answer will be negative. While Didymus is quite comprehensive in his listing of Aristotle's ideas, he could be accused of doing nothing more than that, of listing subject after subject and reducing Aristotle's thoughtful considerations of the many issues needing to be clarified to a long list of brief results. More serious is the fact that Didymus omits an account of the introductory chapters of almost every book of Aristotle's *Pol.*, and in proceeding this way he reveals no interest in the larger or systematic context in which the specifics are placed by Aristotle and should be understood. There is in Didymus nothing of *Pol.* 1.1 which deals with the rank of the *polis* and the method Aristotle wants to pursue. From the introductory chapters 1–5 of *Pol.* 3 which precede the taxonomy of constitutions Didymus mentions only (150.4f.) the definition of the citizen from 3.1 (see above, p. 270; 276). Of the introduction in 4.1 to an expanded treatment of constitutions he mentions again only one sentence

---

[118] The first remarks are given in direct speech, from 148.15 onward the account is marked by indirect speech as a report of Aristotle's views.

[119] See above, p. 271 on the number of citizens.

(151.23f.) (see above, p. 277). The three introductory chapters to the best state 7.1–3 are ignored completely (see above, p. 283). Didymus shows a lack of interest in the philosophical concepts which serve as the theoretical base on which the framework of constitutions is based. The same is true of his remarks on the success or failure of politics, his criticism of other theories and much more. Didymus deals with, and picks out, a few "facts" as if they were not part of a more complex philosophical conception of Aristotle.

Central arguments are overlooked: being in accordance with nature is the one central concept that links the topics of *Pol.* 1.2: the household and its parts and functions, procreation and the relationship between master and slave, the expansion of the household to village and polis are all traced back to the principle of nature. Nevertheless, nature is mentioned by Didymus only as the qualifier of man as a creature that belongs to the city (148.3f.) and as qualifier of one sort of slave (149.1). It is an indication of Didymus' indifference towards the logic of the Aristotelian argument that Didymus cites this remark about man as *physei zōion politikon* in which Aristotle's account of the development of associations culminates (1253a2ff.) *before* he gives that account. In Didymus the statement about man as *physei zōion politikon* is not the result and corollary of the previous build-up of arguments, but is a completely isolated statement, and this was not necessary since Didymus actually provides all the other steps of the argument that lead to this result. However, Didymus does not deal with these two issues, the formation of the city and man as *physei zōion politikon,* in the same context. This separation of issues that belong intrinsically together is one negative side of Didymus' strategy of freely rearranging the material: he isolates statements, separates what belongs together so that the original concepts, taken out of their context, cannot be understood. One could expand on this flaw in Didymus' account: in its highly abbreviated form it could easily be misunderstood—if it is not misleading. We are given a reasonably good idea of the existence of isolated topics but not of the whole.

At the end of this essay, I will use this observation for a different purpose, the question of Didymus' sources. O. Regenbogen wanted to see in Didymus' excerpt a "summary of Peripatetic politics" or "the doctrine of the Theophrastean Peripatos."[120] The only specific argument Regenbogen pro-

---

[120] Regenbogen, *RE* Suppl. VII, 1517.22f.: "in dem Abriß der peripatetischen Politik bei Stob. 148f. Wa."; 1518.62–1519.11 „Lehre des theophrastischen Peripatos." With regard to the political part of Didymus' summary, Regenbogen holds a view that comes close to that von Arnim (1926) had proposed for the ethical part of the summary, a thesis Regenbogen

vides[121] for his thesis that Didymus used a later source is a single term, the use of ochlocracy (150.22f.) for the mistaken form of the rule of the many. This constitution is in Aristotle's taxonomy democracy (*Pol.* 3.7 1279b6) whereas in Didymus democracy is a correct constitution (see above, p. 276). In Greek literature the term ochlocracy is not found earlier than in Polybius.[122] According to Regenbogen, "Theophrastus apparently felt that Aristotle's terminology contradicted the customary usage and therefore included democracy among the correct constitutions and coined for the mistaken form a new word *ochlokratia* which recurs only in Polybius."[123] These conjectures are completely speculative, and the occurrence of ochlocracy in Polybius, who otherwise shows no familiarity with Aristotle's *Pol.*, can be explained in different ways and must not be construed as if Polybius actually used a revised text of Aristotle's *Pol.* as it circulated in the Theophrastean Peripatos.

I do not see enough evidence for postulating the intermediate step Theophrastus or a "summary of Peripatetic politics" between Aristotle and Didymus. If this were the case "the doctrine of the Theophrastean Peripatos" would consist in rearranging isolated Aristotelian arguments in the way described here. Why would Theophrastus have rearranged the material? I explained the rearrangement from the specific conditions of an excerpt that attempts, within the constraints of utmost brevity, at giving a fair impression of the content of the work and, therefore, added from different contexts information that was useful for the subject selected for the summary. Outside of an excerpt I do not understand the need for rearrangement in the way we find it in Didymus. In political theory "the doctrine of the Theophrastean Peripatos" is almost certainly a fiction. It would consist of re-editing the text of Aristotle in order to provide the authoritative doctrine of the school. However, would the elimination of the philosophical content of Aristotle's *Pol.*, as we observed it for the excerpt, have started in the Peripatos as one should assume if Didymus simply reproduced an early revision of Aristotle's *Pol.*? That seems most unlikely.

---

rejects: ibid. 1492.58ff. However, von Arnim 1926, 119, cf, 3, followed Diels and others in acknowledging the closest fidelity of Didymus 147. 26–152.25 to the Aristotelian *Pol.*

[121] Following H. Henkel, *Studien zur Geschichte der Griechischen Lehre vom Staat* (Leipzig 1872), 21.

[122] 6.4.7; 4.7; 57.9.

[123] "T. hat augenscheinlich die Ar.-Terminologie als dem üblichen Sprachgebrauch entgegengesetzt empfunden und darum die δημοκρατία den ὀρθαὶ πολιτεῖαι zugeordnet, für die Entartung ein neues Wort ὀχλοκρατία geprägt, das erst bei Polybios wiederkehrt" (1518.69–1519.5).

Works Cited

Arnim, H. von. 1926. *Arius Didymus' Abriss der peripatetischen Ethik*. SB Wien 204, 3. Wien: Hölder-Pichler-Tempsky.

Fortenbaugh, William W. (ed.). 1983. *On Stoic and Peripatetic Ethics: The Work of Didymus Didymus*. Rutgers University Studies in Classical Humanities 1. New Brunswick, N.J.: Transaction.

Regenbogen, O. 1940. "Theophrastos." In *Paulys Realencyclopädie der classischen Altertumswissenschaft*, suppl. VII. Stuttgart: Alfred Druckenmüller, , 1492–94.

Reydams-Schils, G. (ed.). 2011. *Thinking through Excerpts: Studies on Stobaeus*. Turnhout : Brepols Publishers.

Schütrumpf, E. 1980. *Die Analyse der Polis durch Aristoteles*. Amsterdam: B. R. Grüner.

Schütrumpf, E. 1981. "Kritische Überlegungen zur Ontologie und Terminologie der Aristotelischen 'Politik.'" In Schütrumpf (2009) 36–54.

———. 1989. "Platonic Methodology in the Program of Aristotle's Political Philosophy: *Politics* IV.1." In Schütrumpf (2009) 55–64.

———. 1991. "Aristoteles Politik, Buch I, übersetzt und erläutert." In *Aristoteles Werke in Deutscher Übersetzung*, vol. 9, part I. Berlin: Akademie Verlag.

———. 1996. "Aristoteles Politik, Buch IV–VI, übersetzt und erläutert." In *Aristoteles Werke in Deutscher Übersetzung*, vol. 9, part III. Berlin: Akademie Verlag.

———. 2003. "Slaves in Plato's Political Dialogues and the Significance of Plato's Psychology for the Aristotelian Theory of Slavery." In Schütrumpf (2009) 65–79.

———. 2009. *Praxis und Lexis: Ausgewählte Schriften zur Philosophie von Handeln und Reden in der klassischen Antike*. Palingenesia 95. Stuttgart: Franz Steiner.

Wachsmuth, C. 1884. *Ioannis Stobaei Anthologii libri duo priores qui inscribi solent eclogae physicae et ethicae*. Volumen alterum, editio altera. Berlin: Weidmann.

9

Von Arnim, Didymus, and Augustus
Three Related Notes on Doxography C

Peter L. P. Simpson

1
In Defense of von Arnim on the Theophrastean Origin of the First Sections of the *Doxography*

Let me begin with a longish quotation from the relevant parts of von Arnim's discussion of Arius Didymus' *Doxography* or *Epitome* (translations from the German are my own):[1]

> (Pages 4–6) Before I examine the individual evidence for the prevailing view, which leads to seeing in Arius only a witness for the eclecticism of Antiochus, not at all for the doctrine of the Peripatetics, or at most (if we follow the more moderate view of Diels and Meurer) for the doctrine of the latest Peripatics, wholly sickened in addition by Stoicizing ecclecticism, I would like to stress that the procedure of Arius, as it is presented in accordance with the prevailing view, is a striking and barely comprehensible one. He who devoted a special book in a

---

[1] Von Arnim (1926). In writing "Arius Didymus" I follow the scholarly view that the Didymus in question is the Arius Didymus who was court philosopher to the emperor Augustus. Von Arnim adopts this view.

doxographical work to Platonic, Aristotelian, and Stoic philosophy, obviously does not proceed from the point of view, represented by Antiochus, that these three systems of philosophy agree in the fact of the matter (apart from secondary points) and differ only in manner of expression. Had Arius endorsed the tendency of Antiochus, which emphasizes the commonality of the three systems sprung from the Socratic, he would hardly have chosen this form, which was bound to lead to the presentation three times in three separate books of essentially the same philosophy. This form was better suited to developing the inner coherence of each system and the distinctness of its doctrines. Arius Didymus confessed himself an adherent of the Stoic sect, as the index of Stoics in *cod. Laur.* 69, 35 of Diogenes Laertius shows. If, as an eclectic Stoic, he did hold close to the standpoint of Antiochus, this should have shown itself above all in his outline of Stoic ethics. That this is not the case, that rather only the theory of the old Stoics and not of Panaetius and Posidonius is taken by him into account, is well known. Is it really credible that he would have placed the old Stoic doctrine side by side with the later Academic doctrine of Antiochus and with the later Peripatetic doctrine of Stoicizing Peripatetics? The only section we still have of his book *On the Opinions of Plato* (*Dox. Gr.* p. 447) does not give this impression; the opening words, "How he dealt with the Ideas", show already that the author is claiming to give Plato's own teaching. Antiochus as an Academic, precisely because he maintained the identity of the Peripatetic teaching with the Academic, could not be held by Arius to be a classical witness for the Peripatetic doctrine, which he (Arius) wanted to present in a special book of his *Epitome* as different from the Academic. Hardly could such a fraud by his court philosopher have been kept hidden from the Emperor Augustus. In a Peripatetic school that had been returned by Andronicus to the study of its chief leader [Aristotle] there must have been many men in Augustus' time who knew what was set down in Aristotle's and Theophrastus' own writings. Arius would hardly have dared then to construct his portrayal of Peripatetic philosophy from a non-Peripatetic source.

This argument of von Arnim's constitutes a very strong case for the claim that the alleged Stoicism in the first few pages of the *Epitome* (4–11, 118–24) is apparent only and in fact reflects the teaching of Theophrastus, which teaching may well have been elaborated in opposition to early Stoic teachings and with adoption of Stoic terms, but which would nevertheless count as genuinely Peripatetic and not at all as Stoic. The opinion of Annas,[2] that this development is due, not to Theophrastus but to much later Peripatetics, depends on rejecting von Arnim's argument in favor of the view, argued and defended at length by Pohlenz,[3] that the ancient evidence makes the Stoics and not Theophrastus the origin of the *oikeiôsis* theory. The problem here is twofold: first, to show that Pohlenz's claim that the *oikeiôsis* theory is distinctively Stoic is not compatible with Theophrastus

[2] Annas (1990) 80–96.
[3] Pohlenz (1940).

being the Peripatetic who elaborated a Peripatetic *oikeiôsis* theory in answer in part to the Stoics; second, to identify who these later Peripatetics were. The first point would seem impossible to show, since either account (that Theophrastus did or that he did not develop the Peripatetic *oikeiôsis* theory) seems compatible with Pohlenz' evidence.[4] The second point is harder, for, as von Arnim argues, there are no such later Peripatetics who can plausibly be identified.

> (Pages 6–7) *De Finibus* V contains no complete presentation of the entire Peripatetic ethics, but only the chapter about affinity (*oikeiôsis*) and the highest end in life; and Cicero found in his source (i.e., in Antiochus himself) the claim that Aristotle and Polemo agreed in this teaching (*De Finibus* V 14). He found there also Antiochus' overview of the history of the Peripatetic school, which must have made clear why Antiochus saw only Aristotle and Theophrastus as authoritative in matters of Peripatetic teaching, and took only them for the basis of his own presentation, repeated by Cicero, of the Peripatetic teaching on the highest good. For the exposition in §§13, 14 can have no other purpose in this context, since in it all the scholarchs of the Peripatos after Theophrastus are numbered off in turn and each one blamed individually and set to one side. The authoritative guardians of the school doctrine are, for Antiochus, only the ancients, the "leaders of the sect", and only Aristotle and Theophrastus count as such for the Peripatos in his eyes: "Let us then be content with these. For those after them are better indeed than the philosophers of other schools, but they are so untrue to type that they seem to have given birth to themselves."
>
> … what we get to know from Cicero is only a presentation, constructed from Aristotle and Theophrastus, of the doctrine of the highest good, from which Antiochus gets the proof that it agrees with that of Polemo. It is clear, therefore, that the assumption that Arius constructed his outline from a doxographical presentation of Antiochus as we get to know it in the 5th book of *De Finibus* cannot achieve what it is supposed to achieve for the representatives of the prevailing view, namely to explain why the outline of Arius has absorbed into itself, not only drops, but whole streams of Stoic doctrine… Antiochus, however, as is clear from *De Finibus* V 12-14, had confined himself in his doxographical presentation, which so closely follows Arius' outline, to Aristotle and Theophrastus …

This argument of von Arnim's has not, I think, been given the weight it is due. Perhaps it can be answered, but if so only by probabilities and

---

[4] Pohlenz tried mainly to show that the teaching about *oikeiôsis* in Arius' *Epitome* of Peripatetic ethics makes best sense if it is seen as derivative from Stoic teaching (1940) 13, 26–43. His arguments are powerful but not simply compelling (what Arius says could be derivative from both the Stoics and Theophrastus if Theophrastus was deliberately using Stoic terms in his defense of Peripatetic ethics against Stoic polemic). Pohlenz, however, does not directly confront the counter-arguments of von Arnim quoted here.

conjectures on the other side. No definite refutation of it, not even by Pohlenz, seems forthcoming. So Von Arnim's thesis must be allowed still to stand that Theophrastus could have been the Peripatetic who showed how the *oikeiôsis* theory was fully compatible with, indeed in a sense resulted from, Peripatetic premises. I take it then that von Arnim's case has not been shown to be plainly false nor Annas' plainly true. Either can indeed be allowed to stand, so the case for Theophrastus cannot be ruled out as Annas and other scholars she refers to are inclined to think. In fact Görgemanns, in a nice summary of the scholarly debate,[5] seems to side with Giusta,[6] and is inclined to think that a lot of Arius' material, if not all, does go back to Theophrastus, or even that Theophrastus developed the *oikeiôsis* theme in part in response to and in concert with parallel developments in Stoicism. But I make this point primarily for dialectical purposes. If truth be told, we are probably not in a position to reach a definite decision on the question. Just let us not rule out von Arnim.

2
How Arius Didymus Organized His Peripatetic Materials

David Hahm[7] points out the somewhat disorganized state of the *Epitome* (for both the Stoics and the Peripatetics). A not dissimilar claim has been made specifically for the section on Aristotle's *Politics* by Nagle,[8] although Nagle is inclined to think that Arius tried to produce, and to some extent succeeded in producing, a harmonious whole made up of not altogether harmonious materials. My main reason here for broaching this subject concerns a thesis about the order of books of the *Politics* which, in company in particular with Newman (though not in fact original to him),[9] I have myself also defended, namely that the manuscripts books 7 and 8 should come between books 3 and 4. This view is probably the minority view and one argument against it sometimes given is that Arius seems to have read the *Politics* with books 7 and 8 at the end as the manuscripts have them. My contention will be that, because of the way Arius constructed his *Epitome*, we cannot reliably use it as a guide to the order in which he read the books of the *Politics*. Hence Newman's thesis can emerge unscathed at least from this line of attack.

---

[5] Görgemanns (1983) 166–68.
[6] Giusta (1964–67).
[7] Hahm (1983) 15–37.
[8] Nagle (2002) 198–223.
[9] Simpson (1997) xvii–xx.

My comments will begin with the way Arius has arranged the material on ethics, since we can see better from this arrangement how he generally proceeded. The *Politics* material can then be seen to follow a similar pattern.

Hahm[10] has done some good examination of the ethics material and has plausibly concluded that the division of it, despite a seeming lack of order, does in fact follow an order, that of comparative evaluation of all the constituents of the moral universe, following in this the order of division given earlier in the Stoic *Epitome*. Hahm suggests that the ordering was original to Arius. The thesis is, as I say, certainly plausible and gives some unity to what otherwise seems rather disparate. But whether the order is that suggested by Hahm, or there is no order as others suggest, the order, or lack thereof, is not that of any of the Aristotelian *Ethics* as they have come down to us. A quick summary of the contents will reveal the fact:

1. 1 Ts, 116.19–118.4 Wachs
   Characterization of ethics as derived from custom, about the rational and irrational parts of the soul, of which only the latter is here said to be receptive of virtue, though later it is said briefly that virtues come about in both the rational and irrational part [as is also said briefly in *MM*]
2. 1, 118.5–10
   Sources of virtue: nature, custom, reason [from *EN* book 10]; man midway between god and beasts
3. 1–6, 118.11–124.18
   Extensive discussion of *oikeiôsis* material and the preferable, with discussion of friendship and virtuous friendship [natural sequence as to subject matter, not as to form of treatment in *EN* and *EE*].
4. 6–9, 124.18–128.11
   That the three kinds of goods, those of the body, those of the soul, those external, have an analogy to each other, even though they differ, and the goods of the soul are to be preferred. Political, communal, contemplative deeds. Definition of happiness. The bad go wrong
5. 10, 128.11–128.27
   About virtue in general and the contrast with continence
6. 11, 128.27–129.19
   About things to prefer and things to avoid

---

[10] Hahm (1983) 20–26; see also Nagle (2002).

7. 12, 129.19–130.15
   The sources of happiness—beauty, activity
8. 13–14, 130.15–134.8
   How many parts of good there are, and about the target. Definition of happiness, again, and explained as to its parts; the saying of Solon as to completeness; middling life that is neither happy nor unhappy; vice self-sufficient for misery, and good luck harms the vicious
9. 15, 134.8–137.14
   In how many ways the good is said [mainly from *MM*]
10. 16–19, 137.14–142.15
    About moral virtue, that it is a mean (with division of rational and irrational parts of soul that does not give rise to express distinction into moral and intellectual virtues but the moral virtues are called moral and to these the mean applies), that it concerns pleasure and pain, division of powers and passions and habits; division of virtues according to Theophrastus and *EE*; prudence in relation to virtue
11. 20–21, 142.15–143.2
    About passions of soul [not found in Aristotle, but in Theophrastus?]
12. 21, 143.2–143.18
    About friendship [four differences; not according to Aristotle, but Theophrastus?]
13. 22, 143.18–143.24
    About favor
14. 23, 143.24–145.11
    Ways of life; theoretical life prior
15. 24, 145.11–147.25
    Run through of the virtues à la *MM* and some *VV* and some from elsewhere [Theophrastus?]; gentlemanliness

One thing worth noting about this material is that it borrows heavily from *MM*, more so in fact than from *EE* or *EN*, and that it includes some material and divisions that are not paralleled in extant Aristotelian sources. The facts have long been noted. Nevertheless, although Arius borrows heavily from *MM*, he does not adopt the ordering of topics that we find in *MM* (or that we find in *EE* and *EN*) but an ordering of his own. When we turn to the material on the *Politics* we find the same feature, namely that, despite appearances, it does not really follow the ordering of materials in that work but an ordering of Arius' own. Here then is a summary of the *Politics* material.

1. 26 Ts, 147.26–149.24, Wachs

   An extensive section on the household, taken entirely from book 1 of the *Politics*. But notice that there is nothing from the final two chapters about differences in virtue and about educating women and slaves in virtue.

2. There is nothing from book 2 on regimes considered by others to be best.

3. 27, 150.1–6

   A section from book 1 combined with sections from book 3 about the origin of the polis, and about the definition of citizenship and of city.

4. 27, 150.6–10

   A section from book 7 about the proper size of the city.

5. 27, 150.10–16

   A section from *EE* and *EN* about prudence and its divisions into economic, legislative, political, etc.

6. 27, 150.17–23

   A section from book 3 about the kinds of regimes and the difference between correct and deviant ones [save that democracy is the word Arius uses for what Aristotle calls polity and ochlocracy the word he uses for what Aristotle calls democracy. Note, too, that there is nothing about the division in detail, about ostracism, or about kingship and education from the last chapters of book 3.]

7. 27, 150.23–151.1

   A section from book 4 about a best regime that is mixed from the correct ones. [But the characterization is misleading, since Aristotle's mixed regime is not from the correct regimes but from deviant ones, namely from oligarchy and democracy, and is itself one of the correct regimes, namely polity. Arius' characterization reflects rather what Aristotle says some say about the Spartan regime in book 2, 6.1265b33–40 and what Polybius later says about the mixed regime. And what Theophrastus said?]

8. 27, 151.2–3

   A section from book 5 about regimes changing to the better or the worse.

9. 27, 151.3–5
A section from book 3 and also from book 7 [esp. ch. 13] that the regime thoroughly adorned with virtue is best, the one with vice worst.
10. 27, 151.5–8
A section from book 4, or its final chapters (chs.14–16), about differences between appointment of offices in democracies, oligarchies, and aristocracies. But there is nothing about the several subkinds of democracy or of oligarchy or of the reasons for these subkinds.
11. 27, 151.9–15
A section from book 5 about the origins of faction [but only from the opening chapters; none of the particular details is included and nothing is said about tyranny.]
12. 27, 151.16–22
A section from book 6 (ch. 8) about the several kinds of offices there can be in regimes according to the kinds of regimes [but nothing from the earlier chapters of this book about how to set up democracies and oligarchies]
13. 27, 151.23–24
A section from the beginning of book 4 (1.1289a3–4) about it being a politician's job to correct regimes as well as to found them …
14. 27, 152.1–25
… followed immediately by extensive passages from book 7 about the characteristics of the best regime, as regards people and place and procreation [as if these points are applicable to any regime and not to the best regime only]. But there is nothing from the first chapters of this book about happiness and virtue and that the happy life is the virtuous life for both individual and city [unless we can suppose this point to be implied earlier in the discussion of ethics]
15. There is nothing at all from book 8 [unless remarks in the previous section about the common education can be taken as a brief reference;[11] for these remarks contain, in particular, nothing about music, which however makes up the bulk of the book].

---

[11] A plausible suggestion by Schütrumpf in his essay for this volume.

So we see that Arius starts with book 1, omits book 2, then combines books 1 and 7, then gives a passage from book 7, then a passage from the *Ethics*, then passages from books 3 and 4 and 5 in that order, then a passage combining books 3 and 7, then passages from books 4 and 5 and 6 in that order, then a passage from book 4, then passages from book 7, with book 8 being entirely (or almost entirely) omitted. In other words, whatever order Arius is following in arranging his material, it is not the order of the *Politics* itself.

Brendan Nagle[12] has given an extensive analysis of this part of the *Epitome* that further supports the same claim. He has noted a certain lack of thematic unity, or rather the presence of a certain thematic tension, in Arius' presentation. For if so, and if, as Nagle concedes, the *Politics* does have a thematic unity that Arius seems to lack, then whatever order Arius was following it was not, or not meant to be, the order of the material found in the *Politics* itself.

So on the basis of this evidence we may conclude that nothing definite can be deduced about the order in which Arius read the books of the *Politics*. Perhaps he read them in the MSS ordering as we now have it; perhaps he did not. We cannot say. Therefore, whatever Arius' *Epitome* shows, it does not provide evidence against Newman's thesis that the books of the *Politics* should be reordered to put books 7 and 8 between 3 and 4. A minor point, perhaps, but worth stressing nevertheless.

3
What Arius Didymus Included and What He Omitted in His *Epitome* and Why

More interesting than the previous question about the ordering of the *Politics* material by Arius is the question about the material itself. For Arius omits more than he includes and some of the material he includes is not entirely accurate to Aristotle's text. To begin with, then, something that has not been much noted about the ethical theory as presented by Arius is that it reflects, not just the content, but the orientation too of *MM* and not at all that of *EE* or *EN*. For in particular it downplays, as *MM* does but *EE* and *EN* do not, the so-called intellectual virtues. These virtues or some of them do appear in Arius and also in *MM*, but neither Arius nor *MM* refer to them as intellectual virtues (though Arius does say that there are two forms of virtue, rational and irrational; 1 Ts., 117.18–118.2 Wachs.). Why

[12] Nagle (2002).

the difference? There is a view adopted by a number of scholars[13] that *MM* is an exoteric or popular presentation by Aristotle of his ethical teaching. Popular opinion in Aristotle's day, even respectable popular opinion, seems to have had some suspicion of properly intellectual skills and abilities, associating them with sophistry and the worse kinds of rhetoric. To avoid raising such suspicions about his own ethical teaching Aristotle seems to have deliberately downplayed the intellectual virtues in *MM* while nevertheless obliquely hinting at them.[14] Arius has done the same though he clearly knows of *EE* and *EN* and uses material from them in his *Epitome*. In other words, in presenting a summary of Peripatetic ethics that, precisely as a summary, would seem addressed to a wide and popular audience, he has judged that he should adopt the exoteric or popular orientation of *MM* and not the esoteric or school presentation of *EE* and *EN*. Those who know Aristotle's works could not miss the fact that Arius has followed *MM*'s procedure and not that of *EE* and *EN*. They would be alerted, then, even if others are not, to the possibility that Arius is being as coy as Aristotle was in *MM* about what he really thinks or is really doing.

Lest this claim seem extreme or unmotivated, consider the peculiarities of the *Epitome* of the *Politics* and in particular the things that are omitted and the things that are misrepresented. First, there is a brief mention but no full discussion of distributive justice as the basis for the division of regimes into correct and deviant. There is a brief statement that regimes are correct that aim at the common advantage and those base that aim at private advantage. There is also a statement a few lines later that the regime adorned with virtue is best and the one with vice worst. Aristotle's position is thus correctly but insufficiently described. For, according to Aristotle, only regimes ruled by the virtuous (either by the perfectly virtuous in kingship and aristocracy, or by those with military virtue in polity) aim at the common advantage (for virtue is the common advantage, and only the virtuous pursue virtue properly).

Second there is what is said about the mixed regime, namely that it is mixed from the correct regimes. These Arius has just listed as kingship, aristocracy, and democracy. But what Arius calls democracy Aristotle calls polity, and what Arius calls ochlocracy Aristotle calls democracy. Further, the mixed regime for Aristotle is already one of the correct regimes, for polity is this mixed regime. But polity is not mixed from the correct regimes. On the contrary it is mixed from democracy and oligarchy, and these are

---

[13] For the details see Simpson (2014) introduction, ix–xxviii.
[14] For the details again see Simpson (2014) ix, xii, xxiii–xxiv, 133–35, 154–55, 163–65.

precisely not correct regimes. Admittedly Aristotle allows for varieties of polity, since he allows for oligarchically and democratically leaning polities, the former of which are among those labeled so-called aristocracies while the latter were indeed by the ancients called democracies (*Politics* 4.7, 13.1297b24–25). A so-called aristocracy is a mixed regime, and it counts for Aristotle as a correct regime, but it does not count as an instance of the correct regime Aristotle calls aristocracy. It counts as an instance of so-called aristocracy, which is a combination of virtue, or quasi-virtue, and oligarchy and democracy. It is more like polity than like aristocracy (4.7).

In short, taking all these points together, we can see that Arius is speaking and using terms in a way that is not at all Aristotle's and moreover in a way that makes Aristotle's theory of the mixed regime impossible to state – quite apart anyway from the fact that polity is for Aristotle more properly a middle regime, as founded on the middle, than a mixed regime, *Politics* 4.11.

Notice too that kingship or monarchy is not part of Aristotle's mixed regime although Arius writes as if it is. Aristotle allows indeed that kingship can exist in several regimes (including democracy) but as an office, or a perpetual generalship, and not as constitutive of the regime (*Politics* 3.16.1287a3–8). Monarchy as a regime exists only in kingship proper and in tyranny, which are the best and the worst regimes respectively. In no sense does kingship form part of the mixture that makes the mixed regime for Aristotle. Why then does Arius write in such a way as to confuse these points, or at least to make it very difficult if not impossible to state them?

Third there is what Arius does at 27 Ts., 151.23-24 Wachs. He begins, as noted there, with a section from *Politics* book 4 (1.1289a3–4), about it being a politician's job to correct regimes as well as to found them, and then he follows this section immediately with extensive passages from book 7 about the characteristics of the best regime, as if these characteristics are appropriate to any regime (or to the reform of any regime) and not to the best regime only. The association is not in Aristotle, for the passage about correcting regimes is in the context of his discussion about regimes less than the best (4.1) and not of his discussion about the best regime (7 & 8). Perhaps Aristotle would not deny that one could establish a best regime by reform of some existing regime, but he does not present the material in that way. Why does Arius present it differently?

If we bring all these puzzles together, the following may be suggested. Aristotle's discussion of distributive justice or of the true ground for claims to rule (which Arius admits at least by the by) is revolutionary in character. For it implies that rule is only just when the virtuous rule and is unjust otherwise. Admittedly Aristotle softens the revolutionary implications by allowing that circumstances may be such that rule by the virtuous is hard or impossible so that one must accept a deviant regime instead. But a deviant regime, however unavoidable, is still deviant. Open discussion of distributive justice can be dangerous. Aristotle himself avoids talking of distributive justice in *MM*, which is not surprising if that text is an exoteric or popular one. He only talks of distributive justice in *EE*, *EN*, and then the *Politics*. Arius, who follows the caution of *MM* in his presentation of Peripatetic ethics, does the same in his presentation of Peripatetic politics. Of whom or what was he being cautious? The obvious answer, if the Didymus of the *Epitome* is Arius Didymus the court philosopher of Augustus, is that he was being cautious precisely of Augustus and of the Augustan settlement at Rome. Augustus wanted to restore moral virtue to Rome, but in doing so he implicitly admitted that Rome was not now virtuous. But if Rome is not now virtuous are the rulers, or all of them, virtuous? Is the Senate, who in theory share rule with the emperor, virtuous? Are the people, who also in theory share rule with the emperor, virtuous? If not, should they really share in rule? Should the emperor (if one supposes him virtuous – and Arius could hardly deny he was) rule alone? But for the emperor to rule alone, and to do so openly, would be to undermine the Augustan settlement, which was precisely to preserve Republican forms and at least some semblance of Republican rule under his own leadership.

This suggestion may be supported by what Arius says of the mixed regime. As already indicated Arius does not present Aristotle's theory of the mixed regime. Instead he presents – if only in the briefest of remarks – the theory that the mixed regime is a combination of kingship, aristocracy, and democracy. This theory recalls Polybius rather than Aristotle. Moreover it too neatly fits the Augustan settlement at Rome, which can surely be seen, and which Augustus himself surely saw, as a combination of kingship in the emperor, aristocracy in the senate, and democracy in the people and the army (always fiercely loyal to the emperor). Moreover the emperor was not just military commander in chief but also a member of the senate and, as holder of Tribunician power, the chief representative of the people. Augustus' kind of kingship is thus indeed a sort of regime and not just an office or a perpetual generalship within a regime.

But why would Arius want to present Polybius in place of Aristotle as guide about the mixed regime? An obvious answer is that Arius can thus imply that Aristotle favored the Roman system of government as a mixture of the correct regimes. Of course Polybius was speaking of Republican Rome not Imperial Rome. But Imperial Rome for Augustus, as already remarked, was meant to be, at least in outward form, a continuation of

Republican Rome (for all the old offices continued). The only difference was that one man, Augustus, possessed, and possessed for life, the power of the most important of these offices. Augustus was king in fact but not in name (he carefully changed the name to imperator, or military commander, but history has changed the meaning with the name, for emperor, derived from imperator, means precisely a supreme king).

Aristotle's political thought is thus subtly deprived of its revolutionary elements. For in accord with his exoteric practice Arius avoids saying very much about the principle of merit that should govern distributive justice (and that, in its open form, is an implicit critique, and so an implicit call to the reform or overthrow, of regimes that do not follow that principle). Also, by his subtle and devious presentation of the mixed regime, he presents Aristotle as favoring the Augustan settlement in Rome. Thus Arius downplays the disturbing character of Aristotle's discussion of politics by not revealing too openly, or at all, things that might negatively impact a popular and not a school audience. And since part of this audience was Augustus himself, whose court philosopher Arius was, we have Arius suitably nuancing his presentation to avoid giving Augustus any anxiety about allowing Aristotelian thought, including political thought, a free presence in the empire. Perhaps Arius had that aim as one of his intentions: reveal what is safe, hide what might appear not to be, but not in such a way that readers of the original texts (would these include Augustus?) cannot see the difference and cannot note the prudence of maintaining Arius' qualifications and caution. The mixed regime of Aristotle, which Arius transmutes in subtle ways, into the mixed regime of Polybius, but without naming Polybius, becomes the Augustan settlement of the mixed regime of kingship, aristocracy, and democracy. Accordingly, anything about Aristotle's thought in the *Politics* that might be a threat to the Augustan settlement of the empire is carefully excluded or nuanced away.[15]

So note further that Augustus' settlement at Rome was not the founding of a political system from scratch but the reforming or remaking of one that already existed. In implicit recognition of this fact Arius writes: "It is also a political man's job to correct a regime, which appears much harder than founding one …" (27 Ts., 151.23 Wachs.). But Aristotle himself does not say that it is "much harder" to correct a regime than to found one; he says that it is "no less a job" to correct one than to found one (4.1.1289a3–4).

---

[15] We know that Augustus revised the Sibylline books, removing and burning parts of them, Suetonius, *Life of Augustus* 31.1, quite possibly because he thought these parts subversive.

A slight enough change in words, perhaps, but a great one in effect on the hearer if the hearer was Augustus. The materials that Arius then immediately adds after this remark (27 Ts., 152.1–25 Wachs), and that he takes, not from the context of the remark in Aristotle but from the context of Aristotle's discussion of the simply best regime, commend things that Augustus either did or wanted: the careful management of the population of the empire, the reform of morals or the concern with virtue and the beautiful, the importance of following ancient precedent, the role of religion, the protection of the borders of the empire, the education of the young.

It is not hard, then, to read Arius' misrepresentation of Aristotle's doctrine of the mixed regime and of reform and the best regime, as well as his putting together of material that Aristotle keeps apart, as deliberate rhetorical moves designed, first no doubt to flatter Augustus, but second to encourage and guide him, and third to secure his protection for philosophy. The flattery is obvious: Augustus and his rule are being likened to the best regime of one of the greatest of Greek philosophers, and a philosopher whose works had recently been brought out in a new edition corrected in the light of that philosopher's own recently discovered manuscripts (surely something for the Augustan age to glory in). The encouragement and guidance are no less obvious: the best regime is best because of its concern with virtue and good order and piety and education. If Augustus is to go on deserving praise, let him go on exercising the same concern. The protection of philosophy is now also clear. If the teaching of Aristotle is so favorable to Augustus' own position in Rome, to his settlement of the Roman Empire, to his program of moral reform and careful imperial management, how can philosophy, and in particular the philosophy of Aristotle and the Peripatetics, not be something for the emperor to protect and promote?

Arius, however, has achieved these results through deviation and sleight of hand. He has not presented the Aristotelian doctrine whole and unexpurgated. What if Augustus or one of his friends or aides were to find out? But what would they find out? Difficult reflections on distributive justice whose precise meaning scholars still puzzle over even today; remarks about the mixed regime that are, because of Polybius (and others), so well known that Aristotle must have adopted them (and shifts can be made to show that he did) – or if he did not, his thinking must have been at fault and so he is rightly now corrected; remarks about reform that, first, are a pardonable exaggeration and, second, preface recommendations that no respectable or virtuous man (least of all the publicly moral Augustus) could possibly reject. So even if Augustus himself noted Arius' subtle changes, he could not object to them. Rather he would likely admire them. Arius is carefully sanitizing Aristotle so that the common opinion about Aristotle's thought (as promulgated by Arius himself in the *Epitome*) is no threat. But Arius is doing so in such a way that only careful scholars could notice the sanitization, and also in such a way that scholars who did notice it would notice also the prudence of Arius' procedure. They would thus be taught the prudence at the same time as they are taught the sanitization. Augustus was sane enough and subtle enough as a ruler not to be disturbed by scholars who, if they know subversive things, know also not to act on them.

So further and finally, if we return to the *oikeiôsis* material from the beginning of the *Epitome*, has not Arius thereby shown that Peripatetic philosophy falls fully into harmony with the Stoicism so much embraced by the Romans? Has he not shown how Stoic in the end Peripatetic philosophy really is? Peripatetics and Stoics are made to walk together in praising the *oikeiôsis* that binds all men with all men and so in particular binds together, as Augustus wished, the disparate peoples of the Roman Empire.[16] The *oikeiôsis* doctrine, whatever its origin and whoever its author, is seen to be as compatible with Peripatetic philosophy as it is manifestly compatible with Stoic. What matter if Aristotle did not develop it *expressis verbis*? What matter if Theophrastus did? What matter if some later Peripatetic or even Arius himself developed it or elaborated it? Peripatetic philosophy is in any event brought fully within the scope of the Augustan agenda.

Perhaps, therefore, to recall the first section of this paper concerning von Arnim and the Theophrastean origin of the *oikeiôsis* doctrine in the *Epitome*, we should say that if Arius' aim in that *Epitome* was in part rhetorical and esoteric (to defend philosophy, Peripatetic and otherwise, by subtle changes and insinuations) the question of the origin of that doctrine has no answer—or at least it has no answer that can be derived, as von Arnim and others have wished to derive it, from Arius' intention. For if his intention was rhetorical and esoteric, any answer will do to the question about the source of *oikeiôsis* in the *Epitome*: Aristotle in some lost work, Theophrastus, later Peripatetic borrowings from the Stoics, Arius himself. Certainly, if Arius could be subtly misleading, and deliberately so as it seems, about the mixed regime (at least as it is found in Aristotle) and also about reforming regimes, he could be deliberately misleading elsewhere. Admittedly he would have to keep sufficiently close to Aristotle and Theophrastus that

---

[16] That Arius wanted to present Peripatetic doctrine as favoring a certain cosmopolitan union among all peoples is argued by Nagle (2002), though Nagle also thinks that Arius thereby failed both to present Aristotle's teaching on the household correctly and to develop a cosmopolitanism that could actually work.

his *Epitome* remained recognizably Peripatetic (too great a departure from known truth would not be subtle). But it does remain recognizably Peripatetic (and all the more so if Theophrastus can be seen or implied to be the origin of *oikeiôsis* within Peripateticism). Arius has secured his double aim: to epitomize Peripatetic philosophy, and to defend that philosophy and its continuing study before the unchallengeable authority of the ruler of the Roman world. No mean feat.

Works Cited

Annas, J. 1990. "The Hellenistic Version of Aristotle's Ethics." *The Monist* 73: 80–96.

Arnim, H. von. 1926. "Arius Didymus' Abriss der peripatetischen Ethik." SB Wien 204.3, 3–161.

Fortenbaugh, W.W. 1983. *On Stoic and Peripatetic Ethics, the Work of Arius Didymus*. Rutgers University Studies in Classical Humanities 1. New Brunswick, N.J.: Transaction.

Giusta, M. 1964–67. *I dossografi di etica*. 2 vols. Pubblicazioni della Facoltà di Lettere e Filosofia 15, 3–4. Torino: Università di Torino.

Görgemanns, H. 1983. "*Oikeiôsis* in Arius Didymus." In Fortenbaugh (1983) 165–89.

Hahm, D. 1983. "The Diaeretic Method and the Purpose of Arius' Doxography." In Fortenbaugh (1983) 15–37.

Nagle, B. 2002. "Aristotle and Arius Didymus on Household and Polis." *Rheinisches Museum für Philologie,* n.f. 145. 2: 198–223.

Pohlenz, M. 1940. "Grundfragen der stoischen Philosophie." *Abhandlungen der Gesellschaft der Wissenschaften zu Göttingen.* Philologisch-Historische Klasse. Dritte Folge, nr. 26. Göttingen: Vandenhoeck & Ruprecht.

Simpson, PLP. 1997. *The Politics of Aristotle*. Chapel Hill: University of North Carolina Press

———. 2014. *The Great Ethics of Aristotle*. New Brunswick N.J.: Transaction.

10

Seneca's Peripatetics
Epistulae Morales *92 and Stobaean Doxography C*

Margaret R. Graver

The potential importance of Seneca to the study of Aristotelianism at Rome is easily recognized. It is suggestive, for instance, that the sourcebook compiled by R. W. Sharples includes no fewer than eighteen passages from Seneca's philosophical writings.[1] But the full extent of Peripatetic material in Seneca has never been documented, and the implications of Seneca's knowledge for the history of Peripatetic thought have yet to be worked out. In this paper I supply some details of Seneca's engagement with the issues that are most prominent in the Peripatetic ethical doxography found in Stobaeus 2.7, 116–130W, known to modern scholarship as Doxography C and usually attributed to Arius Didymus. I then proceed, with caution, to draw some inferences as to the provenance of Seneca's information. In so doing I mean to open up the possibility that Seneca might supply us with some indirect and yet valuable considerations that will have a bearing on the study of Didymus' Peripatetic doxography, its antecedents in the

[1] Sharples (2010) For the historical development of Aristotelianism during the Roman period, see also Moraux (1973); Gottschalk (1987); Barnes (1997); Hahm (2007); Gill (2012); Inwood (2014).

Peripatos and the alternatives to it that were still known in the early first century C.E. Along the way, I argue that comparison with Doxography C yields significant benefits for Senecan studies as well, in the form of a better understanding of Seneca's polemical strategies and a more fine-grained account of his positions on some core issues in ethics: the relation between upper and lower divisions of the psyche, the status of the so-called bodily and external goods, and the sufficiency of virtue for happiness.

Of particular interest is the 92nd of the *Epistulae Morales,* a long and meandering defense of Stoic ethics against a series of pointed objections. To my knowledge, this text has not previously been used in Peripatetic studies in any extensive way.[2] The omission is understandable, given that the letter does not give the clear indications that a modern reader would like to have as to the identity of its opponents. Comparison with the Didyman doxography, however, helps to establish that the positions criticized are indeed Peripatetic from start to finish, with one exception that I will address in due course. In view of the range of topics treated and the manner in which they are presented, it is, I think, demonstrable that Seneca in this letter responds point by point to a summary account of Peripatetic ethics that is similar in nature to the version attributed to Arius Didymus. However, I do not argue that he had consulted Doxography C itself, because there are at least two features of the doxography Seneca is critiquing that are not found in Didymus' version. If my inference here is correct, then close scrutiny of Seneca's letter gives access to something that is very much needed for assessing the philosophical content of Doxography C: a near-contemporary comparison text.

1

Let us begin with some general observations about Seneca's working methods. A well-educated man and one who seems to have enjoyed frequent philosophical discussions with similarly well-educated friends, Seneca was undoubtedly capable of explaining doctrines of more than one philosophical school from memory alone. But a man of his wealth and interests must also have owned an extensive library, and mentions of reading and of the contents of specific treatises are frequent enough in his work to suggest that consultation of sources, many of them in Greek, was a regular part of his process of composition. Sometimes, though, he writes in a way that

---

[2] Trapp (2007) 32–35 juxtaposes letter 92, which he calls "a straightforward sermon on the sufficiency of virtue," with the Peripatetic ethics found in Stobaeus, but his remark is of a general nature and does not supply any details.

seems to a modern interpreter to suggest dependence on some kind of written source, but fails to indicate how the material comes to him. Such reticence is easily explained by his literary sensibilities and by the nature of his philosophical project: he mentions a source only when he feels that the name will contribute in some way to the elegance of his artistic product or to the edification of his reader. It is up to us, then, to make such determinations as we can about the works Seneca has consulted, attending first and foremost to such explicit citations as he provides, but also to the presence of characteristically Peripatetic ideas and terminology and to the way such ideas and terms are arranged within a particular context. In addition, we should allow for the possibility that some of his information about Peripatetic thought is taken over at second hand from earlier Stoic authors polemicizing against the school.

One point that strikes the eye immediately when surveying Seneca's works is that his explicit citations of Peripatetic material (where he gives them) do not all follow the same pattern. In the relatively early *De Ira*, his references are always to "Aristotle" or "Theophrastus," never to the Peripatetics, even though the doctrines referred to are recognizably the same as are attributed by Cicero to the Peripatetics.[3] Later on, in the *Epistulae Morales*, doctrines concerning ethics and psychology are consistently attributed to the *Peripatetici*, even on points similar to those mentioned in *De Ira*; letters 58 and 65, however, on substance and causation respectively, speak again of *Aristoteles*.[4] Meanwhile the *Quaestiones naturales*, written at about the same time as the *Epistulae Morales*, refer frequently to Aristotle and Theophrastus and once to Strato, but never to the *Peripatetici*.[5] Such variety in citation practice is just what one would expect to see if, in composing works on different subjects, Seneca consulted works written by different Peripatetic authors or using different systems of reference for Peripatetic material.

The evidentiary value of Seneca's work would be much reduced if it could be shown that his knowledge of Peripatetic ethics had all been derived from Cicero's reportage in the *De finibus* and *Tusculanae disputationes*.[6]

---

[3] Aristotle is named in *Ira* 1.3.3, 1.9.2, 1.17.1, and 3.3.1; Theophrastus in 1.12.3, 1.14.1. Setaioli (1988) 141–52 brings out the important differences between these citations and the actual views of Aristotle and Theophrastus. See also Inwood (2014) 90–103.

[4] *Ep.* 58.9, 65.4–6.

[5] Aristotle in *NQ* 1.1.2, 1.1.7, 1.3.7, 1.8.6, 2.12.4, 6.13.1, 6.14.1, 7.5.4, 7.28.1, 7.30.1; Theophrastus in *NQ* 3.11.4, 3.16.5, 3.25.4, 3.25.7, 3.26.1, 4a.2.16, 6.13.1; Strato in *NQ* 6.13.2.

[6] Inwood (2007) xiv and 218 holds that Seneca has read the ethical writings of 45 B.C.E. and has them in mind while writing. My own view is that while similarities of

But this is not the case, for there are some points reported by Seneca that are not to be found in Cicero. A notable instance is in *Ep.* 85.2, where Seneca discusses the same syllogism as is reported by Cicero in *Tusc.* 3.18, but unlike Cicero also gives the Peripatetic refutation of it. It should be noted also that while Seneca clearly has knowledge of the position in ethics that is attributed by Cicero to Antiochus of Ascalon, the name of Antiochus never appears in his writings; instead, he speaks of the *veteres Academici* (*Ep.* 71.18) or of Xenocrates and Speusippus (*Ep.* 85.18). In studying his reports of this position, we should be open to the possibility that his information about it comes from some author other than Antiochus.

2

Although my central concern will be with the 92nd letter, an important preliminary is to review all passages in Seneca that connect topics treated in Doxography C with an explicit mention of the *Peripatetici*. This overview will supply some useful benchmarks as to the extent of Seneca's knowledge of Peripatetic ethics.

For these purposes, the most important Senecan passages are those concerned directly with the Peripatetic system of value. Both in the *Epistulae morales* and in the *De beneficiis* we find passing remarks indicating some familiarity with the Peripatetics' threefold classification of goods. *Epistulae morales* 88.5 encapsulates the characteristic doctrines of several philosophical schools: as the Epicurean typically "praises civic repose while living amid songs and parties" and the Academic "says there is no certainty about anything," so the Peripatetic "posits three types of goods."[7] *De beneficiis* 5.13.1 is somewhat less transparent, since Seneca there speaks at first of "goods of the mind, of the body, and of fortune" as an element of *Stoic* doctrine; immediately afterwards, however, he correctly assigns that threefold classification to the Peripatetics, adding tendentiously that

---

content can easily be explained by a shared interest in the Greek philosophical tradition, it is much harder to explain why Seneca would have omitted such points as the alternative Epicurean accounts of friendship or the role of Antiochus—matters highly relevant to his own project—if he were aware of them. For present purposes, however, what matters is that even if Seneca knew Cicero's writings, he must have had other sources as well.

[7] *Ep.* 88.5: *modo Stoicum illum faciunt, virtutem solam probantem et voluptates refugientem et ab honesto ne inmortalitatis quidem pretio recedentem, modo Epicureum, laudantem statum quietae civitatis et inter convivia cantusque vitam exigentis, modo Peripateticum, tria bonorum genera inducentem, modo Academicum, omnia incerta dicentem.* All translations from the *Epistulae morales* are those of Graver and Long (2015).

Peripatetici "extend the bounds of human happiness far and wide."[8] The misleading implication that Stoics, too, might recognize goods of the body and of fortune is cleared up later in the paragraph.

Three passages in the *Epistulae morales* show familiarity with arguments used by Peripatetics to support their views. These occur in polemical contexts in letters 85 and 87. In *Ep.* 87.11–12, the Peripatetics challenge the major premise in a Stoic argument that is supposed to prove that externals cannot properly be regarded as goods. The Stoic has claimed that the only things that should be regarded as good are those that make *people* good—that is to say, the virtues. He offers a craft analogy: what is good in musical skill *(in arte musica)* is only what makes one a good musician. The Peripatetics' rebuttal insists that the craft analogy is misused, that in fact some elements of music are good apart from those that make the performer good; good instruments, for instance. Analogously, there are some things in human life that are good for us even though they do not make *us* good.

> Nunc volo paucissimas adhuc interrogationes nostrorum tibi reddere ad virtutem pertinentes, quam satisfacere vitae beatae contendimus.
>> "Quod bonum est bonos facit (nam et in arte musica quod bonum est facit musicum); fortuita bonum non faciunt; ergo non sunt bona."
>
> Adversus hoc sic respondent Peripatetici ut quod primum proponimus falsum esse dicant. "Ab eo" inquiunt "quod est bonum non utique fiunt boni. In musica est aliquid bonum tamquam tibia aut chorda aut organum aliquod aptatum ad usus canendi; nihil tamen horum facit musicum."

> I want now to share with you just a few of the investigations conducted by our school pertaining to virtue, which in our view is sufficient for happiness.
>> That which is good makes people good, just as in musical skill that which is good makes one a musician.
>> Things depending on fortune do not make a person good.
>> Therefore, such things are not goods.
>
> Against this the Peripatetics argue that our first premise is false. "People do not automatically become good from what is good. In music, there are things that are good, for instance a flute, a lyre, or an organ well-suited for playing, but none of these makes a person a musician."

The comparison of non-psychic goods to musical instruments is reminiscent of a type of argument that has its ultimate origin in Aristotle *EN*

---

[8] *Ben.* 5.13, trans. Griffin and Inwood (2011): *Sunt animi bona, sunt corporis, sunt fortunae ... Nec hoc ex nostra tantum constitutione; Peripatetici quoque, qui felicitatis humanae longe lateque terminos ponunt, aiunt minuta beneficia perventura ad malos.*

1.10, 1100b27.[9] According to this argument, at least some non-psychic goods are required as instruments for the activation of the virtues in the same sense as flutes are required for flute-playing or medical instruments for the practice of medicine. This is to say that they are necessary conditions: one cannot perform generous actions if one does not possess at least some of the goods of fortune, and so on. The argument is stated with great clarity by Aspasius, *On Aristotle's Ethics* 24.3–9,[10] and is present also in Stobaean Doxography C, section 12 [129.19–130.12W], where the external goods are compared to the use of tools (τὴν τῶν ὀργάνων χρῆσιν) and are called "necessary conditions" (τὰ ὧν οὐκ ἄνευ).[11]

[9] Because the passage is referred to several times in what follows, I here give the entire segment from 1100b22–1101a8, followed by Irwin's translation: πολλῶν δὲ γινομένων κατὰ τύχην καὶ διαφερόντων μεγέθει καὶ μικρότητι, τὰ μὲν μικρὰ τῶν εὐτυχημάτων, ὁμοίως δὲ καὶ τῶν ἀντικειμένων, δῆλον ὡς οὐ ποιεῖ ῥοπὴν τῆς ζωῆς, τὰ δὲ μεγάλα καὶ πολλὰ γινόμενα μὲν εὖ μακαριώτερον τὸν βίον ποιήσει (καὶ γὰρ αὐτὰ συνεπικοσμεῖν πέφυκεν, καὶ ἡ χρῆσις αὐτῶν καλὴ καὶ σπουδαία γίνεται), ἀνάπαλιν δὲ συμβαίνοντα θλίβει καὶ λυμαίνεται τὸ μακάριον: λύπας τε γὰρ ἐπιφέρει καὶ ἐμποδίζει πολλαῖς ἐνεργείαις. ὅμως δὲ καὶ ἐν τούτοις διαλάμπει τὸ καλόν, ἐπειδὰν φέρῃ τις εὐκόλως πολλὰς καὶ μεγάλας ἀτυχίας, μὴ δι᾽ ἀναλγησίαν, ἀλλὰ γεννάδας ὢν καὶ μεγαλόψυχος. εἰ δ᾽ εἰσὶν αἱ ἐνέργειαι κύριαι τῆς ζωῆς, καθάπερ εἴπομεν, οὐδεὶς ἂν γένοιτο τῶν μακαρίων ἄθλιος: οὐδέποτε γὰρ πράξει τὰ μισητὰ καὶ τὰ φαῦλα. τὸν γὰρ ὡς ἀληθῶς ἀγαθὸν καὶ ἔμφρονα πάσας οἰόμεθα τὰς τύχας εὐσχημόνως φέρειν καὶ ἐκ τῶν ὑπαρχόντων ἀεὶ τὰ κάλλιστα πράττειν, καθάπερ καὶ στρατηγὸν ἀγαθὸν τῷ παρόντι στρατοπέδῳ χρῆσθαι πολεμικώτατα καὶ σκυτοτόμον ἐκ τῶν δοθέντων σκυτῶν κάλλιστον ὑπόδημα ποιεῖν: τὸν αὐτὸν δὲ τρόπον καὶ τοὺς ἄλλους τεχνίτας ἅπαντας. εἰ δ᾽ οὕτως, ἄθλιος μὲν οὐδέποτε γένοιτ᾽ ἂν ὁ εὐδαίμων, οὐ μὴν μακάριός γε, ἂν Πριαμικαῖς τύχαις περιπέσῃ. "However, many events are matters of fortune, and some are smaller, some greater. Hence, while small strokes of good or ill fortune clearly will not influence his life, many great strokes of good fortune will make it more blessed, since in themselves they naturally add adornment to it, and his use of them proves to be fine and excellent. Conversely, if they are great misfortunes, they oppress and spoil his blessedness, since they involve pain and impede many activities. And yet, even here what is fine shines through, when he bears many severe misfortunes with good temper, not because he feels no distress, but because he is noble and magnanimous. And since it is activities that control life, as we said, no blessed person could ever become miserable, since he will never do hateful and base actions. For a truly good and intelligent person, we suppose, will bear strokes of fortune suitably, and from his resources at any time will do the finest actions he can, just as a good general will make the best use of his forces in war, and a good shoemaker will produce the finest shoe he can from the hides given him, and similarly for all other craftsmen. If this is so, then the happy person could never become miserable. Still, he will not be blessed either, if he falls into misfortunes as bad as Priam's."

[10] Sharples (2010) 162, 167–68.

[11] τὴν δ᾽ εὐδαιμονίαν ἐκ τῶν καλῶν γίνεσθαι καὶ προηγουμένων πράξεων. διὸ καὶ δι᾽ ὅλων εἶναι καλήν, καθάπερ καὶ τὴν ἐν τοῖς αὐλοῖς ἐνέργειαν δι᾽ ὅλων ἔντεχνον. Οὐ γὰρ ἐκβιβάζειν τὴν παράληψιν τῶν ὑλικῶν τῆς εἰλικρινείας τοῦ καλοῦ τὴν εὐδαιμονίαν, ὡς

Seneca's Peripatetics: *Epistulae Morales* 92 and the Stobean Doxography C

A closely related line of thought underlies the Peripatetic position reported by Seneca in *Ep.* 85.30–31. Here, too, there is a debate between two speakers, one upholding the Stoic view that only the vices are bad, the other favoring the Peripatetic position that bodily and external circumstances may also be considered bad things.

> "Quod malum est nocet; quod nocet deteriorem facit; dolor et paupertas deteriorem non faciunt; ergo mala non sunt." "Falsum est" inquit "quod proponitis; non enim, si quid nocet, etiam deteriorem facit. Tempestas et procella nocet gubernatori, non tamen illum deteriorem facit." Quidam e Stoicis ita adversus hoc respondent: deteriorem fieri gubernatorem tempestate ac procella, quia non possit id quod proposuit efficere nec tenere cursum suum; deteriorem illum in arte sua non fieri, in opere fieri. Quibus Peripateticus "ergo" inquit "et sapientem deteriorem faciet paupertas, dolor, et quidquid aliud tale fuerit; virtutem enim illi non eripiet, sed opera eius inpediet."

> Whatever is bad does some harm.
> Whatever harms a person makes him worse.
> Pain and poverty do not make a person worse.
> Therefore, they are not bad."

One might say, "The premise you offer is false: it is not the case that whatever harms a person also makes him worse. Wind and storm harm the helmsman, but they do not make him worse." Some of the Stoics respond to this objection as follows. Wind and storm do make the helmsman worse, since he cannot achieve what he set out to do; that is, to hold his course. He is not made worse as concerns his skill, but he is made worse as concerns his activity. To this the Peripatetic replies, "By that reasoning, even the wise person is made worse by poverty, pain, and everything else of that sort, for such things will impede his activities, even though they do not take away his virtue."

Aided by some incautious Stoic dialecticians, the Peripatetic makes effective use of the helmsman analogy to support his own view. Just as the

---

οὐδὲ τὴν τῆς ἰατρικῆς ἔντεχνον δι᾽ ὅλων ἐνέργειαν τὴν τῶν ὀργάνων χρῆσιν. Πᾶσαν μὲν γὰρ πρᾶξιν ἐνέργειαν εἶναί τινα ψυχῆς. ... Τὰ γὰρ ὧν ἄνευ πράττειν ὁτιοῦν ἀδύνατον, μέρη τῆς ἐνεργείας λέγειν οὐκ ὀρθόν. Τὸ μὲν γὰρ μέρος ἐπινοεῖσθαι κατὰ τὸ συμπληρωτικόν εἶναι τοῦ ὅλου, τὰ δ᾽ ὧν οὐκ ἄνευ κατὰ τὸ ποιητικόν, τῷ φέρειν καὶ συνεργεῖν εἰς τὸ τέλος. Happiness is brought about through noble and primary actions; that is why it is wholly noble in the same way that the activity of the flutes is wholly artistic. For the use of materials does not deprive happiness of the purity of nobility, just as the use of tools does not deprive medicine of its wholly artistic activity. For every action is a certain activity of soul. ... The things that are necessary for any kind of action shouldn't be called parts of the activity, for the part is thought of as completing the whole, whereas the necessary things are thought of as productive of it, because they conduce and contribute toward the end. (Text and translation of Doxography C are Tsouni's throughout.) A similar point is made in Doxography A: Stob. 2.7, 46.13–17W.

storm does not make the helmsman worse but does impede the exercise of his craft, so pain and poverty do not keep the sage from being virtuous, but do in a sense make him worse, since they will impede his achievements (*opera eius inpediet*). Again the craft analogy draws ultimately on Aristotle's point regarding the activation of the virtues, where great misfortunes "oppress and spoil blessedness" (θλίβει καὶ λυμαίνεται τὸ μακάριον) not only because they involve pain but also because they impede (ἐμποδίζει) the activation of the virtues (*EN* 1.10, 1100b29–30).

A more cryptic reference to Peripatetic argumentation is found in *Ep.* 87.38. This time the Peripatetics speak first, stating an argument *against* their view, which they claim to be able to refute.

> "ex malis bonum non fit; ex multis paupertatibus divitiae fiunt; ergo divitiae bonum non sunt." Hanc interrogationem nostri non agnoscunt, Peripatetici et fingunt illam et solvunt. Ait autem Posidonius hoc sophisma, per omnes dialecticorum scholas iactatum, sic ab Antipatro refelli …
>
> > That which is good is not made up of things that are bad.
> > But many instances of poverty make up one instance of wealth.
> > Therefore wealth is not a good.
>
> This syllogism is not recognized by our school; it is both devised and solved by the Peripatetics. Posidonius says, however, that this sophism, which has been bandied about among dialecticians from every school, is refuted by Antipater as follows …

Seneca does not explain how the Peripatetics set about refuting the argument; he is more interested in an alternative refutation by Antipater. From our perspective the passage is of interest because of its dialectical format, which is very like that of the two passages just quoted. In all three we see the Peripatetics right in the thick of the fray, challenging premises, turning arguments on their head, and even propounding a bad argument on behalf of their opponents.[12] This is to say that here, at least, Seneca's presentation brings to mind the kind of debates we can imagine taking place in the time of Critolaus. His immediate source in both letters may be Posidonius, who is named also in *Ep.* 87.35, but in that case Posidonius himself must be drawing on an older treatise, since it is he who quotes Antipater.[13] Inwood suggests that refutation by Antipater points to Cri-

---

[12] On the argument, see Sharples (2010) 166; further on the role of Posidonius in *Ep.* 87, see Kidd (1988) 626–37 and (1986).

[13] Posidonius is named in *Ep.* 87.35 and 87.38. His name does not occur in *Ep.* 85, but the manner of presentation, quite different from Seneca's expository style in other letters, carries some weight.

tolaus as the originator of the argument, and the syllogistic construction does seem to recall that philosopher.[14]

In addition to these passages that deal directly with the system of value, there are two passages in the *Epistulae Morales* that connect the *Peripatetici* with a particular doctrine of the emotions. One is *Ep.* 85.3, where "certain Peripatetics" (*Peripatetici quidam*) respond to a Stoic syllogism mentioning imperturbability by stating their own position on that issue: that the wise person does experience emotions, but only "occasionally and in moderation" *(raro perturbatur et modice)*. Similarly, *Ep.* 116.1 says that the *Peripatetici* "restrain" (*temperant*) the emotions, and mentions the term "moderate amount" *(mediocritas)*.[15] We have already noted the resemblance of these doctrines to those attributed in *De ira* to Aristotle and Theophrastus. Moreover, *Ep.* 89.10 shows awareness that Peripatetic authors acknowledged as areas of philosophical study not only ethics, physics, and logic but also politics, household management (*partem quam* οἰκονομικὴν vocant), and "kinds of life" (*de generibus vitae locum*). Finally, *Ep.* 117.11 attributes to the *Peripatetici* a rather subtle claim that a substance such as wisdom cannot be differentiated from the associated predicate such as "being wise," "since each implies the other" (*cum in utrolibet eorum alterum sit*). Nothing much need be said about these passages here; they do, however, have some significance in that they provide further evidence that Seneca possessed an extensive, if rather disparate, knowledge of Peripatetic thought.

3

The overview just given includes all Seneca's explicit references to the Peripatetic school; it does not, however, take in all the passages in which our author knows himself to be repeating Peripatetic doctrines. I turn now to some instances in which Peripatetic influence is evidenced even without explicit citation, either by the content of a paragraph or by the structure of Seneca's argumentation.

That the Peripatetic material in the *Epistulae morales* is in fact more extensive can be inferred from the flow of the argument in two letters that have already been quoted. The more straightforward case concerns letter 87. That letter as a whole has to do with the value to be assigned to wealth. After some anecdotal material concerned with that topic, the issue is stated

---

[14] Inwood (2007) 257–58. On Critolaus' position and methods, see esp. Hahm (2007).
[15] The term is attested in Cicero, *Acad.* 2.135, *Tusc.* 4.46. On limitation and "moderate amounts," see Annas (1993) 59–66.

more formally as that of the sufficiency of virtue for happiness, about which Seneca promises to deliver "some syllogisms of our people" (*interrogationes nostrorum*); that is, of the Stoics. The remainder of the letter comprises a series of six arguments, each followed by an attempted refutation and then a counter-refutation.[16] The first argument is the one quoted above from *Ep.* 87.11–12; there, as we have seen, the refutation is attributed to the *Peripatetici* with their point about musical instruments. The second through fifth arguments are similarly in support of the Stoic view, but are not labeled as such, and the refutations likewise carry no label but are introduced in each case merely with "they say" (*inquiunt*) or "he says" (*inquit*). In *Ep.* 87.15 the interlocutors insist that goods may be possessed by such lowly persons as grammarians; in 87.22, that a good thing, namely financial gain, may come from a bad act such as robbery; in 87.28–29, in a more involved argument, that it is improper to say that wealth is bad merely because the desire for it leads to many bad actions. The fifth Stoic argument is attributed to Posidonius; responding to it, the nameless interlocutor points out that if, as Posidonius claims, riches and the like always produce bad qualities of mind, they should not be counted even as preferred indifferents (*commoda*, 87.36). The sixth argument is the one given above from 87.38; for that one, as we have seen, Seneca notes that both the argument and the refutation originate with the Peripatetics. But Inwood is surely correct in identifying the preceding refutations as likewise reporting Peripatetic views,[17] both because the position represented is consistent throughout and, more specifically, because Seneca's management of the speaking voices here serves in lieu of explicit citations.

The structure of letter 85 is similar in the main to that of its companion piece, but with some meandering that requires close attention to follow. Here too the thesis is stated abstractly at the outset, that virtue is sufficient to fill out happiness, and here too the discussion proceeds as a series of arguments interspersed with efforts at refutation. The first of the refutations has already been mentioned, since it is labeled for the Peripatetics; it is the one concerned with imperturbability and the emotions. Following a lengthy counter-refutation, Seneca returns to the abstract issue and reports two other philosophical views on the sufficiency of virtue for happiness. Xenocrates and Speusippus, he says, hold that "while a person can be made

---

[16] The sixth argument, in *Ep.* 87.38, preserves the pattern even though both the argument and the first refutation are by the Peripatetics. There is then a second refutation by Antipater, followed by a rejoinder in Seneca's own voice.

[17] Inwood (2007) xiv and 218.

happy even by virtue alone, it is still not the case that what is honorable is the only good"; Epicurus "believes that one who has virtue is also happy, and yet it is his view that virtue itself is not sufficient for happiness, since it is the pleasure that arises from virtue that makes one happy, not virtue itself" (*Ep.* 85.18). Epicurus is answered briefly, then Xenocrates' and Speusippus' view is restated ("that a person will indeed be happy through virtue alone and yet not completely happy") and arguments given at greater length against that: for Stoics, "there is no respect in which the happy life can be raised to a higher degree" (*Ep.* 85.19). Immediately thereafter, Seneca proceeds to a second formal argument for the Stoic position, again followed by an attempt at refutation. This time, however, the originators of the refutation are unnamed.

> "Qui fortis est sine timore est; qui sine timore est sine tristitia est; qui sine tristitia est beatus est." Nostrorum haec interrogatio est. Adversus hanc sic respondere conantur: falsam nos rem et controversiosam pro confessa vindicare, eum qui fortis est sine timore esse. "Quid ergo?" inquit "fortis inminentia mala non timebit? istuc dementis alienatique, non fortis est. Ille vero" inquit "moderatissime timet, sed in totum extra metum non est." (*Ep.* 85.24)
>
> Anyone who is courageous is without fear.
> Anyone who is without fear is without sadness.
> Anyone who is without sadness is happy.
>
> This line of reasoning belongs to our school. Trying to refute it, they respond that the premise we take for granted, that anyone who is courageous is without fear, is actually false and controversial. "How's that? The brave person won't fear impending evils? You're talking about someone who is crazy and out of touch, not someone who is courageous. To be sure, the courageous person experiences a very moderate degree of fear, but he is not completely beyond fear."

The third person pronoun implied in *respondere conantur* has no clear referent in what immediately precedes, for it surely cannot refer to Xenocrates and Speusippus. The introduction of the second syllogism marks a new point of departure, returning us to the main argumentative frame of the letter. Now, in two of the three spots in this letter where an attempted refutation directly follows a Stoic syllogism, the speakers are identified as "Peripatetics" (85.3) and "the Peripatetic" (85.31). It seems likely, then, that Seneca considers the letter as a whole to be presenting a debate between Stoics and Peripatetics, despite the intrusion of other philosophical views in 85.18–23. Moreover, the content of the refutation at 85.24 identifies the speakers quite clearly even in the absence of citation, for their position on fear is exactly the one stated for the emotions generally in 85.3.[18]

In both letter 87 and letter 85, then, we see that Seneca sometimes states a Peripatetic position without identifying it as such; the absence of citation does not indicate that he has no specific philosophical school in mind. Where these two letters are concerned, he may imagine that the way he has structured the argument makes it clear where the objection comes from, even if in fact it does not. Or he may not care who owns the objection, since his main interest is in the argument itself. Either way, the omission of citation in these instances should alert us to the possibility that other passages in the *Epistulae morales* may also refer *sine nomine* to views Seneca knows to be Peripatetic.

One such instance is to be found at *Ep.* 71.17. The context is a long explanation of the Stoic position on goods. For Stoics, all goods are equal to one another: as long as one's own behavior exhibits the relevant virtue, winning an election or a battle is not a greater good than losing it, and an honorable life is not a greater good than an honorable death. Realizing that not everyone will accept this view, Seneca explores the consequences of disagreement. If one does not concede that Regulus, tortured by enemies for preserving his honor, is experiencing just as choiceworthy a good as if he had been free of pain, one will be saying in effect that pain is a bad thing: what can diminish a good has to be bad in its own right. Regulus will still have his good, but he will also have an evil, and in fact a great one, since the pain is great. Yet no philosopher has ever been so bold as to say that a virtuous person can be made miserable by adverse circumstances.

> Nam si hanc inaequalitatem receperis ut fortiter torqueri in minoribus bonis numeres, numerabis etiam in malis, et infelicem Socraten dices in carcere, infelicem Catonem vulnera sua animosius quam fecerat retractantem, calamitosissimum omnium Regulum fidei poenas etiam hostibus servatae pendentem. Atqui nemo hoc dicere, ne ex mollissimis quidem, ausus est; negant enim illum esse beatum, sed tamen negant miserum.
>
> For if you accept that there is inequality, even such that you would consider the courageous endurance of torture to be one of the lesser goods, then you will also be regarding it as a bad thing. You will be saying that Socrates was unfortunate in his prison, that Cato was unfortunate when he reopened his wounds even more bravely than he made them, that Regulus was more terribly afflicted than any

---

[18] "A very moderate degree of fear" (*moderatissime timet*) refers to the Peripatetic position on "moderate amounts" (*mediocritates*) of emotion; compare *Ep.* 116.1–3. Sharples (2010) 147 is overly cautious on this point.

of them, in that he kept a promise even to his enemies and paid the penalty for doing so. Yet no one, not even the most fainthearted, has dared to say that: they say that Regulus was not happy yet insist that he was not miserable either.

Who are these "fainthearted" philosophers (*mollissimi*), who say that Regulus was not happy and yet not miserable either? Clearly the position is one held by some historical persons, and these persons cannot be Epicureans, even though *mollissimi* is the kind of polemical epithet Seneca sometimes applies to Epicureans.[19] That they are in fact Peripatetics becomes clear when we compare their betwixt-and-between view with Doxography C, section 14 [133.6–11]:

> Τὸν <δ'> ἀφαιρεθέντα τὴν εὐδαιμονίαν οὐκ εἶναι κακοδαίμονα, καθάπερ τὸν μηδ' ὅλως ἔχοντα ταύτην, ἀλλ' ἔσθ' ὅτε μέσον. Βιοῦν γάρ ποτε καὶ σοφὸν καὶ μὴ σοφὸν τὸν μέσον λεγόμενον βίον, τὸν μήτε εὐδαίμονα μήτε κακοδαίμονα.

> The one who is deprived of happiness is not wretched like the one who doesn't possess it at all, but is sometimes found between the two. For sometimes both the sage and the one who is not a sage live the so-called middle life, which is neither happy nor wretched.

The origin of the view is in Aristotle's statement in *EN* 1.10, 1101a8, that the happy person could never become miserable but is not blessed either.[20] Admittedly "the so-called middle life" may not be quite what Aristotle had in mind. But it is easy to see how someone might have extracted this from the passage, and Solon's dictum, cited just above in 'C', is from the same context.

In *Ep.* 71.18, immediately following the passage just quoted, Seneca brings in some philosophers he calls *Academici veteres*:

> Academici veteres beatum quidem esse etiam inter hos cruciatus fatentur, sed non ad perfectum nec ad plenum, quod nullo modo potest recipi: nisi beatus est, in summo bono non est. Quod summum bonum est supra se gradum non habet, si modo illi virtus inest, si illam adversa non minuunt, si manet etiam comminuto corpore incolumis.

> The Old Academics admit that Regulus was happy even amid such torments, but not to the full and perfect extent of happiness. This is completely unacceptable. If one is not happy, one cannot have attained the highest good. The highest good does not admit of any further degree of goodness, as long as there is virtue in it;

---

[19] Epicurus holds that the tortured sage remains happy (D.L. 10.118); cf. *Ep.* 66.47–48; 92.25.

[20] See n. 9 above.

as long as adversity does not diminish that virtue; as long as virtue remains intact even when the body is maimed.

This is the same position as is given in *Ep.* 85.18–19 to Xenocrates and Speusippus, and as in that letter, Seneca's argument against it targets the notion of a lesser degree of happiness. Here, it stands in contrast to the view of the "fainthearted" Peripatetics, since the Old Academics, like the Stoics, hold that someone like Regulus is happy amid torment. They are criticized only for denying that Regulus is happy "to the full and perfect extent of happiness"; that is, for claiming that there is a "further degree of goodness" that is attainable over and above happiness itself. Interestingly, this "Old Academic" view also has a plausible origin in *EN* 1.10, 1101a8, following a different interpretation of Aristotle's intent. Rather than taking Aristotle to mean that a virtuous person in adversity is neither happy nor miserable, this reading draws a distinction between εὐδαίμων ("happy") and μακάριος ("blessed") and takes the latter to denote a higher degree of happiness. Aristotle would then have said that virtue is indeed sufficient for happiness, but not for the highest degree of happiness.[21]

The pairing of Peripatetic and Old Academic views is perhaps natural; after all, Seneca is looking for views on the sufficiency question that can be compared with his own Stoic view. It is remarkable, though, that both here and in *Ep.* 85.18 we find recognizable but unattributed Peripatetic material supplying the context and introduction for an Old Academic position that is identified as such. The latter, it seems, is something of a curiosity and requires the specific label; after all, Seneca remarks in *Quaestiones naturales* 7.32 that the Old Academic position in ethics had no adherents in his day. By contrast, the Peripatetics are the usual and expected opponents for the core Stoic position in ethics. They will sometimes appear by default, as it were, stating a view Seneca knows is theirs but does not take the trouble to name.[22]

---

[21] For the text see n. 9. Annas (1993) 420–23 presents this reading as an innovation by Antiochus, but Antiochus might just as well have drawn it from an earlier tradition of interpretation. See further n. 35.

[22] For other instances in which Seneca states a Peripatetic position as an unlabeled objection to his own view, see *Ep.* 74.22, where the interlocutor insists that since Stoics recognize "devoted children, good customs in one's homeland, and good parents" as genuine goods, they should also allow for emotional disturbance at the loss of these (*Dicitis enim inter bona esse liberos pios et bene moratam patriam et parentes bonos. Horum pericula non potestis spectare securi: perturbabit vos obsidio patriae, liberorum mors, parentum servitus*); also *Ep.* 118.13, where the objection is that since Stoics make accordance with nature the distinctive property of goodness, they should count everything that accords with nature

4

Comparison with Doxography C is again valuable when we turn to *Epistulae morales* 92. That letter, too, is concerned with the sufficiency of virtue for happiness, and here again the opponents to Seneca's Stoic position are not named. Only by identifying the philosophical doctrines that are assigned to these opponents are we entitled to infer that the letter as a whole contends specifically against the Peripatetics. The survival of Doxography C enables us to make that identification.

Because the case to be made rests upon an ensemble of philosophical claims presented in a rather long and involved text, it will be advantageous to start with an overview of the contents of letter 92. The letter begins with a claim of agreement between Seneca and an unspecified "you"—nominally the addressee Lucilius—on certain points about human nature: that externals are pursued for the sake of the body, that one cares for the body to honor the mind, and that the mind includes both subordinate parts responsible for movement and nutrition and a *principale* or directive faculty. Further, the directive faculty itself is divided into non-rational and rational elements, with the non-rational serving the rational. If there is agreement on all this, Seneca continues, then there should also be agreement on the thesis he means to defend: that the *vita beata* consists solely in perfecting our rationality. His own view of the matter is that reliance on anything outside one's own perfected rationality is incompatible with happiness: to say that anything other than what is honorable is a necessary condition for the happy life would be utterly wrong and absurd.

At the beginning of section 5, Seneca proceeds to say more about the view or views he is arguing against, singling out specific elements and responding to them point by point. The claims are not at first attributed to any philosophical school; we have just "some people" (*quidam*) and the view they take, that "the supreme good is such as to be increased, because it does not attain its greatest fullness when circumstances are unfavorable." There is a brief mention of the Stoic Antipater, saying that he grants something to externals, but Antipater is not the sole or even the principal exponent, since the phrase is *"even* Antipater" (*Antipater quoque*).

---

as a good *("Fateris" inquis "quod bonum est secundum naturam esse; haec eius proprietas est. Fateris et alia secundum naturam quidem esse sed bona non esse. Quomodo ergo illud bonum est cum haec non sint?"*). Cf. *De ira* 1.12.3 (citing Theophrastus); Cicero, *Tusc.* 4.38; Doxography C, sec. 2 [118.15–17]. One additional possibility is discussed in an appendix to this essay.

Next comes further explication of the idea of increasing, first via an analogy to the improvement a candle-flame makes in the light of day, and then by specifying two things that the opponent is bound to want as additions to virtue: either *quies*, or absence of distress, "which the Greeks call ἀοχλησία," or pleasure.[23] Arguments against the inclusion of pleasure carry us through to the end of section 10, with some pungent polemic: pleasure is "the good of a grazing animal" and "a mere tingling in the body"; to add it to virtue is to create a monstrous amalgam like Virgil's Scylla. The earlier addition, *quies*, though it did not supply the mind with anything, at least removed impediments; pleasure, though, actually weakens the mind.

The opponent now responds: if good health, repose, and freedom from pain are not impediments to virtue, will not the Stoic pursue them as well? This point Seneca cheerfully concedes, but without allowing that such objects are therefore to be considered goods. For him, goodness is involved only in that such objects are well selected (*bene eligi*) as being in accordance with human nature. If given an opportunity for selection, the Stoic will prefer health, strength, and so on, but what is good in that selection will reside in the mind, in the propriety of its intention and judgment.[24]

Next, in section 14, an opponent replies with a fuller version of the claim that virtuous knowledge might make one happy yet not perfectly happy. Without some "natural goods" or "tools," among which are included health and soundness of the limbs, one cannot be supremely happy, even though a person who has virtue cannot be miserable. Seneca objects immediately to the notion that one can be happy without being supremely happy: in his view, if the virtuous person's happiness can be diminished at all, adverse circumstances can abolish it altogether. He then compares the happiness of the good person to the light of the sun, which receives not the slightest augmentation from that of a tiny flame or spark. "But," says the opponent, "even the sun has its light blocked by certain things." The cloud, Seneca replies, does not actually prevent the sun from shining, but only prevents us from seeing its radiance; similarly disasters, losses, and unfair treatment have no power against virtue: they can make its exercise less apparent, but not less virtuous.

---

[23] Here at least ἀοχλησία is clearly freedom from *mental* suffering, since this is what the Stoic gets for free as a concomitant to virtue.

[24] In Stoic terminology, "selection" (ἐκλογή) is impulse directed toward a preferred or dispreferred indifferent as such (Stob. 2.7, 85.8–11W; Cic., *Fin.* 3.20). Note that Seneca's phrase *si electio detur* implies that one will sometimes not be able to rationally choose preferred indifferents.

Seneca's Peripatetics: *Epistulae Morales* 92 and the Stobean Doxography C

The paragraph beginning at 92.19 revisits the claim we saw in letter 71, that a wise person who is afflicted in body will be neither miserable nor happy. Arguments against that view occupy Seneca until the end of 92.23. Then in 92.24, the opponent raises the possibility that a long life without pain might be a better life to have; Seneca counters that neither pain nor premature death makes any difference. This raises the question whether the Stoic account of happiness might not be incredible and beyond human nature. Seneca counters this objection by appealing to the testimony of Epicurus in his deathbed letter. If even a hedonist philosopher can consider himself happy in extreme pain, then philosophers who say that the wise person in extreme adversity is neither miserable nor happy come out as "base-minded degenerates" (*degeneres et humillimae mentis*, 92.26).

Finally in 92.27, we get the view that human happiness differs in character from divine happiness. Only the gods possess virtue and a happy life, says the opponent; all humans can get is a "shadow and semblance" (*umbra quaedam ... et similitudo*) of those goods. "We approach, but we don't actually reach them" (*accedimus ad illa, non pervenimus*). As might be expected, Seneca defends the Stoic conception of the divine element in human nature, and the letter ends with an elaborate peroration on disdain for the body.

Side-by-side comparison of this Senecan letter with Doxography C will establish easily that nearly all the specific claims against which Seneca is arguing emanate from the Peripatetic school. The principal target of the letter is a pluralistic account of the *summum bonum* that sees happiness as a combination of virtue with other kinds of goods. That Peripatetics hold just such a combination view of the end is implied throughout Doxography C; it is stated directly, though, in section 8 [126.12–24W], which defines the *telos* as "living in accordance with virtue surrounded by bodily and external goods, whether all of them or the majority and the most important of them" (τὸ κατ' ἀρετὴν ζῆν ἐν τοῖς περὶ σῶμα καὶ τοῖς ἔξωθεν ἀγαθοῖς ἢ πᾶσιν ἢ τοῖς πλείστοις καὶ κυριωτάτοις) and notes also that goods belonging to the body are said to be productive of happiness "by contributing something through their presence" (τῷ συμβάλλεσθαί τι παρόντα).[25] In addition, Didymus' listing of what are meant to be standard Peripatetic doctrines includes all the following points:

---

[25] I take it that the denial in this section that bodily and external goods "constitute" (συμπληροῦν) happiness means only that they do not by themselves make up happiness; i.e., not in the absence of virtue.

- The mind (or soul, ψυχή) has both a rational and an irrational part; each of these is then subdivided into two further parts: section 1 [117.4–118.4W]; cf. Sen., *Ep.* 92.1–2.
- Goods that are choiceworthy for their own sake include pleasure and ἀοχλησία: section 15 [137.4–5W]; cf. Sen., *Ep.* 92.6.
- The goods that are "in accordance with nature" are also called "instruments and equipment," as of a craft: §12 [129.19–130.12W] and §14 [132.19-21W]; cf. Sen., *Ep.* 92.14.
- A good person in adverse circumstances will fail to obtain happiness, but even so "is not wretched like the one who does not possess it at all, but is sometimes found between the two": §14 [133.7–11W]; cf. Sen., *Ep.* 92.19.
- Happiness is dependent on living to an advanced age, since "a short period of time will not make happiness": §13 [131.19–132.8W]; cf. Sen., *Ep.* 92.24.
- Happiness is not the same for a god as for human beings: §14 [132.21–133.2W]; cf. Sen., *Ep.* 92.27.

We see then that even though Seneca does not name the Peripatetics anywhere in the letter, he alludes repeatedly to claims that occur also in Didymus' work, on a miscellany of topics.

The reference to ἀοχλησία and the pungent language about "tickling of the flesh" and "gratification from the trough" have sometimes been taken as indications that the critique in 92.6–10 is directed against Epicurean hedonism.[26] This interpretation should be rejected out of hand. The word ἀοχλησία is indeed used by Epicurus for freedom of pain in the body (*Ep. men.* 127), but it is by no means restricted to Epicurean contexts. It is in fact *lingua franca,* widely attested among philosophers of various persuasions; among Peripatetics; it was favored especially by Hieronymus.[27] As for the polemical phrases, there is no question that they are an attack against hedonism, but not every hedonist is an Epicurean. In this instance, the criticism is leveled specifically against those who bring pleasure in as an addition to virtue with other kinds of goods, producing what Seneca considers to be a hybrid account of the end. The point of the polemical language is

---

[26] As is assumed by Costa (1988) and Préchac (1945–64); see also Inwood (2005) 40.

[27] Among those who included it in their accounts of the *telos* were Speusippus (fr. 77 = Clement, *Stromata* II, 22, 133), the Megarians (Alexander, *De anima* 2.150), Hieronymus (Stob. 1.49, 383.8–10W), and Sextus Empiricus (*PH* 1.10). Its role as philosophical *lingua franca* is well illustrated in Posidonius fr. 187 EK (= Galen, *PHP* 5.6). The term is discussed in White (2004) 397–98.

that anyone who includes pleasure in the end *at all*, even in the smallest degree, is subject to the kinds of criticism usually leveled against Epicureans. Parallels can be supplied for this kind of argument.[28] Only in *Ep.* 92.25 do we see a clear reference to Epicureanism; there, however, the example of Epicurus is invoked *a fortiori* against the Peripatetics, the point being that the Stoic case for sufficiency can hardly be rejected by them as incredible when even Epicureans are found in support of it.[29]

Once these points are established, there should be no hesitation in recognizing letter 92 as the third of three large-scale, unified attacks on Peripatetic ethics within the *Epistulae morales*. With that said, we should also take into account the substantial ways in which the presentation of issues in letter 92 differs from that of letters 85 and 87. Each of those earlier letters takes up a single thesis and treats it in a dialectical manner, with formal arguments for the thesis pulled apart and assessed for the strength of their premises. The subject matter of letter 92 is much more diverse, and the close dialectical argumentation is lacking; in its place, we have a series of loosely related claims offered by the opponent with little or no argumentative support. In a word, the account Seneca criticizes throughout this letter proceeds in a doxographical manner very like that of Doxography C. In particular, it has many points of contact with sections 12–14 of 'C'. However, I do not claim that Seneca has read 'C' itself, but only that he was familiar with a doxographical account of a generally similar kind. There are points of difference to be considered as well, and these are not merely in the ordering and level of specificity within the presentation. They concern more substantive philosophical issues.

5

A point of particular interest is the division of mind (or soul) that is posited in both accounts. Here there are some obvious similarities between our two texts, since both speak of "parts" within a person that are responsible for our various functions, and both prominently mention both "rational" and "irrational" parts. But there are also important differences in the relationship that is established among the parts, reflecting quite different philosophical motivations.

---

[28] The tactic was used by Chrysippus in attacking rival accounts of the *telos* (Cic., *Acad.* 2.138; see White [2004] 401) and also in a polemic against Academic and/or Peripatetic advocacy of the life of contemplation (Plut., *De stoic. rep.* 1033b–c = *SVF* 3.702; for the interpretation, see Bénatouïl [2007]).

[29] Similar arguments are used by Seneca at *Const. Sap.* 16.1 and *Ep.* 66.45–48.

Doxography C posits quite an elaborate partitioning of the psyche. After the initial division into rational and irrational parts, each of those parts is subdivided, the rational into "scientific" (ἐπιστημονικόν) and "deliberative" (βουλευτικόν) parts and the irrational into "appetitive" (ἐπιθυμητικόν) and "spirited" (θυμικόν) parts. The determination of impulse belongs to the irrational part, which is thus also called the "impulsive" (ὁρμητικόν) part, but it is the rational part that deliberates about the objects of desire. Hence it is especially important to note how these parts relate to one another. That the relationship is not entirely harmonious is adumbrated already in section 1 [117.7–10W], where we are told that

> ἄλογον δὲ λέγεσθαι ψυχῆς μέρος οὐ τὸ καθάπαξ ἄλογον ἀλλὰ τὸ οἷόν τε πείθεσθαι λόγῳ, ὁποῖόν ἐστι τὸ παθητικόν, τοῦτο καὶ τῆς ἀρετῆς δεκτικόν.
>
> The part of the soul which is called irrational is not the one that is absolutely deprived of reason but the one which can obey reason; of this kind is the emotional (part of the soul), and, as such, it is also capable of receiving virtue.

This suggests that the irrational or impulsory part is not absolutely subservient to reason. It is indeed capable of obeying reason (οἷόν τε πείθεσθαι), but it actually obeys reason only when virtue is present in it. The potential for conflict between this part and the rational part is explained lower down in section 10 [128.17–25W], which states that emotion and reason "sometimes are discordant, engaging in civil war" (στασιαστικῶς διαφωνεῖν) and that the non-reasoning part exhibits "lack of self control" (ἀκρασία).

The opening of Seneca's letter partitions the *animus* in a way that at first looks quite similar to the Peripatetic doxography. Seneca writes:

> Puto, inter me teque conveniet externa corpori adquiri, corpus in honorem animi coli, in animo esse partes ministras, per quas movemur alimurque, propter ipsum principale nobis datas. In hoc principali est aliquid inrationale, est et rationale; illud huic servit, hoc unum est quod alio non refertur sed omnia ad se refert. Nam illa quoque divina ratio omnibus praeposita est, ipsa sub nullo est; et haec autem nostra eadem est, quae ex illa est. Si de hoc inter nos conuenit, sequitur ut de illo quoque conueniat, in hoc uno positam esse beatam vitam, ut in nobis ratio perfecta sit.
>
> You and I will agree, I think, that one pursues outward things for the body's sake, that one cares for the body in order to show respect for the mind, and that the mind includes subservient parts, responsible for our motor and nutritional functions, which are given to us on behalf of the directive faculty itself. This directive faculty includes both a non-rational and a rational component. The former is at the service of the latter, which is the one thing that does not look to anything else

but rather refers everything else to itself. As you know, divine rationality is similarly at the head of all things, subordinate to none of them; and this rationality of ours, which derives from that divine rationality, is just the same.

Now, if we agree about this, it is only consistent that we should also agree on the other point; namely, that the happy life consists solely in perfecting our rationality …

Again we find the soul divided into heterogenous parts, with one part responsible for reasoning and other, non-rational parts responsible for movement and nutrition. However, we should also attend to what Seneca does not say in this context. He does not say that the lower parts ever cause us to behave in ways that the rational element would not agree to. He certainly does not commit himself to a model of psychic conflict such as we found in Doxography C, in which the part of soul that determines impulse is sometimes at odds with the part that decides what objects ought to be pursued. Rather, he states that the lower elements *serve* the higher, and this not as a fact about the virtuous person only, but as a description of how all human minds are arranged. In his account, then, the lower parts serve the higher not merely when they are so inclined or when they are forced to do so, but always, in their very nature as subordinate parts. It is the rational part alone that determines what the creature should pursue and does pursue. The emphasis falls on the supremacy of reason as the sole element that refers everything to itself.[30]

The partitioning of the *animus* at the beginning of letter 92 has long been an issue in Stoic studies. Why would an author who is elsewhere strongly committed to a single directive faculty allow himself to speak of parts at all?[31] Having now seen that the remainder of letter 92 is targeted

---

[30] Just below, in *Ep.* 92.8, Seneca moves closer to conceding the possibility of mental conflict when he sets up a contrast between two parts within the mind's non-rational part, one "spirited, ambitious, and wayward, consisting in emotions … unruly" *(animosam, ambitiosam, inpotentem, positam in adfectionibus … effrenatam)*, the other "base, idle, devoted to pleasures" *(humilem, languidam, voluptatibus deditam)*. Seneca's point there, however, is that the pluralistic account he is rejecting gets things wrong in terms of its own psychology, by preferring the objective of the mind's lowest part to that of the emotional part.

[31] Seneca generally resists efforts to explain the intransigence of emotion in terms of conflicting soul-parts; see especially *Ira* 1.8.2-3, *Ep.* 116.2, with Graver (2014). Concerning *Ep.* 92.1-2 Setaioli (most recently in [2014] 246. n. 49) agrees with older views favoring Posidonian influence (Posidonius is mentioned on a separate issue in *Ep.* 92.10), but comments that "of course the irrational element must obey the rational one." If it *must*, then either the dualism espoused by Posidonius in, e.g., fr. 187 EK is not at issue, or it has undergone significant modification.

consistently against the Peripatetic position in ethics, we are at last in a position to make some progress on this question. Given the rhetorical aims of his letter, Seneca has good reason to begin with premises he believes his opponents would accept. In effect, he allows his straw Peripatetics to choose the terms of the debate, feeling that he has argumentative resources to defeat them on their own territory. Yet his statement need not be seen as "merely conventional or dialectical," as Inwood has suggested.[32] On the contrary, it is a description of the psyche a Stoic thinker can willingly endorse. For in Seneca's version of the psychic division, the mind's functions are arranged in such a way that the very possibility of disharmony and conflict among the parts is conspicuously absent. Moreover, this account of the mind's structure does not undermine Seneca's Stoic position on the sufficiency of virtue; rather it supports it. For since it is only the reasoning part that determines what objects are to be pursued, there is no reason why anything external to virtue has to be considered good in its own right. The reasoning part can order the pursuit of food and the like for merely instrumental reasons, nurturing and protecting the body and subordinate mind-parts for the support of its own virtuous ends.

Seneca's expressed openness to psychic tripartition thus appears as a deliberate accommodation to Peripatetic thought, but one that has subjected whatever Peripatetic material was at hand to some strategic reshaping. For this reason, there is not a source-critical argument to be derived from the differences between Seneca's statements in *Ep.* 92.1–2 and the psychic partitioning laid out in Doxography C. While Seneca must have been aware that a Peripatetic opponent would favor a division of the mind into rational and non-rational parts, his own Stoic commitments supply him with a motive for adjusting the psychology he found in his Peripatetic source to eliminate the possibility of mental conflict. Thus it is not possible to draw any conclusion about the extent to which that source might have resembled Doxography C in its account of the mind's structure and functions.

6

Matters become clearer when we compare the doxography of Arius Didymus with certain other features of the position Seneca gives to his opponents in letter 92. I have in mind two themes in Seneca's letter which appear to have been taken over from the tradition on Peripatetic ethics, but which could not have originated in Doxography C itself. The presence of these

---

[32] Inwood (2005) 38–41.

themes is in my view quite suggestive as to the nature of Seneca's source, even if no conclusion can be drawn as to its authorship.

Consider first the objection stated by Seneca's opponent in *Ep.* 92.14:

> "Est quidem" inquit "sapiens beatus; summum tamen illud bonum non consequitur nisi illi et naturalia instrumenta respondeant. Ita miser quidem esse qui virtutem habet non potest, beatissimus autem non est qui naturalibus bonis destituitur, ut valetudine, ut membrorum integritate."
>
> "The wise person is happy, to be sure; yet he does not attain the supreme good unless he has some natural tools at his disposal. Thus while someone who has virtue cannot be miserable, one who lacks such natural goods as health and an unimpaired physical condition is still not perfectly happy."

The opponent here concedes that virtuous wisdom is sufficient for happiness, while still insisting that a virtuous person who lacks the bodily and external goods is not supremely happy. He is thus at odds with Seneca, who proceeds to argue against the distinction between "happy" (*beatus*) and "perfectly happy" (*beatissimus*). But he is also at odds with the Peripatetic position that the wise person whose body is afflicted is neither happy nor unhappy (*Ep.* 92.19). On the face of it, his view appears to be identical with the view Seneca assigns in *Ep.* 71.18 to the *veteres Academici* and in *Ep.* 85.18 to Xenocrates and Speusippus.

If this is an Old Academic account, however, then the mention of "natural tools" (*naturalia instrumenta*) comes as a surprise. We have already seen how Peripatetic texts, including Doxography C, sometimes give the term "instruments" (ὄργανα) to bodily and external goods as part of an argument against the sufficiency of happiness. The thought is that just as the crafts require certain instruments to achieve their ends, so virtue cannot be activated without resources external to itself: virtue needs to use those other goods in the same way as a flute player needs to use a flute or a doctor needs to use medicines.[33] This convenient argument is usable by the philosopher who denies the sufficiency of virtue whether or not he also holds that the bodily and external goods are actually constitutive of happiness. The same cannot be said, however, for the philosopher who takes the "Old Academic" line in favor of sufficiency.[34] If bodily and external goods are necessary conditions for the activation of virtue, one can hardly say that virtue is sufficient for happiness even in their absence. For even the

---

[33] For the Aristotelian basis, see above, n. 9.
[34] As implied by the analysis in Sharples (2007) 627–28.

lesser degree of happiness that features in this account requires the possibility of activation.

What then are natural tools doing in the middle of an objection that makes virtue sufficient by itself? It is possible that Seneca has just been careless – that he means to give a Peripatetic flavor to the discussion and imports a phrase characteristic of the school into a paragraph where it does not properly belong. But we should also consider the possibility that the "Old Academic" view might have been framed within a larger Peripatetic position in Seneca's source. For a Peripatetic author, it would represent a kind of fallback position, a place to which a member of his school might retreat under dialectical pressure without giving up anything really important. Sufficiency would have been conceded, but in such a way as to maintain some status for the bodily and external goods. Strictly speaking that would not be the status of instruments but rather of constituents; the Peripatetic author, however, might regard those terms as more or less interchangeable, since he is in the habit of using both to refer to externals.

This is not a theme Seneca could have extracted from Doxography C. In fact Didymus explicitly refuses to take this gambit. We find in sections 13–14 [132.8–21] the following statement:

> Προηγουμένην δὲ τὴν τῆς ἀρετῆς ἐνέργειαν διὰ τὸ πάντως ἀναγκαῖον ἐν τοῖς κατὰ φύσιν ἀγαθοῖς ὑπάρχειν, ἐπεὶ καὶ ἐν κακοῖς ἀρετῇ χρήσαιτ᾽ ἂν καλῶς ὁ σπουδαῖος, οὐ μὴν γε μακάριος ἔσται, καὶ ἐν αἰκίαις ἀποδείξαιτ᾽ ἂν τὸ γενναῖον, οὐ μὴν εὐδαιμονήσει. Αἴτιον δ᾽ ὅτι ἡ μὲν ἀρετὴ καλῶν μόνον ἐστὶν ἀπεργαστικὴ καθ᾽ ἑαυτήν, ἡ δ᾽ εὐδαιμονία καὶ καλῶν κἀγαθῶν. Οὐ γὰρ ἐγκαρτερεῖν βούλεται τοῖς δεινοῖς, ἀλλὰ τῶν ἀγαθῶν ἀπολαύειν πρὸς τῷ καὶ σῴζειν τὸ ἐν κοινωνίᾳ δίκαιον καὶ μήτε ἀποστερεῖν ἑαυτὴν τῶν ἐν ᾗ θεωρίᾳ καλῶν μήτε τῶν κατὰ τὸν βίον ἀναγκαίων. Ἥδιστον γάρ τι καὶ κάλλιστον εἶναι τὴν εὐδαιμονίαν, οὔτε δ᾽ ἐπιτείνεσθαι καθάπερ τέχνην ὀργάνων πλήθει καὶ παρασκευῇ …

> The activity of virtue is (in the definition called) "primary," as it is altogether necessary for it to be surrounded by goods that are in accordance with nature; for the morally good person could make a good use of virtue even among evils but will not be blessed, and even tormented could show a noble character, but will fail to attain happiness. The reason is that virtue in itself produces only noble things, whereas happiness both good and noble. For the latter does not want to endure terrible things but to enjoy good things in addition to preserving social justice and not depriving itself either of the fine things in contemplation or of the necessary things for living. For happiness is the most pleasant and noble thing and it cannot be made greater, as in the case of the crafts, through the number of instruments and equipment …

In contrast to the "Old Academic" interpreters we have just encountered, Didymus here insists that the possession of goods in accordance with nature is "altogether necessary"; that is, altogether necessary for happiness. Being "blessed" (μακάριος) is treated as equivalent to being happy (εὐδαιμονήσει); one deprived of external goods will have neither the one nor the other. Nor is happiness a matter of degree: it cannot be increased (ἐπιτείνεσθαι) by the addition of instruments and equipment—again, of the bodily and external goods. All this reads like a rather emphatic rejection of the "Old Academic" reading of Aristotle. We catch a hint of a controversy that must have gone on at some point in the later Hellenistic period, in which Didymus (or his source) took one position and the Peripatetics later read by Seneca were at least open to the other. Antiochus of Ascalon would no doubt have participated enthusiastically in such a debate; we need not think, though, that the conversation began with him.[35]

A second feature that distinguishes Seneca's Peripatetics from those of Doxography C can be seen in section 6 of letter 92, where the opponent explains why happiness might require ἀοχλησία in addition to virtue.

> Si non es sola honestate contentus, necesse est aut quietem adici velis, quam Graeci ἀοχλησίαν vocant, aut voluptatem. Horum alterum utcumque recipi potest; vacat enim animus molestia liber ad inspectum universi, nihilque illum avocat a contemplatione naturae.

> If you are not satisfied with honorable conduct on its own, you are bound to want the addition of either absence of distress (which Greeks call *aochlēsia*) or pleasure. The former of these is admissible in any case, for the trouble-free mind is not hindered from studying the universe or distracted by anything from contemplating nature.

As we saw earlier in connection with "natural tools," the underlying argument is that virtue cannot be activated unless conjoined with some goods external to itself. In this case, the virtuous activity is contemplation of nature, and the external good is essentially a lack of hindrance. Disturbance (ὄχλος), whether mental or physical, impedes the psyche from carrying out its intention: the mind that is free of such distress is at leisure *(vacat)* and is not distracted *(nihil avocat)*.

As we have seen, the thought that serious misfortunes might impede virtuous activities is present in Aristotle, and has indeed already been treated by Seneca in a Peripatetic context in *Ep.* 85.30–31. But the theme makes an especially strong showing in *Ep.* 92. In addition to the passage

---

[35] Cf. Annas (1993) (above, n. 21). Context for the suggestion made here is supplied in White (2002); Inwood (2002); Sharples (2007); Hahm (2007 and in this volume); Inwood (2014).

just cited, we find it in three other places in the letter, with the impetus coming in each case from the Peripatetic side. In 92.10 it appears again in conjunction with *quies* (= ἀοχλησία), as a less problematic addition to virtue than pleasure would be. "Their other objective, freedom from distress, though incapable of providing the spirit with any positive benefit, would at least remove any impediments" (*Illa utcumque altera quies nihil quidem ipsa praestabat animo, sed inpedimenta removebat*).[36] Slightly different is 92.11, where the interlocutor suggests that good health, repose, and absence of pain might be things to pursue "as long as they are not impediments to virtue" (*si virtutem nihil inpeditura sit*). Here it may be significant that two of the three suggested objects of pursuit are privatives—three, if one thinks of *bona valetudo* as an absence of illness. Finally, in section 17, the interlocutor appears to have a notion of impediments in mind when he objects to Seneca's sunlight analogy.

> Paulo ante dicebam igniculum nihil conferre lumini solis; claritate enim eius quidquid sine illo luceret absconditur. "Sed quaedam" inquit "soli quoque opstant." At sol integer est etiam inter opposita, et quamvis aliquid interiacet quod nos prohibeat eius aspectu, in opere est, cursu suo fertur; quotiens inter nubila eluxit, non est sereno minor, ne tardior quidem, quoniam multum interest utrum aliquid obstet tantum an inpediat. (*Ep*. 92.17)

> As I was saying a bit ago, a spark makes no contribution to the light of the sun; for the sun's brightness obscures anything that might shine in its absence. "But even the sun has its light blocked by certain things." Yet the sun is unimpaired, even when it is obstructed; and even if there is something in between that stops us from seeing it, it is still at work and still proceeding on its round. Every time it shines out between the clouds, it is no smaller or slower than when the sky is quite clear. There is a lot of difference between an impediment and a mere obstruction.

The Senecan response makes it clear how the objection is supposed to work. The opponent allows Seneca's point that nothing external to virtue can make any positive contribution to happiness (the spark does not contribute to the light of the sun) but retains the weaker claim, that some externals can prevent virtue from achieving its ends. The verb *inpediat* belongs to Seneca, but is expressing the position of the objector.

Now, for Aristotle, the capacity of severe misfortunes to impede virtuous activity is a kind of inverse notion to the instrumentality of external

---

[36] The imperfect indicatives recall the prior mention of the concept in 92.6 (*vacat*) and fill in the thought: ἀοχλησία is strictly a privative notion consisting in the removal of impediments.

goods, one that works "conversely" (ἀνάπαλιν) to the way strokes of good fortune are available for fine and excellent use. It takes only a moment's reflection, however, to realize that the philosophical notion of an impediment is in fact distinct from that of an instrument. An instrument, as involved in many of the craft analogies, has properties specific to the purpose for which its use is required: a flute, with its specific properties, is required for flute-playing but not for paddling a boat. An impediment merely prevents: the broken arm that impedes flute-playing also impedes boat-paddling, house-building, and much else. A version of Peripatetic ethics that made happiness consist only in virtuous activity plus a lack of impediments would be quite austere, though still distinct from Stoicism. It would allow that virtue can work with any circumstances that come to hand—a poor person can be generous, a weak person courageous—but it would insist that distress of body or mind can prevent even the best people from activating their virtues. A Stoic might object at this point that the business of avoiding anything that would genuinely impede the activities of virtue is just part of virtuous activity itself. But the austere Peripatetic does not have to allow this, not if he restricts his notion of impediments to Aristotle's "misfortunes like those of Priam"; that is, to events that would plausibly be debilitating to the mind itself.

This kind of position may have been advanced by such Peripatetics as Hieronymus and Diodorus of Tyre, both of whom emphasized ἀοχλησία to the exclusion of the positive external goods.[37] The tradition remembers Diodorus in particular for having conjoined ἀοχλησία with virtue in his account of the end, while Hieronymus, a contemporary of Arcesilas and Chrysippus, is consistently said to have spoken of ἀοχλησία alone. It may be, however, that Hieronymus was falsely portrayed by his opponents as more of a hedonist than he really was.[38] What matters here, though, is that the tendency in letter 92 for externals to be framed in terms of impediments, rather than instruments or positive contributions, cannot reflect the influence of Doxography C itself. Didymus barely mentions impediments. The notion surfaces only once in his account, and then within one of a string of quoted definitions for εὐδαιμονία in section 13 [130.20–21W]. That one definition, in which εὐδαιμονία is «the unimpeded use of virtue among

---

[37] Diodorus *adiungit ad honestatem vacuitatem doloris* (Cic., *Fin.* 5.14), making happiness consist in "living trouble-free and honorably" (ἀοχλήτως καὶ καλῶς ζῆν, Clement *Strom* 2.21.127).

[38] It is of interest that Hieronymus denied that pleasure is intrinsically choiceworthy (Cic., *Fin.* 2.9). See further White (2002 and 2004).

things in accordance with nature» (χρῆσιν ἀρετῆς ἐν τοῖς κατὰ φύσιν ἀνεμπόδιστον) does attest to a notion of unimpededness in at least one earlier version of Peripatetic ethics, but much else in Didymus favors the less austere account, and we can hardly think that such a glancing mention could have provided the impetus for what we find in Seneca.

Thus we have noted two features of the Peripatetic position attacked in Seneca's letter that are significantly different from that laid out in Doxography C: a readiness to make use of the (putatively) Old Academic gambit on degrees of happiness, and a subtle but unmistakeable emphasis on impediments to activation. When these features are taken together with the observations made above (pp. 325–27) concerning points held in common between the two accounts, it is possible to discern at least the broad outlines of the Peripatetic source Seneca must have used. This source must have laid out a fairly comprehensive array of Peripatetic claims, including claims about the structure of the psyche, claims about the non-sufficiency of virtue for happiness, and at least one claim about the nature of happiness itself, viz., that it is different for a god than for a human being. It must have mentioned the possibility that one could be neither happy nor wretched, and it must have argued at some point that external goods are needed as tools for activation, and again that some degree of longevity is required for a complete life. This range of inclusions suggests a doxographical account resembling the one found in Stobaeus and generally considered to be the compilation of Arius Didymus. Unlike Didymus, however, the account known to Seneca made positive use of the "Old Academic" reading of *EN* 1.10; also, it emphasized the austere Hieronyman or Diodoran version of pluralism, allowing only absence of impediments as the adjunct to virtuous activity. In brief, what we meet in Seneca's letter is a second Peripatetic doxography with its own distinctive emphases.

7

Compilers of handbooks are not often credited with any particular philosophical agency. We tend to think of them as reproducing in an unreflective, almost mechanical way the achievements of an earlier, more exciting phase of philosophical discovery. To enliven that picture of the compiler's activity, one needs evidence of variety in approaches taken to a single doxographical task, with possibilities for selection within a disparate body of material and perhaps an element of competition. In this paper I have argued that Seneca's writings provide us with some limited evidence for a second Peripatetic doxographer whose approach was interestingly different from that of Arius Didymus. Like Didymus, the doxographer whose work lies somewhere behind Seneca's 92nd letter undertook to produce an overview of Peripatetic ethics with a grounding in psychic tripartition; he made different choices, however, when it came to the handling of the Old Academic view and to the workings of the activation-based argument against sufficiency. This author cannot have been Seneca's only source for Peripatetic thought: as we have seen, Seneca also knew at least some texts of a dialectical nature, and he may have had other sources as well. But Peripatetic doxographer behind letter 92 is of particular importance for readers of this volume. When we reflect on the choices he (or just possibly she) seems to have made, we gain a new awareness of the kinds of decisions that were open to the doxographer and that were exercised differently by the author of Doxography C.

Appendix
Didymus' πράξεις προηγουμέναι and *Epistulae morales* 66.5

A more tenuous but highly intriguing connection to Peripatetic thought is discernible in the 66th of the *Epistulae Morales,* where Seneca draws a distinction between what he calls "primary goods"—that is, virtuous activities in the midst of preferred indifferents—and "secondary" and "tertiary" goods, which are virtuous activities relating to either dispreferred or neutral indifferents. From a Stoic perspective, the classification is merely for the sake of argument, for the purpose of the letter is to demonstrate that *all* goods are of equal magnitude. No particular opponent is named, but one may suspect that the classification of goods into primary, secondary, and tertiary types is taken over by Seneca from outside the Stoic system. Certainly the Stoic record does not contain any such threefold classification of *goods;* rather, Stoics classify indifferents into preferred, dispreferred, and neutral types, and would argue, as Seneca does in the letter, that no such hierarchy obtains among virtuous activities.[39] A parallel with the usage of προηγούμενος, -η, -ον in three passages in Doxography C may be an indication that its origin is Peripatetic.

Seneca's way of stating the classification is not altogether consistent. As examples of primary goods he at first lists "joy, peace, the safety of one's homeland"; of these, only joy is even a candidate to be considered a

---

[39] For the classification of indifferents see D.L. 7.104–5. That the classification is into precisely *three* categories does not in itself constitute an allusion to the Peripatetic *tria genera bonorum* (cf. Inwood [2007] 158–60). Various threefold classifications of goods are found several other places in the Stoic record, notably in Stob. 2.7, 70.8–9W (where psychic goods comprise virtues, virtuous conditions, and virtuous activities), and in D.L. 7.94–95.

virtuous activity. "Peace" and "the safety of one's homeland" appear to be external goods or, as Stoics would say, preferred indifferents. If that is the intention, however, the classification is poorly arranged, since the examples provided for secondary and tertiary goods *are* virtuous activities. Here is the passage:

> Quaedam, ut nostris uidetur, prima bona sunt, tamquam gaudium, pax, salus patriae; quaedam secunda, in materia infelici expressa, tamquam tormentorum patientia et in morbo gravi temperantia. Illa bona derecto optabimus nobis, haec, si necesse erit. Sunt adhuc tertia, tamquam modestus incessus et compositus ac probus vultus et conveniens prudenti viro gestus. (*Ep.* 66.5)

> It is the position of our school that some goods are primary—for instance joy, peace, the safety of one's homeland—while others are secondary, manifested in unfortunate material, such as endurance under torture or self-control during serious illness. The former goods we choose for ourselves unconditionally, the latter if it becomes necessary. And there are still the tertiary goods, such as a modest walk, a calm and dignified facial expression, and gestures befitting an intelligent person.

The subsequent discussion serves to clarify Seneca's intention regarding primary goods. Joy, or rather rejoicing (*gaudere*) is the preeminent example; such items as "the safety of one's homeland" merely specify the circumstances in which a person might virtuously rejoice.[40] The primary goods are thus articulated exactly in parallel to the secondary goods: in both cases, we have specification of an activity of the virtuous person, whether rejoicing or enduring, and of the circumstances of that activity; for example, one's homeland is safe, one's children are devoted, or one is tortured or afflicted with illness. The clearest formulation is at 66.36–37:

> Ceterum bona quaedam prima existimat, ad quae ex proposito venit, tamquam victoriam, bonos liberos, salutem patriae; quaedam secunda, quae non apparent nisi in rebus adversis, tamquam aequo animo pati morbum, ignem, exilium; quaedam media, quae nihilo magis secundum naturam sunt quam contra naturam, tamquam prudenter ambulare, composite sedere. Non enim minus secundum naturam est sedere quam stare aut ambulare. Duo illa bona superiora diversa sunt: prima enim secundum naturam sunt, gaudere liberorum pietate, patriae incolumitate; secunda contra naturam sunt, fortiter obstare tormentis et sitim perpeti morbo urente praecordia. (*Ep.* 66.36–37)

---

[40] The interest in virtuous activities is stated in the abstract in *Ep.* 66.7, with *quae pro vitae varietate et pro actionibus explicantur*. Joy (χαρά, *gaudium*) is typically listed by Stoics as a eupathic response and hence a virtuous activity; in this letter, though, the response in question differs from the usual account of εὐπάθεια in that it is directed at indifferents.

But there are some goods that it (reason) regards as primary, goods that it approaches deliberately—for instance victory, good children, the welfare of one's homeland—others as secondary, goods that show up only in adverse circumstances—for instance bearing disease, fire, or exile with equanimity—and still others as intermediates, goods which are no more in accordance with nature than they are contrary to nature; for instance, walking sensibly, sitting with composure. For sitting is not more in accordance with nature than standing or walking. The first two types of good differ from one another. The primary goods are in accordance with nature: rejoicing in the devotion of one's children, in the safety of one's homeland. The secondary goods are contrary to nature: courageously standing up to torture and enduring thirst when one's vital organs are parched by disease.

In this, again, the first sentence speaks of the primary goods as if they were merely preferred indifferents. The secondary and tertiary goods are all actions, however (*pati ... ambulare ... sedere*) and in the last sentence quoted the primary goods are as well: for Seneca, at least, the good is that one *rejoices* in the circumstances listed.

Realizing, then, that Seneca's intention is to identify the primary goods as virtuous activities in the kinds of circumstances Stoics call preferred indifferents, one can recognize an essential similarity between those goods and what Didymus designates πράξεις προηγουμέναι or, in one passage, a προηγουμένη ἐνέργεια of virtue. The term appears in three passages in Doxography C:

§8 [126.18–20W]: Ὅθεν ἐνέργειαν εἶναι τὴν εὐδαιμονίαν κατ' ἀρετὴν ἐν πράξεσι προηγουμέναις κατ' εὐχήν ... It follows that happiness is an activity in accordance with virtue expressed in primary actions according to wish.

§12 [129.19–20W] Τὴν δ' εὐδαιμονίαν ἐκ τῶν καλῶν γίνεσθαι καὶ προηγουμένων πράξεων. Happiness is brought about through noble and primary actions.

§13 [132.8–10W] Προηγουμένην δὲ τὴν τῆς ἀρετῆς ἐνέργειαν διὰ τὸ πάντως ἀναγκαῖον ἐν τοῖς κατὰ φύσιν ἀγαθοῖς ὑπάρχειν ... The activity of virtue is (in the definition called) "primary," as it is altogether necessary for it to be surrounded by goods that are in accordance with nature ...

Sharples explains the difficulty scholars have had over this usage of προηγούμενος, -η, -ον.[41] Puzzled by the expression (which after all does not occur in Aristotle), Wachsmuth emended the text at 126.18 to read χορηγουμέναις ("well-stocked") and at 132.8 to read χορηγουμένην. Προηγούμενος does appear in other Peripatetic authors, however, with the meaning "primary" as opposed to "accidental." To throw a ship's

---

[41] Sharples (2007) 633; see further Sharples (2010) 117, n. 22; and Huby (1983) 125–26.

cargo overboard is appropriate in a storm, but only accidentally: weather permitting, one would prefer to convey the cargo to its destination. With the received text, then, the actions of the virtuous person constitute happiness just when they are undertaken in favorable circumstances, in fair weather as it were, or "according to wish." Activities chosen under duress may still be entirely virtuous, but it is not those activities that make a person happy.

Now, the lengthy argument of Seneca's 66th letter definitely presupposes a rival philosophical position that thought of *prima bona* in just the way that Arius Didymus thinks of πράξεις προηγουμέναι. Given the resemblance, I would like to put forward as a hypothesis that Seneca had in fact encountered this primary-secondary-tertiary classification of virtuous activities in some Peripatetic treatise on ethics, or else that Peripatetic content had been transmitted to him by some well-informed intermediary. If the threefold classification did originate in a Peripatetic work, then certain otherwise awkward features of Seneca's discussion can easily be explained. We will then be able to account for what looks like a ranking of goods within a Stoic text: for the Peripatetic author, the primary goods were indeed primary; that is, preferable, rather than only first in order of explication as Seneca tries to make them. We also have a reason for the slippage of *prima bona* between external goods and virtuous activities responding to preferred indifferents. The Peripatetic author had no strong need to insist on a distinction, and Seneca was careless in handling his material. Also unusual for a Stoic author, and unparalleled in Seneca, is the way *gaudium*, rejoicing, is handled in this letter, with a wise mind rejoicing not in goods that are "real and its own" but in things external to it.[42] The Peripatetic author, who thinks differently about the emotions, will have had no difficulty at all in treating χαρά as the proper response to devoted children and the like. And this unprovable hypothesis also offers some illumination to those whose chief interest is in Doxography C itself. When one reads through Seneca's letter looking not for Seneca's position but for the way of thinking about happiness he is seeking to displace, one gains a sense of how the notion of *preferable* activities for virtue might have been developed and expanded in a world where Stoics had already begun classifying the indifferents.

Works Cited

Annas, J. 1993. *Morality of Happiness.* New York: Oxford University Press.

---

[42] *Ep.* 59.2; cf. 23.6 and see n. 40 above.

Barnes, J. 1997. "Roman Aristotle." In *Philosophia Togata*. Vol. 2: *Plato and Aristotle at Rome*. Oxford: Oxford University Press, 1–69.

Bénatouïl, T. 2007. "Le débat entre platonisme et stoïcisme sur la vie scolastique: Chrysippe, la Nouvelle Académie et Antiochus." In *Platonic Stoicism, Stoic Platonism: The Dialogue Between Platonism and Stoicism in Antiquity*, ed. M. Bonazzi and C. Helmig. Leuven: Leuven University Press, 1–21.

Costa, C. D. N. 1988. *Seneca: 17 Letters*. Warminster: Aris & Phillips.

Damschen, G., and Andreas Heil (eds.). 2014. *Brill's Companion to Seneca: Philosopher and Dramatist*. Leiden: Brill.

Fortenbaugh, W. W. (ed.). 1983. *On Stoic and Peripatetic Ethics: The Work of Arius Didymus*. Rutgers University Studies in Classical Humanities 1. New Brunswick, N.J.: Transaction.

Gill, C. 2012. "The Transformation of Aristotle's *Ethics* in Roman Philosophy." In *The Reception of Aristotle's Ethics*, ed. J. Miller. Cambridge: Cambridge University Press, 31–52.

Gottschalk, H. B. 1987. "Aristotelian Philosophy in the Roman World." *ANRW* II.36.2, 1079–1174.

Graver, M. 2014. "Ethics II: Action and Emotion." In Damschen and Heil (2014) 257–75.

Graver, M. and A. A. Long. 2015. *Seneca: Letters on Ethics*. Chicago: University of Chicago Press.

Griffin, M., and B. Inwood, B. (trans./ed.). 2011. *Seneca: On Benefits*. Chicago: University of Chicago Press.

Hahm, D. 2007. "Critolaus and Late Hellenistic Peripatetic Philosophy." In *Pyrrhonists, Patricians, Platonizers: Hellenistic Philosophy in the Period 155–86 BC*, ed. A. M. Ioppolo and D. Sedley. Naples: Bibliopolis, 47–101.

Huby, P. 1983. "Peripatetic Definitions of Happiness." In Fortenbaugh (1983) 121–34.

Inwood, B. 2002. "Comment on Stephen White, 'Happiness in the Hellenistic Lyceum.'" *Apeiron* suppl. 35, 95–102.

———. 2005. *Reading Seneca: Stoic Philosophy at Rome*. New York: Oxford University Press.

———. 2007. *Seneca: Selected Philosophical Letters*. New York: Oxford University Press.

———. 2014. *Ethics After Aristotle*. Cambridge, Mass.: Harvard University Press.

Irwin, T. H. (trans.). 1985. *Aristotle: Nicomachean Ethics*. Indianapolis: Hackett.

Kidd, I. G. 1986. "Posidonian Methodology and the Self-Sufficiency of Virtue." In *Aspects de la philosophie hellénistique: neuf, exposés suivis de discussions*, ed. I. G. Kidd et al. Vandoeuvres-Geneva: Fondation Hardt, 1–21.

———. 1988. *Posidonius*. Vol. 2: *The Commentary*. Cambridge: Cambridge University Press.

Moraux, P. 1973. *Der Aristotelismus bei den Griechen. Von Andronikos bis Alexander von Aphrodisias*. Berlin: De Gruyter.

Préchac, F. (ed.). 1945–64. *Sénèque: Lettres à Lucilius*. Translated by. H. Noblot. Paris: Les Belles Lettres.

Setaioli, A. 1988. *Seneca e i Greci*. Bologna: Pàtron.

———. 2014. "Ethics I: Therapy, Self-Transformation, and 'Lebensform.'" In Damschen and Heil (2014) 239–56.

———. 2007. "Peripatetics on Happiness." In *Greek and Roman Philosophy 100 BC–200 AD*. BICS suppl. 94, ed. R. Sorabji and R. W. Sharples. London: Institute of Classical Studies, University of London, 627–37.

Sharples, R. W. (ed.). 2007. "Peripatetics on Happiness." In *Greek and Roman Philosophy 100 BC–200 AD*. ed. R. Sorabji and R. W. Sharples. BICS suppl. 94. London: Institute of Classical Studies, University of London, 627–37.

———. 2010. *Peripatetic Philosophy, 200 BC to AD 200: An Introduction and Collection of Sources in Translation*. Cambridge: Cambridge University Press.

Trapp, M. 2007. *Philosophy in the Roman Empire*. Aldershot: Ashgate.

White, S. 2002. "Happiness in the Hellenistic Lyceum." *Apeiron* suppl. 35, 69–93.

———. 2004. "Lyco and Hieronymus on the Good Life." In *Lyco of Troas and Hieronymus of Rhodes*, ed. W. Fortenbaugh and S. White. Rutgers University Studies in Classical Humanities 12. New Brunswick, N.J.: Transaction, 389–409.

Subject Index to Chapters 2–10

absence of distress, 324, 326, 333–35
alogical part of the soul: *see* bipartite soul
altruism, 142–49 (or 142–46, 147, 148 n. 50, 149), 157
apical terms, 81
approbation, 149–50, 153–54
appropriate actions, 247–49
appropriation, 83
assessment of Didymus' epitome: strengths, 286–88; shortcomings, 288–89
attraction, 88–91
authorship, 1–3, 69–72, 70–72, 163–64

beauty, beautiful, 81–91, 109–10
behavioral regularity, 95–98, 107–9, 110
best state, 283–86
bipartite soul, 76–81, 91–92, 104, 113

capacities, 78, 83, 93
care and concern, 107
causes of civil war, 279–82
character, 127, 157
chatter, 94–98, 108
choice, 128–29, 131, 134 n. 21
choiceworthy (*haireton*), 128–57, 166–68, 187–88
circumstance/critical moment, 146–51, 231–39, 241–42
city planning, 285f.
classification: *see* Division
cleverness, 100
constitution(s), 229, 260–62, 276
contemplation, 231–32
correct actions, 247–249
courage, 78, 80–81, 83, 92, 104–5, 113, 168, 176, 183, 233, 250, 319
Cyrenaic, 149 n. 51

343

date, 70–72
death/dying, 176, 180–83
deliberation, 82, 84, 233
disposition: *see* intermediate and mean
division, 106, 114
doxography, 69–73, 123–24, 162–64, 189
drinking/imbibing, 178, 234–35

economic and political topic, 255–60
education (moral), 77–79, 85, 96, 229, 249–50
efficient cause, 78
emotion(s), 77–82, 106–8, 114–15, 249–50; moderation in, 317, 320
Epicurean(s)/Epicureanism, 133, 206, 223, 236–37, 321, 326–27
erotic love, 234–35
etymology, 76–77, 85–86
eudaimonia: *see* happiness
external goods, 124, 129–30, 132, 150, 155, 161, 169, 174, 179–80, 189, 192, 195–96, 200, 205–24

fair-commerce, 111
fellow-feeling, 272f.
fine, 80–81, 84, 88–89, 109
friendliness, 107–109
friendship (*philia*), 128, 132–36, 140–42, 146–52

generosity: *see* liberality
good temper, 78, 93, 105
goodwill, 143, 149–50, 152, 154
great souled, 110

habituation, 76–82, 85
happiness (*eudaimonia*), 112, 125, 131, 135, 140, 161–62, 164, 165, 168–76, 179–201, 243–47, 331–36
headings/subheadings, 75–76, 84, 86, 91

hypothetical necessity, 168, 169, 174, 178, 181, 184, 187

impetuosity, 115
impulse, 79–80, 124, 128, 166–67, 328
innate, 114–15
intermediate life, disposition, 165–68, 247–49
intrinsic worth: *see* choiceworthy

justice, 87–88, 92, 104–5, 108, 111–13, 182, 191, 195–97, 201, 302–6

king, 147, 228–30, 262, 302–5

liberality/generosity, 182–84, 185
lives, types of, 145, 176–86, 196–98, 227–52
loquacity: *see* chatter
love: *see* friendship

manner: *see* behavioral regularity
marriage, 233–34, 260–65
master–slave, 264–68, 285
mean–disposition, 91–98
mind, parts of, 323, 326, 327–30; *see also* bipartite soul; tripartite soul
money making, 242–43
moral virtue, 75–114; *see also* practical wisdom; virtue
moral weakness/strength, 85–86

nature/natural, 76–82, 103, 106, 112, 162, 170, 172, 180, 186, 189, 190, 192, 194–201, 209, 243–49, 260
necessary (*anankaia*), 168, 169, 174–75, 181, 187, 196, 198
noble (*kalon*)/nobility, 80–81, 87–88, 98–99, 102, 162, 168–72, 175–77, 182–89, 191–201, 217–19
noble–goodness, 92, 112–14
number of citizens, 272–76

Subject Index

oikeiôsis, 73, 83, 124, 128, 133, 138–39, 141, 153, 155–56, 163, 164, 178, 182, 209–14, 294–97, 307–8
oikonomikos topos, 260–69
Old Academy, 312, 321–22, 331–33

perfection, 76–79, 81–82, 92, 112
piety, 111
pleasure/pain, 92–93, 102–5, 240
polis: definition, 271f.; formation, 270f.
political activity, 146–52, 220–31, 233–34
politikos topos, 258, 270–86
practical wisdom, 98–104, 182; *see also* moral virtue; virtue
praise: *see* approbation
praiseworthy 110, 114
primary action/activity, 176–201, 241
"primary" goods, 337–40
productive/supportive/instrumental, 168–75, 180, 181, 185, 187, 194, 200
progress moral, 112
psychic dichotomy: *see* bipartite soul

reason in moral education, 77, 81–82, 84
reciprocal relationship, 100–101
relatives, 77–88, 93
reputation, 150, 154, 156

seeds, 76–82, 84
slave, 115–19
slow, sluggish, 115–19

soul: and body, 208–10, 213
sources, 73
Stoic, 99–100, 105, 108–9, 124, 126, 129, 131, 133–35, 138, 143, 147, 152, 154, 155–57, 161–63, 166–79, 199, 206, 209, 214–15, 229–30, 248–49, 293–97, 307, 309–40
style, lexical, 131–32, 239–40, 246–48, 251
suicide, 235–39, 246
symplerotic (*symplêroma*), 171, 172, 174–75, 178–80, 200

telos, 100, 161, 163, 164, 165, 171, 173, 174, 178–79, 181, 183, 186–87, 200, 214–21, 325
temperance, 88, 92, 96, 104–5, 108–9, 113
theôria, 182, 196–98, 200–201
training, moral: *see* education
trigeneia of goods, 213, 223
tripartite soul, 77, 80, 160, 330
tyranny, 148, 230, 232

ugliness, 90
useful, 81, 88, 110, 112, 118, 151

virtue, 129–31, 151, 156–57, 206–7, 214–16, 219; *see also* moral virtue; practical wisdom

wealth, 244–45, 317–18
wills, 134, 144
wittiness, 107–8
woman/female, 115–19, 260